THE ROLLING STONE

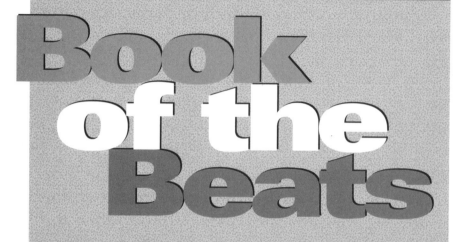

Book of the Beats

THE BEAT GENERATION AND AMERICAN CULTURE

THE BEAT GENERATION

THE ROLLING STONE

Book of the Beats

AND AMERICAN CULTURE

EDITED BY

HOLLY GEORGE-WARREN

NEW YORK

810.9005

ROL

A Rolling Stone Press Book
Editor: Holly George-Warren
Senior Editor: Shawn Dahl
Assistant Editor: Ann Abel
Editorial Assistant: Carrie Smith

Library of Congress Cataloging-in-Publication Data

The Rolling stone book of the Beats: the Beat Generation and American culture /
    edited by Holly George-Warren—1st ed
        p. cm.
    Includes bibliographical references (p.) and index.
    ISBN: 0-7868-6426-5
    1. American literature—20th century—History and criticism. 2. Authors,
American—20th century—Biography. 3. United States—Civilization—20th century.
4. Beat generation. I. George-Warren, Holly. II. Rolling stone (San Francisco, Calif.)
PS228.B6R65 1999
810.9'005—dc21   98-43934
                                                                              CIP
Paperback ISBN 0-7868-8542-4
FIRST PAPERBACK EDITION
1 3 5 7 9 10 8 6 4 2

Original hardcover design by Robert Bull Design

Contents

Introduction

BY HOLLY GEORGE-WARREN

IT WAS BORN IN NEW YORK, GREW up in Mexico City, Tangier and Paris, and peaked in San Francisco. Jack Kerouac named it, then divorced it; William Burroughs always detached himself from it, yet somehow remained part of its very essence. As a cultural phenomenon, the Beat Generation changed us more than any other Twentieth-Century movement; its effects are still being felt today. As a literary movement, the Beat Generation gave us a cacophony of fresh, new American voices; the common thread running through the work was this: to say what hadn't been said in a language as unique as one's own thumbprint.

And so it is the intent of *The Rolling Stone Book of the Beats* to present an equally wide range of individual—sometimes conflicting—voices. To this end, we'll hear from those who lived it, learned from it, studied it, taught it or discovered it through its acolytes. A few are speaking on the subject for the first time; others have made it their life's work.

Why ROLLING STONE? When the magazine started in 1967 in San Francisco, its editors, writers and readers were among the first generation to feel the reverberations of the Beat Generation's quake. In an old printer's loft, across town from the Beat epicenter of North Beach, ROLLING STONE published, along with its music and polit-

Typewriter in William Burroughs's garden,
Lawrence, Kansas, 1996
LEE RANALDO

ical coverage, a smattering of poetry—including poems by Allen Ginsberg, Gary Snyder and Michael McClure; the magazine also frequently reviewed new books by the movement's authors and poets (and later, particularly in the case of Ginsberg, their recordings). Over the years, Beat writers contributed sundry essays to the magazine: among them, McClure on Dylan and Jim Morrison, Ginsberg on the Beatles, Burroughs on the film *Heart Beat* (the latter anthologized here). When Ginsberg testified at the Chicago Seven conspiracy trial in 1970, his testimony ran in ROLLING STONE's pages. Twice, William Burroughs was the subject of "The ROLLING STONE Interview" (an excerpt is reprinted in this book), conducted by the late critic and musicologist Robert Palmer, a longtime contributor to the magazine.

Primarily, though, ROLLING STONE's strongest link to the Beats has been its championing of mavericks like Palmer, as well as such iconoclasts as Hunter S. Thompson, Richard Meltzer and Lester Bangs. Carving out their own territory, these writers clearly were inspired by Beat pioneers. Likewise, the Beat filter has added texture to the recordings of numerous artists whose music gave the magazine its *raison d'être*: from the Beatles, Dylan and the Velvet Underground in the Sixties, to David Bowie, Tom Waits and Patti Smith in the Seventies, to Sonic Youth and Beck in recent years.

Here, you'll find many of these voices: those who knew the Beats, some who were (are) Beats, and those of us whose lives and work have been greatly affected by the Beats. With ROLLING

STONE as a kind of blueprint, the book covers lots of cultural ground—music, film, art, theater, photography—in relation to the Beat movement's beginnings, its major progenitors and its progeny. Some pieces were originally published in ROLLING STONE, a few appeared in other publications or volumes no longer available, and more than half were written specifically for this book. Among the contributors are academics, musicians, memoirists, novelists, poets, photographers, rock critics, record producers, scholars and graphic artists. To complement the text, photographs—a few never before published—and an illustrated narrative offer yet another dimension of the Beat experience.

As a whole, *The Rolling Stone Book of the Beats* should make it clear how such a small group of individualists could affect us so powerfully—how one group could spawn both the Summer of Love and the Blank Generation. As I write, gazing out the window onto West 52nd Street, where bebop clubs like the Three Deuces were ripped down to make way for international banking concerns, it dawns on me that, although certain aspects of today's culture would be unthinkable without the Beats, their world is gone forever. Just as Bickford's and other Beat hangouts have vanished, the days are over when one might bump into Allen Ginsberg at Odessa on Avenue A or steal an upward glance at the Bunker on the Bowery, wondering if William Burroughs is inside. But, of course, what the Beats left behind—the words and philosophies of a forward-thinking and dangerous few—will forever propel us into the new.

Acknowledgments

JUST AS IT IS THE INTENTION of this book to give voice to several behind-the-scenes players in the Beat saga, there are many people whose names you won't find on the table of contents but who really made this book happen. Thanks to Hyperion's Robert Miller, who cheered on

the idea from the beginning, and Leigh Haber, who helped to make it a reality. Our agent Sarah Lazin also gave encouragement from the get-go. The book would not have been possible without my hard-working Rolling Stone Press staff, Shawn Dahl, Ann Abel and Carrie Smith or ROLLING STONE's Jann S. Wenner, Kent Brownridge, John Lagana and Evelyn Bernal. Others who were integral to our endeavors include Tom Gogola, Susan Yusef, Ann Zeidner, Tim Siefert, Fred Woodward, Gail Anderson, Bob Love, M.C. Marden and Irina Reyn. Going out of their way to help us were Ben and Dianne Fong-Torres, John McCormick, Beverly Hennessey, Daphne Holmes, Mellon, Joanna McClure, Brian Hassett, James Austin, Brenda Knight, Billy Altman, Claudio Campuzano, Don Paul, Tom Clark, Jeffrey Smith, Bob Rosenthal, Sterling Lord, James Grauerholz, Tobias Perse and Ted Kim at Kim's Video. And, of course, kudos to the astonishing writers and photographers who have been so enthusiastic about — and inspirational to — this book. On a personal note, I'm grateful to John Everhart for introducing me to the Beat philosophy and work when I was sixteen years old—I've still got my original, dogeared copy of *On the Road!*—to Martha and Alvis George for giving me the Map, and especially to Robert and Jack Warren for traveling the road with me.

—HOLLY GEORGE-WARREN
March 1999

THE ROLLING STONE

Book of the Beats

THE BEAT GENERATION AND AMERICAN CULTURE

PART I

The Birth of Beat

Jack Kerouac (left) and Neal Cassady
(right) with garage mechanic,
San Jose, California, 1952

The City Where the Beats
Were Moved to Howl

BY ANN DOUGLAS

GROWING UP IN NEW JERSEY, I plotted getaways. At seventeen, in June 1959, just after I was expelled from high school, I dyed my hair black, caught a New York–bound train and checked into a YWCA near Times Square under an assumed name. To my eyes, Times Square looked like a party, a party for all the people not invited to the other parties —this was the place where anonymity turned into excitement. When the detective my stepfather had hired found me in my room at the Y a few days later, I was armed with *On the Road*, "Howl" and a Gideon Bible, verging on what I hoped was existentialist psychosis and planning my career as a Beat outcast.

After I returned home, my life took a different direction. In the fall of 1960, I went to Harvard, a place without "beatniks," as authorities had recently informed the *New York Post*, because of "the impossibility of remaining at Harvard and being 'beat' at the same time." But there has always been another life, the one I began near Times Square, which has persisted in reshaping and disrupting my plans. Besides, I wasn't mistaken; being beat did mean making assignations with New York City.

In fact, the founders of the Beat movement, Allen Ginsberg, Jack Kerouac and their first mentor, William S. Burroughs, picked up the word "beat" in Times Square in the mid-1940s, from

Hal Chase, Jack Kerouac, Allen Ginsberg and William S. Burroughs (from left) *hanging out on Manhattan's Upper West Side, circa 1946*
ALLEN GINSBERG COLLECTION

Herbert Huncke, a junkie and, later, a Beat writer himself. They interpreted the word differently— Ginsberg and Kerouac said it meant exhausted, poor, beatific, while Burroughs, a master ironist, used it as a verb, meaning to steal or con. For all of them, however, it spelled a revolution in manners, one that made hitchhiking, jazz, gender-bending, left-wing attitude and high-style low life *de rigueur* for anyone aspiring to hipster status.

Refusing censorship or conventional revision, Kerouac and Ginsberg called their free-form, highly autobiographical style "spontaneous bop prosody" and advertised its affinities with the other path-breaking experiments in expressionist subjectivity going on in the city at the same time —Charlie Parker's improvisational sound, Jackson Pollock's explosive canvases and Marlon Brando's turbulent Method acting. For the Beats, too, art was charisma. They, too, came to New York from the provinces, and found in the city their impetus.

"What a great city New York is!" Kerouac, born to immigrant French-Canadian parents in Lowell, Massachusetts, wrote a friend in 1947. "We are living at just the right time—Johnson and his London, Balzac and his Paris, Socrates and his Athens—the same thing again."

Burroughs was a refugee from the "life-proof houses" of suburban St. Louis. In his novel *Queer*, he explained that he was drawn to New York, as to Mexico City, because it was a "terminal of space-time travel." In other cities, "you are exactly so much dead meat," but "by the fact of being" in New York at all, "you are traveling."

Ginsberg, raised in an immigrant Russian household in Paterson, New Jersey, learned his craft amid the city's "Vast human wilderness/ Houses uplifted like hives off/the stone floor of the world."

When the three men met in 1944, they were just starting their careers. Ginsberg was an eager, intense seventeen-year-old freshman at Columbia; he rushed around the city "in a perpetual sweat of emotional activity," as Kerouac put it,

brimming and flooding over with thoughts, delights, perplexities, catastrophes and discoveries.

The dazzlingly handsome and sweet-natured Jack Kerouac, a star athlete, had dropped out of Columbia at twenty in 1942 to work odd jobs and write. People found themselves telling him their life stories and secret thoughts in minute detail, mythologizing, confessing, sure he would never judge or condemn them. He hoped to capture the "ecstatic tomfoolery" of the age in a series of "true story novels."

Burroughs, at thirty, thin, poker-faced and impeccably eccentric, was studying the city's night life and developing his reputation as a connoisseur of horror. "I'm apparently some kind of agent from another planet," he told Kerouac, "but I haven't got my orders decoded yet." The group soon converged at 421 West 118th Street, the apartment of Kerouac's girlfriend, Edie Parker, where they talked for days and nights at a time, putting on impromptu psychodramas and improvising fresh identities from an intoxicating mix of Spenglerian gloom and absurdist comic timing.

In the mid-1940s, New York City was emerging from World War II, glittering with power, the most important metropolis in the world. For the Beats, however, this public New York, the "capital of capitalism," as the historian Kenneth Jackson has called it, soon to be decked out with dozens of new steel-and-glass, slab-and-square modernist office buildings and caught in a tightening noose of expressways, was the mock-sinister mask of a new, frightening American empire. In his exuberant jeremiad "Howl" (1956), Ginsberg apostrophized it as "Moloch whose buildings are judgment!," a "sphinx of cement and aluminum," devouring its young.

The neighborhoods that gave the Beats their inspiration were the ones then visibly on a downward slide: the Upper West Side of Amsterdam and Columbus avenues, where the first SRO opened in 1939; Harlem's vagrant streets and jazz clubs and, of course, Times Square, once the heart of the posh theater district, but now a honky-tonk of peep shows, seedy all-night cafeterias and porno movie houses, all catering to a host of servicemen, drug addicts, petty thieves and male and female prostitutes.

Interested in downward, not upward, mobility, the Beats were among the first to grasp the nature of the city's new fascination. New York's influence was expanding just as its economic and political health was declining. In 1943 a commission had reported that New York was economically outmoded and overextended, a victim of premature obsolescence, with spreading "ghost" neighborhoods. The growing defense industry favored the towns and cities of the South and the West Coast. Manufacturers, jobs and the white middle classes moved to the suburbs, themselves heavily subsidized by the funds the federal government took away from the cities.

As prosperous whites left, however, poor people of color arrived: 375,000 blacks came to New York between 1940 and 1960, and the number of Puerto Ricans more than quadrupled. East Harlem between 90th and 125th Streets was known as "El Barrio," and Spanish became the city's second language.

Under Mayor William O'Dwyer in the mid-1940s, the rackets took back City Hall. Crime rates soared. This was the Beats' New York, the crossroads of "mongrel America," as Kerouac called it, a *film noir* kingdom rife with farce and catastrophe. In their eyes, the city's vitality lay in its subterranean life of creative decay, its status as a place, in Ginsberg's words, "too vast to know, too/myriad windowed to govern." The Beats aspired to be at the bottom of the world looking up; the angelic could never be separated from the sordid.

Perhaps appropriately, the Beat movement began with a story of ruin and decline, a murder case that made the front page of

the *New York Times* as well as the *Daily News*, and inspired the circle's first literary efforts. About 3:00 a.m., on August 14, 1944, after a night of heavy drinking, a Columbia sophomore named Lucien Carr killed David Kammerer, a thirty-three-year-old gay man, in Riverside Park at the base of 115th Street; Carr stabbed Kammerer in the heart with his Boy Scout knife, then rolled his body into the Hudson River.

Carr, the son of a distinguished St. Louis family, was an intimate friend of Ginsberg, Kerouac and Burroughs. Kammerer was also a member of their circle. On that fateful August night, as the friends entered their favorite haunt, the West End bar on Broadway between 113th and 114th streets, a hit song of the summer, "You Always Hurt the One You Love," was playing on the jukebox.

When Carr turned himself in, no one could believe that this "slender, studious" young man, as he was described in the *Times*, had killed anyone. But Carr re-enacted the crime for the police, and Kammerer's body was shortly discovered floating off 108th Street. Carr spent his time in police custody reading the poetry of Rimbaud and Yeats.

The *Daily News* called the crime an "honor slaying." Kammerer, a former teacher, also from a well-to-do St. Louis family, had fallen desperately in love with the arrestingly handsome Carr when Carr was a student in one of his classes. Although Carr was not gay, in 1943 Kammerer followed him to New York. There, Kammerer drifted toward derelict status, doing odd jobs for the superintendent at 48 Morton Street in Greenwich Village in exchange for a room.

At the trial, Carr, who had a girlfriend at Barnard, claimed self-defense: The older and far larger man was trying to rape him. He pleaded guilty to manslaughter and served two years in an upstate New York reformatory, emerging in 1946 sobered, stouter, with an unbecoming mustache, as if determined to bury his beauty from sight.

Burroughs, a close friend of Kammerer's, had

told Carr not to blame himself—Kammerer "demanded" the fate he met. Yet, while none of his circle thought Carr was homosexual, they noted that he hadn't discouraged Kammerer's attentions. Indeed, the brilliant Carr, a self-declared aficionado of Mephistopheles, took a perverse pride in Kammerer's abject state, taunting him yet never forbidding him his company. "If he doesn't love me," Kammerer asked a friend, "then why is he always around me?"

Although Carr was not himself a writer—he had "the vision," Kerouac realized, "but not the method"—Carr served as a muse to his friends, who at once wrote stories about Kammerer's death. Kerouac and Burroughs collaborated on a hard-boiled, sensational narrative in the manner of Dashiell Hammett, sardonically titled *And the Hippos Were Boiled in Their Tanks,* which no New York publisher would touch.

Ginsberg submitted a chapter of his novel in progress to his writing professor at Columbia, only to find himself summoned to the office of the dean, who expressly forbade him to write on the subject. Columbia wanted no more bad publicity. James Baldwin's second novel, *Giovanni's Room* (1956), was partly inspired by the case, but the accounts of Kerouac, Burroughs and Ginsberg remain unpublished, part of the city's secrets. (Carr went on to become a reporter and an assistant managing editor for United Press International in New York; he is now retired. He is the father of the novelist Caleb Carr.)

New York afforded the Beats more than scandal. In 1948 Ginsberg moved into El Barrio, to a brownstone apartment at 321 East 121st Street (a block later razed to make way for John S. Roberts High School and the Robert F. Wagner Houses, a public apartment complex). Less than a year before, he had reluctantly authorized the lobotomy of his hopelessly psychotic mother, Naomi, at Pilgrim State Hospital on Long Island; Naomi would be the subject of his

greatest poem, "Kaddish" (1961). Engaged in a painfully frustrating affair with Neal Cassady, Ginsberg had not yet finished his course work at Columbia; friends felt he was beginning to crack.

One July afternoon, as Ginsberg was lying on his bed by the open window, masturbating and reading Blake, he heard a prophetic, tender voice. He knew at once that it was Blake speaking, telling him to "cultivate the terror, get right into it." A series of intolerable, bright visions began; "the top of my head came off," he said later, "letting in the rest of the universe." The buildings outside his window, the entire city, became a living thing.

At the Columbia Bookstore the next day, a fresh revelation hit him: "Everybody knew. Everybody knew completely everything." Everyone was aware of the "great unconscious running between all of us," but adopted masks to hide it. Convinced that he had seen God, he called his psychiatrist to tell him what had happened; the doctor hung up on him. Ginsberg had embarked on what would become a major career as a poet-provocateur, remixing the sacred and the profane, seeking the leverage to pry his society loose from its destructive self-deceptions.

Ginsberg stayed in Manhattan, where he died of cancer in April 1997 at the age of seventy in his East Village apartment, but his first and closest friends did not stay there with him. Burroughs, who achieved international fame in the early 1960s with the publication of his novel *Naked Lunch,* settled in 1981 in Lawrence, Kansas, after decades of living in Tangier, Mexico, London and New York; he died in August 1997 at eighty-three in Lawrence.

Kerouac began to travel around the country in 1947. When he was in the city, he spent more and more of his time in Queens with his mother, Gabrielle, first at 133-01 Cross Bay Boulevard in Ozone Park, then at 94-21 134th Street in Richmond Hill. Manhattan still thrilled his soul, he said, but it had begun to "mortify" his heart.

Neal Cassady, whom Kerouac immortalized as Dean Moriarty, the exuberant, fast-talking "jailkid" from Colorado in *On the Road* (1957), first looked him up in Ozone Park in the winter of 1947. When Kerouac opened the door, Cassady plunged into intimacy: "I've come to ask you to show me how to write," he said.

In 1951, standing on Cross Bay Boulevard before the window of a bakery (still there today), Kerouac discovered "sketching," a way of achieving "100 percent personal honesty" by writing down what was right before him, on the spot, as it happened. It was in Queens that Kerouac wrote or rewrote some of his best novels, including *On the Road*, *Visions of Cody*, *The Subterraneans* and *Maggie Cassidy*. Fittingly, on October 23, 1969, the Historic Landmarks Preservation Center of New York placed a plaque with his name on it on 133-01 Cross Bay Boulevard. Despite the enduring devotion of Ginsberg and Carr, Kerouac died of alcoholism in Florida in 1969, a bitter and defeated man. He was forty-seven.

Yet Kerouac always remembered the first days in New York as the happiest of his life. He left a wonderful "true story" vignette of them in *The Town and the City* (1950), his first novel. It is 1946. Kerouac has just come back to town, and Ginsberg is eager to give him a demonstration of the insanity of the postwar city, the result of the "atomic disease" now afflicting America. Radioactive fallout has turned the population into "zombies," Ginsberg says, "locked up in the sad psychoses of themselves." His experiment is to be performance art, madcap mayhem undertaken in the interests of metaphysical hunger and social prophecy.

Ginsberg and Kerouac get on the subway at Times Square. Once seated, Ginsberg holds a newspaper in front of his face and pretends to be reading it. He has torn a hole in the middle of the page, however, and a melancholy old gentleman seated opposite him with his small grandson is soon aware of the "glittering eyes of a madman burning triumphantly into his." Ginsberg has told Kerouac that his "victim" will show signs of "paranoid persecution," and in fact, under Ginsberg's unrelenting gaze, the old man becomes extremely uneasy. Others in the car look pointedly away or assume expressions of outraged indignation.

But, contrary to Ginsberg's prediction, several people, including a man coming home from work, a young student and the grandson, are transfixed with delight at his antics. The little boy jumps up, sticks his face in the hole and stares, pop-eyed, back at Ginsberg. Then he claps his hands and cries, "Do some more, Mister, do some more!"

Soon everyone in the car is laughing. Ginsberg's experiment has apparently backfired; he's been outwitted. But he's not upset. He needed collaborators, not victims, people ready to drop their preconceptions at divine folly's cure, and in New York he has found them.

As a girl, I ran away to be part of the world the Beats were inventing, and living in Manhattan today, I still feel them, co-conspirators with its creative chaos, riding the electric connections that turn the city into a hive of overlapping purposes and fantasies. Catching the hope-and-fear rhythms of their time and place, they paced the streets, "digging" everything one day, bushed and mute on a park bench the next—in Kerouac's words, "storing up for more belief."

VISIONS of PARADISE: "KEROUAC in N.Y.C."

written & illustrated by Rick Bleier

A FOOTBALL SCHOLARSHIP HAD BROUGHT KEROUAC to N.Y.C. in 1939, BUT BY THE EARLY FORTIES, DISENCHANTED with COLUMBIA UNIVERSITY, he BEGAN TO PURSUE MORE *TRENCHANT* EXPLORATIONS in the COMPANY of a UNIQUE GROUP OF INDIVIDUALS.

THESE CHARACTERS, SOON TO BE RECOGNIZED by the WORLD AS the NUCLEUS OF THE BEAT GENERATION, WERE BEGINNING to NURTURE SOME STARTLING (AND WELL-NIGH *HERETICAL*) IDEAS — CHIEF AMONG WHICH was the NAKED/UNBIASED PERCEPTION & EXPERIENCE of both the BEAUTIFUL AND HORRIFIC, FUELED BY a SYSTEMATIC DERANGEMENT of the SENSES...

JACK HAD ALREADY DONE A CONSIDERABLE AMOUNT OF WRITING IN FAIRLY CONVENTIONAL STYLE, BUT NOW BEGAN TO FEARLESSLY BREAK THROUGH ESTABLISHED LITERARY BOUNDARIES TO FORGE A WHOLE NEW SPACE. INFLUENCED BY THE ADVENTUROUS AND OPEN-ENDED SOLOING OF THE NEW JAZZ PIONEERS, SUCH AS CHARLIE PARKER & DIZZY GILLESPIE, KEROUAC RIFFED ON: "FIRST THOUGHT, BEST THOUGHT."

Another aficionado of this music was Denver's own Neal Cassady, a rawboned and rakish young saint who himself aspired to be a writer. Con artist and mad seducer of women and men, car thief and ex-con who'd read Proust in jail, Neal had a brilliant mind and a gentle soul.

KNOCKED OUT BY NEAL'S STREAM-OF-CONSCIOUSNESS LETTERS AND EXTENDED SPEED RAPS, KEROUAC FELT HIS OWN PERCEPTIONS ABOUT WRITTEN EXPRESSION STRETCH FURTHER STILL...

THE TWO BECAME GREAT FRIENDS QUICKLY, RUSHING AROUND the CITY from the VILLAGE TO 52nd STREET and UP TO HARLEM, BLASTING BIG BOMBS OF WEED and DIGGING THEIR HEROES...

YAS! O, BIRD, YOU SWEET SONOFABITCH!

BLOW!

AND NEAL COULD DRIVE; WAS IN FACT the ULTIMATE PURVEYOR of JACK'S DREAMS of the GREAT AMERICAN ROAD: A RUSH to EXPERIENCE the BIG SWOLLEN HEART of EVERYTHING at NERVE-JANGLING & in fact DEATH-DEFYING SPEEDS. NEAL WOULD BECOME DEAN MORIARTY in "ON THE ROAD," a SHINING, GALVANIC MOMENT of LITERARY INSURRECTION that would have UNPRECEDENTED CONSEQUENCE in POSTWAR AMERICA...

AND SO, APART FROM ANY POSSIBILITIES the SITUATION MAY HAVE PRESENTED, AND OF COURSE ATTENDANT KICKS NOTWITHSTANDING, I TOLD HER "I CAN'T HEEL & TOE, I'M DOUBLE-LEFT!" — AH, YOU STILL WITH ME SON?

RIGHT BEHIND YOU, CAP'N!

ALLEN GINSBERG, A YOUNG POET FRIEND of KEROUAC'S from COLUMBIA U., HAD BEEN STUDYING VISIONARY THEOLOGICAL TEXTS WHEN he had a LIFE-CHANGING SATORI — THE VOICE of WILLIAM BLAKE CAME TO HIM, CLEAR & RESONANT, as he GAZED OUT the WINDOW of HIS EAST HARLEM APARTMENT...

"Ah, Sunflower! Weary of time who countest the steps of the sun..."

THESE GUYS SOON ENCOUNTERED ONE WILLIAM S. BURROUGHS, A LACONIC MISSOURIAN and HARVARD GRADUATE WITH A PREDILECTION for GUNS and NARCOTICS. BILL, POSSESSED of a SARDONIC DRY WIT, INTRODUCED JACK and ALLEN TO THE SEAMY UNDERBELLY OF LIFE...

...as exemplified by HERBERT HUNCKE, a CHARMING ADDICT and GAY HUSTLER who'd RECENTLY ENDED A STINT as SEAMAN on an OLD TANKER. HE'D CONNECTED with BILL, WHO NEEDED to UNLOAD a MACHINE-GUN and some MORPHINE SYRETTES.

...THEY'D GATHER AT TIMES SQUARE'S ALL-NIGHT BICKFORD'S, WHERE HUNCKE'D HOLD FORTH AT SOME LENGTH REGARDING HIS DOWNTRODDEN CONDITION...

GENTLEMEN, I AM FUCKING BEAT.

HUNCKE STASHED THE SPOILS OF A RECENT HEIST AT GINSBERG'S YORK AVE. APARTMENT; GINSBERG WOUND UP IN A STOLEN CAR WITH HUNCKE'S FELONIOUS PARTNERS, PURSUED AT WHITE-KNUCKLE SPEEDS by the POLICE.

LORD, GOD OF ISRAEL, ISAAC and ABRAHAM!

THE RESULTS OF THESE EVENTS WERE A 5-YR. SENTENCE FOR HUNCKE and A STINT IN A MENTAL INSTITUTION for ALLEN. It was HERE, AT COLUMBIA-PRESBYTERIAN HOSPITAL, that GINSBERG MET CARL SOLOMAN, to whom HE WOULD DEDICATE HIS GREATEST POEM: "HOWL."

DAY ROOM

O, WELL, YOU'RE NEW HERE.

WAIT AWHILE, GINSBERG, YOU'LL MEET SOME OF THE OTHER REPENTANT MYSTICS.

JACK WOUND UP INCARCERATED AS WELL:

IN AUGUST '44 HE PACED THE CELL OF BRONX COUNTY JAIL, MATERIAL WITNESS TO A SORDID CRIME AND UNABLE TO PERSUADE HIS FATHER TO BAIL HIM OUT.

13

... THE CRIME: — JACK'S PAL LUCIEN CARR, ATTEMPTING TO FEND OFF THE VIOLENTLY AMOROUS MINISTRATIONS OF HIS BOYHOOD SCHOOL-TEACHER DAVID KAMMERER, STABBED THE OLDER MAN TO DEATH AND ROLLED HIS WEIGHTED BODY INTO THE DARK WATERS OF THE HUDSON RIVER. HE THEN VISITED JACK, WHO HELPED HIM DISPOSE OF THE MURDER WEAPON AND KAMMERER'S EYEGLASSES...

OK, WE'RE CLEAR—DROP IT!

Edward G. Robi—
BUY THE BES—

TWO DAYS LATER CARR TURNED HIMSELF IN.

JACK'S WAY OUT: $2500 BAIL-MONEY from the family of his gal EDIE PARKER, IN RETURN FOR WHICH a QUICK MARRIAGE CEREMONY was PERFORMED—FOLLOWED by a PERIOD of EXEMPLARY DULLNESS at the HOME OF HIS NEW IN-LAWS in GROSSE POINTE, EDIE'S MOM BUGGED HIM incessantly...

JACK, YOU WORK SO HARD AT THIS — BUT, I MEAN, DO YOU THINK YOU'LL EVER BE A BEST-SELLING AUTHOR LIKE, SAY, PEARL BUCK?

AGAIN SHE HITS ME WITH PEARL BUCK!

WAS JAIL REALLY SO BAD?

THO KEROUAC FELT COMPELLED TO INVESTIGATE THE "DENSE BALZACIAN HIVE IN A JEWEL POINT," MOST AMERICANS PLEDGED FEALTY TO MORE PROSAIC NOTIONS. HE WOULD ONE DAY WRITE ABOUT THE BLUE-LIGHT SQUARE OF THE UBIQUITOUS TV SCREEN THAT HOVERED IN THE WINDOW OF EVERY MIDDLE-CLASS DWELLING HE PASSED IN THE NIGHT.

JACK FELT HUNCKE'S WORD "BEAT" IMPLIED A RAGGED KIND OF ILLUMINATION, A "STATE OF GRACE" FOR THE DISENFRANCHISED. SURELY SOME HARD-TACK RECOGNITION MUST BE AFFORDED THOSE WHO'D BEEN BEAT BLOODY & LOW...

JACK RETURNED TO NEW YORK, AS HE WOULD CONTINUE TO DO FOR MUCH OF THE REMAINDER OF HIS LIFE. AND AFTER THE BENZEDRINE JAGS AND WEEK-LONG DRUNKS ON THE STREETS OF THE CITY, THERE'D ALWAYS BE THE SANCTITY OF MÉMÈRE'S SWEET LITTLE KITCHEN OUT IN OZONE PARK. HE'D SIT AT THE TYPEWRITER, LISTENING TO TRUCKS BOOM BY IN THE LONG ISLAND NIGHT, KNOCKING AWAY AT A NEW MANUSCRIPT...PERHAPS A SEPULCHRAL CRY, AN UNREQUITED SONG OF LOVE...

BUT AS HE HIMSELF WOULD LATER WRITE, "EVERYTHING BELONGS TO ME BECAUSE I AM POOR."

JACK HOPPED A FREIGHT OUT of L.A.

ON THIS PARTICULAR TRIP TO SAN FRANCISCO KEROUAC MET A QUIET LITTLE BUM WITH WHOM HE SHARED HIS TOKAY WINE; THE OLDTIMER RECIPROCATED WITH A PRAYER BY SAINT TERESA, in which SHE PROMISED ETERNAL SHOWERS OF ROSES FOR ALL LIVING CREATURES.

JACK WAS HEADED FOR A NIGHT OF EPHEMERAL DREAMS ON A LONELY SANTA BARBARA BEACH, FOLLOWED BY A BENNY-ZAPPED 70-MILE-AN-HOUR HITCHHIKE RIDE WITH A GREAT BLONDE IN A JUICEY-RED MERCURY —

...and then the City.....

VISIONS OF PARADISE —
"KEROUAC in SAN FRAN...SCO"

Written & Illustrated
by RICK BLEIER

16

SAN FRANCISCO IN THE EARLY '50s HAD BECOME A MECCA for the NEW SUBTERRANEAN CULTURE, A GREAT BLASTING CONFLUENCE of YOUNG POETS, ARTISTS and HIPSTERS — AND, MUCH TO JACK'S SURPRISE and DELIGHT, OTHER ASPIRING BUDDHISTS; HE'D BELIEVED HIMSELF TO BE ALONE in his APPRECIATION of THESE PREVIOUSLY ARCANE TEXTS and SUTRAS...

GARY SNYDER LIVED A MILE AWAY FROM THE ROSE-COVERED BERKELEY COTTAGE JACK & ALLEN SHARED. HIS BOUNDLESS ENERGIES & PROLIFIC ENTHUSIASMS ENCOMPASSED ANIMALS & INDIAN LORE, MOUNTAINCLIMBING & ORIENTAL MYTHOLOGY AND A SHARP RECOGNITION OF THE OLD WAYS.

HIS TWINKLING EYES LOOKED WITH BEMUSEMENT UPON EVERYTHING AS HE SWUNG HIS BICYCLE AROUND THE HILLS OF THE CITY or LEFT TO A CRAZY LITTLE WINE-INSPIRED JIG: A TRUE MYTHIC *RAPSCALLION* LIKE **OLDMAN COYOTE**...

JACK SPENT HOURS IN SNYDER'S LITTLE SHACK, DRINKING GREEN TEA AND WATCHING IN FASCINATION AS THE YOUNG SCHOLAR TRANSLATED THE THOUSAND -YEAR OLD "COLD MOUNTAIN" POEMS OF HAN SHAN.

SEE HERE, HE SAYS: "NOW MORNING I FACE MY LONE SHADOW, I CAN'T STUDY WITH BOTH EYES FULL OF TEARS."

YEAH. ...YEAH! THATS GREAT!

SNYDER ALSO CHALLENGED JACK TO FORSAKE HIS VOW OF CELIBACY BY INTRODUCING VENTURESOME YOUNG WOMEN WHO WERE EAGER TO PARTICIPATE IN GAMES OF YABYUM.

BUT, UH — PRETTY GIRLS MAKE GRAVES!

O, CMON, KERACKY! LOOSEN UP THAT BUDDHIST SPHINCTER!

SNYDER and KEROUAC WERE PRESENT AT A HISTORIC POETRY READING, tho JACK LIMITED HIS PARTICIPATION to COLLECTING WINE MONEY and HOLLERING ENCOURAGEMENT to his COMPADRES...

GO! GO! GO!

EVERYONE IN ATTENDANCE AT THE 6 GALLERY READING ON OCT. 13 1955 FELT THAT THESE YOUNG 'ARCHITECTS OF THE NEW POESY' HAD TRULY UPPED THE ANTE ~ IT WAS A PIVOTAL MOMENT FOR AMERICAN LETTERS, CHARACTERIZED MOST DRAMATICALLY BY GINSBERG'S DYNAMIC PERFORMANCE OF "HOWL"...

"I SAW THE BEST MINDS OF MY GENERATION DESTROYED BY MADNESS..."

~ OVER IN NORTH BEACH ON COLUMBUS AVENUE, POET AND PAINTER LAWRENCE FERLINGHETTI HAD OPENED THE CITY LIGHTS BOOK-STORE, THE VERY FIRST SHOP TO SELL PAPER-BOUND BOOKS EXCLUSIVELY. LAWRENCE PUBLISHED MANY OF THE "NEW RENAISSANCE" POETS —INCLUDING ALLEN GINSBERG & GREGORY CORSO— AT AFFORDABLE PRICES.

CITY LIGHTS BOOKS

BOOKS

OTHER EXUBERANT VOICES WERE PART OF THE WEST COAST POETRY SCENE AT THE TIME. MICHAEL McCLURE, WHO KEROUAC DESCRIBED AS HAVING THE HANDSOMENESS OF "A MYTHIC BILLY THE KID," HAD BEEN INFLUENCED BY ABSTRACT EXPRESSIONISM AND WOULD WRITE WILD LYRICAL POESY in "BEAST LANGUAGE."

PHILIP WHALEN, GARY'S PAL FROM OREGON, WOULD BECOME A ZEN MONK, AND WRITE HIS POEMS FROM THE PARTICULARITY OF THAT PERSPECTIVE. . . .

HIS STATED VISION WAS TO FREE THE WORD 'FUCK' FROM ITS CHAINS. . .

CITY LIGHTS' PUBLICATION OF "HOWL" RESULTED IN A WELL-PUBLICIZED "OBSCENITY" TRIAL WHICH VINDICATED ALLEN & LAWRENCE — BUT THIS, IN ADDITION TO A "LIFE" MAGAZINE PROFILE THAT DEALT SHALLOWLY WITH THE BEATS AND THEIR WORK, ENGENDERED CARICATURES & DERISIVE ATTENTION — BUSLOADS OF TOURISTS CAME TO SAN FRANCISCO TO SEE THE "BEATNIKS"

This was a happy time for Kerouac, as evidenced by his participation in Snyder's "Rucksack Revolution". The two climbed Matterhorn, and Kerouac would capture the breathless spirit of the adventures on the mountain in "The Dharma Bums".

C'MON, TIGER — "WHEN YOU GET TO THE TOP OF A MOUNTAIN --- KEEP CLIMBING!"

OH MAN, THIS IS TOO DAMN HIGH!

...Those passages fairly ring with the borderless possibilities of rock & sky, climaxing with Jack's great "Zen" revelation:

YOU CAN'T FALL OFF A MOUNTAIN!

AFTER GARY SNYDER LEFT SAN FRANCISCO to STUDY at a JAPANESE MONASTERY, KEROUAC HIKED OFF to WASHINGTON to TAKE GARY'S OLD GIG as a FIRE LOOKOUT on DESOLATION PEAK. ~ LIKE HIS ARTISTIC FOREBEARS VINCENT VAN GOGH and THOMAS WOLFE, KEROUAC BELIEVED HIS MOST PROFOUNDLY WROUGHT ACTIVITIES to EXIST ONLY in the MARGINS of OTHER PEOPLE'S LIVES. ~

FOR A MAN SO LONELY as JACK KEROUAC, a GREAT and PROLIFIC ARTIST WHOSE PASSIONS for LIFE REMAINED UNREQUITED, a SEASON of "DESOLATION in SOLITUDE" WAS DEEPLY DISTURBING... a COMBINATION of ECSTATIC VISIONS and WAKING HORRIFIC NIGHTMARES...

JACK GAZED at the DARK LOOMING PEAK of NEIGHBORING MOUNT HOZOMEEN and SAW the BLACKEST PART of HIS OWN SOUL. ~~

JACK WOULD RETURN to THE CITY.
the RELEASE of "ON THE ROAD" WOULD BRING HIM INOTORIETY as "KING of the BEATS"...

BUT the RESPECTABILITY & ACCEPTANCE he LONGED FOR, recognition as a HARD-WORKING & VISIONARY MAN of LETTERS, WOULD ELUDE HIM FOR THE REST of HIS LIFE.

Abstract Expression:
From Bird to Brando

BY BRIAN HASSETT

Fire lights and smoking nights
And splashes of dripping paint;
Jazz explosions and constant commotions
Leave It to Beaver this ain't.

—B. H., July, 1998

IT WAS THE HALFTIME SHOW OF THE CENTURY!
1945 to 1955.
"We're gonna rock the rock in the second half."
Or we're all gonna die.

Life was pretty uncertain after two world wars and two
atomic bombs in too little time. By 1945, it could go
either way and everybody knew it. Edward R. Murrow was
on the wireless delivering poetic nightly accounts of the
bombing of Europe. Centuries-old nations were tumbling by
the month. Blackouts, rationing and depression were a way of
life. The end was surely near. But leaning forward into this tension wind were some courageous artists transforming their
media into gloriously honest expressions of the furthest and
sometimes most beautiful reaches of our mind.

Through a door opened by Freud and into a room lit by
Jung, Reich, Stanislavsky, Breton and others, the expression of
the subconscious self, the center, the soul, the truth, became
the new goal of artists all over the world, some who happened
to be drinking together, and others who were drinking alone.

During the same years that Jack Kerouac was blowing
apart the novel and Allen Ginsberg the poem, Jackson Pollock
was exploding canvases on Long Island, Charlie Parker was
breaking the sound barrier on 52nd Street, and Marlon
Brando was ripping his chest open on Broadway. In nextdoor
Midtown, it was television's Golden Age with *Your Show of
Shows* inventing live sketch comedy and *Kraft Television Theatre*

*Charlie Parker Quintet gigging at the Three Deuces on
West 52nd Street, New York City, fall 1947; Tommy Potter,
Parker, Miles Davis, Duke Jordan* (from left)

FRANK DRIGGS COLLECTION

live weekly drama. Surfing the last of the vanishing vaudeville nightspots, Lord Buckley and Lenny Bruce were cutting their teeth before cutting the edge of stand-up comedy. And several new publications began appearing, from the *Village Voice* to *Playboy*, bringing the edge to the middle of the country.

In 1945 Jackson Pollock moved away from the nightly Village bar scene—with Franz Kline, Willem de Kooning, Frank O'Hara and roomfuls of other boozehounds—and out to the seclusion of a farmhouse in Springs, Long Island, to begin his dripping live-action paintings. Where he came up with the idea is anybody's guess, since the tormented alcoholic abstractionist was notoriously uncommunicative about his process. His sculptor-friend Constantine Nivola could at least explain the lead-up: "It was the Surrealists, such as Breton, who had the idea of releasing the tension in painting without any preconceived notions, letting the spontaneity do the actual painting." Pollock just took the idea to outer space. Or inner space. If you stand in front of one of his dripping paintings and stare into it for a while you can take a long, strange trip without ever leaving the gallery. Somehow in the subconscious rhythms of Pollock's trance dance, he created a mirror of our mind, patterns out of chaos and motion out of stillness.

"It was great drama," photographer/filmmaker Hans Namuth said of watching him work. "The flame of explosion when the paint hit the canvas; the dancelike movement; the eyes tormented before knowing where to strike next; the tension; then the explosion again."

"When I am *in* my painting, I am not aware of what I'm doing," Pollock once said. When another brilliant Abstract Expressionist Hans Hofmann asked him about the use of nature in his work, he answered, "I *am* nature."

It was this firm belief in the natural flow of self that was propelling so many of these daring young artists in their flying seat pants. And remember—this was an era when gray was the color, vanilla the flavor, conformity the goal and McCarthyism the disease. To many of those in this newly military-trained generation, the slightest deviation in hair length or hemline meant you were a communist.

In November 1945, the same month Pollock moved into the barn on Long Island, Charlie Parker moved into the WOR Studios in Midtown Manhattan to lay down some abstract expression of his own in what Savoy Records not unjustly called "the greatest recording session in modern jazz." The first session ever under Parker's own name featured a little combo including Dizzy Gillespie, Miles Davis and Max Roach.

What Bird, Diz, Miles, Thelonious Monk and others had been working on the last few years of Monday night jam sessions at Minton's Playhouse in Harlem and the clubs along 52nd Street was the first big break in jazz since Louis Armstrong stretched the solo in his Hot Five and Hot Seven sessions in the mid-Twenties. By improvising a new melody line based on the existing chords of thirty-two-bar popular songs like "I've Got Rhythm," "Sweet Georgia Brown" and "How High the Moon," and often playing at double the tempo of the rhythm section, these bop-blazers created an unprecedented "skidilibee-la-bee you,—oo,—e bop she-bam," as Doctor Kerouac so accurately diagnosed it in his essay "The Beginning of Bop."

Considered "almost telepathic" by even the most reserved jazz journals, Bird's frenetic speed carried him into the unknown every night, relying on the same subconscious instinctual current that Pollock was channeling. And this complete commitment to intuition was about to revolutionize American theater.

Get this: The original 1898 production of Chekhov's first play, *The Seagull*, bombed so badly he vowed never to write another play. Then a young director named Konstantin Stanislavsky came along with some wacky new idea about actors improvising from their own experience to fully convey the psychology of the characters, and begged Chekhov for the rights to re-stage the play. This pivotal production heralded the birth of both the Moscow Art Theatre and the Stanislavsky "Method," while giving the playwright Anton Chekhov the encouragement to go on and write a few more plays you may have heard of.

Flip ahead to December 1947, New York City, and *A Streetcar Named Desire* with Marlon Brando is opening on Broadway. *This* pivotal Elia Kazan production heralded the birth of both the Actors Studio and the Method in American theater, while giving the playwright Tennessee Williams the encouragement to go on and write a few more plays you may have heard of.

Stella Adler described *Streetcar's* lead and Greenwich Village resident Brando as "the perfect marriage of intuition and intelligence," but she could have been talking about any of these ice-breakers of the American art-ic.

Stanislavsky's tenet was: "You must live the part every moment you are playing it." Like Bird, Jackson and Jack. Rather than rely on perfect diction or posture, actors were encouraged to channel the center of their soul. The frame of dialogue was only a canvas to fill in from the actor's own experience.

And this same self-reliant philosophy was taking hold all over New York City. In 1950, with network television barely five years old, Sid Caesar and a few friends came up with this wild idea to do a funny ninety-minute skit-driven show on Saturday night *live* on NBC. For the next four years, televised sketch comedy was being pioneered on *Your Show of Shows,* with such writers as Woody Allen, Neil Simon and Mel Brooks first getting their pens wet.

That same year, Lord Buckley, the wailinest Beat comedian there ever was, was getting ready to hit the road after five years of developing his improvisational hipster style in New York's dives and dying vaudeville halls. Telling stories in his hipsemantic rap he'd "recast incidents from history and mythology into a patois that blended scat-singing, black jive and the King's English," in the words of biographer Oliver Trager.

"Lord Buckley's a secret thing you pass under the table," Ken Kesey once explained of Buckley's lack of name recognition, even though his influence ranges from George Carlin to Jerry Garcia. "Lord Buckley and Grateful Dead philosophy merge in a certain irony of viewpoint," Garcia told Trager. "The way he did his show was very dramatic. It would start off like a regular stand-up routine, but . . . it really turned into kind of a primal experience. A very powerful style with a lot of magic. You can't act it. You have to think of yourself as 'Lord Buckley.' "

In December 1950, Kerouac received "The Big Letter"—Neal Cassady's famous thirteen-thousand word Joan Anderson/Cherry Mary epic (brought jazzily to the screen in 1997 as *The Last Time I Committed Suicide*)—which would change Jack's approach to writing. "I have renounced fiction and fear," he wrote Cassady right back. "There is nothing to do but write the truth." And within a few months he'd finished *On the Road* in a single twenty-day stretch on a single roll of tracing paper in a single paragraph.

To best describe the derivation of his technique, Jack honored his friend Allen's request to write his "Essentials of Spontaneous Prose":

> *Time being of the essence in the purity of speech, sketching language is undisturbed flow from the mind of personal secret idea-words, "blowing" (as per jazz musician) on subject of image ... Write "without consciousness" in semi-trance (as Yeats's later "trance writing") ... Begin not from preconceived idea of what to say about image but from*

jewel center of interest in subject of image at "moment" of writing, and write outwards swimming in sea of language to peripheral release and exhaustion ... Struggle to sketch the flow that already exists intact in mind. Don't think of words when you stop but to see picture better.

And speaking of seeing better: That same year, the revered *Brave New World* author, Aldous Huxley, first took mescaline and wrote a vivid and valuable account of it in *The Doors of Perception*. Louis Armstrong was an old teahead of time, Bird a heroin addict, Jack, Jackson and Tennessee hard liquor drinkers, but this was a whole new trip. Huxley's detailed and "inexpressibly wonderful" account of exploring the amplified mind opened The Doors for the psychedelic revolution shimmering just around a corner on Haight Street.

In 1953 yet another scholarly study appeared, sparking an even better revolution—Dr. Alfred Kinsey's *Sexual Behavior in the Human Female*—whispering in science that a quarter of all married women had extramarital affairs and most women had multiple premarital partners. Ozzie was aghast and Harriet blushed, but the secret was out. Sex *was* happening. As part of his research, Kinsey met with Tennessee Williams, went to see *Streetcar* and studied the actors' sexual backgrounds. Earlier, for his *Sexual Behavior in the Human Male* (1948), he even employed the Beats' number-one hustler Herbert Huncke, to round up subjects, two of which were Ginsberg and Burroughs. Too bad Cassady lived in San Francisco.

In 1954, a nineteen-year-old Elvis Presley passed through the doors of the Sun studio and the whole world snuck in behind him. Brando won an Oscar for *On the Waterfront* the same year he appeared nationwide as the leather-clad leader of a motorcycle gang called the Beetles in *The Wild One*. The possibilities of commercial acceptability were changing forever.

By '55, the rockets of the renaissance began going off like fireworks: James Dean's disaffected hipster goes drag-racing with trouble in *Rebel Without a Cause*; Rod Serling's "Patterns" wins an Emmy as he begins tweaking the summit of our imagination; the *Village Voice* and a new journalism appear; Chuck Berry goes cruisin' with "Maybellene," Little Richard lets everybody know he's "Tutti Frutti" all rootti and *Billboard* begins tracking its first Pop chart; Marilyn's white dress goes whoosh in *The Seven Year Itch* and the first birth-control pills start working; Jack writes *Mexico City Blues* in a month, giving it the inscription, "I want to be considered a jazz poet blowing a long blues in an afternoon jam session on Sunday"; Burroughs starts nibbling on his *Naked Lunch*, Ferlinghetti snaps a few *Pictures of the Gone World*, Ginsberg begins to "Howl" at the Six Gallery reading; and the *On the Road* fame train is still two years away.

From Pollock's swirling strokes to splashing color screen-savers, from Brando reaching New York audiences with *A Streetcar Named Desire* to Bravo reaching nationwide living rooms with *Inside the Actors Studio*, from Jack's punctuation-liberated prose to the abbreviated brevity of online language, from Ginsberg freely howling to Richie Havens howling "Freedom," the commitment to spontaneous subconscious expression of this pivotal mid-century decade intuited our new millennial lives in ways still being improvised.

Beat Jazz:
The Real Thing

BY JOHN SWENSON

WHILE COLUMBIA UNDERGRAD Jack Kerouac was partying in a 118th Street apartment with Allen Ginsberg, William Burroughs and Lucien Carr in 1944, developing the "New Vision" that would later define what Kerouac called "the Beat Generation," a revolution in black American music was taking place down the block at Minton's Playhouse, a club on 118th Street next to the Cecil Hotel, a popular spot for visiting black entertainers.

The Minton's Monday house band, started in 1941 by former bandleader Teddy Hill and powered by the radical all-out polyrhythmic drumming of Kenny "Klook" Clarke, playing the compositions of the visionary Thelonious Monk and featuring what amounted to gladiatorial combat among many of the greatest soloists in jazz history, including alto saxophonist Charlie Parker and trumpeter Dizzy Gillespie, had upset the apple cart of swing music and ventured into a brave new world with the disarmingly comic name of bebop. At Minton's, and in the midtown clubs centered around 52nd Street —the Spotlight Club, the Three Deuces, Birdland etc.— bebop transformed jazz from the mainstream pop music it had been during the war to an occult science.

The Beats would go on to embrace bop as the soundtrack to their own revolution. Though the backgrounds of the two groups of people were far different, their goals were similar. In the aftermath of a World War II culture that made nonconformity a crime, the beboppers and the Beats shared a revulsion for the status quo, a desire to challenge the artistic complacency of the era and the new ideas to do something about it.

That same year, 1944, another student arrived in New York with new ideas and a fondness for jazz. Miles Davis was an eighteen-year-old trumpeter from a well-to-do East St. Louis black family. Davis came to New York to study at Juilliard, but his real education was going to come from bop pioneers Dizzy Gillespie and Charlie Parker.

Davis found out right away that Minton's was "the black jazz capital of the world . . . It was the music laboratory for bebop. After it polished up at Minton's, *then* it went downtown to 52nd Street —the Three Deuces, the Onyx and Kelly's Stable —where white people heard it," said Davis. "But what has to be understood in all of this is no matter how good the music sounded down on 52nd Street, it wasn't as hot or as innovative as it was uptown at Minton's. The idea was that you had to calm the innovation down for the white folks because they couldn't handle the *real* thing. Now, don't get me wrong, there were good white people who were brave enough to come up to Minton's. But they were few and far between."

Kerouac, who lived across 118th Street from Minton's, certainly could handle the real thing. He had come to New York with an ear for rhythm and an advocate's enthusiasm for jazz. In 1940, while he was a student at Horace Mann prep school in Riverdale, Kerouac arranged to interview jazz critic George Avakian at a nightclub in Greenwich Village and went to see the Jimmy Lunceford Orchestra at the Apollo.

One of Kerouac's first published pieces was a review of *The Decca Chicago Style Album* in the

Dizzy Gillespie recording, 1945
FRANK DRIGGS COLLECTION

Horace Mann school paper. "Most of today's swing is a sensationalized carbon copy of jazz!" Kerouac complained. "It lacks both purity and sincerity."

Kerouac's description of "real jazz" reads like an auto-analysis of his own prose style: "Music which has not been pre-arranged—free-for-all ad lib. It is the outburst of passionate musicians, who pour all their energy into their instruments in the quest for soulful expression and super-improvisation."

If it were a *Jeopardy* question, followers of Beat culture would say that Kerouac was writing about Charlie Parker. But it was Lester Young, the profoundly influential tenor saxophonist with the Count Basie band, who epitomized "real jazz" to Kerouac at the time.

Kerouac's romanticized vision of jazz drew some justified criticism that he was being patronizing to dedicated artists who had hammered out a new form of great technical complexity. Jazz wasn't just random emotion any more than Kerouac was just blindly hitting the keys on his typer and hoping words would come out. Nor was Parker's art just energy—the young Parker was thrown out of a jam session in Kansas City for not having his chops together. Yet he was a spontaneous compositional genius at his best, as another anecdote related by Miles Davis in his autobiography proves.

Davis was recounting a gig at the Three Deuces on 52nd Street in 1947. Though Parker was the band leader, he hadn't shown up for any rehearsals the week before the gig.

"When it's time for the band to hit, he asks, 'What are we playing?'" Davis recounts. "I tell him. He nods, counts off the beat and plays every motherfucking tune in the exact key we had rehearsed it in. He played like a motherfucker. Didn't miss one beat, one note, didn't play out of key all night. It was something. We were fucking amazed. And every time he'd look at us looking at

him all shocked and shit, he'd just smile that 'Did you ever doubt this?' kind of smile."

At this time, 1947, bop was going like mad all over America ... bop was somewhere between its Charlie Parker "Ornithology" period and another period that began with Miles Davis. And... I sat there listening to that sound of the night which bop has come to represent for all of us...
— JACK KEROUAC

In his masterful biography of Kerouac, *Desolate Angel*, Dennis McNally gave a perfect description of the influence black music had on Kerouac's psyche. "Blues truth seized Jack," McNally wrote, "ripped him out of the white world, made him companion to Ishmael and Huck Finn, thrust him into the twilight land between the races."

In *Kerouac*, Ann Charters offered an excellent description of Kerouac's artistic relationship to jazz. "Jack...identified more with musical geniuses like Bud Powell, Charlie Parker, Billie Holiday, Lester Young, Gerry Mulligan and Thelonious Monk than he did with any established literary scene, and of all the books he ever wrote, *Mexico City Blues* is most directly related to jazz. Bop was to Kerouac a new art form that had broken through to eloquence. His own method of spontaneous composition was meant to do the same thing with words that he heard bop musicians doing with their instruments. When Miles Davis played, Kerouac heard his trumpet sounding long sentences like Marcel Proust."

Jazz illuminates *On the Road*, which features numerous references to specific shows Kerouac attended and records he and others were listening to. Most important, the music is contextualized in a wide range of emotional responses. When Kerouac encounters the Okie family at harvest time he expresses the scene in a musical image:

My mind was filled with that great song "Lover

Man" as Billie Holiday sings it; I had my own concert in the bushes. "Someday we'll meet, and you'll dry all my tears, and whisper sweet, little things in my ear, hugging and a-kissing, oh what we've been missing, Lover Man, oh where can you be ..." It's not the words so much as the great harmonic tune and the way Billie sings it, like a woman stroking her man's hair in soft lamplight. The winds howled. I got cold.

Later, Kerouac writes about listening to a wild bop record, "The Hunt," a saxophone battle between Dexter Gordon and Wardell Gray. The record is a metaphor for the renewed vitality of adventure associated with his reunification with Dean Moriarty. In New York, Kerouac and Dean go to see George Shearing at Birdland, a show reviewed vividly in the book:

Shearing came out, blind, led by the hand to the keyboard. He was a distinguished-looking English-

man ... the bass player leaned to him reverently and thrummed the beat. The drummer, Denzil Best, sat motionless except for his wrists snapping the brushes. And Shearing began to rock; a smile broke over his ecstatic face; he began to rock in the piano seat, back and forth, slowly at first, then the beat went up, and he began rocking fast, his left foot jumped up with every beat, his neck began to rock crookedly, he brought his face down to the keys, he pushed his hair back, his combed hair dissolved, he began to sweat. The music picked up ...

The classically trained Shearing used a unique locked-hand technique in which he phrased chords without changing the spatial relationship between his left and right hands, as all syncopated piano players did. Kerouac brilliantly describes the moment of recognition in the audience when Shearing's trademark approach takes over:

Shearing began to play his chords; they rolled out of

BEBOP DISCOGRAPHY

The following recordings are representative of the bebop Kerouac, Cassady and their buddies were digging.

Count Basie	*The Original American Decca Recordings (1937-39)*	GRP, 1992
Ornette Coleman	*The Shape of Jazz to Come*	1959; Atlantic, 1996
John Coltrane	*My Favorite Things*	1960; Jazz Hour, 1992
Miles Davis	*The Birth of the Cool*	1948–50; Blue Note, 1998
Slim Gaillard	*Slim's Jam*	1945–46; Drive Archive, 1996
Stan Getz	*Diz and Getz*	1953; Verve, N.A.
Dizzy Gillespie	*Groovin' High*	1945–53; Savoy, 1996
Dizzy Gillespie	*Shaw 'Nuff*	1946; Musicraft, 1987
Lionel Hampton	*Midnight Sun*	1946–53; GRP, 1993
Billie Holiday	*Billie Holiday's Greatest Hits*	1944–49; Decca Jazz, 1995
Jimmie Lunceford	*Swingsation*	1934–38; GRP, 1998
Jay McShann	*Blues From Kansas City*	1941–43; GRP, 1992
Charles Mingus	*Mingus at the Bohemia*	1955; Original Jazz Classics, 1990
Thelonious Monk	*The Complete Blue Note Recordings*	1947–57; Blue Note, 1994
Charlie Parker	*Bird: The Complete Charlie Parker on Verve*	1946–54; Verve, 1988
Charlie Parker	*Complete Dial Sessions*	1945–47; Stash, 1993
Cecil Taylor	*Unit Structures*	1966; Blue Note, 1989

the piano in great, rich showers, you'd think the man wouldn't have time to line them up. They rolled and rolled like the sea. Folks yelled for him to "Go!" Dean was sweating; the sweat poured down his collar. "There he is! That's him! Old God! Old God Shearing! Yes! Yes! Yes!" And Shearing was conscious of the madman behind him, he could hear every one of Dean's gasps and imprecations, he could sense it though he couldn't see. "That's right!" Dean said. "Yes!" Shearing smiled; he rocked. Shearing rose from the piano, dripping with sweat; those were his great 1949 days before he became cool and commercial.

Kerouac continued his jazz odyssey in San Francisco with this description of Slim Gaillard:

Slim Gaillard is a tall, thin Negro with big sad eyes who's always saying "Right-orooni" and "How 'bout a little bourbonorooni." In Frisco great eager crowds of young semi-intellectuals sat at his feet and listened to him on the piano, guitar and bongo drums. When he gets warmed up he takes off his shirt and undershirt and really goes. He does and says anything that comes into his head ... Dean thought Slim was god.

At the end of Part Two of *On the Road*, San Francisco impressed Kerouac, and he wrote: "I never saw such crazy musicians. Everybody in Frisco blew. It was the end of the continent; they didn't give a damn." Across the bay they were "hitting Negro jazz shacks in the oil flats . . ." but the road beckoned. "It was the end; I wanted to get out."

Part Three begins with Kerouac wandering Denver in the spring of '49, "wishing I were a Negro, feeling that the best the white world had offered was not enough ecstasy for me . . ."

The road took Kerouac past "San Francisco alto man Ed Fournier," past Dean Moriarty's definition of "IT," past Chicago and the unidentified young bopper, "self-indulgence written in his eyes" and "a tone just like Lester Young himself," through Anita O'Day's club and Detroit, where

they spent a "wild bop night . . . spending a good part of the morning in Negro bars and chasing gals and listening to jazz records on juke boxes."

At the end of Part Three Kerouac strikes a wistful note as the sojourners approach New York and are heartened by the sound of Symphony Sid on the radio, "with all the latest bop."

On the Road also encompasses the sense of implosive loss that follows the exhilaration of freedom, and Part Four is imbued with a gathering poignance. There's Dean exulting to the sounds of saxophonist Gator Tail Jackson; Lester Young at Birdland, "eternity on his huge eyelids," and Stan Getz, Young's spiritual heir.

But when Moriarty insists "I have not myself changed over the years and continue with that policy," the reader is aware that all the writer can think of at that moment is how profoundly *everything* has changed. Despite listening to Dizzy Gillespie and assorted bop records, a change has occurred in Kerouac himself that has robbed him of the joy with which he began his excursions. The curse of William Blake has struck— the tiger of experience has slaughtered the lamb of innocence. In the final section of *On the Road* Kerouac has tickets to Duke Ellington at the Metropolitan Opera and a Cadillac to take him there, but his world-weary thought is "I sure wish I didn't have to go to the concert . . . for which I had no stomach whatever."

Later in his life Kerouac continued to go to clubs, hitting the legendary Lower East Side jazz club the Five Spot to hear Ornette Coleman and Don Cherry and befriending the pianist Cecil Taylor. These musicians were far beyond bop, reconfiguring the most basic approaches to jazz arrangement and performance in an open-ended search for freedom of expression. That freedom drew Kerouac even when he no longer enjoyed the freedom of the road, and that freedom fires the music of Coleman, Taylor and their followers to this day.

Painting Beat by Numbers

BY MICHAEL McCLURE

1. I ARRIVED IN SAN FRANCISCO FROM Tucson on December 31, 1954. My first night, New Year's Eve, I was thrown out of a club onto Columbus Avenue, across from City Lights, for trying to make it with a girl on the bandstand. I was drinking and blurred on benzedrine —I didn't notice it was a lesbian bar. Earlier in the day, with two old high school friends, I ate with chopsticks for the first time at Sam Wo's rickety, four-floored Chinatown restaurant. I had come to San Francisco from Tucson to study abstract expressionism, and to inform my poetry with its action philosophy, but Mark Rothko and Clyfford Still had already left town.

2. Allen Ginsberg and I met at a party for famed and graying English poet W. H. Auden, early in 1955. The wallflowers at the academic party, Allen and I spotted each other and began talking about the Nineteenth-Century mystic poet William Blake. Allen was a skinny, vividly intelligent New Yorker who had experienced visions of William Blake. I was twenty-two years old, and from Seattle by way of Kansas and Arizona. At age seventeen, I dreamed I *was* William Blake.

3. Allen and I got together from time to time, and he told me about his friend Jack Kerouac, whose letters and enclosed poems Allen read to me. I liked the spontaneity and intensely casual word music of those poems, which turned out to be the choruses of Jack's epic poem "Mexico City Blues."

4. In 1955, there was no lack of art and adventure in San Francisco and it was underground. The greatest paintings I'd ever seen were tiny, transcendental smears and daubs by Jay DeFeo that were hanging on the walls of The Place, the North Beach artists' and poets' bar. Her work was better than anything I imagined was in Paris. Soon, to accompany Allen's poems, Robert LaVigne did flower paintings, which were exhibited at The Place. Located on Grant Avenue, a back street in an Italian neighborhood, the bar was run by painters who served draft beer and wine by the glass. I moved into a small flat on narrow and shady Hargrove Alley half a block up Telegraph Hill above The Place. (Jay DeFeo's huge painting from the period, "The Rose," was the centerpiece of the 1995 Whitney Museum show of Beat art. During her lifetime, Jay shunned publicity.)

5. In the Fifties San Francisco was a cross between Cowtown, USA, and Harbortown, USA. It was a small city, the tallest building

The last gathering of North Beach poets and artists, 1965, in front of City Lights Books: Robert LaVigne, Shig Murao, Larry Fagin, Leland Meyezove, Lew Welch, Peter Orlovsky (front row, from left); *David Meltzer, Michael McClure, Allen Ginsberg, Daniel Langton, Ginsberg's friend Steve, Richard Brautigan, Gary Goodrow, Nemi Frost* (center row, from left); *Stella Levy, Lawrence Ferlinghetti* (back row)

LARRY KEENAN JR.

was sixteen stories high, and there were fog and foghorns and harbor smells.

6. The 1950s were mean, Cold War and conformist; the promotion of the "American Way" (the tract home and big Buick) was an endless flood of propaganda via black-and-white television and *Time* and *Life* magazines. Citizens were secretly tortured by their toothy and smiling indifference to each other, and many turned to the new pharmaceuticals, especially Thorazine, to ease the psychic strain. Even in San Francisco the harsh Cold War persisted, but there was North Beach—a "reservation" for poets, philosophers, artists, bohemians, wierdos, radicals and free-thinkers.

7. In those days, there were possibly twenty people in San Francisco with the nerve in a public place to call themselves poets. That was like announcing you were a fairy and asking to be hung to a lamppost. Burly gray businessmen with military crewcuts stared and yelled, "Queer!" at us, regardless of our sexual preferences. As our hair grew longer, we were inventing a style. North Beach was located between Chinatown and the Italian district, and you could feel the tolerance there.

8. Anarchist philosopher/poet Kenneth Rexroth held an open house one night a week. With the right credentials, you could drop in. Philip Lamantia, a dashing surrealist poet, took me over to Rexroth's flat located in the windy avenues. From Rexroth we learned about anarchist working-class circles still active in the city, and about moving poetry off the page with the voice. We found we could as easily relate to Asia and the Pacific Rim as to New York and Paris. Rexroth promoted serious Buddhism, Eskimo poetry, radical social movements, physics

and even esoteric Christianity. He was a mountain climber, a hiker, and he knew how to fix his own car.

9. Back in Wichita, a few years before coming to San Francisco, I was tight with Kansas City beboppers and went to jam sessions in black nightclubs. In San Francisco, when I could afford it, I'd go to hear Miles Davis or Chet Baker at the Black Hawk. There, I first met Tim Leary, who was wearing a gray suit, necktie and hearing aid. He was beginning to become expansive. Lalo Shifrin was playing piano that day. Mostly, I listened to recordings by Scarlatti, Monk, Miles, Anita O'Day and Ornette Coleman.

10. I was poor—everyone was poor. I'd climb into my old station wagon, the door tied shut with a piece of rope, and drive for forty minutes from San Francisco to the top of Mount Tamalpais. Muir Woods was on its slope, and there were cliffs looking out onto the Pacific Ocean. Sometimes several of us got together and drove four hours south to Big Sur, where we might spot Henry Miller; once we stayed for dinner at Miller's. Monterey was a fishing village, and Carmel had a sandy beach where you could sleep before driving home. Going inland, there was desert and Death Valley, which was wildly painted with flowers after the spring rain. While high, driving through Titus Canyon, we saw walls sculpted with gigantic carvings of gods and heroines. Back home we could ocean-swim beside the Golden Gate Bridge in the icy surf at Baker Beach, which was empty except for Samoan anglers and a barking dog.

11. One year I worked taking the Census in the black district (before white city planners dreamed up "Urban Renewal"). I discovered that black people in San Francisco lived much like we did—with their family or friends in big, inexpensive, high-ceilinged flats, furnished with furniture that friends had passed on. In my flat there was an ongoing show of assemblage art by Bruce Conner, George Herms and Wallace Berman. Assemblage was a new form that I loved: a ladder with worn-out brightly colored shoes nailed to it, or a painting with photo collage and doll heads attached and jammed into a nylon stocking. This art was as new as we were. Riding on a homemade swing in the flat, my toddler daughter would sing songs with no words. The art on the walls seemed to be about the same things as her songs . . . the celebration of consciousness and discovery of a world.

12. The Six Gallery reading on October 7, 1955, has been called the first Beat poetry reading. That night, I met Gary Snyder and Philip Whalen, Jack Kerouac was in the audience, and Allen Ginsberg debuted "Howl." It was the first poetry reading for Allen, Gary, Phil and me. Kenneth Rexroth was our master of ceremonies, elegant in a handsome thriftshop suit.

13. The Six Gallery was an automobile repair garage in the Marina District converted into an exhibition space by artists drawn to San Francisco to express their edge-driven ideas. The door of the gallery was open to poetry, and earlier that year master poet Robert Duncan had presented there a staged reading of his play *Faust Fucked,* for which I'd had a role. When I was asked in August to organize a reading at the Six I said okay, but then, too busy, I asked Allen to do it. Meantime, Allen met Snyder and Whalen at Kenneth Rexroth's. With Philip Lamantia back in town from Mexico and Rexroth volunteering to MC, that's all we needed. The sizable gallery was mostly raw walls and concrete floor, with a low stage.

14. About 150 people arrived for the reading. Allen's comic/serious mailer announced a "remarkable collection of angels on one stage reading their poetry." Showing up were elderly women professors in fur coats, bearded anarchist carpenters, painters and sculptors, conscientious objectors from Oregon's CO camp who had settled in Frisco, serious young people looking for ideas, and the poet and publisher of City Lights Press, Lawrence Ferlinghetti—an audience consisting of an almost secret, semi-outlawed slice of America. This was the age of official censorship: In his novel *The Naked and the Dead*, Norman Mailer had to use the word "fug" to replace *fuck*. Also banned were meaningful nonconformist, anti–Cold War, pro social and environmental speech and action. The Six Gallery audience was standing up, listening intently, then began saying, *yeah*, or laughing with the poems. As the evening wore on, many sat on the floor or leaned against the gallery walls and corners. The then-unknown traveler Jack Kerouac began a collection for wine and went out and bought homemade Italian red, eighty-five cents a gallon. Somewhere during Allen's reading of "Howl," Jack started yelling "Go!" like at a jazz club. Nobody had heard anything like this poem, though we knew exactly what it was about and because we were living it, had lived it or knew friends who had. We wanted its statement to be made and wanted the freedom to do something about it. Allen read in an intense, creaky, bardic voice. "Howl" drew a social position that we had already taken or would be taking.

15. Equally well-received was Gary Snyder, bearded and laughingly intense, reading his nature poems of logging and forest fire, huckleberries and bear shit on the trail, love-making and the trickster god Coyote. Gary knew at first breath how to read words of his lore directly into the ears of the cheering listeners. Presently, Gary is a world-class environmentalist and deep ecologist, as well as a figure of renown in American Buddhism and poetry.

16. One of the poems I read that night condemned the brutal murder of one hundred whales by American servicemen stationed at an airbase in Iceland. Another was "Point Lobos: Animism," about the most mystical wild beach I'd ever seen and about the dark shadow side of it gleaming in the sun. Another poem's subject was our oneness with all life and Buddha's Fire Sermon. As a way to go beyond the social machine left over from two world wars and the Korean debacle, I was working with sight, sound, taste, touch, smell and subjectivity. I was in personal revolt and wanted to start the art of poetry and living over, *for real*!

17. Philip Whalen had just arrived from Oregon, and his humor was a bolt of big intelligent laughter. Whalen's poems fusing Zen structure and cool hipness were spoken with ironic casualness. Whalen's writing makes American cartoons with deep Buddhist knowledge; it's all grafted onto his huge appetite for hiking and for Chinatown. His knowledge of nature and history fills the poems with jewels of wit. One of his poems, as he spoke it, created an arguing married couple that turned into a quarrelsome pair of blue parakeets, jerking their tail feathers as they ranted. It was a comic vision. Twenty-five years ago, Philip was ordained a Zen priest, and later he received Dharma Transmis-

sion from a Zen master. Recently, Whalen retired as abbot of the Zen center in San Francisco's Castro district.

18. The day after the reading, Allen came over, bringing Jack to visit. With an air of modesty, Jack was good-looking in a rugged, athletic way. He was the only person I'd met who was more self-conscious than I was. Watching him, I guessed that his head had creaked on his neck when he walked across the high school cafeteria. I knew about that.

19. There has been no shortage of women poets among the Beats. In the early days, Lenore Kandel faced a censorship trial regarding her erotic poem "The Love Book." Diane di Prima was widely active in New York, then moved to San Francisco in the early Sixties, and is presently at the cutting edge. Joanne Kyger is one of the most refined poets of nature and Zen. Joanna McClure had the most sensitive ear for sound. Anne Waldman is known for powerful performances and for her collaborations with Allen Ginsberg.

20. The Beats can be split into two segments. The first was in the Forties and early Fifties in New York, where Allen, Jack and William Burroughs created an outspoken, urban style of writing, defined by alienation and self-exploration. Centered around the Village, Columbia University and Times Square, the scene included Herbert Huncke, and Gregory Corso bloomed in it as well. Kerouac and Ginsberg came "West" thanks to their friend Neal Cassady, a mad driver and epic talker. *On the Road* is a spin into the West, a first exploration. The Beat Generation was a guy-centered, urban thing but emphasized the urge to get out, *to get on the road*.

21. At the Six Gallery reading, the Beats broadened into another incarnation and a new layer came into being. "Howl" transcends urban literature, becoming a poem about life and mind as if speaking about nature—and they *are* nature. Snyder's poems were adventurously about mountains and trails and what is now called deep ecology—nonhuman-centered nature. My poems were nature poems whether about the murder of whales or the intensity of love. Whalen's writing was essentially Buddhism and nature.

22. After a stay in the woods of nearby Mill Valley, Kerouac left, but soon returned to try firewatching in the mountains and to hike and study Zen with Gary Snyder. He wrote *The Dharma Bums* about a new vision of life's possibilities. Sometimes Ginsberg wrote poems about landscape and wild flowers, as well as about his intensified politics. Gregory Corso came to San Francisco and wrote "Bomb"—a great comic ode centering on the atomic destruction of nature and the world.

23. Soon after the Six Gallery reading, Lawrence Ferlinghetti's City Lights Press brought out "Howl" in the Pocket Poets series. The new poetry—and the accompanying dissent—began to be heard across the country. At the same time, North Beach became a stage for people thinking they were Beats. Typically, they wore berets, goatees and sandals made from car tires, and they sat in cafes drinking their wine as it warmed. As newspapers and magazines covered the scene, the Beats were misrepresented and tourists were attracted. For one reason or another, most of the Beat poets and artists moved out of North Beach.

24. We went back to meet in North Beach at The Place or the Coffee Gallery or City Lights Books. The streets began to fill with tour buses of people watching the "beatniks" playing bongo drums in front of the open-air cafes. About the same time, Poetry and Jazz opened in the basement jazz club the Cellar. David Meltzer worked at the scene deeply, writing new poems for every night's performance. Ruth Weiss, an orginator of the scene, made herself heard as a performing jazz poet. The stars of the new art form were Rexroth, Ferlinghetti and the visionary, musically sensitive Kenneth Patchen, who cut an album with Charles Mingus.

25. Early in the Fifties, *Life* magazine ran an article presenting the new poets of the Bay Area—in it I was called "a careful craftsman." It was pleasant and sounded supportive. But a few years later, *Life* ran a major feature presenting us as contemptible, dangerous, slovenly madmen. *Life* wanted to cajole the public into some tarring and feathering. After seeing what was printed about me, I expected FBI agents to crash through the windows, swinging on ropes. Scores of millions believed the magazine was the voice of truth. In fact, as a group we were more "dangerous" than *Life*'s fabrications— we were *more* outspoken and serious than the magazine made us out to be.

26. The "Howl" obscenity bust resulted in a nationally watched trial that attracted much attention to poetry, City Lights and Allen. Ferlinghetti and City Lights manager Shig Murao won the case. Poetry seemed to be free. But even now "Howl" cannot be read over the radio—the FCC has tightened up. (Though the printed word has shed government censorship, the issue today is the insidious censorship by corporations and the "marketplace.") Next, Barney Rosset, owner of Grove Press, carried the censorship challenge a step further and published D. H. Lawrence's banned *Lady Chatterley's Lover,* a novel with frank sexual scenes. Rosset won that case, then Grove published William Burroughs's *Naked Lunch.* There were a number of cases and Rosset won them. The novel and poetry were beginning to be free of censorship at that point.

27. My play *The Beard* was confronted by theater censorship. In *The Beard* Billy the Kid met Jean Harlow in a blue-velvet eternity. While writing the play I believed the characters were really there and that I functioned as a scribe, writing it down. A play about the nature of human mammals, *The Beard* was charged with violation of obscenity laws and its actors were arrested in San Francisco, Berkeley, Vancouver and Los Angeles, where there were arrests on fourteen consecutive nights. It was a front-page battle during the L.A. run; on opening night the sky was full of searchlights and the audience filled with the Hollywood elite. The *Los Angeles Times* ran two editorials condemning the play while it was in rehearsal.

28. *The Beard's* censorship-fighting heroes were the actors Richard Bright and Billie Dixon, plus Alexandra Haye, who played Harlow in Los Angeles. The audience stayed each night to watch the police arrest the actors, who, as they were led to a waiting police car, received a second standing ovation. The language spoken between Harlow and the Kid went beyond anything yet produced on the modern stage, and there was a graphic representation of sex. We saw the play as beautiful, serious and comic, and we discovered it was shaking the chains on language and theater. In a way, it was our answer to the Vietnam War.

29. *The Beard* received two Obie awards in New York and high praise in London reviews. During the three years of censorship trials, I kept my balance by remembering Lenny Bruce's destruction—and self-destruction—during the police persecution of his genius.

30. Nancy Reagan, wife of then-governor Ronald Reagan, and Charlton Heston (current president of the National Rifle Association) denounced *The Beard* while it was on trial. Robert Dornan (recently a right-wing congressman from Southern California) sued me over a *Beard*-related issue. The California legislature's criminal committee attempted to enact a law against "obscene" plays and specifically named *The Beard.* The actors and I believed our play was art and that we'd win, which we did in all cases, thanks to the ACLU and many others.

31. In August 1960 there was a parade of three old station wagons down the coast to Big Sur to meet Kerouac. Ferlinghetti, Beat nature poet Lew Welch and I were driving. My wife of the time and our daughter were along. Victor Wong (now a film actor) was making art with colored ink pens in a big sketchbook, drawing everyone and the landscape as we drove. Phil Whalen was in outrageously entertaining form in his old pre-priesthood drinking days. Big Sur in August is all sun blare, a glaze of flaring light over everything as it comes off the ocean. Ominous feelings can rise from the the ultra-rugged scenery and raw Western forest. Jack had been suffering from d.t.'s on the East Coast. Now he was back to nature to rest and dry out in Ferlinghetti's cabin at the mouth of Bixby Creek under a high bridge on the seacoast.

32. At Ferlinghetti's cabin we read our poetry to each other and talked about art and experience and what we had been reading and where our lives had been going. As night got nearer, I read my new long poem "Dark Brown." It closes with a graphic sexuality unheard of in the Fifties. In his novel *Big Sur*, Jack called "Dark Brown" "the most fantastic poem in America," and he tried to find a publisher for it. A great narrator, Jack read aloud the ending of *Doctor Jekyll and Mister Hyde*, making each vowel and consonant rich in sound, but keeping the words' natural, normal shape. It was not fanciness, but playing with words like a jazzman plays with sound. He told us about a new long poem where he was writing down what the ocean said to him as he sat listening.

33. Later that night, in the beach darkness, Jack led us by lantern light up to the little cliff where he would listen to the ocean and write his poem "Sea." We scrabbled over gravelly sand and rock dunes, rustling against beach plants in the yellow, shadowy lantern light. As we sat down in the sand, there was a cold Big Sur wind in our ears and uncountable stars in our eyes. Jack proceeded to read the great nature poem that the ocean spoke to him. Such a poem could only come from an urban man who had been transfixed by the beauty and the awfulness of Big Sur. It didn't echo Wordsworth but found its root in James Joyce's stream of consciousness.

> ... Which one? the one? Which
> one? The one ploshed—
> the ploshed one ? the same,
> ah boom—Who's that ant
> that giant golden saltchange
> ant magnifying my mountain
> of feet? 'Tis finder, finding
> the change in thought to join
> the boomer hangers in the
> cave a light ...

Jack read the poem for many minutes. Night-

flying seabirds passed over. I was awed by the doubleness of what was happening. The waves below continued speaking as Jack spoke his poem for them, and he read it to them as well as to us. It was a complex and mystical moment.

34. Later it dawned on me that what is called the Beat Generation is, in fact, the literary wing of the environmental movement. We began to write poems about the crisis that was so apparent to us, and we studied and spent time with people who could show us more of what was going on. This part of our movement is getting lost in what has become academic literary criticism and sentimental fascination with the urban aspect of Beat consciousness—that's as accurate as calling the bearded bongo players in the open-air cafes Beat poets.

35. Years later, in 1972, in Stockholm, at the first United Nations Conference on the Environment, there was a "counter-conference" of poets and social activists speaking for biodiversity and for Native peoples and against overpopulation. Gary Snyder and I were busy there. I wrote an article titled "Death of All Flesh," covering the conference for ROLLING STONE.

36. Today, I'm doing what I did at the Six Gallery—reading my poetry. Sometimes I read solo and sometimes with Doors keyboardist Ray Manzarek, who plays piano while I perform poems. We play music clubs, colleges, festivals. Ray's improvisational genius is derived from black Chicago music, Miles Davis, mystic Russian composers and his own head and fingers. Ray was onto Beat poetry early, then worked with our friend Jim Morrison. Together, we hope to create a deep experience for our listeners and audience and to help leave footprints on the war agencies as well as a corporation or two.

Beat Queens:
Women in Flux

BY JOYCE JOHNSON

I N 1922 MY NINETEEN-YEAR-OLD mother Rosalind Ross went on the road. For nearly a year, in her family's effort to improve her marital prospects, she was shipped from cousin to cousin—from Cleveland to Baton Rouge, from Baton Rouge to Little Rock, from Little Rock to Los Angeles. She was the youngest and prettiest of three sisters, a proud and withdrawn girl who dreamed of singing Schubert on the stage of Carnegie Hall. My aunts, who were in their early thirties, still lived with their mother in Bensonhurst; one was a bookkeeper, the other a stenographer. They had no prospects whatsoever. "Stay away as long as you can," my mother's eldest sister Anna wrote her. "There's nothing for you here." My mother saw the Grand Canyon and posed for a snapshot outside the gates of the Fox Pathé studio, but she returned to Brooklyn without a proposal. She gave up her voice lessons and became a secretary. Ten years later she married my father, an auditor in a tobacco firm. In 1935, when I was born, her brother Uda wrote her: "At last you have something of your own!"

After my mother died, I found a

Elise Cowen flanked by Gregory Corso and Allen Ginsberg, Washington Square Park, New York City, 1957

BURT GLINN/MAGNUM PHOTOS INC.

small manuscript typed on onion skin among her papers. It was a record one of my childless aunts had kept of entertaining episodes from my earliest years. I was interested to learn that at age four, I had developed an adventurous streak and had persistently agitated to be allowed to cross our street on my own and go to the candy store on the opposite corner. My mother's response to me, which my aunt also jotted down, seemed so characteristic that I had the sensation of recalling it word for word: "Why would you want to do that? There's nothing there." It seemed to epitomize our lifelong conflict. My need for experience that inescapably involved risk; her need to insist there was nothing out there in order to keep me tied to her.

My mother chose the all-girls schools I attended in New York City—Hunter High School and Barnard College. In the late Forties and early Fifties, they were rather grim institutions in which bright girls were rigorously educated in ironic preparation for limited futures. Except for an aged elevator operator, not one male was visible inside the gray Gothic building that housed Hunter High. Within the conventlike precincts, however, there were adolescent nonconformists. Red-diaper babies who marched in May Day parades, lesbians who were having affairs with their teachers. Audre Lorde and Diane di Prima, two sixteen-year-old poets who would later make their mark, were running *Argus*, the Hunter literary magazine, where I published my first story. Diane was then writing imitative rhymed verse, but Audre wowed us all in that era of Bomb consciousness with her daring riposte to T. S. Eliot: "This is how the world ends. / Not with a whimper but with a BANG!"

My rebellion began at thirteen with my first sip of that forbidden beverage coffee in a diner two blocks from Hunter. Soon I was sneaking off to Greenwich Village on Sunday afternoons with my classmate Maria Meiff. We played the guitar and sang folk songs in Washington Square Park

with a bohemian crowd that was much too old for us, but actually quite harmless. We peered in the windows of bars like the San Remo and Fugazzi's, which were hangouts of Allen Ginsberg, Jack Kerouac and other subterraneans at the time. Condemned to be observers, we felt shielded from what we considered "real life" by our embarrassing jailbait status. Yet we had inklings that real life could be a scary proposition. A black ex-convict named Billy became obsessed with Maria, who looked seventeen; Maria was rather fascinated by the situation, but refused to go out for coffee with him in the Waldorf cafeteria unless I came along for protection. When we left Washington Square one Sunday, Billy started following us so we gave him the slip by ducking into Minetta Lane. There we saw a man bashing another man's head against the curb; blood was everywhere. We ran away to the uptown subway as fast as we could, but I knew that what we had just seen was good material. I wrote up the fight in a paper for my English class and got a C. "Write about what you know," the teacher reprimanded me in red ink.

What did "real life" mean to a middle-class adolescent girl in 1950? I yearned for it and thought I'd recognize it when I saw it, but could not quite define it. I was sure real life was sexual, though my ignorance of sex was profound. Since no information could be extracted from grownups, and my friends knew little more than I did, I pursued my forbidden research in the dictionary and in the steamy passages of historical novels, trying to connect the dots. At fifteen, I probably knew less than today's average eight-year-old. Until I entered Barnard College in 1951 and took a freshman orientation course called Modern Living, I did not have a very clear idea of how babies were born, nor did many of my classmates. I would meet Jack Kerouac only six years later.

The postwar period was an age of enforced innocence in America. Ground that women had won in the Jazz Age and during the war years was suddenly gone, as if society had deliberately contracted amnesia. Women who had worked were now relegated to the home, and girls were sent to college to get their MRS. Sexual intercourse was reserved for married couples.

It was unusual in the early Fifties for a young woman to get her own apartment, and if she did, it was a sign that she would be up to no good there. The only proper way for a girl to achieve independence from her family was to put herself under the protection of a husband.

In a journal entry written in September of 1951, when she was a sophomore at Smith, Sylvia Plath voiced the despair and frustration that many rebellious young women felt:

> ... I have come to the conclusion that I must have a passionate physical relationship with someone—or combat the great sex urge in me by chastic means. I chose the former answer. I also admitted that I am obligated in a way to my family and to society (damn society anyway) to follow certain absurd and traditional customs—for my own security, they tell me. I must therefore confine the major part of my life to one human being of the opposite sex ...

For unmarried young women, sex was more than adventure, more than a broadening of experience; it was a high-risk act with sometimes fatal consequences, given the inadequacy of birth control. To get a diaphragm in those days from the Margaret Sanger Clinic, an unmarried woman would have to appear wearing a wedding ring (purchased at the Five and Ten) and be prepared to fill out a form detailing the number of times a week she had intercourse with her fictitious husband. "Don't discuss your marriage with your classmates," a friend of mine who married at nineteen was warned by a dean at her college.

For Fifties women, all this repression made sex a very charged and anxious thing. You were breaking the rules. You could lose your place in the world, you could even lose your life. With so

much at stake, feelings became very heightened. In contrast, relationships between young people in the Nineties seem so easily entered into and so casually ended, that the novel of love, as Vivian Gornick has noted, is dying out.

The neighborhood around Columbia University and Barnard College was the birthplace of the Beat Generation, the meeting ground in the early 1940s of Jack Kerouac, Allen Ginsberg, William Burroughs and Lucien Carr. The group included two unusually adventurous young women—Edie Parker, Kerouac's first wife, and Joan Vollmer Adams, who had a common-law marriage with Burroughs. As I would be in the next decade, both were drawn to charismatic men who lived the larger lives denied to women, and who offered them little in the way of security or protection. Edie was from an affluent Grosse Pointe, Michigan, family; when her mother discovered that her daughter and Kerouac were living in sin in Joan Adams's apartment, Edie's checks from home were cut off. Determined to stay on in New York with Jack, come what may, Edie worked as a longshoreman for eighteen months loading Liberty ships; after that, she worked as a cigarette girl at 21, earning $27.50 a week. Some of her earnings went to supporting Jack and other early members of the Beat circle who crashed in Joan Adams's famous apartment.

When Edie Parker was nineteen and Kerouac was away at sea, she discovered she was pregnant. Edie knew Jack's fear of familial responsibility, so she had a horrendous abortion by forced labor at five months in the kitchen of a Bronx apartment; the baby, a perfectly formed boy, was dropped into a bucket. Edie survived but was never able to have children. Joan paid even more heavily for the chances she took. She went too willingly where Burroughs led her—she accepted his homosexuality, followed him into experimentation with drugs and became addicted to Benzedrine; she died in 1951, when her husband attempted to shoot a cocktail glass off her head and missed. Like Carolyn Cassady, who later married Kerouac's friend Neal, these Forties women seemed content to define themselves as wives of geniuses. Although Joan was said to be brilliant and could hold her own in intellectual discussions with the men, she left behind no writings of her own.

Edie Parker didn't read any of Kerouac's novels until after his death in 1969; she was surprised to find bits of herself all through his work—from *The Town and the City* through *The Vanity of Duluoz*. She remained married to Kerouac in her mind years after they'd split up. When she looked me up in the Eighties, she told me that she believed Jack would have ultimately returned to her and that the annulment of their marriage in 1945 had never been valid. "Do you know who you look like?" she asked me, as we sat in the Chinese restaurant where we had agreed to meet. "Didn't Jack ever tell you? You look just like Joan!"

Like Edie and Joan before us, Elise Cowen and I were a disaffected duo, neither of us quite fitting in at Barnard. We both found the austere, rather militaristic brand of feminism preached by Dean Millicent McIntosh quite useless and unappealing. The Dean made much of the fact that she had been a commander of the Waves during the war. She inveighed against promiscuity and sexual experimentation. Women were to remain chaste until marriage, and if they had an occupation, no allowances were to be made for any special needs they might have at work. For those who were especially ambitious to prove they could do a man's job, the Waves had a recruiting office right on campus. McIntosh's success as a superwoman seemed unduplicatable— Dean of Barnard, married to a medical specialist, mother of five. In her Modern Living course, she somehow neglected to tell us about the household help she must have had, the boarding schools her children were sent to.

Like me, Elise had hung around in the Village and was attracted to what we then called bohemianism. I had entered college at sixteen; Elise was two years older. The summer before her freshman year, she had actually gone all the way with a boy she was crazy about, who had rejected her soon after—a pattern in Elise's relationships. Nice young men found Elise off-putting. She was too intellectual, too intense; eruptions of acne flared on her face like evidence of her seething emotions. Elise cared little about making herself pretty. She'd stand in a corner at a freshman dance defiantly rolling her own cigarettes. The aspirations she had, she kept to herself. She was obsessed with T. S. Eliot, but majored in psych. I'd show her the stories I was writing, but she'd never show me her poems. "I'm a *mediocre*," she told me, pronouncing the word in an odd hollow French way.

The Beats have often been accused of having no respect for creative women. But in truth this lack of respect was so pervasive in American culture in the postwar years that women did not even question it. One exception was Elizabeth Hardwick, who wrote in "The American Woman as Snow Queen," an essay published in *The Prospect Before Us* in 1955 about the contempt of male intellectuals for what she called "the culture-hungry woman." In his posthumous memoir, *When Kafka Was the Rage*, the critic Anatole Broyard, a contemporary of Kerouac's who was very jealous of the Beat writers' success, complained about girls "who wore their souls like negligés that they never took off." No wonder an intellectual young woman like Elise felt so little confidence.

I felt surer than Elise about what I wanted to be. Certainly I would write—it was the only thing I was good at—though my belief in my powers could momentarily be deflated by a cutting remark from a man. "Quite the little existentialist, aren't we?" a male professor wrote sneeringly on one of my papers. Another teacher,

John Kouwenhoven, who had just made his reputation as a critic of popular culture, told a roomful of girls that if they really wanted to be writers, they wouldn't even be enrolled in his class—they'd be out in America hopping freight trains. Since it was inconceivable in 1953 that a young woman would open herself up to such experience, and since all we had to write about was what Kouwenhoven called our "boring little lives," there was obviously no hope for us. I remember feeling angry and confused, yet the notion of challenging the professor's remark seemed unthinkable. A few years later, during my relationship with Kerouac, I found an unexpected source of encouragement when I showed him the novel I was working on. Jack was critical only of the way I was arranging my life. Instead of wasting so much of my time on the dreary secretarial jobs that supported me, why didn't I go for broke the way he had—see the world, put all my energy into writing, try to become great. I couldn't respond to his question; the answer was too humiliating: Because I was a woman. Because I didn't see how I could survive without a safety net. Yet oddly enough, I never expected that a man would provide me with one.

In some important ways my upbringing had been rather unconventional. My mother had grown up in a fatherless household; her sisters had gotten their first jobs when they were in their teens. She always told me I would have to make my own way in the world. My mother mistakenly believed I would eventually write musical comedies that would be produced on Broadway and advised me to defer marriage (in other words, to continue living under her thumb) until I had established this career. Meanwhile I might have to work in offices, so she enrolled me one summer in a secretarial course where I learned typing and shorthand. These were the skills that later kept me afloat. My mother did not realize that she had equipped me to leave her, that I was only biding my time.

By nature I was rebellious but innately cautious, never questioning the need for a safety net of my own making. Elise proved to be more like Kerouac—unable to find one, not even really trying to.

It was Elise who eventually led me to the Beats, first by introducing me to her experimental psychology instructor Donald Cook, who had been a classmate of Allen Ginsberg's. Donald had a shabby ground-floor apartment near Columbia where the door was always open—interesting people who later became literary figures kept passing through: John Hollander, Richard Howard, Robert Gottlieb, Allen Ginsberg, even William Burroughs. The phonograph played jazz and Mahler. There were trips to Birdland, solemn experimentation with smoking grass. Elise began sleeping with Donald, painfully accepting the fact that he was not hung up on her. But she would soon fall in love much more deeply with Allen Ginsberg—at last she had found someone who could read her soul. She would remain in love with Allen—a one-sided passion—until her suicide in 1962. Allen, who was still painfully working out his sexual identity, saw in Elise a resemblance to his mother, Naomi, that both attracted and disturbed him.

In 1952 Elise and I read John Clellon Holmes's article "This Is the Beat Generation" with great excitement, recognizing the name John Kerouac that we'd heard in Donald's apartment, and finding a stirring affirmation of our own sense of being outsiders.

"There are those who believe that in generations such as this," wrote Holmes, "there is always the constant possibility of a great new moral idea, conceived in desperation, coming to life. Others note the self-indulgence, the waste, the apparent social irresponsibility, and disagree." Surely this Beat Generation was the one we really belonged in, not the gray, bottled-up Silent one. Soon we read Holmes's novel *Go*, fascinated by the Dostoyevskian intensity generated by Holmes's "boy gang," but we were incapable of asking ourselves why Holmes's female characters were always relegated to the backseat. That sort of analysis would have to wait until the next decade.

For some doctrinaire feminists in our own time, *On the Road* has been a deceptively easy target. Choosing to ignore the social context in which *On the Road* was written, they deplore the macho posturing of Dean and Sal and the way Kerouac depicts their transient, totally irresponsible sexual relationships with women. Reading Kerouac now, they find nothing in his work that speaks to female readers. Yet, in 1957 when *On the Road* was published, thousands of Fifties women experienced a powerful response to what they read. *On the Road* was prophecy, bringing the news of the oncoming, unstoppable sexual revolution—the revolution that would precede and ultimately pave the way for women's liberation. It was a book that dared to show that men too were fed up with their traditional roles. It suggested that you could choose—choose to be unconventional, choose to experiment, choose to open yourself up to a broad range of experience, instead of simply duplicating the lifestyle of your parents.

Kerouac seemed to realize how mired in the status quo women were; he saw the intrinsic sadness in lives of quiet desperation. "What do you want out of life?" Sal Paradise asks the pretty little waitress Rita Bettencourt who is "tremendously frightened of sex." "'I don't know,' she said. 'Just wait on tables and try to get along.' She yawned. I put my hand over her mouth and told her not to yawn. I tried to tell her how excited I was about life. . . ." Later Sal asks the same question of a country girl in Michigan. "I wanted to take her and wring it out of her. She didn't have the slightest idea what she wanted. She mumbled of jobs, movies, going to her grandmother's for the summer, wishing she could go to New York and visit

the Roxy, what kind of outfit she would wear. . . . She was eighteen and most lovely, and lost."

When I read these passages in late August of 1957, I thought of my mother and her sisters, but Kerouac's lost girls did not remind me of myself—it was Sal, passionately impatient with the status quo, with whom I identified.

By then I had begun my relationship with Kerouac, but even before that, I'd had my immersion in real life. I'd defied my parents to have a painful affair with Donald Cook, left home, broken with my family, found jobs, had an abortion and had my first taste of despair. Still, I wouldn't have turned back if given the choice. At twenty-one I felt I'd gone to the bottom and floated up; I had the lightness of feeling there was nothing left to lose, so I'd let Kerouac come home with me the first night I met him. Quite the little existentialist, as my Barnard professor once wrote. Or perhaps my state of mind approached the original definition of Beat.

"Come on down, I'm waiting for you," Jack had written to me from Mexico City that July. "Don't go to silly Frisco. First place, I have this fine earthquake-proof room for 85¢ a night for both of us, it's an Arabic magic room with tiles on the walls and many big round whorehouse sex-orgy mirrors (it's an old 1910 whorehouse, solid with marble floors)—we can sleep on the big clean double bed, have our private bath . . . it's right downtown, we can enjoy city life to the hilt then when we get tired of our Magian inwardness sultan's room we can go off to the country and rent a cottage with flowerpots in the window— Your money will last you 5 times longer & in Frisco you wouldn't be seeing anything *new & foreign & strange*—Take the plane to Mexico City (bus too long, almost as expensive too), then take a cab to my hotel, knock my door, we'll be gay friends wandering arm-in-arm . . ."

How could I resist such an invitation? I immediately quit my secretarial job at Farrar,

Straus and Cudahy and gave up my apartment. Jack and I were going to live forever on the five-hundred-dollar advance I had just gotten from an editor at Random House for my first novel, but unfortunately I didn't move fast enough. By the time I was ready to leave for Mexico City, Jack, too depressed and shaky to stay alone in that sultan's room, was on his way to his mother's house in Florida. From there he wrote me asking for a loan of thirty dollars, so that he could take a bus to New York in time for the publication of *On the Road*. Being a witness to Jack's collision with sudden, unexpected fame would soon turn into one of the most profoundly educational experiences of my life.

Looking at Beat women in a paper she read at the 1994 Beat conference at New York University, Alix Kates Shulman saw merely passivity, pathos and victimization. Of course, she didn't take into consideration the heady excitement of taking part in the cultural revolution ushered in by the Beats. Nor did she acknowledge the courage required to venture into what was then new territory for women. As Hettie Jones succinctly put it in her memoir *How I Became Hettie Jones*, "Sex hadn't made us *bad*." When Hettie dared to cross the color line to marry the poet LeRoi Jones, her family considered her dead. Like Elise, Hettie would become my comrade and close friend; years before the concept of sisterhood became fashionable, we found in each other the emotional support we could not get from our men or our parents. "We shared what was most important to us," Hettie wrote, "common assumptions about our uncommon lives. We lived outside, as if. As if we were men? As if we were newer, freer versions of ourselves?"

In our downtown scene in the East Village there was an interesting role reversal going on—women were often the breadwinners so the men would be free to pursue their creative work. I had a taste of this the first night I met Kerouac, when I bought him frankfurters and beans at Howard Johnson's because he was absolutely broke. I had never done such a thing before. Interestingly enough, it did not make me feel exploited but strangely grown up. During our relationship, whenever he passed through New York, each of the three apartments I lived in from 1957 through 1958 served as a base for him. Homelessness had become Jack's way of life; even the house he bought in 1958 with his royalties from *On the Road* was more his mother's than his.

In the LeRoi Jones household, it was Hettie who paid much of the rent. Her small salary from her job at *Partisan Review* not only helped to support her husband, but fed numerous other young writers who hung out at their Chelsea apartment, which rapidly turned into a Beat salon. With what was left over, Hettie and LeRoi published the literary magazine *Yugen*.

"It's perfectly possible to live with a male chauvinist and not be oppressed," Joanna McClure, whose husband Michael was one of the leading figures in the San Francisco Renaissance, observed in 1982 on a women's panel at a Naropa Institute Conference commemorating the twenty-fifth anniversary of *On the Road*. It all came down to what kind of male chauvinist you were with. The men Hettie and I found suffocating were the bourgeois, conventional ones. Men like LeRoi and Jack somehow gave us the breathing space we needed. "You'll end up in Mamaroneck with Marjorie Morningstar," a lawyer boyfriend of Hettie's had once predicted. "What unforeseen catastrophe would send me up the river," she'd wondered, "to decorate a home in Westchester?"

"But you *suffered!*" I can imagine a feminist critic like Shulman interrupting accusingly. "Don't forget that!" Yes, indeed, we suffered. We were poor, sometimes even hungry; we had holes in our black stockings and wore thriftshop clothes; whenever Consolidated Edison turned off the electricity, we were plunged into darkness. At times we were frightened. We had orphaned ourselves by becoming "bad women," so we had no one to fall back on. We took terrible chances with our bodies when we had illegal abortions. We were afraid our restless men would leave us, and usually they did, even when we tried to put up with their affairs. Most of us never got the chance to literally go on the road. Our road instead became the strange lives we were leading. We had actually *chosen* these difficult lives for good reasons; we hadn't fallen into them by default, or been kidnapped into fifth-floor walkups in the East Village. We couldn't take on the task of transforming relationships between men and women because it took such an over-whelming amount of effort to come as far as we had; our most consuming struggle was the break with the mores of our parents' generation. We experienced the thrill of being part of a move-ment that changed life in America, and we endured the hard times that came with making something new. Many of us discovered we were tougher and more resilient than we'd imagined we could be.

Would Hettie have become a writer herself if her marriage hadn't broken up? How long would I have lasted as Mrs. Jack Kerouac, coping with Jack's heartbreaking alcoholism and his jealous Mémère? Sometimes the unhappy endings of love stories turn out to be the right ones.

The subject of Beat women is currently rather fashionable. Two anthologies of the women's writings have recently been pub-lished, and I keep hearing about scholars who are working on papers. There is particular attention paid to Elise Cowen, but too much of it is mor-bidly centered upon her suicide, as if she is the prime victim even the admirers of Beat women have been looking for.

Elise was remarkable because of her intellect, her absolute honesty and her capacity for devoted friendship. The poems she left behind are rough and unfinished but have the power that comes when a writer holds nothing back. Elise's obses-sive love for Allen Ginsberg set her on an impos-sible course—as if she had to prove herself worthy of him by living as he did. She even emulated him sexually—entering into an affair with a Barnard classmate when Allen became involved with Peter Orlovsky. I remember feeling very worried about her in 1957 when she set off for San Fran-cisco on a Greyhound bus with only a few dollars in her pocket. As usual, she was unable to hold a job. She ended up in a North Beach skid row hotel and came to grief when she found she needed an abortion and couldn't afford one. By the time she found a psychiatrist who signed the papers permitting her to have a clinical abortion, she was five months pregnant. The operation was traumatic for her.

Elise had been subject to depression even back when I first met her and had slit her wrists when we were in our junior year at Barnard. She had a toxic relationship with her parents, espe-cially with her father who was far too emotion-ally involved with her. She began taking speed around 1960 and deteriorated very quickly. Her parents had her committed to a mental hospital and then had her released in their custody even though she was far from stable. In our last conver-sation, she spoke of radios listening in on her; her parents were planning to take her to Miami Beach, of all places. A few weeks later, I heard about her death.

"I wonder how I'll wear my hair when I'm thirty," I remember her saying. But she never found out. I've often thought Elise was born too soon. In a time with more tolerance for noncon-formist behavior in women she might even have survived. Elise could never conceal what she was. She could never put on a mask as I did and pass in and out of the straight world.

When I was writing my memoir *Minor Characters,* I went, for research purposes, to the twenty-fifth reunion of my Barnard class of 1955. Few of the renegades I'd known were there. Most of the women present had followed the traditional Fifties path, marrying soon after or even during college, becoming housewives in the suburbs. Some, judging by their nametags, had married two or three times. Now with their children grown, they were wondering how to get into the job market. They had difficulty describing themselves—"I live in Scarsdale," they'd say, or "I have a son at Yale." One of them went up to one of the few members of the class who had never married, peered at the single name on her nametag, and said, "What's the matter? Didn't anyone *like* you?" These women looked old to me. How had vibrant girls turned into these matrons? I felt grateful that I had escaped this fate.

I thought of Elise as I stood on the Barnard lawn drinking punch. When the 1955 yearbook was passed around, I looked for her picture. I found a blank rectangle with her name printed underneath.

Hettie Jones (left) *and Joyce Glassman (later Johnson) at the Artist's Club, New York City, March 10, 1960*

FRED W. McDARRAH

Babes in Boyland

BY HETTIE JONES

I N 1994, AT THE FIRST NEW YORK UNIVERSITY conference on the Beats, a question was addressed to me after a panel on "Women *and* the Beats." "In an earlier discussion," came a male voice from the back of the room, "someone said your role was actually insignificant, that you were just the typist. Can you address this?"

In the silence that followed, I struggled to get past my astonishment. The very idea, I went on to explain, assumed that *Yugen*, the magazine I published with LeRoi Jones (Amiri Baraka), had appeared in bookstores and on library shelves on the wings of song. Whereas, to the contrary, without the typist there'd have been no magazine at all, since the early issues of *Yugen,* as well as some of our Totem Press books, were, well, hand jobs. Put together on the kitchen table. And indeed I did the typing. In those pre-computer days, on a rickety, erratic IBM with "proportional spacing"—which meant typing a piece repeatedly until it approximated print. Centering Michael McClure's capitalized verses, organizing Hubert Selby's dense prose into justified lines. Besides typing I also handled the "press type"—peel-off display lettering you could buy on a sheet and then lay onto an original for photo offset. *Yugen* was subtitled *a new consciousness in arts and letters,* and, as I wrote in my memoir *How I Became Hettie Jones,* my consciousness was definitely raised by press-typing—and squaring over a makeshift light box—every letter of those words.

Insignificant?

I think the real—and unasked—question was, Why was the typist there? Why was she involved? Why, if her specific interests, as we know them today, were represented only marginally among the Beats if at all? Why was I willing to do all this work after eight hours on my day job? Why was I willing to buy paper, pay the offset printer and the rent on the typewriter? Arrange for distribution, fill orders, solicit ads and then throw a party for the people who came to do the collating?

Why were most of us babes even in that Boyland?

Sex of course—let's start with this and get it out of the way. Most, though not all, of the guys wanted us there for sex. And we ourselves were expecting it. Like some young women in every generation, some of us did have sex in the Fifties. You could have sex anywhere then—basement, backseat, haystack—as long as you remained silent about it, didn't live as if it were part of your life and didn't get caught or pregnant. With the Beats, though, we had escaped to a place where women could admit, or at least take for granted, their desires. Sort of. Sometimes. Here's a poem of mine from the Seventies, "Homage to Frank O'Hara's Personal Poem":

> Over and over the mind returns
> to the bent shoulders of the young woman
> who types, over and over, the poem
> until it is perfectly placed
> on the page, the name
>
> of her husband, the name
> of her lover
> the guilty thrill
> of juxtaposition as
>
> each gives
> to the poet

what he keeps
in his pocket

in her arms she holds them
over and over

But you had to have more than sex to keep you in Boyland with your pride intact. You had to be brave and resourceful. It had to be worse where you came from. As the narrator in one of my short stories says, "We women had all left bloodstains." You had to believe, as a woman, that stirring things up in general would eventually define a new life for you in particular. You had to believe in the transformative power of art, in the word, and you had to believe yourself part of that process.

This is not exactly how we've been remembered. Early on in the current revival of interest in the Beats, a college student came to interview me. Clearly anxious for some instant reassurance, she blurted out her first question—"You weren't just Beat chicks, were you?"—and was much relieved to learn that we'd been more than black stockings on spread legs. That we'd danced, painted, acted, and, yes, there were writers among us. And some who weren't writing—or if writing not publishing—did eventually write and publish. And others remained in the business of publishing, continuing a love of literature that had, in the first place, brought them to the scene.

The Beat Scene. The heat was great, I'll admit, but for me the core was the work. It was challenging, a lot of it was good, and I simply assumed that the best of what we published would eventually be recognized for its literary value. Making sure of that was another job for the typist. From 1957 to 1961 I was the girl [sic] in the office of the *Partisan Review*. *Partisan*'s distributor, Bernhard DeBoer—one of only a few distributors for the handful of literary magazines around in those years—agreed (because he liked us) to send *Yugen* across the country. Piggybacked on the old guard, it made its way onto midwest campuses and into West Coast bookstores. Despite its far-out focus and its few little offset pages stapled at the spine, despite the fact that it looked nothing like *Partisan* or *Kenyon* or even *Dissent*, it went to places like Brown and Purdue and Northwestern and Idaho State.

As Joyce Johnson tells it, Jack Kerouac went to sleep one night and woke up the next day famous. Similarly, to that Fifties Affluent Society, the Beat Generation seemed a pop-up surprise, an overnight, tailor-made threat. How hidden and feared were the worlds exposed in Ginsberg, Burroughs, Kerouac, Selby. And just as feared, I soon learned, by those who held tight to American letters. The Spring 1958 issue of *Partisan* featured "The Know-Nothing Bohemians," a review of *On the Road* by Norman Podhoretz, who trashed the book and what it celebrated: "The spirit of hipsterism and the Beat Generation," he wrote, "strikes me as the same spirit which animates the young savages in leather jackets who have been running amok in the last few years with their switchblades and zip guns."

That quote has staying power. Consider what might have happened had we not been in that spirit at that time.

But how do we speak to *this* time?

In the fall of 1995, when the Whitney Museum in New York presented "Beat Culture and the New America," like many I was skeptical at first about such an exhibit. But then I looked at the display of *Yugen* and other self-published magazines and broadsides, and felt not only sentiment but respect. Taking up where the Whitney left off, the New York Public Library in 1998 mounted "A Secret Location on the Lower East Side: Adventures in Writing, 1960–1980," celebrating some four hundred of these informal publications and crediting *Yugen* as one of the progenitors of an indie movement that has continued to influence American literature, poetry in particular.

Forty years before, bent over my drawing board cutting and pasting, I'd longed to make pretty books, like those from Auerhahn Press and City Lights, with real print that would honor the work. But *Yugen* and its equally funky contemporaries had done that, I realized, and were as worthy as any outsider art that exists because of the will of its creator, and not because of any immediate prospect of recognition or reward.

Nevertheless, that was then. The point, now, is not only to ensure that the spirit that moved us keeps its forward motion, but also that it survives to find its own future. Today, as then, established presses publish established writers ("presses" being an obsolete reference when what's meant is "corporation"). The NEA, created in the Sixties, is continually threatened in the Nineties, state-level lending hands are tied, and the recent Supreme Court "decency" decision has tightened the rope. It's discouraging to watch things come full circle, especially since, at the same time, interest in poetry and diverse voices seems to have grown. And since there are always talented new writers—as a teacher I collect evidence—I wonder, given the price of paper and the daunting task of distribution, whether what we did is at all possible or whether the Internet, with its incredible reach but ephemeral nature, is all there will be.

I am of two minds about this. The idea of reaching so many people is awesome to someone like me who dealt in such small numbers. Still, remembering those beautiful objects at the Whitney, I remain convinced that here today is not necessarily gone tomorrow if you are a magazine or a book or even a stapled-together collection of pages. Not long ago I came across these words on a poster: "The material record of the past in the form of objects, art and text continues to shape our identity," yet "this record is a mystery . . . transient, changing with each generation." One can only *hope* to be understood by the future. But

as part of that material record, you'll at least stand a chance to be there, in each object complete with its humanity—not only the writers and the cover artist and the editor and the typist, but everyone at the collating party, the music in their ears and the very dark horse they rode in on.

In this regard, I think it's best to urge respect for the original texts before they get lost in the impulse to explain decades in sound bites. A review of the CD-ROM "The Beat Exprience" described it as an "elegant, if incomplete, multimedia tour of the period," and after looking long and hard at the illustration of the Beatpad, and noting the couch and the rug, I decided it all seemed upscale to me, nostalgia wearing off the hard edge. Although we frequently had a wonderful time, arrests for obscenity and other scares were not pleasant. We also made a lot of passionate mistakes, and wrote plenty of bad poems. If I were a young person genuinely curious about the era, I'd want the whole story, not someone's version of the "experience."

Nor should anyone be fooled into thinking, simply because women have now established their presence among the Beats, that it was all too terrific to be the typist. Many, myself included, wanted far more of ourselves than we ever produced. I've been asked how women in that group got published, and the answer, with some notable exceptions, is "if men wanted to include them." It's true that there weren't too many demanding, since most of us were still at home, petting our washing machines or pretending to. The real lives of women, like the real lives of those "savages in leather jackets," were nowhere near the official story. Only a few of us knew how bad off we were. When I went back to original sources to research my memoir, the repression we'd resisted amazed me, and it was a relief to understand that, given where I'd come from, I'd summoned whatever consciousness I could.

To my suggestion that readers go to the original texts I'd add that the *body* of work of these writers be considered. This is especially important regarding women, not only because much of our contribution came later, but because our position in that outsider life remains equivocal: from "Women and the Beats" in 1994 we progressed to *Women of the Beat Generation* (Conari Press, 1996) to *A Different Beat* (Serpent's Tail/High Risk, 1997). Beware: If you're going to suggest Beat Women, you'll have to accept that redundancy, Beat Men.

Though in many ways now is not then, it's still easy to draw parallels between that moment at mid-century and now, at its end. We're still debating women's roles, and again in fear of art that points fingers. "What does not change / is the will to change," wrote Charles Olson. That will keeps alive the necessity for change. It seems as important as ever to hang in and encourage our children—and there certainly are a lot of them by now—hippies, punks, even the new little wannaBeats, who have been handed a world of real trouble along with their cyberspace. But at least, now, *everyone* is typing.

The Beat Generation and the Continuing American Revolution

BY JOHN TYTELL

Although it does seem difficult to believe, as late as the end of the 1960s, the Beats were regarded more as rabblerousers than writers of merit. While there had been enormous coverage in the media, in places like 'Time' and 'Life' magazines, it was more like bear-baiting than criticism, a taunting ridicule of a lifestyle that seemed incomprehensible or incorrigible to many whose values had been formed during the yawning complacency of what I like to call the frozen Fifties.

Even the more adventurous academic critics like Leslie Fiedler had no good words for the Beats. In fact, in academia, they were reviled and almost unanimously despised. Most scholars viewed the Beats as philistines without a viable literary past—a noisy species of distasteful and aberrant contemporary anomaly.

Many established writers seemed threatened by the quality and character of Beat writing, appalled as Allen Tate was by Burroughs's scatological sexuality, his scenes of sadistic terror presented in a scary moral vacuum. Randall Jarrell, accepting the National Book Award in 1960, castigated Kerouac, arguing that the quality of personal revelation in 'On the Road' was more suitable to successful psychoanalysis than fiction. Others, like Norman Podhoretz in his 'Partisan Review' essay "The Know-Nothing Bohemians," impugned Kerouac's ebullience, his romantic declaration that the writer should accept his original notation, that revision was a subtle form of censorship, an accommodation to satisfy an editor or public taste. Except for Gilbert Millstein in the 'New York Times'—a music critic who reviewed the novel during the summer when the regulars were away—most reviewers disparaged the manners of the characters in 'On the Road.'

The early reviews of "Howl," the first major publication by a Beat writer, and a book that changed the direction of American poetry in the mid-Fifties, document the awful initial reception of Beat writing. John Hollander, writing about his own Columbia classmate in a spirit of evident distrust for what he saw as modish avant-garde posturing, complained in 'Partisan Review' of the "utter lack of decorum of any kind in this dreadful little volume." James Dickey, in 'Sewanee Review,' established Ginsberg as the tower of contemporary Babel, finding the poem full of meaningless utterance.

An aspiring James scholar just out of the graduate program at NYU in 1968, I reviewed Kerouac's last novel, 'Vanity of Duluoz,' for the 'Catholic World,' and Bruce Cook's 'The Beat Generation,' a thin, insubstantial assessment of the Beats, for 'Commonweal.'

Also, while completing my thesis on Henry James's enormous changes in narrative strategy during the 1890s, I edited for Harper & Row 'The American Experience: A Radical Reader,' perhaps the first collection of countercultural writing. About as far as one could get from James's mannered gentility, the controversial book included writing from Norman Mailer, Timothy Leary, Malcolm X and Lenny Bruce, as well as Ginsberg.

In 1970 I was an untenured assistant professor in an English department with lots of star players at Queens College, considered the jewel of the CUNY system. Many of the young people of Queens were finally outraged by the interminable war in Southeast Asia, and they were demanding changes, sitting in corridors and occupying buildings, refusing to take spring semester final exams. Singing "We Shall Overcome!" with an inebriated revolutionary passion, over a hundred of them lay on the boiling pavement of the Long Island Expressway. To placate the students, the college devised what it called the Last Lecture Series, inviting prominent faculty members to address students as if this would be their last chance to say something meaningful in a university setting.

Perhaps because of the notoriety surrounding my 'Radical Reader,' I was asked to speak. Aware that students would not be interested in the fastidious euphonics or the leisure-class morality of Henry James, I decided to talk about the Beats, whom I had read eagerly as an undergraduate when their books first appeared.

When I reread 'On the Road,' 'Naked Lunch,' "Howl" and the poetry of Gary Snyder, I appreciated those works even more than on earlier readings. More than ever, I realized how misunderstood, maligned and patronized the Beats had been by critics and academics since the 1950s, and I decided to write an essay exploring their origins and importance. I also added Beat literature to my poetry and fiction classes. At the time, it was somewhat anomalous and certainly risky to begin teaching these figures in Queens, then a conservative, lower-middle-class, very white section of the city. I had to endure the dour condescension of some of my older colleagues who reminded me that I had been hired to teach James and the novel of sensibility—not a bohemian tradition of dubious distinction.

When in 1974 I proposed a course exclusively on the Beats, the committee in charge shuffled papers for a few semesters, and eventually let me do it in the evening. An overflow of enthusiastic students sent an immediate signal, making it apparent to me that the Beats were generational spokesmen, Zeitgeist writers who spoke directly to the needs of my students in ways that the authors on the ordained syllabus could never hope to approach.

In the meantime, realizing what the Beats needed most was intellectual credibility in the world of letters, I submitted my Last Lecture essay to 'The American Scholar,' the venerable publication of Phi Beta Kappa, the most prestigious honor society in America. The magazine held onto the piece for a very long time, almost eight months, and I later learned there had been a ferocious in-house squabble about whether they should publish it.

When it appeared, in the spring of 1973, I sent it to Allen Ginsberg. He responded enthusiastically, declaring that my essay would change the reputation of the Beats, and he sent copies to William Burroughs, John Clellon Holmes and others. I also sent the essay to Joyce Johnson, who had been Jack Kerouac's lover in 1957, the year 'On the Road' was published. Graciously receptive but a demanding editor, she was working at McGraw-Hill, which then had an active trade division, and she encouraged me with a contract for 'Naked Angels,' which would become the first comprehensive appraisal of Beat literature when it appeared in 1976.

Much of "The Beat Generation and the Continuing American Revolution" (most of which follows) found its way into the beginning of that book. At that time, except for Ann Charters's biography of Kerouac, there was virtually nothing of a secondary or scholarly nature that was useful on the subject. Now there is a small library with more than eighty general treatments, and another forty books about Kerouac alone.

I am not surprised by this. Over two decades ago, I predicted that the Beat Generation would in the long run arouse more interest worldwide than the 1920s Lost Generation of Hemingway and Fitzgerald because it was more coherent and had more clearly defined spiritual imperatives. "Howl" *and Lawrence Ferlinghetti's 'A Coney Island of the Mind' are the two most widely read books of poetry written by Americans in our time. 'On the Road' is in print in more than twenty countries and has sold over three million copies, sixty thousand in the United States each year. Now the Beats are taught in universities all over America. The 1995 Whitney Museum Beat Culture retrospective show, the 1996 exhibition of Burroughs's paintings at the Los Angeles County Museum of Art, the 1996 Venice Film Festival, which featured thirty Beat-related films, and the 1997 Beat conference at the Roosevelt Center in Holland are recent signs of the international vitality of this interest.*

—J.T., AUGUST 1998

THE RECEPTION AFFORDED TO WRITERS IS one index of cultural health. And when writers dare to voice political ideas, the relationship of audience to artist becomes an even more significant measure of a society's vitality. Since the European surrealists, no literary group has been as conscious of the political situation as the members of the Beat generation. Such fears as William Burroughs's projection of a "thought-control mob," or Allen Ginsberg's awareness of dangerous military excesses—concerns that once were regarded as mere hysteria by hostile critics— now seem to share the gift of prophecy.

During the vacuum of silence that embalmed the early 1950s the Beats stridently proclaimed a humanistic ideology and dramatized the beginnings of a new lifestyle, only to be greeted by scorn in official circles and the distortions of sensationalism in the media. Nevertheless, the romantic ideals and unconventional attitudes of Beat writers informed the generation of the 1960s with a vision of what was most perilous about American life. Rejecting the glut of postwar materialism and an obsessive national conformism, the Beats proposed a creed of individuality and a commitment to the life of the spirit with a passion that recalls the struggles of the American Transcendentalists—Emerson, Thoreau and Whitman. William Burroughs's *Naked Lunch*, Allen Ginsberg's "Howl," Jack Kerouac's *On the Road* and Gary Snyder's poetry provide a view of the intentions and accomplishments of an especially revealing literary movement.

One of the anomalies of the quiescent Fifties was the vociferous presence of the Beats as they fashioned a worldview that opposed the dominant values of their time. Few periods in our history have presented as much of an ordeal for artists as the decade of the Fifties. Norman Mailer, for example, in *The Prisoner of Sex*, wonders how he survived those years without losing his mind. What Allen Ginsberg has called the Syndrome of Shutdown began in the early Fifties: the move toward a closed society where all decisions would be secret; the paralysis caused by the use of technological devices to invade privacy; the perfectly paranoid atmosphere of McCarthyism; the increasing power of the Pentagon with its military bases designed to contain a new enemy supposedly (and suddenly) more threatening than the Nazis. The hysteria of rabid anticommunism was far more damaging than any native communism; the patriotic blood-boiling became a convenient veil assuring a continued blindness to domestic social conditions that desperately needed attention. An internal freeze gripped America in the Fifties, an irrational hatred that created intense fear and repression, and since any repression feeds on oppression as its necessary rationalization, the red witch-hunts, the censorship of artists and filmmakers, the regimentation of the average man began with unparalleled

momentum and design. The contamination caused by this psychic and moral rigidity has been discussed by Allen Ginsberg in a spring 1966 *Paris Review* interview:

The Cold War is the imposition of a vast mental barrier on everybody, a vast anti-natural psyche. A hardening, a shutting off of the perception of desire and tenderness which everybody knows ... [creating] a self-consciousness which is a substitute for communication with the outside. This consciousness pushed back into the self and thinking of how it will hold its face and eyes and hands in order to make a mask to hide the flow that is going on. Which it's aware of, which everybody is aware of really! So let's say shyness. Fear. Fear of total feeling, really, total being is what it is.

With the exception of the Civil War period, never before had the sense of hopefulness traditionally associated with the American experience been so damaged. The Fifties were times of extraordinary insecurity, of profound powerlessness as far as individual effort was concerned, when personal responsibility was being abdicated in favor of corporate largeness, when the catchwords were coordination and adjustment, as if we had defeated Germany only to become "good Germans" ourselves. The nuclear blasts in Japan had created new sources of terror, and the ideology of technology became paramount; science was seen as capable of totally dominating man and his environment. And the prospects of total an-nihilation through nuclear explosion, of mass conditioning through the media, only increased the awesome respect for scientific powers of the Fifties.

The Beats expressed hypersensitive concern for these conditions. In "The White Negro"—the first philosophical manifesto on the Beat

Jack Kerouac (left) and Allen Ginsberg poring over Proust's 'Remembrance of Things Past,' 1959
JOHN COHEN

movement—Norman Mailer suggested that America was suffering from a collective failure of nerve, and that only a new breed, the hipster, was prepared to forge a new nervous system. At the same time, Ginsberg flatly stated, in his essay "Poetry, Violence and the Trembling Lambs," that America was in the process of a nervous breakdown (the McCarthy hearings were, retrospectively, a visible symptom). Ginsberg argued that a vast conspiracy to impose one level of mechanical consciousness on mankind existed, that drugs were one force powerful enough to rupture that conditioning, and that a huge police bureaucracy would aid in the national brainwash and would persecute those spreading illumination.

Nowhere was the fear of institutional power more pronounced than in the nightmarish collage of *Naked Lunch*. Burroughs, assisted by Ginsberg, who helped him assemble the fragments he had been writing, pictured a future possibly far more dismal and terrifying than Orwell's *1984* or Huxley's *Brave New World*, a dystopia where technology strangles all vestiges of freedom, a police state where the human attributes of love and community are stripped away and defiled. *Naked Lunch* is an hallucinatory vision of the very worst expectations of the Fifties. Burroughs's central figure is the junkie, the weakest, most despised and vulnerable citizen, a Western version of India's untouchable caste. Ginsberg has written that to be a drug addict in America is like having been a Jew in Nazi Germany, and Burroughs reflects this idea of fascist control, magnifying its horror through the distorted lens of a junkie. The view of the drug experience is harshly antiromantic. Clinical, detached, almost scientifically cinematic, *Naked Lunch* is an educative warning against the horrors of addiction. It relentlessly parodies our institutional life, and at the same time makes apparent the deconditioning effects of drugs, which, like Dr. Benway's cures, are an end in themselves. Rarely has any novelist managed so explosive a struggle between the demands of total

control and the nihilistic impulse to defeat those in control. The ensuing combat is so ferocious that the novelist, ordering experience, seems distant and lost, especially to the reader already distracted by Burroughs's experimental bias.

If there is an intellectual center in *Naked Lunch*, it will be found in a pervasive suspicion of the dangers inherent in technology:

> *The end result of complete cellular representation is cancer. Democracy is cancerous, and bureaus are its cancer. A bureau takes root anywhere in the state, turns malignant like the Narcotics Bureau, and grows and grows, always reproducing more of its own kind, until it chokes the host if not controlled or excised. Bureaus cannot live without a host, being true parasitic organisms. (A cooperative on the other hand can live without the state. That is the road to follow. The building up of independent units to meet the needs of the people who participate in the functioning of the unit. A bureau operates on opposite principles in inventing needs to justify its existence.) Bureaucracy is wrong as a cancer, a turning away from the human evolutionary direction of infinite potentials and differentiation and independent spontaneous action to the complete parasitism of a virus.*

This passage exaggerates a social awareness into political ideology, pointing to the new communalism advocated by Ginsberg and Snyder. It is important because it is one of Burroughs's rare projections of anything that might resemble an ideal, for Burroughs's mood is a disgust so intense, so voluptuously vicious as to make any ideal seem false and impossible, and—American ideals, especially—precariously incompatible with the realities of world power.

Burroughs's disdain for future possibilities and his staunch antiromantic bitterness make him an exception among the Beat writers. He represents a logical fulfillment of the despair of T. S. Eliot's "The Waste Land." Curiously enough, the backgrounds of the two writers are similar: Both were born in St. Louis, both were descendants of

Cadets read "Howl": Virginia Military Institute, February 19, 1991. © GORDON BALL old American families (the Burroughs Adding Machine Company, ironically, in Burroughs's case), both attended Harvard, where Burroughs received a master's degree in anthropology. Both writers, especially in "The Waste Land" and *Naked Lunch*, share a destructive attitude toward form and structure. Burroughs's use of the "cut-up" method—an arbitrary juxtaposition of randomly selected words and phrases—is part of an attempt to restructure the grammar of perception; the new linguistic order that Burroughs invents initiates the Beats' assault on the conditioning influences of language.

Burroughs takes the motif of the unreal city from "The Waste Land" and compounds it with a nauseating imagery of hideous physical disintegration and degradation that promises a state of future plague. His hanged men episodes in *Naked Lunch* are grotesque parodies of the talismanic material Eliot himself parodied with the grail legend in "The Waste Land." Burroughs presents these horrors with an unsettling calm, a cold earnestness reminiscent of Swift, a view of the psychological transformations latent in fantasy close to Kafka, and a picture of man as helpless victim that reminds us of Sartre, Beckett and Genet. Entering the absolute nadir of existence, Burroughs's fiction defines a purgatory of endless suffering—Beat in the sense of beaten, oppressed and dehumanized. Yet, Ginsberg's and Kerouac's pathway to beatitude stemmed from Burroughs's nightmare of devastation.

Burroughs's affinity with Eliot's objectivity and impersonality raises an aesthetic issue that is crucial for the Beats; because of this affinity, Burroughs, in an interview that appeared in a fall 1965 issue of the *Paris Review*, denied belonging to the Beat movement, and emphasized the differences in form among writers he considered more as friends than literary compatriots. The effect of Burroughs's vision on Ginsberg and Kerouac—who both frequented Burroughs's apartment near Columbia University in the late 1940s—cannot be denied; Kerouac, for example, makes Burroughs an oracular source of the wisdom of experience as Bull Lee in *On the Road*. But Burroughs's fiction, while capable of diagnosing what the Beats saw as threatening about American values—especially the worship of technology—did not project a sense of self strong enough to counter the debilitating apathy of the culture. In this respect, Burroughs is in accord with Eliot's notion that the artist's progress is measured by how well he transcends personality and private emotion.

Conversely, Ginsberg and Kerouac made personality the center and subject of their work. In the Fifties, when the voice of personality seemed so endangered by an anonymity of sameness, the Beats discovered a natural counter for the silence of the day in a new sense of self, a renaissance of the romantic impulse to combat unbelievably superior forces. The Beats crashed through the restraining mask of the removed artist in a search for what Ginsberg termed "Unified Being." The objective camera eye of "The Waste Land" would be replaced by the "I" of the personal in "Howl;" the difference can be felt simply by listening to the sound of Eliot reading his work—dry, unemotional, ironic, distant—and comparing that to Ginsberg's impassioned, arousing, rhapsody of voice.

The Beats' denial of the artistic mask had extraordinary implications for the nature of language in literary art and the quality of experience to be expressed. Prematurely conscious of the potentials for lying on a national scale, the Beats raised the standard of honesty no matter what the artistic consequences. Art is created by the polar tensions of spontaneity and artifice, improvisation and contrivance, and the Beats passionately embraced the extreme of uncontained release and denounced superimposed and confining forms. Kerouac, in "Essentials of Spontaneous Prose," attacked the concept of revision sacred to most writers as a kind of secondary moral censorship imposed by the unconscious, and compared the writer to the jazz saxophonist in search of language as an undisturbed flow from the mind. In a sense, the nitrous oxide experiments of William James and Gertrude Stein at Harvard, which resulted in automatic writing, anticipated Kerouac's denial of the artist's traditional selectivity.

Ginsberg has addressed this question in his spring 1966 *Paris Review* interview with great clarity:

> ... what happens if you make a distinction between what you tell your friends and what you tell your Muse? The problem is to break down that distinction: when you approach the Muse to talk as frankly as you would talk with yourself or with your friends. So I began finding, in conversation with Burroughs and Kerouac and Gregory Corso, in conversations with people whom I knew well, whose souls I respected, that the things we were telling each other for real were different from what was already in literature. And that was Kerouac's great discovery in 'On the Road.' The kind of things that he and Neal Cassady were talking about, he finally discovered were the subject matter for what he wanted to write down. That meant, at that minute, a complete revision of what literature was supposed to be, in his mind, and actually in the minds of the people that first read the book.... In other words, there's no distinction, there should be no distinction between what we write down, and what we really know to begin with. As we know it every day, with each other. And the hypocrisy of literature has been—you know like there's supposed to be a formal literature, which is supposed to be different from ... in subject, in diction and even in organization ... our quotidian inspired lives.

The goal of complete self-revelation, of nakedness as Ginsberg put it, was based on a fusion of bohemianism, psychoanalytic probing and Dadaist fantasy in "Howl" that dragged the self through the slime of degradation to the sublime of exaltation. While the idea of self is the Beat focal point, it represents only a beginning, an

involvement to be transcended. The movement in Ginsberg's poetry is from an intense assertion of personal identity to a merger with larger forces in the universe. The ensuing tension between the proclamation of self—evident in a poem like "America"—and an insistence upon man's eternal place in time creates a central dialectical opposition in Ginsberg's poetry. Believing that consciousness is infinite, and that modern man has been taught to suppress much of his potential awareness, Ginsberg attempted to exorcise the shame, guilt and fear that he sees as barriers to self-realization and total being. Ginsberg's work, generally, is an outgrowth of the tradition begun by Coleridge: to search for the source of dream, to release the unconscious in its pure state (avoiding literary simulation), to free the restraints on imagination and seek (as Blake did) the potency and power of the visionary impulse.

Ginsberg saw his poetry as transmitting a sacred trust in human potentials, and he spoke in the *Paris Review* interview of how his mystical encounter with Blake in 1948 revealed to him the nature and direction of his own search as a poet. Ginsberg, then living in New York's East Harlem, suddenly heard a voice reciting Blake's "Ah! Sun-Flower" and "The Sick Rose." Ginsberg said that the resulting feeling of lightness, awe and wonder catalyzed him as a poet, making him see that his role would be to widen the area of consciousness, to open the doors of perception, to continue to transmit messages through time that could reach the enlightened and receptive.

Ginsberg's poetry is characteristic of the Beat desire *to be*, affirming existence as a positive value in a time of apathy. The quest for experience is as obsessive and all-consuming in "Howl" as it is in *On the Road*. Whether these experiences are destructive or not is of less importance than the fact of contact, especially the kinds of experience that allow an individual to discover his own vulnerability, his humanness, without cowering. As Gary Snyder argued in his essay "Why Tribe," to follow the grain of natural being "it is necessary to look exhaustively into the negative and demonic powers of the Unconscious, and by recognizing these powers—symbolically acting them out—one releases himself from these forces." This statement points to the shamanistic implications of Beat literature; "Howl," like *Naked Lunch*, is an attempt to exorcise through release. While Burroughs's novel futuristically projects into fantasy, "Howl" naturalistically records the suffering and magnanimity of a hipster avant-garde, a group refusing to accept standard American values as permanent. The experiences in "Howl," certainly in the opening part of the poem, are hysterically excessive and frantically active. It is the sheer momentum of nightmare that unifies these accounts of jumping off bridges, of slashing wrists, of ecstatic copulations, of purgatorial subway rides and longer journeys, a momentum rendered by the propelling, torrential quality of Ginsberg's long line, a cumulative rhythm, dependent on parallelism and repetition of initial sounds, that is biblical in origin.

Ginsberg's poetry ranges in tone from ecstatic joy to utter despair, soaring and plunging from one line to the next, confident, paranoid, always seeking ways to retain the ability to feel in numbing times, always insisting on a social vision that stresses transcendence and the need for spirit in the face of a materialistic culture. No wonder Bob Dylan remarked that Ginsberg's poetry was for him the first sign of a new consciousness, of an awareness of regenerative possibilities in America. That Dylan shares Ginsberg's surrealistic imagination is evident in early recordings like "Subterranean Homesick Blues," but even more, Dylan participates in the Beat affinity for the road, the symbol of an attitude toward experience that braves anything as long as movement is encouraged.

The first account of this sensibility is found in Norman Mailer's 1957 essay "The White Negro." Mailer announced the appearance of a new man, whom he termed the "hipster," who found an existential model in the danger felt by the black man every time he walked down an American street. Seeking, sometimes psychopathically, the "rebellious imperatives of the Self," the hipster rejected the conformity of American life, and spread a "disbelief in the words of men who had too much money and controlled too many things." The hipster sought an apocalyptic answer to the demands of adjustment in the American pattern; he would become, Mailer promised, the thorn in an emerging totalitarian society. The hipster, in a constant attempt to change his nervous system, would always express forbidden impulses and actively violate social taboos; like Elvis Presley, Lenny Bruce, even Rojack in Mailer's *American Dream*, he would release primitive energies before a repressive society. Responding to a "burning consciousness of the present," the hipster stressed the energy of movement and magnified Hemingway's concentrated formula of "grace under pressure" to confront a state of perpetual crisis.

The new forces perceived by Mailer form Kerouac's ideological focus in *On the Road,* a novel that seems characteristically American in its search for a fluid, unshaped life, free of preimposed patterns, fearing most the horrors of stasis, of staying in the same place without the possibility of change. The reviewers misread the novel almost without exception, finding it incoherent, unstructured, unsound as art and unhappy as prophecy. Instead of seeing Dean Moriarty as a genuine picaresque center, and thereby a source of unity in a novel about turbulence, the reviewers attacked the sensibility of nihilism. It is, perhaps, easier to see Dean today as a remarkable fusion of desperation and joy, as the "ragged and ecstatic joy of pure being" to borrow Kerouac's description, an utterly rootless individual who careens from coast to coast on sudden impulse, a man whose incredible energy makes a mockery of the false idol of security. The sign of Dean's freedom is his infectious laughter. In the novel, laughter—even in the presence of despair—becomes a kind of life-force, a token of spirit; merely to laugh at the world, like the existentialist ability to say no, becomes a valuable source of inspiration for Kerouac. Dean has been in jail and reads Proust; but his defining quality is speed—in conversation, in a car, in his lifestyle. Kerouac, depicting Dean as a function of speed, has saliently tapped the distinguishing strain of American life in the second half of the Twentieth Century. This speed is reflected in an extraordinary hyperactivity that determines the atmosphere of the novel:

> The only people for me are the mad ones, the ones who are mad to live, mad to talk, mad to be saved, desirous of everything at the same time, the ones who never yawn or say a commonplace thing but burn, burn, burn like fabulous yellow roman candles exploding like spiders across the stars.

All the Beat writers—and Gregory Corso is an especially good example of this—use madness as a source of wonder, as a way of breaking through the apathy that they found so asphyxiating in the Fifties.

But Kerouac himself, through the figure of his narrator, Sal Paradise, tried to offer a check on Dean's exuberant anarchism. And Sal is inevitably drained by the momentum of experience, always aware of growing older and saddened by this; like Kerouac, he is an outsider, an imperfect man in an alien world, brooding, lonely, seized by moments of self-hatred. The refrain in On the Road of "everything is collapsing" is a reminder of the effects of disorder, of Kerouac's own vision of uncontained release, on himself. Clearly the endless celebrations, the pell-mell rushing from one scene to the next, create an hysteria that makes Sal want to withdraw from the world. This conflict between the demands of Self as expressed by Dean, and the need to extinguish Self as expressed by Sal, becomes the pivot of Kerouac's fiction; with The Dharma Bums, his next novel, and the influence of Gary Snyder, the movement toward union with nature begins.

In The Dharma Bums, Kerouac dramatized a crucial shift in the Beat sensibility; instead of continuing to seek escape from boredom and the spiritually corrupting emphasis on materialism and careers through desperate activity, Kerouac began an inward search for new roots. The Dharma Bums replaces the hysteria of On the Road with a quietly contemplative retreat toward meditation. Like On the Road, it is a very personal novel based on Kerouac's experiences; in this case living with Allen Ginsberg (Alvah Goldbook in the novel) in Berkeley during the early Fifties, and meeting Gary Snyder (Japhy Ryder in the novel). Kerouac, not always generous when depicting his friends, offers an extremely favorable account of Snyder studying Chinese and Japanese, reading Pound, exploring the tenets of Zen Buddhism, emulating the ascetic Buddhist poet Han Shan; taking Kerouac into the mountains on camping trips, teaching him a new independence, a new pride in the body; acting with charity, giving gifts spontaneously in contrast to Western acquisitiveness; generally preparing Kerouac for transformation of his values by isolating him in nature, creating in Kerouac a more profound sense of his own vulnerability than hitchhiking ever provided.

The warmth that Kerouac described in the character of Japhy Ryder, the overflowing ebullience, the need for affirmation in spite of a deep sense of doom in Western culture, the contagious vitality and love for life, all find ample reflection in Snyder's poetry. His main subject has always been nature—whatever threatens or enhances it.

Like Thoreau, Snyder withdraws to nature for substance, and to regain a sense of what is essential for life. Thoreau, who warned that the Western reliance on mechanical means would end with man becoming a "tool of his tools," offered a perception that is repeated in Snyder's observation, in his 1969 essay "Poetry and the Primitive," that "a hand pushing a button may wield great power, but that hand will never learn what a hand can do. Unused capacities go sour." Snyder's vigils as mountain lookout on Sourdough Mountain and Glacier Peak are confluent with Thoreau's watch at Walden Pond; ironically, like Whitman's unfortunate experience with the Department of the Interior after the Civil War, Snyder was discharged by the Forestry Service as a security risk during the Fifties. Thoreau and Snyder used hermetic withdrawal as purification, as a detoxification of social poisons; each acted in the surety that vulnerability to nature leads to the fullest expression of one's humanity, and permits the natural passions to flow without corruption.

Snyder uses nature to see the direction of our civilization more clearly; he has stated that for him the wilderness is the equivalent of the unconscious, and in his sentient communion with nature there is much to admire. In *Myths and Texts*, Snyder employs his knowledge of logging and hunting to separate himself from the destructively parasitic relation to nature that characterizes our past. Snyder writes of trees being cut for suburbs, of choking creeks and dying trout with a passion that makes it obvious why the ecology movement has discovered him.

As a nature poet, Snyder's imagination has been honed and clarified by his study of Zen Buddhism, which has given him the ability to cut through to essentials "like a blade which sharpens to nothing," to borrow one of his own images, and to see the vital interrelationship of man and nature. He never uses his Buddhist lore sentimentally or naively, but always with a practical accommodation to Western needs that again makes us think of Thoreau. He has written that his involvement with Zen has taught him two things that seem central to the Beat quest: the virtue of poverty as a way of avoiding the materialism that has depleted the soul of the West, and the virtue of wandering, that is, no confinement whether spiritual or physical. He has voiced the same prophetic concern for the American Indians, seeing how our domestication of the wilderness began with our wars against them. Snyder's interest in Indian and nomadic cultures is part of an attempt to find a more universal basis for understanding the peculiarities of Western existence. As a poet, his fascination with Indians and with the East (he trained with Buddhist monks, spending nearly a decade in Japanese monasteries) has resulted in a departure from the exclusive reliance on classical and biblical myth that has dominated Western poetry. Instead, Snyder has been stimulated by legends of primitive peoples all over the world, and his vision has been fortified by an awareness of forty thousand years of human existence. Snyder's experience has been broader than that of many of his contemporaries, and he seems far less rigid, less dogmatically bound by Western conditioning.

Traditionally, one indication of the vitality of a literary movement has been the following it attracts among writers, the degree and quality of literary imitation. But the issue of literary genealogy is hardly as crucial with the Beats as past movements. One reason for this is that the Beats' experiments with open forms, in poetry and fiction, encourage formal variety and difference, and therefore make them less apparent as a school. Their unity, indeed their very identity, is a function of shared attitudes rather than one of common form. The American ancestors of the Beats are men like Thoreau, essentially conservative in his distrust of industry and its machines, protecting the natural in aristocratic isolation (reading his Homer at Walden Pond), and men like Whitman, optimistically proclaiming with egalitarian gusto the newness of America, joyously celebrating the potential of the common man.

The real descendants of the Beats may not be writers at all, but a growing number of young people who share the essential quest initiated by the American transcendentalists. The Beats, deconditioned by their defeats and the shocks of romantic experience, began to raise such possibilities again in an era of ominous malaise. They have vigorously sustained their attacks on the Moloch of industry, on the regimentation of the bureaucratic state, and by eliminating the separation between an artist's work and his life, they have made of themselves living symbols. Suddenly, in the Sixties, what had been merely literature became social action. The seed planted by Beat literature is an awareness of what is significant in life. While it may be too soon to measure the extent and degree of change, it is certain that the quality of life in America has been profoundly affected. Rarely has any literary group enjoyed such an impact on its times, but then hardly any other literary group has made as concerted an effort to cause such change.

D1718

THE NEW NOVEL BY

JACK KEROUAC

AUTHOR OF

ON THE ROAD

THE DHARMA BUMS

The sensational bestseller
about two reckless wanderers
out to scale the heights
of life...and love

A SIGNET BOOK COMPLETE AND UNABRIDGED

Another Superficial Piece
About 158 Beatnik Books

BY RICHARD MELTZER

What Beat is. What Beat isn't. Who it is and isn't. Stuff like that.

TEN, TWELVE YEARS AGO I WAS talking to some small-press jerk, a publisher of pamphlets and broadsides and occasional forty-page books and such, who didn't much care for the Beats. His idea of a Real Poet was somebody like James Merrill. Artaud to him was not a poet, and Wallace Stevens was vastly preferable to Ezra Pound, who in turn was preferable to William Carlos Williams. His bottom line on Beats was they had nothing much to offer beyond the ambiguous (libertine) gushings and spoutings of any other bohemian lit cult, and his only interest in 'em—historically—was that much of their early work saw its first light of print in venues much like his (though his own whimsical notion of publishing destiny was more on the order of being absorbed someday as an imprint of Knopf than spreading/thriving mushroom-like, City Lights–like, on its own enduring compost patch of back-catalog populism).

Anyway, we're talking, and he's asking me, challenging me, to come up with one example of something (anything!): a single bookwrit perception by a Beat living or dead that a non-Beat of equivalent mettle would've found impossible—or at least difficult—to come by. So I think for a sec and I mention this scene late in *The Dharma Bums*, which I was reading at the time, where Jack Kerouac, backpack-weary on a strange dark street in Eisenhower frontlawn suburbia, flashes on how dogs bark at pedestrian footfalls but not hissing, squealing automobile tires—how maddening— and he, the jerk, says, "Okay, that's something." Gee, that was easy. (Where even *I* didn't think— and don't think—that was v. much in the way of an actual New Offering.)

WENT to this party back in high school, few weeks after the '60 elections, an idiot teen "beatnik party," my first, though they'd been having such events for at least a couple years by then. Sweatshirts, berets, sunglasses. Drawn-on goatees. Rock & roll of the moment. No jazz. (No reefer.) Bongos notwithstanding, after an hour I was feeling kind of down, y'know?, 'cause it seemed to me even then that beatnik meant something, man, something more than a roomful of bullshit, something on the order of, well—dig it—Kennedy. Or something.

THIS guy I know who makes low-budget horror films is always trying to make a case for Maynard G. Krebs as a beatnik, a *real* beatnik, to which I tell him: Maynard G. Krebs was a ROLE played on the *Dobie Gillis* show by Bob Denver, the basic thrust of which was I-hate-work/what-can-I-pretend-*this*-week-is-totally-absurd-enough-to-call-groovy? If you wanna go so far as to declare such shtick (qua shtick) Beat, you might as well call the Fonz (even Springsteen) punk rock. You can, but what's the payoff? Thin it out that much, why bother?

If you're gonna have parodies, I'd sooner accept insider parodies like Ed Sanders. Or second-raters who seem as shallow as Maynard, and maybe even *are*, but at least are so ingenuously, like Jack Micheline or Carl Solomon. And Beats as hipsters: *what* hipsters? You could get by

—and tell no lie—describing them all as a bunch of squares. Hip is but one of the myriad parameters of experience—vectors on being—Beats embraced. Kerouac may get off on Lester Young in *On the Road*, but he also does a number on Beethoven's *Fidelio*.

Inclusive vs. exclusive: That *they*—the originals—were wildly inclusive resources of input doesn't mean *you* should include (as fellow travelers) every heavy-outlined cartoon, every cardboard-mounted EXPLOITATION that came down the pike. Even "endearing" (and enduring) ones like Maynard.

Still, there's occasionally something not wholly unappealing about the cliché qua *litrachoor*. Which is to say (for inst.) that Beatnik Poetry Contests *can* have their charm, are in any event *not always* thoroughly loathsome. Where a Pre-Raphaelite Poetry Contest (or Hemingway Parodython) would be inconceivable in any remotely similar context—among the real-time-make-your-own-fun crowd, let's say—Beat is (perhaps) the most recognizable of literary affiliations, the most tip-of-tongue topical, the most (even if ironically/sarcastically) "enjoyable" qua text—groovable, and (within limits) imitable—by a total outsider (literary neophyte) (functional illiterate).

Which means what—beatnik art is "democratic"? "Double-open"? "Transcultural"? Don't ask me, I'm still fishing.

In grocery-listing what Beat might possibly be "about," it would be too easy to push buttons that are ultimately Hippie, which I really can't see Beat as precursor of—*the* precursor of—nohow. I mean it is/isn't, but mostly—and most crucially—it is not, any more than Elvis is the Grateful Dead—and I don't even mean in a "generational," decade-referenced "zeitgeist" type of way. Hippie, if you wanna play such cards, was

simultaneously the more- and the less-concrete Actual World version of certain prominent/superficial (genuine/imagined) aspects of Beat Writ Large. Had more to do with rock & roll, and different drugs (differently *defined* drugs), anyway.

In *my* dumb retrospect, it's more like the substance and tenor of Beat skipped a generation. Beat seems much more like, has at heart much more to do with, Punk (hey—it wasn't hedonism, it wasn't flowers, it was more, y'know, *beat*). It's also arguable that those Beats who played a participatory role in early Hippie (with the exception of Neal Cassady, who was just *digging it*—while fucking and chauffeuring it—and Sanders, who was young enough to have his own band), e.g., Allen Ginsberg, Gary Snyder, Michael McClure, were simply SEDUCED by its paradise-now easy ride (not to mention the elder-statesman preeminence it for ten minutes afforded them—before casting them in the over-thirty geezer slag heap with everybody else), but this seduction had no more basis in Universal Oompah than kids voting for McGovern over Nixon (f'rinstance), like why the hell not?

Reading Beat literature calms (soothes) me the way Buddhism—or let's say Buddhist literature—or even Walt Whitman—can't (or doesn't). Or maybe I don't let it, but I let Beat. Soothes me the way watching the rain can. Or a cat washing himself.

Okay—first stab—what separates the Beats from other "writing scenes" is its undivided insistence: Let's get naked (for five minutes) and tell the truth (let's at least *try*, okay?) . . . and this at a Time, a Place, when/where, said Ginsberg, "the suppression of contemplative humanity [was] nearly complete." Which is not even to say, *hmm*, Let's get honest—if we're really naked, the truth'll just fucking ooze out, can't help but ooze out: writing as emanation of a writer's buck-naked soul (speaking by turns loud/soft/thudding/purring/silent), not even an art-on-a-pedestal "transcription" of such stuff: real lifeblood, real mammal sweat, real sweet-dream vapor.

(Which eliminates John Updike.)

The intersection of kicks and cellular concern?
The neat and the sloppy?

The roster.

Since there *is* no such thing as Beat Style—it's a wild pluralism that escapes simple taxonomy—Kerouac made book on the forge of first-draft automatic writing; William Burroughs purloined (and cut up) pre-existent texts; Snyder was influenced by haiku and Robinson Jeffers; Philip Whalen has acknowledged his debt to Gertrude Stein, of all people—Beat writing is best approached as no more, no less than writing by any and all Beats. To qualify as a Beat, for this piece anyway, it's enough to be a friend (at the very least: friend of a friend) of a Beat, specifically of Kerouac, Ginsberg, Burroughs . . . some finite interpersonal extension of one or more of these three. Don't mean to sound fatuous, or again beg the question, but friendship, along with the (lingering, intertwining) friendships, plural, between/among the writers involved, is the very content—the meat—of much of their poetry and prose; all the references and homages to each other, down even to the merest namedrop, seem more heartfelt (and necessary) than traditional writerly protocol would require; their literary interplay (the cross-feeding, the trial-and-error, the shared open-lab environment) is vital and immense; the projected (still ongoing) sense of "literary community" is perhaps more authentic (for its size) than any there has ever otherwise been.

But of course (thankgod) it's a 360-degree deal: Love, hate and indifference make the whole

thing (for want of a better expression) existentially real to the short hairs. Looking for a little betrayal? Check out five pages from the end of *On the Road*, where Dean Moriarty (Neal) leaves Sal Paradise (Jack) fevered and delirious in Mexico City . . . and five pages later Jack toasts him as a grand wink of the planetary Night.

If for no other reason than that he was basically a loner (though you could certainly come up with plenty of others), Charles Bukowski was *not* Beat: no!

Apropos of nothing (and everything), in multifarious nonfrivolous ways, Kerouac, Ginsberg and Burroughs are to Beat what Charlie Parker, Dizzy Gillespie and Thelonious Monk were to bebop. Parker and Kerouac: universe blazers, stripminers of personal pneuma and easily the finest (most consistently exciting) soloists. Ginsberg/Gillespie: the behavioral flamboyance, the scene-manifesting definition-starts-here show-and-tell, scene-steering sometimes to the point of trivialization, of horseshit on dotted lines as hokey as any their respective scenes were born to kill—but still, much work of seminal muscle and technical brilliance. Burroughs and Monk: the odd men out, stylistically and attitudinally different enough to be "not really Beat," "not really bop" (just majorly, transcendentally significant and "of the time"), reassessors, dynamiters of prevailing form (and challengers of audience forbearance).

Okay, some Beat books I've read . . .

The standard line on Kerouac, *a* line, common enough, is *On the Road* is his masterpiece, while its mandated sequel, *The Dharma Bums*, is simply not in its class. I see it a little different. *On the Road*, good as it is, is far from Jack's high-water mark, no better than his fifth or sixth best, and *Bums* isn't far behind. There are even days when I'll reverse the pecking order. It's mainly a question of whether you wanna read about Neal (Dean Moriarty) or Snyder (Japhy Ryder), or about the late-Forties Jack as opposed to the mid-Fifties installment. The prose in *Bums* is maybe a little more bite-size, less willfully rambling and nutty, but the basic fictional premise— the film of my life, take it or leave it—is identical.

His actual bloody masterpiece, and one of the great, great works of the English language, is *Big Sur*. The great first-person now-I-begin-to-die novel, it documents a few weeks of horror as Jack was pushing forty at Lawrence Ferlinghetti's cabin overlooking the Pacific, where L.F. had convinced him he could dry out (he'd been drinking heavily for years) and write nature poems and whatnot and never have to drink again. He does nature and poems for a couple weeks, hitches back (or tries to—a failure so traumatic he would never hitch again) to San Francisco, meets and greets old faces, new faces, and puts a down payment on his terminal drunk. In the course of things, he yells "fuck you" at a Michael McClure only asking for (as promised) the address of Jack's editor, has his last civil encounter with Neal, during which he is "given" the last in a long string of women Neal would for various reasons dump on him (he falls for her, unfalls for her, then tries to stir up trouble between her and Mrs. Neal, his own erstwhile slumbermate Carolyn), wakes up drunk in a park with the saintly Philip Whalen watching over him (last documented instance of a saint doing such for him), steps all over the generosity of Lew Welch and Lenore Kandel— friendships stretched to their limit—*snap*—as much an explanation for why he then/there began to *officially* pack it in as any. Finally, sick from all the cheap swill he's been drinking, he returns to the cabin for the third or fourth time, d.t.'s rampant, to hallucinate Neal's woman's kid as the (literal) devil—after which he sucked it up,

went home to mom and sat down and wrote it, raking himself over coals even he (the self-loathe champ) had never dreamed of, and seven years later he was dead (so it took a while).

A notch down is *The Subterraneans*. Written in three days on speed in the fall of '53, it's as good as it gets for a three-day novel—or a lost-love-tearing-my-guts-out novel of any gestation. Of all the early-to-midfilm-of-my-life works ("the Duluoz Legend"), as hot a read as most of it tends to be, only *The Subterraneans* stands out as an *ur*-expression of topical etcetera—the tale told as Screaming Literature—and it isn't really until *Big Sur* ('62) and *Vanity of Duluoz* ('68) that he manages to come up with a Different Kind of Statement, a breakaway, then another, to the Other Side of Writing, a pair of fully focused New Ways of telling tales at all—above and beyond the fact of write-ing them—and this at a time when the overall level of his writing—qua writing—was at its peak, its zenith, never better, never stronger— am I lost yet?—talking 'bout the life and times of *The Subterraneans* . . . or some such. Anyway: the story of Jack and Mardou—a black woman, played in the film version by Leslie Caron (!)— who eventually fucks Gregory Corso (not in film). George Peppard played Jack; everybody lives hap ever aft at film's end—and real-life Jack had yet another alibi for drinking till his esophagus hemorrhaged.

Vanity of Duluoz is the sleeper, last one to come out while he was still alive, some bios even label it lousy, or pass over it as the feeble output of a dying man, but it's one of his very best. In form, it's kind of I've-got-this-to-say-and-that-to-say (listen well or walk out—but you'll miss some *surprises*)—a cross between Ring Lardner and Thucydides? No more Buddhist humility (and a few quarts down from his normal quota of "compassion"), it's a take-off-the-gloves affair, not too kind to Ginsberg (or even Burroughs for that matter). Covers a lot of autobio space/time not touched on elsewhere, for ex, Jack, football star (with rude comments 'bout his college coach, Lou Little), his buddy Lucien Carr's stabbing of Dave Kammerer.

A couple of shorties, *Tristessa* and *Visions of Gerard*, 96 and 150 pages, respectively, also deserve wider recognition. The former, consisting of two time-separated takes on the march to the Abyss of a heroin-addicted Mexican prostitute, is possibly his best single-subject hunk of prose writing. The latter, a meditation on the death of his older brother from rheumatic fever (Jack was four at the time), presents the author in a windy world of pain and incomprehensible grownup protocols, and contains probably his longest third-person run, a multi-page fantasy about his father and his poker buddies.

Pull My Daisy is the script from the film of the same name—Jack's voice-over, improvised in two sessions while he watched the visuals—camera follows a roach to a piece of cheese, it's a "cheese roach."

Maggie Cassidy, story of a high school romance, goes on and on, a not-unbearable melodrama—'bout him not getting laid—until the last two chapters, which end it like a Faulkner (years pass, home from the wars, he tries to get off her panty girdle—change of narrative voice—no go): not bad. Also: We learn that he did in fact drive alone (or says he did) (only evidence in any of the books), working nights at a garage in hometown Lowell, Mass.

Lonesome Traveler is a collection of odds and ends with a travel tie-in, many of which had been published in *Holiday* and *Escapade* and whatnot, and most of which could've been recycled into early to mid novels, as inserts or whatever, but weren't (or cover turf previously covered anyway). "The Railroad Earth" and "Piers of the Homeless Night" are pretty good. In "New York Scenes" he mentions Robert De Niro's artist father.

Even *Doctor Sax* and *Pic* ain't half bad if you read 'em with Jack's reading voice in mind, for which the Rhino three-disc box set, *The Jack Kerouac Collection*, is (in spite of its glitzy gosh-oh-gee booklet) invaluable. *Sax*, the only one of his novels written entirely (or close) on marijuana, doesn't really make it as, in Jack's words, "Faust Part Three," or even as much of a childhood-is-*so*-scary *roman à reefer*, but it has its moments. The much-maligned *Pic*, a twenty-year-old manuscript dusted off and fussed with (minimally) toward the end, though not soon enough to be issued before he was dead, doesn't play at all if you read it as an African-American dialect joke—natch—but if you read it as *Jack* reading the joke . . . hey, there's some real warmth and tenderness there (believe it).

Then there are the clunkers. Only thing worth a damn about *Book of Dreams*, the sole Kerouac published by City Lights during Jack's lifetime (they passed on *On the Road*), is the cover shot of Jack sleeping . . . tells you something about Ferlinghetti's taste. *Mexico City Blues*, consisting of "242 choruses"—y'know, jazz—has a couple-few good things, or let's call 'em *interesting*, in most cases they're about death (24, 57, 184), but mainly it's just page after page of lesser (much lesser) "Beat poetry"—his best poetry (and he was the best Poet of the whole dang bunch) is in his prose. In *Satori in Paris*, about an aborted Sixties trip to find his family's trail in dusty French archives (mostly he gets drunk and decides to chuck it), he isn't sure himself that anything especially eye-opening (satori: "kick in the eye") actually happened. *Desolation Angels*, which covers the period from the end or so of *Dharma Bums* to the release of *On the Road*, should've been a good'un but it's really the shits. At one point, en route to California with his mother (Mémère)—the light of his life, bane of his being and only woman he ever took on the road—he comments that if you can't dig it, "tell it to Mao."

Even guest appearances by Lafcadio Orlovsky—Peter's brother—and Alan Watts don't ultimately redeem things.

Call me a heretic, call *my* mom a whore, but I find *Visions of Cody*, his "nonlinear" Cassady book, largely unreadable and not just because every edition I've seen has had a miniscule typeface. Opening with a shitload of viable, but increasingly monotonous, unconnected "sketches" (lonely ladies in the rain . . . a pork chop in Hartford '41 . . . following Lee Konitz into a music store), it slowly but surely reveals itself as a top-heavy (bottom-heavy) (all-heavy) four hundred pages without much payoff—*Moby Dick* without an Ahab to take everybody to hell. Even Jack's voice, his and Neal's combined, can't save it, and what Ginsberg, McClure, et al., rave about is (I'm guessing) what they'd like to IMAGINE it is (it isn't!) . . . the kitchen sink, ma! (has lots o' leaks). Verbatim transcripts of actual taped conversations between Neal and Jack—or alternating monologues—only serve to underscore the difference (and distance) between verbatim spoken and verbatim written. Jack's stream of vocal consciousness was *less* interesting than his unedited stream of writerly etc. (or: his ear for *recollected* speech beats the hand as originally dealt), and Neal's vocals here are less hot, less "on," than the voice in his letters. Some of the black stuff even seems racist this time (racist as a non-ironic I'm-pure-so-I-can-use-the-word-*nigger*, racist as this-is-*America*-and-I-can-say-what-I-want provocation). Occasional patches of good content, tho: Neal's report on Burroughs in Texas, Jack talking 'bout meeting Lucien and Kammerer and Burroughs . . . getting blown by his first wife . . . quitting football 'cause he heard Beethoven's Fifth one day just as it was time for practice.

Soon after Jack died, City Lights put out *Scattered Poems*—no great shakes. Later, *Heaven & Other Poems* came out on Grey Fox—ditto.

Since his third (and final) wife kicked it, some more substantial new stuff has appeared. *Selected Letters, 1940–1956* is a real roller-coaster ride: Jack at his most hopped up, guileless, unaffected, then (turning on a dime) flip, pompous, even academic (imagine: treating Alfred Kazin—!—as a co-conspirator) . . . and back again. In a letter to Ginsberg, January 18, 1955, he accepts as fact his paternity to daughter Jan and claims (contrary to how this usually gets told) that it's wife number two who "doesn't want me to see her." *Pomes All Sizes*, titled and intended for publication during his lifetime, has more variety (and less self-consciousness) than *Mexico City Blues*, but still the best stuff is about death: "If I die the dying's over—if I live the dying's just begun." Its first printing by City Lights didn't have his name on the binding, the final revenge (one surmises) of Ferlinghetti for Jack's having once called him a "genial businessman." *Book of Blues*, a step up, is in general more prosey ("MacDougal Street Blues": "I mean/This is prose/Not poetry") and a good deal more gripping. *The Scripture of the Golden Eternity*, a series of sutras encouraged by Snyder at the time of the action covered in *Dharma Bums*, is a better version of the Buddhist folderol in the opening section of *Desolation Angels*—less annoying, jus' plain better. *Some of the Dharma*, a four-hundred-plus-page multiform assault on same, is better still (p. 221: "Every day is Saturday"—umpteen years before "Weekend" by the Dictators). *Old Angel Midnight*, originally in *Big Table* mag, is the most entertaining of Jack's attempts at a *Finnegans Wake* sort of "goofy language" spew. *Good Blonde & Others* is the best (so far) of the odds 'n' ends collections. Title piece (from *Playboy*) is real good, "In the Ring" is a neat little whatsit on his father as wrestling promoter, and "Essentials of Spontaneous Prose" and "Belief & Technique for Modern Prose"—classics long out of print in any form—are always nice to have around. And there's this other one from 1990, one of those little ones from Hanuman Books, a bunch of fragments of interviews and stuff—if you missed it you'll live—*Safe in Heaven Dead.*

(Oh, I've never read *The Town and the City*, his "pre-Beat," traditionally linear, Thomas Wolfean novel. Tried, but I've never gotten very far. Third person, kind of dreary, with Jack's persona split among a bunch of brothers.)

Of the Kerouac bios/memoirs, the standouts are still *Memory Babe*, by Gerald Nicosia, and *Jack's Book*, by Barry Gifford and Lawrence Lee. The former, over seven hundred pages, has a lot of data not in any of the rest (details of twenty years' worth of fall-down drunks, including one with painter Willem de Kooning; the numerous times he had sex with men, especially after he decided his dick was too small; a bad acid trip in Florida as late as '69; phone calls to first wife Edie toward the end, allegedly asking her to get back with him; partial transcript of a tape made drunk with the radio playing, also toward the end, Jack singing along, improvising dirty lyrics, funnier and more revealing than any of the tapes in *Visions of Cody*); and more textual critique of Jack's books than the others put together. *Jack's Book* consists of the oral reminiscences of anybody living ('78) who'd had anything to do with Jack and was still willing to talk it, which is more people than were willing to talk to Robt. Reisner while he was compiling *Bird: The Legend of Charlie Parker*. The participants, quoted in bits ranging from a paragraph to several pages at a clip, are fascinating as much for their own strut as for whatever light they shed on, y'know, Jack. Highlights include: Neal's first wife, LuAnne, on who was fucking who which week, Lenore Kandel on the external look and feel of Jack's last crazy night at Big Sur, Gore Vidal insisting Ginsberg once told him that Mémère had told *him* she suspected her husband, Jack's father, was a "pansy"—something Allen himself denied ever hearing/telling.

While some people I know consider *Minor Characters*, by Jack's one-time gal Joyce Johnson (née Glassman), a sour-grapes insider-becomes-outsider book, I see it as a pretty dispassionate examination of Jack, the Beats and how they treated women (like shit). It's also got the best theory yet on the origin of the Jack–Mémère *relationship* (Mémère taking him into her bed—clinging to him—following the death of Gerard), an analysis of Jack's *Weltschmerz* as not-too-subliminal mom-hate, and some of the most detailed depictions of his continuing (late Fifties) friendship with Lucien. An excerpt appears in *Women of the Beat Generation* (edited by Brenda Knight), the single best item in which is a poem by Glassman's friend Elise Cowen ("Who will slap/my backside /When I am born/again/Who will close my eyes /when/In death/They see"), who went out with Allen during his brief fling at heterosexuality, had a role in Allen introducing Joyce to Jack, and later jumped out a seventh-story window—our perfect segue now to Allen . . .

Although Ginsberg's total page count as a published poet is probably less than the total for a couple-three Kerouacs—heck, the bulk of his poems can be found in three currently available books, *Collected Poems 1947–1980*, *White Shroud* and *Cosmopolitan Greetings*—I've probably only read about half of 'em—who except students reads entire books of poems?

The stuff that's great is great ("Howl," "Kaddish," "A Supermarket in California," "Death to Van Gogh's Ear," "Wichita Vortex Sutra," "Please Master," "On Neruda's Death," "White Shroud," "First Party at Ken Kesey's with Hell's Angels," "Don't Grow Old," etc., etc.), appearances by Jack, Neal, Bill and the rest of the gang are always fun ("Two Sonnets After Reading Kerouac's Manuscript *The Town and the City*," "On Neal's Ashes," "On Burroughs' Work," "Gregory Corso's Story," "G.S. [Gary Snyder] Reading Poesy at Princeton"), and the rest of it, at least starting

FROM THE PAGAN DEPTHS OF FRISCO'S BOHEMIAN BARS TO THE DIZZYING HEIGHTS OF THE SNOW-CAPPED SIERRAS...

THE DHARMA BUMS

This is the story of two sensation-seeking hipsters and their jet-propelled search for Experience.

Here are their "yabyum" sexual orgies...their marathon wine-drinking binges...their wild careening mountain-climbing sprees...their skyrocketing poetry–jazz bouts—as only Jack Kerouac, the author of ON THE ROAD, can reveal them.

JACK KEROUAC was born in Lowell, Massachusetts. He played football at Columbia, served in the Marines and has explored the United States and Mexico by foot, bus and car. His bestselling novel **ON THE ROAD** is also available in a Signet edition. The higher priced edition of **THE DHARMA BUMS** was published by The Viking Press.

PUBLISHED BY THE NEW AMERICAN LIBRARY

Cover Printed in U.S.A.

from the time of "Howl" ('55), I certainly *could* read if you gave me a couple months (which is something I could never do with James Merrill)—I mean he changed the face of poetry-as-dealt as decisively as anybody ever has—right?—but I still have to say even the great stuff is sometimes a little . . . um . . . clunky. For images he's ace, metaphor mountains, tops, his momentum module, ditto—forward, *go*—poetry as the conscience of man up the old wazoo, self-consciousness as NO SIN (now and forever), but when you read (in *Composed on the Tongue*, for inst.) this biz about how "Howl" was modeled rhythmically on "Lester Leaps In" (Lester Young) you gotta wonder what kind of ear he has: duh duh *dah* dah, *dah* duh-da dah duh DAH dah—now where in "Howl" is that? (He doesn't have Jack's ear.) Perhaps I quibble.

Then there's that coffee-table beast: *Howl: Original Draft Facsimile, Transcript & Variant Versions, Fully Annotated by Author, with Contemporaneous Correspondence, Account of First Public Reading, Legal Skirmishes, Precursor Texts & Bibliography*—actual title, not subtitle. Sixteen tons of archival impressiveness, single-spaced and double-spaced typescripts, Allen leading you through time-coded crawl paths of creation, a selection of verse he feels like designating the Roots (Christopher Smart, Shelley, Apollinaire, Mayakovski, Kurt Schwitters, Artaud, Garcia Lorca, Wm. Carlos Wms., Hart Crane), a complete "Howl" bibliography (twenty-four languages), an interesting (all-too-typical) all-but-nothing '86 statement by Carl Solomon (full original title: "Howl for Carl Solomon") plus *his* complete bibliography (two books), nice paper, nice photos—but 'tis all a little precious, *n'est-ce pas?* Cover price, $22.50—original price on City Lights was what, like less than a buck? As Jake LaMotta says of an overcooked steak in *Raging Bull*, an endeavor like this kinda defeats its own

purpose. (The purpose of "Howl"!!) (Did he say *porpoise?*)

In *Composed on the Tongue* he talks about such arcana as Kerouac's brief ('40–41) flirtation with Marxism—who'd've thunk it?—and Burroughs's mockout of the '48 election campaign. *Straight Heart's Delight* has a series of (typed in progress, typos and misspellings left alone) "sex experiments" involving himself and Peter Orlovsky ("I continue jerking him off, his cock has a slight bend"). In *Gay Sunshine Interview* he discusses the "Matterhorns of cock, Grand Canyons of asshole" line from " Kaddish." *Allen Verbatim* (edited by Gordon Ball), contains the presentation of his research to the Institute for Policy Studies on the CIA's involvement in the heroin trade (1971—before too many people were on to that one); his response, on a live college radio show, upon hearing of the death of Ezra Pound. *The Visionary Poetics of Allen Ginsberg* has a long section where he recalls (for author Paul Portugués) the specific drugs he took during the writing of such and such major poems (lot more morphine than might be assumed) (also, he was real spooked by acid—felt obligated to keep taking it for the higher sake of Evolving Consciousness); in the section on Tibetan Buddhism, he advances an argument re Hubert Humphrey and Vietnam that sounds incredible coming from anyone but a card-carrying Democrat (hindsight and aging can do that). In *The Visions of the Great Rememberer*, restored to its full length as preface to the most recent edition of *Visions of Cody*, he wonders whether Kerouac was right when he accused Allen of stealing from him—verse—and decides yes, all these years later, Jack was right after all. *As Ever* is the collected correspondence of Allen and Cassady—amazing how much of this stuff was preserved (toward the end Neal is incoherent, but in the early days he more than holds his own). *Journals Early Fifties Early Sixties* lists all the books he read (or intended to read) in January, June and

July of '54 (incl. *Winesburg, Ohio* and selections by Kant). *Journals Mid-Fifties* contains the poem "To Huncke in Sing Sing," purportedly reworked into "The Names" (*Collected Poems*, p. 176), though they have almost nothing in common. *Indian Journals* has gruesome beggar photos. *Photographs* has the full Burroughs–Kerouac couch shot cropped for the cover of Viking's *Portable Beat Reader*; one of Neal and Natalie Jackson under a marquee hyping *The Wild One*; a two-page spread of the life-beaten Orlovsky clan; and a *very* scary pic of Jack in '64 "shuddering in mortal horror, grimacing on D.M.T." (giving it to his dear buddy at that point—the half-hour concentrated version of LSD—had to be the meanest thing Allen ever did) (or did and documented).

Ginsberg's principal biographers (Barry Miles, Michael Schumacher, Jane Kramer) all suffer from the same problem—they eat his "image" whole, take his role as America's Sartre (or something) as a *fait accompli* and deal with him at too many stages of things as an undebunkable sacred cow. This is most bothersome when it comes to the Psychedelic Sixties. The assertion by all three, for example, that their subject was a beacon in the night for spiritually starving contempo youth, that he indeed served as an actual—not metaphoric, not imagined—leader, y'know, "guru," for masses of folks under twenty-five or twenty-seven or twenty-nine, is just flat-out absurd—like the kind of dumb take on things you might get from TV news. To wit: They picture him prodding/coaxing numerous groups, from Be-In dopers to Hell's Angels, into joining him in assorted Eastern chants—wholeheartedly—from Hare Krishna to just plain Om.

As demographics go, I could be counted as a member of that age & culture group, and lemme tell ya we wasn't starving nohow. Maybe Prague kids were in '65, but us 'Merican young'uns had enough Culture/Nurture of our own by '66–67 (y'know: rock und roll—its healthiest period ever), thanx. To even the more hip and book-learned among us, Allen was at most a reborn curiosity, as in, "Hey, looks like Ginsberg's shuffled himself back in," and that largely because he seemed to covet the limelight, couldn't long endure without it—seemed as forced an act as Tiny Tim, y'know? Even on a drug level—that he'd "been there" first—such hokum gave him no more cachet than it would've Huxley (had he not been three years dead). A couple things to bear in mind about young louts and their preferences through the late Sixties: (1) there really wasn't all that much (maybe 6–7 percent) Eastern flavoring in the overall mix, *honest*, and the very notion of "guru" was almost instant self-parody; and (2) when anybody on stage at rock shows—celebrity or not—would try during a break to get a chant going, maybe a couple people would comply out of embarrassment, it happened, but *many* people would yell out, "Fuck *you*!"

(And now that I think of it, *no*: In spite of his "Punk Rock Your My Big Crybaby" poem, in spite of his having played with the Clash, Ginsberg was *not* a Beat who translated well into Punk.)

The biographers also fail to mention what an amazing NERD the young Allen was. Fail, that is, to underline it ('cause it's certainly there). The biggest nerd ever to emerge as a major writer (which is COOL—don't get me wrong)? One would think.

In terms of the "evolution of the novel" (y'know: *that* old warhorse), William Seward Burroughs is probably the most important figure since the heyday of Faulkner—certainly more than Kerouac (even if not "as good a writer"), who was more about the genesis of personal (old-fashioned) art. We're talking "form" here, not "storytelling"—as a storyteller, Bill's voice is probably more old-fashioned than Jack's. Anyway, historically more vital, more *necessary*, than Kerouac, but he doesn't have a single work as start-to-finish words-on-a-page exemplary as, say,

Big Sur or *The Subterraneans*—his import (again, even more than that of Kerouac, who thought about *his* long haul well in advance) is in his whole entire oeuvre: the whole mess (and it often *is* one).

For the sake of not-so-dumb analogy, just as Faulkner can be seen as the full extension/realization of some weighty implications of the mystery pulp (units of fictive text, from the sentence on up, as THEMSELVES existing in a state of mystery: a *universal* "Who said what . . . what did *that* mean . . . what the suffering hell is going on???"), Burroughs is the extension (and "art" appropriation) of science fiction, specifically a dystopian sci-fi whose universe is one of menace, terror and Control—viral, genetic, corporate and otherwise. Operating from various "possible"—imaginable—space/time coordinates at which the conventions and rites of sequential, linear fiction have little or no sway, he has managed, from *Naked Lunch* on, to not just nibble at nonlinear, but to BE it. Before or after, what's the difference? First person versus third? No functional, no *useful* distinction (so deploy them in the same paragraph). Dialogue vs. voice-neutral narrative: ditto. An aesthetic that shuns repetition? Repeat ad infinitum. All art, all language, representing Control, the Mission is to come up with a technology of decontrol, to debunk the notion of the unitary "artist" (and his goddam Mission). Voila: the cut-up and fold-in (by which anyone can make or unmake literature, turn it into a document found in a bottle on Venus); the establishment of safe zones for "bad writing" (intentional, unintentional, readymade, synthetic, etc.: anything goes and it *doesn't have to play* . . . at all!).

The individual novels, because there's so much overlap (both style and content), are hard to separately rate or even separate . . . better to just chronologically group them. First you've got *Junkie* (a.k.a. *Junky*) and *Queer*, from the early Fifties—the linear novels. No cut-ups yet; "routines" run not as bald narratives but as framed real-time verbal performances by Burroughs's stand-in character. *Naked Lunch*, *The Soft Machine*, *The Ticket That Exploded* and *Nova Express*, from '59 to '64, constitute the first big serving of Black Meat (the '66 revision of *Soft Machine* being my own favorite—densest with cut-ups—or maybe I remember wrong). *The Wild Boys* (great chapter: "The Frisco Kid"—material introduced, cut, shuffled, mixed, matched until he gets it right), *Exterminator!* (nice poem on p. 13: "Come and jack off . . . 1929") and *Port of Saints*, '71 to '73, are more of same with some new faces and stylistic mixes. *Cities of the Red Night* (my favorite Burroughs of all—his longest—almost Dickensian in spots), *The Place of Dead Roads* (my vote for his worst—takes about a hundred pages to get going—the most linear of the late ones) and *The Western Lands* (more antimonotheistic than Ishmael Reed, with a very heavy ending: Writer tries to write his way out of death, fails—if *Big Sur* is the great now-I-begin-to-die book, *Western Lands* is Burroughs's now-I-am-dead book—with the entropy and detritus of his life as a writer; recycled lesser cut-ups; fewer new cut-ups—writing is something you do from *within life*, not apart from it—you get old, they're too much present-tense bother), '81 to '87, are the end of his novelistic road. (A road the EQUAL of Faulkner's, or Beckett's, after all is said and done.)

In addition to the above, there's *The Yage Letters*, an "epistolary novel" (with some ten pages of participation by Ginsberg), the first part of which ("In Search of Yage") dates from the time of *Queer*; *Interzone*, a book's worth of very funny scraps (oh, did I forget to mention he's funnier than *any* of your standard stand-up humorists—Twain, Lardner, Nabokov, etc.?) from the time *Naked Lunch* was being pieced together; and *My Education* (like Kerouac's *Book of Dreams*, only edited and organized with Burroughsian malice—a fusillade upon the "reality" shuck). *And the Hippos Were Boiled in Their Tanks*, a collaborative novel cowrit with Kerouac somewhere in the

Forties, is supposed to still exist but has never been published.

Then come his shorties: *Roosevelt After Inauguration* (on abuses of political power; '79 edition has a section on Anita Bryant, Senator Briggs and Proposition 6—remember?), *White Subway* (works in progress, stillborn works, "experimental" leavings), *Cobble Stone Gardens* (the stink of childhood St. Louis remembered), *The Last Words of Dutch Schultz* (delirium as natural generatrix of nonlinearity), *The Book of Breeething* (on Egyptian hieroglyphics and the Tut tomb death curse—illustrated), *Blade Runner, a Movie* (from which *the* movie title was lifted, otherwise no resemblance), *The Retreat Diaries* (dream notes and such from two weeks without a typewriter on a Buddhist retreat not totally his idea), *Early Routines* (incl. the time he cut off the end of his finger), *The Four Horsemen of the Apocalypse* (speech delivered to an Outer Space conference in '88: dreams not spaceships for exploring the sucker), *Tornado Alley* ("For John Dillinger—In hope he is still alive"), *Painting & Guns* (his own work in the former, recommendations on the latter), *The Cat Inside* (one of his finest efforts—believe it—best of all cat books—cats as the Other—declares his current mission their protection), *Ghost of Chance* (more animal-love, this time for Madagascan lemurs).

The Adding Machine—his grandfather invented it (true)—is an organized collection of essays/lectures, chock full of surprises (e.g., he loves the work of Scott Fitzgerald, hates Beckett). In "On Jack Kerouac," he credits Jack with not only naming *Naked Lunch* (he also named "Howl," according to some accounts) but getting him to write at all. "Bugger the Queen" (same time frame as the Sex Pistols' "God Save the Queen") is an antimonarchist delight.

The Job is a series of early-Seventies interviews of Bill by Daniel Odier ("And what of money, ownership, property?") with illustrative experiments and routines. *The Third Mind*, with Brion Gysin, actual father of the cut-up, is an exegesis

on such methods, but (disappointingly) not a textbook, not exactly much of a read. Victor Bockris's *With William Burroughs: A Report from the Bunker*, which feels (ho hum) like a Burroughs issue of *Interview*, features pix with Patti Smith and Christopher Isherwood, texts of dinners with Susan Sontag (more venom on Beckett) and Debbie Harry, drinks with Terry Southern.

The Letters of William S. Burroughs, 1945–1959 (ed. Oliver Harris) is a fantastically great 472 pages, spilling such shit as Bill's will to become a writer (far earlier/stronger than generally presumed), his thoughts on cheap farm labor, his high level of paranoia as the publication of *Naked Lunch* approached, his indecision on how to market it (pro-heroin? anti?—back and forth). Most fascinating of all, perhaps, is a letter to Ginsberg following the latter's announcement of intent to be reprogrammed as a heterosexual. Bill tells him he's been "laying women for the past 15 years . . . [B]etter than nothing, of course, like a tortilla is better than no food. But no matter how many tortillas I eat I still want a steak," to which his wife, Joan (four months before he would shoot her), has added in pencil, "Around the 20th of the month, things get a bit tight and he lives on tortillas" (touché!). Hepcat parody on p. 121: "Get with those technicolor peyote kicks Daddy O and shoot me that solid address."

Cassady, Neal. Kerouac's buddy and early muse, jester, asshole, con man for the ages. The first third of his only book, *The First Third*, is pretty damn good, the rest good enough. Only in his letters, tho, do you get that here/there/everywhere fevered discontinuity that became one of the staples of Jack's "post-Wolfean" modus operandi. For bulk letters there's *As Ever* (him to Ginsberg), *Grace Beats Karma: Letters from Prison* (mostly to wife Carolyn) and some things to Jack in the *Beat Reader* (ed. by Ann Charters, editor also of the *Kerouac Letters*, as well as author of one of the earliest, and in my opinion

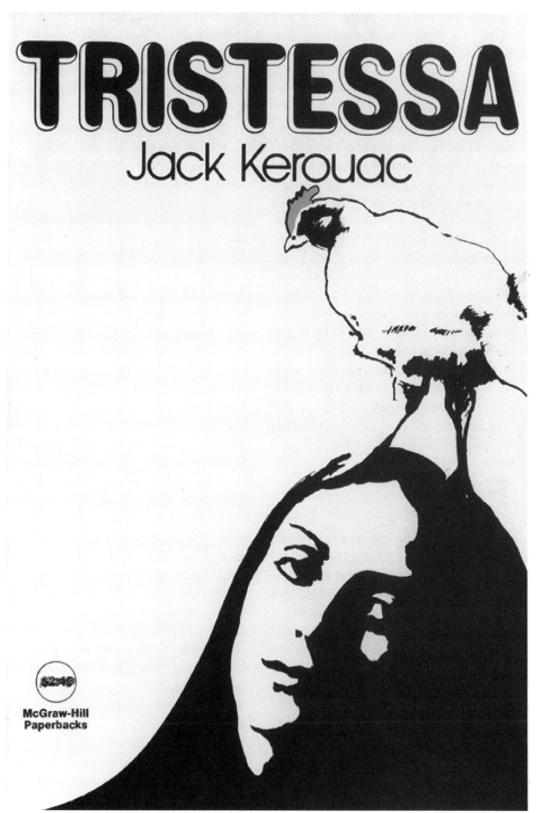

the least, Kerouac bios). A Ken Kesey mostly picture book, *The Further Inquiry*, transcribes some Neal monologues and has a flip-page sequence of Neal, shirtless, in Sixties motion. And for Jack-filtered snatches of Neal's oral discharge, there's always *On the Road* and *Visions of Cody*.

Cassady, Carolyn. She plays it less coy in *Heart Beat* (partial source of the film of the same name, as awful in its own right as the George Peppard *Subterraneans*), but in *Off the Road: My Years with Cassady, Kerouac, and Ginsberg* she either doesn't quite "get" things or is one of the bigger bullshit artists since Nixon. So much that happened, that the world knows happened—even Nixon knows happened—she acts like she didn't notice. An insider pretending to be an outsider, as straight as Pat Nixon. Sexist it may sound to say this, but say it I will: She was arguably a third of the reason (would you settle for a sixth?) Neal never wrote much except the letters, and while in no way a source of, or contributing factor to, his assholeness, a contributing unmaker of its positive dimension—although fuck him, he certainly had his complicity in this biz.

Faster . . .

Gregory Corso is the great Brat of Beat (Elf, Imp). An innocent? a primitive? In *The Beat Vision* (ed. Arthur & Kit Knight) he calls himself "poor simple human bones," gets in a fight with Gary Snyder (too "intellectual" for him), is the only one at a writers' convention who doesn't find "I fall upon the thorns of life, I bleed" irredeemably corny. In *The Subterraneans*, he's the one whose sex act with Mardou precipitates the end for Jack. Has poems titled "God Is a Masturbator" (in *Elegiac Feelings American*) and "Don't Shoot the Warthog" (*Gasoline*). "Columbia U Poesy Reading–1975" (*Herald of the Autochthonic Spirit*) is a lively debate

between Gregory's capital-M Muse and drug of choice heroin. In "Bomb" (*The Happy Birthday of Death*) he thumbs his nose, says (from the death mire of the Fifties) what-*me*-fear-annihilation? (Anti-nuke demonstrators once threw shoes at him.)

Although basically an outsider (slumming? no, but just dropping in), John Clellon Holmes wrote the first Beat novel published, *Go* ('52), which pissed Kerouac off (two reasons: jealousy—natch—his own teletype rolls were then dying on the vine; Holmes has his Kerouac character go to bed with the Holmes wife character, which never happened in life, as cover for Holmes's own real-life infidelity), the first Beat piece in the mainstream press ("This Is the Beat Generation," *New York Times* '52, reprinted in *Nothing More to Declare*) and the first Beat think piece in the mainstream "lively arts" media ("Philosophy of the Beat Generation," *Esquire*, Feb. '58, a month before Jack's piece of the same name, now in *Good Blonde & Others*; the Holmes piece also in *Declare*). The *Times* article is exactly the sort of two-sided/no-sided glibspeak you find in the *Times* now as then, but at least he acknowledges Beat's spiritual dimension. The *Esquire* thing goes out of its way to give credit where due (to Jack for coming up with the term "Beat Generation," for defining it as religious to begin with). *Go* is simply an itchy, tired-of-the-whole-thing-before-it-even-happened neo-Dostoyevskian calisthenic that feels at best like a New York genre novel—where virtually all of Jack's own writings completely transcend place. Best (and inadvertently silliest) image in the book (p. 306): ". . . where a few squalid bars forlornly gathered the discontented into gaudy islands of warmth and alcohol." Although he and some biographers claim he and Jack remained "lifelong friends," he only does a couple-few cameo turns in Jack's earlier novels.

Herbert Huncke is the street hustler, junkie

and petty thief from whom Jack had gotten "beat" (w/out the generation). The character based on him in *Go* is a model of vile pus and scum with about a week to live. He outlived its author (eleven years his junior) by eight years. In his amiable 1990 autobiography, *Guilty of Everything*, Huncke gets back at Burroughs (for overstating, in *Junkie*, how skinny Huncke's neck looked in its collar) by detailing how quaint and fastidious Bill had been about his v. first shot of morphine; describes what a nervous wreck Ginsberg was behind bars—his "woebegone expression," "saying Jewish prayers"—the time they got busted together for stolen goods in Allen's apartment; and claims Edie divorced Jack because he "wasn't too successful with her sexually." His image of "awful red stone brick" (p. 46) is the polar opposite of Jack's ubiquitous "redbrick America." *The Herbert Huncke Reader* is a big posthumous stack of very open, reader-friendly narratives from (mostly) the scuzzy side—or let's jus' say the *street* side—of the street. "Courtroom Scene" has the great sequence "Fuck my writing. Fuck me. Fuck the world."

Carl Solomon, who met Ginsberg in the loony bin Allen opted for in lieu of actual jail time (Solomon was in for more psychologically pressing reasons), was not only the dedicatee of "Howl" but, working for his publisher uncle, the man who got *Junkie* signed to Ace Books (he rejected *On the Road*). In his two books of prose, *Mishaps, Perhaps* and *More Mishaps* (their innards scrambled and resequenced, possibly in toto—it's hard to tell—in *Emergency Messages*, along with some new material including an interview that repudiates the oft-quoted shuck that he saw Artaud perform in Paris in '47), he reads like a lumbering lummox—sorry—a lovable lummox. A typical wheeze: "The Story of Syphilitic Minnie—Vietnik Communist, F.B.I. Lesbian." (Hey, he doesn't cause cancer.)

Even more ingenuous is Peter Orlovsky, gentle soul love-mated to Ginsberg—for better and worse—from '54 to, I dunno, somewhere in the Eighties. Though it's conceivable that only at Allen's behest did he ever write poem one (title: "Frist Poem" [*sic*]), his sole collection, far as may be knowed, *Clean Asshole Poems & Smiling Vegetable Songs*, is my single favorite object from the wide world of book things. Really bearable, uncorrected misspellings and all. "Lepers Cry" is reprinted in both *Beat Reader* and *Beat Vision,* but my own favorites are "Frist Woman Lay" [*sic* again] ("3 times/in the night in Paris—at her place"), "High on H" and "Dick Tracy's Yellow Hat."

And who am I? The reason we're all still here . . . this is my beatnik party. On to California . . .

Poets Gary Snyder, Philip Whalen and Lew Welch went to Reed College together, and when Jack, Allen and the New York contingent hooked up with them (or the first two of 'em, at first) and *their* loosely defined crowd in the mid-Fifties Bay Area, whatever it was that Beat *was* was suddenly national.

Snyder I have trouble figuring out. The way I've always had him pegged is as a young smartypants nature poet who in forty years still hasn't taken it especially far—never an academic, but still not much danger *in the verse*. He raves about these Zen lunatic mountain men for a whole half-a-book (the "Cold Mountain" part of *Riprap and Cold Mountain Poems*), but he isn't one himself. Even the young stuff is not young. Never celebrates—revels in—his own wildness, except from the vantage point of many calm yrs' separation (in "Cartagena," also in *Riprap*, recalling whores of his late adolescence). In "Four Poems for Robin" (*The Back Country*) he waxes on about skin and heat and gal-nakedness, relinquished in pursuit of "what my karma demands"—that about says it all. "I Went into the Maverick Bar" (*Turtle Island*), an account of drinks and vibes in redneck New Mexico, is Kerouac without the joy, Ginsberg without the bite. "Sherry in July" (*Left Out in the Rain*) is the closest he comes to humor. If Kerouac hadn't captured him *externally* (in *Dharma Bums*) at a moment of still-ebullient whippersnapperhood, how else would we know he was any fun at all?

But maybe this is a bum rap, 'cause actually there are a couple Gary poems I could see myself reading again—"The Bath" (*Turtle Island*), about bathing his son in the sauna, and "Painting the North San Juan School" (*Axe Handles*), which reads like Wm. Carlos Wms. with but the *eensiest* jot of hey-this-is-poetry to make you forget it isn't. And there's no denying the, uh, validity of everything he SAYS ABOUT THE PLANET in his eco-essays ("The Politics of Ethnopoetics" in *The Old Ways*, "Notes on Poetry as an Ecological Survival Technique" in *Earth House Hold*, most everything in *The Practice of the Wild*). And give him some points for what he says about Bukowski in *The Real Work*: Yes, Bukowski is a nature poet—"eating, drinking, farting. What could be more natural?" But none of his poems about Lew Welch (read on, reader) are *good enough*.

Reading Philip Whalen may not be as easy as falling off a log, but it's close. The most appealing, the least ax-to-grind, of why-we-keep-on-keeping-on poets. From *On Bear's Head*, "Prose Take-Out, Portland 13:ix:58"—sun rises—fuck even mentioning it—last jerk awake, everyone else faded (memory of Kerouac, a nonfader, evoked)—inch left to the wine "& the cigarets few" . . . makes me wanna move to Portland. In "For Kai Snyder"—star of "The Bath"—from *The Kindness of Strangers*, he forgets how to do a somersault—shit—then remembers, does three ("Age 46 years 6 months 37 days"). Bukowski without hemorrhoids? From *Decompressions*, "The

Madness of Saul": "Everybody takes me too seriously./Nobody believes anything I say." Most rudely undersung of living poem-makers (true—but don't take my word for it); currently (last time I looked) an actual bona fide Zen monk.

From *Off the Wall*, a great, uplifting (ah, fuck me) series of interviews, we learn he's possibly the only Beat writer who doesn't type . . . peyote saved his life . . . *non*topical poetry is revolutionary (and he means it with a HAMMER).

A novel from '67, *You Didn't Even Try*—domestic push-pull and divorce—is nothing to write home about.

The story of Lew Welch is, for my money, the most fascinating True Beatnik Tale, more than Jack and Mémère, more than Bill, Joan and William Tell, you name it. The long version, well not that long, it ends at age forty-four, is told parallel to that of the other major Beat players in Aram Saroyan's *Genesis Angels: The Saga of Lew Welch and the Beat Generation*, my pick for the best-written literary bio of anybody, ever. The short version: Grandfather, a surgeon with an operation in the morning, doesn't drink, drives BARRY GOLDWATER'S MOTHER (who does) home from a party, is killed in a collision (Mrs. G. unharmed); young Lew works writing ad copy, comes up with the line "RAID KILLS BUGS DEAD," hates it, hates the life, drops out to join his Reed poet buddies in San Francisco, starves, takes other crummy jobs for which he hates himself, the compromises, drinks too much; two drives across the country with Jack, Lew (a surrogate Neal) at the wheel, a crucial figure the last gruesome night of *Big Sur*; time marches (still drinking), the adjustments too great, tries living alone in the wilds, squirrels maim his cat, fuggit, the pain, the pain, until finally: writes his greatest poem, "Song of the Turkey Buzzard" (his favorite beast), in which it is asked that no one grieve, that his remains be placed on a rock, hail sweet buzzard, he then disappears in the mountains with his revolver, never to be seen again, Snyder sends out a posse but they never find a trace, no one does (this was '71), the theory being: hiked remote, shot and left himself to be entered into the food chain—quick—direct—et by his friends the buzzards, become nonmetaphoric ONE WITH NATURE, one with nullity/eternity . . . whew.

"Buzzard" can be found in *Ring of Bone: Collected Poems 1950–1971*, as can such hotsos as "Wobbly Rock," "Barbara/Van Gogh Poem," "Brown Small Bird," "Supermarket Song" and "Not Yet 40, My Beard Is Already White." Lew's poems are all so consistently *of his voice* that to pick up any one is to hear *him* in it—as distinctive as a line, a phrase, a held note by the most recognizable jazzmen. And it all has his SMILE.

Evergreen Review #17 has a prose fragment from *The Man Who Played Himself*, a third-person fictional send-up of hip, that reads something like Terry Southern, but it's still got Lew's smile.

Okay, now let's sort the rest out and get this party *over* . . .

Bob Kaufman and John Wieners are the greatest of the nonscene Beat poets, whatever that means—the social second unit?—people who didn't spend *scads* of time with the frontrunners. They're also two supreme sufferers, and Kaufman, in particular, swallowed more broken glass than all the others combined. His mastery of Ameri-*surrealist* word-spew is evident in "Secondless" (in *The Ancient Rain: Poems 1956–1978*): "MINUTE AGES OF TIMELESS TIME & CLOCKLESS CLOCKS, & COCKLESS COCK." Only Beat writer, poetry or prose, who pegged jazz really, *totally* right: "Bird with Painted Wings" (*Solitudes Crowded with Loneliness*). Wieners's "A Poem for Cocksuckers" and "The Ages of Youth" ("And with great fear I inhabit the middle of the night"), from *Selected*

Poems (Black Sparrow), are intense, to say the least. Kaufman's "Ginsberg" (*Solitudes*) and Wieners's "For Huncke" (*Selected Poems*, Grossman) are as great a pair of tributes as ANY of these guys ever paid one another.

Diane di Prima is good enough. She'll do. The percentage of her poetry that's pap is no worse than for your average superstar academic. She writes decent travel stuff ("Two from Gallup," "Brief Wyoming Meditation," "Ramada Inn, Denver") and occasionally gets one off like "I hope/you go thru hell/tonight/beloved/I hope you choke to death/on lumps of stars," in "More or Less Love Poems" (all in *Pieces of a Song: Selected Poems*). Her *Memoirs of a Beatnik*, the only Beat exploitation novel by an *insider*—wait, no, there's also Ed Sanders—is a nice functional hunk of smut. Toward the end she fucks Kerouac (verified in the Dennis McNally bio *Desolate Angel*).

LeRoi Jones (Amiri Baraka), father of one of her kids, is Beat's only triple threat: passable fiction, poetry, drama. *The System of Dante's Hell* is the finest novel by any Beat other than Kerouac or Burroughs. *Preface to a Twenty Volume Suicide Note* is as good a first book of poems as you got in those days ('61). *The Toilet* is the best play I ever saw live ('64). Hettie Jones (née Cohen), mother of two of *his* kids, is the author of the best Beat spouse memoir, *How I Became Hettie Jones* (the "skinny" on di Prima is pretty good).

For such a gung-ho nature muhfuh (and unrepentant mammal), Michael McClure tiptoes through the tulips a little, um, daintily, y'know? There's also something very *Aryan* about much of his shit—very "stags in the meadow"—or English Protestant church musicy. And these page-centered symmetrical repetition poems seem like ideal fodder for (perish the thought) computer fun and hilarity—but does he ever get the hilarity? *Scratching the Beat Surface* is a dry, dry, dry monograph—so straight, *its* surface so unbroken.

"Peyote Poem" is okay, though, and *Ghost Tantras* has a great werewolf cover, and *The Beard* was the quintessential late-Sixties smash-the-boundaries-of-stage-decorum theater event. (Mixed reviews for the pretty boy.)

His role as publisher/bookseller notwithstanding, as a writer Lawrence Ferlinghetti is the least interesting of the frontrunners. He's such a square that hipsterism when he wears it (like in *A Coney Island of the Mind*, which isn't even his title, it's Henry Miller's) seems ludicrous. Yet most of his square stuff doesn't play either. *Tyrannus Nix?—his* putdown of Nixon—who cares?

We're outta beer, outta wine . . .

Ted Joans is the poet (black) who said of his friend Jack, "I know a man who's neither white nor black/And his name is Jack Kerouac." His ending to "God Blame America!!" (*A Black Manifesto in Jazz Poetry and Prose*) follows "America . . . FUCK YOU!" with "MAY I?" The direct *friendship* link between Kerouac and Charlie Parker.

In the introduction to Jack Micheline's *River of Red Wine*, which Troubadour Press agreed to publish only if he could get "somebody famous" to write a prefatory, an obliging Kerouac says, "I like the poetry of Jack Micheline. See?" and I don't mind it either. It's meant to be read, is easy to read, and in fact only when read—aloud—does it seem like much. Title poem ('82) from *Imaginary Conversation with Jack Kerouac* opens with "Wacky Daky Doo," moves on to "Yippie Yippie Loo," finishes with "Long Live Harold Goldfinger!"

Of the five people who read at the historic Six Gallery whozis, S.F., '55—Ginsberg (unveiling "Howl"), Snyder, Whalen, McClure, Philip Lamantia—the one with the least currently in print under his own name is Lamantia (who didn't read his own verse that night anyway): nothing. (Listed in the City Lights catalogue, but I've never seen him even in the artso specialty stores.) Only five short things in the *Beat Reader*, all with a fair quota of self-conscious nuttiness. The image "reality sandwiches" ("Fud at Foster's") recurs as (is the source of?) the title of a subsequent Ginsberg City Lights collection.

Ray Bremser is a jailbird who willed himself into a poet, hooking up via mail with Ginsberg, Corso, LeRoi Jones while serving six yrs. for armed robbery. *Beat Reader* has something of his, "Funny Lotus Blues . . . ," with a lot of parentheses and gratuitous variable indents, verse-critiquing Nat King Cole, Rosemary Clooney and Thelonious Monk, image-dropping Tanu Tuva, pubic hair and Nero Wolfe. *Troia: Mexican Memoirs*, an excerpt of which also appears in the *Reader*, is a conspicuously Kerouacian account by wife Bonnie (Brenda Frazer) of their flight (with baby Rachel) from the law, written while Ray was serving another five-year stretch. In Elias Wilentz and Fred McDarrah's *The Beat Scene* ('60) there's a great snap of him reading with shades on.

Tuli Kupferberg, the best mind of his generation to have jumped off the Brooklyn Bridge and lived (vaguely cameoed in "Howl"), once asserted (in *The War Against the Beats*): "Listen Square—You may kill the Beatnik but you will not kill the Beatnik in yourself." In 1964 he and Ed Sanders (plus Ken Weaver) formed the Fugs, the bulk of whose greatest work has been reissued on two Fantasy CDs, *The Fugs First Album* and *The Fugs Second Album*. In the mid-Seventies Sanders, responsible for the term "peacecreep," put out a great country-western parody album, *Sanders' Truckstop*, with its unforgettable "Polaroid spread shot" refrain ("The Maple Court Trajedy"), but his principal calling is words on paper. "Elm-Fuck Poem" ("in to the oily crotch/place dick") and

"The V.F.W. Crawling Contest" (*Thirsting for Peace in a Raging Century: Selected Poems, 1961–1985*) are good samples of his poetic craft. *Tales of Beatnik Glory* starts pretty funny, but the knee-jerk ha-ha of its prose is a little tough to sustain for 543 (revised edition) pages.

Says the cover blurb to Lenore Kandel's second book, *Word Alchemy*, that bk. and her first, *The Love Book*, "openly celebrate sexual love"—you could say so. "Invocation for Maitreya": "sweet cunt-mouth of world serpent Ouroboros girding the universe/as it takes in its own eternal cock."

There's a famous photo from North Beach of Ginsberg, McClure and Bob Kaufman with Harold Norse and Jack Hirschman, so I guess you should include H.N. and J.H. Hirschman translated Artaud for City Lights ("Shit to the Spirit" is especially juicy). In 1986 I read with him in L.A., and he was so intense he actually drooled—very impressive. "The Halls of Academe" (*Endless Threshold*) is as vigorous and thoroughgoing a slam of said haunts as y'may ever encounter. Harold Norse's *Beat Hotel* is a first-rate cut-up/ellipsis novel from his days at that Parisian hostelry, where he met Gysin and Burroughs. Good grim poem in *Karma Circuit*: "Another Form of Junk." His *Memoirs of a Bastard Angel* spends less time on Beat than some might prefer, more on superstars he hath known (Tennessee Williams, Chester Kallman, Truman Capote).

Likewise, the black & white of David Meltzer with McClure, Lamantia, John Wieners, S.F. '58, argues strongly for *his* inclusion. (And the name is right.) From *Bark, a Polemic*: "Pass around pics of chicks in black patent-leather boots, pink bras, fucked by wolfhounds, German shepherds, St. Bernards. Motel-room camera gets it all"—I would certainly hope so.

Time to mop up.

Let's see. Aside from *Beat Reader, Beat Scene, Beat Vision, Women of the Beat Gen.*, let's see what's left.

The Beat Generation & the Angry Young Men (ed. Gene Feldman, Max Gartenberg) clearly doesn't know what Beat is—1958—classifying Anatole Broyard and Chandler Brossard as Beats alongside Jack, Ginsberg, Burroughs and Solomon—pshaw. *The Beats*, Seymour Krim's 1960 beatsploitation anthology, has lots more real stuff, but it also has pieces by Broyard and Brossard, plus Norman Mailer (and not even Mailer's dick-driven criticism—"The White Negro" is in both the above collection and *Beat Reader*—but excerpts from *The Deer Park*, prefaced by Krim's comment that "Mailer is moving these days, carving out his own version of beat vision"—Mailer *as* Beat!) and an early upchuck by that Beat-bashing pigfucker Norman Podhoretz, "The Know-Nothing Bohemians."

The New American Poetry (1960, ed. Donald Allen) contains a ton of items not in the *Beat Reader*. The revised edition, retitled *The Postmoderns* ('82, Allen w/George F. Butterick), has a ton, but a different ton (notable deletions: Stuart Perkoff, Kirby Doyle). In *Whitman's Wild Children*, Neeli Cherkovski does in-depth treatments on ten poets who have taken "to the open road both spiritually and physically," seven of them Beats, including Bob Kaufman, John Wieners and Harold Norse (spotlighting Norse's poem "I'm Not a Man": Powerful ain't the word), who rarely get such credit. In Ekbert Faas's *Towards a New American Poetics*, the split is only two poets in six, and the two are Ginsberg (who it turns out didn't really "study" Whitman until after "Howl") and Snyder (amused the Beats had to take so much shit for being crazed—while the Anne Sextons and John Berrymans are *really* out there).

All in the family: Jan Kerouac; Louis Ginsberg; Wm. Burroughs Jr. Imagine

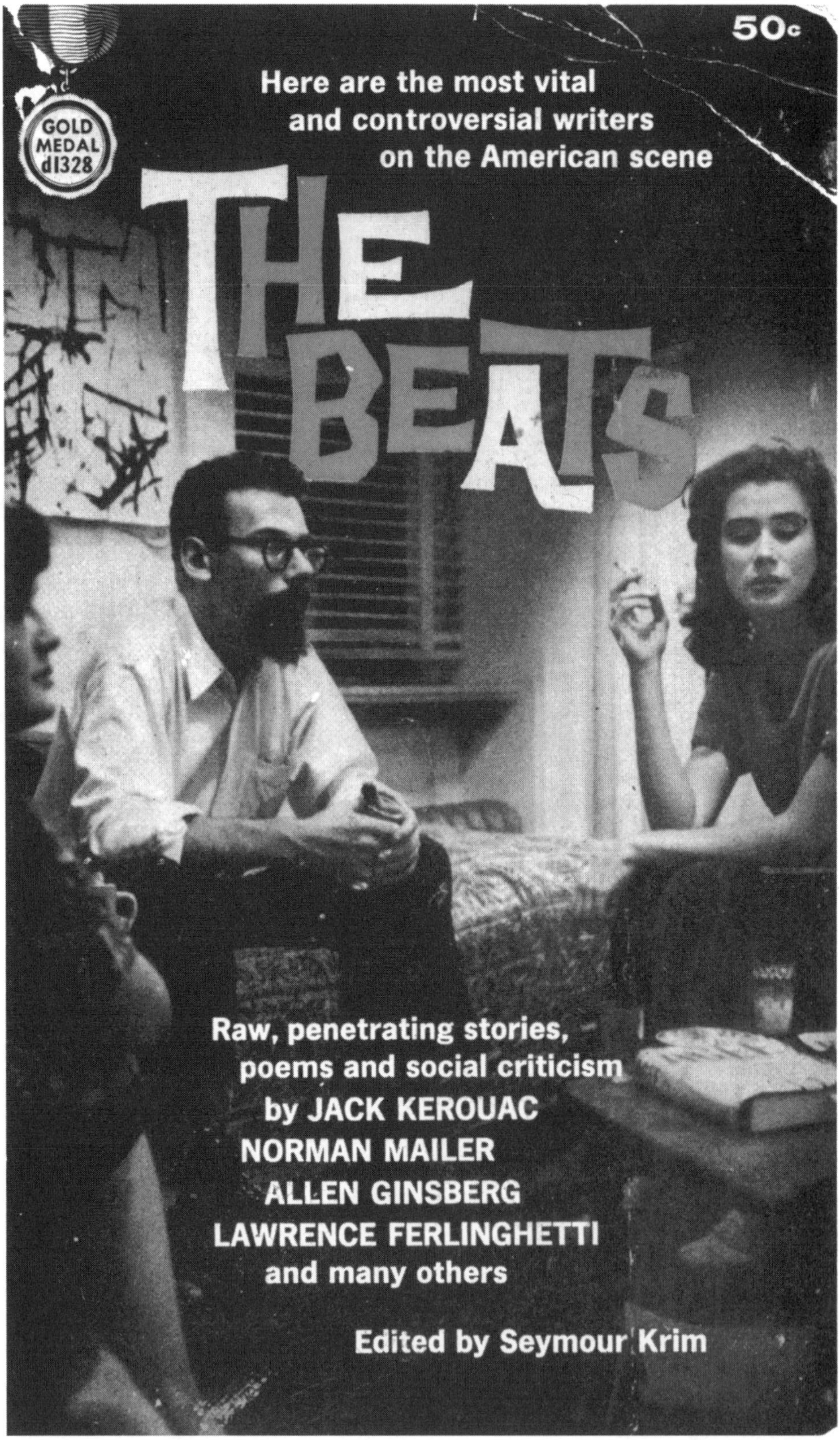

HOLLY GEORGE-WARREN COLLECTION

a daughter of Jack opening a novel—her first—with an epigraph from a PAUL SIMON song—*Baby Driver*—if that don't beat all. In "Now a Satellite" (*Morning in Spring and Other Poems*), Allen's father rhymes "risen" and "prison," "an ion" and "Orion." *Speed*, Bill's son's first, is funny, grim as life itself, non-derivative of dad, no b.s., but with his next (and last), *Kentucky Ham*, he's already out of things to say.

File under Beat: Bob Dylan; Anne Waldman; Lester Bangs. Dylan's an easy choice, although the lyrics Ann Charters picked for *Beat Reader* ("Blowin' in the Wind," "The Times They Are a-Changin'") are more Woody Guthrie than Ginsberg-and-beyond (why not "Positively Fourth Street" and "Memphis Blues Again"?). His *Tarantula*, especially in the A. J. Weberman pirate edition, is everything you could want from a Beat novel (cameo appearance by Ernest Tubb). Waldman I'll accept although she's the same age as I am, if only because everybody else accepts her (based mostly on her connection to Ginsberg at Naropa), and if you give me a minute I'll find something to endorse . . . hmm . . . okay, "Queer Heart" ("Kiss pussy, Mother Country") in *Fast Speaking Woman*. Lester is younger than me, much younger—the dead don't age—but he ate all these guys for breakfast, along with the Benzedrine inhalers, and *Big Sur* is as good a blueprint, at least a cipher, for his death at thirty-three, thirty-four, whatever it was, as any you could offer. I thought "Women on Top: Ten Post-Lib Role Models for the Eighties" (in the posthumous *Psychotic Reactions and Carburetor Dung*) was incredible—weirder and weirder misspellings while drinking Romilar—until I read Kerouac's *Old Angel Midnight*. Now I know what he was aiming for.

Floating Universities: The Power of the Collective in Art

BY BRIAN HASSETT

Give me your befuddled masses, your rejection slips, pink slips, verbal slips, all. Knock down the gates, throw open the bars, the artists are having a ball. Teach me, show me, let me in. Challenge me, push me, help me win. Athletes have their team and suits can wear the firm, but making art keeps you home alone, and the tavern's the place you turn. Solo suffering totally blows, so into the sea you dive, searching for souls who swim like you and act at least vaguely alive; with deep sea wails you plunge the depths, with freshwater poets you school, with coral reefers you spark the sea, drinking in dreams from the pool.

— B. H. AUGUST 1998

O UT OF THE ONE GROW MANY, AND out of many grows the One. The "It." The Ahhh. The Unspoken Thing. And from this desire for oneness, togetherness, the whole, artists from the Beat poets of the Fifties to the women songwriters of Lilith have collaborated, cajoled and consoled each other into movements and generations.

The "so-called" Beat Generation—as some members like to say when push comes to interview and now that it's carved into history—may never have had a single unified voice any more than Generation X does, but their range of harmonies ended up blending into a pretty inspiring choir.

The term was coined by Jack Kerouac, expounded upon by John Clellon Holmes in the *New York Times Sunday Magazine*, and endlessly championed by Allen Ginsberg, partly because the prior "generation" of disaffected visionary American writers had come up with the convenient "Lost Generation," thanks to Mama Stein. Hemingway—another pretty shrewd self-promoter—dropped her phrase as an epigraph to his first novel, *The Sun Also Rises*, and suddenly F. Scott Fitzgerald, Hart Crane, John Dos Passos, e. e. cummings and so on were no longer a bunch of struggling writers, but a *generation*. "Yeah, that's it, we're a generation. Yeah." We're talkin' 'bout my g-g-generation. Suddenly lone authors joined a *team*, and instead of remaining disparate spindly voices drowned out by a raging torrent of daily fads and fixations, each of their challenging visions became buoyed by the others.

And in this supportive spirit a loosely defined Beat community became a very interdisciplinary affair as they freely mingled and collaborated with Abstract Expressionist painters, jazz musicians, Living Theater actors, playwrights, photographers, cartoonists, dancers, mystics and poets from other New York Schools. In smokin' Greenwich Village joints like the Cedar Tavern, the San Remo and the Artist's Club, something more than ideas were being exchanged.

"We were sharing the holy light," said composer David Amram, Kerouac's principal musical collaborator and the jazz laureate of the Generation. "The Artist's Club was a beautiful get-together run by artists for artists, with talking, philosophy, arguments and discussions by the

Allen Ginsberg, Peter Orlovsky and Gregory Corso (from left) *on the set of 'Pull My Daisy,' 1959*
JOHN COHEN

hour by serious and brilliant people. Then afterwards we'd all go over to the Cedar Tavern and continue the rap. It was like a floating university."

The Cedar Tavern, now woven vibrantly into the quilt of New York City history, was the collective comfort zone for Jackson Pollock, Willem de Kooning, Franz Kline, Larry Rivers, Frank O'Hara, various art critics and the Beats as they emerged on the scene. Located originally on 8th Street and University Place, it was a tiny tavern with no jukebox or TV, deep in the heart of the Village when it still was one.

"We had a lot of love and a gigantic extended family of friends," Amram said of the Cedar scene. "You could sit at any table and hear the most inspiring conversations about art, theater, music, baseball, everyday living. It was an oasis, a mecca.

"There was a communal sense; we all helped each other rejoice in the struggle rather than despairing by always encouraging and paying attention to each other and trying to give that love and respect and interest, and also honest opinions and criticisms."

Nowhere is this more visually animated than in the 1959 film *Pull My Daisy*, the single most illuminating Beat collaboration. Narrated by Kerouac's best twenty-eight minutes on tape, captured in early cinema verité by evocative still photographer Robert Frank, playfully scored by the classically trained Amram who also appears as the boppin' French hornist Mezz McGillicuddy, and starring Ginsberg, Gregory Corso and Peter Orlovsky as themselves, this Lower East Side home movie is the only existing footage of the Beats in their prime other than a few scattered TV clips. Coproduced by painter Alfred Leslie and shot in his canvas-filled loft, featuring painter Larry Rivers in the role of Neal (who was, sadly, imprisoned in San Quentin at the time), with art dealer Richard Bellamy as the bishop antagonist, and financed by Wall Street libertine painter Walter Gutman, it's a film made by painters about poets narrated by a novelist.

Another inspired collective on the path were the writers and artists of the Black Mountain College of North Carolina, an experimental Appalachian art school whose faculty included poets Charles Olson, Robert Creeley and Robert Duncan. Flourishing between 1950 and 1957 (when the school went bankrupt), their manifesto was Olson's 1950 essay "Projected Verse" that emphasized the transferral of energy between a poem's creator and reader. The group's influential *Black Mountain Review* was one of the first regularly published collections of the wide-ranging free-verse voices of the new American poetry movement, with Creeley, William Carlos Williams and Denise Levertov appearing alongside Ginsberg, Kerouac and Gary Snyder. In 1952 the Black Mountaineers produced *Theater Piece 1*, America's first "happening," which teamed Olson's unfettered poetry with the work of artist Robert Rauschenberg, avant-garde musician John Cage and choreographer Merce Cunningham.

Also dancing in the klieg lights of collective freedom was the Living Theater, the iconoclastic company founded by Julian Beck and Judith Malina, who began their playful, interdisciplinary association in Greenwich Village in the late Forties. In their first years of production (1951–1952), they staged plays by such diverse contemporary artists as Pablo Picasso, T. S. Eliot, Gertrude Stein, Kenneth Rexroth and John Ashbery. Rather than acting within the confines of conventional theater, the company practiced street theater, confrontational theater, interactive theater, wholly *living* theater. As longtime member Steve Ben Israel described their evolving method: "When you're an actor, you're waiting for a playwright to get an idea, or a director to do a play, or a producer to produce a play.

And here we were, actors *creating* all of that—producing, directing, writing and acting it together with *our* specific message."

This same blessing of community has been felt by artists ranging from the High Renaissance in Florence to the also fairly high Poetry Renaissance in San Francisco. Most of the groundbreaking geniuses of Florence circa 1500 belonged to some regimented guild or patron's stable, so many of the artists like Michelangelo, Leonardo, Filippo Lippi and Rustici, along with architects, storytellers and poets, would also gather in their own mock confraternities. In one of the more wacky images in art history, picture several of these blazing masters meeting as the Company of the Cauldron for lively drunken dinners around a giant cooking pot in one of their sculpture studios where they'd begin creating murals not with paint but with chicken legs, sausages, cheese and jelly. Even though their quarrels were nearly as colorful as their art, never has a generation of artists advanced their media so quickly. "Hi! I'd like you to meet my friend, *David*."

In San Francisco in the 1950s a community of poets began a similarly inspired coffeehouse collective, meeting and reading in the nooks and bookstores of North Beach. Embracing the Platonic adage, "To good men's parties good men flock unasked," the cultural outlaws from around the nation who'd gathered in this traditionally liberal port city were starting to notice the same faces on the same stages night after night. Poets like Gary Snyder, Michael McClure, Lawrence Ferlinghetti, Robert Duncan, Kenneths Patchen and Rexroth, assemblage artists like Bruce Conner and Wallace Berman and filmmakers like Kenneth Anger and Harry Smith all began an enthusiastic crossover of interdisciplinary collaboration that was breaking society's birdbrained habit of pigeonholing artists. A lush flower garden had burst into bloom and it wasn't long before the psychedelic paisley ran wild.

In a sunshower of Day-Glo paint, Ken Kesey and his Merry Pranksters had a great notion to take the collective to an even higher level. Incubating in pools of acid on the edge of Stanford University, Kesey was forming an ever-expanding coterie of authors and intellectuals that would eventually encompass Neal Cassady, the Grateful Dead and cherry Kool Aid. As Intrepid Traveler Ken Babbs put it, "The Pranksters are a collective of that American spirit that's been passed on from the founding fathers through Melville, transcendentalism, Whitman, Faulkner, the Beats and *zoom* into the Pranksters where it took a wild turn of spontaneity in tribal dance, uninhibited jazz, nonsensical word raps and any other unfettered reaching of the spirit toward newfound freedoms."

A healthy dose of this Prankster ethic came from the pranksterish Dadaists who were trying to overthrow not only the rigidity of the fine arts in the 1910s and '20s, but civilization itself. By staging pranks in public places like cathedrals in the middle of a service, this gang of offbeat artists and authors had a collective effect on history rather than simply getting arrested as solo psychos.

And out of their inspired playfulness grew the more serious subconscious exploration of the Surrealists. Founded by the psychologist and poet André Breton, and including Salvador Dali, Joan Miró and René Magritte, the Surrealists strove to fuse our dreamscapes with reality, creating "an absolute reality, a surreality." Blending psychology, poetry and painting into a collage of the subconscious, the Surrealists were on a dedicated search for the meaning of life in the mysteries of the mind that Freud had only recently begun to unveil. Their direct channeling of the subconscious through trance-like states and automatic writing appealed to many artists of the time.

Painter, occasional Burroughs collaborator and regular cut-up Brion Gysin joined the Surrealists in Paris, as did future Beat poet Philip Lamantia in New York, who also helped edit their magazine *View*. But joining this group had a disturbing caveat: Namely, you could actually get expelled from it by Breton—as both Dali and Gysin were—for hanging with the wrong people or changing your mind, which is a curious condition for a mind-based movement.

But along the way, the group had a lot of fun poking a carrot in the eye of the snobby Parisian art world as they painted green apples on faces and eyes in the middle of baked hams. Now picture Monty Python's cartoons of a head popping out of a foot, or a naked man playing an organ in a field. The Surrealists expanded on the illogical juxtaposition of thought earlier espoused by the French poets Apollinaire and Lautréamont and the line of their legacy is still being doodled.

And that's the great thing: As much as these cool collectives were happening in the recent past, many are thriving today. From communal artists' hearths like New York's Nuyorican Poets Cafe and Knitting Factory to attention-getting rockfests like Lilith Fair and the Tibetan Freedom concerts, groups of likeminded people are still working together for the collective better.

"It's good for the soul, for one thing," Sheryl Crow said of joining the Lilith tour. "I mean, it's what religion's based on—that commune, the community, the solace and the fellowship of people who have a kindred spirit."

Whether it's painting the walls with dinner in Florence or breakfast in bed for four hundred thousand at Woodstock, coming together stretches the horizon beyond the sun of its parts. And you don't have to be half-a-million strong. As George Harrison put it of his much smaller group, "That was the good thing about being four together. Not like Elvis, you know. I always felt sorry for him later 'cause he was on his own. He had his guys with him, but there was only one Elvis and nobody else knew what he felt like. But for us, we all shared the experience."

Being together counts. Even a collective of two. Supporting someone who is supporting you is the seed of a generation.

From Beat
to Beatnik

BY HENRY CABOT BECK

"Hey Man, don't knock my clothes. I'm a symptom."
"A symptom of what?"
"Of the Beat Generation ..."

—MAYNARD G. KREBS (1959)

EVEN TODAY, WITH THE BENEFIT OF college courses, exhibitions, elaborate film studies programs, books, CDs and some considerable historical perspective, it is a bit difficult to define "Beat." The very origin and meaning of the word was changed several times by those who devised it in the first place. And when one takes into consideration the range of literature and lifestyles, from Neal Cassady to Paul Bowles and beyond, it becomes ever more difficult to place the "Beat Generation" within a rigid set of parameters. But in 1959, anybody with a television, a subscription to *Life* or access to a drive-in theater could describe a "beatnik" in great detail. And nine out of ten would probably have said his name was Maynard.

Maynard (the "G" stands for Walter), who ended the above declaration on *The Many Loves of Dobie Gillis* with a little tepid scat singing, was right. He really *was* a symptom of the Beat Generation. But as far as America was concerned, all Bob Denver as Dobie's boho sidekick needed was a goatee, a torn sweatshirt and a petrified frog to fix forever the image of the One True Beatnik.

These were the days when Liberace was straight, Ricky never cheated on Lucy and fatuous bus drivers from Brooklyn never really sent their wives to the moon, or the hospital. On the evening that Julius and Ethel Rosenberg were executed for treason, folks were home watching *Ozzie and Harriet.* Beatniks were right at home in the tail end of a parade of culture: Davy Crockett

and Elvis, Doris Day and Little Richard, Tennessee Ernie Ford and Tennessee Williams. The period was riddled with eccentricity: hula-hoops, Tiki lounges and Purple People Eaters.

Very few in Middle America were savvy enough to recognize that teenaged Maynard was really a beatnik wannabe. Maynard saw the best minds of HIS generation destroyed by Social Studies. And had anyone suggested that Maynard borrow Jack Kerouac's copy of *The Brakeman's Handbook* and spend a season laboring on the railroad earth, his time-honored howl would have certainly been "WORK!?!"

Krebs and Kerouac were worlds apart, but on television they were separated by less than twenty-four hours. In November of '59, Kerouac was a guest on Steve Allen's show on Monday, *Dobie* was on Tuesday, and two days later hepcat John Cassavetes starred in *Johnny Staccato,* describing on one episode a coffeehouse as "...a second home for the beatniks, avant-garde artists, the plain unlabeled lost souls of the Village." Like wow.

Kerouac didn't look much like your typical TV beatnik—nobody would be looking to the author of *On the Road* for tips on goatee grooming. Beatnik style and sensibility were already in place before "Howl" and *On the Road.* Aspiring beatniks had, by that time, a fairly fixed idea of how to look and act the part, and no one could dissuade the Maynards-in-training from seeking dingy cellars to spew free-form poems and guzzle

enough bitter java to shake their nerves and rattle their brains.

The first real glimmer of onscreen Beat attitude, in fact, had come a decade earlier by way of Robert Mitchum, far more the hipster Everyman than any other postwar personality. Nobody could drop a line like "Baby, I don't care" with such perfect cool. And it doesn't require much imagination to picture the ex-hobo, pot smoker and former chain-ganger hanging with Neal Cassady.

But while Mitchum provided an entrance point, he was too established by then, and certainly too adult to start the parade. That job fell to Marlon Brando, slouching toward Beat Bethlehem in the daddy of all motorcycle gang films, *The Wild One* (1954). As biker Johnny, Brando was more narcissistic than fashionably nihilistic and too numb to really rebel against anything, but when Lee Marvin entered the picture as Johnny's Neanderthal nemesis, the two men stood at either end of the Beat spectrum, Brando stupefied and Marvin frenzied, opiate versus amphetamine. (Legend has it that former Hell's Angels leader Sonny Barger later stole Marvin's striped-shirt costume from the studio's wardrobe department.)

In the Fifties Paramount announced its interest in a production of *On the Road* starring Brando, but it never came to pass. Instead, Brando brought the same Method-internalized bearing to his snakeskin-clad drifter, Val, in *The Fugitive Kind* (1959) and in the Western *One-Eyed Jacks* (1961), where Brando was Beat in the Saddle. His final truly great performance, as the expatriate Paul in *Last Tango in Paris* (1973), was Beat in everything but era, including Brando's improvised dialogue and Gato Barbieri's jazz-tango score.

James Dean followed Brando, but Dean was

A scene from 'The Subterraneans'
JAMES AUSTIN COLLECTION

more interesting for who he was (like Mitchum) and how he died than the roles he played. While his movies were undeniably important, it was the image of Dean shuffling down empty Manhattan streets and playing congas that spoke loudest to a generation that saw Dean's red-jacket cool as an ideal way to cope with a world in a gray flannel suit. When he took his Porsche out for a last spin in 1955, Dean became the first real pop martyr of his generation.

That same year, Robert Aldrich directed Mickey Spillane's *Kiss Me Deadly*, which was so deliriously perverse William Burroughs could have scripted it. In this extremely stylish and violent movie, dumb-as-a-fence-post detective Mike Hammer (Ralph Meeker) races with a psycho-Beat waif for the possession of an atomic-bomb-in-a-box, referred to as "the great whatsit." If ever there was a film pointing the way to the collision of Beat sensibilities with pop culture and bomb paranoia, this was it. The picture had a tremendous influence on the French New Wave, and had more than a little in common with David Lynch's recent *Lost Highway*.

As Aldrich influenced the French, so too did the French inform Stanley Donen's *Funny Face* (1957). The film featured Audrey Hepburn as a clerk in a "sinister" Village bookstore called Embryo Concepts, whose dream is to travel to Paris to join the bearded, black-clad "empathicalists," who inhabit the subterranea of the Left Bank, staring dreamily at the clouds in their Pernod. Here, Hollywood was already having a go at parodying the burgeoning bohemia. "We're not inhibited by outmoded social conventions," she tells fashion photographer Dick Avery (Fred Astaire), as she commences to dance with abandon in the center of her dingy French hangout, dressed head to toe in black. As a footnote, the music she dances to is pretty much the same kind of post-bop stuff the adults are asking Vince Everett about in *Jailhouse Rock* (1957), causing

Elvis to snarl and say, "Lady, I don't know what in the hell you talkin' about." But then, Elvis probably never told a girl that love was "too plebian."

It was at about this time that fashion fadism began to overwhelm what the Beat writers were bringing to the party. Taking cues from the Sartre-approved singer/actress Juliette Greco, Euro/Russo intellectuals, bebop jazz musicians and the cool stylish angularity of jazz dance (created by Jack Cole, Bob Fosse and others, in Fifties movies and plays like *The Pajama Game*), the new bohemians were now getting all dressed up with nowheresville to go.

On the Road was published the same year that *Funny Face* was released. The next year, San Francisco columnist Herb Caen stole the "nik" from the Russian Sputnik and pasted it onto the Beats, effectively separating counterculture and subculture like egg whites and yolks.

John Van Druten's Broadway play *Bell, Book and Candle* was adapted to film in 1958 and featured a coven of very hip Greenwich Village witches who spent their evenings listening to jazz in a little underground club called the Scorpio. James Stewart and Kim Novak, fresh from *Vertigo*, were reunited as the downtown Darren and Samantha, with Jack Lemmon as Novak's kooky bongo-playing brother, Nicky. Novak's novocaine acting was perfect: "Don't you ever wish that you weren't — what we are?" she muses, "that you could spend Christmas Eve in a little church somewhere, listening to carols instead of bongo drums?" It's a point that would be reiterated over and over in the next few years, that whatever value there might be in trying to be different couldn't possibly compare to some rarified suburban Stepford bliss.

The yang to Kim Novak's yin that same year was Susan Hayward as the bad-girl-gone-worse in Robert Wise's *I Want to Live!* The *Dead Man Walking* of its time, sans nun, the movie told the story of real life convicted murderess Barbara Graham, who partied her way to the electric chair. In the film, Graham has a fatal passion for jazz, and one scene, at a place called the Frisco Club, features Gerry Mulligan's band, bongos and some marijuana. Crazy, dad.

The music of West Coast Jazz Cool Schoolers began turning up on the soundtracks of films like *I Want to Live!* and *The Subterraneans* (1960). Leith Stevens's score for *The James Dean Story* (1957) teamed alto saxophonist/flautist Bud Shank with trumpeter Chet Baker. Chico Hamilton's jazz group had been an important part of *The Sweet Smell of Success,* a picture starring Burt Lancaster and Tony Curtis, released the year before. As a promotions man in the glistening Manhattan of 1957, Tony Curtis was as much hipster as he was hustler, planting reefers in poor Martin Milner's pockets to make a few points with a powerful columnist. The film's soundtrack by Elmer Bernstein contributed greatly to a vision of a city that operated in secret, with a language all its own. It may not have been beatnik, but it was very Beat.

Throughout the latter part of 1958 into 1959, beatniks were all the rage, as well as a topic of controversy: Articles in *Life*, *Newsweek* and *Time* reported on their arrival in a way that suggested that mothers should pull their children from the streets. Beatniks would from this point on be available in both clean-cut and funkier varieties.

Indeed, 1959 saw the beginning of a long trend in beatnik exploitation films, low-budget cheapies designed to give couples something to ignore while they made out at the drive-in. Most of the filmmakers were just switching motorcycle jackets and duck-ass pompadours for berets and beards, presenting hipsters as killers or crazies, or worst of all, insufferably pretentious poetry-spouting morons.

Most guilty of this was a movie naturally entitled *The Beatniks* (1960), which featured a gang of convenience-store thieves led by a Vince Edwards look-alike named Eddie who doesn't realize that any clever talent agent lucky enough to catch him singing "Sideburns Don't Need

Your Sympathy" would not immediately want to make him a star. The film's main beatnik caricature is Eddie's best friend, who is more hophead than hipster. *The Beatniks* was written and directed by Paul Frees, the actual voice of Boris Badenov (of "Rocky and Bullwinkle") and hundreds of other cartoon characters, including two of the Beatles on their animated show. He also wrote the unforgettable song.

Albert Zugsmith, who had produced pictures by top-shelf auteurs like Douglas Sirk and Orson Welles, put director Charles Haas at the helm of *The Beat Generation*, which, in true exploitation style, had little or nothing to say about the Beats except that they were no good. In Zugsmith's own novelization of the film, he refers to beatniks as "phony-baloney" and "moldy figs." That had to hurt. Zugsmith's characters make their and his position very clear: "Phony intellectuals, most of them. Jumping on a gravy train of rebellion. They bore me." Maybe so, Albert, but in spite of the presence of Mamie Van Doren, Vampira and Louis Armstrong, this picture does the same. (And as for gravy trains, Zugsmith spent the latter part of his career making awful films like 1960's *Sex Kittens Go to College*, where Mamie got to play a genius-turned-stripper. At least that film had Conway Twitty fronting a jazz combo.)

Zugsmith had also thrown a Beat scene into the previous year's far more entertaining *High School Confidential!*, in which a woman reads the poem "Tomorrow Is a Drag, Man." Featuring Russ Tamblyn posing as a high school student out to bust pot and heroin dealers, the film's best moment (besides the close-up of Mamie Van Doren's skin-tight sweater and bullet bra) is Jerry Lee Lewis performing the title track on the back

'A Bucket of Blood': Beat meets B movie gore
JAMES AUSTIN COLLECTION

of a pickup truck. KIX WITH CHIX, HIX, STIX AND A FIX, was how the *Variety* review headline might have read.

Considerably more entertaining as Beat-pastiche is Roger Corman's 1959 *A Bucket of Blood*. When people talk about beatnik movies, this one is always near the top of the list. The movie opens when a large, loud beatnik with a face like a bearded carp, looms over the screen and declares loudly, "What is not creation is Graham Cracker!" In typical Corman fashion, the movie was shot in probably less time than it takes to watch, and it introduced the world to Dick "One-Take" Miller as Walter Paisley, a table-clearing nebbish at a joint called the Yellow Door. After Walter accidentally stabs a cat with a butcher knife, he covers the stiff carcass in plaster. When he presents his creation to his gang of vacant posers, he is suddenly deemed an artist. This new acceptance goes to his head to the extent that he naturally begins killing people to make new art.

What is wonderful about *A Bucket of Blood* is that by mistake or design the movie is rather leisurely paced, with the characters growing more likable. Even when Walter's ego shoots through the roof, and he begins to look as though he's prepping to understudy Burgess Meredith as the Penguin, he's a very sympathetic lunatic. Hell, the poetry and the folk singing are scarier than the murders.

Literature professor Herschell Gordon Lewis was still three years away from his first gore-splattered feature when he directed 1960's *The Prime Time,* about a wanton teen and her cop boyfriend who use a beatnik's pad for their rendezvous crib. Unfortunately, nobody sees much action in this tired excuse for a couple of skinny-dipping scenes, not even the young Karen Black, who does double duty in a few shots. The film's one redeeming virtue is a band called the D-Cups, who perform "Teenage Tiger."

England and France meantime were launch-ing films truer to the spirit of this new international Zeitgeist with very little outright parody. Great Britain had its Hammer Horror films and Carry On series, and Brigitte Bardot had become a major export from France, but at the same time, new, youth-oriented adult films were changing the face of world cinema in ways that America, particularly Hollywood, would take years to catch on to. In 1957, Louis Malle used Miles Davis for the soundtrack of *Ascenseur pour L'Echafaud (Elevator to the Gallows)*; in 1959, Jean-Luc Godard took his first steps to rewrite cinematic structure in *A Bout de Souffle (Breathless)*, starring the young American actress Jean Seberg; and in 1960, François Truffaut was gearing up for his Antoine Doinel series with *Le Quatre Cent Coups (The Four Hundred Blows)* and was about to direct *Jules et Jim*. These experiments had much in common with work by independent American directors Cassavetes and Shirley Clarke.

Britain was producing such "angry young men" films as 1959's *Room at the Top* and 1960's *Saturday Night and Sunday Morning*, which are often classified under Beat, sociologically and aesthetically, since they attacked class and social conventions. With James Bond only a couple of years away, the Brits also managed to turn out less ambitious gems like 1960's *Beat Girl* a.k.a. *Wild for Kicks*, which was England's answer to both the beatnik and the Bardot crazes, and was directed by a Frenchman, *naturellement*. The movie features some wonderful pre-007 jazzy-twangy music by John Barry, a couple of dandy strip sequences, the requisite underground coffee cellar, the Offbeat, and a lot of snappy patter: Beat Girl Jenny says to her perplexed dad, "Next week: VOOM! Up goes the world in smoke! And what's the score? Zero!" The kids in the film also refer to beatniks as "hopeless and soapless . . . a gimmick from America."

Hollywood couldn't have done more at this time to show its full unbridled disdain for Beat lit than to produce a version of *The Subterraneans*

(1960) in which Kerouac's black lover was portrayed by Leslie Caron. In the novel, Mardou Fox is described as being: "a little thin brown woman disposed to wearing dark clothes, poor beat subterranean clothes . . ." What MGM exec wouldn't immediately slap his head and exclaim, "Leslie Caron! Of course—she's perfect!"? Others were tackling sensitive racial issues at the time, from Luis Buñuel (1960's *The Young One*) to Cassavetes's *Shadows* (1960) and Shirley Clarke's *The Connection* (1961), so for Hollywood to pass on the opportunity to make the first great interracial love story, and perhaps the first real Beat film, only added insult to injury. *The Subterraneans* did have a fine soundtrack featuring Gerry Mulligan and other West Coast jazz stars, with the exception of a cheerfully inane summation of the Beat set in the song "Coffee Time," performed by Carmen McRae: "Coffee time/My dreamy friend it's coffee time/Let's listen to some jazz and rhyme/And have a cup of coffee/Let me show/A little coffee house I know/Where all the New Bohemians go/To have a cup of coffee."

This would be the first and only time that a Kerouac novel would be adapted to the big screen, although several unsuccessful efforts have been made to get a version of *On the Road* produced, most recently by Francis Ford Coppola.

There were other fun films in the late Fifties–early Sixties that took a crack at the beatniks, notably 1959's *The Rebel Set*, starring Maxwell Smart's Chief, Edward Platt, as a crook with a coffeehouse, and 1963's *Greenwich Village Story*, directed by Jack O'Connell, which was certainly the most affectionate, least clichéd of all the beatnik movies of that time. That it followed the

end of the Beat era added a poignancy that would be all too rare in most films of its kind. In some ways it closes the door on the real Beat world, and leaves all the subsequent portrayals to be seen as ludicrous afterthoughts—which isn't to say that these ludicrous afterthoughts couldn't be fun. One of the best, 1964's *The Flesh Eaters* finds Omar the beatnik (Ray Tudor) arriving on a raft on an island (a nightmare version of Gilligan and his gang), mere seconds away from having his sandals and feet eaten by tiny glowing monsters that live in the sea. "The geek can't get me," he says, part rockabilly goofball, part neo-hippie, "Omar's got the love weapon." One interesting footnote about *The Flesh Eaters* is that its soundtrack features Anita Ellis, the vocalist on the title song of Robert Frank's *Pull My Daisy*.

The Fat Black Pussycat (1964), a cop drama set among beatniks and goofy intellectuals, stars a cross between Mannix and Casey Kasem as a hero who gets assaulted at a party by bad poetry and abstract expressionism (literally) and wakes up in a neighbor's apartment whose female resident claims to be pursuing an "anthropological approach to beatniks." The cop's partner becomes a star at the local coffee joint by reciting traffic law: "Parking in a hospital zone is strictly prohibited . . . man."

If there is a definitive cinematic endpiece to the Beats, it is the 1965 British film *Catch Us If You Can* (a.k.a. *Having a Wild Weekend*), directed by John Boorman. Doubtless intended to make the Dave Clark Five as competitive with the Beatles on film as they were in the charts, the film took a perversely opposite approach, removing the comic touches and satirical bits of Richard Lester's *A Hard Day's Night*, becoming as bitter and aggressively cynical as the Beatles' picture was whimsical. In one scene, Steve (Dave Clark) and his girlfriend accidentally stumble upon a deserted village where they find themselves in the company of a group of vagabonds who look like a lost tribe of Deadheads or the roadies from the

'The Beat Generation,' the movie
JAMES AUSTIN COLLECTION

last Velvets tour. Drugged out, mumbling and thoroughly stupefied, one of the group asks Steve if he has any "spliffs" or "horse." Steve's girl is fascinated: "Are you *on the road*?" she asks with delight. Steve calls them a "load of Beats" and they tell him "that's a dead word—a word for thicks." If this scene had been clipped and pasted into any number of the Altamont-era counterculture films, including *Easy Rider*, it would hardly have played any differently. Long hair, drugs, ennui and arrogance, the beached detritus of two generations in a single decade.

It seemed to be an unwritten rule in the 1959 to 1966 television seasons that most of the dramatic series and a lot of comedies had to feature a beatnik character—if not in the series, then in at least one story. The West Hollywood hipster-type could be found on 77 *Sunset Strip* as Gerald Lloyd Kookson III, or "Kookie." It's a little difficult to think of Kookie as a beatnik, mostly because he wasn't really very, well, kooky. As played by Ed Byrnes, he was blond and beardless and (as Neal Cassady sometimes did) parked cars for a living. He was like a finger-snapping Jan looking for a Dean. His record "Kookie's Mad Pad" did reveal that his apartment was furnished with "plaid light bulbs," "feathers from Birdland" and "alpaca lampshades," adding fuel to the tabloid rumors that Kookie had been spotted shopping on Hollywood Boulevard with Ed Wood Jr.

Staccato debuted in fall 1958, with the *Johnny* added later. John Cassavetes played a New York tough guy who just happened to play jazz piano in a little MacDougal Street joint. Staccato, like *Peter Gunn* and *Mr. Lucky*, was Phillip Marlowe with some swing, some cool, some jive. The Manhattan exteriors added a nice touch, as did the fact that Staccato got to meet a lot of swinging chicks, doe-eyed blondes in Capri pants, including his future wife Gena Rowlands. In one episode, Cloris Leachman played a knife-happy

pacifist, and the future Samantha Stevens, Elizabeth Montgomery, managed to show more skin in one half hour than either Darren would ever glimpse. Staccato wasn't a beatnik but lived in their world and they in his, and it was refreshing to see real musicians like Milt Holland and Barney Kessel performing in the show.

Peter Gunn (starring Craig Stevens) also hung out in a jazz club, getting tips from his beatnik pals, and *Mr. Lucky* (starring John Vivyan) had a lot of interesting friends. Steven Hill, later of *Law and Order*, did some nice beatnik work on *Ben Casey*, and George C. Scott, who took a turn in the same series as a doctor-turned-junkie, played a hip character called "The Baron" in a show called *The Delinquent, the Hipster, the Square*. Alfred Hitchcock introduced one of his episodes, "The Big Kick," in Beat threads: "Like, good evening." The story, written by Robert "*Psycho*" Bloch, had a couple of hustling down-and-out beatniks being done in by a young, serial-killing Wayne Rogers who would go on to do less objectionable things with sharp instruments as Trapper John on *M*A*S*H*.

In a 1966 episode of *The Man from U.N.C.L.E.*, titled "The Pop Art Affair," an artist (Mark Harris) ran a beatnik gang for THRUSH. One of the sculptures featured in the episode is credited to Ward Kimball, and it's reasonable to hope that this was the same eccentric individual who worked as an animator for Disney, and who co-created the 1953 Oscar-winning cartoon "Toot, Whistle, Plunk and Boom," which was loaded with beatnik and bebop moments.

Other cartoon studios hopped on the beatnik bandwagon: Warner Bros. resident genius Friz Freleng created 1957's "The Three Little Bops," which told the animated story of a trio of jazz pigs and one very unhip trumpet-playing wolf with some singing by perennial parodist Stan Freberg. Most of these shorts, like Paramount's "Miceniks"(1960) and "Boppin Hood" (1961), were simply bad cartoons loaded with beatnik clichés. Then again, "Rocky and Bullwinkle" featured a coffee dive managed by Boris Badenov and Beat Queen heartthrob Natasha Fatale. "Like, allow me to introduce myself, man."

One rather wonderful cartoon was Bob Clampett's "The Wildman of Wildsville" starring Beany and Cecil. It featured a brief introduction by Lord Buckley and the voice of Scatman Crothers as "Go Man Van Gogh," a psychedelic Tarzan who lives on the "Hungry I-Land" surrounded by Jackson Pollock backdrops. Cecil the Seasick Sea Serpent and his pals are trying to capture the elusive swinger, but eventually they're all overcome by the Wildman's manic exuberance: "If you can't beatnik 'em, join 'em," they declare, donning shades, berets and goatees, and launching into a chorus of "Twinkle Twinkle Little Beatnik."

The only television program that actually had a Beat pedigree of sorts was *Route 66*, which kicked off in 1960. The show starred Martin Milner, fresh out of reefers, and George Maharis as a Hell's Kitchen escapee. Tod (Milner) was straight, and Buzz (Maharis) was streetwise, and together they roamed the countryside in Tod's convertible Corvette, looking for adventure and whatever came their way. Kerouac was convinced, and with good reason, that *Route 66* had been stolen from his writings, but, like Maynard, the show was less cause than symptom. What it had going for it was some fancy cinematic footwork—most or all of the episodes were actually shot on location—and the show fit rather smugly into a spate of new series that didn't shy away from sensitive issues and downbeat endings. In retrospect, however, Milner's constant stiff perplexity and Maharis's tortured, too-hip gaze are

nearly intolerable. In one show, Robert Duvall plays a junkie with roughly the same breathtaking realism that Frank Fontaine brought to Crazy Guggenheim. Buzz, of course, knows a junkie with an IQ of sixteen when he sees one, and a look of sad recognition creeps over him as he says, "You don't know what's buggin' him. He's got a birdcage on his foot; he's all strung out behind H." As kids from the era used to say, spare me.

Finally, the Sixties television show that deserves an honorable mention as perhaps the best beatnik series, but, finger-snapping notwithstanding, without ever once identifying the cast as such, was *The Addams Family*. Kooky, perhaps, but hardly creepy, Gomez, Morticia and the rest of the Addamses were a society apart, a Bizarro culture that made its own rules, but which deliberately took a stance that opposed everything the world embraced as normal. The difference between this group and the plastic TV and movie beatniks was that there was no rancor, no neurosis, no bitter rejection of the world outside. They were sexy and good-natured, and so comfortable in their skin that they invariably made the straight world seem out of place, not just in their presence, but altogether, as if their only possible avenue of redemption would be to embrace the values of the Addamses. Maynard seemed like a lost cousin.

Wolcott Gibbs wrote an introduction to an early collection of cartoons by Charles Addams, creator of *The Addams Family*, in which he may be defining, as well as providing an epitaph for, Beat and beatnik alike: ". . . As if God had shrugged His shoulders [and] presently our civilization will once again belong to the misshapen, the moonstruck, and the damned."

PART II

King of the Road

Jack Kerouac

Jack Kerouac, 1963

Jack Kerouac, Columbia University football player, circa 1940
FRANK DRIGGS COLLECTION

The American Journey
of Jack Kerouac

BY DOUGLAS BRINKLEY

A N ODD MOMENT OF CULTURAL history took place in September 1968 when the forty-six-year-old Jack Kerouac appeared on William F. Buckley Jr.'s talk show *Firing Line* to discuss hippies, flower power, Vietnam, underground literature and other phenomena of the time. After all, his novel *On the Road*—which was then selling thousands of copies a year in paperback—was said to have inspired the 1960s countercultural rebellion against the military-industrial complex. There was just one glitch: The seemingly apolitical Kerouac was in fact himself a nonvoting Eisenhower Republican and frequent admirer of Buckley's *National Review* and its wry conservatism. "Now Bill Buckley," Kerouac gushed to a friend when the pretaped program aired, "there's a guy I admire. I know him from way back."

And so it was: Kerouac and Buckley had been friends in the early 1940s, when Jack was a freshman football player at Columbia University about to live out the romantic novels of Thomas Wolfe, and Buckley a young aristocrat at Yale University fascinated with the British monarchy. The pair had gotten together for champagne at the Plaza and double dates in Times Square; now they reunited on television to dissect an America in upheaval, with the ghettos of Los Angeles and Detroit on fire, Martin Luther King Jr. and Bobby Kennedy in their graves, and a beleaguered President Lyndon Johnson on the ropes and refusing to seek reelection.

Kerouac's literary friends, or at least those like poet Allen Ginsberg—who had a stake in keeping the Beat ethos alive—pleaded with Kerouac not to appear on *Firing Line* for good reason: Repub-

lican presidential candidate Richard M. Nixon was claiming to represent the great "Silent Majority" of Americans fed up with the Sixties' social chaos. Ginsberg feared that Buckley would bait his erstwhile friend and badmouth the Beats on national television. Kerouac, of course, ignored the appeal, seeing the program as an opportunity to disassociate himself from Ginsberg's advocacy of social anarchy and left-wing politics.

When he arrived at the Manhattan studio for the *Firing Line* taping, he happened to encounter his literary nemesis, Truman Capote, occupying a dressing room down the hall. "Hello, Jack," Capote assayed. Kerouac—long annoyed that the famed author of *In Cold Blood* had called *On the Road* "typing" rather than writing—responded with, "Hello, you queer bastard" before walking over to shake Capote's hand, continuing, "You've been saying bad things about me, but I have nothing against you." Kerouac *did*, however, have an ax to grind with Ginsberg, who against his fervent entreaties had accompanied him to the Buckley show.

Once the cameras were rolling, a besotted Kerouac joined underground poet and editor Ed Sanders and sociology professor Lewis Yablansky in discussing contemporary issues with Buckley. Throughout the program, Kerouac ardently denied that he was "the Father of the Psychedelic Sixties" as Sanders had suggested. Yet, when Buckley asked whether the Beat Generation had ever been "pure," Kerouac responded, "Yes, it was pure—my heart." Midway through the show the cameras panned to a fidgety Ginsberg sitting in the audience stroking his beard, then cut over to show Kerouac giving the premier Beat poet an unmistakable thumbs down. Earlier that year he had vehemently denounced Ginsberg as a fraud in the *Paris Review;* Kerouac—whose long jazz lines of prose had so influenced Ginsberg's confessional free verse—had thus already broken ranks with his Beat Generation cronies. He may have provided the titles for Ginsberg's signature poem "Howl" and Burroughs's defining novel *Naked Lunch,* but Kerouac had no interest in maintaining any literary associations with them when they denounced the U.S. government and sneered at average, working-class Americans.

After the Buckley show ended, a saddened Ginsberg hugged Kerouac and whispered, "Goodbye, drunken ghost." Years later Ginsberg told the *Firing Line* story as he chose to see it: that alcohol had ravaged Kerouac's once poetic mind, and insinuating that his conservatism was actually a side effect of this. What the ringleader of the counterculture refused to accept was that his friend had in fact bid him an intellectual goodbye a decade before.

As convenient as it may have been for the New Left to claim that alcohol had addled Kerouac into irrelevance, the truth was that, despite frequent blackouts, the self-proclaimed "conservative Catholic" had maintained lucidity in his prose. While Ginsberg opted to see Kerouac as a "drunken ghost" because of his support for Main Street values and the Vietnam War, he actually had changed little since that August day in 1942 when he joined the merchant marine, carrying a duffel bag full of classic novels to read at sea. Not that he followed America's living classic writers Ralph Ellison, James T. Farrell and John Dos Passos in signing pro-war petitions, or that he engaged in friendly correspondence with President Johnson like John Steinbeck; instead the paradoxical Kerouac took the middle of the road and stood against the immoral war while maintaining that it was plain wrong not to support the American soldiers, like his nephew, who were dying in the rice paddies under clouds of Agent Orange in Southeast Asia. (In the spring of 1943 Kerouac had been discharged form the U.S. Navy for announcing he would never kill anyone, even in self-defense.) Having been attacked by the Right in the 1950s for his bohemian lifestyle and by the Left for his middle-American politics, Kerouac didn't even try to bridge the cultural schism but remained an island unto himself, informed and guided by the blue-collar values he had learned as a boy in Lowell, Massachusetts.

Born on March 12, 1922, the youngest of three children in a French-American family who had come to Lowell from Canada in 1914, by the age of ten Jack Kerouac was aiming to become a writer. His father ran a printing shop and published a local newsletter called *The Spotlight,* so young Jack learned about layout at an early age in an atmosphere made intoxicating by the smell of printer's ink. Although French had been his first language, Kerouac's facility with English manifested itself early; before long he took to writing and producing his own weekly sports sheet, which he sold on the streets of Lowell. He attended both Catholic and public schools and won athletic scholarships to the Horace Mann prep school in the Bronx and then to Columbia University in 1940, where he soon fell in with Allen Ginsberg and William S. Burroughs. A broken leg put an end to his college football career, and Kerouac quit school his sophomore year to join the merchant marine, beginning the restless wandering that would characterize both his literary legacy and the greater part of his life.

He wrote about his merchant marine trip to the Arctic in a still-unpublished first novel, *The Sea Is My Brother,* at age twenty; he also started faithfully keeping a diary, which he would continue doing almost until the last year of his life. After his discharge from the merchant marine as a "schizoid personality," Kerouac began a diligent study of Keats, Yeats, Shakespeare, Pascal, Tolstoy—the whole of the Western literary canon—

in dead earnest. He took his working motto from Middle America's champion novelist Sinclair Lewis, whom he greatly admired: "The first rule of writing is to put the seat of your pants to the seat of your chair." This Kerouac did, and better. Beat Generation bohemianism aside, he not only was—but strove to be—first and foremost an old-fashioned *craftsman*, and struggled to achieve the colloquial rhythm in his prose that would capture the uplifting essence of America as did Aaron Copland with music in 1945's "Appalachian Spring." For every day he spent "on the road" gathering material over the next twenty years, Kerouac toiled for a month in solitude, handwriting, polishing and typing his various novels, prayers, poems and meditations.

To Kerouac, "Beat" was not about politics but art. The thirty books he wrote between 1946 and 1969 give evidence of a downright workmanlike, if spontaneous, "sketching" technique whereby he would jot down every impression that coursed through his consciousness in the exact order of its occurrence. Taken together, these novels, including *On the Road,* comprise Kerouac's more or less autobiographical Legend of Duluoz—a study of a particular lifetime, his own, in the manner of Honoré de Balzac's *Human Comedy* or Marcel Proust's *Remembrance of Things Past.* But Kerouac tried to go one better than Balzac and Proust with a new prose technique influenced by both modern jazz and an architect friend, Ed White, who urged him to sketch New York in his pocket notebooks as White did buildings on his oversized pads.

Kerouac's mania for jazz cannot be overstated: He honestly believed that Charlie "Bird" Parker, Thelonious Monk and Dizzy Gillespie were the modern American equivalents of Bach, Beethoven and Brahms, a notion that earned him much ridicule from New York's cultural elite. "When I first heard Bird and Diz in the Three Deuces I knew they were serious musicians playing a goofy new sound and didn't care what I

thought," Kerouac would write in 1959. "In fact I was leaning against the bar with a beer when Dizzy came over for a glass of water from the bartender, put himself right against me and reached both arms around both sides of my head to get the glass and danced away, as though knowing I'd be singing about him someday, or that one of his arrangements would be named after me someday by some goofy circumstance."

Improvisational jazz spurred Kerouac to avoid writer's block by the same means: recording the very process of crafting prose, a creative method legitimized by the automatic writing of William James, the trance poems of William Butler Yeats, the first "happening" at Black Mountain College and the paint drippings of Jackson Pollock, with whom Kerouac used to drink in Greenwich Village. But Kerouac picked Kansas City's Bird as his true mentor, a "tenor man drawing breath and blowing a phrase on his saxophone till he runs out of breath, and as he does, his sentence, his statement's been made . . . and that's how I separate my sentences, as breath separation of the mind." To date, no writer has waxed more enthusiastic about jazz than Kerouac, particularly in his underrated *Mexico City Blues*—242 poetic choruses presented as a long Sunday-afternoon jam session. Yet Kerouac was not a serious jazz scholar like Ralph Ellison or Albert Murray; his unsophisticated critiques of musicians were based on emotional fandom rather than a classical comprehension of the new rhythms, harmonies, textures and structures of bop.

Given his infatuation with the spontaneity of jazz, it is not surprising that the fastidious Kerouac preferred the image of a natural-born, wild-eyed Rimbaud-like genius rather than an exacting cobbler of words in the careful manner of John O'Hara. Thus Kerouac set out to become the quintessential literary mythmaker of postwar America, creating his Legend of Duluoz by spinning what he called "proletariat tall tales" about his revelatory road adventures. At a time when Norman Mailer was astutely playing sociologist by studying "White Negro" hipsters, Kerouac wanted to create a myth around his fascinatingly inchoate friend Neal Cassady as the modern-day equivalent of Old West icons Jim Bridger, Pecos Bill and Jim Bowie combined. Like the young Lowell boy he never left behind, Kerouac saw football players and range-worn cowboys as the paragons of the true America; his diaries teem with references to "folk heros" and praise for Zane Grey's honest drifters, Herman Melville's confidence men and Babe Ruth's feats both on the diamond and in the barroom. Thus Kerouac brought Cassady into the American mythical pantheon as "that mad Ahab at the wheel," compelling others to join his roaring drive across Walt Whitman's patchwork Promised Land.

While gathering material for *On the Road* in 1949, crisscrossing America in search of kicks, joy and God, he stopped off in the eastern Montana town of Miles City, and wandered around in the February snow, temperature registering at 20 degrees below. Soon Kerouac had one of his many epiphanies. "In a drugstore window I saw a book on sale—so beautiful!" he wrote in his journal. "*Yellowstone Red*, a story of a man in the early days of the valley, and his tribulations and triumphs. Is this not better reading in Miles City than *The Iliad*? Their *own* epic?" Kerouac was intent on creating his own Yellowstone Red story, only in the modern context, where existential jazz players and lost highway speedsters would be celebrated as the new vagabond saints.

On the Road protagonists Dean Moriarty and Sal Paradise were intended as the automobile-age equivalents of Butch Cassidy and the Sundance Kid. "Beyond the glittery street was darkness and beyond the darkness the West," Kerouac wrote in 1951. "I had to go." In the avant-garde circus that was the Beat culture, populated by whores, swindlers, hipsters, horn players, hobos and char-

latans, Kerouac saw himself as the F. Scott Fitzgerald of the post–Jazz Age, whose frantic stories would bring their unorthodox exploits before the Eisenhower era's public at large. But spinning yarns about deviant characters was dangerous business in the days of Joe McCarthy's philistine witch hunts: In 1954, for example, John Steinbeck's own hometown of Salinas, California, launched an effort to keep H. G. Wells's *Outline of History* and Bertrand Russell's *Human Knowledge* out of the public libraries. In San Antonio, where Davy Crockett and 184 other patriots had given their lives for liberty at the Alamo, an effort was underway to tack SUBVERSIVE labels to more than 500 books by 118 writers including the likes of Thomas Mann and the Fourteenth Century's Geoffrey Chaucer, while the state of Texas passed a law requiring textbook authors to sign a loyalty oath to the U.S. government. Alabama took censorship yet another step further: Its law required textbook writers not only to state whether or not they were communists but to declare the same of every author they cited. Elsewhere the matter took an even sillier turn: The Indiana Textbook Commission, for example, demanded the excision of all references to Robin Hood and the Quaker religion because of their communist leanings.

In this bizarre Red Scare atmosphere Kerouac was either extremely naive or wildly courageous to claim that *On the Road*'s car thief and con artist Dean Moriarty was "a new kind of American Saint," and Cassady's criminal bent a "wild-eyed overburst of American joy." In an era when Zen Buddhist teachings were considered communist propaganda, Kerouac's quest to make heroes out of hoodwinkers and hoodlums was bound to raise critics' eyebrows and concerns at the FBI.

But it was Kerouac's peculiar genius to find the heroes of Western dime novels in Catholic saints, Zen Buddhist masters and Levantine holy men. He had a gift for paradoxical mixtures of characters: quipster W. C. Fields and navel-gazing memoirist Marcel Proust; the comics' Li'l Abner and French Symbolist Louis-Ferdinand Céline; Yankee slugger Mickey Mantle and Japanese Zen philosopher D. T. Suzuki. Combining TV cowboy Hopalong Cassidy with St. Francis got him Neal Cassady, melding Johnny Appleseed with Buddha turned out Gary Snyder. Filtered through Kerouac's fertile imagination and populist view of American cultural history, even Burroughs became an old-time "Kansas Minister with exotic phenomenal fire and mysteries." The result in his books was a parade of divine outlaws, desolate angels, holy goofs and subterranean prophets, every one of them unmistakably American. It is through such characters that Kerouac approached in *On the Road* one of the central questions of postwar Western literature: "Whither goest thou, America, in thy shiny car in the night?"

The biblical lingo was no accident. Although Kerouac only hints at his fixation on the death of Christ in his letters, his diaries are another matter entirely. The pages are strewn with drawings of crucifixes or teem with pleas to God to forgive his wayward carnal sins. (Kerouac's most impressive oil painting is a colorful portrait of Cardinal Montini.) Examined as a whole, Kerouac's diaries are nothing so much as a portable confessional, with every other page a Mass card, and every repent a votive candle lit to another saint. From childhood until death, Kerouac wrote letters to God, prayers to Jesus, poems to St. Paul and psalms to his own salvation. In fact, he coined the very term "Beat" one rainy afternoon while praying to a statue of the Virgin Mary at Lowell's St. Jeanne d'Arc Cathedral, which triggered a teary vision: As Kerouac described it, "I heard the holy silence in the church (I was the only one there, it was five p.m., dogs were barking outside, children yelling, the fall leaves, the candles were flickering alone just for me), the vision of the word Beat as being to mean 'beatific.'"

A more down-to-earth, but related, defini-tion of "Beat" in the sense of "beaten down" appears in *On the Road*: "Because I am poor the world belongs to me." But in Kerouac's view the earth stood to be inherited not only by the meek but also by the other downtrodden in his Legend of Duluoz narratives—the drifters, hobos, migrant workers and prostitutes—which he turned into heroic angels in his own version of Jesus' holy work. After all, it was one thing to paint a halo on Eleanor Roosevelt for her good deeds, but quite another to transform a Bowery bum into St. Christopher—alchemy that seemed to work only when Kerouac brooded alone at night with his cats and his mother, to write to the chapfallen rhapsodies of Billie Holiday across the scratches on a 78. In this amort atmosphere it seemed logical that if Jesus loved Barabbas on the cross there was no reason why he shouldn't love Herbert Huncke for robbing stores, Cassady for stealing cars or Ginsberg for homosexuality. Often while writing, Kerouac would take breaks and draw "pietas" in his diaries accompanied by psalms asking for the "Lamb of God"—that is, mercy—to fill every sinner's heart. "Poetry is Lamb's dust," Kerouac was fond of saying. It is a testament to the depth of Kerouac's faith in the holy outcast and proletarian saint that his romantic visions of Cassady in *On the Road* and Snyder in *The Dharma Bums*, among others, have now sent four generations on a quest for spiritual awakening.

The most enduring myth about Kerouac, which his diaries and journals partially dispel, is that he wrote *On the Road* in April 1951 in a three-week frenzy fueled by Benzedrine and coffee. According to the legend, one day Kerouac, inspired by his raucous travels with Cassady over the previous three years, stuck a roll of Japanese tracing paper into a typewriter at his apartment on West 20th Street—so as not to distract his concentration changing paper—turned on an all-night Harlem jazz radio station, and produced a modern masterpiece. Kerouac's archives in Lowell tell a different story from his claim that between April 2 and April 22 he wrote all of *On the Road*, averaging six thousand words a day, logging twelve thousand the first day, and fifteen thousand the last. The thirty-five-year-old author said he "blew out" his holy words like Lester Young on his midnight saxophone those nights, writing fast because the "road is fast." Revisions were for hung-up squares and the culturally constipated, too afraid to dig the natural rhythms of their own minds. Once the Benzedrine ran out and *On the Road* was finished, Kerouac allegedly scotch-taped the twelve-foot sheets of paper together and delivered the hundred-foot "scroll" to Harcourt Brace editor Bob Giroux, who, instead of gushing, bellowed at the author, "How the hell can the printer work from this?" Insulted, Kerouac stormed out of the office, although he would later claim that Giroux compared the work to Dostoyevsky's and called Kerouac a literary prophet ahead of his time. (Kerouac continued to admire Giroux's skills as an editor. In November 1956 Kerouac wrote a still-unpublished thirty-five-chorus poem, "Washington, D.C. Blues," which included a salute to R. G. Giroux, while staying at the Capitol Hill home of poet Randall Jarrell.)

This tale of *On the Road* as the product of a fevered burst of divine inspiration is exaggerated. That the manuscript Kerouac typed in Chelsea in April 1951 was the outcome of a fastidious process of outlining, character sketching, chapter drafting and meticulous trimming is clearly evident from even a cursory glance at what he called his "scribbled secret notebooks." Not only did he have a coherent and detailed one-page plot line for most chapters, but portions of the dialogue had also been written before April. Journal entries were incorporated directly into the manuscript in the famous marathon typing session, during which he also used a list he had kept of key phrases to be worked into the text denoting ideas

that Kerouac would paraphrase from T. S. Eliot, Mark Twain, Thomas Wolfe, William Saroyan, John Donne, Thomas De Quincey and many others. A writer looking for an academic model of how to prepare for a novel could do worse than emulate Kerouac's methods for *On the Road*.

The most consistent factor throughout the novel's various drafts was the depiction of Cassady in some guise as the wild Western protagonist of the saga. The real Cassady was such a marvelous character—a point continually reconfirmed whether he cropped up as the secret hero of "Howl" or as the sledgehammer-flipping, speed-rapping, manic driver of the Day-Glo bus labeled "Furthur" in which novelist Ken Kesey "unsettled" America—Kerouac sketched him truthfully, if with the occasional Hollywood touch of Beat-like actors such as Humphrey Bogart and Montgomery Clift. Kerouac also clearly set out to "celebrate" Western towns like Butte, Truckee, Medora, Fargo, Spokane, Denver and Salt Lake City, which he felt had not been given their due in American literature. As for his own alter ego Sal Paradise—the narrator of *On the Road*—he originally had been named Ray Smith, Chad Gavin and then Red Moultrie, in any case a hypocrisy-free American Adam with a scholarly bent.

What the working files for *On the Road* make clear is that Kerouac, far from clinging soley to the romantic notion of the spontaneous eruption of prose, had already drafted portions of *On the Road* between 1948 and 1950 and typed it onto the Japanese tracing paper nearly verbatim. Kerouac denied the care he took largely because it went against the Legend of Duluoz he was creating around himself as a "bop-prosody" genius. Kerouac exaggerated his act of literary creation, which was admittedly intense for those high-octane weeks, to prove that he was as spontaneous with words as the blind pianist George Shearing, the existential trumpet player Chet Baker and jazz guitarist Slim Gaillard were with music. Just six weeks after finishing *On the Road*, Kerouac wrote to Cassady that his next novel would be *Hold Your Horn High*, the ultimate romanticization of a "hot jazz cat."

Kerouac's prolific output, in other words, was the result of constant "sketching," creative self-discipline, and spontaneous prose. This is further manifested in the meticulousness with which Kerouac maintained his vast archives. "Hemingway has nothing over me when it comes to persnicketiness about 'craft,'" he wrote an editor. "Nor any poet." When it comes to literary productivity, he nearly matches Norman Mailer and Henry Miller, as his copious diary volumes of all shapes and sizes prove, filled as they are not only with regular observations but with chapter drafts, false starts and random character profiles as well.

Of course, these revelations about Kerouac's actual work methods are not entirely new. Throughout the 1950s and 1960s, Viking's Malcolm Cowley, who served as editor for *On the Road*, went on record claiming that Kerouac had written versions of his masterpiece before April 1951 and done major rewrites before its eventual publication in 1957. Some of the confusion stemmed from the peculiarity that over the years Kerouac had shown editors two different manuscripts titled *On the Road*. The second was an experimental, "spontaneous prose" portrait of Cassady that Kerouac wrote in 1951–52 and retitled "Visions of Neal"; it was published in 1972 as *Visions of Cody*. Still, "*On the Road* was good prose," Cowley recalled. "I wasn't worried about the prose. I was worried about the structure of the book. It seemed to me that in the original draft the story keeps swinging back and forth across the continental United States like a pendulum." Cowley urged Kerouac to consolidate episodes, shorten chapters, rewrite passages and throw out dead-end tangents. "Well, Jack did something that he would never admit to later," Cowley maintained. "He did a good bit of revision, and it was very good revision. Oh, he would never, never admit to that, because it was his feeling that the

stuff ought to come out like toothpaste from a tube and not be changed, and that every word that passed from his typewriter was holy. On the contrary, he revised, and revised well."

And so did Cowley. Worried that Kerouac would reinsert excised passages back into *On the Road*, the editor never sent him galleys, only a box of finished books. His concern was justified: Cowley had tweaked sections of the intricate novel without even informing the author, who complained bitterly to Ginsberg, Peter Orlovsky and Allen Ansen on July 21, 1957, "He yanked much out of *On the Road* . . . without my permission or even sight of galley proofs! Oh Shame! Shame on American Business." It left an even bigger bruise on Kerouac's ego when Cowley read some of his other manuscripts—*Doctor Sax*, *Tristessa* and *Desolation Angels*—and rejected them all, fretting that Kerouac had "completely ruined" himself as a "publishable writer" by embracing "automatic or self-abuse writing." Cowley believed that Kerouac's first book, 1951's *The Town and the City*, an extremely well-written, Wolfe-inspired paean to growing up in America, was better than anything in this new spate of jazz- and Buddhist-influenced stuff.

In addition to his struggles with Cowley, Kerouac's *On the Road* journals also reveal how he tussled to devise the right title for his confessional, picaresque novel. Enamored with Jack London's *The Road* and Walt Whitman's "Song of the Open Road," at various points between 1948 and 1957 Kerouac toyed with "Souls on the Road," "American Road Night," "Rock and Roll Road," "Home and the Road," "Love on the Road" and "Along the Wild Road," among other possible titles. *On the Road*, the simplest and best, won out, and just a few weeks after Gilbert Millstein reviewed it glowingly in the *New York Times* on September 5, 1957, Kerouac's audacious work made the best-seller list for several weeks, alongside Ayn Rand's *Atlas Shrugged* and Grace Metalious's *Peyton Place*.

Virtually overnight, *On the Road* made Kerouac into the "avatar" of the Beat Generation, appearing on John Wingate's TV show *Nightbeat* to tell millions of viewers he was "waiting for God to show his face." Bright women bored with *Ozzie and Harriet* domesticity swooned over this new James Dean with brains, while literary lions like Nelson Algren, Norman Mailer and Charles Olsen dubbed Kerouac a Great American Writer. Marlon Brando commissioned him to write a three-act play so the Academy Award winner could play Dean Moriarty. PEN—the International Association of Poets, Playwrights, Editors, Essayists and Novelists—invited him to join, but he declined. The Village Vanguard nightclub had him read jazz poetry, and TV talk show host Steve Allen provided piano accompaniment as Kerouac read passages from *On the Road* on Allen's popular program. "Jack was on top of the world," his musician friend David Amram recalled. "Everybody wanted to meet him, to hang with him." Russian artist Marc Chagall wanted to paint the first Beat's portrait with angels fluttering around his head. Photographer Robert Frank asked him to write the introduction to his book of elegiac photographs, *The Americans.* Jackie Kennedy, wife of the future President, said she had read *On the Road* and loved it. Instead of the "little magazines," Kerouac was now commissioned to write articles for *Playboy, Esquire, Escapade, Holiday* and the *New York World and Sun* explaining the Beat Generation. In a letter to Cassady, a bewildered Kerouac reported that "everything exploded."

And there stood the handsome Jack Kerouac with his penetrating blue eyes and football player's build, the victim of his own mythmaking, and unsure how to act under the spotlight as who the media wanted him to be. Never before had an American literary icon seemed so utterly confused and ill-equipped for fame, and certainly nobody could have guessed from reading *On the Road* that the shy Beat author was afraid of cars.

"[I] don't know how to drive," he admitted, "just typewrite."

But the fast-track adulation died down quickly. *On the Road* stayed on the bestseller list for only a few weeks. Warner Bros. withdrew its $110,000 offer for the film rights, a punishing blow. Kerouac wrote a long letter to a Hollywood producer explaining how *On the Road* could be made into a fabulous feature film. "Put a camera in front seat of car, show the widescreen color road winding into the car like an enormous dangerous snake," Kerouac wrote Jerry Wald in January 1958. "Just show Sal's feet to the right propped up on dashboard, let the dialog [*sic*] roll; let the road or the desert, the mountains, the narrow road, freeways, roll into the audience, all the way thru the picture." Unfortunately, Kerouac's enthusiasm was soon extinguished.

"Hollywood ain't buying my book probably at all," Kerouac complained to Ginsberg. "Brando is a shit, doesn't answer letters from the greatest writer in America and he's only a piddling King's clown of the stage." Kerouac also now deemed Millstein, who had raved about *On the Road* in the *New York Times,* "evil," just a hype-happy spoke in the corroded wheel of Madison Avenue, where the blasphemous dollar reigned. Sick of being criticized, Kerouac wrote to a friend in December 1957, "I'm just an old moth-eaten storyteller of America asking no more than a living so that I can eat my bread in sorrow from the sweat of my face."

As Kerouac prepared for the publication of *The Subterraneans* in 1958—brought out by Grove Press—he started to pull away from his Beat friends, and they from him. "Allen never loses track of me even when I try to hide," he complained to a former wife in early 1957, even before *On the Road* was published. The attention-seeking Ginsberg may have reveled in New York fame, but the painfully aloof Kerouac instead became more introspective and inclined to spend more time with his mother. Kerouac's mother

Jack Kerouac passing corner bar Avenue B & East 7th N.Y.; we went out for a walk along Tompkins Park, September 1953

Allen Ginsberg

Jack Kerouac, 1953

ALLEN GINSBERG

Gabrielle—whom Jack (and later his wife Stella) dutifully cared for at home—was reluctant to allow the bearded, revolutionary Ginsberg into the house. In fact, at one point she sent the poet a letter—at her son's prodding—threatening to report him to the FBI for engaging in anti-American activities. She wrote similar letters to Burroughs, telling him to steer clear of Jack or face her wrath. "My God!" Burroughs concluded. "She really has him sewed up like an incision."

"No wonder Hemingway went to Cuba and Joyce to France," Kerouac wrote a San Francisco poet friend. "I was in love with the world thru blue purple curtains when I knew you and I now have to look at it thru hard iron eyes." As so often happens when a persona-driven writer hits the publishing jackpot, Kerouac, as his friend John Clellon Holmes observed, "no longer knew who the hell he was supposed to be." So the fresh-minted literary icon numbed himself with whiskey to cope with his exploding stardom; Old Crow became his "liquid suit of armor, my shield which not even Flash Gordon's super ray gun could penetrate."

Matters turned even worse when the cultural elite, inspired to destroy the notion of Dean Moriarty as a saint, began attacking *On the Road*. Few critics gave the novel objective, fair, serious reviews. Herbert Gold mocked the book in *The Nation* as vulgar gibberish, writing, "when you take dehydrated Hipster and add watery words to make instant Beatnik, the flavor is gone but the lack of taste lingers on." Cultural mandarin Diana Trilling sneered at *On the Road's* "infantile camaraderie," insinuating that Kerouac was the victim of marijuana. Norman Podhoretz, in a stinging jeremiad in the *Partisan Review* titled "The Know-Nothing Bohemians," completely missing the spirituality of the narrative, claimed Kerouac's psychopathic motto was "kill . . . kill . . . kill."

The devoutly Catholic author was devastated by these vehement attacks: The notion that he promoted violence was 180 degrees off the mark.

A worshipper of St. Francis of Assisi, Kerouac loved *all* earthly creatures—criminals included. The gentle writer raised cats, denounced hunting for sport and practiced nonviolence, refusing to swing back at barroom provocateurs who wanted a piece of the King Beat. Still, thanks to tabloid-style journalism, every strange murder or youthful act of violence reported was now attributed to *On the Road's* supposed promotion of juvenile delinquency. Beatniks, the Republican right claimed, were ruining America. In fact, former President Herbert Hoover, speaking at the 1960 GOP convention in Chicago, blamed the "communist front, and the beatniks and the eggheads" for destroying the social fabric of the nation. These charges stung Kerouac, particularly since he objected to the Soviet prohibition on celebrating God or owning Bibles. "It is not true that *On the Road* is an evil influence on the young," Kerouac insisted in a June 22, 1965, letter to a friend, "it's simply a true story about an ex-cowboy and an ex-football player running around the country looking for pretty girls to love. If this is evil send it back to Eden & Mother Kali."

Later, Snyder took offense at Kerouac's portrayal of him in *The Dharma Bums* as Japhy Ryder, intimating that he considered it a pack of lies and writing to the author that his tongue should be cut out in hell. Bewildered by such harsh denunciations of books he had "written in heaven" with a joyous heart, Kerouac began hiding from the Beat scene, renting a house on Long Island's North Shore, drinking too many highballs while taking care of the love of his life, his mother, and bitterly watching *The Many Loves of Dobie Gillis*, which debuted in 1959, as no royalty checks rolled in. Rather than being respected as a herculean wordsmith like F. Scott Fitzgerald, Kerouac watched himself and his characters become a pop-culture joke, in the ridiculous TV caricature of Maynard G. Krebs. Depression hit Kerouac like a runaway train. Subsequent installments of the Duluoz Legend such as *Big Sur* (1962) and

Desolation Angels (1965) received mostly poor reviews from critics who wrote only about the author's persona and not his art. "I discovered spontaneity," Kerouac complained to Ginsberg. "I discovered a new Beat Generation a long time ago, I hitchhiked and starved, for art, and that makes me the Fool of the Beatniks with a crown of shit. Thanks, America."

Instead of playing the Beat role, Kerouac took refuge in work. By the early 1960s, he had gone out of his way to disassociate himself from Ginsberg and Burroughs, denouncing their public gestures and refusing to be included in anthologies that contained their homoerotic work. Most of all, it was Ginsberg, whom he now called a "hairy loss," who infuriated his sense of decency. In the 1940s Ginsberg did teach Kerouac about Hart Crane, William Blake and the New York Underground, while Jack, ever the American intellectual, taught Ginsberg the joy of Whitman, Wolfe, comic books and "the countryside glance." Kerouac had always loved Allen as a glorious con man and Whitmanesque bard, but was appalled that his friend had developed what he considered dangerous messianic tendencies. Their final break came shortly after the Kennedy assassination, when Ginsberg returned from India talking "pro-Castro bullshit" and wearing a "long white messiah shirt." As Kerouac wrote to his agent Sterling Lord, "I'm refusing any idea of his forever."

Just how disenchanted Kerouac had become with Ginsberg and, to a lesser extent, Burroughs can be seen in one occurrence in 1964 when he was stone broke and couldn't afford a headstone for the Orlando grave of his sister, Nin: He turned down three thousand dollars to appear in a Beat film with Ginsberg. Similarly when Nando Pivano, an Italian translator of American literature, wrote Kerouac a letter asking permission to include him in a Beat poetry anthology to be published in Milan, Kerouac refused. "What these bozos and their friends are up to now is simply

the last act in their original adoption and betrayal of any truly 'beat' credo," he wrote to Pivano, insisting that he would not be published alongside Ginsberg and company. "Now that we're all getting to be middle-aged I can see that they're just frustrated hysterical provocateurs and attention-seekers with nothing on their mind but rancor towards 'America' and the life of ordinary people. They have never written about ordinary people with any love you may have noticed. I still admire them of course, for their technical excellence as poets, as I admire Genét and Burroughs for their technical excellence as prose writers, but all four of them belong to the 'keep-me-out-of-the-picture' department and that's the way I want it from now on."

Kerouac wanted to be considered an individual American writer like Melville or Steinbeck, not as part of an insidious antiestablishment Beat cabal devoted to mocking the New Testament and bedeviling common decency. "Beware of bums of the anti-American variety," Kerouac wrote a friend. "I'm only Buffalo Bill." Tirades were unleashed at Pavlov, Freud, Marx and Ignorance—what he saw as the "Four Horsemen of the Modern Apocalypse" bent on condemning the old-fashioned sweetness of American innocence. As he put in a letter to one of the few Beat writer friends whose company he still enjoyed—John Clellon Holmes, who had become a creative writing instructor at the University of Arkansas—he himself *was* the American grain, not some radical flaming against it. He desperately wanted to escape the tag of archetypal City Lights Books pocket poets and be held in the same critical esteem as William Saroyan, Conrad Aiken, Eudora Welty and Pearl Buck.

Throughout his last years Kerouac continued his prodigious literary output, remaining to the end what Jack London earlier called a "workbeast." Given this unfailing ethic it is hardly surprising how it annoyed him to no end that the Sixties coffeehouse poets were hungrier for publicity than for education. By eschewing libraries, his young imitators seemed not to understand that Miles Davis practiced his trumpet ten hours a day, and that before he launched into action paintings Jackson Pollock had worked to become an ace draftsman and studied with Thomas Hart Benton. And during the 1950s, when he was writing *Some of the Dharma* (1997) and *Wake Up*, his biography of Buddha, Kerouac himself had spent months in libraries, poring over ancient texts to master the principles of Hinayana and Mahayana. The ensuing spread of "Pop Buddha" he had helped trigger irked him. "Buddha was right," Kerouac wrote Snyder. "Zen is a corruption of his truth."

One element in these admonishments was, of course, the sour grapes of a middle-aged writer who had lost touch with the erupting youth culture. But it remained his unwavering conviction that Madison Avenue packaging had ruined the flourishing art scene of the late 1950s and destroyed genuine artists and celluloid icons such as Elvis Presley, James Dean and Marlon Brando. Modern America, Kerouac lamented, had grown sterile and had forgotten neighborly gestures of kindness and respect, soft summer nights and delicate laughter by winter's firelight. Abstract Expressionist painters such as Robert Motherwell and Mark Rothko, he maintained, *could* lift their viewers up to where Daniel blew his joyful trumpet. Andy Warhol's pop art, on the other hand, was to Kerouac a nihilistic sham that offered neither love nor hope. It was not that Kerouac disdained modernism. On the contrary, his admiration for James Joyce grew over the years. But he loathed cynical modernism and its black humorists who believed the function of art was to ridicule instead of uplift.

It further angered him that the Kerouac wannabes of the so-called "Soaring Sixties," pouring lambs' blood on tanks and sticking daisies in gun barrels, had misread *On the Road* and created from it a "soaring hysteria." Filled with avuncular concern for uncouth hippies, he wished they would wise up and abandon Ginsbergian hype for tranquil afternoons reading Cervantes or just meditating under an old oak tree. He blamed Ginsberg for playing Pied Piper to these gullible youth, parading around in bizarre costumes at the 1967 March on Washington, the San Francisco Be-In, the 1968 Democratic Convention and Warhol's Factory. Meanwhile, nobody seemed to appreciate Gregory Peck, read Carl Sandburg, listen to Frank Sinatra or applaud Chuck Berry, the latter of whom Kerouac deemed better than all the British Invasion pop groups combined.

It is a tribute to Kerouac's workbeast endurance that he never stopped writing prose or poetry and never abandoned his quest to unravel the mysteries of his interior life as St. Augustine had in his *Confessions*. "I've got to keep busy with my Legend," Kerouac wrote, "or die of boredom." He had grown into Jack Kerouac the Elder, his fiction taking on a bittersweet tone like that in Wolfe's *You Can't Go Home Again*. As Kerouac wrote to a student, "I'm middle-aged now and no longer an enthusiastic college boy lyrically feeling America. As Joyce says, First comes the Lyric, then the Dramatic, then the Epic—I hope for me too." He knew that alcohol was ravaging his body, but he had fun drinking and comforted himself in the knowledge that Fitzgerald had written *The Last Tycoon* after his bibulous crack-up. Most of all, it was the prospect of completing the Legend of Duluoz saga that drove Kerouac on week after week; he so wanted to do for Lowell what Faulkner had done with his mythical Yoknapatawpha County. His last three books were *Satori in Paris* (1966), about his June 1965 journey to France to trace his Cornish ancestry; *Vanity of Duluoz* (1968), a coming-of-age story about his emergence as a football player–writer; and *Pic* (1971), an updated version of a 1950 story about a black ten-year-old North Carolina jazz enthusiast named Pictorial Review Jackson.

Vanity of Duluoz, published in February 1968,

ranks among Kerouac's most enjoyable works. Brimming with spontaneous prose, Shakespearean dialogue, humorous juxtapositions and a Wolfe-like faith in old-fashioned American values, it drew raves from *Time* as Kerouac's best novel, while the *Atlantic Monthly* showed its enthusiasm by excerpting an unpublished section as a short story titled "In the Ring." But only days after the triumphant publication, Kerouac received the devastating news that Cassady had died on February 4, 1968, just short of his forty-second birthday, beside some railroad tracks near San Miguel de Allende, Mexico.

The last time Kerouac had seen Cassady was in the summer of 1964, when Ken Kesey and his Merry Pranksters made their cross-country bus trek to explore America with a New York visit to Kerouac high on their list of pilgrimages. After all, Cassady was behind the wheel of "Furthur," Kesey's Day-Glo-painted 1939 International Harvester. If Kerouac had been the avatar of the Beat Generation, Kesey was the John the Baptist of the Neon Revolution. The "Furthur" crew extended an invitation to Kerouac to attend their Madison Avenue party, where the idea was to spiritually link the two "youth generations," which would on cue emerge as one. He accepted, anxious to spend time with his buddy Cassady as well as the talented Kesey.

That evening Kerouac was aghast to find the Merry Prankster party a media circus of Warholish proportions: glaring floodlights, tape recorders, movie cameras and a grinding, grating acid-rock band thrashing about euphorically. It saddened Kerouac to see his beloved outlaw Cassady performing like a dancing bear for such an unworthy crowd; he also worried that LSD and amphetamines were destroying his friend. "Dig this, Jack," Cassady raved, "the tape recorders and the cameras, just like we used to do, only this time professionally!" Instead of joining the psychedelic bash, Kerouac walked over to a sofa draped with

an American flag, folded Old Glory military fashion into a perfect triangle, and sat down.

When Kerouac heard the news of Cassady's death, he refused to believe it, taking the Mark Twain approach that the reports were greatly exaggerated. "Whoever made up that story of old Neal's cashing out, oughta be tarred and feathered," he snapped to Charles E. Jarvis, a literature professor friend from Lowell. "Guys like Neal just don't do things like that."

"You mean like dying?" Jarvis asked.

"That's right," Kerouac responded. "I mean, not at this point. Neal is in his prime. If I know that devil, he probably gave out the story of his death just to see me cry my eyes out. Well, I ain't gonna do it—because any day now, I'll get a letter from Neal wanting to know if I'm wearing a black band around my arm!"

It was impossible for Kerouac to believe that his proletariat superhero, his personification of both sainthood and cowboy myth, could perish from the earth. And in fact he didn't: By sketching Cassady as Dean Moriarty in *On the Road* and as Cody Pomeray in *Visions of Cody*, Kerouac had transformed his friend into an enduring character as vivid as Mike Fink, the renowned half-alligator Mississippi River keelboat-poler, or Casey Jones, the brazen Kentuckian train conductor who simply refused to put on the brakes.

Death had long haunted Kerouac; it was as if he poured so much of life into his books in order to bat the grim reaper into the shadow lands of his growing despair. By creating a legend for himself, Kerouac believed he would be immortalized, an American Giant with tousled hair and Canuck charm who told some of the best stories of his generation. What is astounding is that Kerouac never wavered from this mission launched in boyhood, staying beholden only to his mother; he was a big, raw, irrepressible talent who followed Thoreau's guidelines and marched to the beat of his own drum. That he was misunderstood had to be expected from a Cold War America in the throes of an anticommunist crusade. Kerouac in essence was an unconscious revolutionary, not in the political sense like Ginsberg but by celebrating the nation's underculture, the tenderloin districts and midnight cafés, smoking marijuana and writing about interracial sex, challenging the New York intellectual set with a spontaneous bop-prosody that showed America a way out of its stultifying, puritanical complacency. Kerouac never meant to insult but always to uplift, in the undying hope that the joy of Thomas Wolfe's lost America could somehow be recaptured.

If his appearance on the Buckley show in September 1968 demonstrated the conservative side of Kerouac, his struggles with alcoholism and his growing intolerance of change, it also gave testimony to his bulldog insistence that an artist should stick to his guns no matter the cost. "Walking on water," he quipped, "wasn't made in a day." Just a year after his appearance on *Firing Line*—on October 21, 1969—Kerouac died in St. Petersburg, Florida, survived by his mother and his wife Stella. For defending a drunken disabled Air Force veteran, he had been pummeled by the manager of the Cactus Bar; but while a massive hemorrhaging that resulted from the beating was the cause of death, alcohol was the real culprit.

In the last article Kerouac wrote, syndicated in the *Chicago Tribune* and in other papers in August 1969, he claimed he had never been of either the GOP right or Yippie left but simply an average working-class citizen, a "Bippie in the Middle." At that time he was also writing a novel called *The Spotlight*—after the little Lowell newspaper his father had printed in the 1930s—as the final installment in his Legend of Duluoz. He had planned to tell the story of how skyrocketing fame could destroy any artist, of his own struggles

to write ecstatic novels after *On the Road* when all the media wanted was to stamp him BEATNIK like a box of soap flakes. *The Spotlight* would explain that American "success" meant "you can't enjoy your food anymore." Lampoons of the tabloid culture had been sketched out in his journals, story lines and chapter headings already in place. It would be a humorous yet sad tale, showing that even the vipers of Madison Avenue would lose to the honest individual artist in the end.

The Spotlight would also have taken swipes at the *New York Times*, ABC, NBC, *Time*, the *New York Post* and, yes, even William F. Buckley Jr. "It will complete the 'Legend' up to now and may very well be my most exhausting writing experience," Kerouac wrote to Sterling Lord, "since the story is so fraught with imminent peril, men, women, dogs, cats, cornpones, agents, publishers, poolsharks, TV directors calling me a 'drunken moron,' celebrities, boozers, bookies, phew, wait till you see it."

To the bitter end, Kerouac stayed true to his notion that true liberation came from spontaneity of expression. And there is no doubt about it: Kerouac's "first-thought-best-thought" writing technique had a liberating effect during the Cold War, from the Molotov-cocktail hurlers of the 1956 Hungarian Revolution to the young intellectuals avoiding police during the 1968 Prague Spring to the 1989 East German John Henrys swinging their sledgehammers to bring down the Berlin Wall, as seen on CNN in living rooms around the world. The Eastern European youth movement against totalitarianism was not seeking democracy per se: They were demanding rock & roll, jazz and Kerouac's Beat poetics. Few writers get to fulfill their goals to the fullest, and as Kerouac had sworn in an August 1944 journal entry: "I promise I shall never give up, and that I'll die yelling and laughing. And that until then I'll rush around this world I insist is holy and pull on everyone's lapel and make them confess to me all."

This Song's for You, Jack:
Collaborating with Kerouac

BY DAVID AMRAM

UST FIND ONE PERSON AND PLAY for that person all night long, Dave," Charlie Mingus told me in the fall of 1955, when I had just arrived in New York and was fortunate enough to be chosen by him to play French horn in his quintet. "All you need is one person in your whole life to really be listening."

Jack Kerouac was one of those people who listened and observed as well as he wrote and performed. Jack and I first began performing together—his words backed by my playing—in 1956. Collaborating with Kerouac was as natural as breathing. That is because the breath and breadth of Jack's rhythms were so natural that even the most stodgy musician or listener or reader could feel those rhythms and cadences, those breathless flowing phrases, the subtle use of dynamics that are fundamental to the oral (i.e., spoken) and aural (i.e., to be listened to) tradition of all musics and poetic forms of expression.

Whoa, you might say. Why such a long sentence? Because Jack himself spoke, wrote, improvised and sang in long flowing phrases, like the music of Franz Schubert, George Gershwin, Hector Berlioz, Joseph Haydn, Charlie Parker, Lester Young and Billie Holiday, like the poetry of Walt Whitman, Dylan Thomas, Baudelaire, Langston Hughes and other lyric artists whose work we both loved and admired.

The 1950s were the pinnacle years for great conversationalists and great rappers, the last generation to grow up reading voraciously, traveling by extension of the thumb and trusting the Great Creator to get you to your destination. Part of your requirement for being a successful hitch-hiker was to engage your patron saint of the moment—the person who picked you up—in conversations about anything and everything.

Forty years ago, storytelling was still practiced as a people-to-people activity. TV and the Internet were not part of the picture. Entertainment and communication came from the interaction of people with one another. Many of the greatest poets, authors and jazz artists, whether reading or playing in public, could carry on for hours for an audience of one other person—as Mingus suggested. Our expectations and goals were to achieve excellence, with the hope that once we did, someone out there would dig it.

I participated in incredible jazz gigs, jam sessions, poetry-music readings, classical music concerts and dance events where it was more or less expected that the performers usually outnumbered the audience. On the rare occasions when there was a large audience, that sense of intimacy remained the most important goal. Our universal motto was "Be for Real."

At BYOB parties, often held at painters' lofts, guests would bring wine, beer, Dr. Brown's Black Cherry Soda, sometimes just paper cups or potato chips, graham crackers or a musical instrument, a new poem, a monologue from Shakespeare or Lord Buckley's latest comedic-philosophical rap, a song or simply their unadorned selves, looking for romance, fun, excitement and a chance to celebrate Friday and Saturday night, where you could stay up till dawn, because you didn't have to go to your day job!

This was the part of New York where Jack and I each felt most at home, in an environment that was inclusive, almost rural, temporarily created for a few hours in the midst of the vast skyscrapered metropolis, where we miraculously found temporary cocoons of warmth and camaraderie. These party environments made for magical, spontaneous gatherings, similar to back-

porch Luckenbach, Texas, picking parties in the summer, or Lowell, Massachusetts, get-togethers over beer with Acadian accordions and singing of old songs, or great jam sessions in the South, like the ones with Charlie Parker and Dizzy Gillespie in my basement apartment in 1951–52 in Wash-

ington, D.C., before I met Jack. Years afterward, Jack talked about our New York all-night week-end bashes, but when we first performed together over the course of an evening, we hardly said a word to each other. Just as I related to Thelonious Monk, Sonny Rollins, Mary Lou

David Amram at the Five Spot, 1957
BURT GLINN/MAGNUM PHOTOS INC.

Williams and scores of other great musicians with whom I was blessed to play who never said much and let their music do the talking, Jack and I had that same musician's ESP. It was an unspoken communication that came to us naturally. I could play while he read or improvised words, and I knew exactly what to do. When I made up a throwaway topical rhymed rap at 3:00 a.m. and he banged on the piano accompanying me, we related in the same way. We both knew how to LISTEN, to lay back, to breathe together, to curb aggression and search for harmony, to tune into one another and surrender ourselves to the particular rhythm and pulse of the evening. That rhythm and pulse were always connected to the Native American drum we both felt so strongly, the African drum that permeated all the great music of our time and the drum of the Middle East, as well as the soulful song-stories, prayers and chants of the Catholic Church Jack had in his bones and the Jewish liturgical wailing of ancient songs that reverberated in my subconscious. As soon as our performance ended, we gave each other a wink, a nod, a smile and became part of the party, flirting with young women and searching for food, drink and adventure. *On the Road* was not yet published, so the terrible pressures of celebrity hadn't arrived in Jack's life.

Jack and I had first begun to know each other as fellow transplanted hicks—Jack from Lowell, Massachusetts, and I from Feasterville, Pennsylvania—trying to relate to Golgothian New York City. Even though we had both seen a lot of the world, we bonded as outsiders in sophisticated Manhattan, searching for something we knew was there. Jack told me how being a football player had opened the doors for him to leave Lowell for an Eastern prep school followed by a stint at Columbia University, playing football had resulted in breaking his leg, but not his spirit. I told Jack about my childhood growing up on a Feasterville farm, dreaming of being a musician. I described the trauma of moving to Washington, D.C., at age twelve and deciding to become a musician and composer, the joy of my job as a part-time gym teacher at a French school, then getting drafted into the army and beginning my travels around the world.

We found we shared a mutual interest in sports and speaking fractured French, which often annoyed the 4:00 a.m. stoned-out customers at Bickford's greasy spoon, where we congregated late at night to eat hamburgers with fried onions and mayonnaise on English muffins, while drinking coffee and planning our conquest of New York.

After several months of frequently crossing paths at nocturnal gatherings, my weekend party excursions temporarily came to a halt when I began an eleven-week stint with my quartet at the Five Spot. This funky Bowery bar was the hangout for artists like Franz Kline, Willem de Kooning, Joan Mitchell, Alfred Leslie and Larry Rivers. The Five Spot was also crowded with actors, composers, authors, poets, moving men, postal workers, winos, office workers, off-duty firemen—just about anyone and everyone was welcome at the Five Spot, where you could get a huge pitcher of beer for 75 cents. My quartet was sometimes joined by as many as eighteen musicians (one evening the whole Woody Herman Band sat in with us). Late at night, poets and actors would recite poetry or improvise verse while we played music. Never planned in advance, it just happened, partly because as the leader of the quartet, I was open to it. Jazz was about sharing and spontaneity—*in*clusive, not *ex*clusive.

Jack was often there, and we in the quartet could feel his presence the minute he arrived. Often sitting alone, like a wayward meditative Canadian lumberjack in his plaid red-checkered

work shirt, he exuded a special energy. We could telepathically feel his power as a listener, just as we could feel his observational power, reflected in his dark, brooding eyes—he was that one special person Mingus alluded to, the one person we always knew we could play for. Soon, I began performing *with* Jack as well.

In November of 1957, he and I, along with drummer-poet Howard Hart and San Francisco poet Philip Lamantia, gave the first-ever jazz poetry reading in New York City at the Brata Art Gallery on East 10th Street. There were no posters and no advertising—just a typed, mimeographed handbill that we gave away at our various meeting places—the Cedar Tavern, the Five Spot, the Cafe Figaro, the Kettle of Fish, the White Horse Tavern and the San Remo bar.

The Brata was packed that night. We did what Jack and I had already done at parties. Even so, we felt a tremendous spirit, as if we were doing something for the very first time. We didn't know it then, but seeds were being sown. Shortly after, we performed at the Circle in the Square Theater. The theater's lighting designer improvised with us throughout the night. He must have used everything in his experience, flashing all the colored lights, dimming and brightening every lamp at different angles and tempos, blinking and pulsating, contrasting the hues, creating instant blackouts and beaming lights in the audience's faces from time to time, all synchronized to the rhythms of the poetry and music (this was ten years before so-called psychedelic lighting came into existence). Jack and I had told the lighting designer to watch, listen and do what he felt the poetry and music told him to do. He did it and the audience loved it.

When Jack, Howard and Philip disappeared during intermission to celebrate and drink Thunderbird with their fans at tiny Sheridan Park across from the theater, I had to fill time till they returned from their "break." So I played the piano and made up rhymed scat-songs, based on audience's suggestions. That's how my signature performance style got its start—sometimes, desperation is the mother of invention.

We gave several more readings in 1958 and spent time hanging out whenever Jack was in New York. Whether he was reading, singing or scatting, I never knew what was written down beforehand or what was made up on the spot. It was all spellbinding and fun.

In 1959 Jack and I collaborated on the Robert Frank/Alfred Leslie film *Pull My Daisy*. In addition to appearing in the film as Mezz McGillicuddy, the deranged French horn player in the moth-eaten sweater, I composed the score for the film and wrote the music for the title song, with lyrics by Jack, Neal Cassady and Allen Ginsberg. Jack provided an improvised narration for the film, as I played piano and French horn. I made a second score two weeks later, performed by my jazz quartet and a small chamber ensemble.

The idea of making a film based on Jack's work was easier to discuss than to actually accomplish. Many people felt the experience of reading *On the Road* was like watching a film, projected on the screen of your mind, as you devoured the pages of his classic adventure story–poem–novel. Jack's writing, like his spontaneous raps, conjured up kaleidoscopic imagery that made you feel you were a cast member in a great documentary about quintessential America. Like most of the high-energy musicians, poets, painters and assorted dreamers we hung out with, Jack relished each precious moment of every day and night. His books were sight and sound journeys told in the style of a great jazz solo, to be shared with readers, accompanying him on his endless odyssey. Never thinking of ourselves as members of the Beat Generation,

Jack and I considered ourselves as part of a group of wildly diverse people who wanted to see doors opened and hearts filled with energy and hope. We wanted to acknowledge and appreciate the joy and genius of many of America's unsung heroes and heroines.

Today, as a composer—of classical music as well as jazz—I'm still setting Jack's words to music, in both a new choral composition and a work for narrator and orchestra. Jack's words still tell me what to do. Sometimes when I'm composing a score, I spend a whole day writing and rewriting just one measure of music to make it perfect, paying attention to every tiny nuance: tempo change, metronome marking, precisely notated dynamic and phrase. But the music—the breathing, living, human, mystical, mysterious part—comes together *naturally*, which is what Jack and I celebrated when we performed together. Working alone, we each created formal works (his books and my symphonies) inspired by the natural energy of real-life experiences. When we performed together, we celebrated the moment, dealing with the informal and daring to improvise like tightrope walkers. We wanted to create formal works—built to last—that retained this same energy. That's what we were all about and what formed the basis of our friendship and collaborations.

As I approach the age of seventy, feeling blessed and lucky to still be here, I try every day to share the joy of seeing my own dreams in music finally coming true. I also try every day, in some small way, to share with everyone I meet the gift of Jack's spirit, energy and human kindness. A giant of Twentieth-Century letters, Jack Kerouac created a body of work that has enabled new generations to look back on the second half of this century and see the Beauty.

With Jack Kerouac in Hyannis

BY ANN CHARTERS

ON A HOT AUGUST MORNING I drove to Kerouac's house. He had mailed me directions to his home in Hyannis, Massachusetts, earlier in the month. Located close to Joseph Kennedy Memorial Skating Rink, it was easy to find—a brown-shingled, one-story house in a modest neighborhood of recently built Cape Cod and ranch houses separated by small yards with no sidewalks. It was August 16, 1966.

Kerouac had written me, "This will be fascinating. I myself am beginning to need a bibliography. And I look forward to meeting a scholar and a gentlewoman." In his second letter, he penciled a postscript: "Throw these instructions away, rather, that is, bring 'em with you—'Beatniks' look like Spooks in my mother's poor door at midnight—You understand."

After collecting Kerouac's books for three years, I was compiling his bibliography for a Contemporary Writers series published by the Phoenix Bookshop in New York. At that time he was receiving very little respect as a writer, but he was well known as an alcoholic recluse.

I arrived at Kerouac's front door at noon after a seven-hour drive from New York's East Village. When he opened his front door, I mistook him for his father. Dressed in a rumpled white V-neck T-shirt and baggy chinos, he looked much older and heavier than in his photographs.

He introduced me to his mother, Gabrielle, who came from the kitchen wearing the kind of bib apron my mother used to wear. "Wait a minute, Charters is your married name. What's your real name?" Jack asked me. I told them and

they had a quick exchange in French Canadian. I understood enough to say, "Yes, that's right, I'm Jewish." "Oh, you know what we're talking about. Then we'll talk in English," Jack said.

Kerouac took me into his study, actually the third bedroom in the house. His mother's bedroom was on one side of it, and his bedroom was down the hall, separated from the study by the bathroom. He told me to sit at his desk when we started to catalogue the "A" section of the American editions of his novels for his bibliography.

He sat in a rocking chair beside a window next to the single bed, directly in front of a small electric fan. A can of malt beer was open on the top of the bookshelf beside him and a juice glass of Johnny Walker Red beside that. The bottle of scotch was in the kitchen. He went there to refill his glass, always stopping first in the bathroom.

While we worked, Kerouac took many trips down the short hallway. Once his mother followed him back carrying a tray of baloney and egg-salad sandwiches and pickles and potato chips and hot coffee. Jack didn't eat any sandwiches but he took some potato chips and drank steadily.

Jack kept passing me books so I could measure them and note their dimensions. After we'd been working for about three hours, he offered me half a benny. "I've taken one, it's keeping me going. I'll give you one too." I said no, I never used them. "Then okay, don't have any now." But I asked for some scotch and he brought me a

Jack Kerouac high on D.M.T., 1964
ALLEN GINSBERG

small shot in a juice glass, straight. Later, when I asked for it, he brought me another.

All afternoon through the open windows the faint cries of children were among the sounds we heard filtered across Jack's narrow front lawn and its half-grown pine trees. Apparently we were on the flight path to the Hyannis airport. Once the noise of a jet filled the study and Jack said, "The *Caroline*. It's the only jet that comes here. It's Sargent Shriver flying off to Washington. Fuck them."

Kerouac sat at the window that faced the house next door, one spindly tree between him and his neighbor. The other study window looked out on a backyard enclosed by a tall red-wood fence where his mother was looking after my dog, an Irish setter I had brought along for company. Jack told me that he and Gabrielle had lived in the house only four months.

Before that, it had been a "bigger house" in St. Petersburg, Florida, filled, I suppose, with the same maple and chintz furniture, the mahogany spinet piano, the television set and the same two framed pictures on the living room walls—a photograph of Jack as the handsome young author of *The Town and the City* over the sofa and a large drawing by James Spanfeller of Kerouac's dead brother, Gerard, as a boy feeding the birds, one of the illustrations in *Visions of Gerard*, over his mother's favorite armchair.

Bookshelves lined three of the four walls of Jack's study. The upper shelves of the one near the desk contained paperbacks in French—Balzac, Celine, Flaubert, Hugo. Beside the desk, by the shortwave radio and Hermes portable typewriter, were more books: Shakespeare's tragedies, Emily Dickinson's poems, Balzac's *Quest of the Absolute*, Joyce's *Ulysses*, Boswell's *Life of Samuel Johnson LL.D*, Christopher Smart's *Poems* and the *Complete Rabelais*.

Tacked to the walls over the desk and bookcases were large pages from an illustrated Japanese calendar. On one of them Jack had drawn a

teacup and penned a haiku to Spring. Over the light switch near the door were magazine cutouts of American Indians and four bird feathers arranged in a semicircle like a war bonnet. Jack had found the feathers on his lawn. He admired the Indians, he said, because his mother's family was part Indian.

There were religious pictures cut out of magazines tacked above the bed and on the back of the door. Somebody had thumbtacked to the wall above the desk a small red-felt pennant with *Hyannis* lettered on it. The new pennant and the magazine cutouts and the narrow maple bed made me feel like I was in a kid's room, but Jack's dedication to his writing was unmistakable.

Lined up neatly on the shelves were rows of foreign editions of Kerouac's novels, with well-thumbed copies of American editions alongside. His manuscripts and correspondence were organized just as carefully in manila folders in a tall green filing cabinet in one corner. Deep drawers in a built-in dresser contained little copybooks and notebooks and carefully rolled teletype paper covered with typewriting—the raw material of Jack's books grouped in separate bundles and tied with string and rubber bands.

Jack untied the string and showed me the first draft of *Doctor Sax* written in pencil on both sides of small, cheap notebook pages. Why, I asked, did he use such small notebooks? They were small enough to be slipped into his shirt or pants pockets, he told me. Then he could carry them and write anywhere. He flipped the pages carefully to show me that here and there in the *Sax* notebooks some lines were crossed out. "When I typed the book for the publishers, I wouldn't type what I crossed out. Now I don't cross anything out when I write."

I asked him why he used the rolls of white paper in his typewriter. "You know why you use a roll like that? So you don't have to change pages. The secret of narrative—Fielding, Richardson, Defoe, Dickens knew that—is that you get hot when you get disgusted. That's the time *not* to stop. Just roll along."

The tidy piles of books, magazines and papers on the bed, the bookshelves, the radio, the bureau, the portable TV were the result, Jack told me, of having "worked a week" to stack everything up neatly for his bibliography. He wanted it to be complete, "maybe a hundred pages," so that he could "be like that fellow in Cambridge, Edmund Wilson, always giving a little pamphlet away." He had kept copies of "99.5 percent" of his published work, and he spent hours organizing "the neatest records you ever saw."

This surprised me, since I'd gotten the impression from his books that he lived a chaotic life, especially *Satori in Paris,* just published in *Evergreen Review.* But then, at forty-four, Kerouac seemed full of contradictions. He was the lover who had come back to his mother's house in Queens for breakfast every morning during the passionate affair he had described in *The Subterraneans* a dozen years earlier.

Around 7:30 that evening I took Jack back on the road. I told him my dog needed a run on the beach before it got dark, and he said he'd come along to pick up something at the liquor store. There was a whispered conference with his mother in the kitchen about cashing a check, but finally everything got straightened out. I greeted my dog in the backyard and put her in my dusty orange Volkswagen Beetle.

Still talking to Gabrielle, Jack emerged from the house a few minutes later and got into the car. Right after he sat down he popped open another fresh can of malt beer. The metal flip-top was on the floorboards as a souvenir the next morning. I hadn't seen him palm it out of the refrigerator, but then fresh cans of beer kept appearing at his side all afternoon, like a W. C. Fields sleight-of-hand trick.

The beach was a few miles away through the center of Hyannis. Jack knew the stretch of road near his house, but closer to the ocean he became disoriented and asked me to put on the headlights to read the sign for beach parking. He had worn reading glasses in the study—"Never used to need 'em, but now I'm getting old"—but he'd left them at home.

I stopped the car in the middle of a deserted parking lot. We got out, the dog raced onto the sand toward the splashing waves, Jack stopped on his side of the car to take a leak, and I slipped off my sandals so I could walk more easily on the beach.

In the twilight, the deserted beach reminded Kerouac of Tangier. That's where William Burroughs had told him that Whitman and Melville were both "homos" (Jack's term). He threw out his arms: "Here's how Burroughs did it." Jack pulled at the neck of his T-shirt, where the gold chain from his religious medal shone against his chest. His gray-blue eyes got very big and round.

"That's how Whitman came on with little boys. While Melville, he'd sidle up to them in a dark slouch hat." Jack hunched his shoulders up to meet his Indian-black hair and narrowed his eyes. "He'd chuck them under the chin and whisper, 'How'd you like to come with me?' " I protested about Melville and Jack scowled. "Yes, he was a queer. Burroughs showed me a poem he'd written in Italy, a love poem to a boy."

We plodded through the soft sand to sit on some rocks and listen to the waves as the lights disappeared. I asked him about the form of his novels. He answered impatiently. "I tell you the novel is as dead as Queen Victoria coming down the street in Hyannis. I wrote only one novel, *The Town and the City.* That's according to what they taught me at Columbia. Fiction. Then I broke loose from all that and wrote picaresque narratives. That's what my books are. You know what that is? Picaresque narratives."

Abruptly he stood up and shouted at me, "You know the difference between me and those boys Ginsberg, Burroughs, Snyder, Corso, Duncan? I'm the only one who laid down my life for my country. I'm still a Marine, you know, and that's why I don't mix with those beatniks. All those guys carrying signs for peace on their shoulders. Not me."

It was dark when we left the beach. "Just a minute, I'll meet you at the car. I want to take a leak." Jack walked away and stood on the hard sand near the water. Back in the car he seemed subdued, not saying much, and I wondered aloud about the chicken pie his mother was baking for dinner. "Naw, don't worry about her. Wait—we're passing the best bar in Hyannis. Stop the car, let's go in. I want to show it to you."

Suddenly he was in high humor. "You know, it's a funny thing about being famous. They don't believe you're you. You go into a bar and they say, 'Aw go on, get out of here.'" The bartender was a blond young man in his early thirties whom Kerouac introduced as Al Hill. "So you're a writer, huh," Hill said to Kerouac. "Anything published?" Jack nodded, pouring Budweiser into his glass.

The bartender pushed a little. "How much do you make a year?" Kerouac screwed his eyes and hesitated only a moment. "About as much as you do. Maybe nine thousand dollars." Hill replied with friendly scorn, "That's nothing. If you've published all them books you told me about, how come you don't make more?" He moved a little further down the bar to serve another customer.

Jack leaned over his beer, finished it quickly, left for the toilet, bought cigarettes and reappeared. "Buy me another beer, please," he asked me. I did and he looked around the room. "This is the best bar in Hyannis. When I first came here to look for a house, I was so happy to be back in New England I got drunk and they arrested me twice. But the cops are good here. They didn't bring me in. Both times I only got a warning."

The bartender moved back. "Yes, you were so drunk the first night you came in here, I wouldn't serve you. You looked bad, too. You hadn't shaved." Kerouac raised his chin, grandstanding: "I shaved today for this lady here." The bartender continued, "And you were wearing a funny hat." "Yes, my big straw hat. I found it in the swamps in Florida," Jack said. "What were you doing in the swamps?" asked Al. "I was taking a short-cut to the supermarket," Jack told him.

Somebody started to play a World War II song on the piano. Kerouac took my arm, "Come on, they have a piano bar." The pianist was a middle-aged blonde who looked tired. Jack asked me, "Isn't she good?" I nodded. "What would you like her to play?" I said anything she wanted. Jack kept looking at me. "Wait a minute, you remind me a little of Joan Crawford. The movie star. I wrote a story about her once, 'Joan Rawshanks in the Fog.' You know it?"

Near Kerouac's house we made one more stop at the liquor store so he could pick up some champagne. ("My mother likes champagne. It's the only thing she can drink anymore.") Jack told me he wanted to celebrate the bibliography—he was having a good time. He made only one small pass during the two days we spent together, a shy kiss on my arm the next afternoon while I sat near him on the bed in his study looking at some book contracts.

The rest of the time he repeatedly asked the question, "You don't love your husband, do you?" I always answered, "Yes, I told you, I love him very much." At the end of the second afternoon, he said to shock me, "I don't need you anyway. I can do it to myself. Tell me, what does detumescence mean, my dear?" I replied, "To come down off of?"

That was the only thing I said to Jack that he thought was funny.

Kerouac
Retrospective

BY ERIC EHRMANN

LESS THAN 300 PEOPLE SHOWED up at Jack Kerouac's funeral. Today, if you surf him on the net, you'll get 30,000 hits. It's a testimony to the extreme velocity of information that he loved, then watched haplessly as it zoomed by him in the end.

ROLLING STONE'S coverage of the funeral was one of the defining moments in the magazine's evolution from an underground broadsheet to an authoritative chronicle of cultural change. Jann [Wenner] wanted to capture the emotion of the event, and the piece weighed in with more feeling than what *Time, Newsweek* and the venerable *New York Review of Books* offered. It sent the publishing world a message that there was now a place where those who lived and created on the edge could get equal time.

Sam Shepard once said that alcohol was the medicine of the World War II generation. And it was booze that killed Jack. The slam poets and performance artists who are his legacy weren't even born yet. The beatniks had been eclipsed by the Beatles, Vietnam and the civil rights movement and, unlike others, a stubborn Kerouac chose not to reinvent himself.

To a young writer, his death and the circumstances surrounding it were emotionally draining, a reminder of how lonely the business of writing can be. Kerouac had been something of a hero and role model to many who came of age on the cusp of the Beat and hippie generations. Selected recently as one of the hundred most influential English-language books of the Twentieth Century by the Modern Language Association, *On the Road* was a blueprint for breaking out of white-bread, *Ozzie and Harriet* America.

The Beat lifestyle was a road less traveled, blazed not only by the icons-in-waiting but by thousands of restless ex-GIs and other World War II vets who went on the road long before the movement was discovered. Out to the coast, down to Mexico City and over to Paris, searching and escaping and "making the scene" much as Kerouac and his crowd did. Oklahoma-born jazz trumpeter Chet Baker was a typical example.

Reading *On the Road* in senior English at Shaker High School in 1964 I got the message that beatniks were cool, and cool was good. Every time I looked at Kerouac's poster-boy photograph on the back of the book it challenged me to write. Then, five short years later, I found myself touching the corpse of the man who got me in touch with my own feelings, and it sent me in another direction.

I filed my last story for ROLLING STONE in 1971. A year later I was in Europe, writing about politics, not pop culture. Heidelberg, five years in Paris. Four years in Buenos Aires when Argentina was transitioning from dictatorship to democracy. Not sure if I was running from Kerouac or running from myself. I'm still not sure.

Kerouac's death increased the body count in the killing fields of the literary world. Covering the funeral I learned one of the unwritten rules of the writing profession, namely, that when somebody wants to check out, friends honor boundaries and rarely intervene. Nobody stopped Ernest Hemingway from pulling the trigger. Nobody stopped Jerzy Kosinski from doing himself in. Or Tennessee Williams from guzzling the booze and pills. And nobody stopped Jack. Sterling Lord, Kerouac's agent, dodged the issue at the burial. The best he could offer was "Jack liked his scotch." If the Sixties was a decade of big black cover-ups, this was a little white one.

Kerouac's family wanted it known that in the end, he was a good boy, and Father Armand Morrissette, who gave the eulogy, kindly obliged. But like Hemingway, Kerouac's greatness overshadowed his drinking, his anger and his propensity for womanizing. For years, he denied being the father of his daughter, author Jan Kerouac, who died of kidney failure in 1997 at age forty-

three. One would never assume that the handsome face glancing out at America in the much publicized "Kerouac wore khakis" ad was that of a deadbeat dad.

Kerouac's own troubled childhood unfolded in an old Yankee mill town laid low by the Great

Depression. It took another child of those lean years, columnist Jimmy Breslin, to provide the quote that gave the ROLLING STONE piece its turning point.

I was surprised to see Breslin walking down the steps of Eglise St. Jean le Baptiste after the mass. He was someone who was detached from the Beat scene. So much of the piece focused on emotions and descriptions and there was Breslin, putting it all into perspective. He remembered Kerouac not only as a writer, but as a harbinger of cultural change, someone who opened doors for other scribes of his generation.

The example Kerouac and his work offer today's aspiring writers has less to do with style and content than with the ability to develop self-confidence and to believe in your work. He was fearless in running the gauntlet of self-censorship imposed by publishers during the dark days of the McCarthy era. Finally, in 1957 he made it. James Dean had already shocked America in *Rebel Without a Cause*, but he was acting. In *On the Road,* Kerouac *was* a rebel without a cause and he had the guts to tell the world.

The irony of Kerouac, the literary antihero, is that much of his mental toughness came from football. After all, it was the pigskin sport, not writing, that got him a ticket out of Lowell. One glorious end run and it was on to the Big Apple and a football scholarship at Horace Mann, an elite prep school. His jock status then enabled him to pick up what most working-class kids could only dream of, a scholarship to Columbia University.

Columbia's coach, Lou Little, was a creator of all-Americans and NFL stars. And if he hadn't suffered a bad leg injury, Kerouac might have become one. After a run-in with the coach, he lost interest in football, then lost his scholarship. He started hanging around Broadway and 112th

Jack Kerouac singing to himself, 1959
JOHN COHEN

with Ginsberg and Huncke. He tuned in, turned on and dropped out a quarter of a century before a former Army major named Timothy Leary did. The competition he learned in football was now starting to drive his writing.

This same sense of competitiveness can be seen today at poetry slams at college bars and coffeehouses: poets of the new millenium building on a tradition established by Kerouac and the Beats, a throwback to the Forties and Fifties when bebop musicians would gather with poets and writers and have multimedia jams. You can hear it in their droning voices, and see it in the berets and goatees that frame their faces. Some of them are wannabes. Others want to be tops in the slam. But one thing's for certain: They're taking the spoken word into the Twenty-First Century with a bang, and Jack Kerouac is up in heaven, smiling finally, maybe even wearing khakis.

There Is Really Nothing Inside

BY ERIC EHRMANN AND STEPHEN DAVIS

[ROLLING STONE 47, November 29, 1969]

LOWELL, MASSACHUSETTS — A small placard in the front hallway of the A. Archambault & Sons Funeral Parlor, one of a string of funeral homes along Pawtucket Street in this dreary mill town, directed mourners to the back room where the wake for Jack Kerouac was being held.

Jack Kerouac's people were all there in their Sunday best, sharp-featured French-Canadian people. Old ladies gushed and moaned in French *patois*, their heads bobbing up and down as they gossiped about what Father Morrissette had told the young Kerouac many years before. They were cordial enough.

One led the way down a small hallway and around a corner to meet one of Jack's friends, Allen Ginsberg, who sat comforting Kerouac's wife Stella. Peter Orlovsky, Ginsberg's constant companion and fellow poet, was taking a drink from the electric water cooler. A small toothless man in a gigantic blue overcoat paced nervously about, his thick black hair tousled, blue sunglasses peering anxiously about. It was Gregory Corso, the poet who had been right there, in New York and San Francisco and everywhere, with Kerouac and Ginsberg and the others, from the start.

Arms pressed tight to his body, head down, shoulders hunched, Corso stalked the room in perfect 1950s Beat style, as if he still lived that crazed agony. He kept aiming those "What should I do now?" looks at Ginsberg.

Orlovsky and Ginsberg led the way to have a look at Kerouac. "You must see him," Ginsberg said. "He looks like a happy clay buddha."

Jack Kerouac, dead at forty-seven of a massive abdominal hemorrhage, on October 21. He symbolized an era. Whether or not his friend John Clellon Holmes was first to call it the Beat Generation in print, Holmes later attributed the term to Kerouac. "You might say," Kerouac told Holmes in 1948, "we're a Beat Generation." Nobody was in a better position to know.

They had laid out his body in a grey houndstooth sports jacket (at least one size too small), a yellow shirt and red bowtie with white pin dots. His face, heavily madeup, waxy and dull, had been molded into a cheery, vacant smile. The silver rosary clutched between his hands was faintly discolored by the heavy makeup caked upon his fingers.

"Touch him," said Ginsberg. "There's really nothing inside."

Not surprisingly, Kerouac's forehead was quite cold to the touch.

"This," Ginsberg continued, "is exactly the way he wanted it. Listen." He read aloud from Kerouac's *Mexico City Blues*. Ginsberg's manner was entirely reverent: This was his service over the body. Orlovsky fought back the tears.

Among the wreaths was a very special one that Ginsberg and Orlovsky had brought. A typical wreath, really, except for the senders, whose names—*Bill*, *Terry*, *Allen* and *Peter*—were spelled out in glittery sequins. (William Burroughs, Terry Southern, Ginsberg and Orlovsky.)

As Ginsberg departed the bier, Corso came over, ill at ease, that same wild Lower East Side–Brooklyn huckster rap from the coffeehouse poetry readings of the Fifties, and asked: "What are the young people saying about Jack?"

He shuffled back and forth, talking more than he listened. The old Village style. For Corso, the young people are another group—a set of people he does not know. He does not know what they are saying about Jack. The *young people* have rock & roll and their common shared experience. Kerouac and Corso and Ginsberg broke on through to the other side, kicked out the jams, long before any of those ideas ever passed through the heads of Jim Morrison or the MC5 or the Rolling Stones. They were on the road and turning on a decade before the drop out/tune in/turn on litany was first sounded.

The following morning, Friday, was the day of the funeral, in the Eglise St. Jean le Baptiste. The weather was unseasonably cold for the New England October: In fact, it was the coldest day in months. The pallbearers (Kerouac's relatives, Ginsberg and a man dressed as an Italian gangster who was uptight at the sight of so many cameras, from Gregory Corso's Bolex to about twenty Kodak Instamatics and Brownies that kept flitting about) all wore overcoats. Corso was filming the entire funeral, panning up and down the sub-Gothic facade of St. Jean and back to Ginsberg carrying the coffin. He said he was doing it for himself.

One missing figure at the funeral was Lawrence Ferlinghetti, whose City Lights bookstore was Kerouac's mailing address during the quintessential San Francisco years of Beat. "I don't like funerals," Ferlinghetti said later. "I've been asked by all sorts of big publications to write something about Jack. I can't do that. I don't write about dead men. They should have done something for him two years ago, when he needed it."

The gunmetal black casket was trundled toward the altar on a good-sized coffin dolly with the trademark *Eureka* embossed on its side. A nice touch.

Father Armand Morrissette celebrated mass for Kerouac's soul in front of a congregation whose majority hadn't been inside a church in years, except to see an avant-garde play in the basement. During the offertory, someone quietly speculated whether the body had been flown up from Florida, where Kerouac had died. A writer from a Cambridge weekly said that he had heard that the corpse had to be forcibly restrained from hitching up the coast by itself.

It might seem out of character for one of the Beat Generation's most renowned sons to be the object of the church's traditional religiosity. But Kerouac had always walked with Jesus, in his way. The Jesus of Sunday school atonement and redemption. "Horrors of the Jesus Christ of passion plays," wrote Kerouac in *Doctor Sax,* "in his shrouds and vestments of saddest doom mankind in the Cross Weep for Thieves and Poverty—he was at the foot of my bed pushing it one dark Saturday night (on Hildreth & Lilley second floor flat full of Eternity outside)—either He or the Virgin Mary stooped with phosphorescent profile and horror, pushing my bed."

In his address to the congregation, Father Morrissette said, in part, "Jack Kerouac embodied something of man's search for freedom: He refused always to be boxed in by the pettiness of the world. He had what Allen Ginsberg called 'the exquisite honesty,' the guts to express and live his ideas. Now he is on the road again, going on further, as he said, 'alone by the waters of life.' Our hope and prayer is that he has found complete liberation."

During his last days in Lowell, before he moved to St. Petersburg, Florida, to look after his invalid mother, he would walk into Mello's Bar and bellow at the top of his lungs—"I'm Jack Kerouac!"—as if he had to prove it to himself. He had never played along with the beatnik hype that the media lavished upon some of his cronies.

Now, nearing his fiftieth year, Kerouac had become a lonely, embittered man, increasingly unsure of himself and upset with the world he saw around him. He was cut off. A dreadfully corny middle-aged gag word—"bippie," from TV's *Rowan & Martin's Laugh-in*—even figured in the title of his last published writing. It was called, "I'm a Bippie in the Middle," it was published in the *Washington Post*, and it spoke his nightmare vision plainly if not clearly:

> I think I'll drop out—Great American Tradition—Dan'l Boone, U. S. Grant, Mark Twain—I think I'll go to sleep and suddenly in my deepest inadequacy nightmares wake up haunted and see everyone in the world as unconsolable orphans yelling and screaming on every side to make arrangements for making a living yet all bespattered and gloomed-up in the nightsoil of poor body and soul all present and accounted for as some kind of sneakish, craft gift, and all so lonered.

In his last years, his wife says, Jack Kerouac became a heavy drinker, a steady dope-smoker and tended to flip out often. There is a definite sense in his novels—in *On the Road, The Subterraneans, Doctor Sax* certainly—that Kerouac was a free man. But he lost that freedom. He was almost totally alienated from the free generation of the 1960s that he had, in a way, prophesied during the 1950s; the hippies and the dope freaks pissed him off. He grumbled in "I'm a Bippie in the Middle":

> Really, so what's new if they would like to see to it that under Timothy Leary's guiding proselytization no one in America could address a simple envelope or keep a household budget or a checkbook balanced or for that matter legible . . . Ah, so what if they don't believe in the written word which is the only way to keep the record straight.

As the mourners poured out of the church into the blinding reflection of the sun on the stone steps, Corso filming every move, a reporter sidled up to Jimmy Breslin and asked him what the reaction was to Kerouac's death in New York. Breslin said he didn't really know. But Breslin had some definite ideas about Kerouac the writer. "Yeah," he said, "you can say he opened a lot of doors for a lot of people. Tom Wolfe. Mailer a little bit. Nobody was publishing his kind of stuff in the Fifties and then all of a sudden in '57, *On the Road* hit. He opened a lot of doors."

By now the cortege was pulling away for the cemetery. But the supposedly inviolate single file of cars, lights on, was quickly broken up by a huge oil truck making a quick turn to catch a light. The driver didn't seem to like the beatniks, so he stayed in line.

TV cameras caught the action at graveside: the cranes lowering the casket into the freshly dug earth. Corso filmed it, too, right on top of it, two feet from the grave. He tilted the big sixteen-millimeter camera right down into the hole, all the way, until Kerouac's casket settled into place.

Ginsberg lofted a handful of dirt onto the coffin as workmen shoveled away. A few other mourners followed with *their* handfuls, but most simply watched. The TV crews were packing up, the daily-press men were departing, and it seemed like it had really ended a long time ago.

Allen Ginsberg, himself a model for various characters in Kerouac's works, had already said it a couple of days earlier. Speaking to an audience at Yale, Ginsberg said that Kerouac "broke open the fantastic solidity in America as solid as the Empire State Building—that turned out not to be solid at all. His vision was what the universe as we will experience it is—golden ash, blissful emptiness, a product of our own grasping speed."

Elegy for
a Desolation Angel

BY LESTER BANGS

[ROLLING STONE 47, November 29, 1969]

MY WOMAN CALLED AND woke me early this morning, pulling me from strange diffuse dreams to tell me Jack Kerouac had died of a hernia at the age of forty-seven. I rolled over and stared at the wall; I had dreamed this very night of finding a portfolio of Kerouac's unpublished manuscripts in a dusty pawn shop.

Jack was in so many ways a spiritual father of us all, as much as Lenny Bruce or Dylan or any of them. He was among the first artists to broadcast to the world this new sensibility aborning these last two decades, a sensibility that first began to take shape about the time many of us were born. He describes it in "The Origins of the Beat Generation": "Anyway, the hipsters, whose music was bop, they looked like criminals, but they kept talking about the things I liked, long outlines of personal experience and vision, nightlong confessions full of hope that had become illicit and repressed by War, stirrings, rumblings of a new soul (that same old human soul) . . . By 1948 it began to take shape. That was a wild vibrating year when a group of us would walk down the street and yell hello and even stop and talk to anybody that gave us a friendly look."

The first hipsters were a far cry from the affected zombielike "cool" stance that came to predominate later. Like the best aspects of the Sixties' hip movement and Kerouac himself, they represented the apotheosis of American individu-

Jack Kerouac at Allen Ginsberg's East 7th Street apartment, New York City, 1953

ALLEN GINSBERG

ality and rascally exuberance, "a wild yea-saying overburst of American joy." In the Forties Kerouac fell in with a group of these madmen at Columbia University. Their names were destiny: Allen Ginsberg, William Burroughs and the greatest, wildest yea-sayer of them all, Neal Cassady, a legendary car-thief, baller and sometime speedfreak who rushed about seeking experience with an exhilaration and thirst for life that seemed superhuman. Cassady was the "Dean Moriarty" of Kerouac's great book *On the Road*, an American classic whose hero, like a Twentieth-Century Huck Finn, races back and forth across America with blond carhop pickups in stolen jalopies, through Rocky Mountain dawns and neon New York midnights, a wild gleam of unquenchable excitement in his eyes as he tears off great raw chunks of experience and devours them whole, shouting "Yes, yes, yes!" at each new revelation.

It was Cassady who served as the primal prototype for a whole generation of mad meat-joy hipsters and hippies, but it was Kerouac who gave this prototype to the world in his writings, as when he compared the dropout folk-hero Cassady to the cynical New York intellectual crowd that included Burroughs and Ginsberg: "But Dean's intelligence was every bit as formal and shining and complete, without the tedious intellectualness. And his 'criminality' was not something that sulked and sneered; it was a wild yea-saying outburst of American joy; it was Western, the West wind, an ode from the Plains, something new, long prophesied, long a-coming (he only stole cars for joy-rides). Besides, all my New York friends were in the negative, nightmare position of putting down society and giving their own tired bookish or political or psychoanalytical reasons, but Dean just raced in society, eager for bread and love; he didn't care one way or the other, 'so long's I can get that lil ole gal with that lil sumpin down there tween her legs,

boy,' and 'so long's we can *eat* son, y'ear me? I'm *hungry*, I'm *starving*, let's *eat right now!*'"

It was this heart-pounding intoxicated love of life that represented the precious essence that was the best of both the Beat and the Hip movements, and which has today become so rare as we move into the renaissance's jaded aftermath of mindless political violence and the drug-drenched numbness of psychic overload. But not even its avatars could sustain this joy through the cold pudding of the Fifties and the psychic dislocations of the Sixties. Kerouac himself went on to write a string of beautiful but little-recognized books: *The Subterraneans*, which he wrote in three days (and Kerouac was the first and greatest of those to write literature akin to the sound and feeling and spirit of rock & roll), was the tender and achingly poetic account of a love affair with a spade chick in San Francisco. *Doctor Sax* and *Visions of Gerard* were impressionistic of the sweet nightmares of childhood, where Kerouac's beautifully drawn deities were Dr. Sax, the sinister shrouded slouch-hat dwarf who slinks through the rainy night of old horror movies laughing that crazy Shadow laugh "mwee hee hee ha ha haaa," and saintly Gerard, his older brother who died at the age of nine and contributed much to Kerouac's gentle Catholic mysticism. *The Dharma Bums* described the early Eastern-religious-and-meditation scene in San Francisco, while *Big Sur* and *Desolation Angels* recorded Kerouac's own disenchantment with and departure from the entire fabric of Hip/Beat society; perhaps most graphically in the latter book, where he described the scene in Tangier:

> *And just like New York or Frisco or anywhere, there they are all hunching around in marijuana smoke, talking, the cool girls with long thin legs in slacks, the men with goatees, all an enormous drag after all and at the time (1957) not even started yet officially with the name of "Beat Generation." To think that I had so much to do with it, too, in fact that very*

moment the manuscript of 'Road' was being lino-
typed for imminent publication and I was already
sick of the whole subject. Nothing can be more
dreary than "coolness" (not [Allen's] cool or [Bur-
roughs'], or [Peter Orlovsky's], which is natural
quietness) but postured, actually secretly rigid *cool-*
ness that covers up the fact that the character is
unable to convey anything of force or interest, a kind
of sociological coolness soon to become a fad up into
the mass of middleclass youth . . . Later I'm back in
New York sitting around with [Allen] and [Peter]
and [Gregory Corso] . . . and now we're famous
writers more or less, but they wonder why I'm so
sunk now, so unexcited as we sit among all our pub-
lished books and poems . . . A peaceful sorrow at
home is the best I'll ever be able to offer the world,
in the end, and so I told my Desolation Angels
goodbye. A new life for me.

Kerouac published few books in the Sixties, his inspiration declining along with his subject matter and the excitement of his prose, and in 1967 he finally gave up the road and all the rest of it to marry a woman who owned a laundro-mat and settle down in New England. Burroughs and especially Ginsberg are now world-famous, almost more for the legends that have grown up around them than their writings, but only Cassady pushed the high hot lifestyle that the group of them pioneered on to a final crackup—as a member of Ken Kesey's acid-pioneering Merry Pranksters, his legend billowed in the underground all over again, but Cassady was now a man in his forties, still going like some berserk V-8 cylinder cranking on to eternity, which finally received him in February 1968 when his heart stopped forever by a railroad track in Mexico.

Not long after that, *Cheetah* magazine ran a full-page picture of Kerouac with his new bride accompanied by a cruel article describing Cassady's death and accusing Kerouac of selling out, going soft and deserting the historic dream they had created. Jack, his French-Catholic soul as gentle as it had ever been since childhood, never replied, and this week he joined Neal in the vast incalculable silence which must claim all our forefathers as the decades fall past like dominoes into bookless eras of daily apocalypse. Good night, Jack—may Gerard and all your white-robed angels sing you tenderly upward-borne forever.

A Chicken-Essay

BY VICTOR-LÉVY BEAULIEU

Editor's note: The following is an excerpt from the book 'Jack Kerouac: A Chicken-Essay,' originally published in French in 1972. The book documents Quebec novelist Victor-Lévy Beaulieu's obsessive analysis of Kerouac and his work. Beaulieu suggests that Kerouac's conflicted relationships with women (including that with his mother) and his fear of death may be linked to his Roman-Catholic French-Canadian upbringing.

IN THE END THE THING IS FAIRLY simple: Even during the Beat period the only place where Jack felt comfortable was his mother's house—All his books follow the same scenario: a summer spent running around, philosophizing and getting drunk with the usual old buddies, followed by a winter of writing up the summer, *beneath Mémère's benevolent look*. I write benevolent deliberately because what could Jack's mother understand about the dealings of her son the writer? To comprehend what I mean, read this section of *The Dharma Bums*, a very beautiful bit and important because it sheds light on everything I've just said; it even heralds the ultimate Jack, the one who would end his life in St. Petersburg:

> *At nine o'clock I was stomping with full pack across my mother's yard and there she was at the white tiled sink in the kitchen, washing her dishes, with a rueful expression waiting for me (I was late), worried I'd never even make it and probably thinking, "Poor Raymond, why does he always have to hitchhike and worry me to death, why isn't he like other men?" And I thought of Japhy as I stood there in the cold yard looking at her: "Why is he so mad about white tiled sinks and 'kitchen machinery' as he calls it? People have good hearts whether or not they live like Dharma Bums. Compassion is the heart of Buddhism."*

And it's no coincidence that Jack's best Buddhist meditations and ecstasies are the ones that came to him in his Mother's house—he was alone there without really being alone and the subtle protection of the clan allowed him to dig around in his interior world. If he had to, Jack could have gone without reading a single Buddhist book (or meeting a single beatnik) and his reflections on life and the human condition would have been the same. The ghost of his Uncle Mike is behind all his thoughts—(Ancestral inheritance is a devastating kind of conditioning)—And too bad if Jack pretended not to know it! Not always, though, because he often had moments of cold lucidity that led him, inexorably, to the old world of Lowell, to childhood religious habits, to the Bible, to Saint Paul, whom he re-read with fervor in his mother's little house, underlining certain significant phrases such as: "Let him become a fool, that he may become wise," and "Already are ye filled, already are ye become rich. The saints shall judge the world"—Jack had a passion for that, different from "all the poetry of the new San Francisco Renaissance"—It is because Jack discovered in Saint Paul the memory of his Forefathers and the fatalism of Uncle Mike, that dear dislocated Canuck: "Meats for the belly, and the belly for meats; but God shall bring to naught both it and them."

[But if the reader is in a hurry he shouldn't be surprised if the 1963 reader paid more attention to the Beats' sexual and mystical prowess than to Jack's thinking—*Big Sur* is the book to read on the subject.]

For Jack, meditating was a return to the happy period of childhood, it meant entering into the secret dream of his brother Gerard—Very striking similarities between certain chapters of *Visions of Gerard* and *Dharma Bums*—You can see in them the same profound desire for knowledge and the kind of despair in the face of the futility of all knowledge:

> What does it mean that I am in this endless universe, thinking that I'm a man sitting under the stars on the terrace of the earth, but actually empty and awake throughout the emptiness and awakedness of everything? It means that I'm empty and awake, that I know I'm empty, awake, and that there's no difference between me and anything else. In other words it means that I've become the same as everything else. It means that I've become a Buddha. . .

I've become Buddha, Jack writes, meaning that he has been transformed into Gerard, that he is living the life of all the dead, of his dead father, his dead uncles, what he calls "the truth that is realizable in a dead man's bones and is beyond the Tree of Buddha as well as the Cross of Jesus"—In these passages of Jack's there is a kind of high voltage (Jack wanted words to be liberated from what he was and to transmute him from within, which is the whim of a writer hibernating in the warmth of his illusions)—Neither Jack's literary Buddha nor his Christ could bring him ultimate peace—The nightmares returned with the spring, and Jack took to the road again in order to flee them, proud of the thick nailed soles Mémère had put on his boots—But he meets Japhy and wants to tell what he has discovered in his winter meditations and the cutting retort doesn't fail to come—Japhy tells Jack that it's just words, nothing but words and that he doesn't want to hear words recounting what he has built so preciously

with words, nothing but words—What counts, Japhy adds, is action—Act, then, which was the opposite of what Jack was—Don't be surprised if Japhy's retort made him feel the need to go away from his companions so he could take total refuge within himself, in the disillusionment of his anguished spirit, which was a way of speaking because Jack wrote (and in this respect he makes me think of the great Thomas Wolfe who was too much a man to be a real novelist):

> Then I suddenly had the most tremendous feeling of the pitifulness of human beings, whatever they were, their faces, pained mouths, personalities, attempts to be gay, little petulances, feelings of loss, their dull and empty witticisms so soon forgotten: Ah, for what? I knew that the sound of silence was everywhere and therefore everything everywhere was silence. Suppose we suddenly wake up and see that what we thought to be this and that, ain't this and that at all? I staggered up the hill, greeted by birds, and looked at all the huddled sleeping figures on the floor. Who were all these strange ghosts rooted to the silly little adventure of earth with me? And who was I?

[*Who was I?* This simple question to which we can give only derisory answers marks the objective of Jack's work at the time of the Beats—And that alone is important to me, I leave to others the rest, which is only an anecdote about Jack (for the revolution is nothing if not interior)—Now Jack knew that the word doesn't go so far, that it is always extremely fragile and perhaps is finally addressed only to oneself—The inevitable superficiality of speaking and the impossibility of being totally inside one's words]—Write twenty thick novels and then die. Shit on the beatniks, old or new, who don't understand anything about that, about that religious madness. Write twenty thick novels and then die in St. Petersburg in the thickness of your disillusion, in a fog of alcohol and stomach ulcers—(Jack, the rotted old Canuck) Shit.

Another blank page to fill with words for

Jack—I wouldn't want it to be just an imposition or an anecdote about him—

Having made that clear, I look through the marine telescope left to me by my Uncle Ulric, old treasure-hunter in the Gulf of St. Lawrence. And what do I see in my telescope? A boat sailing on the frothy Ocean—On the bridge, hands in pockets, Jack is dreaming that he's left his New York friends and will soon be seeing Burroughs again—But old Jack is sad, stupefied and twisted like an old nail by his weariness with life—In the middle of the Ocean he suddenly understands that he no longer has anywhere to go—For it is in the middle of the Ocean that he realizes he has been tragically deluded about himself for years: His travels, deliciously juvenile at first, have become routine, monotonous, so that on the way to Tangier he feels in a state of "total disgust"; having for his experience of the world only "a repulsion in every sense of the word"—Taking his bearings on the last months (his adventure as a forest ranger in the woody solitude of Oregon,

and his reclusion in Mexico City, later dragged away by Allen), he realizes he no longer has an appetite for such things, that he's weary, despondent and most of all, alone as he has never been before—PAINFUL REPORT OF SPIRITUAL BANKRUPTCY—Could Jack's quest for the Holy Grail end up any other way?—And my left eye plastered against the telescope, I see again that there is a storm on the Atlantic, that Jack's boat is bobbing like a cork—Everything is heaving and pitching as Jack looks out, terrified, everything is rolling,

crashing, whirling, turning yellow—Jack, sick as a dog, reflects:

All I had to do was stay home, give it all up, get a little home for me and Ma, meditate, live quiet, read in the sun, drink wine in the moon in old clothes, pet my kitties, sleep good dreams . . .

Instead, he was risking losing his skin on this damned solitary boat in the midst of a storm! (Yes, I know it hurts, but what can I do? I'm only Uncle Ulric's telescope—Lying wouldn't solve anything)—Anyway, the boat has just come into port, Tangier at last and old Will withdrawn into his Casbah—What draws Jack to Will is obviously this insane solitude, which is expressed for the first time in *Naked Lunch*, an atrocious book, Jack says, so atrocious that "when I undertook to start typing it neatly doublespace for his publishers the following week I had horrible nightmares in my roof room—like of pulling out endless bolognas from my mouth, from my very entrails, feet of it, pulling and pulling out all the horror of what Will saw, and wrote"—

Jack of course didn't understand why Will had gone so far in his book and said so many truly horrible things—Between two promenades in Tangier he felt a need to settle the question with Will—Their conversation is rather sublime because of Jack's naiveté and Will's insane replies, he who in his clouds of dope took himself to be an agent in the service of another planet, whose Leaders had given him instructions that he hadn't completely decoded—Obviously it was all Greek to Jack, he didn't understand a thing and, coming back to *Naked Lunch*, he asked Will this question, a foolish one because after all the novel is perfectly clear: "But why all the vile rheum?"—Will answers: "I'm shitting out my educated Middlewest background for once and for all. It's a

Jack Kerouac on East 7th Street, New York City, 1953
ALLEN GINSBERG

matter of catharsis where I say the most horrible thing I can think of—Realize that, the most *horrible* dirty slimy awful niggardliest posture possible—By the time I finish this book I'll be as pure as an angel, my dear. These great existential anarchists and terrorists so-called never even their own drippy fly *mentioneth*, dear—They should poke sticks thru their shit and analyze *that* for social progress"—Morally, Jack found it very hard to accept, he couldn't permit so much excess—And so he asked like a dumb schoolboy: "But where'll all this shit get us?"—And Will answers: "Simply get us rid of shit, *really Jack.*"

Then in between two pipes of opium they began to wait. Will cried. He cried because Allen, adrift somewhere on the Ocean in Yugoslavian freighter, had not yet arrived in Tangier—Now Will was in love with Allen, and it went back to 1954, as Jack tells us in *Desolation Angels*—He was living with his mother at the time and Will often came to the house (sometimes Mémère even had to pay for the taxi and perhaps that was one of the reasons she disliked Will and wanted so much for her Ti-Jean to get away from him, just as she would have liked him to break with Allen whom she hated because one day he'd said something bad about a Catholic priest who had helped him)—Will didn't go to the Kerouac house because of Jack's beautiful eyes but because he was corresponding with Allen—So thanks to Jack, then, Will had some hope of starting a romantic liaison with Allen—Jack wrote: "The reason he'd come to my house, he admitted in Tangier in his bored but suffering tomes, was, 'Because the only connection I had at that agonized time with Irwin was thru *you*, you'd been getting long letters from him about what he was doing in Frisco. Laborsome human prose but I had to have some connection with him, like you were this great bore getting big letters from my rare angel and I had to see you as secondbest to *nothing*'"—

And when Jack heard that he said nothing, he didn't even feel insulted. He adds: "I knew what he meant having read *Of Human Bondage* and Shakespeare's will, and Dmitri Karamazov too . . . I loved Hubbard so for just his big stupid soul. Not that Irwin wasn't worthy of him but how on earth could they consummate this great romantic love with Vaseline and KY?"

That's pretty strong coffee, eh? And yet that's what Jack was like, a little miserable on the edge of his affections and scrupulous as an old maid (considering homosexuality to be a fault, a sin, a vice, and I don't know what else!)—(And again to add to Jack's record—Imagine! The Pope of the Beats was as sick as a dog every time he took drugs!)—And Jack had to go all the way to Tangier to understand, that under the patronage of holy Opium he dreamed: "*And I realized how my mother was waiting for me to take her home, my mother, my mother who smiled in her womb when she bore me.*"

This, particularly, is significant in *Desolation Angels*, it expresses very well who Jack was; the rest is only literature—(Even Will's madness when Allen arrived in Tangier)—"I'll cook big goldfish for supper, yum yum!"—After a dozen Beat years there was nothing left but the debasement of Jack, who was tired of his legend and wanted nothing but the peace of Lowell—*Mémère peeling potatoes, Poppa smoking his big wet cigar and Gerard slowly sinking into death*—"I was fed up with that story!"

That explains Jack's short trip to London and France (we still haven't got to *Satori in Paris*) and the poor vagabond doesn't understand anything he sees in these strange and highly alcoholic places—And soon he returns to *my own bleak France*, in other words America, a total trap, Florida, inner madness and Paradise of dispossessed Zulus, thundering and despondent like Canuck Jack. There's no more sun at Big Sur.

Anyway, there were years when Jack knew that at the end of the road the only thing left to find was death . . . death . . . yes, Jack died on October 21, 1969 . . . and you???

Beat Book Reviews

BY MICHAEL ROGERS

[ROLLING STONE 132, April 12, 1973]

Visions of Cody by Jack Kerouac, McGraw-Hill, 398 pp., $8.95

The Fall of America by Allen Ginsberg, City Lights Books, 188 pp., $2.50

W E'RE BACK ON THE ROAD again: one last time, with the travel-worn ghosts of Jack Kerouac and Neal Cassady, and one more time with the undeniably lively presence of Allen Ginsberg. Kerouac and Ginsberg—two long-time buddies who have managed together to put a considerable twist into the literary and social consciousness of the last two decades. And here they are represented by long works that reflect both the best and the worst of each.

A truly rabid Kerouac fan is one who will insist that Kerouac quality is relatively consistent and that one stretch of bop-prose is, within limits, just about as good as any other. My own approach to Kerouac, either the poetry or the prose, is more along the lines of take-what-you-need-and-leave-the-rest—a philosophy I'm certain that at least the younger Kerouac would have deemed eminently sensible.

Sensible and necessary, for a first cut at *Visions of Cody*, Kerouac's posthumously published paean to Neal Cassady, which manages in the course of its four hundred pages to run the gamut from absolutely impenetrable pseudo-Joycean incoherence to passages of crystal-clear observation and lyric emotion. Kerouac could write like a no-fooling sumbitch, and he could write with all the self-conscious pretension of a college sophomore terminally overstuffed with the mystique of Literature. And when Kerouac set about to get down his all-American hero—the last rugged

individualist, the lonely manic cowboy who herds '49 Hudsons coast-to-coast in forty-eight hours—he pulled out all the stops.

Kerouac can describe the "*shiny food*" on the counter of a New York cafeteria—"as brilliant as B-way outside!"—with an eye so sharp and language so vivid that by the end of the paragraph there is no other conclusion possible but his own: The counter, "showering like heaven," is "an all out promise of joy in the great city of kicks." Or the behavior of people parading up Sixth Avenue, or a single girl eating alone in a restaurant, delineated with such precision that a photograph would not only be redundant, but pale by contrast. Or young Cody's early days in the Denver pool-hall scene; the characters, the atmosphere, the electric promise of manhood so fully realized that when Cody cries "Damn! Lessgo!" the reader can hardly wait. The pure verbal energy in passages like these is hard to match anywhere in American literature.

But for every passage of "Damn! Lessgo!" there are probably four of "Where the hell are we?" Probably the heaviest of the bogs in *Visions of Cody* lie in the tape transcriptions of long and irredeemably stoned-out conversations between Kerouac and Cassady/Cody. Truman Capote's now-classic observation about *On the Road*—that he always thought there was a difference between typing and writing—is overly harsh, because Kerouac was a determined artist and the way he chose to write is more fairly considered technique than simply passed off as sloth. Yet Capote's jab, on a scale of one to ten, makes a good deal more sense than the long defense of those interminable transcriptions that Allen Ginsberg presents (in uncharacteristically organized fashion) in the introduction to *Visions of Cody*. The fact that the lengthy dialogues are *real*, or that twenty years later Andy Warhol studied Campbell Soup cans, really doesn't justify the massive presence of so much detail that in the end sheds so little light on anyone involved.

The question of detail, in fact, may be just where the Kerouac style grows most directly—and most murkily—from content. Kerouac's prose is an unceasing mania for detail, both psychic and physical, a relentless recounting of exactly how each thing was—trivial or not; and no matter how fleeting or spurious. Getting It All Down—no filters, no judgments, no editorial grid. It may be the vision of the Beat, but it is also the vision of the alien: the observer who has no real idea what's at stake or what's going on and who hence describes every detail he sees, in the hope that some combination of them will finally make sense.

"America," Kerouac wrote in *Visions of Cody*, "is the impersonal nighttime at crossings and junctions where everybody looks both ways, four ways, nobody cares . . ." It's a place where a man goes to college and is "deprived of his one time innocent belief in his own thoughts that used to make him handle his own destiny." And it's where Kerouac watched a successful young executive step off a plane, and realized suddenly that "nothing in the world matters; not even success in America but just void and emptiness await the career of a soul of a man." And there, past the frantic exuberance, is the source of his energy: When nothing matters, through a simple reversal of the image, everything can be made to matter. And if void and emptiness are in fact all that await, then there's certainly no reason not to fill up the spaces with just as much noise as you can possibly make.

Allen Ginsberg's America as sketched first in *Planet News* (City Lights Books, 1968), and now in *The Fall of America*, is on the surface somewhat less joyous than Kerouac's, but beneath, finally, considerably more affirmative.

The Fall of America chronicles the last days of the crumbling fascist empire, state by state, town by town, from the center of Chicago to the padded seats of a jetliner to the flowering hills of Big Sur.

> Black Magicians screaming in anger Newark to
> Algiers
> How many bottles and cans piled up in our
> garbage pail?
> Space age children wandering like lost orphans
> Thru a landscape filled with iron—
> Their grandfathers sweated over forges!
> Now all they know is all them rockets they see
> Silvery
> Quivering on Television.

"The President at home in his swinging chair on the porch / listening to Christmas Carols" as the tacky car radio announces that "The Ally Cease Fire Will Not Be Extended."

Ginsberg is clearly the most burdened with the contradiction of automated firestorms abroad and the faces of decadence and decay at home; ecologic breakdown, the isolation and alienation of the American people. Even the golden rural retreat has a sour edge: "The Farm's a lie! / Madmen growing giant organic zucchini," while "Marie Antoinette had milkmaid costumes ready, / Robespierre's eyeball hung on his cheek / in the trumbril to the guillotine."

The chronicle pours out of car radios, television newscasts, the pages of magazines—bits and pieces of the media clipped, arranged, inset among the lines of rolling and powerful language that have always distinguished Ginsberg's work. But by the end the reader may feel that the pull of Ginsberg's conscience—the poison of the War—has rendered a portion of *Fall* too obsessional; too many references and facts and figures that divert the mind from the roll of each line, away from the feeling of the time and back instead to visions of the *New York Times* and *Ramparts*. And Ginsberg is too good a poet to settle for connections as easy as these.

There are many fine poems in this six-year collection, however: a heroic portrait of Che Guevera ("One radiant face driven mad with a rifle/Confronting the electric networks"), of Cassady, of a nineteen-year-old Marine describing Vietnam killings; fine pastoral poetry, and some hermit-hut musings on America's first moon landing.

"Common Sense, Common law, common tenderness & common tranquillity /our means in America to control the money munching war machine / bright lit industry," Ginsberg writes early in this collection. And if that doesn't work? "What do I have to lose if America falls?" he asks, "my body? My neck? My personality?" All of them conceivably, and if not those, then at least one of the most convoluted subjects that has ever tugged and nagged at the poet's muse.

Kerouac's Ghost

BY DAVID L. ULIN

Lowell, Massachusetts, October 21, 1989

JACK KEROUAC DIDN'T DRIVE. All those years, all those cross-country journeys, all that traveling back and forth from East Coast to West, from Massachusetts to New York to North Carolina to Texas to Mexico City to San Francisco, he rarely ever spent time behind the wheel. For a man so associated with the freedom of the open road, he always left the driving to someone else—to Greyhound, to the strangers who picked him up hitchhiking and, of course, to Neal Cassady, who, in the late 1940s, once did Denver to Chicago in seventeen hours, devouring the twelve hundred desolate miles of blacktop between the two cities as if pursued by the hounds of hell.

That's a small fact, on the face of things, insignificant almost, just another way the truth about Kerouac diverges from the myth. But I can't stop thinking about it because today, *I am* the passenger, sitting full of ambivalence as my friend Stu drives north on Route 27 toward Chelmsford, Massachusetts, where we will pick up Route 110 for Lowell. Outside, the trees have turned brown and lost their leaves; it is a crisp morning, with air that smells like wood smoke, and a light dusting of frost lying in eddies on the ground. All the years I lived in New England, I used to love days like this, used to love the sallow quality of their light, the darkness creeping across the fields at the end of the afternoon, the shadows disappearing into the long Northeastern night. As Kerouac himself wrote in his first novel, *The Town and the City*, "when the sun of October slopes in late afternoon, the children scurry home from school, make footballs out of stuffed socks, [then] leap and dash in the powerful winds and scream with delight."

Like his friend Allen Ginsberg, Jack Kerouac would be some kind of literary elder statesman if he were alive today; instead, Stu and I are on a pilgrimage to his grave on the twentieth anniversary of his death. At the time of his funeral, Kerouac was largely dismissed as a serious literary figure, only three of his books—*On the Road*, *The Dharma Bums* and *Book of Dreams*—still in print. Now, there is a monument for him in downtown Lowell and a creative writing program—the Jack Kerouac School of Disembodied Poetics—established in his name at the Naropa Institute in Boulder, Colorado. Just a few months prior to this trip, I attended a Sunday afternoon marathon reading of Kerouac's long poem *Mexico City Blues* at a jazz club in Greenwich Village (honoring his intention "to be considered a jazz poet blowing a long blues in an afternoon jam session on Sunday"); virtually all his surviving Beat counterparts, from Ginsberg to Herbert Huncke to Gregory Corso to Carl Solomon, were there, trading off choruses of his work while a trio of sax, bass and drums jammed behind them. All in all, Kerouac is a larger presence on the American cultural landscape than he has been in nearly a generation, a figure of mythic proportions on spoken word scenes coast-to-coast, where his ideas on sponta-

Bob Dylan (left) *and Allen Ginsberg take a break from the Rolling Thunder Tour to visit Kerouac's grave, 1975*

neous writing and his sad-eyed quest for kicks and experience are invoked by poets and scenesters who were themselves barely alive, if at all, when he died.

As we make the turnoff onto Route 110 and head into Lowell, neither Stu nor I say very much. Although I spent three years attending boarding school in Andover, less than twelve miles away, I've never been here, and my first impression is of how much Lowell resembles every other mill town in the area—squat, blocky red brick cities built at the turn of the century, quarried out of hillsides and the rocky banks of the Merrimack River, full of heavy stone constructions thrown up against the cold, thin light of the Massachusetts sky. I remember prowling the streets of Lawrence as a student, discovering warehouse districts littered with broken glass and mortar that looked like photographs of the Great Depression; today, I feel the same way I did back then, as if the simple act of squinting my eyes might be enough to reconfigure time. Driving through these blank industrial streets, it's hard to know where memory ends and imagination begins.

We leave Stu's car in an ash-gray concrete parking structure on the edge of downtown, and exit into the Saturday morning hush. The sidewalks are empty, the sun pale and weak, casting little heat. At a newsstand, I buy a copy of the *Lowell Sun*, where Kerouac once worked briefly as a sportswriter; afterwards, Stu and I walk down the block to a storefront diner with faded vinyl chairs and Formica tables that look as if they haven't been replaced in fifty years. We order eggs, toast and coffee, and scan the paper, but there is no mention of Kerouac's name. Briefly, I think about the photos I've seen of Kerouac at the end of his life—bloated, boozy, face florid and eyes small black pinpricks floating in a rheumy sea—and compare that with the popular perception of the rebel angel, the dark-haired saint of the underground. For a decade or

longer, I've struggled to reconcile these images, and now I'm hoping that, by paying my respects, I can achieve some kind of resolution, that by making this visit to Lowell, I can, once and for all, put Kerouac into perspective, escape the weight of his romantic myth.

There have been times in my life when I measured everything against Jack Kerouac, times when his words have been so strong within me that my own voice was all but drowned out. For obvious reasons, this has left me deeply wary of being overwhelmed. Nonetheless, I continue to respond to Kerouac in a way I never have with other writers or cultural icons, his influence a fundamental aspect of how I define myself. On a rational level, I can see the man for what he was—a contradictory, often bitter figure who retreated into the bottle when the burdens of his life became too much—but in my imagination, he is forever young and lean, his face as chiseled as a piece of New Hampshire granite, charisma literally rolling off him in waves. By the same token, I'm aware of the uneven quality of his work, but ever since I first came upon Kerouac in my early teens, his idiosyncratic mix of sadness and euphoria, of irony and exuberance, has represented, for me, at least, the epitome of cool, a way of engaging the world while remaining slightly on the outside. It's a position I have always found attractive, one to which I am naturally drawn.

Over the last several years, my fascination with Kerouac has ebbed and flowed like the tides, advancing and receding in my consciousness according to some internal rhythm I can't quite understand. As an adolescent, sitting in my boarding school room sneaking furtive puffs of pot, I dreamed of partaking in my own version of the Beat experience, hitting the highway to discover a place more elemental than the one in which I found myself, more concerned with spirit and substance, where the petty concerns of my friends and parents—grades, popularity, college—would be subsumed in favor of something more profound. It was a stereotypical perspective, but no less potent for being so, and given my sheltered, upper-middle-class upbringing, the appeal it held still makes a lot of sense. If you buy the myth, after all, Kerouac stood in opposition to every received notion I was being encouraged, often against my own private judgments, to accept. He turned his back on an Ivy League education, opting instead for the bhikku's backpack and the mystery of the open road. He wrote what he felt like, when he felt like it, creating an "original classic literature," that celebrates the transitory nature of existence and laments the inevitability of death. He traveled with a group of outcast geniuses who glorified each other's exploits until they had created the ultimate in-group, their reports from the fringes the cultural equivalent of an atom bomb. He was impulsive, extemporaneous, a creature of intuition. More than anything, he was not tied down.

Yet the problem with the Kerouac myth, I've come to understand, is that it is precisely that: a larger-than-life archetype reducing the author to a two-dimensional version of himself. For Kerouac *was* tied down; he spent most of his life sharing quarters with his mother, and until the end was so frightened of her wrath that if she called a house where he'd been drinking, he would automatically sober up before coming to the phone. He was a reactionary, a supporter of the war in Vietnam, who barely acknowledged his only daughter Jan while he was alive. He was an alcoholic, a barroom brawler, a romanticizer of skid row bums, who destroyed his talent with cheap wine and Scotch and died of massive esophageal hemorrhaging (what biographer Gerald Nicosia has called a "classic drunkard's death") at the age of forty-seven. He was also, for a period of about seven years in the early and mid-1950s, one of the most startlingly original

and diverse writers in the history of American letters, a man who, by his own admission was "blowing such mad poetry and literature that I'll look back years later with amazement and chagrin that I can't do it anymore."

That "mad poetry and literature" has everything to do with why I've decided to come to Lowell today, why I need to connect these conflicting impulses into a more cohesive vision of Kerouac and his work. It's all part of that ebb and flow, the rise and fall of his voice within my head. Lately, I've been obsessing about him as much as I ever have, hearing the admonishing textures of his broad New England accent each time I revise a sentence, or begin a story that's not completely rooted in the truth. Years ago, when I was taking my first, tentative steps toward becoming a writer, Kerouac's first-thought-best-thought theories of spontaneous composition seemed to me a fundamental means of breaking through my own polished surfaces, of opening myself up to whimsy, to improvisation and jazz. I remember my sense of discovery the first time I read *Mexico City Blues*, how I came away from the experience with a new appreciation of what poetry could do, of the relationship of music, of rhythm, to meaning in a literary work. Of course, spontaneous writing is a lot harder than it looks; you have to turn off every bit of critical reflex in your mind, and just let the words and associations find their way across the page. In fact, it's taken me until this past summer, two months prior to visiting Lowell, to write *Cape Cod Blues*, a blues poem of my own, after better than a dozen attempts to pull it off.

Now, though, the strain of derivation has become too much. Over the summer, when I was writing *Cape Cod Blues*, with *Tristessa* on my night table and Nicosia's biography *Memory Babe* in my bag for the beach, Kerouac was such a presence that to try and get a handle on him by visiting his tomb seemed like the most logical thing I could do. What better way, after all, of making him physical, of defusing his mythological impact, of somehow placing him within the world? Yet several times in the last few weeks, I've picked up the phone to call Stu and cancel the trip, and on the train ride up to Massachusetts, I watched the question marks crawl across my face in the darkened window glass, as I wondered whether I was getting in too deep. During my three years at Andover, I always resisted making this journey, even though most weekends, one group of friends or another would take the bus to Lowell and spend a couple of hours sitting on the cemetery grass, passing a jug of red wine, pouring a little into the earth over Kerouac's head each time it was his turn. Maybe it was reticence, maybe a desire to maintain whatever distance I could, but the only time I've even seen the gravesite was in an old issue of ROLLING STONE, where a photograph captured Bob Dylan and Allen Ginsberg taking a break from the Rolling Thunder Revue tour to pay their respects, sitting on crossed legs surrounded by bare trees of autumn, singing and chanting to the dead man's bones. Once, that picture filled me with excitement, with the surety that here was the place I was seeking, where poetry and music was common currency, and society was what you made of it, not the other way around. That, however, was many years ago, and thinking about it today is enough to raise the hackles of my ambivalence all over again.

Stu and I finish our breakfasts, and move out of the diner in the direction of downtown. By now, the sidewalks are starting to fill up; it is getting on to late morning, and the stores of Lowell are open for business, just like any other Saturday. The city's central corridor has a refurbished look; the ancient industrial buildings scrubbed, ruddy, their facades freshly painted, as if they were monuments in a historic district like the South Street Seaport or Faneuil Hall. For a moment, the whole thing almost seems like a photograph, caught in some strange suspension of time, but ultimately, the streets are too clean, too well-attended for the illusion to hold. I try to see Kerouac in such a landscape, try to remember his descriptions of Galloway in *The Town and the City*, or Pawtucketville in *Doctor Sax*. Those were living places, full of grime and mystery; if they were faces, they would be etched deep with creases, pockmarked, weatherbeaten, lined with wear and age. But Lowell this morning is like a matron with a facelift, all her history erased in favor of this newly polished look, and I can't help feeling that I could be anywhere, any town with a few vintage structures and an aggressive Chamber of Commerce eager to redirect the past.

After checking out the heart of the city, Stu and I ask a couple of passersby how to get to the Kerouac Memorial, dedicated with great fanfare only a couple of years before. One after another greets our request with a blank stare. "Kerouac?" a man asks. "I don't think I know that name." Finally, we wander over to the offices of the Lowell Historical Society, where we pick up a map and directions to both the Memorial and other Kerouac landmarks scattered throughout the town. When Stu inquires about commemorative activities, though, the woman behind the counter gives us a long scowl. "Here in Lowell, we prefer to mark Kerouac's birth, not his death," she tells us, as if she's heard the question once too often. And all of a sudden, I get a glimpse of Stu and myself through her eyes—just two more acolytes of the King of the Beats, me with my earrings and long hair, Stu all dressed in black. It's exactly the image I'm seeking to distance myself from, and the idea of being seen this way makes my stomach clench. Once again, I start thinking that maybe this whole thing isn't such a good idea.

But good idea or no, Stu and I have both come a long way, so I swallow back my doubts, and we set off for the Kerouac Memorial, trying to decipher the grainy Xeroxed lines of the map.

Even with directions, the Memorial is nearly impossible to find, and by the time we get there, Stu and I have seen most of the available markers of Kerouac's life. We pass Lowell High School, stop at the church where Kerouac's funeral took place, cross the threadbare span of the Moody Street Bridge to Pawtucketville and stare from street level at the fourth floor apartment in which he lived as a teenager. Finally, after an hour or more of meandering back and forth along the same stretch of road, we discover what we're looking for, an arrangement of marble slabs engraved with excerpts from Kerouac's books, erected in a small park on the banks of the Merrimack. For both of us, the day has long since taken on a surreal quality, as if we are living in one reality and everybody else in another, so we are not especially surprised that we have walked by this spot a number of times. We make a circuit of the park, sit down in the shadow of the stones. I read the words; Stu takes a couple of pictures. We are all alone.

If there were ever an appropriate moment for me to resolve my relationship with Kerouac, this would probably be it. But life does not imitate art, and this afternoon in Lowell, there is no instant of revelation, no sign that will somehow clear up all this ambivalence and put everything in its place. Actually, confronted with the monument, I find myself confused all over again, at how the living flesh of Kerouac's language seems so out of place preserved upon the static surface of the rock. When this memorial was built, Norman Podhoretz, once Kerouac's classmate at Columbia University, complained that it sent the wrong message to honor someone who had led so many people's lives astray. At the time, I thought Podhoretz was just being contrary, that his comments were additional proof of how poorly served Kerouac had been by the terms of his own myth. Sitting here, however, I can't help but think that this fails to serve Kerouac either, that immortalizing his words in marble is exactly

the wrong way to go. It's such a seeming contradiction—the middle-class values that inform the monument versus the avant-garde sentiments etched on its polished sides—that it only works to heighten my discomfort, transforming the ethereal textures of Kerouac's writing into something solidly respectable, and dead. Twenty years later, is this what Kerouac's "spontaneous bop prosody" has become, a series of tombstones, proscriptions, laws?

The wind picks up off the Merrimack and blows a swath of dirt across the park. Dust rasps in the empty spaces between the facades of jutting marble, sifts in the letters of Kerouac's name. Stu turns up his collar, stands and stomps his feet. "You ready?" he asks. I nod.

So we turn away from the monument, and beat a path back into downtown Lowell. By now, foot traffic is thin again; the streets emptying like a river as the light slowly fades from the sky. Stu and I retrace our footsteps, past the Historical Society, past the diner where we had breakfast so many hours ago. In a certain sense, it feels as if we are rewinding time, as if we are not just covering old ground but moving backwards, as if, in the last thirty minutes, we have slipped some kind of boundary, and can actually retrace the past.

That feeling comes on even stronger when we arrive at Edson Catholic Cemetery, where Kerouac is buried beneath a simple marble marker laid flush to the ground. As we pull through the gates and open the windows to ask directions to the tomb, the sky reddens to a dusky shade of plum, and our breath is visible in wisps of precipitation. The caretaker gives us a map of the grounds; Stu puts the car in gear. Edson Cemetery is laid out like a city, with numbered streets and avenues, all paved and wide enough for two-way traffic. For a couple of blocks, we see nothing but shadows lengthening across the ornate Victorian monuments and through the keening, bare-ribbed trees. Then we take a left, and Stu's headlights flicker against a shadow dance of movement, a scraggly band of people clustered around a solitary grave.

Stu stops the car about twenty feet away. He cuts the ignition and the lights, and for a second, the only sound is the ticking of the engine as it cools. I roll down my window, take a deep breath of sharp fall air. From up ahead, I can smell marijuana, and see a bottle of wine making the rounds. Periodically, someone spills some of the dark liquid into the ground. At first, I'm not quite sure what's happening, but then I understand that, like my boarding school friends, whoever's out there is marking Kerouac's place in the circle whenever it comes around.

And watching them, I start to feel a little telescoped, as if it *is* my teenage buddies sitting there upon the grave. My mind flashes back to the photo of Dylan and Ginsberg, and all of a sudden, I am drawn to that circle, to the romance of it, the illusion of camaraderie so strong that it's almost as if, by sheer force of will, these people could resurrect Kerouac from his premature demise. As the light continues to slip, a tall, stocky teenager stands up in the middle of the pack. From here, it's all I can do to make out his silhouette, like a ghost in the gloaming, and it takes me a minute to notice the book in his hands. I lean out the window, peering at the cover; outside, someone lights a cigarette, and in its glow, the title becomes momentarily clear. *Visions of Cody.* An odd choice, I think, and wonder what he's doing, until the wind changes direction, and his low, droning intonations sweep over me like a storm.

For he is reading. "It's been so long since I've heard the sound of the Merrimack River washing over rocks in the middle of a soft summer's

night," he mumbles, his voice marked by the broad vowel sounds of the region, not very different from Kerouac's own. The pull of those syllables is contagious, and in the thrall of their rhythms, I remember the Kerouac Monument and its silent letters, think about the contradictions at its core. To tell the truth, I had expected to find something similar here, but what fills the cemetery instead is Kerouac's living language, his words soaring like birds in the darkening air. "It's our work that counts, if anything at all," he told *The Paris Review* in 1967, and this ragtag tribute is nothing if not a testament to that. I make a move to open the car door, but then, as if I was a teenager again, something stops me, keeps me apart. This is, after all, the thing I was most afraid I might end up confronting, and the idea that it is somehow attuned to what Kerouac was really all about just adds a final layer to all the mixed emotions my trip to Lowell was supposed to dispel.

So, as usual, I wait. I wait until everyone has returned to their cars and driven slowly out of Edson Cemetery, calling "Goodnight, Jack" as their tail lights fade away. I wait until Stu and I are the last people left, until between the cracks of night's descent, the caretaker's truck begins to make its rounds. I wait until there's no one left to give witness, before I finally extricate myself from Stu's passenger seat and approach the grave. Standing there, I observe a moment of silence, then take out my notebook and scrawl something suitably ambivalent, one of my favorite quotes from Kerouac, which I leave upon the stone:

"Perhaps nothing is true but everything is real" . . .

Heart Beat:
Fifties Heroes as Soap Opera

BY WILLIAM S. BURROUGHS

[ROLLING STONE 309, January 24, 1980]

The question I should really like to have answered, although I don't expect an answer to in this lifetime, is why, in the course of nailing the frame of a film together, so much energy and thought are invariably expended, and have to be expended, in a sort of contest between a superficial reasonableness and a fundamental idiocy. Why do film stories always have to have this element of the grotesque? Whose fault is it? Is it anybody's fault? Or is it something inseparable from the making of motion pictures? Is it the price you pay for trying to make a dream look as if it really happened?

—RAYMOND CHANDLER

THERE IS A KIDNEY-SHAPED swimming pool in the courtyard of the Tropicana motel on Santa Monica Boulevard. On the patio are rusty metal tables, deck chairs, palms and banana trees: a rundown Raymond Chandler set from the 1950s. One expects to find a dead man floating in the pool one morning or to hear a voice from an old detective film intoning: "You see, the killer forgot just one thing when he drowned this joker in the bathtub: swimming pool water contains more chlorine . . ."

This is actually my second visit to Hollywood. The first time was in 1971, when Terry Southern and I were trying to sell a script of *Naked Lunch*. Everything started out propitiously, with first-class plane tickets and a Daimler to meet us at the airport. We were taken to meet the Man from the Studio and his secretary. "Believe it or not, her name is Keester," said the driver, and right then I had a premonition. Sure enough, two days later our Daimler had shrunk to a two-seater, spelling out the native dialect: "The studio doesn't like the script."

This time I am in Los Angeles to cover the filming of *Heart Beat*, a movie based on Carolyn Cassady's memoirs of life with Neal Cassady and Jack Kerouac. My editors think that because I knew Kerouac, Cassady and Allen Ginsberg in the Fifties, I can get a Beat angle on this film.

Hollywood is still the image of the capital of the world, which is to say, the world center for time travel. At the studio in Culver City, I find a San Francisco tract house carefully furnished in 1950s style, with period magazines on the coffee table. Even the canned goods in the kitchen are period priced. Time travel requires these sets to be recreated with the utmost precision.

Time travel also requires time travelers—astronauts, in fact. I meet the stars: Nick Nolte, who is playing Neal Cassady; Sissy Spacek, who is Carolyn Cassady; and John Heard, who is Jack Kerouac.

The scene they are shooting involves Neal and Jack coming home drunk with a black woman and trying to smuggle her past Carolyn into the attic. The clowning is uncannily realistic, since I remember Jack and Neal's amatory escapades as being more of an act than real sexual exploits. They were always on set. So of course they stumble all over the children's toys, making enough noise to raise the dead . . . CUT. On a good day, with take after take, they may get four minutes on film. Two minutes is standard. Nick Nolte finally does a spontaneous pratfall on the last take, and that's it for the scene. A two-minute day.

I have lunch with Nolte at a dark restaurant nearby. From time to time I have the eerie feeling that it is Neal sitting there beside me in his cheap 1950s suit with the sleeves pushed up. So I ask Nolte whether he has experienced any, uh, psychic manifestations in the course of filming. Yes, he answers: In a scene in which Neal and Carolyn invite some square neighbors over for dinner, Neal blows it and finally has to go out on the porch and smoke a joint. After the neighbors had gone, Nolte picked up a toy pistol and pointed it to his head, just playing around. This was not in the script. Watching this on the set, the real Carolyn Cassady said, "My God, that's exactly what Neal did, the one time I saw him play with a toy gun."

We discuss the challenge of acting the role of someone from the recent past, like Neal: There are thousands of words written about and by him, there are photos and tapes and films. The actor is swamped with data. Nolte feels that the actor should not attempt to duplicate details like hair color, accent, mannerisms. Such details are not important for the overall picture. The actor needs to maintain a spontaneous flow that will permit such inventions as the toy pistol incident, and to open himself up to possession by the character; once this took place, Nolte could let Neal Cassady speak for himself.

Jack and Neal are listening to a baseball game in the kitchen of the tract house. Carolyn comes back with the groceries to report that Ira Streiker's poem "Rage" has been seized by the police: an obvious reference to Allen Ginsberg's "Howl."

"What do you mean by *seized*?" asks Jack suspiciously.

"*You* know. *Seized!*" Carolyn repeats.

Neal, looking over the report in the paper, says, "It'll never stick. All it's going to do is make him famous, the poor bastard."

Here, John Heard perfectly portrays Jack's capacity for being sullen without being hostile.

"So what's so wrong with being famous?" he asks.

Neal says, "Are you kidding? We all gotta serve, my friend . . ." (he meditatively licks the joint he has rolled) ". . . but the famous got to serve as an example."

Jack walks out of the room. The scene is an inspired re-creation of what Jack and Neal and Carolyn might have said under the circumstances, and for a moment the past hangs in the air.

At lunch in one of the worst Thai restaurants I have ever experienced, I talk to John Heard and Ray Sharkey, who is taking the part based on Allen Ginsberg—under the name Ira Streiker, since Ginsberg did not want his name used. This script's conception of Allen is rather more bumptious and outrageous than Allen himself. I cannot imagine Allen shouting out in a Chinese restaurant: "Waiter, there's a *turd* in my soup!" Just not his style.

John Heard tells me he turned down the lead in Joseph Wambaugh's *The Onion Field* because he wants to get out of Los Angeles for a while. He would have played a young cop; either one of them could have played the role.

Heard has the hardest part to play in *Heart Beat*, since Kerouac was a writer, and most of the action for any writer takes place inside his head. In Kerouac's case, there was a lifelong incompatibility between his uneasy surface presentation—of a nice guy, regular American who likes beer and mom and TV and baseball, works as a brakeman, wants to settle down with Carolyn and give up writing—and the spy in his body, the writer whose status as a normal guy is belied by the obsessive need to write about it. And his life so written becomes a sham that barely conceals the writer himself.

> People keep seeing destruction or rebellion in Jack's writing, and "Howl," but that is a very minor element, actually: It only seems to be so to people who have accepted standard American values as permanent. What we are saying is that these values are not really standard or permanent, and are in a sense I think ahead of the times. . . . Only way out is individuals taking responsibility and saying what they actually feel—which is an enormous human achievement in any society. That's just what we as a "group" have been trying to do. To class that as some form of "rebellion" in the kind of college-bred social worker double talk misses the huge awful point.
>
> —ALLEN GINSBERG

I reflect on the awesome power of the word. Kerouac's *On the Road* sold millions of Levi's and created thousands of espresso bars to serve their wearers. His book launched a children's crusade to Paris, Tangier, Katmandu, Goa, Mexico, Colombia, winning converts everywhere.

"Hello, Johnny, you want opium, hashish, cocaine? Horse maybe?" The boy whinnies and paws the air and lets his eyes drop significantly. "*Muy fuerte, muy bueno. . . .*"

If Kerouac felt like the sorcerer's apprentice in his later years, for my part I saw no basis for this ethical unrest. Rather, let determined things to destiny hold unbewailed their sway. I reflect on the awesome power of a kidney shape from the 1950s. Forgot just one thing. Horse maybe? The boy paws the swimming pool water significantly.

Kerouac's writing is an inextricable mixture of so-called fact and fiction that calls both into question. It is generally assumed by his readers that he is talking about actual events and actual people. In the sense that his characters do have counterparts—that Neal Cassady, Allen Ginsberg, Carolyn Cassady existed—this is true. But once written into his books, they are fair game. He can equip me with a trust fund I never had, and depict Neal as a compulsive talker. I have driven for eight hours with Neal Cassady, in the course of which neither of us said a word.

When I protested to Jack that he had endowed me with a nonexistent trust fund and married me a White Russian countess, he replied mysteriously that I would understand it all by and by. Did he mean that his fiction would produce somehow a magic trust fund and evoke a slinky countess with a fur coat down to her Russian boots? I think not. He meant that I would come to understand that fiction is more enduring than fact, and that history books are full of it. And readers are convinced that everything in his books actually happened in so-called real life exactly as he describes it.

As time passes and eyewitnesses die off, it becomes more and more difficult to determine what really happened and what Jack invented or pieced together—because his inventions are usually composites. For example, I actually built an orgone box in Texas, where Jack never visited me, so he transports the box to New Orleans.

I was not in San Francisco during the time covered by *Heart Beat,* so I can't say firsthand how things were. I was, however, presumably off stage in a Mexico City scene in which Jack is typing on the toilet as a Mexican junkie vomits into it. You see, Jack said once that he wrote *Doctor Sax* in *my* toilet in Mexico City. I recall that, on occasion, he would retire to the toilet to write if there were too many people in the apartment and too much talk. At other times he wrote at the kitchen table or in the front room or sitting on a bench somewhere. My apartment was a small, clean, modern, two-room flat at 210 Orizaba. I would never have tolerated cockroaches in my living quarters as the script suggests. Old Dave was my supplier at the time, and is undoubtedly the basis for the "Mexican" junkie in the scene. The only time he ever vomited, however, was when he was sick from lack of junk, not when there was opium to burn.

So, the question is not, "Did it happen like that?" but, "How would Jack have *written* it?" The Mexican scene is not true to life, but it is true to Jack.

In short, Jack Kerouac wrote *his* version of Neal, Allen, Carolyn, and of himself as well. This film is based on Carolyn's version of the same events, and informed by a familiarity with Kerouac's story. But fictional characters are expendable. No trouble, no story. No death, no life. If birth is the cause of death, in the world of fiction the contrary is true, and death is the beginning of life. "They lived happily ever after" ends the story. But death leads to just another episode. Will *Heart Beat* be a box-office hit? Will *On the Road* follow? Will nostalgia for the Beat Fifties inundate us all? Will not the escalating rate of change

mean a shorter and shorter nostalgia distance until we are all playing ourselves in period yesterday?

From the script: Jack to Neal, who is holding a copy of *On the Road*, embarrassed: "So. Who'd have guessed, man? You go for a ride with a guy and ten years later they publish a book about it!"

Each writer creates his own universe. When you buy a book, you are buying a ticket to travel in the writer's time. Here on the set of *Heart Beat* we see Jack Kerouac's universe painstakingly recreated: the lumpy sofa, the wobbly lamp, the TV, the beer, the T-shirts, the kitchen table, the whole middle-class set. Not to mince words, *Heart Beat* is a soap opera.

So, what's wrong with soap operas? They are the heartbeat of America. But the film can also be seen as a detective story. Who killed Neal Cassady? Dean Moriarty killed Neal Cassady; he died of exposure. And who killed Jack Kerouac the man? A spy in his body known as Jack Kerouac the writer.

The Blind Follow the Blind

BY CAROLYN CASSADY

"Does any one drink much wine? Do not say that he does ill, but that he drinks a great deal. For unless you perfectly understand his motives, how should you know if he acts ill? Thus you will not risk yielding to any appearances but such as you fully comprehend."

—EPICTETUS

THE TITLE "KING OF THE BEATS" with which Jack Kerouac was crowned in the 1960s became a major factor in his vow to drink himself to death. Like Jack's coronation, the "Beat Generation" was an invention of the media and Allen Ginsberg; neither Jack nor my husband, Neal Cassady, fit into their prescribed category of rebellion, yet their forced involvement contributed to their early deaths. Having known both these men intimately for twenty years, I often disagree with many of the "theories" other writers put forward in an attempt to explain or judge Jack's and Neal's actions and beliefs. The general practice of grouping individuals by labels has always been regrettable to me, and when writers copy other writers' surmises, truth is obscured and/or distorted. They select a stereotype into which they fit their subject. My own conclusions may be wrong—there is never an "absolute" truth—but over and over I must read the judgments of writers who never knew the men but are very familiar with the stereotypes and the opinions of other authors.

The problem with judging people by socially categorized models (or by ourselves?) is that allowance is rarely made for subconscious drives, conditioned attitudes, hopes, fears or motivations. These should be carefully researched from available sources such as letters or friends, as do some biographers, but in the case of Kerouac and Cassady, not very many. Some consult psychologists who pass on acquired knowledge of their predecessors. An author of a recent "portrait" of Kerouac consulted a Freudian psychologist, even though Freud has been largely discredited by later scientists. Hence we are treated to a lot of Freudian clichés. The "Oedipus Complex" has always been a handy explanation of men who seem too attached to their mothers, and this author is pleased to apply it to Kerouac and his mother. Kerouac himself embellished the notion ("I always fall in love with my mother"), but I wonder why, then, he found it easy to leave her alone so frequently. There may be some Oedipal features in his relationship with her, but based on our discussions when she and I exchanged notes in his letters, another possibility seems to me equally valid: Jack was painfully self-conscious and extremely ill at ease in company. When sober, he was shy and gauche with strangers. Any public attention had to be met fortified with drink. With us he found a degree of unguarded expression, but he still must have felt some constraint in remembering his manners and keeping aware of others' needs. With his mother, on the other hand, he could relax completely and be truly himself any way he felt, knowing her love was unconditional.

When Jack's travels were interrupted by visits to us, he enjoyed our household because he could experience most of the pleasures of family life without being held responsible for it. Although he has often been criticized for being irresponsible, he, like nearly every other male

before the Sixties (even Allen Ginsberg!), expected to one day be head of household with a wife and children. In time Allen found he was not suited to that role, but Jack continued to dream of the kind of home he desired. We often discussed these dreams with him. He explained that he wasn't cut out to work at a steady job, stay in one place and support a family as Neal could (who also is universally condemned for being irresponsible), and he'd have to wait until he could earn enough from his writing. To us this conviction indicated a deeper sense of responsibility, especially when compared with attitudes of today. I learned firsthand how opinionated Jack was about child-rearing. He felt very strongly about the circumstances essential to being a good father and had fixed ideas of how parents should behave. He often made comments on our performance, both complimentary and advisory, but I could sense the strain at times when he disapproved of my methods. He was far too kind to criticize, but he might offer a suggestion.

Therefore, I was not surprised when he panicked once he was forced to accept that his daughter, Jan, by his second wife, Joan, was his child and not sired by Joan's lover. There was no way he could have handled the task of raising her without his strict criteria in place. Nor could he face the failure and the extra helping of guilt that failure would have produced in him. Everyone I have heard or read condemns Jack alone for the self-destructive life Jan led; not once has it been suggested that perhaps her mother might have had some influence on her as well—and Jan adored her mother. No, it's all Jack's fault that she made the wrong choices, merely because she didn't have him with her as a

Carolyn Cassady and Jack Kerouac with
Carolyn's daughters Cathy and Jami,
in front of the Cassady home on Russell Street,
San Francisco, 1952
CAROLYN CASSADY COLLECTION

father. Need I point out how many millions of boys and girls must live and grow without one? They don't all reach such depths.

In the early Fifties when Kerouac lived with us, we would never have imagined that Jack and Neal's friendship would be the impetus for some future "movement." Kerouac firmly believed in his own talent as a writer and envisioned himself in the near future as a respected literary figure, acclaimed by academia and the public alike. So did we all. He had to write, and in his case, to do so he had to be mobile and free—free of responsibilities that would tie him down until he became a success. He was somehow driven to record any and all of Life as he observed it, yet much of the time he remained semidetached, self-absorbed, in a world of his own. Many of the Beat heroes were vociferous in their damnation of society's faults (it's easy to see what's *wrong).* In contrast, Jack and Neal were less politically or socially oriented; they were deeply concerned with seeking an understanding of the *purpose* of life and of their lives in particular. Kerouac's appeal was his joyous celebration of Life in whatever form or condition he found it, giving us descriptions so intimate, intense and colorful, few others have matched his gift. These two men were unusual in their comprehension that we are not merely the flesh and blood of our physical form, that our minds are not just in our brain but in every cell, that there are levels of consciousness above the third dimension, even without the enhancement of drugs. Most of the other "Beats" had their feet firmly planted on the *terra firma* of this planet— Ginsberg was the most materialistic person I've known. He embraced a faith that teaches eternal life as did Jack, yet both were convinced that "death" was an end. Ginsberg was keen to insure a future on earth by seeking renown and accumulating wealth and property—far from Buddhist teachings—even if he shared a large portion. For example, he had no notion of the cause of his guru's downward plunge. He became skilled in the language and superficial precepts he chose to embrace as he impressed (and silenced) us with his chanting.

Kerouac probably had deeper instinctual insights into the message of Buddha; much of the appeal was in the imagery and the reflection of his own compassionate and tender feelings. One of the primary attractions was the concept that everything material was an illusion, temporary. Sensory desires cause suffering; they must be transcended. This much was compatible with his indoctrination into Catholic dogma, but the church did not explain it in such benevolent terms. He could thus understand his suffering, but he could not find the release from it. Such was the root of Neal's failure as well: Like Jack, he was raised a Catholic.

When very young children living grimy, deprived lives are ushered into a Catholic church, they must be stunned by the lofty interior, the color, the richness of fabric, paint and gilt, which is enhanced by light through stained glass and by candles, with all the graven images of saints, the bleeding miserable Jesus on the cross, the priests in their elaborate robes, the glorious but melancholy music. It isn't difficult to understand what a deep and lasting impression this must make on their inexperienced minds and imaginations. Add to this the constant grim pronouncements that they are miserable sinners no matter what they do. They must spend their lives in penitence, denying any pleasure of the senses if they wish to look forward to reward *after* they die. This, of course, had no relativity to the message of their "Lord," Jesus Christ, or the New Testament; it is sheer Churchianity, not true Christianity. In vain were the efforts Jesus made to demonstrate there is no death; the Church declared death meant utter annihilation of one's identity in a void.

Kerouac's constant question was "Why are we born if only to die?" or a refrain repeated over and over, "We're all gonna die." Yet, strangely enough, he often lapsed into memories of past lives, finding that possibility sensible. Further investigation of that heresy was too frightening in his safe cage of Catholicism, the bedrock beneath every attitude held by Jack and Neal, even if unconsciously.

From reading Jack's musings on Buddhism, *Some of the Dharma,* it dawned on me that Jack's major dilemma was this dichotomy of his nature. He was so keenly aware and appreciative of sensory delights, most of which he viewed with reverence (as did Jesus and Buddha), but Catholic threats made such feelings mortal sins. His guilt compounded, and he became more and more desperate to get away by himself. When he succeeded, he was tormented even more. We all told him he wasn't suited to solitude, and he never realized what he was trying to escape was simply temptation—the temptation of enjoying all of Life. The overpowering guilt is nurtured in childhood and grows ever stronger, as both men displayed. Eventually it killed them both. Although you can't fight one force with another force, both men tried their damnedest to conquer their excessive sensory desires. Naturally, the urges became stronger. In the end (and often in between), they would despair in their failure to achieve the control they sought and acted on the old saying "Got the name—play the game." In their last few years, they both gave up the struggle and masochistically exaggerated these actions that had caused their self-loathing, indulging in a kind of flagellation, compatible with that as prescribed by the Church.

The eager accusations today of their being homosexual are too inane to be considered seriously and can be easily explained otherwise. Even if the accusations were true, none of the accusers take into consideration the condition of the men at the times of the encounters they describe. These incidents in Jack's life only illustrate the extent of his fall; they do not make him a homosexual, even if it actually matters what he did in bed. There is nothing wrong in being homosexual, Jack and Neal didn't happen to be of that mold in spite of so-called evidence to the contrary.

Another fallacy being perpetrated is that Kerouac was cruel, merciless, manipulative, insensitive, uncaring, selfish. Such a totally misguided judgment tells us more about the judge than it does Kerouac. Anyone who reads his books or letters can't help but feel the compassion, the high ideals, the glorious plans. His nickname was "the Heart." He responded to most things emotionally at first and blurted out whatever thought that emotion created, depending on his mood of the moment. Everyone knows how often he maligned Allen Ginsberg. Allen understood that Jack didn't mean it personally or permanently and knew Jack's love for him was unconditional. I don't mean to whitewash Jack's conduct, some of which in his last years was disagreeable in the extreme. For one thing, Jack didn't have the kind of smarts to be manipulative had he wanted to—that was Neal's province, although never with malice.

In addition to reacting emotionally, Jack operated mostly from a right-brain focus. He was impractical and ungrounded in worldly affairs. Rather than thinking logically or analytically, his head was in the clouds. Anyone who reads his letters can see how many hundreds of "definite" plans he made, none of which came to fruition. Neal, on the other hand, was more left-brain oriented. Very logical, he loved analysis, always asking "Why?" "What is my purpose here?" "What is life all about?" He agreed with Emerson that all life is an exercise in cause and effect; Neal sought those causes with a passion, especially "what you sow, you reap." Neal wanted a faith to follow that would be practical and change him in his everyday living, not a vague future state of bliss. Neal's late confession was "I fully believe intellectually that there is a divine core in each of us; my tragedy is that I cannot *know* it and act upon it." This again can be put down to his Catholic conditioning and the enormous burden of guilt he carried. The Church had not told him that Jesus said "Ye are gods; anything I can do you can do better." Both men talked or wrote about their beliefs and endlessly proselytized, but most of it was an effort to convince themselves.

Kerouac did not possess Neal's exceptional personal magnetism that drew devotion from nearly everyone who knew him, even if some had felt abused by him; Jack's appeal came through his words on paper. Both sought higher insights; otherwise both would not have so eagerly grasped at a form of spiritual teachings for further enlightenment in their desperate search for "IT."

Those of us who admire or have been touched by Neal and/or Jack might try to appreciate the good in them, rather than condemn the failings for which they themselves already suffered so dreadfully. Although it is common to draw conclusions based on selective memory or information reinforcing what we want to believe, let's not make up our minds from ill-informed opinions based on hearsay, inaccuracies, distortions and a desire for personal gain.

PART III

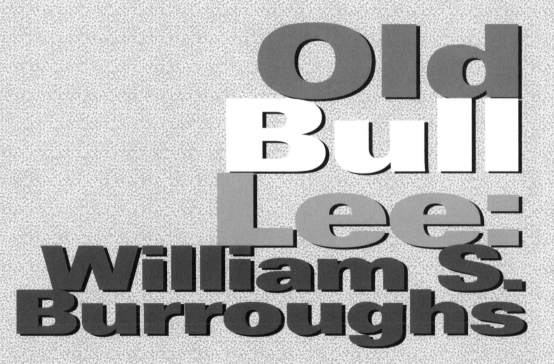

Old Bull Lee: William S. Burroughs

William S. Burroughs in front of the Burroughs Corporation executive headquarters, 1975

GERARD MALANGA

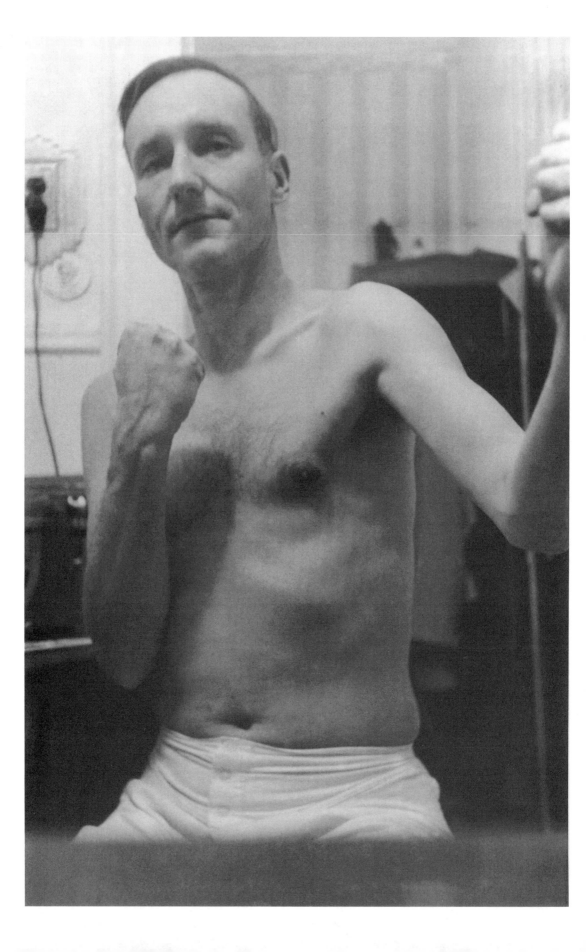

William S. Burroughs (1914-1997)

BY LEWIS MacADAMS

[ROLLING STONE 769, September 18, 1997]

O F ALL THE BEAT GENERATION writers, William S. Burroughs, who died on August 2, 1997, at the age of eighty-three, was the most dangerous. Not only was he the dark tutor of the young Allen Ginsberg and Jack Kerouac, but his entire life's work maintained a sustained, vitriolic—and hilarious—attack on the values held dear by mainstream society. In his trademark suit and snap-brim fedora, he was anarchy's double agent, an implacable enemy of conformity and of all agencies of control—from governments to opiates.

The publication of his novel *Naked Lunch* in the United States, 1962, and the ensuing obscenity trial led to a landmark court victory in the battle to end censorship in this country. In 1973, Burroughs returned to the United States after two decades of self-imposed exile and continued in his renegade's role. He wrote books (*Nova Express, Exterminator!*), acted in movies (*Drugstore Cowboy, My Own Private Idaho*) and created his riotously deadpan stage presence in readings and performances. He collaborated with U2, Kurt Cobain and Tom Waits. Burroughs came to embody a Luciferian spirit to generations of musicians, from Lou Reed to David Bowie to Patti Smith to Trent Reznor. Bands like Steely Dan and the Soft Machine named themselves after his images. Though in his later years he lived a mostly quiet life with his three cats in a small house in Lawrence, Kansas, Burroughs's presence at a public event, in a music video, even a Nike

William Burroughs in New York City, 1953
ALLEN GINSBERG

ad, stamped it with genuine and undeniable hipness.

William Burroughs was born on February 5, 1914, into a respectable St. Louis family. Although much has been made of the fact that his paternal grandfather was the inventor of the first accurate adding machine, by 1929 the family had sold all of its stock in the Burroughs Adding Machine Corporation, and young Bill grew up in a slightly straitened upper-middle-class existence. His parents made ends meet by running a genteel suburban gift shop called Cobblestone Gardens.

Burroughs was not a popular child. "That boy smells like a sheep-killin' dog," a parent of one of his childhood friends said of him. At age eight, Burroughs wrote his first work, a ten-page opus called *Autobiography of a Wolf.* "You mean *biography*, don't you?" his family suggested. No, Burroughs insisted. Burroughs's older brother, Mort, was the "good" son. He went to Princeton, became an architect and spent his entire career at General Electric. William was bred to a harder calling. He dropped out of Los Alamos Ranch school just two months before graduation, depressed over being rejected by a boy in his class with whom he was infatuated. He managed, though, to get himself admitted to Harvard and graduate in 1936 without honors—known principally among his peers for the live ferret he kept in his room.

For the next fifteen years, Burroughs's life seemed to unravel as he drifted slowly downhill, a washout from his class and from his sex. He studied psychiatry at a Viennese medical school and took a series of dead-end jobs. He moved to

Chicago at the beginning of 1939 to attend a series of lectures by Count Alfred Korzybski, the author of *The Theory of General Semantics*, a work that takes issue with Aristotelian notions of duality. Burroughs worked as an exterminator, lived in a boardinghouse on the near North Side, hung out with lowlifes and masterminded great crimes in his imagination. In 1942 he was drafted into the army but was quickly rejected when it came to light that he'd spent a month in New York's Bellevue and Payne-Whitney hospitals after slicing the last joint off the little finger of his left hand to impress a wayward boyfriend.

In the summer of 1943, Burroughs moved to New York, where a friend from St. Louis, Lucien Carr, had enrolled at Columbia. It was Carr who introduced him to future Beat writers Jack Kerouac and Allen Ginsberg. In the summer of 1945, the three moved into an apartment at 419 West 115th Street, along with Kerouac's girlfriend, Edie Parker, and Joan Vollmer, a suburban rebel from upstate New York who would become Burroughs's common-law wife and with whom he would eventually have a son, William Burroughs II.

One cold January night in 1946, Burroughs, hoping to unload a sawed-off shotgun and a batch of stolen morphine Syrettes, knocked at the door of a railroad apartment with yellow-and-black walls under the Manhattan Bridge. The late Herbert Huncke, junkie, thief and mesmerizing raconteur, answered, and the Beat Generation was born. Burroughs introduced Ginsberg and Kerouac to Huncke, Times Square, heroin and Benzedrine. Burroughs shepherded the young men on a tour of the dark side, picking up a fifteen-year addiction to heroin, a habit so powerful that in 1954 he sold his typewriter in London and wrote in longhand.

Burroughs wrote thirteen novels, the best known of which is one of his earlier works, *Naked Lunch*. Throughout his career he remained

an adamant outsider, but he lived long enough to garner literature's most coveted accolades, to hear himself praised by Norman Mailer as "the only American novelist living today who may conceivably be possessed by genius." In 1983, Burroughs was inducted into the American Academy of Arts and Letters, an honor he accepted with characteristic suspicion. In his biography of Burroughs, *Literary Outlaw*, author Ted Morgan recorded Burroughs's reaction: "Twenty years ago, they were saying I belonged in jail. Now they're saying I belong in their club. I didn't listen to them then, and I don't listen to them now."

Besides the singularity of his vision, what is thrilling about Burroughs's work is his certainty in the power of language. "I do definitely mean what I say to be taken literally, yes," Burroughs told an interviewer in 1970, "to make people aware of the true criminality of our times, to wise up the marks." His words, he wrote, were weapons "against those who are bent—by stupidity or design—on blowing up this planet."

One day in 1951, Burroughs was in an apartment in Mexico City, drinking whiskey with Joan Vollmer and several other American expatriates while waiting for a man to whom he was hoping to sell a used handgun. Seemingly out of the blue, Burroughs announced to Vollmer that it was time for their "William Tell act." As he took the .380 automatic out of his overnight bag, she balanced her glass of gin and *limonada* on her head, giggling, according to one party guest: "I can't watch this—you know I can't stand the sight of blood." The gun shot low, and she was killed instantly. Not until 1984, in the preface to his novel *Queer*, was Burroughs able to write directly about the incident. Vollmer's death, he explained, "brought me in contact with the invader, the Ugly Spirit, and maneuvered me into a lifelong struggle, in which I have had no choice except to write my way out."

His family bought his way out of prison, and he spent the next twenty-two years as an expatriate. It's no coincidence that his breakthrough work, *Naked Lunch*, was typed in Tangier, an international colony governed, in effect by no one—a place he called Interzone. "To speak is to lie," he wrote. "To live is to collaborate." With his longtime creative partner, Brion Gysin, he discovered a technique for forging new connections: the cut-up method, which involved the arbitrary recombination of pieces of syntax. Burroughs's goal in using cut-ups was never anything less than a "breakthrough in the gray room," he said, a rethinking of the human mind.

Not long after returning to this country from London, in 1973, Burroughs met James Grauerholz. At first a lover, Grauerholz soon became Burroughs's manager and helped to set the writer on a course that brought him not only fame but also a decent income. Burroughs, with Grauerholz's guidance, embarked on a series of reading tours, flogging his vitriol and his outrageous characters such as *Naked Lunch*'s mad surgeon,

Dr. Benway, and the gay gunslinger Kim Carsons, from *The Place of Dead Roads* and *The Western Lands*, to a growing public. The drawling, acerbic humor that had always been a part of Burroughs's work started to seep into the mainstream. By 1981, Lauren Hutton would introduce Burroughs to millions of *Saturday Night Live* viewers as America's greatest living writer. His genius had begun to shape the culture, to influence people who had never read a single page of his work.

In his later years, in movies like Gus Van Sant's *Drugstore Cowboy*, Burroughs came to represent the man who called bullshit on the culture because, as he wrote, he "didn't want to be caught short in a gray-flannel suit when the shit-house went up." In *What Happened to Kerouac?*, a film I codirected in 1989, Burroughs approvingly quotes Kerouac: "I am a spy in someone else's body, and all my credentials—from my birth certificate to everything I've written—is just completely unreal." From that point of view, Burroughs himself may well have been his own most inspiring creation.

Visiting with William Burroughs in Mexico, 1950

BY LIZA WILLIAMS

THE HOUSE WAS PALE, OR WHITE, or had been white, it crouched in the middle of the street, crouched because the top was bigger than the bottom, the heavy red tile lay over the roof, lay like a shawl over the roof, over the top of the house with its windows shaded, then the walls sliced inwards and the bottom was narrow, dark, the door hidden behind a bush, the steps cracked. We rang the bell, waited, rang again, waited. We could hear steps, the door opened a little bit, letting out a slice of light, *sí?* The voice was hesitant, the face, the part of face we could see, dark eyes moist and brown, questions unspoken in the voice, *sí?* Is this the home of Mr. Burroughs? I asked . . . silence, then, *sí,* said the voice and shut the door. We waited, Lucien laughed, shit he said, Mexico, he said, and started to rap on the door. Stop that! said a voice from the inside of the house, fuck off said the voice, crap, said the voice, and we could hear feet coming down steps, who is it the voice said, for Christsake Carmelita who is it. The door opened again and the small brown face looked at us. Who? It's Lucien, I said. The door shut and the girl shouted inside the house, Lushen. Now we could hear the change in the steps of the man inside, a hurrying sound, a loud sound as he hauled open the door, came out suddenly and almost knocking me over grabbed at Lucien, Oh for Christsake he said, shook him, grabbed his arm, dragging him into the house, leaving me to follow holding our sleeping bags under both arms.

Joan Joan, it's Lucien the man was yelling upward, up the stairs which curved out of sight, he was standing at a table in the middle of the room pouring transparent liquid into glasses, Carmelita he said, between calling to the woman above, make food. The girl was young and silent, she hesitated everywhere, hesitated to look at me, hesitated over the stove, hesitated over a box of meat on the sink, hesitated to turn to move, to be.

That's Lizzie, Lucien said, we are in love, he didn't turn toward me, he might have been speaking about the table in front of him. Hello the man said, glad you could come, they both laughed at that, the man grabbing Lucien's arm again, peering at him, looking into his eyes, examining him, still calling out to the invisible woman above, it's Lucien he yelled, hey Joan it's Lucien. There was a funny smell in the room, a sweet cloudy smell, a strange smell I didn't know but it wasn't completely strange, I had smelled it before somewhere, or caught the edge of its flavor, somewhere. I kept looking toward the stairs, where any minute I expected to see the woman who would be called Joan, and who would, perhaps be glad to see me, as women are to other women, and would ask me if I was tired and wanted to wash or have some food and show me where we would sleep and say how fatiguing travel was. Two small children came down the stairs, edged down the stairs, crept down the stairs, sliding their bodies against the wall, softly stepping, not saying anything. The man saw them, Carmelita, for fucksake get the kids out of there, the girl stopped in her slow movements at the sink, put down the bowl she had been stirring and went to the children still without a sound, and took them up the stairs, silently all three of them, up the stairs slowly, silently, up into the whatever there was where, because of his insistent calling, a woman, a woman who must after all be their mother, was doing, or at least present, though silent, perhaps crouching just beyond the turning of the stairs, listening, sensing us below, waiting for her, waiting for her to come down and do . . . what.

I'm tired, I said to Lucien, I don't want a drink, I want to go to bed. She's tired he said to the man, she doesn't want a drink, she wants to go to bed. She's tired the man yelled, Hey Joan, she's tired, she doesn't want a drink, she wants to go to bed. Oh, said the man, after we all waited for some answer from the silence above, oh, well, I guess you must be tired, I suppose I can show you where you can sleep can't I, but he stood at the table, drinking from the pale blue glass, rubbing his fingers over the grease spots on the wood, pushing remains of food on plates with a spoon, making patterns in the dried beans. That's okay, I said after a while, how long, a while in the stillness with Lucien looking at the wall and the man moving only his long thin finger through the debris, it's okay, I can find a place, don't trouble yourself.

I could hear myself talking, sounding like a demented Emily Post in a vacuum, don't trouble yourself, my voice shouted back at me, don't trouble yourself? Whose self, which people, who are they, where are we, is that the man, the man we have come to see, hurrying over mountains like insane goats, hurtling through heat, swinging across space, blinded by dust and fatigue? He was tall, thin, had rivers and islands of skin on his face and eyes that shone in the day like pebbles, he had lank hair that clung to his head strand by strand, he was so thin he was made of paper, he was so tall that he walked doubled even in the forest, he was so so loving that he couldn't stop touching Lucien's arm. And Lucien, Lucien had turned to silk, to Victorian elegance, shrouded beauty, Lucien stood on the platform and performed magic tricks, and now ladies and gentlemen, presenting the marvelous beauty of Lucien and he

made himself visible, turned his fine head on his fine neck, let the lights shine from his eyes. I went up the stairs by myself, up the stairs to the brightly lighted hall where three closed doors blocked out whatever there would be.

The light woke me, the bars of sun across the floor, and finally across my face, I opened my eyes to the blank walls and the piles of paper and the shutter still swung half to on its pin. Lucien slept, he snored, he winced, he moved his hand across the bed, across his body, he turned, the shirt catching under him, pulling the row of buttons askew, wrinkles slid toward the sides, the collar sagged against his shoulder, the top button of his trousers was undone and the zipper halfway down, a piece of white cotton underpants was caught by the nickel teeth. I got up, climbing out of the bag, moving over Lucien, hoping he would waken, not wanting him to know I had wakened him, not wanting to bear the burden of waking him for myself. He didn't open his eyes, lids almost transparent, lashes curved against the skin, over the grayish smudge, over the bone of the cheek, the lips opened once, for a moment, and I could see a fleck of tobacco on his tooth, but the lips shut again, it was a magic show.

I went down the red stairs to find food and found Carmelita sitting by the radio, sitting with her ear close to the woven cloth of the speaker, her brown face pressing its curves against the brown wood curves of the radio, her hands patting her lap where a picture love-story magazine lay open. She stood up when she saw me—though I smiled, said—don't it's okay, smiled and tapped my foot to the music which I could not really hear. Sometime later Lucien got up, Bill got up, the children were gone, school? I didn't ask, the woman named Joan didn't come downstairs, but the drifting sweet smell filled the house again.

And then in the evening, after a meal, Carmelita placing bowls of food on the table, Lucien staring into his tequila glass, turning it between his hands, turning it the way English gentlemen turn snifters of brandy, slowly, Bill staring out the window at the houses across the street, raising his pistol, wow, zip pop rat tat tat. Shot that hole, he said, pointing to the ceiling, shot clear through the ceiling. The rug above, the roof—zip, crash, thud, he said, love to shoot, it scares Joan he said (was that why she stayed in their room?) I never miss.

Then Joan, sitting on a chair, receiving us into her silence. I stand there, just inside her bedroom door, hello. Yes, she said, that's the proper word. Her children, small and silent standing in front of her, watching her delicate maneuverings with a match and a teaspoon of white powder, watching her heat it, it melt to liquid, watching her pour it into the syringe, watching her examine her arm (where like freckles the puncture marks danced on her skin), watching her push the needle in, watching the fluid join her body, watching her pull the needle out, watching the bubble of blood rise from the puncture. Lick it, she said to her son, lick it, it tastes just like roast beef.

We left the house, two days later, in the middle of the afternoon, with Bill standing in the kitchen waving his gun at us, farewell he said, blat blat, and Carmelita just behind him silently watching us go, and the children clinging to the stairs, against the wall, and upstairs, in the white sweetness, Joan, silent in her room, with the door closed.

The 1972 ROLLING STONE Interview:
William S. Burroughs

BY ROBERT PALMER

[ROLLING STONE 108, May 11, 1972]

William Burroughs lives in a sparsely furnished flat near Piccadilly, in London. The neighborhood is comfortable, but Burroughs works and lives with a minimum of encumbrances: typewriter, table, plain chairs, bed, books, a cassette machine. Brion Gysin, Burroughs's friend and long-time collaborator, lives upstairs in surroundings that include Moroccan rugs, a few of Brion's paintings of Marrakesh and the desert, a stereo, two Uhers and an extensive library of sounds that Brion recorded in Morocco. It's a quiet place for a man who has made some of the biggest waves in contemporary literature: from the early auto-biographical 'Junky' through the influential 'Naked Lunch' and early experimentation with psychedelics, lightshows and the surreal cut-up writing technique.

The interview took place in Brion's flat, which he recently occupied after an extended residence in Tangier. Tapes of trance music, Fifties rock & roll, Sun Ra and Coltrane, furnished by Brion, [writer] Charlie Gillett and myself played in the background, and various young people, many of whom Burroughs met while teaching at the University of the New World in Switzerland, were in and out. The picture of Burroughs and Gysin with the Dreamachine [pages 184–5] was taken at the home of Ian Sommerville, their friend since the days of the Beat Hotel in Paris.

The first question I asked Burroughs concerned infrasound, air vibrations that oscillate at less than ten Hertz, or ten vibrations a second, below the range of human hearing. Professor Vladimir Gavreau of Marseilles has developed and patented a "Death Ray" using these inaudible sounds, but Burroughs has suggested other uses for them. He gave me, as explanation, a clipping from the 'National Observer'; he had underlined the following passages:

"… the team built a giant whistle, hooked to a compressed air hose. Then they turned on the air."

" 'That first test nearly cost us our lives,' Professor Gavreau says. 'Luckily, we were able to turn it off fast. All of us were sick for hours. Everything in us was vibrating—stomach, heart, lungs. All the people in the other laboratories were sick too.' "

You've mentioned the possibility of using this infrasound in music. Could you expand on that?

The point is that here it has been developed as a weapon. Now there are possibilities, say at the borderline of infrasound, experimenting with very slow sounds, that you could produce rhythmic vibrations that would not necessarily be fatal or unpleasant; they might be quite the contrary. In other words, it would be another step toward producing—as all music, all writing, all art is really attempting to do—is to produce very definite psycho-physiological effects in the audience, reader, viewer, as the case may be. Of course they've never been completely successful in that. If they had, they would have taken over years ago. But if they were successful, presumably you could kill a whole Shea Stadium full of people in their seats.

There's been a great deal of work done

recently in automatic shaping and brain waves—people now being able to reproduce brain waves and to learn to control heartbeats, etc. That is, people can now learn in ten hours what it takes a yogi twenty years to learn, if they want to. They have a battery now that they can plug people into which records brain waves, blood pressure, heart beat, resistance, tension, etc. As far as I know, no experiments have been done along these lines while listening to certain music to see what the actual physiological and psychological correlates of that music are and what happens when someone listens to it.

So I wanted to suggest the possibility of very precise musical experiments.

How would that relate to Moroccan music? How precise do you think Moroccan trance music is at producing definite states?

Certainly Brion knows a good deal more about that than I do, but I would suggest the same experiments be carried out. If you knew what a state of trance was, what the brain waves, the blood pressure, heart beat and so forth was, then you'd have some idea as to how to go about producing it, and also you'd know when you are producing it and when you're getting close.

What about your experiments with projections?

I've said quite a lot about that in *The Job*. Antony Balch and I did an experiment with his face projected onto mine and mine onto his. Now if your face is projected onto someone else's in color, it looks like the other person. You can't tell the difference; it's a real mask of light. Brion was the first to do this at the rue Dragon in Paris, and no one would believe how it was done. They thought it was all a film.

Jan Herman was here with his little video camera outfit and we did quite a precise experiment, which was: Antony brought up the Bill and

William Burroughs in London, 1972
CHARLES GATEWOOD

Tony film, I sat there, and he projected it onto my face, which was rephotographed on the video camera, but that faded in and out so that it would be that face, then fade back to the now face, so that you got a real-time section. We wanted to project it onto the television screen from the camera, but we couldn't because the cycles were different; Antony and Jan Herman were fooling around and they managed to fuck up the television. But even seeing it on a little view screen, it was something quite extraordinary.

Another experiment that Antony and I did was to take the two faces and alternate them twenty-four frames per second, but it's such a hassle to cut those and resplice them, even to put one minute of alternations of twenty-four frames per second on a screen, but it is quite extraordinary. An experiment I always wanted to make was to record and photograph very friendly and very unfriendly faces and words and then alternate them twenty-four frames per second. That should have quite an upsetting effect, I think; you don't know until you actually do it.

What about your story in 'The Job' about the Buful Peoples projecting baby faces on their audiences and making them run out and shit in the streets? Is that your idea of what the effects of such an experiment might be?

They could be. It's a question of getting a sufficient degree of precision. If I really knew how to write, I could write something that someone would read and it would kill them. The same way with music, or any effect you want could be produced if you were precise enough in your knowledge or technique.

How would that work with writing?

Exactly the same way. What is a writer trying to do? He's trying to reproduce in the reader's mind a certain experience, and if he were completely successful in that, the reproduction of the experience would be complete. Perhaps fortunately, they're not that successful.

Can words actually be that successful?

I think so. I think words possibly above all.

Back to music: Do you feel that a pop group's dependence on costly equipment and establishment media makes it difficult for these groups to disseminate an antiestablishment, anticontrol message?

I think the dividing line between establishment and nonestablishment is breaking down. People tend to say that if an underground paper succeeds and makes money, that it is now part of the establishment, or if pop singers make a lot of money and their records make a great deal of money for big companies that they are now part of the establishment, but the underground or any movement is not going to succeed by not succeeding. If you publish an underground paper that nobody reads or produce music that nobody listens to, there's no point. And if people do read your paper or listen to your music, then you are subject to make money.

Do you think the force and amplitude of rock can make it a force for liberation, regardless of the lyric content?

I would say so, very definitely. And potentially a tremendous force, in view of the experiments that I have suggested.

Do you think a group that's operating its own record company has a freer hand than a group that must operate through a conglomerate?

I do not know enough about the music business to answer that question, but a similar question: Do you think that writers would have more effect if they published their own work? Definitely no. Because the publisher is set up to distribute just as the record company is. If you're going to try to do all that yourself—for one thing it's going to take up all your time, and you're not going to do it as well.

The media are really accessible to everyone. People talk about establishment media, but the establishment itself would like to suppress the media altogether. There was a program on television the other night where they came right out and said that showing wars and riots on television can produce wars and riots. There's never been a comparable situation, where whatever is happening anywhere people can switch on their televisions and see it. I recall in Chicago, the riot pictures were shown in the convention hall live as they were happening, and then all sorts of similar incidents broke out in the convention halls. Cops blackjacked delegates . . .

What about the many references to popular songs in your books, especially some of the sequences in 'The Soft Machine' that are made up of song titles and lines?

In writing, I see it as a whole set. It's got a script, it's got pictures, and it has a good soundtrack. And very often the soundtrack is musical. I've used quite a bit of these techniques actually—that is, a sentence to be sung to a certain tune.

Do remembered tunes call up stronger and more specific associations than images that aren't related to tunes?

Very definitely, yes. That's what tunes are all about. I think it's pretty well established pragmatically that music is more precise in evoking a scene, particularly a past scene, than, shall we say, a neutral soundtrack of words. But I notice that they are tending, at least in the Jajouka record [*Brian Jones Presents the Pipes of Pan at Jajouka*], toward deliberately using some of the background noise: shouts, dogs barking in Joujouka, the chauffeur snoring in another reference. That's something I think that has to be done with a very precise hand. In practice, the music is played on a location so that there will be background noise as well.

Would you like eventually to put out books with accompanying records? Having the musical and sound references along with the writing?

I had not thought of that. I think that is a very brilliant idea, because people have put out books with a record. I even did that, but the record simply consisted of a spoken tape of the book, which in this case was a short book. But to me, spoken tapes, you can just take so much. It's a different operation than reading. The idea of spoken books is completely unworkable. But I hadn't thought of a soundtrack, which could actually be quite carefully prepared, have some of the dialogue, etc., but be principally musical. Or some of the sound effects that people haven't heard, for example, like howler monkeys, the noise that howler monkeys make. It's like wind in the trees, but not quite, because there's nothing quite like it. And listening to it for a few seconds is much more precise than talking about it.

You wrote in 'The Job,' "It is now possible to decondition man from the whole punishment–reward cycle."

I simply mean that if we had sufficient knowledge we could—any neurosis, any hangup resulting from past conditioning must express itself in actual physiological reaction patterns. Now recent experiments have indicated the possibility of simply reprogramming reaction patterns, as you would reprogram a computer. Scientists have attached an ape's brain to a computer, so that the electrical impulses from the ape's brain were giving orders to the computer—that is, setting programs which could then be fed back the other way. Now undoubtedly they could get to the point of simply reprogramming, and they might be able to do that in a matter of hours. We don't know, because it has never occurred in history, what a completely deconditioned human being would look like, or act like.

What about the giant black centipede the deanxietized man turned into in 'Naked Lunch'?

I have no reason to think that the result would be . . . of that nature. [*Laughter*] And if it is, what the hell, I mean we're all black centipedes at heart, so why worry about it.

You've talked about hieroglyphic or picture writing. Do you feel that we're living out the end of the age of literacy, that people are going to be reading more and more picture books?

Well, that is not at all certain, because the actual picture magazines are all going out of business—*Life, Newsweek* and all of them. There are ideas that I had which have not been borne out. Like when I said in the Academy Series, "recommend that the daily press be discontinued." Remember that the Academy Series was all predicated as occurring in 1899, and it was my feeling that if certain measures had been taken then, the present mess might have been avoided, that being an arbitrary date when it might have been possible. But that is 1899, and this is 1972. I would certainly not recommend it now.

You're working on a comic book?

Yes. It is a comic book in that it has whole sequences of action in pictures. But there are also about sixty pages of text, so it's something between a comic book and an illustrated book.

Malcolm MacNeil is doing the artwork. It is most closely similar to the actual format of the Mayan Codices, which was an early comic book. There'll be pictures in the Codices, and sometimes there'll be three pages of text in writing that we can't read. We can read some of it, and we can read the dates. A great deal of it was dates. The story concerns someone who has discovered the control secrets of the Mayan books.

Is the fact that Mayan books were a control system, able to control the people very precisely by having the calendar dates and knowing what stimuli were going to be applied on any one day, your main interest in the Mayan civilization?

Yes. It was a control system that required no police, working on psychological controls. The priests were only about 1 percent of the population. Priests and artisans would certainly not come out to more than 5 percent. And how did they keep them working?

A good question.

Yes, come to think about it. [*Laughter*]

You don't feel, as McLuhan does, that print is on the way out?

Well, no. What does he think is going to take its place? We know that physics and mathematics have whole nonverbal communication systems.

Apparently he thought electronic media, spoken words and pictures were going to take the place of print.

Well, you still have the problem of the actual prose. Now I see that in this book I'm doing with Malcolm, there are lots of sections which go just like film. But the text is really still essential. There are sixty pages of text; we're already having problems with translating that into images—not the problem that we can't do it, but the problem that it would take three hundred pages to do it all. If we took every sentence and translated it into pictures, we'd have a huge book that would be way out of our budget. And there are things really that there's no point in translating into pictures, since they are much clearer in prose. There's another point where a page of prose can't do what a picture can.

Well, when you said, "Rub out the word," was that another way of saying, "Learn to use words instead of being used by them"?

That's one I will have to think about, because I've been thinking about a whole field theory of words. I don't think when I said that I had any clear idea as to what it would involve, or even what words were. I have a much clearer idea now as to what would be involved, but it's something pretty drastic. Of course it was Brion's suggestion originally ... Let's say you would have to first have some idea of what the word is and how it operates.

I predicate that the word is an actual virus, and a virus that has achieved equilibrium with the host and therefore is not recognized as a virus. I have a number of technical books on that subject, and there are other viruses that have achieved this. That is, they replicate themselves within the cells but they don't harm the cells.

Are you thinking of something like the proliferation of responses to Mailer's one article about Women's Lib?

Not precisely. I mean that a phrase can replicate itself and jump all over the world. It usually is a pretty simple formula. An example: Years ago I found out that a cure for the common cold was Vitamin A in massive doses. I've used it for years, and it definitely does work. Well, someone seems to have a vested interest in the common cold, because Vitamin A was completely ignored and they started this Vitamin C bit. And Vitamin C is absolutely worthless for a cold. Now time and time again I've told people about Vitamin A and they immediately say, in exactly the same tone, "You mean Vitamin C." No, I don't mean Vitamin C, I mean Vitamin A. I got exactly the same tone of voice from a number of people that I spoke to about this Vitamin A. It's a turn-off on Vitamin A.

Do you have any information on the introduction of weight heroin into Harlem and into the ghettos during the Forties, which seems to have been the beginning of the current problem?

I don't. You see, I was there in the late Forties and early Fifties, and the agents then were just beginning to bother addicts. Before that they'd been more interested in pushers.

Why did they start bothering addicts rather than pushers?

In order to spread it. That kept the pushers continually looking for new markets.

Do you see that as a very conscious attempt to spread it for certain, say political ends, or as a tendency of bureaucracies to perpetuate themselves?

Both. The tendency of bureaucracies is to increase personnel, of course. If you've got one person who isn't doing anything, then he gets five or six subordinates in, and so it goes. They tend to make themselves necessary.

Well, they're really cracking down on grass and psychedelics now, and causing lots of kids to turn to downers. They called last year the year of the downers, and none of my friends who used to take acid, say, once or twice a week, have had any in the last year and a half.

Brion Gysin: Did you get uncomfortable physical side effects from acid?

No. Some uncomfortable psychological effects occasionally, but never a bad trip or anything like that.

Well, I had two bad trips, and I would never touch it again. So really my considerations on acid are pretty personal. I think it's horrible stuff.

Why do you think it's horrible stuff?

So far as I'm concerned, it has absolutely nightmare reactions—symptoms of an extreme and depressing nature. I felt as if I was on fire.

Do you think it can have value for some people?

It seems to, but then it's very dubious, because lots of people that take it all the time, *they* think they're benefiting, but I don't, as an observer.

Gysin: Oh, but I think everybody should have taken it at least once. I don't think that anybody has to take it more, in fact. Essentially very square people have taken it just once, and it's made an astounding difference in their lives and their outlook.

Burroughs: But couldn't they have done the same with majoun [a preparation of hashish]?

Gysin: I don't think so. It doesn't take you quite as far out.

Burroughs: Not quite as far, but at least there I'm in an area that I can control . . .

Gysin: No, but the experience is to get into an area that you can't control and realize that you can go there and come back again.

Burroughs: I find both mescaline and yage, which has never been circulated, though it could be—it's just a question of chemical analysis—much more interesting. Peyote made me terribly sick, so sick I couldn't get enjoyment out of it.

Of the drugs people take to get high—say, barbiturates, speed, cannabis, psychedelics—which ones do you think have some value?

Cannabis, I think, has the most value.

Amphetamines, absolutely none. Barbiturates, absolutely none. I just can't see anything that could possibly result from either barbiturates or amphetamines that could be considered desirable from any point of view.

How about for going to sleep?

The worst thing possible, because all you're doing is further interfering with the cycle of sleep and waking.

Do you think cannabis has any effect on sleep or keeping you awake?

No, the only result that I have noticed from cannabis is that if you smoke a lot of cannabis, you won't dream as much. Now there it's quite obvious that you're doing your dreaming while you're awake, and therefore you don't dream as much while you're asleep. Now if I've been smoking a lot of cannabis and not dreaming, and then I suddenly don't have any cannabis, I'll have very vivid dreams every night.

Let's delve into the past a little. Where and what was the "Beat Hotel"?

Gysin: The Beat Hotel was in Paris at 9 rue Gît-le-Coeur, just off the Place Saint Michel in the Latin Quarter. For a lot of young people in Paris it was more than a home. That's where the Beat scene in Paris was born. A Dutch painter turned Allen Ginsberg onto it in 1956, I am told. I didn't get there myself until 1958 when I ran into Burroughs on the street, and he told me he lived in Room 15.

The hotel was run by a wonderful Frenchwoman named Madame Rachou, who might have made herself rich and famous if she had laid away just a few of the manuscripts of what was written under her roof or collected some of the pictures painted in her hotel. She was a funny mixture of peasant shrewdness and hardness along with the most disinterested generosity. She would do anything to help anyone just coming out of jail, no matter who they were or what they had been in for. She had her own ideas about who she wanted in her so-called hotel and some people waited forever, buying drinks at her little zinc-covered bar. I remember her telling an American that there would be a room ready in ten minutes. From behind her bar, she could see the municipal undertakers going up the stairs to take out a poor old French pauper who'd died in his rent-controlled room. Americans pay more, even beatniks. On the other hand, the better-off anyone looked, the more likely she was to turn them away, and she certainly preferred young people—even troublesome young people—to old.

Were you working on 'Naked Lunch' at that time?

I wasn't doing all that much at that time, actually. Girodias of Olympia Press, the eventual publishers, had turned the manuscript down the first time, around two years before that, and I just wasn't doing that much work.

Had you written 'Naked Lunch' in Tangier, then?

Right.

Gysin: In a hotel we called the Villa Delirium, which was another great spot, near the beach in Tangier. It had a garden and . . .

Burroughs: Another memorable Madame . . .

Gysin: The lady from

Saigon. The number of people who revolved through those two hotels is really remarkable. All the Beats . . .

Burroughs: . . . and so many people who have really gone places since then. That young film-maker, for example . . .

Gysin: Oh, Melvin Van Peebles.

William Burroughs (right)
and Brion Gysin with the
Dreamachine, London, 1972
CHARLES GATEWOOD

Burroughs: Terry Southern, Mason Hoffenberg . . .

Gysin: The list is really endless. An enormous number of musicians. The place was always bubbling with music, whether being produced on instruments or being played on tapes or records. Mezzrow's son lived there . . . Mezz Mezzrow!

My God, he was a fantastic cat. He was around the hotel quite a lot. I remembered one day in winter. It was very, very cold, and I opened the door, and here was this big, fat black woman complaining about something. She really put on such a scene that I just told her, "I don't know, I don't know" and I slammed the door, and she went banging on the next door, which was Gregory Corso's, across the hall. And I think it was Gregory who cracked up and said, "But Mezz, what are you doing?" The old man had got himself into drag, put some kind of makeup on his face and he went through the entire hotel until somebody said, "What is that you're doing?"

Was it during this time that you discovered the cut-up technique?

Gysin: I had a big table on which I worked very often with a Stanley blade, and I had cut up a number of newspapers accidentally. They had been underneath something else that I was cutting. The pieces sort of fell together, and I started matching them up, and I thought, Wo-o-o-ow, it's really very funny. And I took some of them and arranged them in a pattern which was visually pleasing to me and then typed up the results, and I have never laughed so heartily in my entire life.

The first time around,

doing your own cut-ups and seeing the results, there's a sort of feeling of hilarity.... But it doesn't happen again. It's a oner, a single sensation that happens just that one first time, it seems to me. But I was really shocked by that. And it had exactly the same effect on him. But I must say that I had thought of it as a rather superior amusement, and was very impressed by William's immediate recognition that here was something extremely important to him, that he could put to use right away, and did.

With great excitement we put together a book, and the title was really pulled right out of the air. It seems to me we were standing in the doorway to my Room 25 when someone said, "Hurry, hurry, there's only minutes to go!" and I said wow, that's the title obviously.

What was it you saw in the cut-ups initially, after you stopped laughing?

Well, I saw the possibility of permutations, particularly of images, which is the area in which it has worked best over a period of time. A book of Rimbaud's poetry or any extremely visual text will cut up and give you new combinations that are quite valid new images. In other words, you are drawing a whole series of images out of this page of text.

Does this technique relate to Twentieth-Century painting?

Gysin: A whole lot. Look at it like this: Twentieth-Century painting ceased being representational, gave up storytelling and became abstract. Today, only squares can stand in front of a work of art whining: "But what does it *mean*?" Confronted with a piece of writing, that is the only question that readers still do ask. Perhaps there could be abstract literature, as abstract painting. Why not? We wanted to see.

We began to find out a whole lot of things about the real nature of words and writing when we began to cut them up. What are words and what are they doing? Where are they going? The cut-up method treats words as the painter treats

his paint, raw material with rules and reasons of its own. Representational painters fucked over their paint until they made it tell a tale. Abstract painters found that the real hero of the picture is the paint. Painters and writers of the kind I respect want to be heroes, challenging fate in their lives and in their art. What is fate? Fate is written: "*Mektoub*," in the Arab world, where art has always been nothing but abstract. "*Mektoub*" means "It is written." So, . . . if you want to challenge and change fate . . . cut up the words. Make them make a new world.

Within weeks of stumbling on the cut-ups, I came across the Divine Tautology in Huxley's *Heaven and Hell*. I am that I am. I took a long look at it and found that the design of the phrase did not please me at all. I decided to make it more symmetrical by displacing the words. The biggest block was that, so I decided to leave it in the middle. My first move was to put at each end the word I. It read: I am that I am I. That sounded more like a question. What had been one of the most affirmative statements of all time had become a question, and a poignant one, simply by changing the word-order around.

As I began to run through some of the other one hundred and twenty simple permutations of these five words, I heard the words running away by themselves. That I am I am, am I that I am? Et cetera. They went on asking and answering themselves like the links of a chain, jingling against each other as they fell apart and changed places musically. I heard them. I actually heard the words falling apart. I fell back on my bed in Room 25, hearing this strange distant ringing in my ears like Newton said he heard the music of the spheres when he stumbled on the laws of gravitation. I was as high as that. All that period in the Beat Hotel was one enormous intellectual high, wasn't it, William? I have a whole book of permutated poems I've never been able to get published. Ian Sommerville put them through the Computer for me. In 1960 I gave a program of them on the BBC and they have come out on records issued by Henri Chopin for his review, *Ou*.

William, would you encourage people to read 'Minutes to Go' before reading your subsequent books? Is it important for people who want to understand what you're doing?

Burroughs: I think it's quite an important book, and it does give a much clearer indication as to what I'm doing and the whole theory and development of cut-ups.

Where do you feel you've used cut-ups to greatest advantage?

I would say in sections of *The Soft Machine*, *The Ticket That Exploded* and in *Nova Express* as well. In certain sections it has worked. I feel that in all those books there was too much rather undifferentiated cut-up material, which I eliminated in *The Wild Boys*. The cut-up technique has very specific uses.

Brion, what about your Dreamachine? You've both used it?

Gysin: Yes. It's a stroboscope, in one word. But regulated to produce interruptions of light at between eight and thirteen flashes a second, complementing the alpha rhythms in the brain, or eventually bringing the two into phase, and at that moment, immediately, one begins with sensations of extraordinary, bright color and infinite pattern which is quickly elaborating itself into fields that appear at 180 degrees to begin with and eventually seem to be occurring around 360 degrees. There are several different areas of color, of intensity and changes of pattern, which follow each other in apparent random order, and then give way, at a certain point, to things recognized as dream images, imaginary events occurring at a certain speed, much like a speeded-up movie. But depending on one's own state, or the length of time one watches, they become like the most elaborate, highly structured sort of dreams. I've had science-fiction dreams. I've imagined that I was swimming over what seemed to be an ocean

bottom opened up and that big mollusks at the bottom opened up and through them appeared swimmers in Leonardo da Vinci–type helmets.

There seems to be no end to it. I've watched for literally hundreds of hours, and things never repeat themselves. Patterns do. Apparently they can eventually be learned and recognized. Some of the people who've investigated them, including a group in Germany, have identified a great many of the elements of design all over the world, found in weaving or in pottery or in archaeological objects elements of these patterns. All of them have been related to the sort of visions that one has with the Dreamachine. But there just haven't been many of these machines around; it's never been possible to have them made. We struggled for years to try to get someone to manufacture them, and nothing has ever come of it.

Did you say something about someone doing some of the first light shows during this Beat Hotel period?

Gysin: Yes, they were invented by us in the Beat Hotel, by Ian Sommerville and me. And with the very small amount of electricity we were allowed by Madame Rachou, who—like all Freanch hotel keepers—rationed it out with a fuse box down in her bistro. If you started using too many watts, you'd blow a fuse, so we used to sometimes hook up two or three rooms together to get things going. We put on shows that most of the people who later went into the thing as a business were turned on by—those shows we did in Paris with projections and tapes and sound poetry.

Does the writing technique in 'The Wild Boys' differ from that of the previous four novels?

Burroughs: Yes, I think that in *The Wild Boys* I was really quite deliberately returning to older styles of writing. Quite a bit of it is really Nineteenth Century. It's a different style of writing.

Did you use cut-ups in 'The Wild Boys'?

Yes, but sparingly, and very carefully selecting the phrases from the cut-ups, sifting through them many, many times. I didn't use it to the extent it was used in *The Ticket That Exploded* and *The Soft Machine* and *Nova Express*, nowhere near.

Has there been a progression in your writing to using them more sparingly and with more precision and control?

Yes. And also there are literary situations in which they are useful, and others in which they are not. Now, in recreating a delirium, they're very good, because that is what is happening. In high fever the images cut in, quite arbitrarily. So I used that in the dream section where the Boy is dying in the jungle.

Is the 'The Wild Boys' closely connected to your previous novels, or does it stand by itself?

I think it stands by itself. There's no carryover of characters as there are in the other books. *Naked Lunch*, *The Soft Machine*, and to some extent *The Ticket That Exploded* and *Nova Express* even, were all part of about a thousand pages of manuscript. And then I had to get together one book for Girodias in two weeks. And I did. That is how it happened. I thought, which chapter goes where is going to be very complicated, but it came back from the printers, and Sinclair Beilles took one look and said, "Why don't you leave it like this?" And we did. That's just pure chance, as the chapters were going in as we typed them out.

That was *Naked Lunch*. Then I had lots of material left over, and I started writing *The Soft Machine* after that, from this material. But there were no cut-ups as such used in *Naked Lunch*.

How far does that material go back?

The actual notes for *Naked Lunch* started, I think, around 1955 or '54. They piled up over a period of years, and I sent one version to Maurice Girodias, who didn't want it at that time. A few years later I was in Paris, and he sent Sinclair Beilles over to say that he wanted to publish it within two weeks. And a month from his saying that he wanted it, it was out on the bookstands.

Eric Mottram calls your first four novels "The Tetralogy." Is a similar grouping emerging from your new work?

Yes, everything I'm doing now is connected with *The Wild Boys*. The comic strip is using one of the same characters, as well as the other book . . .

What does this other book have to do with?

It concerns an incestuous family of father, mother, two brothers and two sisters—completely interchangeable sexual combinations. And they succeed because they are incestuous, liberated from all their inhibitions.

Succeed at what?

Well, by selling short during the Depression, they're able to fill a swimming pool with gold dollars.

Is that the last or the next Depression?

The last one; it's set back. What they do, in a sense, is make capitalism work. That is, they buy up the Dust Bowl, so they keep people there on the land and turn them all into incestuous family groups in completely interchangeable sexual combinations. So not only are they happier, but they're much more efficient, and nobody could compete with these families.

So this is a very different scenario sexually from 'The Wild Boys,' but it's approached in the same way?

Yes. I thought it might have more popular appeal. . . . And that of course brings them into conflict with the sinister forces of Big Money; they're subverting the whole meaning of money.

We haven't talked about your teaching gig in Switzerland. Were you applying the deconditioning process we talked about earlier?

Hardly. My impression of the University of the New World was that while the general idea was good, there was not a clear enough concept as to what the education process was supposed to bring about. You must have some idea as to the product you wish to turn out before you can go about taking the necessary measures. And there didn't seem to be a clear enough idea in this case of what they were going to teach people to do. I was vaguely teaching "Creative Writing." There's a question in my mind as to whether writing can be taught. There are techniques of writing, but I don't think any writer has ever lived long enough to really discover these, or codify them. I gave two talks, and I had twenty to thirty students in each talk.

I don't see how you could bring about any deconditioning in two talks. If I was running such a university, I would teach people very definite things, like how to make change, even in a street crap game, how to get service and so on. How to do things. I would set up a number of dummy situations, and I think that would teach them to transport themselves, etc., efficiently, or as efficiently as possible. Of course, I went into these ideas in *The Job* and in the Academy Series.

All of those things mentioned could be taught, and would be extremely beneficial. Now, by product I mean, for example, the English public schools were set up to turn out these old school ties, English gentlemen who ran the Empire when they had one. There's not much point in that now, but at least they knew what they were trying to do, so therefore they knew how to go about doing it. Now, the general proposition of all these free universities is they're to teach people to think for themselves, whatever that may mean. But it all has to be quite precise when it comes to actually giving courses. And I think that's where that university, and many others that were formulated on a similar basis, have broken down.

If you were running such a university, would you offer the synthesis of Eastern/mystical and Western/technological disciplines you proposed in the Academy Series?

Well, personally I've always drawn very much of a blank on yoga, and I feel that in view of electric brain stimulation and autonomic shaping, I would not be inclined to spend much time on

slower methods for accomplishing the same thing. It's questionable in my mind whether these Eastern disciplines do have very much to offer. I mean, after all these thousands of years, where is India? If we're thinking now in terms of possible new mutations into more efficient forms, certainly nothing of the sort is taking place in the East. In other words, their statistics are not all that good. If they were able, through yogic disciplines, to achieve the level of awareness that they claim they're able to achieve, it would seem odd that their area is in such a complete mess. They haven't come up with solutions to the overpopulation, soil exhaustion, etc.

You've often pointed out attitudes and styles shared by young people all over the world—they dress similarly, use cannabis and other consciousness-expanding drugs, hear the same music. Are these generational ties more binding than national, cultural, family ties?

Yes, I would say so, very definitely. And one reason that they are is, of course, media.

Do you foresee these ties eventually unifying the world's youth to the point where they can destroy the control machine being perpetuated by their elders?

Certainly. They will become their elders, and therefore make the changes. Now in twenty or thirty years all the Wallace folks, etc., will have died. Well, who's going to take their place? Occupying all those positions that are now occupied by their elders, either occupying all those positions or nullifying them, you're bound to have a whole different picture. I mean, if they've got some cool, pot-smoking cat as president, he's not going to make the same kind of decisions or impose the same policies. Now the question of whether the control machine, as you said earlier, would impose certain necessities on anybody that used it—that's another consideration, and to some extent it would. But they certainly would be more willing to listen to the idea of basic alterations, and perhaps change it.

The control machine is simply the machinery—police, education, etc—used by a group in power to keep itself in power and extend its power. For example: In a hunting society, which can only number about thirty, there's nothing that could be called a control machine in operation. They must function effectively as a hunting party in order to survive, so leadership is casual and you have no control machine. Now as soon as you get an agricultural society, particularly rich in land, you will tend to get inequality. That is, the advantage of slave labor then becomes apparent and you may have, as with the Mayans and Egyptians, workers and priests—in other words, stratification, repression, and you have a control machine. As I said, the ancient Mayans had almost a model control machine through which about 1 or 2 percent of the population controlled the others, without police, without heavy weapons. The workers all had such weapons as were available, stone axes, spears, etc. So it was pure psychological control.

Is the modern control machine's dependence on heavy weapons a sign that psychological control is breaking down?

Yes. Of course, the whole concept of revolution has undergone a basic change with the introduction of heavy weapons. Now anybody can go down into his basement and make a sword or a spear, and they can make some approximation of small arms. But they can't make automatic weapons, tanks, machine guns, planes and so on. So with heavy weapons, 5 percent can keep down 95 percent by just sheer force, if they have to. Of course, no government has ever survived for any length of time anywhere by sheer force, because of the personnel they would have to have. They would have to have constant surveillance, unless they used some form of psychological control like electric brain stimulation. But the problem that you see in all guerrilla warfare of occupying a territory where the governed are hostile, or even a good percentage of them, of course, is terrific and

ultimately insoluble. The French had to get out of Algeria; they'll all have to get out of Vietnam.

Now, as to the effectiveness of street fighting in a revolutionary context, you must remember that America is not in a state of revolution. It is not even in a state of pre-revolution, and any guerrilla movement, in order to survive, must have supplies from the outside. The liberals in the Colombian civil war had seized an area that bordered Venezuela, so they were getting their arms in through Venezuela. In Vietnam they're getting their arms from the North. Without something comparable to that, no guerrilla movement is ever going to be able to survive. They may talk about the guerrilla movements in the large cities, but they're just not talking in realistic terms. In Algeria the rebels occupied the mountains, and therefore could not supply their guerrillas in the cities. And also an underground army must have popular support. They don't have the potential for much support in America.

So that would not seem to be a viable tactic at present. I don't take back what I said in *The Job*, that there should be more riots and more violence, because at the time—May 1968—they were indicated. They accomplished something, there's no doubt about it. If there had been no riots, no violence, they wouldn't pay nearly as much attention to militants or their demands as they are paying now.

You also wrote in 'The Job,' "Once a problem has reached a political-military stage, it is already insoluble."

Yes, because it's not meant to be solved. This is a game universe. Basically there's only one game and that game is war, and we just have to keep it going, if we're to have political/military units.

But a new generation might not be interested in such things. They've got all those countries on the west coast of South America, countries like Colombia and Peru—they all have armies and they all consider that Peruvians are bad people, or Ecuadorians are bad people. And that, of course, is kept going by the military and by the very wealthy people. Otherwise, there'd be no reason for their existence. Now if a generation took over that just wasn't interested in maintaining these states, there'd be no reason for these countries to have any boundaries, or armies, at all.

What would you say to young people who want to change things through street fighting?

The only context in which street fighting would become important would be in the wake of some catastrophe, possibly an atomic war. In the chaos following an atomic attack on America, street fighting is a very important factor. I've already pointed out that I don't think that street fighting is at all a viable tactic, or a revolutionary tactic in the States. It is not in any country once it reaches a certain technological stage.

There are, of course, weapons that anyone can make in their basement, if they know how, and those are biological and chemical weapons. I have a reference, commenting on the discovery of the synthetic gene, from the science representative of one of America's major embassies: "This is the beginning of the end. Any small country with good biochemists can now make the virus for which there is no cure. Someone will do it." That means, of course, any small country or private group with a good biochemist and a small laboratory. It could be done in a place as small as this room. If they can make life particles, they can make death particles. They can make a virus to order, a virus that will do what you want it to do.

But how do you protect yourself from it if there's no cure?

No cure for the attack. Usually they develop antitoxins at the same time. It would be quite possible, for example, to develop a plague that would attack only whites. And incidentally, any college physics major, with that much technical knowledge and about $300,000, can turn out a low-yield nuclear device and take out New York from Times Square to Central Park. Nothing big, you understand . . .

The thing about virus weapons is that they need not be recognized as such. It could just come on as paralyzing depression. Everyone just feels a little worse and a little worse until they can't get out of bed, and the whole thing founders.

Do you think any particular dissatisfied group in the society might be most inclined to use this kind of weapon? Say, the right wing?

I think the right wing more than the left. The left is still back there with Che Guevera and barricades and bullets. But to hesitate to use them I think would definitely be foolish.

You and Brion have described your collaborations over the years as the products of a "third mind." What's the source of this concept?

Burroughs: A book called *Think and Grow Rich*.

Gysin: It says that when you put two minds together . . .

Burroughs: . . . there's always a third mind . . .

Gysin: . . . a third and superior mind . . .

Burroughs: . . . as an unseen collaborator.

Gysin: That is where we picked up the title. Our book *The Third Mind* is about all the cut-up materials.

The book is a statement, in words and pictures, of what the two of you have achieved through your collaborations?

Burroughs: Yes, exactly that, from the very first cut-ups through elaboration into scrapbook layout, cut texts and images.

Brion, what did you mean when you said "Rub out the word"?

Gysin: "Rub out the word" was essentially to do with the fact that all the religions of the "peoples of the book," that is the Jews, the Christians and the Moslems, all these three religions are based on the idea that in the beginning was the word. Everything seems to be wrong with what was produced from those beginnings, and so let's rub out the word and start afresh and see what really is going on. The methods were first of all a disruption of the time sequence, as William said a few minutes ago, produced by the cut-ups, and one had the idea of rubbing out the word itself, not simply disrupting its sequential order, and finding out some other way. There are other ways of communication, so an attempt at finding them would begin by rubbing out the word. If the whole thing began with the word, well then, if we don't like what was produced, and we don't, let's get right to the root of the matter and radically alter it.

Burroughs: Rubbing out the word would probably entail considerable psychological alterations in the whole structure. The reason apes can't talk is because their inner throat structure is not set up to do so. We can imagine that the word could have occasioned the alterations in the inner throat structure that then made the words possible, and that this alteration was then genetically conveyed. Now, rubbing out the word could make objective alterations in the actual physio-psychological structure. What these alterations would be we have no way of knowing.

What precisely is the desirability of not verbalizing?

Well, verbalization has got us precisely where we are: War is a word. The whole war universe is a verbal universe, which means they've got us in an impasse. And in order to break out of that impasse it would seem desirable to explore alternative methods of communication.

How would you compare exploring these avenues to exploring more precise manipulation of words?

Well, it would certainly be a step in the same direction. The more precise your manipulation or use of words is, the more you know what you're actually dealing with, what the word actually is. And by knowing what it actually is, you can supersede it. Or use it when you want to use it. Most people never stop talking—"talking to themselves," as they call it. But who are they actually talking to, and why? Why can't they simply lapse into silence?

In my case, because I have just a couple more questions. I've seen the 'Naked Lunch' film script which Brion adapted from the book. What is the current state of your movie-making project?

Gysin: The shooting script is finalized and budgeted. All we need is half a million dollars to finance it. Have you got any ideas?

Ummm ... just one more question: William, what are your thoughts on the future of writing?

Burroughs: The future of writing is to see how close you can come to making it happen.

Beat Godfather Meets Glitter Mainman:
Burroughs and David Bowie

BY CRAIG COPETAS

[ROLLING STONE 155, February 28, 1974]

William Seward Burroughs is not a talkative man. Once at dinner he gazed down into a pair of stereo microphones trained to pick up every munch and said, "I don't like talk and I don't like talkers. Like Ma Barker. You remember Ma Barker? Well, that's what she always said. 'Ma Barker doesn't like talk and she doesn't like talkers.' She just sat there with her gun."

This was on my mind as much as the mysterious personality of David Bowie when an Irish cabbie drove Burroughs and me to Bowie's London home on November 17, 1973 ("Strange blokes down this part o' London, mate"). I had spent the last several weeks arranging this two-way interview, I had brought Bowie all of Burroughs's novels: 'Naked Lunch,' 'Nova Express,' 'The Ticket That Exploded' and the rest. He'd only had time to read 'Nova Express.' Burroughs, for his part, had only heard two Bowie songs, "Five Years" and "Starman," though he had read all of Bowie's lyrics. Still, they had expressed interest in meeting each other.

Bowie's house is decorated in a science-fiction mode: A gigantic painting, by an artist whose style fell midway between Salvador Dali and Norman Rockwell, hung over a plastic sofa. Quite a contrast to Burroughs's two-room Piccadilly flat, decorated with photos of Brion Gysin—modest quarters for such a successful writer, more like the Beat Hotel in Paris than anything else.

Soon Bowie entered, wearing three-tone NASA jodhpurs. He jumped right into a detailed description of the painting and its surrealistic qualities. Burroughs nodded, and the interview/conversation began. The three of us sat in a room for two hours, talking and taking lunch: a Jamaican fish dish, prepared by a Jamaican in the Bowie entourage, with avocados stuffed with shrimp and a beaujolais nouveau, served by two interstellar Bowieites.

There was immediate liking and respect between the two. In fact, a few days after the conversation Bowie asked Burroughs for a favor: A Production of 'The Maids' staged by Lindsay Kemp, Bowie's old mime teacher, had been closed down in London by playwright Jean Genet's London publisher. Bowie wanted to bring the matter to Genet's attention personally. Burroughs was impressed by Bowie's description of the production and promised to help. A few weeks later Bowie went to Paris in search of Genet, following leads from Burroughs.

Who knows? Perhaps a collaboration has begun; perhaps, as Bowie says, they may be the Rodgers and Hammerstein of the Seventies.

Burroughs: Do you do all your designs yourself?

Bowie: Yes, I have to take total control myself. I can't let anybody else do anything, for I find that I can do things better for me. I don't want to get other people playing with what they think I'm trying to do. I don't like to read things that people write about me. I'd rather read what kids have to say about me because it's not their profession to do that.

People look to me to see what the spirit of the Seventies is, at least 50 percent of them do. Crit-

David Bowie and William Burroughs at their London summit meeting, 1973

TERRY O'NEILL

ics I don't understand. They get too intellectual. They're not very well versed in street talk; it takes them longer to say it. So they have to do it in dictionaries and they take longer to say it.

I went to a middle-class school, but my background is working class. I got the best of both worlds, I saw both classes, so I have a pretty fair idea of how people live and why they do it. I can't articulate it too well, but I have a feeling about it. But not the upper-class. I want to meet the Queen and then I'll know. How do you take the picture that people paint of you?

Burroughs: They try to categorize you. They want to see their picture of you and if they don't see their picture of you they're very upset. Writing is seeing how close you can come to make it happen, the object of all art. What else do they think man really wants, a whiskey priest on a mission he doesn't believe in? I think the most important thing in the world is that the artists should take over this planet because they're the only ones who can make anything happen. Why should we let these fucking newspaper politicians take over from us?

Bowie: I change my mind a lot. I usually don't agree with what I say very much. I'm an awful liar.

Burroughs: I am too.

Bowie: I'm not sure whether it is me changing my mind, or whether I lie a lot. It's somewhere between the two. I don't exactly lie, I change my mind all the time. People are always throwing things at me that I've said and I say that I didn't mean anything. You can't stand still on one point for your entire life.

Burroughs: Only politicians lay down what they think and that is it. Take a man like Hitler, he never changed his mind.

Bowie: *Nova Express* really reminded me of *Ziggy Stardust*, which I am going to be putting into a theatrical performance. Forty scenes are in it and it would be nice if the characters and actors

learned the scenes and we all shuffled them around in a hat the afternoon of the performance and just performed it as the scenes come out. I got this all from you, Bill . . . so it would change every night.

Burroughs: That's a very good idea, visual cut-up in a different sequence.

Bowie: I get bored very quickly and that would give it some new energy. I'm rather kind of old school, thinking that when an artist does his work it's no longer his. . . . I just see what people make of it. That is why the TV production of *Ziggy* will have to exceed people's expectations of what they thought *Ziggy* was.

Burroughs: Could you explain this Ziggy Stardust image of yours? From what I can see it has to do with the world being on the eve of destruction within five years.

Bowie: The time is five years to go before the end of the earth. It has been announced that the world will end because of lack of natural resources. Ziggy is in a position where all the kids have access to things that they thought they wanted. The older people have lost all touch with reality and the kids are left on their own to plunder anything. Ziggy was in a rock & roll band and the kids no longer want rock & roll. There's no electricity to play it. Ziggy's adviser tells him to collect news and sing it, 'cause there is no news. So Ziggy does this and there is terrible news. "All the Young Dudes" is a song about this news. It is no hymn to the youth as people thought. It is completely the opposite.

Burroughs: Where did this Ziggy idea come from, and this five-year idea? Of course, exhaustion of natural resources will not develop the end of the world. It will result in the collapse of civilization. And it will cut down the population by about three-quarters.

Bowie: Exactly. This does not cause the end of the world for Ziggy. The end comes when the infinites arrive. They really are a black hole, but

I've made them people because it would be very hard to explain a black hole onstage.

Burroughs: Yes, a black hole onstage would be an incredible expense. And it would be a continuing performance, first eating up Shaftesbury Avenue.

Bowie: Ziggy is advised in a dream by the infinites to write the coming of a starman, so he writes "Starman," which is the first news of hope that the people have heard. So they latch onto it immediately. The starmen that he is talking about are called the infinites, and they are black-hole jumpers. Ziggy has been talking about this amazing spaceman who will be coming down to save the earth. They arrive somewhere in Greenwich Village. They don't have a care in the world and are of no possible use to us. They just happened to stumble into our universe by black-hole jumping. Their whole life is traveling from universe to universe. In the stage show, one of them resembles Brando, another one is a black New Yorker. I even have one called Queenie the Infinite Fox.

Now Ziggy starts to believe in all this himself and thinks himself a prophet of the future starman. He takes himself up to incredible spiritual heights and is kept alive by his disciples. When the infinites arrive, they take bits of Ziggy to make themselves real because in their original state they are anti-matter and cannot exist on our world. And they tear him to pieces onstage during the song "Rock and Roll Suicide." As soon as Ziggy dies onstage the infinites take his elements and make themselves visible. It is a science-fiction fantasy of today, and this is what literally blew my head off when I read *Nova Express*, which was written in 1961. Maybe we are the Rodgers and Hammerstein of the Seventies, Bill!

Burroughs: Yes, I can believe that. The parallels are definitely there, and it sounds good.

Bowie: I must have the total image of a stage show. It has to be total with me. I'm just not content writing songs, I want to make it three-dimensional. Songwriting as an art is a bit archaic now. Just writing a song is not good enough.

Burroughs: It's the whole performance. It's not like somebody sitting down at the piano and just playing a piece.

Bowie: A song has to take on character, shape, body and influence people to an extent that they use it for their own devices. It must affect them not just as a song, but as a lifestyle. The rock stars have assimilated all kinds of philosophies, styles, histories, writings, and they throw out what they have gleaned from that.

Burroughs: The revolution will come from ignoring the others out of existence.

Bowie: Really. Now we have people who are making it happen on a level faster than ever. People who are into groups like Alice Cooper, the New York Dolls and Iggy Pop, who are denying totally and irrevocably the existence of people who are into the Stones and the Beatles. The gap has decreased from twenty years to ten years.

Burroughs: The escalating rate of change. The media are really responsible for most of this. Which produces an incalculable effect.

Bowie: Once upon a time, even when I was thirteen or fourteen, for me it was between fourteen and forty that you were old. Basically. But now it is eighteen-year-olds and twenty-six-year-olds—there can be incredible discrepancies, which is really quite alarming. We are not trying to bring people together, but to wonder how much longer we've got. It would be positively boring if minds were in tune. I'm more interested in whether the planet is going to survive.

Burroughs: Actually, the contrary is happening; people are getting further and further apart.

Bowie: The idea of getting minds together smacks of the Flower Power period to me. The coming together of people I find obscene as a principle. It is not human. It is not a natural thing as some people would have us believe.

Copetas: What about love?

Burroughs: Ugh.

Bowie: I'm not at ease with the word "love."

Burroughs: I'm not either.

Bowie: I was told that it was cool to fall in love, and that period was nothing like that to me. I gave too much of my time and energy to another person and they did the same to me and we started burning out against each other. And that is what is termed love . . . that we decide to put all our values on another person. It's like two pedestals, each wanting to be the other pedestal.

Burroughs: I don't think that "love" is a useful word. It is predicated on a separation of a thing called sex and a thing called love and that they are separate. Like the primitive expressions in the Old South when the woman is on a pedestal, and the man worshipped his wife and then went out and fucked a whore. It is primarily a Western concept and then it extended to the whole Flower Power thing of loving everybody. Well, you can't do that because the interests are not the same.

Bowie: The word is wrong, I'm sure. It is the way you understand love. The love that you see, among people who say, "We're in love," it's nice to look at . . . but wanting not to be alone, wanting to have a person there that they relate to for a few years is not often the love that carries on throughout the lives of those people. There is another word. I'm not sure whether it is a word. Love is every type of relationship, every type of relationship that you can think of.

Copetas: *What of sexuality, where is it going?*

Bowie: Sexuality and where it is going is an extraordinary question, for I don't see it going anywhere. It is with me, and that's it. It's not coming out as a new advertising campaign next year. It's just there. Everything you can think about sexuality is just there. Maybe there are different kinds of sexuality, maybe they'll be brought into play more. Like one time it was impossible to be homosexual as far as the public were concerned. Now it is accepted. Sexuality will never change, for people have been fucking their own

particular ways since time began and will be continue to do it. Just more of those ways will be coming to light. It might even reach a puritan state.

Burroughs: There are certain indications that it might be going that way in the future, real backlash.

Bowie: Oh yes, look at the rock business. Poor old Clive Davis. He was found to be absconding with money and there were also drug things tied up with it. And that has started a whole clean-up campaign among record companies; they're starting to ditch some of their artists.

I'm regarded quite asexually by a lot of people. And the people that understand me the best are nearer to what I understand about me. Which is not very much, for I'm still searching. I don't know, the people who are coming anywhere close to where I think I'm at regard me more as an erogenous kind of thing. But the people who don't know so much about me regard me more sexually.

But there again, maybe it's the disinterest with sex after a certain age, because the people who do kind of get nearer to me are generally older. And the ones who regard me as more of a sexual thing are generally younger. The younger people get into the lyrics in a different way; there's much more of a tactile understanding, which is the way I prefer it. 'Cause that's the way I get off on writing, especially William's. I can't say that I analyze it all and that's exactly what you're saying, but from a feeling way I got what you meant. It's there, a whole wonderhouse of strange shapes and colors, tastes and feelings.

I must confess that up until now I haven't been an avid reader of William's work. I really did not get past Kerouac to be honest. But when I started looking at your work I really couldn't believe it. Especially after reading *Nova Express*, I really related to that. My ego obviously put me on to the "Pay Color" chapter, then I started dragging out lines from the rest of the book.

Burroughs: Your lyrics are quite perceptive.

Bowie: They're a bit middle-class, but that's all right, 'cause I'm middle-class.

Burroughs: It is rather surprising that they are such complicated lyrics, that can go down with a mass audience. The content of most pop lyrics is practically zero, like "Power to the People."

Bowie: I'm quite certain that the audience that I've got for my stuff don't listen to the lyrics.

Burroughs: That's what I'm interested in hearing about. . . . Do they understand them?

Bowie: Well, it comes over more as a media thing and it's only after they sit down and bother to look. On what level they are reading them, they do understand them, because they will send me back their own kind of write-ups of what I'm talking about, which is great for me because sometimes I don't know. There have been times when I've written something and it goes out and it comes back in a letter from some kid as to what they think about it and I've taken their analysis to heart so much that I have taken up his thing. Writing what my audience is telling me to write.

Lou Reed is the most important definitive rocker in modern rock. Not because of the stuff that he does, but the direction that he will take it. Half the new bands would not be around if it were not for Lou. The movement that Lou's stuff has created is amazing. New York City is Lou Reed. Lou writes in the street-gut level, and the English tend to intellectualize more.

Burroughs: What is your inspiration for writing, is it literary?

Bowie: I don't think so.

Burroughs: Well, I read this "Eight Line Poem" of yours and it is very reminiscent of T. S. Eliot.

Bowie: Never read him.

Burroughs: [*laughs*] It is very reminiscent of "The Waste Land." Do you get any of your ideas from dreams?

Bowie: Frequently.

Burroughs: I get 70 percent of mine from dreams.

Bowie: There's a thing that just as you go to sleep, if you keep your elbows elevated that you will never go below the dream stage. And I've used that quite a lot and it keeps me dreaming much longer than if I just relaxed.

Burroughs: I dream a great deal, and that's because I am a light sleeper, I will wake up and jot down just a few words and they will always bring the whole idea back to me.

Bowie: I keep a tape recorder by the bed and then if anything comes I just say it into the tape recorder. As for my inspiration, I haven't changed my views much since I was about twelve, really, I've just got a twelve-year-old mentality. When I was in school I had a brother who was into Kerouac and he gave me *On the Road* to read when I was twelve years old. That's been a big influence.

Copetas: *The images both of you transpire are very graphic, almost booky in nature.*

Bowie: Well, yes, I find it easier to write in these little vignettes; if I try to get any more heavy, I find myself out of my league. I couldn't contain myself in what I say. Besides if you are really heavier there isn't much more time to read that much, or listen to that much. There's not much point in getting any heavier . . . there's too many things to read and look at. If people read three hours of what you've done, then they'll analyze it for seven hours and come out with seven hours of their own thinking . . . where if you give them thirty seconds of your own stuff they usually still come out with seven hours of their own thinking. They take hook images of what you do. And they pontificate on the hooks. The sense of immediacy of the image. Things have to hit for the moment. That's one of the reasons I'm into video; the image has to hit immediately. I adore video and the whole cutting up of it.

What are your projects at the moment?

Burroughs: At the moment I'm trying to set up an institute of advanced studies somewhere in Scotland. Its aim will be to extend awareness and alter consciousness in the direction of greater range, flexibility and effectiveness at a time when traditional disciplines have failed to come up with viable solutions. You see, the advent of the space age and the possibility of exploring galaxies and contacting alien life forms pose an urgent necessity for radically new solutions. We will be considering only nonchemical methods with the emphasis placed on combination, synthesis, interaction and rotation of methods now being used in the East and West, together with methods that are not at present being used to extend awareness or increase human potentials.

We know exactly what we intend to do and how to go about doing it. As I said, no drug experiments are planned and no drugs other than alcohol, tobacco and personal medications obtained on prescription will be permitted in the center. Basically, the experiments we propose are inexpensive and easy to carry out. Things such as yoga-style meditation and exercises, communication, sound, light and film experiments, experiments with sensory deprivation chambers, pyramids, psychotronic generators and Reich's orgone accumulators, experiments with infrasound, experiments with dream and sleep.

Bowie: That sounds fascinating. Are you basically interested in energy forces?

Burroughs: Expansion of awareness, eventually leading to mutations. Did you read *Journey Out of the Body*? Not the usual book on astral projection. This American businessman found he was having these experiences of getting out of the body—never used any hallucinogenic drugs. He's now setting up this astral air force. This psychic thing is really a rave in the States now. Did you experience it much when you were there?

Bowie: No, I really hid from it purposely. I

was studying Tibetan Buddhism when I was quite young, again influenced by Kerouac. The Tibetan Buddhist Institute was available, so I trotted down there to have a look. Lo and behold, there's a guy down in the basement who's the head man in setting up a place in Scotland for the refugees, and I got involved purely on a sociological level—because I wanted to help get the refugees out of India, for they were really having a shitty time of it down there, dropping like flies due to the change of atmosphere from the Himalayas.

Scotland was a pretty good place to put them, and then more and more I was drawn to their way of thinking, or non-thinking, and for a while got quite heavily involved in it. I got to the point where I wanted to become a novice monk and about two weeks before I was actually going to take those steps, I broke up and went out on the streets and got drunk and never looked back.

Burroughs: Just like Kerouac.

Bowie: Go to the States much?

Burroughs: Not since '71.

Bowie: It has changed, I can tell you, since then.

Burroughs: When were you last back?

Bowie: About a year ago.

Burroughs: Did you see any of the porn films in New York?

Bowie: Yes, quite a few.

Burroughs: When I was last back, I saw about thirty of them. I was going to be a judge at the erotic film festival.

Bowie: The best ones were the German ones; they were really incredible.

Burroughs: I thought that the American ones were still the best. I really like film. . . . I understand that you may play Valentine Michael Smith in the film version of *Stranger in a Strange Land*.

Bowie: No, I don't like the book much. In fact, it is terrible. It was suggested to me that I make it into a movie, then I got around to reading it. It seemed a bit too Flower-Powery and that made me a bit wary.

Burroughs: I'm not that happy with the book either. You know, science fiction has not been very successful. It was supposed to start a whole new trend and nothing happened. For the special effects in some of the movies, like *2001*, it was great. But it all ended there.

Bowie: I feel the same way. Now I'm doing Orwell's *1984* on television; that's a political thesis and an impression of the way in another country. Something of that nature will have more impact on television. I don't believe in proper cinema; it doesn't have the strength of television. People having to go out to the cinema is really archaic. I'd much rather sit at home.

Burroughs: Do you mean the whole concept of the audience?

Bowie: Yes, it is ancient. No sense of immediacy.

Burroughs: Exactly, it all relates back to image and the way in which it is used.

Bowie: Right. I'd like to start a TV station.

Burroughs: There are hardly any programs worth anything any more. The British TV is a little better than American. The best thing the British do is natural history. There was one last week with sea lions eating penguins, incredible. There is no reason for dull programs, people get very bored with housing projects and coal strikes.

Bowie: They all have an interest level of about three seconds. Enough time to get into the commentator's next sentence. And that is the premise it works on. I'm going to put together all the bands that I think are of great value in the States and England, then make an hour-long program about them. Probably a majority of people have never heard of these bands. They are doing and saying things in a way other bands aren't. Things like the Puerto Rican music at the Cheetah Club in New York. I want people to hear musicians like Joe Cuba. He has done things to whole masses of Puerto Rican people. The music

is fantastic and important. I also want to start getting Andy Warhol films on TV.

Burroughs: Have you ever met Warhol?

Bowie: Yes, about two years ago I was invited up to The Factory. We got in the lift and went up and when it opened there was a brick wall in front of us. We rapped on the wall and they didn't believe who we were. So we went back down and back up again till finally they opened the wall and everybody was peering around at each other. That was shortly after the gun incident. I met this man who was the living dead. Yellow in complexion, a wig on that was the wrong color, little glasses. I extended my hand and the guy retired, so I thought, "The guy doesn't like flesh, obviously he's reptilian." He produced a camera and took a picture of me. And I tried to make small talk with him, and it wasn't getting anywhere.

But then he saw my shoes. I was wearing a pair of gold-and-yellow shoes, and he says, "I adore those shoes." He then started a whole rap about shoe design and that broke the ice. My yellow shoes broke the ice with Andy Warhol.

I adore what he *was* doing. I think his importance was very heavy, it's become a big thing to like him now. But Warhol wanted to be cliché, he wanted to be available in Woolworth's and be talked about in that glib type of manner. I hear he wants to make real films now, which is very sad because the films he was making were the things that should be happening. I left knowing as little about him as a person as when I went in.

Burroughs: I don't think that there is any person there. It's a very alien thing, completely and totally unemotional. He's really a science-fiction character. He's got a strange green color.

Bowie: That's what struck me. He's the wrong color, this man is the wrong color to be a human being. Especially under the stark neon lighting that is in The Factory. Apparently it is a real experience to behold him in the daylight.

Burroughs: I've seen him in all light and still

have no idea as to what is going on, except that it is something quite purposeful. It's not energetic, but quite insidious, completely asexual. His films will be the late-night movies of the future.

Bowie: Exactly. Remember *Pork*? I want to get that onto TV. TV has eaten up everything else, and Warhol films are all that are left, which is fabulous. *Pork* could become the next *I Love Lucy*, the great American domestic comedy. It's about how people really live, not like Lucy, who never touched dishwater. It's about people living and hustling to survive.

That's what *Pork* is all about. A smashing of the spectacle. Although I'd like to do my own version of *Sinbad the Sailor*. I think that is an all-time classic. But it would have to be done on an extraordinary level. It would be incredibly indulgent and expensive. It would have to utilize lasers and all the things that are going to happen in a true fantasy.

Even the use of holograms. Holograms are important. Holograms will come into use in about seven years. Libraries of video cassettes should be developed to their fullest during the interim. You can't video enough good material from your own TV. I want to have my own choice of programs. There has to be the necessary software available.

Burroughs: I audio-record everything I can.

Bowie: The media is either our salvation or our death. I'd like to think it's our salvation. My particular thing is discovering what can be done with media and how it can be used. You can't draw people together like one big huge family, people don't want that. They want isolation or a tribal thing. A group of eighteen kids would much rather stick together and hate the next eighteen kids down the block. You are not going to get two or three blocks joining up and loving each other. There are just too many people.

Burroughs: Too many people. We're in an overpopulated situation, but the less people you have does not include the fact that they are still

heterogeneous. They are just not the same. All this talk about a world family is a lot of bunk. It worked with the Chinese because they are very similar.

Bowie: And now one man in four in China has a bicycle and that is pretty heavy considering what they didn't have before. And that's the miracle as far as they're concerned. It's like all of us having a jet plane over here.

Burroughs: It's because they are the personification of one character that they can live together without any friction. We quite evidently are not.

Bowie: It's why they don't need rock and roll. British rock and roll stars played in China, played a dirty great field and they were treated like a sideshow. Old women, young children, some teenagers, you name it, everybody came along, walked past them and looked at them on the stand. It didn't mean a thing. Certain countries don't need rock and roll because they were so drawn together as a family unit. China has its mother-father figure—I've never made up my mind which—it fluctuates between the two. For the West, Jagger is most certainly a mother figure and he's a mother hen to the whole thing. He's not a cockadoodledoo; he's much more like a brothel keeper or a madam.

Burroughs: Oh, very much so.

Bowie: He's incredibly sexy and very virile. I also find him incredibly motherly and maternal clutched into his bosom of ethnic blues. He's a white boy from Dagenham trying his damnedest to be ethnic. You see, trying to tart the rock business up a bit is getting nearer to what the kids themselves are like, because what I find, if you want to talk in the terms of rock, a lot depends on sensationalism and the kids are a lot more sensational than the stars themselves. The rock business is a pale shadow of what the kids' lives are usually like. The admiration comes from the other side. It's all a reversal, especially in recent years. Walk down Christopher Street and then you wonder exactly what went wrong. People are not like James Taylor; they may be molded on the outside, but inside their heads it is something completely different.

Burroughs: Politics of sound.

Bowie: Yes. We have kind of got that now. It has very loosely shaped itself into the politics of sound. The fact that you can now subdivide rock into different categories was something that you couldn't do ten years ago. But now I can reel off at least ten sounds that represent a kind of person rather than a type of music. The critics don't like to say that because critics like being critics, and most of them wish they were rock and roll stars. But when they classify they are talking about people *not* music. It's a whole political thing.

Burroughs: Like infrasound, the sound below the level of hearing. Below sixteen Hertz. Turned up full blast it can knock down walls for thirty miles. You can walk into the French patent office and buy the patent for forty pence. The machine itself can be made very cheaply from things you could find in a junkyard.

Bowie: Like black noise. I wonder if there is a sound that can put things back together. There was a band experimenting with stuff like that; they reckon they could make a whole audience shake.

Burroughs: They have riot-control noise based on these soundwaves now. But you could have music with infrasound, you wouldn't necessarily have to kill the audience.

Bowie: Just maim them.

Burroughs: The weapon of the Wild Boys is a bowie knife, an eighteen-inch bowie knife, did you know that?

Bowie: An eighteen-inch bowie knife . . . you don't do things by halves, do you. No, I didn't know that was their weapon. The name Bowie just appealed to me when I was younger. I was into a kind of heavy philosophy thing when I was sixteen years old, and I wanted a truism about cutting through the lies and all that.

Burroughs: Well, it cuts both ways, you know, double edged on the end.

Bowie: I didn't see it cutting both ways till now.

Undercover

BY GREIL MARCUS

[ROLLING STONE 239, May 19, 1977]

Junky by William S. Burroughs, Penguin, 158 pp., $1.95

Cobble Stone Gardens by William S. Burroughs, Cherry Valley Editions, 49 pp., $3

JUNKY, THE MEMOIRS OF A heroin addict, originally appeared in 1953 as *Junkie* by "William Lee." Printed back-to-back with the memoirs of a narc, it was William S. Burroughs's first book. It is essentially a day-to-day meditation on the possibilities of estrangement; its story is plainly told in an unsettlingly flat tone of voice. It insists always on the ordinary if slowed-down normality of the junkie's world; it is clinical. The author chooses a life, and he argues without stridency that his life makes sense.

Everything moves according to a predetermined pace here; the most lurid incidents are denied any trace of sensationalism. The result is a work of very remarkable creepiness—a mid-Twentieth-Century version of "Bartleby," that story in which Herman Melville set forth the proposition that the human contact necessary for temporal salvation is simply impossible.

Certain scenes in *Junky* remain horrifying, more than twenty years after they were written; the difference time makes is that they no longer seem artless.

There is a type person occasionally seen in [junk] neighborhoods who has connections with junk, though he is neither a user nor a seller ... His place of origin is the Near East, probably Egypt. He has a large straight nose. His lips are thin and purple-blue like the lips of a penis. The skin is tight and smooth over his face. He is basically obscene beyond any possible vile act or practice. He has the mark of a certain trade or occupation that no longer exists. If junk were gone from the earth, there might still be junkies standing around in junk neighborhoods feeling the lack ... So this man walks around in places where he once exercised his obsolete and unthinkable trade. But he is unperturbed ...

What is his lost trade? Definitely of a servant class and something to do with the dead, though he is not an embalmer. Perhaps he stores something in his body—a substance to prolong life—of which he is periodically milked by his masters.

Burroughs's latest book, *Cobble Stone Gardens*, is written in the form of a childhood memoir, but it veers off almost immediately into images of pedophilia, murder and dismemberment. The book is dedicated to Burroughs's parents—"We never know how much we learn / From those who never will return," Burroughs quotes E. A. Robinson—and is illustrated with Burroughs's family portraits and photos drawn from the public life of the 1910s and 1920s (Burroughs was born in 1914). Despite the fundamental violence of the book, the lines from Robinson are not used for irony, because Burroughs long ago passed beyond irony, if indeed he ever bothered with it.

The prose, inevitably, is far more self-consciously spontaneous than that of *Junky*; waves of hallucination rush across the pages. But the continuity with Burroughs's first book is there, and,

tracing it, one can see that his work, so often understood as a negation of bourgeois life (which it is) is also utopian: a search for a forbidden city of the senses, an attempt either to retrieve that paradise from a past as distant as that adhering to the repulsive Egyptian, or to invent it. The problem is that Burroughs is certain that there is an inverse relationship between his desire for paradise—some final, permanent orgy on the edge of death, or perhaps the very moment of death eternally maintained—and his ability to achieve it. This might be the source of the revulsion that fragments Burroughs's descriptions of utopia (he hates that Egyptian, but also loves him, would become him if he could): The more palpable Burroughs's goal, the more acute his understanding that his black paradise is only a sort of primal memory. Thus the need to go back to beginnings, to childhood.

Still, the subversion of childhood in *Cobble Stone Gardens* is as brutal as Burroughs can make it. Like Alice, Burroughs cannot get through the door, and rage takes over the story: Even if one can see through all the episodes of castrating South American border guards and flesh-eating insects to the little boy who lies somewhere behind them, one also feels that even Burroughs's return to his childhood is a form of pedophilia: The man eats the child alive.

It is, in the end, the strongest sort of reaffirmation and intensification of the sense of displacement that is at the heart of all of Burroughs's work. Recalling the Egyptian and his all-but-forgotten trade, Burroughs writes in *Cobble Stone Gardens*: "Messages in the lost tongue of a vile people cut off in a mountain valley by towering cliffs and a great waterfall. The inhabitants are blond and blue eyed." This is a complete image, as that of the Egyptian is not: It combines the lure of James Hilton's Shangri-La with the most ominous parody. And it is this image of childhood that Burroughs is determined to leave us with. As he notes, summing up the passage: "It may be that you are in locations or circumstances that will be dangerous at some future time."

Self-help: *How to Save Your Own Life*, a novel by Erica Jong (Holt, Rinehart and Winston): In which the author of *Fear of Flying* combines the ambitions of *Portrait of a Lady* with the imaginative power of the classified section of the *St. Louis Post-Dispatch*. —G. M.

William Burroughs, New York City, circa 1980
STEPHANIE CHERNIKOWSKI

Portrait of the Artist
as an Old Man

BY DAVID L. ULIN

Editor's note: David L. Ulin conducted one of the last extensive interviews with William Burroughs before his death. Ulin's assignment was to question the writer about his paintings, which were being exhibited in a show at the Los Angeles County Museum of Art in July 1996. This piece originally ran, in a somewhat different form, in the August 1996 issue of 'Detour.'

WILLIAM S. BURROUGHS IS A well-insulated man. Partly, that's because, for the last fifteen years, the eighty-two-year-old author, painter and all-around iconoclast has lived in Lawrence, Kansas, a college town just a couple of hundred miles from his boyhood home of St. Louis, exactly in the middle of the United States. Lawrence is a difficult place to reach, requiring a three-and-a-half-hour plane ride to Kansas City, and another hour behind the wheel of a rental car. Flying in for the weekend from California, I watch as the deserts and mountains of the West yield to a patchwork quilt of country roads and irrigation ditches, all laid out in large square plots of farmland and crops as if the earth itself were a giant collage. In the distance, small dots of houses give way to clusters of towns. The Friday morning sunlight glints in sharp reflection off the metal rooftops, and the entire landscape recedes into flatness as far as I can see.

It's not enough just to get to Lawrence, however; once I arrive, I have to navigate my way through the appropriate channels, setting up appointments, confirming plans. I check into the Eldridge Hotel, a five-story 1920s-era brick and stone structure that is one of the tallest buildings in town, and call James Grauerholz, Burroughs's long-time secretary, business manager and confidante, to let him know I'm around. Grauerholz is polite, although he sounds tired, as if this interview is something that he'd rather not arrange. I can't say I blame him: As he explains when we meet late in the afternoon for the short drive over to Burroughs's house, something like twenty requests for interviews or meetings come in every week, not including the people who just show up, pleading, "I've got to see Mr. Burroughs," to which he replies, "But why does Mr. Burroughs have to see *you*?" It's a lot to ask of a man who, Grauerholz tells me, now lives in "pretty much full retirement," spending his time painting and shooting, or looking after his six cats and the goldfish pond in his backyard.

The problem, of course, is that Burroughs is no longer just a writer, but a pop-culture icon, a shadowy, wraithlike figure infiltrating our collective consciousness, a literal ghost in the machine. Over the past half century, he has been associated with, or an influence on, nearly every significant underground movement to come along in the arts. Gentleman junkie, Beat progenitor, friend and mentor to Allen Ginsberg and Jack Kerouac, he's crossed all measure of boundaries, from membership in the American Academy and Institute of Arts and Letters to his titular position as the de facto godfather of punk. As a result, there's almost a proprietary edge to the way his fans think of him, a perception of ownership, as with the guy on the Internet who calls himself Willy

Lee, co-opting Burroughs's nom de plume (Lee was his mother's maiden name, under which he published his first novel, *Junky*, in 1953) in an act of identification or presumption, depending on your point of view.

In recent years, that's all been exaggerated as Burroughs's public persona has continued to grow. Since the early 1980s, he's been introduced as "the greatest living American writer" by Lauren Hutton on *Saturday Night Live* and appeared in movies like *Drugstore Cowboy*. He's made records with Kurt Cobain and R.E.M., shared the bill at readings with Stephen King. He's also done advertisements, most notoriously a series of television spots for Nike, which cast him as a talking head on a video monitor, pontificating about the future. Grauerholz defends this decision as representing "basically just a permeation, a further avenue into the culture. It's a source of earnings to support his comfortable old age, and I think it brings people to the work." To be fair, it *does* seem of a piece with Burroughs's own vision; in a 1965 *Paris Review* interview with Conrad Knickerbocker, he suggests, "I see no reason why the artistic world can't absolutely merge with Madison Avenue. Pop art is a move in that direction. Why can't we have advertisements with beautiful words and beautiful images?"

Still, Grauerholz admits, "a lot of people who profess to think highly of him and his work haven't really read it, and the more exposure that he gets, and the more curiosity draws more people to the work, this has remained a large factor, and maybe even become larger." So it's no great shock that, as we pull into Burroughs's driveway, he turns to me and says, "I wish there was some kind of magic you could put in your piece to stop people from coming anymore."

What's immediately striking about William S. Burroughs is the extent to which he has become an old man. There's no getting around it, no way to squint away the years and make him something he is not. He answers the door of his house wearing a fatigue jacket, a pair of jeans, and brown Rockport walkers, his back hunched, hair clumped in wispy tufts on his head. He is thinner than I expected, smaller; it is as if, in age, he has begun to collapse in upon himself like an imploding star. But there is an energy that comes off him also, a kind of vibrancy—when he walks, he bops from foot to foot, reminding me of nothing so much as a bantam rooster, and even standing, he cannot keep his body still.

Grauerholz introduces us, and Burroughs shakes my hand. "Come in, come in," he says in a gravelly whisper, waving his arm toward the living room and leading me inside with his bouncing half-hop of a walk. The house is small, single-story, with a sagging, half-reconstructed porch out front and five cozy rooms. By the door, atop an old, enclosed bookcase, sits a stone slab engraved with the words, "It is necessary to travel. It is not necessary to live." Further back, there is a small living room, with an eating table and a beat-up couch. On the coffee table is a copy of *S.W.A.T.* magazine ("Special Handgun Issue"); a *TV Guide* featuring the stars of *The X-Files*; a Quality Paperback Book Club omnibus edition of *Junky*, *Queer* and *Naked Lunch*; and a catalog offering antique drug paraphernalia for sale. Burroughs's own artworks hang on the walls, and down a narrow hallway, a second bedroom has been converted into a painting space, with pictures spread out across the small single bed, and paints, brushes and other tools lining the surfaces of a nondescript furniture set.

Once we get settled, Grauerholz asks Burroughs how he's feeling and whether he did any painting today. There is an easy camaraderie between them, but it is marked by a certain midwestern formality, a slight elevation of language and manners that charms me even as it surprises me, so contrary is it to my expectations, to the author's reputation for eschewing the conventions of social intercourse in any form. It is as if, I think, the Burroughs image represents some kind of defense mechanism for the individual, as if the icon exists, at least in part, to protect the man inside. That sense is heightened when I listen to Burroughs and Grauerholz discuss a recent inter-

view in which the author has been described as physically frail; although Grauerholz argues that the overall portrait is sympathetic, Burroughs can't get the image out of his mind. "An elegant wreck," he complains, "but a wreck nonetheless," and I am struck by the thinness of his armor, the way he has taken this small thing to heart.

After a few minutes, Burroughs goes into the

kitchen, where he pours himself a drink. Grauer-holz offers me one also, but the only thing in the house is vodka and Coca-Cola, so I decline.

"Do you want something else?" Grauerholz asks, looking at me with a host's concern.

"It's okay. Don't go to any trouble . . ."

"No trouble," he says. "Are you a scotch drinker?"

"Actually, scotch would be great."

"Let me get you some." He stands up. "William? Do you want anything from the store?"

Burroughs's head pops through the kitchen door, bouncing gently up and down. "Yes, yes," he whispers, the syllables long and sibilant, as if their meaning were a function of sound.

"Well?" Grauerholz asks, when Burroughs refuses to say any more. There is a moment of something between them, some strange suspended eye contact, before Burroughs says, "I've written it down."

For a second, I feel like I'm witnessing a kind of role reversal, with Burroughs gone all coy and quirky like a little boy. In the living room, Grauerholz shoots me an indulgent grin and heads for the kitchen, where Burroughs points at a yellow legal pad. I hear Grauerholz exclaim, "I think that's a fine idea," before he moves to the door. An instant later, Burroughs comes hopping around the corner, and disappears into the back of the house.

I wait for a second, just to make sure. Then, slowly, quietly, I walk into the kitchen and steal a look at the pad. On the top sheet of paper, in a quavery old man's script, is written a single sentence: "Is it all right to bring out a joint?" From somewhere deep in the house, I hear Burroughs's footsteps, and I return to the living room. As I sit down, he emerges with a neatly rolled reefer, which he lights and draws from, deeply, before he passes it to me.

Smoking dope with William S. Burroughs is a very strange experience. It's not that the pot is particularly potent—Burroughs, in fact, apologizes that it is not—or that it affects me in a truly mind-altering way. It's just

William Burroughs at home in Lawrence, Kansas, 1996
LEE RANALDO

that, after all these years of admiring Burroughs's work, the act of sharing a joint takes on a kind of funhouse aspect, as if this were some kind of movie I am acting in and watching at the same time. Burroughs, after all, has been an icon of mine ever since I read *Junky* as a college freshman in 1981. Or no—not an icon, since this is a notion I don't believe in anymore. But either way, the fact remains that, in a world of fakes and poseurs, Burroughs is one of the few literary heroes I have.

Even so, there are all these contradictions, all these areas in which Burroughs and I diverge. For every revelatory idea or pronouncement, there's a more reactionary notion with which I cannot reconcile myself. I've always had trouble with his unapologetic misogyny, for instance, his notion that women are a biological mistake. And his ongoing fascination with guns and weaponry also makes me uncomfortable, not least because I've never been quite sure just how much of it is genuine and how much is calculated for effect. (Later in the weekend, when the subject comes up, he pulls a small five-shot .22 handgun out of his jacket pocket and shows it to me. "I go out," he says, "I always take this with me. It can be quite deadly in the head or the neck or the heart.")

Thus, when Burroughs invites me to go shooting the following afternoon, I have to demur. I tell him that I'd planned to interview him tomorrow, and that Grauerholz has told me we might visit the one-room cabin they share at a local lake. Burroughs insists again that he wants to go shooting; then, he looks at me across the table and suggests we do the interview now.

"Now?" I sputter. "But I don't have my tape recorder."

"You got your memory," he growls.

The comment brings to mind Burroughs's description of the writer as a "recording entity," whose sole purpose is to describe, not interpret, what he has seen. That, of course, is what I am here for, but sitting in his living room, I feel almost completely off my guard. Burroughs and I might occupy the same physical setting, after all, but it's a stretch to say we're here together, and when he gets up to set out a couple of dishes for the cats, he neither tells me to stay put nor to come along. For a moment, I linger at the table, before following him into the kitchen, and from there, out to the backyard to feed the fish. Standing on the bank of his small man-made pond, watching Burroughs rock back and forth on his heels, I am struck by how much he resembles my mother's father in the last years of his life: the same sharp stoop; the same jutting features; the same impression of all extraneous meat having been whittled away, leaving behind only bones and gristle—the most elemental kind of physical essence. My grandfather's obsession was his rock garden, but I could see him here, staring into the still, murky water, talking for hours about the fish.

Then Burroughs gestures at a boxy, chest-high metal structure just behind the fish pond that looks not unlike a half-size coffin stood on end. "Orgone accumulator," he says. "Although I don't use it much anymore." And with that, he launches into a discussion of the theories of Wilhelm Reich, as the image of my grandfather slowly fades.

An hour or so later, I am standing with Burroughs in his painting room, going through his latest efforts, commenting on the images that appear ghostlike in the swirls of paint he's applied to paper, sophisticated and childlike all at once. In recent years, he's essentially stopped writing, and painting has become his primary means of expressing himself.

"That looks like some of Brion Gysin's stuff," I suggest, invoking the name of Burroughs's close friend and collaborator, who died in 1986. I point out the delicate latticework of uneven black lines that overlay one painting like a screen.

Burroughs nods intently. "I inherited Brion's

roller," he says, and seems to look at me—really to notice me—for the first time. He reaches over to a side table, picks up a small, handled cylinder scored with delicate crosshatched squares; together we examine how the ridges have worn down from constant use. It is as close as we come to a moment of intimacy, here in this small room with the door closed against the cats. I see a face amidst all the color; Burroughs suggests the outline of a pair of shoes.

"Why shoes?" I ask. "Do you put certain things in on purpose?"

"No," Burroughs tells me, hunching over yet another picture and peering close. "There's no intention at all. They emerge. Why they emerge so clearly or why they take definite forms—shoes, faces, feet in general—I just don't know. I don't have any idea of draftsmanship at all; I can't paint a chair, draw a chair or a tree or anything. But I am interested in how clear images emerge."

As Burroughs speaks, I find myself noticing certain parallels between his writing and his art. From the beginning of his career, he has not only experimented with various visual media, but also borrowed techniques from nonliterary disciplines like film and painting and adapted them to his work. In the late 1950s, for instance, he collaborated with Gysin to pioneer the use of cut-ups, a linguistic application of collage. "Life is a goddamn cut-up," he says when I ask him to explain the theory behind this notorious technique. "Every time you look out the window, or answer the phone, your consciousness is being cut by random factors. Walk down the street—bam, bam, bam. It makes you realize that your awareness is much wider than you ordinarily think." Even before that, however, Burroughs was exploring similar material in what he calls his "scrapbooks"—little datebook calendars where, during the 1950s and 1960s, he pasted up pictures, newspaper headlines, and odd fragments of type, creating small multimedia collages that seek links in the randomness of juxtaposition, looking

for definitions between the lines. Burroughs's scrapbooks feature everything from notes for novels to washes of ink to a chart that assigns each letter of the alphabet a specific color, often overlapping words and images in a way that casts into question the meaning of both. "There's no clear distinction between painting and writing," he says. "The word is an image. It's useful for conveying certain information, that's all."

With this as a defining aesthetic, it's not a far reach from the scrapbooks to the paintings that Burroughs and I peruse in the dusty silence of his back room. In fact, if you begin with these images, you can trace a line backwards that extends all the way through his oeuvre. When you factor in Burroughs's various pronouncements on the subject of language, there's an undeniable logic to the progression, as if it were somehow inevitable that—as an artist, at least—he should finally reach a point beyond verbal expression, where words don't create meaning anymore. Among his most fundamental beliefs has long been the notion that "language is a virus," that, in order for the human race to evolve, we have no choice but to "rub out the word." In *The Job*, a volume of interviews he did with the French journalist Daniel Odier, he frames the issue with typical directness: "You must learn to exist with no religion, no country, no allies. You must learn to live alone in silence." Now, watching as he identifies unconscious images with a finger, I decide that in this room I am confronting the terminus of that line of thinking, a self-contained world, beyond words or interaction, in which Burroughs has become almost a creation of his own mind. It's a victory of sorts, although, in the end, it may be a lonely one; as he wrote to Allen Ginsberg nearly forty years ago, "I am getting so far out, one day I won't come back at all."

Still, what's compelling about this is the way it reveals just how much of a conscious artist Burroughs remains, the degree to which his work continues to be bound up in the exploration of certain beliefs, from his ideas about language to his fascination with the substance and application of dreams. Some of his most effective cut-ups—in novels like *Nova Express* and *The Ticket That Exploded*—have a dreamy, repetitious logic, and the best of his painting also draws you in to an indefinable visual universe, where lines and colors suggest certain connections that you develop in your own mind. "Art," he says as he turns to another drawing and begins to point out the shapes that arise there without any conscious intention on his part, "makes people aware of what they know but don't know they know. What they see but don't know that they are seeing. But you cannot make them see. They have to, on some level, know something already. Everybody who lived on a seacoast in the Middle Ages, they knew the earth was round. They *believed* the earth was flat because the Church said so. When Cézanne's pictures were first exhibited, people were so enraged—some of them—that they attacked them with umbrellas. They didn't realize that this is the way an apple actually looks when seen from here and there and here, in different lights, at different times. They couldn't get it through their heads, some of them. Later, it became accepted as part of the general cultural awareness. And it's closer to the facts of your own perception, that's the point."

Saturday afternoon, Grauerholz picks me up at the Eldridge and we go get Burroughs for our trip to the lake. Driving down his street, we pass by a succession of quiet suburban homes with their yards and flags. Up ahead, a young father on a bicycle pulls his sleeping baby in a cart; to the right, a middle-aged woman weeds a garden while her husband mows the lawn. Briefly, I wonder what these people must think about having Burroughs as a neighbor, if they know what goes on in his books, or if they have identified the metal structure in the back-

yard as an orgone box. Then I look at the old man sitting in the front seat, army surplus cap on his head, and recall his description of himself as "looking like a retired farmer." He's absolutely right, and when I think of him that way, it gives his residence here a context it might not otherwise have.

On the way out of town, we pass through low rolling hills, past valleys and streams, and the ubiquitous farms. It's a surprise, all this gentle swelling, and it makes the earth seem somehow voluptuous, reminiscent of a blanket someone has shaken out but forgotten to smooth. At one intersection, a tractor waits at a red light, while off to the side, a farmer in bib overalls works in his fields. From the front seat, Burroughs keeps up a running commentary, pointing out birds and flowers, and a police shooting range nestled far back off the road, in a hollow between two ridges of land.

At the lake, as we make our way slowly down the uneven concrete steps to the cabin, Burroughs cautions me about keeping my center of gravity back so if I fall, I won't tumble all the way to the bottom of the stairs. Again, I am reminded of my grandfather, who spent his final years obsessed with safety, cataloging everything that could possibly go wrong.

Yet inside the cabin—once I set up my microcassette recorder and turn it on—the old man fades away a bit, leaving in his place the shadow of a shy and uncomfortable boy. Indeed, as soon as the tape starts rolling, Burroughs stiffens, staring straight ahead through the open screen door and out across the lake, banging his walking stick on the floor with a soft, insistent thud. He answers my questions forthrightly, but his responses are less than effusive, and I can't help thinking of Charles Platt's comments in Ted Morgan's biography *Literary Outlaw*: "Burroughs turns out to be almost as difficult to talk to as I feared. He is polite and perfectly willing to tolerate my presence, but many of his remarks are dismissively brief, as if the questions bore him. . . . Typically, he makes a brief categorical statement, then stops and regards me with his pale eyes as if waiting to see if I really intend to ask any more dumb questions." To me, it appears more a matter of nervousness, as if, despite all Burroughs's experience, going through with this, or any, interview is a painful ordeal.

Burroughs isn't the only one who's nervous. All weekend, I've avoided thinking of this moment, when he and I would sit down for the formal interview. Partly, it's because I doubt the efficacy of the process; interviews tend to be structured for pronouncements, and Burroughs appears to have nothing like that in mind. His attitude, in fact, seems unchanged from when he wrote in *Junkie* that "basically no one can help anyone else. There is no key, no secret someone else has that he can give you." He has no thoughts, for instance, on his iconic status, and when I ask him about the militia movement (with whom, I suspect, he'd have a sneaking sympathy, if only for their rabid antigovernment stance), he tells me that the subject is "too complex."

Then there's the matter of all the Burroughs interviews already in existence, the vast array of territory that has been previously mined. Because of this, I've decided not to talk with him about his wife, Joan, whom he accidentally shot in the head during a drunken 1951 game of William Tell, or their son, Billy, who died in 1981 of cirrhosis and self-abuse at the age of thirty-three. In addition, I stay away from the subject of heroin, and avoid asking about the Beats, a movement he's long since disavowed. There are so many questions Burroughs has answered so often that his responses have become a kind of routine, a shield composed of anecdotes, of moments turned to legend by familiarity and time. As early as 1968, in a brief "Author's Foreword" to *The*

Job, he notes that "as Monsieur Odier asked questions I found that I had in many cases already answered these questions in various books, articles and short pieces. So instead of paraphrasing or summarizing I inserted the indicated material."

Consequently, when the ubiquitous joint comes around, even though I'm supposed to be working, I figure, what the hell. I take a couple of hits and pass it to Burroughs, looking through the window to the tree leaves fluttering in the breeze. By the time we finish, Burroughs seems to have undergone a nearly physical transformation, becoming, if possible, more fully himself. Gone are the uncomfortable silences, the tapping of the cane; gone the old man's hunch in his back and the vacant look in his pale blue eyes. Now, he sits up straighter and makes eye contact, his gaze no longer rheumy but focused, the blue of his irises translucent going to clear. Even his face seems to grow fuller, more defined, as if ten years have been washed away. Emboldened by the change, I ask about mortality and his sense of the afterlife, and he leans forward and confides that it's always been an ongoing concern. "I remember when I was in camp in New Mexico," he tells me. "I had very much of a concern with the idea of mortality. I was fifteen, fourteen years old."

"That's a long time ago," I say. "How have your ideas evolved?"

"They haven't changed very much. In the first place—and I shocked Allen Ginsberg and a lot of other people by saying this—I believe in God and always have. I don't know how anyone could read my books and think otherwise. For example, 'Kim had never doubted the existence of God or the possibility of an afterlife.' I say it as simply as that, but people just don't, won't, can't believe that I mean what I say." To illustrate the point, he picks his cup up from the table before us and waves it in my direction. "Now," he says, "this glass or cup made of paper—very much what you're made of—it doesn't move itself. Something has to move it. In other words, in the magical universe, nothing happens unless some power or something wills it to happen. It's as simple as that. It comes down to the Big Bang Theory. Somebody triggered the Big Bang."

"But what about death? Are you frightened of it?"

For a moment, Burroughs doesn't seem to breathe. Then he begins to speak quietly, his words slow and meticulous, as if he is choosing them one by one. "Everybody's frightened of it," he says. "Because we don't know it. We can't." He stares out through the open door, oblivious to the fact that I am here.

Toward the end of the interview, there's a disconcerting moment, an oddly portentous interaction that could come straight from Burroughs's work. We've been talking about extra-sensory perception, and Burroughs's long-held belief that it exists. "The evidence is overwhelming," he says. "For one thing, our perceptions are limited, particularly in Western society." Apropos of this, he mentions Count Alfred Korzybski, the Polish lecturer and author whose theory of General Semantics he studied in Chicago in 1939. "One of the noble truths that Korzybski brought to light," Burroughs proclaims, "is that either/or is the great fallacy of Western thought. It's almost always both/and. So the message is to keep your eyes open. Dali said that anyone who *doesn't* believe in extra-sensory perception simply hasn't kept his eyes open because it happens all the time."

Given this attitude, I ask Burroughs what he thinks about demonic possession. It's a loaded question, for he has written at length about the subject; in fact, he's often attributed his wife's death to this very process, suggesting in the introduction to his novel, *Queer*, that "the death of Joan brought me in contact with the invader, the Ugly Spirit, and maneuvered me into a lifelong struggle, in which I have had no choice except to write my way out." Although his explanation has been derided in certain quarters as a cop-out, a way of deflecting responsibility for the tragedy onto something over which he had no control, Burroughs has never sought to deny his own complicity in events. In the same introduction, he admits that, "[l]ike a virus, the possessing entity must find a port of entry," and today, he says simply, "There's no such thing as an accident. Just how arbitrary is arbitrary? Questions I don't have the answers to."

Still, as soon I mention the Ugly Spirit, Burroughs clams up. "To some extent," he says, when I ask whether his possession by the entity is demonic in nature, and after that, he stops and purses his lips, as if determined to say no more. I pose another question, but even as he answers, I catch a glimpse of the interview tape spinning loosely on its spindle like a broken limb. When I pop it out of the recorder, I see that it has torn clear from the reel.

Burroughs keeps talking, while I sit there and wonder how much of the conversation I have lost. At the same time, bits and pieces of the weekend's dialogue start drifting back to me like cut-ups of their own. In the *Queer* introduction, Burroughs writes of the telepathic, or revelatory, qualities of the cut-ups, citing one in particular—"Raw peeled winds of hate and mischance blew the shot"—that, years later, provided some subconscious insight into the circumstances of Joan's death. Now, I think of his admonition that "You got your memory," and consider the timing of the break. If there are no accidents, there are only reasons, and if there are only reasons, than somehow, on some level, everything connects. I feel a raw peeled wind blow through me, as I reach for another tape.

Late in the afternoon, we return to the house, where Burroughs's assistant Brad prepares a meal of pork chops, couscous and broccoli, and Burroughs sits and opens the mail. I'm still thinking about the broken tape, so I don't say much, just jot down notes every couple of minutes, trying to reconstruct the interview in my head. Grauerholz drifts in and out, reminding Burroughs about some upcoming projects, mostly the planned audio adaptations of *Junky* and *Queer*. It's a busy life for a retired writer, and I wonder to what extent it takes its toll.

During dinner, Grauerholz and I talk a bit about computers, and the projected movie version of *On the Road*. Burroughs has a drink and then another one, not really seeming to listen, making an occasional comment, but for the most part lost in that inner world of his own. After a while, he starts to drift off, and as his face relaxes and his eyes close, he takes on that grandfatherly aspect again. Grauerholz looks at his watch: 8:30. "We should go," he says.

We make our goodbyes around the table, and Burroughs accompanies us out to the porch. In the glare of the electric lights, he looks impatient, glad at the prospect of being left alone.

Grauerholz nods, and I shake Burroughs's hand, then move down the steps and across the slender grass to the car. As I spring open the door, though, I am stopped by the sound of Burroughs's distinctive deadpan, rumbling like thunder across the silence of the Midwestern night.

I look up; Burroughs is still on the porch, standing at the rail.

"*Vaya con Dios*," he tells me. "Go with God."

My Burroughs:
Postmortem Notes

BY RICHARD HELL

BURROUGHS WAS THE REAL Rimbaud, or at least the one who stayed the course. Rimbaud's program to banish the ego and undo the controlling, classifying brain ("derangement of the senses" in order to "become a seer"—AR) was self-evidently desirable to Burroughs. "The ego is excess baggage," he wrote. (AR: "I is another.") Burroughs's life was one long cultivated coma.

Writing was another way of subverting that which would control him. As a writer, he was also utterly unpretentious, workmanlike, scientific. ("What is Art," Ginsberg asked him in the Forties. "'Art' is a three-letter word.") He postulated the Word—language—itself as the ultimate form of control: a virus that turns the cells of its host into factories for copying itself; and intended to mess with all the ways he could find that writing would influence people and their realities. Writing was a way out of his ego's control as well: He always described himself as recording rather than writing; much of his material came from his own dreams. ("An artist is in fact transcribing from the unconscious." AR: "I am a spectator at the flowering of my thought.") He further subverted any egoistic function of writing with his cut-ups, as well as exploiting and exploring the technical magical/inoculative/therapeutic possibilities of writing—neutralizing horrors by revealing and describing them, looking for prophesies and new realities in the cut-ups. . . .

William Burroughs at the West End bar,
New York City, 1974
MELLON

©MELLON 1998

He spent his workdays in the mines—his dreams (drug nods), others' writings (which supplied many of his lines), cut-ups.

The first thing that always hits me in his writings is his fearless unattachment. He has no vested interest in how things are or the nature of his own responses to them. I remember when I was a teenager being stunned to learn from Burroughs's writing the concept of the hidden "vested interest"—the doctor's vested interest in disease, the cop's in crime, the general's in war. . . . He treated himself as a specimen. The value he held highest seemed to be minding your own business. "The mark of a basic shit is that he has to be *right*." It's like he was a detective sent back from death. He had nothing to prove, only to discover. His detachment from his own humanness, his unsentimentality, was outrageous. He did not want to be human (earthlings are "insect servants"). But neither did he want to die. He even resented mortality as a form of control. He wanted to write his way out of it all.

What is the meaning of his narcotics addiction? Many people don't realize that he was an addict till the end. The Lawrence years were spent on methadone—synthetic heroin. Well, it's who he was, you can't get around it—it's not the sort of thing you'd call incidental about a person. I think it's got to be called the central fact. It gave him his metaphor. To the actor all the world's a stage; to Burroughs it was a torture chamber of alien manipulations to his organism (and he wanted to escape it).

He was a kind of classic addict type—a person who despised himself, found the world greatly paining, and who wanted out. He said that he'd always felt that within himself "there was a basic wrongness somewhere," that "other people are different than me and I don't really like them," and he felt great guilt and self-hatred for "mistakes too monstrous for remorse"—killing his wife, never visiting his mother in the nursing home, his neglect of his son. "I have crippling depressions. I wonder how I can feel this bad and live. Very few people are ever in contact with that area of human despair. I've survived by confronting it. I let it wash through me." He described repeated occasions throughout his life of being overcome, broken down, by final relentless sadness, in freezing convulsive sobs, usually from loneliness and guilt at having failed others. I think he himself feared that deep down he really was the "sheep-killing dog" that he was said to resemble—by the father of a schoolmate—before he was twelve years old. Addicts tend both to hate themselves for their self-absorption and emotional distance (tending to be "sensitive," but to their own feelings, not others'), and to exacerbate these problems by the flight from them into narcotics. Hair of the dog. It's complicated.

And of course addiction makes for a complicated attitude toward addiction. It seems to me Burroughs was confused about how to conceive of narcotics use. He would affirm the citizen's right to use drugs, mocking and cursing governments' efforts to control, while at the same time he would describe addiction as a horrible control—the very model of control—and depict it as following from mere proximity to a substance. There was also a lot of death and misery around him wherever he went, and no doubt much of that was due to vulnerable souls taking Burroughs as a model and trying to live up to the metaphysical glamour of his "nothing is true, everything is permitted" program. Burroughs was a soulful and decent guy—an old-school gentleman, a "Johnson"—and he shouldn't be held accountable for the weaknesses and cluelessness of some of his followers. Still it's useful to remember that a lot of what you hear when you listen to Burroughs comes from bottomless despair and narcotics. Thing is, it makes a lot of sense, little as he wanted to.

Then again, maybe this is obvious and I'm just muttering to myself. His writing is beautiful and of course hilarious: meticulously seen, sawn and nailed, deadpan, fearless, matchless ear. He's among the most select (Joyce, Beckett) in having a style so refined that you can generally recognize him in a sentence. But just as great is that freedom from ties, from debts to, from vested interests in virtually anything. When you're coming from no assumptions, not even of the virtue of human existence, what you see here on earth could well make pain-killing dream-inducing drugs a preferred option, no matter what the sacrifices. Think about it, or as Bill'd say, "Wouldn't you?"

ps/alm 23 revisited
for william burroughs

BY PATTI SMITH

The word is his shepherd
he shall not want
he spreads like the eagle
upon the green hill
boys of the Alhambra
in vivid sash
serve him still
your orange juice, sir
your fishing pole
accepting all
with tender grace
and besting us
with this advice
children never be ashamed
wrestle smile walk; in sun
thank you, Bill
your will be done
God grant you
mind and medicine
we draw our hearts
and you within
moral vested
Gentleman

*Patti Smith visiting William Burroughs on her
twenty-ninth birthday, December 30, 1975*

KATE SIMON

Remembering
Burroughs
August 1997

[ROLLING STONE 769, September 18, 1997}

We would cut up these speeches by Eisenhower and works by Rimbaud and Shakespeare, and we'd combine them. He taught me it would work if the eye catches something. It was pure magic. Burroughs was one of the most beautiful and intelligent men I met in my life. I was so lucky to know him—it was like meeting Appolonius of Tyre or Pythagoras. Of the Beat Generation, Burroughs was kind of the captain of the ship. Ginsberg would've been the radio operator; Kerouac, the first mate; and I would have been a passenger. But there was Burroughs, steering in a great cargo.

—GREGORY CORSO

William Burroughs was the person who broke the door down. When I read Burroughs, it changed my vision of what you could write about, how you could write. He broadened people's conception of what makes humanity. In that way, he really was an American hero, a hero writer, and also just a great man. I am sad not to have him writing anymore.

—LOU REED

Before I met Burroughs, I was already a beatnik, living that life. I had always assumed James Dean and I kind of started it, emulating Marlon Brando, but that's how the Beats touched everything, how Burroughs's influence was. Burroughs took everybody back onto the street, into the realm of the senses to write about those inner dark places. He broke barriers, opened paths.

—DENNIS HOPPER

Burroughs is the true godfather of outlaw artists. He was always hovering in the shadows, always suspicious of human nature and authority. Burroughs made us look for what masks the truth. He was always suspicious about movies, saying the truth can't possibly be found in twenty-four frames a second. In the greatest sense, Burroughs made me think about what's supposedly permissible in art.

—JIM JARMUSCH

William had a fine taste for handguns, and later in life he became very good with them. I remember shooting with him one afternoon at his range on the outskirts of Lawrence. He had five or six well-oiled old revolvers laid out on a wooden table, covered with a white linen cloth, and he used whichever one he was in the mood for at the moment. The S&W .45 was his favorite. "This is my finisher," he said lovingly, and then he went into a crouch and put five out of six shots through the chest of a human-silhouette target about twenty-five yards away.

Hot damn, I thought, we are in the presence of a serious Shootist. Nicole had been filming it all with the Hi8, but I took the camera and told her to walk out about ten yards in front of us and put an apple on her head.

William smiled wanly and waved her off. "Never mind, my dear," he said to her. "We'll pass on that trick." Then he picked up the .454 Casul Magnum I'd brought with me. "But I will try this one," he said. "I like the looks of it."

The .454 Casul is the most powerful handgun in the world. It is twice as strong as a .44 Magnum, with a huge scope and recoil so brutal that I was reluctant to let an eighty-year-old man shoot it. This thing will snap back and crack your skull if you don't hold it properly.

But William persisted.

The first shot lifted him two or three inches off the ground, but the bullet hit the throat of the target, two inches high. "Good shot," I said. "Try a little lower and a click to the right." He nodded and braced again.

His next shot punctured the stomach and left nasty red welts on his palms. Nicole shuddered visibly behind the camera, but I told her we'd only been kidding about the apple. Then, William emptied the cylinder, hitting once in the groin and twice just under the heart. I reached out to shake his hand as he limped back to the table, but he jerked it away and asked for some ice for his palms. "Well," he said, "this is a very nasty piece of machinery. I like it."

I put the huge silver brute in its case and gave it to him. "It's yours," I said. "You deserve it."

Which was true. William was a Shootist. He shot like he wrote—with extreme precision and no fear. He would have fired an M-60 from the hip that day, if I'd brought one with me. He would shoot anything, and he feared nothing.

—HUNTER S. THOMPSON

PART IV

Beat's Poet laureate

Allen Ginsberg

Allen Ginsberg at home
New York City, 1969
DAVID GAHR

Allen Ginsberg: 1926-1997

BY MIKAL GILMORE

[ROLLING STONE 761, May 29, 1997]

Allen Ginsberg typing "Howl," 1955
ALLEN GINSBERG COLLECTION

FOR MANY OF US, ALLEN GINSBERG'S death came with such suddenness, it proved to be a mind-stopping jolt. But Ginsberg had been contemplating death's inevitability for nearly the entirety of his writing career. In 1959, in "Kaddish," his narrative-poem about his mother's decline and death, Ginsberg addressed her memory: "Death let you out, Death had the Mercy, you're done with your century. . . ." And in 1992, he wrote of himself:

> Sleepless I stay up &
> think about my Death
> —certainly it's nearer. . . .
> If I don't get some rest I'll die faster

As it turned out, it was only seven days before his death that Ginsberg learned the illness of his last few years had turned worse—that it was now inoperable liver cancer. Hearing the news, Ginsberg returned to his apartment in New York's East Village, and proceeded to do what he had always done: He sat down and wrote a body of poems about the experiences of his life—in this case, about the imminence of his end. One of these poems—a long, hilarious and heart-affecting piece called "Death & Fame"—ran in *The New Yorker* the week following his demise. In the poem, Ginsberg envisioned hundreds of friends, admirers and lovers gathered at his "big funeral," and he hoped that among the eulogies, someone would testify: "He gave great head."

In those last few days, Ginsberg also talked to friends—his lifetime compeer, author William S. Burroughs; his lover of several decades, Peter Orlovsky; poet Gregory Corso, among others—

and he wrote a letter to President Bill Clinton (to be sent via George Stephanopoulos, another Ginsberg friend), demanding, in jest, some sort of medal of recognition. At one point during his last week, he sang along with a recording of "C.C. Rider" by 1920s blues vocalist Ma Rainey—the first voice Ginsberg said he remembered hearing as a child. By Friday he had slipped into a coma. Surrounded by a few close friends, Ginsberg died early Saturday morning, April 5, 1997.

A quiet closing to a mighty life. Not since the 1977 death of Elvis Presley and the 1980 murder of John Lennon has a certain segment of popular culture had to come to terms with the realization of such an epochal ending. Allen Ginsberg not only made history—by writing poems that jarred America's consciousness and by insuring that the 1950s Beat movement would be remembered as a considerable literary force—but he also lived through and embodied some of the most remarkable cultural mutations of the last half-century. As much as Presley, as much as the Beatles, Bob Dylan or the Sex Pistols, Allen Ginsberg helped set loose something wonderful, risky and unyielding in the psyche and dreams of our times. Perhaps only Martin Luther King Jr.'s brave and costly quest had a more genuinely liberating impact upon the realities of modern history, upon the freeing up of people and voices that much of established society wanted kept in the margins. Just as Dylan would later change what popular songs could say and do, Ginsberg changed what poetry might accomplish, how it could speak, what it would articulate, and who it would speak to and for. Ginsberg's words—his performances of his words and how he carried their meanings into his life and actions—gave poetry a political and cultural relevance it had not known since the 1840s' Transcendentalists (Ralph Waldo Emerson and Henry Thoreau, among them) or since the shocking publication of Walt Whitman's 1855 classic, *Leaves of Grass*. Indeed, in Ginsberg's hands, poetry proved to be something a great deal

more than a vocation or the province of refined wordsmiths and critics. Ginsberg transformed his gift for language into a mission—"trying to save and heal the spirit of America," as he wrote in the introduction to fellow poet Anne Waldman's *The Beat Book*. In the process, he not only influenced subsequent writers like Dylan, Lennon, Lou Reed, Patti Smith and Jim Carroll, but Ginsberg's effect could also be found in Norman Mailer's *Advertisements for Myself*, in the writings and deeds of Czech President Václav Havel, in the lives and exploits of 1960s insurrectionists like Timothy Leary, Tom Hayden and Abbie Hoffman. One can also hear Ginsberg's effect on such current artists as Sonic Youth, Beck, U2 and several of our finer hip-hop poets.

Ginsberg was also, of course, simply a man—at turns generous and competitive, self-aware yet self-aggrandizing, old in his wisdom, juvenile in his tastes and affections, and relentlessly promiscuous though deeply faithful. More than anything, however, Ginsberg was someone who once summoned the bravery to speak hidden truths about unspeakable things, and some people took consolation and courage from his example. That example—that insistence that he would not simply *shut up*, and that one should not accept delimited values or experiences—is perhaps Ginsberg's greatest gift to us. Today there are so many artists who have carried on in that tradition that Ginsberg's death does not rob us of unfulfilled possibilities, as happened in the horrid deaths of Kurt Cobain, Tupac Shakur and the Notorious B.I.G. That's because Ginsberg's entire life was a process of opening up himself (and us) to possibilities. Still, the loss of Ginsberg remains enormous. There is no question: We have seen a giant pass from our times. It is only fitting to look back on what he did for us and for our land.

Allen Ginsberg was born in 1926, the son of politically radical Jewish parents (Allen's older brother, Eugene, was named after labor organizer Eugene V. Debs; Ginsberg also recalled that the music of Ma Rainey, Beethoven and Bessie Smith filled the family's home in Paterson, New Jersey). Allen's father, Louis, was a published and respected poet. Louis and Allen would have many arguments over the years regarding poetry's language and structure, though in his father's last few years, the two men often shared stages together, exchanging poems and genuine respect and affection.

But it was Ginsberg's mother, Naomi, who proved in many ways to have a more profound and haunting effect on her son's life, mentality and writing. By 1919, she had already experienced an episode of schizophrenia. She recovered for a while and returned to her life as an activist and mother, but when Allen was three, Naomi had an intense relapse. She committed herself to a sanatorium, and for much of the rest of her life, she moved from one psychiatric institution to another. During the times she returned home, she would often declaim frightened fantasies about a pact between her husband, Hitler, Mussolini and President Franklin D. Roosevelt, all involved in an attempt to seize control of her mind. Also, she took to walking around the house nude. Allen—who was kept home from school to take care of his mother on her bad days—would sit reading, trying to ignore Naomi's nakedness and ravings.

Growing up witnessing painful madness and missing the attendance of a loving mother had a profound impact on Ginsberg. For one thing, it taught him a certain way of preparing for and dealing with hard realities. In Jerry Aronson's film *The Life and Times of Allen Ginsberg*, Ginsberg stated: "I've had almost like this screen built, so I could hear people dying and get on with it. . . . I could survive without tears, in a sense, so that the tears would come out in a poem later, rather than in an immediate break-up of my world. My world already was broken up long ago."

Naomi's problems—and her absence from the home—also brought out a neediness and uncertainty that stayed with Ginsberg in many ways throughout his entire life and that affected how, as a child, he made connections between erotic incentives and emotional fulfillment. Ginsberg often related how, during the lonely nights when his mother was away, he would cuddle up against his father, Louis, Allen rubbing his erect penis against the back of his father's leg while Louis tried to sleep. Finally, Naomi's mental problems also made Ginsberg both more afraid of his own possible madness and also more sympathetic about the troubles of others—and it left him with a fear of shadows and ghosts. By the time he was eleven, Allen was already writing about these visions in his early journals, and he discovered something that gave him a certain comfort and strength: Words, unlike so much that surrounded him as a child, were something he could have dominion over, something that could express his thoughts, something he could take pride in.

But for all the loneliness and fearfulness that characterized his childhood family life, Ginsberg also inherited his parents' clear intelligence and much of their political compassion. By the time he was sixteen, he was also coming to the realization that he was attracted to men sexually; in particular he worshipped a high school hero who left Paterson for Columbia University, in New York City. In 1943 Ginsberg received a scholarship from the Young Men's Hebrew Association of Paterson, and he promptly headed for Columbia.

Ginsberg arrived at the university planning to study to become a labor lawyer, but two differing intellectual milieus changed that course. The first was Columbia's formidable English department, which then included Pulitzer Prize–winning poet Mark Van Doren and Lionel Trilling; Ginsberg became enamored of these men as mentors, and soon changed his major to literature. During the course of the next year or so, Ginsberg also met another group of men—some of them fellow Columbia students, closer to his own age—and it

was this fraternity that turned his life around and that would function as a secondary family for much of the rest of his life. Among these men were William S. Burroughs, Lucien Carr and a football star with literary aspirations named Jack Kerouac. The bond that developed between them transformed not only their own destinies, but also those of future generations. In particular, Ginsberg and Kerouac seemed to share a special connection. Both were haunted by their childhoods—Kerouac had an older brother, Gerard, who had died young and Kerouac's mother used to hold Jack as a child and tell him, "*You should have died, not Gerard.*" But the most important thing these men shared was a sense that, in the mid-1940s, there were great secrets lurking at America's heart, that there were still rich and daring ways of exploring the nation's arts and soul—and that there was a great adventure and transcendence to be found by doing so. Indeed, America *was* about to change dramatically, but the significance of that change wouldn't fully be understood or reckoned with for another twenty years. In 1945, the nation emerged victorious from the horrors of World War II and would enter a long era of new prosperity and opportunity; the new American life, many politicians and critics declared, was now the world standard of the *good* life. But all this came at unexpected psychic costs: The knowledge of the possibility of nuclear devastation changed all the possibilities of the future. Plus, for all the nation's victories abroad, there were still many battles unwaged at home—including the delicate question of minority rights. Ginsberg, Kerouac, Burroughs and the rest of their crowd were beginning to be drawn to some decidedly different ideals and hopes. They heard the music of bebop alto saxophonist Charlie Parker and pianist Thelonious Monk, they

Allen Ginsberg on his Cherry Valley, New York, farm, Labor Day 1973

MELLON

tasted the visions of marijuana and Benzedrine, they prowled the reality of Times Square. A new world—a world still largely underground—was being born, and they had keen eyes and a keen need for it.

The friendship that developed among them was complex, sometimes tense, sometimes loving, but what held it together for so long was a shared desire to inquire—in matters of the mind, of aesthetics and of the senses. In time, this group became the nexus for a literary and artistic community known as the Beat Generation—the first countercultural movement that would have a major impact on America's popular culture. But all this was still years away, for before Beat became a movement or style, it was simply the way Ginsberg and his friends chose to live their lives, to examine their own experiences and their view of things both internal—like the spirit—and external, like the night and music and sex. Sometimes these men related to each other sexually (Ginsberg later told stories of him and Kerouac jacking each other off after a night of drinking; years later, Ginsberg also had an affair with Burroughs). Mainly, the group would spend nights consuming alcohol and mild drugs (though Burroughs soon turned to heroin), staying up until dawn, talking about the poetry, visions and madness of Blake, Whitman, Rimbaud, Dostoyevski, Celine, Genet and Baudelaire; about how language might learn from jazz; about what was truly holy and what was allowed in one's life. Along the way, the group derived a certain ethos and aesthetic that they called the New Vision. It relied on stretching one's experiences, finding truths in distorted realities, in sexual pursuits, finding spirituality in the lower depths of life and, most important, in making a commitment to an extemporized manner of living, writing, talking and risking. Somewhere along the line another friend of the group, a bisexual junkie prostitute, Herbert Huncke, referred to them as "beat," meaning *beat down, wasted.* Kerouac saw in the word another possibility: *beatific*. In time, the term went both ways: Beat came to stand for the idea that to discover one's true self and the self's liberation, you first had to descend into some of the most secret, used-up and bereft parts of your heart, soul, body and consciousness. Consequently, Beat became hard-boiled and loving at the same time, erotic and spiritual. Later, Ginsberg would write to Kerouac: "I can't believe that between us . . . we have the nucleus of a totally new historically important generation."

But the budding movement also could lead to costly excesses. In August 1944, Lucien Carr stabbed to death a friend of his, David Kammerer, after a night of drinking and arguing. Carr was a beautiful young man, and Kammerer had been obsessed with him, and he relentlessly pursued and pushed Carr. After the stabbing, Carr went directly to Burroughs's apartment and admitted what he had done. Burroughs advised Carr to turn himself in to the police. Carr then went and awakened Kerouac and repeated his confession. Kerouac helped Carr get rid of the knife. In a few days, Carr turned himself in to the police, and Burroughs and Kerouac were arrested as material witnesses. Ginsberg, as well, was castigated for being part of such a dangerous crowd. In truth, though, Ginsberg felt that in some way the group's "libertine" attitudes had helped make the tragedy possible—and that understanding made Allen much more careful, in years to come, about any excesses that might lead to violence. Eventually, Carr was sentenced to twenty years in prison (he served two years), and for a short time, the old crowd dispersed. A few months later, Ginsberg was found in his Columbia dormitory in bed with Kerouac; for that infraction, and for having written offensive graffiti in the dust of a windowsill, Allen was suspended from the university for a year. Things went up and down for the group for a few years. People drifted in and out of New York, and then in 1949, Ginsberg got

involved in the life of Huncke, the drug addict and thief. That association later resulted in Ginsberg's arrest for possessing stolen property, and his being committed to the Columbia-Presbyterian Psychiatric Institute—a turn of events that would, in time, have great effect on his poetry.

Prior to that, though, in late 1946, a new figure showed up in the Beat circle—and his involvement with the crowd had a seismic impact on both Ginsberg and Kerouac. Neal Cassady was a sharp-featured, handsome, fast-talking, brilliant, natural prodigy. He didn't so much write (in fact, he wrote very little), but he did live his life as if it were a novel. He drove across America relentlessly, loved to masturbate frequently each day and also fucked a good number of the beautiful women (and some of the men) he met along the way. He became involved with a woman named Carolyn Robinson, and the couple eventually settled down in Denver for a time. Kerouac was taken by Cassady's intense, fast-clip language—like a spoken version of bebop—and with Cassady's willingness to go as far as he could with the sensual experience and sensory rush of life. Ginsberg was impressed by the same traits, but he was also entranced by Cassady's beauty. One night, following a party, Ginsberg and Cassady found themselves sharing the same bed. Ginsberg was scared of his own desires, he later admitted, but Cassady put his arm around him and pulled him close, in a gentle motion. It was the first time in his life that Ginsberg felt truly loved, and it was also his first passionate sexual experience.

Ginsberg fell in love with Cassady, and his pursuit of that love—and the intensity of how wrong it all went—proved a key episode leading to his development as an artist. Cassady, meantime, started to discourage the attraction, but Ginsberg was undaunted and followed him to Colorado. Though the two still had sex on occasion, Ginsberg soon realized that it meant little to Cassady. Devastated by his rejection, Ginsberg returned to New York, where he went on to fall into trouble with Huncke.

By the early 1950s, Ginsberg had gone through severe pain over his loss of Cassady and had also gone through psychiatric treatment. He didn't know what he wanted to do with his life and was working in an advertising agency in Manhattan. One day, discussing this matter, Ginsberg's therapist asked him what he *really* wanted to do with his life. Ginsberg replied: quit his job and write poetry. The therapist asked, "Well, why don't you?" Then, in 1954, the old crowd started to reassemble in the San Francisco Bay Area. The Cassadys had moved to San Jose, California, and Kerouac settled in for a visit. In San Francisco itself, a poetry movement was burgeoning, inspired in part by the success of local poets Kenneth Rexroth and Lawrence Ferlinghetti. Ferlinghetti had just opened the nation's first all-paperback bookstore, City Lights, and had started to publish local poets. Ginsberg headed for San Jose. He was thinking about poetry, but he was also still thinking about Neal Cassady. One afternoon, Carolyn returned home to see Neal and Allen in bed, Ginsberg sucking Cassady's penis. She ordered Ginsberg from their home, drove him to San Francisco, gave him twenty dollars and left him there.

It was the best thing that ever happened to Ginsberg. He soon fell in with the poetry crowd in San Francisco's North Beach area, and he met a man with whom he would stay involved for decades, Peter Orlovsky. The hopes and visions that had formed years before in New York were starting to come to fruition for some of the old crowd—especially for Kerouac, who had finished two novels, and for Ginsberg, who was working steadily, ready for something to break loose in his poetry. One afternoon, in August 1955, Ginsberg sat down at a typewriter in his tiny apartment and attempted to write a poem for his own ear, a poem that would catch the free-flowing style that he had seen Kerouac hit upon in his own recent writing. Ginsberg wrote the whole day, thinking about many things: his lost loves, his found loves, the discarded people of America, the discarded promises of America, the fear that was just behind him, the fear that lay ahead for all.

Two months later, in October, Ginsberg—with help from Kenneth Rexroth—organized a poetry reading to be given at a cooperative art gallery, the Six Gallery, to showcase a handful of the scene's poets. Six poets read that evening—including Gary Snyder, Michael McClure and Philip Lamantia—to a crowd of maybe a hundred to two hundred people, with Kerouac sitting on the gallery's floor, drinking and tapping out rhythms on a wine jug, urging "Go! Go!" to the cadences of the poets' words. Ginsberg was the last to read, and as he began "Howl"—the poem he had written in one sitting two months earlier—the crowd was transfixed from the first lines:

> I saw the best mind of my generation
> destroyed by madness, starving
>   hysterical naked
> dragging themselves through the negro streets
> at dawn looking for an angry
>   fix,
> angelheaded hipsters burning for the
> ancient heavenly connection to the
>   starry dynamo in the machinery of the night.

Ginsberg went on to describe the fearsome evil that he saw America becoming—"Moloch whose blood is running money! Moloch whose fingers are ten armies"—and when he finished, the crowd exploded in applause. "All of a sudden," Rexroth later said, "Ginsberg read this thing that he had been keeping to himself all this while, and it just blew things up completely. Things would never be quite the same again."

"Howl" was one of the most incandescent

events in post-World War II literary history or popular culture, and its arrival later insured the Beats their place on the map of modern time. Also, because "Howl" was a poem that had such force when read aloud by Ginsberg, it marked a return of poetry to the art of vocalization. But most important, "Howl" was the first major American work of the era that spoke for the outcasts, for the mad and the lost, and about what would soon happen in the nation's soul. In the context of those times, in the midst of a frightened new patriotism that was being defined by fears of socialism and communism and a desperate need to believe in the assurance of the family structure and traditional mores, "Howl" battered at the heart of the American ideal of civilization. It was a heroic work on many levels. America was hardly prepared to admit that homosexuality might be anything other than a form of insanity; for a poet—for anybody—to declare pride or pleasure to be queer was to run a monumental risk. To talk about—to cherish—those who "let themselves be fucked in the ass by saintly motorcyclists, and screamed with joy" was no small matter. In effect, it meant aligning oneself with madness, with inexpressible values. To find grace and worthy companionship and celebration in the company of junkies, prostitutes and black jazz revolutionaries only upped the ante more. Something opened up in America's culture and in its future the day that Ginsberg gave utterance to these thoughts with "Howl." The following year, working from quite different quarters, Elvis Presley in his own way helped push the gates open as well. "We liked Elvis," Gregory Corso later said of the night he and Kerouac watched Presley on *The Ed Sullivan Show*. "We identified with the sexual wiggling of his body."

"Howl" and Presley. Nothing would ever be

Peter Orlovsky with basil, Cherry Valley, New York, 1973

MELLON

the same after that. America's libido, America's likelihood, had been ripped wide open.

This isn't to say that "Howl" was immediately or widely read, or praised. Quite the contrary: The reaction of some people was that "Howl" should *never* be widely read. In 1957 Lawrence Ferlinghetti (who published the first editions of "Howl") and a City Lights bookstore employee were arrested for knowingly selling obscenity and put on trial. The prosecutor was a Bay-area district attorney, Ralph McIntosh, bent on closing down porn shops and prohibiting the sale of magazines with nudity. The American Civil Liberties Union, Grove Press, *Evergreen Review* and poet Kenneth Patchen, among others, offered their support to Ferlinghetti, Ginsberg and "Howl." Among those testifying on behalf of the poem's serious merits were Rexroth and author Walter Van Tilburg Clark. In his final argument, McIntosh asked Judge Clayton W. Horn: "Your Honor, how far are we going to license the use of filthy, vulgar, obscene and disgusting language? How far can we go?"

Horn ruled that "Howl" was not lacking in social importance, and therefore could not be ruled obscene. In delivering his decision, Horn also offered what may be the single best—and most succinct—review that "Howl" received: "The first part of 'Howl' presents a picture of a nightmare world; the second part is an indictment of those elements in modern society destructive of the best qualities of human nature; such elements are predominantly identified as materialism, conformity and mechanization leading toward war. The third part presents a picture of an individual who is a specific representation of what the author conceives as a general condition . . . 'Footnote to Howl' [the final section of the poem] seems to be a declamation that everything in the world is holy, including parts of the body by name. It ends in a plea for holy living."

Though Ginsberg was vindicated and suddenly famous, he was determined not to arrive as the Beats' sole writer hero. Over the years, he helped Jack Kerouac in his long quest to publish *On the Road*—a book about Kerouac's adventures with Neal Cassady (who was called Dean Moriarty in the published text)—which had been turned down by numerous major publishers since 1951. The book was finally published by Viking in 1957, as a result of Ginsberg's efforts. It is now recognized as a milestone novel in modern literature. Ginsberg also championed the cause of William S. Burroughs—a much tougher sell, because Burroughs was a drug user who wrote radical prose (such as *Junky*), and because he had killed his wife in a shooting accident in Mexico in 1951. Ginsberg understood that his old friend felt tremendous guilt and Ginsberg also believed Burroughs might never redeem himself unless he could concentrate his soul and mind on his writing. Ginsberg later helped Burroughs assemble the final draft of *Naked Lunch* and worked tirelessly until the book was published in the United States. (Which resulted in *Naked Lunch*'s own obscenity trial and another ruling that the book could not legally be considered obscene.)

The Beats were—at least for a brief time—a force in American arts and letters, but there remained many who were incensed by their words and beliefs. In 1960 FBI Director J. Edgar Hoover stood before the Republican Convention and declared that "beatniks" were among America's major menaces. In addition, Norman Podhoretz—an old classmate of Ginsberg's at Columbia and by 1958 the editor of *Commentary* magazine—asserted that the Beats were an affront to the nation's central ideals. By the end of the decade, the Beats had been sidelined, declared a silly aberration by moralist critics on both the right and left. But despite all the resistance and disdain, Ginsberg continued to grow and thrive as a poet—and to remain undaunted in spirit. At the conclusion of one of his most defiant works,

"America," he wrote: "America I'm putting my queer shoulder to the wheel."

Then, in 1959, after a night of taking Benzedrine, listening to the rhythm & blues of Ray Charles and walking New York's streets, Ginsberg sat down to write "Kaddish." It was his tribute to his mother, Naomi, whose mental pain had grown so horrifying that, in 1947, Ginsberg had signed papers allowing doctors to perform a lobotomy on her. Ginsberg never truly got over the guilt of that decision, and he would never enjoy the union and relationship with his mother that he'd longed for his entire life. In 1956 Allen sent Naomi a dittoed copy of "Howl." Naomi died shortly thereafter. A few days after learning of her death, he received her last letter: "I received your poetry," she wrote, "I'd like to send it to Louis for criticism. . . . As for myself, I still have the wire on my head. The doctors know about it. They are cutting the flesh and bone. . . . I do wish you were back east so I could see you. . . . I wish I were out of here and home at the same time you were young; then I would be young."

In "Kaddish," Ginsberg remembered everything about his mother—tender things, scary things, the amazing perceptions that sometimes blazed through her madness—and with enormous love and compassion, he finally found her place in his heart (and recognized his in hers) and let her go to her death. It was most likely Ginsberg's finest moment as a poet, and it is impossible to hear any of his readings of that work and not be moved by how profoundly "Kaddish" measures just how much people, families and nations can lose as their hopes and fates unwind.

For the next three decades, Allen Ginsberg would remain an important artist and active force. Indeed, more than any other figure from the Beat era, he made the transition from the styles and concerns of the 1950s to those of the decades that followed. Jack Kerouac died in 1969, after living an embittered and alcoholic final few years at his mother's home in Massachusetts (his mother hated Ginsberg and came between the two men's friendship whenever possible). Neal Cassady went on to become a popular figure in San Francisco's mid- and late-1960s Haight-Ashbury scene; he became the driver for Ken Kesey and the Merry Pranksters' legendary cross-country bus trek, and he also became a driver and companion to the Grateful Dead. But perhaps Cassady pushed his spirited self too hard. One day, in 1968, after leaving a wedding in a small Mexican town, Cassady collapsed while walking alongside some railroad tracks. He died the next day, just short of his forty-second birthday.

Ginsberg not only survived but kept pace with the spirit and needs of the times, with the permutations of youth culture; also, he kept faith with the humane and impassioned ideals that had made "Howl" so powerful in the first place. In 1965 he became friendly with the Beatles and Bob Dylan. Ginsberg's and the Beats' work already had meaning and effect for these artists. Dylan recalled that after reading Kerouac and Ginsberg, he realized that there were people like him somewhere in the land—and, indeed, when he made his startling transition to the electric, free-association style of music found on *Highway 61 Revisited* and *Blonde on Blonde* (and again later with *Blood on the Tracks*), Dylan was taking the language, cadences and imagery of the Beats and applying them to a new form. The impact of this melding on 1960s music—like the effect of Ginsberg's "Howl" on the 1950s—was colossal. (In fact, one of the early proposed cover photos for *Blonde on Blonde* showed Dylan standing with Ginsberg and poet/playwright Michael McClure.) In addition, John Lennon had read the Beats in his years as an art student in Liverpool, England, and changed his spelling of the group's name, Beetles, to Beatles, in part as tribute to the spirit of their inspired artistry. Dylan and the Beatles changed not just a specific art form—that is, rock & roll—but also transformed the perceptions and aspirations of youth and popular culture at large. But without the earlier work of Ginsberg and Kerouac, it is possible that these 1960s artists might not have hit upon quite the same path of creativity—or at least might not have been able to work in the same atmosphere of permission and invention.

Ginsberg also became increasingly involved and influential in the political concerns of the 1960s and thereafter—though he did so in a way that made plain his own conviction in the politics of nonviolence and joy rather than of destruction and hatred. In some ways, in fact, the 1960s culture of the hippies and radicals amounted to the realization of what the Beats began to envision and prophesy in the late 1940s (interestingly, hippie was a term first coined by the Beats, meaning "half-hip," and the phrase "flower power" was first verbalized by Allen Ginsberg). In the summer of 1968, Ginsberg helped the Yippies organize Chicago's Festival of Life (along with Abbie Hoffman, Jerry Rubin, Tom Hayden and members of the Black Panthers), in protest of the Democratic Party's promotion of the Vietnam War and as a rebuke to Hubert Humphrey's capitulation to the party's hawkish elements. But when the events of those few days turned suddenly brutal and bloody—with policemen clubbing young people, old people, anything in their path and demonstrators tossing bricks at, and taunting, the already enraged cops—Ginsberg became sickened and horrified. On one occasion, as police raged through a crowd bashing protesters, a policeman came upon Ginsberg seated in the lotus position, softly chanting. The policeman raised his club to crash it down on Ginsberg's head. The poet looked up at the officer, smiled and said: "Go in peace, brother." The cop lowered his club. "Fucking hippie," he declared, then moved on. In 1969, when several of the key Chicago activists—known as the Chicago Seven, including Hayden, Hoffman and Rubin—were brought up on federal charges of conspiring to riot, defense attorney William Kunstler called Ginsberg to the witness stand. At Kunstler's request, Ginsberg recited parts of "Howl." When he reached the poem's climax—"Moloch the vast stone of war! Moloch the stunned governments!"—he turned in his chair and pointed at Judge Julius Hoffman, who had been so hostile to the defendants. (Ironically, this was the same judge who years earlier declared *Naked Lunch* not obscene.)

In addition, Ginsberg became a key player in the 1960s argument over such psychedelic drugs as LSD. He had, of course, taken several drugs in his days with the Beats and already had some psychedelic experience. But in the early 1960s, Ginsberg heard about a Harvard professor, Dr. Timothy Leary, who was conducting authorized research at the university and was sharing the drug psilocybin with his project's volunteers. Ginsberg contacted Leary and arranged for a visit to experiment with the drug. Leary and Ginsberg struck up an immediate friendship and had considerable influence on each other's thinking. Ginsberg believed strongly (in contrast to most of Leary's cohorts) that it would be a good idea to move psychedelics from the domain of a small elitist group and share them with writers and artists—and he arranged for Leary to do so with Robert Lowell, William S. Burroughs, Thelonious Monk and Jack Kerouac, among others. But Ginsberg's biggest contribution to the era's emerging drug ethos was what became known as "the egalitarian ideal": Psychedelics, Ginsberg convinced Leary, could be a way of empowering people to inquire into and transmute their own minds, and he suspected that it was young people who were most open to such an experience.

Ginsberg later forswore psychedelics, but his friendship with Leary continued off and on for more than thirty-five years. During the last several weeks of Leary's life, the two men spoke often. Leary knew that Ginsberg had planned a trip to Los Angeles, in July, to attend an art show featuring Burroughs's work. Though Leary's health was daily diminishing as his body succumbed to prostate cancer, he hoped to live until Ginsberg's visit and made the date the last mark on his calendar. Leary would die without seeing his friend one last time. But in the hours preceding his death, Ginsberg's Buddhist teacher, Gelek Rinpoche, managed to reach Leary, uttering a final prayer for his passage into death.

Ginsberg stayed active in politics, arts and popular and renegade culture for the remainder of his life. In the mid-1970s, he toured with Bob Dylan and his Rolling Thunder Revue, singing and reading poetry. A few years later, Ginsberg released his own sets of songs and collaborations with such artists as Dylan and the Clash—and it proved as exhilarating as his best poetry had a generation earlier. Throughout the Seventies, Eighties and Nineties, Ginsberg befriended and encouraged many other poets, punk musicians and rap artists.

Of course, as time went along, the role of the renegade grew more acceptable, assimilated to some degree in mainstream culture. What was shocking in the Fifties was less shocking in the Seventies; what was disruptive in the Seventies was commonplace and profitable by the Nineties. Ginsberg understood this inevitable progression of how radical works and impulses are first resisted, then gradually diffused, and in his own way he had fun with that fact and mocked it a bit. He took to wearing suits and ties as he grew older. In part, it gave his pronouncements more authority, more respectability, for some critics, but the other thing was: Ginsberg looked *great* in suits and ties. But for all his venerability, there was a part of Ginsberg that would never be domesticated, much less silenced. In 1979 the National Arts Club awarded him a gold medal for literary merit. At the awards dinner, according to Burroughs's biographer, Ted Morgan, Ginsberg bemusedly read a poem called "Cocksucker Blues," to the genuine consternation of his audience. He also remained a relentless supporter of author Burroughs. In the late 1970s, after his own 1973 induction into the rarefied ranks of the American Academy and Institute of Arts and Letters, Ginsberg began a campaign to have Burroughs inducted as well. Ginsberg met with a great deal of refusal—Burroughs was *not* a writer several of the other fine authors wanted in their company—but the poet persisted. It took six years, but Ginsberg won Burroughs's entry into the Institute, in 1983. Also, Ginsberg remained a fierce advocate of free speech. In recent years he even took up a defense of NAMBLA, the North American Man-Boy Love Association, an organization dedicated to lowering the age of consensual sex between men and boys. Ginsberg's involvement with the outfit outraged many of his longstanding admirers, but Ginsberg would not be cowed. "It's a free-speech issue," he said repeatedly, pointing out that to stifle the ability to discuss such a matter in a free society was perhaps its own kind of outrage. Also, apparently he stayed as sexually active as he could. In "Death & Fame" in *The New Yorker*, Ginsberg boasted about the many men he had seduced throughout his lifetime, and he detailed what it was he liked about his sexual intimacy with these partners. But for all that Ginsberg did or attempted to do, to this day "Howl" still cannot be played over America's airwaves during the day, due to the efforts of Jesse Helms and the Federal Communications Commission.

And so he is gone. In the days since Ginsberg's death, I have seen and heard countless tributes to his grace, power, skills and generosity—but I have also seen and heard just as many disparaging remarks: what a shoddy writer he was; what a failure the legacy of his Beat Generation and the 1960s generation turned out to be; what an old lecher the guy was. Perhaps all this vitriol isn't such a bad thing. Maybe it's another tribute of sorts: Allen Ginsberg never lost his ability to rub certain nerves the wrong way when it came to matters of propriety, aesthetics, morality and politics.

But I also know this: Allen Ginsberg won—against the formidable odds of his own madness-scarred childhood, against all his soul-crippling doubts of self, against all those stern, bristling, authoritarian forces that looked at this man and saw only a bearded radical faggot they could not abide. Ginsberg won in a very simple yet irrefutable way: He raised his voice. He looked at the horror that was crawling out from the American subconscious of the 1950s—the same horror that would later allow the nation to sacrifice so many of its children in the 1960s to a vile and pointless military action—and he called that demon by its name: "Moloch!" He looked at the crazed and the despairing, those people hurting for a fix, for a fuck of love, for the obliteration of intoxicated visions, and he saw in them something to adore and kiss, something to be treasured and learned from. And Ginsberg looked at himself, and for all his hard-earned pride, lust, vanity and audacity, he would not shut up even in the face of his own vulnerability. In one of his best poems, 1992's "After Lalon," Ginsberg wrote:

I had my chance and lost it,
many chances & didn't
    take them seriously enuf.
Oh yes I was impressed, almost
    went mad with fear
I'd lose the immortal chance,
    One lost it.
Allen Ginsberg warns you
    dont follow my path
    to extinction

In an evening, long ago—an evening caught between two Americas, the America of the past and the America that was to follow, an evening where America was truly found, realized and celebrated—a nervous, young homosexual Jewish man stood before a crowd, and he raised his voice. He said things that nobody had ever said before to a crowd in this nation—filthy things, beautiful things—and when he was finished, he had become a braver man. He had, in fact, in that hour, transformed himself into the most eventful American poet of the century. When Lawrence Ferlinghetti—who was in the room that night and who brought "Howl" to the world—heard that his old friend was dying, he wrote the following: "A great poet is dying / But his voice won't die / His voice is on the land."

Ginsberg's voice will never leave us. Its truths and purposes will echo across our future as a clarion call of courage for the misfits, the fucked-up, the fucking and the dying. And we—all of us, whether we understand it or not—are better for it.

Goodbye, Allen Ginsberg. Thank you for illuminating our history—thank you for the gentle yet fierce slow-burning flame you ignited on that evening so long ago. Thank you for what you brought to our times, our nerve and our lives.

Go in peace, brother. Your graceful, heavy, loving heart has earned it.

A One-Man Generation

BY GORDON BALL

Editor's note: This essay was adapted from a paper given at the 'Legacy of the Beat Generation' symposium at New York University in May 1994, and was originally published later that year in the chapbook 'Beat Legacy, Connections, Influences' by White Fields Press.

A KEY TO THE BEATS, AND TO the fact that they've given us a large, multi-dimensional and ever-growing legacy, is their ability to absorb the form and vitality of many different literary and aesthetic traditions. It's as if they took to heart Henry James's nostrum "Be one upon whom nothing is lost"—and so we find ourselves today, still in the midst of opening and discovering their gifts. Allen Ginsberg, in particular, drew richly (sometimes to the point of apparent contradiction) from an almost unlimited range of source and inspiration. And he left a legacy rich and diverse, in shape and subject.

What were the greatest influences on Ginsberg? At the heart of Ginsberg there's Kerouac: Ginsberg was inspired to write spontaneously (and frequently) by Kerouac's example, as well as by his manifesto, "Essentials of Spontaneous Prose," and his *Book of Dreams*. Equally important, he was inspired by the *sound* of Kerouac's prose and poetry, the "wopbopgooglemop," which Kerouac derived in part from *his* eclectic mix of interests: William Shakespeare and Thomas Wolfe, the American workaday vernacular he both heard and used, the American musicalized vernacular of Lester Young and Charlie Parker, as well as his model for vocal phrasing (for full-mouthed enunciation of individual words), Frank Sinatra. When we read, in Ginsberg's "Notes for 'Howl' and Other Poems," that the poem was "writ for my own soul's ear and a few other golden ears," we know the most golden of all were Kerouac's.

In mid-Fifties San Francisco, Ginsberg and Kerouac and other young poets were reading R. H. Blyth's four-volume collection of *Haiku*; for Ginsberg, in his own words, "the crucial discovery of haiku and ellipsis in haiku . . . serves as the [syntactic] base in 'Howl.'" As he wrote in his journal from that period:

> Study of primary forms of ellipse, naked haiku,
> useful for advancement of practice
> of western metaphor
> "hydrogen jukebox"

At the same time, his study of the ellipse—or ellipsis as he later called it—may also have evolved from attention to Paul Cézanne. As he once noted, "I am like Cézanne, sketching." "Howl," Ginsberg later claimed, was "an homage to Cézanne's method," and his study of the artist returned him to another influence, his 1948 William Blake epiphany, as he sought to convey in words and the spaces between them a sense of the transtemporal state of his Blakean "auditory illuminations." Ginsberg has also spoken of the importance of Buddhist studies and surrealism to his use of ellipsis.

So the signal stylistic feature of "Howl" may well have evolved from several quite different points of contact. *And* the fact that the spirit of something as radically condensed in form as the haiku appears on page after page of a *long* poem of *long* Whitman-like lines is extraordinary.

Numerous other influences, sometimes almost violently joined, abound in this epoch-making poem. Dozens of important sources are identified in Barry Miles's *Annotated "Howl,"* ranging from Christopher Smart and Kurt Schwitters, through numerous Beat colleagues and their personal anecdotes and "eyeball kicks," to Fritz Lang's *Metropolis,* peyote and the Sir Fran-

cis Drake Hotel. Ginsberg's inclusion of anecdotes is especially interesting, not only because by using them he violated a critical credo of the day —not to write directly of personal experience— but also because he gave us, let's say, Herbert

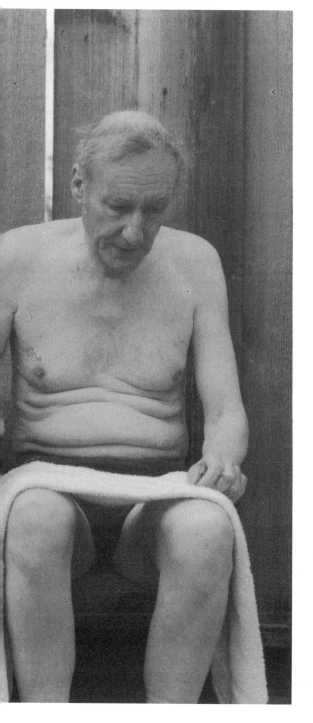

Huncke shoulder to shoulder with Herman Melville. And the poem takes as its first locus for its "best minds" the "negro streets" of what was then an even more segregated America. Partially due to Kerouac's influence, much of Part One has a subtle presence of African America, which is later yoked with a different ethnic tradition in the phrases "bop kaballah" and "eli eli lamma lamma sabachthani saxophone cry."

In his later *Kaddish*, we find a majestic amalgam of the canonical and noncanonical, of the literary and nonliterary: personal family history, public history, ethnic folklore, Hebraic scripture, prosaic inspiration from Louis Ferdinand Celine, Thomas Wolfe and Kerouac; poetic inspiration from William Carlos Williams's "particularity and diction" and Ray Charles's "Blues Chant & Shout" as well as from Percy Bysshe Shelley, Hart Crane, Tristan Tzara, Kit Smart and Samuel Greenberg's "Dear Daniel." *And* we find an influence from a younger poet, Edward Marshall, who'd written a significant poem at age twenty-three: His "Leave the World Alone" is a long narrative depicting the hospital confinement and deterioration of his own mother through gists and fragments of family history. (It's especially characteristic of Ginsberg to be profoundly affected not only by old masters and peers but by the young: Another instance would be his being moved to tears after his return from India in 1963, when Al Aronowitz played him a song, "Masters of War," by a new kid in the Village.)

Sometimes influences arrived in the form of a strange challenge. In 1971, not long after shaving off his beard on a dare from his guru-to-be Chogyam Trungpa, he began improvising poetry

Allen Ginsberg, Philip Whalen and William S. Burroughs (from left), *swimming pool area, Varsity Apartments, Boulder, Colorado, July 1976*
© GORDON BALL

and blues onstage: Trungpa had baited him, "You're bored reading your poems—why don't you improvise like the great poets like Milarepa did?" That was the genesis of Ginsberg's extended investigation into and re-creation of blues forms from Furry Lewis to Bob Dylan. Its results were seen in performance and heard on numerous recordings, as Allen accompanied himself not only with his Benares harmonium and his finger cymbals, but with what he called "the oldest form of human poetics," yerkallah song sticks from his contact with Aborigines in Australia.

Sometimes the influences are quiet, not so well known. An example is "objectivist" poet Charles Reznikoff, whose work reinforced Ginsberg's recognition that "the poetic" can be found in the most humble, everyday "unpoetic" material—an idea that gave some of Ginsberg's later poems an especially familial and Jewish emphasis. As Ginsberg wrote me in 1990, Reznikoff enhanced "the sense of Jewish anecdotal family tale immigrant greenhorn richness in my own background." One example is the magnificent poem "White Shroud," where the prosaic depiction of Ginsberg's mother Naomi as a homeless bag lady corresponds to images of age and decrepitude in Reznikoff going back to 1920. Yet, within six months of writing another Reznikoff-like poem, 1976's "Don't Grow Old," Ginsberg was adapting Blake's Miltonic line while composing the long "Contest of Bards."

A word about Ginsberg's concept of the poet: Although much of his work equals the finest of *belle lettristic* writing, he was in no way a poet in only the strict sense, no more than as a Buddhist he was concerned with only his own spiritual advancement. Although his scholarship was formidable, Ginsberg was not a scholarly recluse but was out there in the world, putting his life on the line, as activist, bard, social critic, Hebraic prophet and scholar (challenging even the CIA, through his scholarship). Though he characterized himself as "basically a coward," Norman Mailer once described him as "the bravest man in America."

So Ginsberg took much, from many sources. What are we taking from *him*?

To begin with, American poetry. American poetry as composed, presented and received is not as it was in the 1950s. From the Beats' insistence on talking to each other in the Forties and Fifties, intensely and without qualm, and their resulting coffeehouse and gallery declamations, came a revival of our recognition that poetry is *not* principally something that exists flatly, two-dimensionally on a printed page, but is projected from within a human organism, within a human community. It can be, as Ginsberg maintained, "composed on the tongue."

I don't mean to say that today all poetry is so composed, simply that it's no longer *de rigeur* to follow accepted forms of the past. Today, a poet is less likely to be asked the question a colleague of Robert Creeley's took at a reading a generation ago: "Was that a *real* poem, or did you just make it up yourself?" The Cold War of Poetic Forms is over, and we—Open Form—won. Rather than domination by the New Critical preference for the short lyric, what we have today is a great multiplicity of form and subject matter. A simple measure might be the changing status of Walt Whitman: In "Notes Written on Finally Recording 'Howl,'" Ginsberg claimed that Whitman's form had "rarely been further explored," that Whitman was a "mountain too vast to be seen," that with few exceptions his line was taken as "a big freakish uncontrollable necessary prosaic goof." Today, as we survey poets from Galway Kinnell to June Jordan to Ed Sanders to James Tate, we find it's no longer so.

And poetry today is presented differently. Ginsberg's locating the poem in human tongue and breath, his linking it to music, has helped give us verse with a much greater emphasis on oral delivery and performance, mixing artistic media: Patti Smith, Laurie Anderson, Anne Waldman and Arrested Development come to mind. Poetry is no longer the nearly exclusive province of the academy, no longer just for sissies and stiffs.

Consequently, poetry is received differently. A generation ago, poems were often studied by sober explication, as if they were something like crossword puzzles. They might've been scanned, sometimes laboriously, but I wonder how often they were read out loud for joy. T. S. Eliot's legacy of impersonality, as appropriated by the New Criticism, was worlds removed from Diane di Prima's reaction on first encountering "Howl" late in 1956. As she tells us in her *Memoirs of a Beatnik,* "... we read 'Howl' together, I read it aloud to everyone."

In that winter of 1956–1957, Ginsberg's former Columbia schoolmate, the poet Louis Simpson, was coediting *New Poets of England and America,* an anthology of contemporary verse. Ginsberg gave Simpson a large collection of poems by Robert Duncan, Gary Snyder, Denise Levertov, Philip Whalen, Frank O'Hara and Kerouac. But when the anthology's first edition appeared, it contained no works by any of those poets or by Ginsberg. Today, Allen's works and those of his colleagues appear in numerous anthologies and syllabi, and classes specifically on the Beat Generation are found at many colleges, and even some high school classes are studying the Beats. Years before his death in 1997, Ginsberg became a member of the American Academy of Arts and Letters and an honorary fellow of the Modern Language Association; "Howl" and "Kaddish" were the subject of two special sessions at MLA conventions, in 1986 and 1991.

How much of this poetic shift was purposely engineered by the Beats? According to Ginsberg:

There was some conscious intention to make a cultural breakthrough, to talk in public as we talked in private.... How we behave in private is actually the ultimate politics. So the original literary inspiration was to behave in public as we do in private.

Kerouac wrote Ginsberg early in the Fifties that their group's distinguishing feature was their practice of honestly confessing to each other their deepest feelings. Their candor and openness—in an age of denial!—surely had *something* to do with the fact that today national debate includes as legitimate topics for discussion such subjects as homosexuality and heroin addiction. In the snow of winter 1964–1965 Ginsberg carried POT IS FUN and POT IS A REALITY KICK placards in New York City demonstrations; two years later his landmark article "The Great Marijuana Hoax: First Manifesto to End the Bringdown" appeared in the *Atlantic Monthly.* According to Michael Aldrich, an early member of LeMAR (a marijuana legalization group), Allen literally remade the language in which people considered such issues.

The obscenity trials of the books *Howl* and *Naked Lunch,* along with many other legal skirmishes of the Beats, have contributed to greater freedom of life and letters in the United States. Has such influence been felt abroad? Let's consider Eastern Europe. In the eyes of some poets and scholars, the Whitmanic candor of Ginsberg's life and works helped with the peaceful downfall of Communist regimes at the end of the last decade. Ginsberg's being chosen King of May in Prague 1965 may have been a prelude. He was already admired within Prague's literary world, student population and cafe society, as was evidenced in Czech translations of his work and performance of his poems. When Ginsberg revisited Prague in 1990, his crown, taken from him by the Communists, was returned.

A young Polish student of Ginsberg's has

written of how Polish academics were not idle (or, "academic") in their appreciation of the Beats, whose literature gave them added heart to challenge the literary and cultural conditions they faced. In the personal experience of this young Pole, Ginsberg's poetry was ballast against the Polish police state when he returned there in the mid-Eighties from a year in the United States. After barely escaping Polish jail for reported illegal and immoral behavior—homosexuality—while in America, he wrote that only reading poetry, most especially Ginsberg's "Howl," relieved some of the crush of his alienating homeland: He loved Ginsberg's poetry because "it created a little world of freedom for me." Such a comment is a microcosm of what Ginsberg meant to readers throughout much of Iron-Curtained Europe for the span of a generation. As Nobel Prize–winning poet Czeslaw Milosz said of Ginsberg in a 1991 tribute, he is a "great poet of the murderous century."

In the Soviet Union, poet Yevgeny Yevtushenko reported:

After the grim McCarthy era and the witch hunts in Hollywood, the appearance of the beatniks was that sigh that had been trapped in the chest of American society. It was not for nothing that we were attuned to the slightest reverberation of that sigh. The young poets of Moscow passed around issues of 'Evergreen Review.' The generation of beatniks and our generation in Russia are inseparable.

Finally, there's one specific element in the collective psyche of the Beats that I'd like to explore. Kerouac late in the 1950s gave "beat" the sense of "beatific." Ginsberg in 1968—when an American political revolution seemed at hand—said, "If the revolution isn't spiritual, it's not worth it." This spiritual base, which I see as the center of the Beat Generation, may redeem the woeful American legacy projected by Walt Whitman 125 years ago, as he considered manifestations of "Moloch" in his day. In 1870 Whitman wrote in *Democratic Vistas*:

… I say of all this tremendous and dominant play of solely materialistic bearings upon current life in the United States … that they must be confronted and met by at least an equally subtle and tremendous force-infusion for purposes of spiritualization, for the pure conscience, for genuine aesthetics, and for absolute and primal manliness and womanliness— or else our modern civilization, with all its improvements, is in vain, and we are on the road to a destiny, a status, equivalent, in its real world, to that of the fabled damned.

The Beats *are* that "subtle and tremendous force-infusion" Whitman called for. Over five decades, Allen Ginsberg wrote, spoke, agitated, meditated, dreamed and sang to bring about the spiritualization of America. As Richard Hell once said, "He's a one-man generation."

A Beat Book Review

BY JOHN GRISSIM JR.

[ROLLING STONE 33, May 17, 1969]

Planet News (1961–1967) by Allen Ginsberg, City Lights Books, 114 pp.

ALLEN GINSBERG IS THE FRANK Zappa of American letters — older perhaps but nonetheless gloriously profane, hairy, benevolent, perverse and without question a first-rate artist. Angry and outspoken in the Beat Fifties, he became the conscience-eye of a country, tribal elder to the war baby generation, and almost by chance, a multimedia presence.

There he is in *life*, having coffee with cornbelt coeds at the University of Kansas, looking academic and residential or standing in the background of *Don't Look Back*, talking to someone while the protagonist deals cut cards in syncopation to "Subterranean Homesick Blues." He is advisor and confidant to the Hell's Angels, a roly-poly celebrant at the mammoth Golden Gate Park Be-in, a correspondent at the Democratic convention flashing a V-sign to watching millions. They love him on the *Merv Griffin Show* and hate him at the Department of Defense—a ubiquitous, benign Brooklyn uncle Santa Claus—Americans' most important poet.

Planet News is a collection of forty-one poems written during seven years of the Sixties. All have been previously published in scattered periodicals throughout the world, but several have been revised "in a manner similar to manicuring grass, that is, the removal of seeds and twigs, ands, buts, ors, especially ofs that don't contribute to getting the mind high." The resulting syntactical cleanliness enhances the strange godliness of Allen Ginsberg. Sharing his vision, even in its sometimes irrational fragmented form, is rewarding.

The chronological order of the poems supplies the book's only linear dimension—a reflection of Ginsberg's unceasing travels. The voyage begins in New York, stops briefly in the Mediterranean, the Sea of Galilee and India; then to Asia to be interrupted by movements of intense self-realization on a Tokyo-bound train. A six-month tour of Soviet-bloc countries is followed by a stay in London, then a long sojourn from the West Coast through Kansas, back to New York, on to Wales, and a final, fitting, return to North American shores to exorcise the evil presence within Pentagon walls.

Mood and style vary considerably, shifting from lucid, tactile description to rambling and introspective associations. The book's featured poems, "Television Was a Baby Crawling Toward That Deathchamber" and "Wichita Vortex Sutra," embody both characteristics. Each work is monumental in significance. Less staggering but no less vivid are moments excerpted from a party at Ken Kesey's, a Warsaw cafe, Carmel Valley and the author's own hypnogogic landscape.

The most successful poems really do get the mind high. Ginsberg has a remarkable ability to share sensation so completely that the eye is unaware of its dependence on the printed word.

> Still night. The old clock Ticks half past two.
> A ringing of crickets awake in the
> ceiling. The gate is locked
> on the street outside—sleepers, mustaches,
> nakedness, but no desire. A few mosquitoes
> waken the itch, the fan turns slowly—
> a car thunders along the black asphalt

a bull snorts, something is expected—
Time sit solid in the four yellow walls . . .
> —From "Last Night in Calcutta"

The Ginsberg vision is polished, precise and funny in "Portland Colosseum":

Apparition, four brown English
    jacket christhair boys
Goofed Ringo battling bright
    white drums
Silent George hair patient
    Soul horse
Short black-skulled Paul
    wit thin guitar
Lennon the Captain, his mouth
    a triangular smile,
all jump together to End
    some tearful memory song
    ancient two years. . . .

Yet that same vision encompasses the spectre of a sick, paranoid society in "Television Was a Baby Crawling Toward That Deathchamber," written in 1961. It is lengthy, prophetic and disassociative—a ghastly portrait of "America for All" formed by the steady, almost hypnotic accretion of detail, often incomprehensible, yet brought to clear focus in its totality. The executions of Julius and Ethel Rosenberg and Caryl Chessman elicit a bitter, anguished denunciation:

the Soul of America died with
    Chessman—strange
saintly average madman driven to
    thing for his own
Killers, in his pants and shirt with
    human haircut,
said NO to—like to Cosmic NO—
    from the One
Mouth of America speaking life or
    death—looked
in the eye of America—

While "TV Baby" excoriates a depraved society, Ginsberg is no less inclined to come to terms with himself. In "The Change: Kyoto-Tokyo

Express," he conveys a sense of dialectic in his own spirit. Penumbras of cosmic energy alternate with fetid public descriptions. Humanity is recapitulated in the mind—a reservoir of archetypes of a collective unconscious. It is a comedown—an introspective, almost solipsistic poem—not clearly perceived, but somehow communicated.

It all comes together in "Wichita Vortex Sutra," not a vision of America, but a tragic reality. Ginsberg describes it as "a mind collage and keystone section of progressively longer poem on 'These States.'" But it stands by itself, a carefully pieced together mosaic of Kansas—the fertile heartland that yields its harvest of youth to the mill of the gods:

While the triangle-roofed Farmer's
Grain Elevator sat quietly by the
side of the road
    along the railroad track
American Eagle beating its wings
over Asia
    million dollar helicopters
    a billion dollars worth of marines
    who loved Aunt Betty
        Drawn from the shores and
        farm shaking from the high
        schools to the landing barges
        blowing the air through their
        cheeks with fear
            in Life on television . . .

The road to Wichita is traveled slowly. Each image, each sound burns leisurely into consciousness. The momentum builds until the city appears gradually on the far, flat horizon, not a miasmic phantom skyline, but a real, almost touchable entity at the center of a vast continental vortex:

Is this the land that started war
    on China?
This be the soil that thought Cold
    War for decades?
Are these nervous naked trees &
    farmhouses
        the vortex

of Oriental anxiety molecules
that've imagined American Foreign
                          Policy
and magick'd up paranoia in
                          Peking
and curtains of living blood
      surrounding far Saigon?

In its honesty and immediacy, "Wichita Vortex Sutra" is the cry of a generation. Allen Ginsberg is a poet of the first magnitude. And as a book, *Planet News* is a beautiful experience in sharing one man's vision of humanity.

A Beat Book Review

BY MARSHALL ROSENTHAL

[ROLLING STONE 69, October 29, 1970]

Indian Journals by Allen Ginsberg, City Lights Books, 210 pages, $3 paper

ALLEN GINSBERG IS A TRAVELER. Whether sitting cross-legged and still beneath Howrah Bridge or watching the dead bodies burn in Indian ghats, he moves along the edge of life, and in ancient journalistic fashion reports the news to us.

He reports that it took him five years to transcribe, edit and publish this "lonely handiwork of self keeping record of self's consciousness, the old yoga of Poesy," that is now known as *Indian Journals*. In temporal terms, the *Journals* begin November 1961, and conclude May 1963. But Allen's words transcend time to explore the depths of thought, dream and spiritlife.

"Remembering as a child on Haledon Avenue I said to a girl (with her armful of books coming home from School #12) my what a big bust you have—and she hit me and chased me home, her face red with annoyance and embarrassment—and that silly drama must have been the Greatest Freudian Trauma that turned me against girls ever since—sort of a silly denouement of decades of homosexuality—a scene like that really bugged me out and I was always ashamed of—my naiveté—to have such a lasting effect on me—yet that's about all there is to it—this girl in [tonight's] dream acting the opposite in such a nice way I woke thinking by god look what I've been missing!"

And not many writers, except the few poets among us, would acknowledge self-doubt as Allen did on July 8, 1962.

". . . as my mind development at the year moment seems blocked so also does my 'creative' activity, blocked, revolve around old abstract & tenuous sloppy political sex diatribes and a few cool imagistic photo descriptions (which contain some human sentiment by implication)—

"I really don't know what I'm doing now.

"Begin a new page."

The *Journals* are a book of dreams, reveries, letters, snatches of poems, chants, doodles and ravings. At one moment he is "scribbling in a vast book of blank pages, hoping my death will make sense of chaos notations." He pens a will, leaving all to Peter Orlovsky. At another time he transcribes a note by Jean Arp which affirms that Tristan Tzara "discovered the word *dada* on the 8th of February 1916, at 6 o'clock in the evening . . . at the Cafe de la Terasse in Zurich and I [Arp] had a roll of bread up my left nostril."

This is Ginsberg the Journalist—our Man in the Interior reporting on the Struggle to Endure, to Exist, to find peace and meaning. It is a reporting that is free of fad and fashion and provides energyfood for our survival.

After reading the *Journals*, you might be reminded of the prayer Jack Kerouac said in *The Dharma Bums*. He'd name each of his friends, and after each name add, "Equally empty, Equally to be loved, Equally a coming Buddha."

You might recall Kerouac saying it for Allen Ginsberg.

A Beat Record Review

BY LESTER BANGS

[ROLLING STONE 60, June 11, 1970]

Songs of Innocence and Experience, recorded by Allen Ginsberg, Verve/Forecast FTS-3083

HERE'S AN INTERESTING PRESS RELEASE: "Allen Ginsberg and William Blake cut an album for MGM's Verve/Forecast label titled *Songs of Innocence and Experience*." Wow! What longevity!

Well, old Bill may have been misrepresented by MGM, but he has certainly received justice from Allen Ginsberg. This album contains a cycle of twenty-one of Blake's most affecting (and least obscure) poems, set to simple melodies and sung by Ginsberg himself. It could have been a ponderous disaster, but Allen's unfailing intuition has kept the musical setting simple, augmenting his concert combination of ethereal voice and droning harmonium with sweetly blending flute, double bass and occasional understated uplift from such jazz giants as Don Cherry and Elvin Jones.

The result is an oddly moving album that manages to sound amateurish and pure at the same time. Ginsberg is no singer, but the distinctive sinuousness of his reedy voice is one of the set's most compelling qualities. Nothing here sounds strained or pretentious, which should make it the last word in concept albums. It sounds, rather, like a labor of love, a salute from a young visionary to an ancient sage, executed with delicacy and charm in a vocal style reminiscent of an Anglo-American muezzin. The melodies are nothing special, yet each sounds intuitively *right* for the words it's been built around—no small achievement when one is working backwards from words to music. One reason it works so well is that the method of approach was implicit and organic, as natural as drawing a breath and speaking. As Allen says in the liner notes: "The purpose of putting them to music was to articulate the significance of each holy and magic syllable of his poems; as if each syllable had intention—I tried to follow natural voice tones up or down according to different emphases and emotions vocalized as in daily intimate speech."

Well said, Allen, and a fine job. Now how about electric transpositions of some of your own thundering verbal music—say, "Howl"?

Elder Statesman, Unrepentant Rebel:
A Chat with Ginsberg

BY BARRY ALFONSO

Allen Ginsberg lived to achieve the rare feat of becoming an elder statesman while remaining an unrepentant rebel. The young man who howled at the walls of Caucasian conformity in the 1950s was still beyond the pale in the family values–obsessed 1990s. This gay Jewish Buddhist bardic visionary never stopped demanding his place in the American conversation, and never fully traded in his outsider credentials despite the literary honors he received in his latter years.

Growing up in the Seventies, I entered high school in time to study Ginsberg's work in my English classes, and to notice his unmistakable influence on the music of Bob Dylan, John Lennon and other artists I admired. Later, as a songwriter and journalist, I kept encountering his presence all over the cultural landscape, from the antiwar and psychedelic upheavals of the Sixties through the morality wars of the Twentieth Century's closing days. One of his accomplishments was to blur the boundaries between art and social activism—you had to deal with his life and work in all its phases as a whole.

In June 1994, I had the pleasure of interviewing Ginsberg by telephone in connection with the release of his CD box set 'Holy Soul Jelly Roll.' He had a great deal to say about the interplay between poetry and music, and the blending of "high" and "pop" culture. It was very much classic Allen Ginsberg: synthesizing extremes, merging the traditional and the radical. The Beat enfant terrible lived on inside the sage, as the following remarks will show.

—B. A., SEPTEMBER 1998

What is your method for combining spoken poetry and music? Would you make a distinction between that and writing/performing songs?

Yes and no. It depends. The progression (for me) was, when I came back from India in '63 I was chanting mantras. I switched over to composing tunes for Blake's *Songs of Innocence and of Experience* because Blake himself sang them—the first biography by Gilchrist says that Mr. Blake sang his songs of innocence and of experience in his friends' parlors accompanied by instru-

Allen Ginsberg leading the tribes at San Francisco's Human Be-In, Golden Gate Park, 1967
LISA LAW

ments of the day, which are probably not very far from my harmonium. It also said that the scholar/professors of the day failed to notate his melodies. The poem "Little Lamb" is actually a paraphrase of a Wesleyan hymn; Blake borrowed the form and even the imagery from the hymn. So we have some idea of what it could be like. Country/Western, really, Appalachian music . . . the hymns, . . . Southern spiritual singing.

What I did was—after many years of chanting monochordal mantras—I began discovering that there was a second chord possible. I had played the harmonium, but with one chord. In doing the Blake songs, I began discovering that I needed to change a chord for some bending of the melody. In 1969 I recorded a complete album of Blake. The same year I began listening to folk music more, though I'd listened to a lot of Lead-belly and blues since I was a kid in grammar school, Ma Rainey and Bessie Smith particularly . . . and Josh White, Woody Guthrie and Burl Ives.

So having recorded the Blake songs, one day I was doing some improvising at NYU with Peter [Orlovsky] at a big reading, and Dylan was sitting there in the back. He called me up later at my house—he'd heard us improvising on the subject of "why write poems on paper when you have to cut down trees, why not put it into the air?" That was Peter's theme, and I picked up on it. And we had about ten musicians, amateurs and friends [there], and it was kind of like a jamboree. So Dylan called and said, "Can you always do that?" And I said, "Yeah, Kerouac and I used to make up lyrics walking in the silence."

Dylan came over to the house and we began jamming together—he wanted to see what I could do. And then he showed me there were more than two chords [laughs]. He showed me the three-chord sequence. I didn't quite understand it, but I got the idea that there's a regular sequence, finally. It was funny. He advised me to get an instrument, and by then I was borrowing Peter's harmonium.

So that led to my going to folk concerts at the Peace Church in Greenwich Village with Happy and Artie [Traum] and the Woodstock band they had around 1970, [and] imitating their folk style. I began writing regular song lyrics. Usually I would write the lyric and then cook up a melody out of my one or two or three chords.

Then in 1971 I was recording with Dylan, and I wanted to have something worthy of working with him. So I sat down and wrote a long poem called "September on Jessore Road." I wrote the words and music simultaneously. I asked somebody for a third chord that fitted the first two. The first two chords—F minor, B flat—are from a very lugubrious mantra that was taught to me by a Tibetan lama. I composed the whole

thing in one night and a half, with some relative yakking at me the whole time. I was totally fixed on it, each note and each word simultaneous. This was one of the few times I was inspired to do both. I wanted to give Dylan something that would make him cry, so I finished and gave it to him, and he came back the next day and said that he'd cried. I was trying to get something long and serious like "Sad Eyed Lady of the Low-lands," that and one Blake song, "On Another's Sorrow." The rhyme scheme and the stanza form are similar.

Do you think that your poetry helped to make the work of songwriters like Dylan possible?

Among others. I think that, between Kerouac and myself and Burroughs, there was quite an impact. Dylan told me that—I know Kerouac was a major inspiration for him as a poet.

I think it's those chains of flashing images: "the motorcycle black madonna two-wheel gypsy queen and her silver-studded phantom lover" come out of Kerouac's rhetoric. I think Dylan came to Burroughs later—after the Rolling Thunder tour he began digging Burroughs a great deal. And Burroughs has influenced everybody from Soft Machine to Steely Dan up to Kurt Cobain. So there seems to have been some influence. . . . The Beatles named themselves partly out of "Beat."

During Christmas '65, I taught Phil Spector "Hare Krishna" at his house. I was singing it and he was giving me piano accompaniment. It was Christmas Eve, and he was all alone in his house, and Peter and I were keeping him company. He took us up there in his limousine, and we jammed "Hare Krishna" for a while. We did it again in '71 with John Lennon in Syracuse.

Did it strike you as unique that a literary figure like yourself would have this commonality with pop musicians?

Well, no, because I grew up on folk music and blues, and I've always thought that blues lyrics were among the treasures of American lyric poetry. My father was a lyric poet. "Lyric" means "with a stringed instrument," a lyre. When they say song "lyrics," the word originally came from Sappho and her lyre. So the most venerable form of poetry is lyric poetry, like Shelley and Sappho, and they sang. Music and poetry were always together.

Do you hear the link with your own work and with Kerouac's in Dylan's songs?

Well, Beat writing has been in the air for quite a while, from the late Fifties on. But I wouldn't claim credit, particularly. That long verse line with many nouns and adjectives and interesting combinations of words, like "fried shoes" or "hydrogen jukebox"—that was a genre drawn from Whitman, from Surrealism, from European poetry of the Twentieth Century, from the Dadaist poets, from the Russian poets, from Lorca. Sort of an international style of unobstructed breath. Dylan has fantastic breath, great wind, like a blues singer of the West. When I first heard Dylan's records, I heard that instantly, and I was knocked out. I thought, "Well, at least we're not a dead end."

You were recording your poetry as early as the late Forties....

John Clellon Holmes had a paper-tape recording machine. They used paper tape at that time. There are recordings that Holmes made of Kerouac reading Shakespeare among those early things. And Neal Cassady had a tape recorder. If you read *Visions of Cody* by Kerouac, there's about a hundred pages of verbatim tape transcripts between him and Neal. That's actually the first really perfect tape transcription, with all the "uhs" and the syntactical breaks and the ambiance of actual tape. And then [in *Visions of Cody*] Kerouac went on to write an imitation of the tape in Joycean language. On that same tape recorder I did some recording at Neal's house.

What enabled you to develop your skills as a reciter?

Lots and lots of poetry readings. In thirty-five

years of poetry readings, you learn something. I learned a lot from Kerouac, from his first tapes, when he's pronouncing Shakespeare very beautifully—I never will forget, though I never heard it again, him reciting something from *Hamlet*, sitting on the steps wondering about himself, with beautiful inflections. And Kerouac said he learned a lot from Frank Sinatra, who learned a lot from Billie Holiday.

So the musical connection was there from the beginning?

Yeah. Particularly the pronunciation of the long-voweled sentences that you get in Herman Melville's "Pierre." Kerouac noticed how good a poet Burroughs was way back in the early Fifties: "motel motel motel loneliness moans across still oily tidal waters of east Texas bayous / motel motel motel loneliness moan." It's the vowel, the musical assonance, the tone leading the vowel, as Pound calls it, that Kerouac gets from Thomas Wolfe and from Melville, and that I get from Kerouac and Hart Crane and Blake.

And pop musicians, in turn, have become more like poets?

Well, the Beatles were pure poets. Lennon's "A Day in the Life" is a great poem, as good as Apollinaire. Dylan, I think, is a major poet for this half of the century, if not *the* poet for eloquence, exuberance, energy and prolificness. He is a poet's poet.

I've learned from Dylan, but also from Bono and [Lee] Ranaldo and the others. If you don't learn from younger people, who are you going to learn from? Older and younger people. But there was always this respectful transmission of poetry from generation to generation. Kerouac was always interested in Wolfe and Hemingway and Melville, and I was in contact with William Carlos Williams as a kind of mentor. And I'm happy that younger people have looked back and found a lot of our work as workable for them as ground to take off from. And doubling back and teaching us something.

You've had an affinity with the punk rock movement ...

There was a lot of eros involved there, all these kids bouncing up and down with naked chests with wild abandon, the Dionysian element to the mosh pit. And I also lived with a band, Denise Mercedes and the Stimulators. She was Peter [Orlovsky's] girlfriend for ten years. They were one of the earliest kickass women's bands. They played around, at CBGB's and all over New York. I performed with them at St. Mark's Poetry Project a couple of times. Her nephew Harley [who was the drummer] is the head of the Cro-Mags. I'm sort of a godfather to Harley—I wrote a preface to his poetry picture book when he was seven or eight.

Do you feel much in common with the punks' outlook on life?

Well, with the rebellion against authority and underclass hell. The subtlety from rock to punk to grunge has become increasingly refined, with intellectuals like Lee Ranaldo—that group [Sonic Youth] comes out to poetry readings. An appreciation of the decline of the West, the decline of the Empire, the ecological fix and the beginnings of spiritual wisdom and Eastern thought are increasingly present. They're absorbing the work of Philip Glass, because a lot of grunge is influenced by Glass also, as well as the monochordal material from Charlie Mingus and [John] Coltrane.

You don't seem to make a distinction between pop culture and high culture. You tend to break those barriers down ...

Historically, "Lord Randall" or any of those Elizabethan or earlier ballads and songs, are they pop or are they high culture?

Perhaps they were created before the distinction was made.

Right. And certainly the lyrics of Ma Rainey were created before such a distinction could be made too, but they're among the great American poems. "I'm gonna buy me a pistol just as long as I am tall / kill my man and hit the cannonball / you won't have me, you won't have any girl at all"—that's as good as anybody's lyrics.

That's still a controversial idea in academia ...

In academia, but not among poets. But even academia is starting to have little courses on Cole Porter and Gilbert and Sullivan. The lyrics in songs like Elizabeth Cotton's "Freight Train" are just exquisite on the page. But the one who taught me blues the most was Richard "Rabbit" Brown—"I'll give you sugar for sugar / you'll get salt for salt / but if you don't love me, it's your own damn fault." It ends: "sometimes I think that you're too sweet to die / other times I think you ought to be buried alive." That's great poetry.

Since Susan Sontag and Warhol, there's been a breakdown between pop culture and high classical. After all, Stravinsky wrote to jazz and Kurt Weill's "Mahagonny" is perhaps *the* opera of the century.

Do you think that your audiences have gone beyond these distinctions?

Well, I'm conscious that if I do "Meditation Blues," I'm using the tune from "I Fought the Law." I've adapted it to, "I found the dharma and the dharma won." I use some form of the music, but I change it a bit.

What do you think of the revived interest in the Beats?

I think it's inevitable. Let us say that the spiritual and natural [themes] that were being proposed during the Beat Generation were somewhat bypassed during the political aggression of the Sixties from the New Left, who went off in an ideological direction. Then the culture went through the counter-reactions of the Reagan/Bush era till the country was bankrupted, and the country itself was beat financially, and people had to look around when they didn't have that prosperity anymore. By then, what was important were values of some sort, Eastern thought, the residue of psychedelic intelligence, meditation practice, gay and sexual liberation.

Gay lib in "Howl" and *Naked Lunch* opened humor about it and exuberance rather than fear.

[There's been a] realization of the decline of the West, the decline in Empire—everything you find in Burroughs's *The Wild Boys*, the prophecies of universal anarchy and innercity turmoil and Bosnian massacres. The border guards you find in *Naked Lunch* are amazingly prophetic of today. The whole "Interzone" thing has almost come true in Rwanda and Zaire and Bosnia.

So the themes were, let us say, some kind of new planetary consciousness, awareness of ecological destruction and some impulse toward reconstruction if possible, some desire to save the world, maybe a little too late, and how to relate to chaos in a generous way when it comes, Eastern thought, [and] the whole drug theme, the realization of the government scam and how much government is involved in drug-running from cocaine to heroin. That's all [been] written up by Burroughs and by me many times.

Oliver North is like a Burroughs character ...

Oh, very much so. Some kind of a hustler with a queasy grin. And so is pompous, bullfrog-like Jesse Helms. There's a whole lot of replicas from Burroughs let loose.

So there's been this penetration of the cut-up and spontaneous prosody, and the integration of Negro rhythms and culture into white culture, which goes along with a lot of other popular trends, from rhythm and blues to Presley. Bebop [went] into Kerouac's prose—that is, bebop was originally modeled on people talking to each other through their horns, syncopations of street speech, and Kerouac heard that in Harlem, and began to try to write that down in words again. So speech went into horn-breath and came back to cadence-sentences.

Did you imagine how much resonance poems like "Howl" would have when you started writing them?

Well, before "Howl," I said (in "The Green Automobile"), "All time is eternity in the one light of this poem's radio/we'll sit behind forgotten shades, harkening the lost jazz of all Saturdays." But it's not really magical knowledge, it's imaginative exuberance and hyperbole and some shrewdness. Just the poetic imagination.

Innerview

BY HARVEY R. KUBERNIK

Through much of his life, Allen Ginsberg formed creative relationships with musicians, collaborating with artists ranging from Ornette Coleman to Bob Dylan to the Clash. Music played an important part in Ginsberg's life. When Ezra Pound was in an asylum, Ginsberg visited him with a copy of the Beatles' 'Sgt. Pepper' and played it for Pound, who began tapping his cane. Allen Ginsberg's life has been lived over a variety of musical settings. Blues, jazz, folk, rock, punk and rap have been melded with his voice and words.

On October 14, 1996, I sat down with the then-seventy-year-old Brooklyn College professor to discuss his musical collaborations. Ginsberg had just released a rocking protest song, "The Ballad of the Skeletons" b/w "Amazing Grace," with the lyrics rewritten as an ode to the plight of the homeless. "The Ballad of the Skeletons" was initially published in 'The Nation,' in November 1995. As a word/rock merger excoriating the corporate-political establishment, the recording was produced by Lenny Kaye and featured multi-instrumental support from Paul McCartney (a hang buddy) and composer Philip Glass. The disc was issued on Mouth Almighty/Mercury Records, which released the full-length Ginsberg recording, 'The Lion for Real,' in 1989. The 1994 four-disc box set 'Holy Soul Jelly Roll: Songs and Poems (1949–1993)' (WordBeat/Rhino) features Ginsberg's work with Dylan and the Clash, his musical teaming with David Amram and Elvin Jones, material from Ginsberg's John Hammond–produced sessions and a version of his "Kaddish" poem produced by Jerry Wexler and originally released on Atlantic Records. Ginsberg's other recordings, some of which were reviewed upon release by ROLLING STONE, include 'Hydrogen Jukebox,' a 1993 work with Philip Glass, issued by Elektra Nonesuch.

In the mid-1990s Ginsberg performed with Sonic Youth's Thurston Moore and Lee Ranaldo, recorded with U2 in a studio in Ireland and filmed a video for "The Ballad of the Skeletons" directed by Gus Van Sant. Even in the last years of his life, Ginsberg's voice remained rich and full.

A portion of the following interview originally ran in 'Hits' magazine.

—H. K., AUGUST 1998

What about poetry readings and performances? Is it different reading with a musician next to you?

I have to focus on my text. I'm still pointing toward the tornado.

You still read from text onstage—do you ever read from memory?

I rarely read from memory. I can sing "Father Death Blues" and "Amazing Grace" from memory, but I don't know what lines are coming, so I have to refresh myself. I'm not particularly interested in memorizing perfectly 'cause I think it distracts from interpreting the text differently each time. I think you have to have all the dimensions at once, the book thing, the poetry thing, plus the performance, plus the musical accompaniment, and if you have all of them, and they're all in a good place, that's fine. Certain cadences are recurrent and certain intonations are recurrent, but on the other hand, if I don't memorize it, there's always the chance that putting it a little differently will bring out a meaning that I didn't realize before. So I prefer to have the text in front of me and interpret it new each time.

Was there ever a conflict between the original writ-
ten page and audioland?

We wrote in the tradition of William Carlos
Williams's spoken vernacular, comprehensible
common language that anyone could understand,
coming from Whitman through Williams
through bebop. We were built for it. I can talk.
I'm an old ham.

Does the vision change once it leaves the paper?

No. It doesn't make much difference. The
method of my writing to begin with is that I'm
not writing to write something: I suddenly notice
something I have thought of when I wasn't thinking of writing, and then I write it down if it is
vivid enough. And as far as the choice of whether
or not to write it down, if the slogan is vivid, it is
self-selecting. So in a sense, the method is imper-
vious to influence by the audience because I'm
just thinking to myself in the bathtub.

So even if it's the most private, it's the most
public, because as Kerouac said in *Pull My Daisy*,
"Everybody is interested in their secret scatological doodlings in their private notebooks." I mean,
what do people really think about?

As far as performance and poetry readings,
when you read before a house, aren't you
trying to keep the same original text's meaning and not
really expand or bring in heavy theatrical elements?

I like to stick to something that is grounded in
anything I could say to somebody, that they
wouldn't notice I was really saying it as poetry—
intense fragments of spoken idiom, with all the
different tones of the spoken idiom, which is
more musical than most poetry. Most poetry by
amateurs is limited to a couple of tones, a couple
of pitches, instead of an entire range. The poetry
I do fits with the music because it has its pitch
consciousness—the tone reading the vowels up
and down.

What do music and beat do to voice and text?

Well, a whole mish-mosh. First of all, I grew
up on the blues, Ma Rainey and Leadbelly. I lis-

tened to them live on radio station WNYC, back
in the late Thirties and early Forties. So I have a
blues background. There's some sort of Hebrewic
cant relation to the blues that I've always had. So
the first thing on my box set is "When the Saints
Go Marching In" that I made up a capella when I
was hitchhiking, and recorded in Neal Cassady's
house a year later. Then things my mother taught
me—"The Green Valentine Blues"—just coming
from everyone who likes to sing in the shower.
Then there was the poetry and music, King Pleasure, and the people who were putting together
bebop, syllable by syllable, like Lambert, Ross and
Hendricks. I knew them in 1948. We used to
smoke pot together in the Forties, when I knew
Neal Cassady, around Columbia, when I was living on 92nd Street.

You know, I originally felt about your early writing
that there really wasn't any musical influence or instru-
mentation behind or around your words. Yet the first
track on this box set recorded in the late Forties in Neal
Cassady's crib actually has the radio playing in the
background on the tape.

The first cut has a jazz background, because
the whole atmosphere from 1940 on was permeated with bebop and [New York's WJZ DJ] Symphony Sid. Around 1944, '45, Kerouac and I
were listening to Symphony Sid, and I heard the
whole repertoire of Thelonious Monk—"Round
Midnight," "Ornithology" and all that. I actually
saw Charlie Parker, weekend after weekend a few
years later at the Open Door. And in the Sixties,
I went night after night to hear Thelonious Monk
at the Five Spot, where I actually gave him a copy
of "Howl," and got his critique on it two weeks
later when I saw him again. "What did you think
of it?" He said, "Makes sense."

In 1960 I delivered some psilocybin from
Timothy Leary to both Thelonious Monk and
Dizzy Gillespie. And Monk said later, "Got anything stronger?" Then I spent an evening with
him at what's now called Charlie Parker Place
around 1960.

Also in San Francisco, in the mid-Fifties, there was a music and poetry scene at The Cellar. Mingus was involved with Kenneth Rexroth and Kenneth Patchen. And Fantasy Records documented some of that. By that time, I didn't know how to handle it, so I never did much of that myself 'cause I was more into funky, old-fashioned blues. I couldn't cut the mustard with free jazz.

What happens when the beat or the music collides with your words and voice?

Elvin [Jones] has a very interesting attitude.

He feels that he's not there to beat out the vocalist. He's there to put a floor under them. He's there to support and encourage, and give a place for the vocal to come in, not to compete with the vocal, but to provide a ground for it. He's very intelligent as a musician. We did it once together

in 1969 on my [William] Blake album—there was a military-type drum—and then again on this recent rap song. I've got some other stuff we haven't put out with Elvin. I've rarely found opposition to the music because the musicians were very sensitive, and built their music around the dynamics of my voice.

You write something on a piece of paper. Other people, musicians, come invited to participate and collaborate. Does the original intention become a different trip once the music and other elements are involved?

Well, it widens it into a slightly different trip, but the words are pretty stable, and they mean what they mean, so there is no problem. The interesting thing is adjusting the rhythmic pattern and the intonation to the musician's idea of what is there. That's pretty good, because I'm good as an improviser, I can fit in, as you can hear on "Birdbrain" where I can take a long line or a short line and fit in sixteen bars without worrying about spaces and closed places.

Do you enjoy going into the recording studio?

I'm understanding the recording process more. I'm basically the poet, I have tunes I come up with. I have ideas, but I still can't make a song with a bridge [*laughs*]. As far as recording, I had to supervise my own recordings at first, and it was very simpleminded—the *William Blake's Songs of Innocence and Experience* tuned by A.G. on MGM Records. I thought there were good musicians on it, and it may be coming out again.

Can we talk about John Hammond Sr., perhaps the A&R man of the century?

Well, I think I first ran into him in the early Sixties. He knew my poetry quite well. But it was around the Rolling Thunder Revue with Dylan that we got more intimate. I had already made

Allen Ginsberg making music on the streets of San Francisco, with a pair of unknown buskers, circa 1970
ALVAN MEYEROWITZ

one recording, the Blake album, in 1968, with some very good musicians, including Julius Watkins on French horn, Don Cherry, Elvin Jones and also Herman Wright, a bassist who was suggested by Charles Mingus. Mingus encouraged me to do the Blake. So I had something to play. It disappeared when Mike Curb bought MGM and denounced all the dope fiends who were on his roster and wanted to ban them, so then we reissued it with a beautiful cover, with a picture of Judge Julius Hoffman, on their archive series. I was on the Rolling Thunder Tour, doing a little singing, and I had a whole bunch of new material I had done with Dylan in 1971 when we went into a studio and improvised. I had forty minutes of music with him. The [original] idea was that it was going to be put out by Apple [Records]. [John] Lennon had encouraged it and I paid for the thing. So I brought that to Hammond in 1975, after the tour. And I had a bunch of new songs and he said, "Let's go in the studio and make an album." I had some musicians who had been with me since the 1968 Blake recording plus David Mansfield from the Rolling Thunder Tour, and a wonderful musician, Arthur Russell, who Philip Glass has just put out posthumously on Point Records. Arthur Russell lived in my apartment building, upstairs, and had accompanied me across country on tours, and managed the Kitchen in New York. We had a good little group of musicians.

So we got together at CBS Studios and did another forty minutes of music, and later, John Hammond put the two together. He had left Columbia and started his own label, Hammond Records, to be distributed by Columbia. So he not only put out what he did with me, he put out a double album, and he got Robert Frank, who had done the *Exile on Main Street* album cover, who's an old friend, to make a composite for our cover, and there was a really good playlist inside, and the text was a good deduction. However, the

record didn't sell. Before I had a chance to rescue the ten thousand copies [Columbia] had left, they shredded them, so they were gone, and a rarity now. I visited Hammond in the hospital, on his deathbed, years ago, and our final conversation was about Robert Johnson and Bob Dylan. In the Sixties, Dylan taught me the three-chord blues pattern. I began singing mantras in India, and I began transferring the sacred music idea to Blake, and began transferring that to folk music. I was influenced by Happy Traum and Ramblin' Jack Elliott, whom I've known since the Forties, and Derrol Adams. So finally, the amalgam got together and it was very simpleminded blues. Also, improvisation was important.

My four-CD box set is a summary of all the studio recordings I did, plus a lot of other stuff that was never done in a studio, but done at readings, plus another album with Blake, including Dylan on Blake, and a duet with Elvin Jones, including some work with Dylan out in Santa Monica in 1982 in his studio, the live Clash cut and an excerpt from the opera I did with Philip Glass. So the range runs from a capella up through folk, punk, dirty blues, classical, collaborations with Dylan, some rap, percussion and vocal with Jones. David Amram is on it as well. Some of it is uproarious and funny, and very hilarious, joyful yodeling.

Fugs guitarist Steven Taylor has been playing guitar on tours and recordings with you since 1975. What are his strongest assets as a musician, guitarist, collaborator?

He can play funky blues and can improvise. He was born in England, and came to America when he was ten. I invited him to the Hammond sessions in 1976. We toured Europe together with Peter Orlovsky, and in 1982, we ended up in Dylan's studio in California with David Mansfield. We played together at Woodstock around 1980. Ed Sanders saw us and said, "You've got a fantastic accompanist. Get yourself a band and go around the world." He's very supportive. Two years ago, Steven dropped out of the punk garage band False Prophets to go to Brown University to get his Ph.D. in ethnomusicology, influenced by the great ethnomusicologist Harry Smith. Harry Smith, before he died, came out to Naropa, where he was the resident ethnomusicologist and philosopher. He won a Grammy in 1991, the year he died. Harry recorded me for Folkways, produced by Samuel Charters. *First Blues*, it's still in print through the Smithsonian Institute.

Do you feel that documenting your development on record is important for future poets?

My background was William Butler Yeats, and seeing the sequence of his development, maturation and growth over the years was really interesting to me—how he began as a vague, misty-eyed young 1890s devotee of Irish mythology, and how he wound up, this tough old guy who put a skin on everything he said. So I like the idea of seeing the development of the mind, or of the voice, or of the thought, or of the poetic capacity, and I want to leave that trail behind for other poets so they could see where I was at one point, or where I was at another. My oration, my pronunciation, my singing, my vocalization differs, and it builds.

As I get older, it gets more interesting with more and more tones, and more and more breath, and deeper and deeper voice and higher and higher voice. But still the original rhythms and the original ideas are from the original text, so you've still got a chronology going. So people could see the development of the mind. I'm not writing about the external world. I'm writing about what goes through my mind. So, at a certain period I'm interested in this kind of sex, another period, this kind of politics, another period, this kind of meditation. And I like people to be able to dig that there's a development, and not a static process.

I know you worked with the Clash on Combat Rock. How did your box set's "Capitol Air" come together?

Well, it's an accident. I wandered into a place called Bonds, which at that time was a big club in New York. The Clash had a seventeen-night run, and I knew the sound engineer, who brought me backstage to introduce me, and Joe Strummer took one look at me and said, "Ginsberg, when are you going to run for President?" And then he said there was some guy they'd had trying to talk to the kids about Sandinistas and about Latin American policy and politics, but they're not listening. They were throwing eggs or tomatoes at him. "Can you go out and talk?" I said, "Speech, no, but I have a little punk song that I wrote that begins, 'I don't like the government where I live . . .' So, we rehearsed it for about five minutes during their intermission break, and then they took me out onstage. "Allen Ginsberg is going to sing." And so we improvised it. I gave them the chord changes. It's a kind of Clash-like good anthem. The guy who was my friend at the soundboard mixed my voice real loud so the kids could hear, and there was a nice reaction, because they could hear common sense in the song. You can hear the cheers on the record.

"Capitol Air" was written in 1980, coming back from Yugoslavia, oddly enough from a tour of Eastern Europe, realizing that the police bureaucracies in America and in Eastern Europe were the same, mirror images of each other finally. The climactic stanza is "No Hope Communism, No Hope Capitalism. Everybody is lying on both sides."

What inspired you to start doing the jazz-backed readings?

Hal Willner had the idea of going back to the old jazz poetry thing. Hal Willner got some musicians like Bill Frisell, Arto Lindsay and others, Lounge Lizards, people from the Knitting Factory, and assembled those people and he saw me, not singing, but as a vocalist, reciting. And so he had me come into the studio and make a four-hour tape of the favorite pieces of all those musicians who read my books. Then I made a list of what I should recite, and I did that in the studio, with him present. Then I went home to work on full texts, lead sheets, compositions, ideas and came back to the studio, and did it live—all together in the studio. They already had my dynamics from the tape, but I did it again, live. So I finally graduated from lines ballad, or folk, to irregular-verse-spoken poetry. Before that, I made one experiment with the Glue-Ons, a garage band from Denver that really worked—"Birdbrain." It was the first time that I found a way to incorporate free verse lines into a primal sixteen-bar structure by extending my rant fast or slow.

Run down "The Ballad of the Skeletons" recording.

Well, the whole project has been a collaboration with a lot of geniuses, really. When you get Philip Glass and Paul McCartney along with [guitarist] Marc Ribot and [producer] Lenny Kaye and [mixer] Hal Willner, and [violinist] David Mansfield. There's a seven-minute version, as well as an edited, clean four-minute version for radio.

What was the genesis and development of "The Ballad of the Skeletons" poem and printed context?

I started it because of all that inflated bullshit about the right wing and family values, the Contract with America, Newt Gingrich and all the loud-mouth stuff on talk radio—Rush Limbaugh and all those other guys. It seemed obnoxious and stupid and kind of sub-contradictory, so I figured I'd write a poem to knock it out of the ring.

Were there any inherent music or melodic rhythms in the poem when it was first written?

Yes. I had a riff, "Dum. Dum. Dum." "The *New York Times* . . ." I first thought of singing it,

but then I thought it better to speak it with that riff behind it. It got printed in *The Nation* with illustrations by Eric Drooker, and it came out in a book I did called *Illuminated Poems.* The next stage was a benefit somewhere in a New York club where I did a reading with Amiri Baraka, and I ran into guitarist Marc Ribot there. I had worked with him before on an album, *The Lion for Real.* I asked Marc if he would accompany me, and I sang him the riff. He added a little instrumental in between, but he made it dramatic. The next step was a benefit I did for Tibet House at Carnegie Hall that Philip Glass organized. I called David Mansfield, who was going to accompany me at Carnegie Hall, and Lenny Kaye was there with Patti Smith, and David asked Lenny if he could play bass, and he did a knockout job with David. And it was a big hit of the evening 'cause it was the one rocker—everything else was classical or softer.

Then I went to Princeton to give a reading by myself with my harmonium. When I got picked up by the limousine, there was Gus Van Sant. He had done a lot of work with Burroughs and met him many times. When we got out of the hotel, he pulled out a guitar, and I said, "Do you play guitar?" And he replied, "I have a band in Portland." So I said, "I don't have an accompanist tonight. Can you accompany me, after your lecture and during my reading?" So he said yeah. We rehearsed it and played it.

Then I had a gig at Albert Hall in London. A reading. I had been talking quite a bit to McCartney, visiting him and bringing him poetry and haiku, and looking at Linda McCartney's photographs and giving him some photos I'd taken of them. So, McCartney liked it and filmed me doing "Skeletons" in a little 8mm home thing. And then I had this reading at Albert Hall, and I asked McCartney if he could recommend a young guitarist who was a quick study. So he gave me a few names, but he said, "If you're not fixed up with a guitarist, why don't you try me? I love the poem." So I said, "It's a date." It was last November. We went to Paul's house and spent an afternoon rehearsing. He came to the sound-check and we did a little rehearsal there, again. And then he went up to his box seat with his family. It was a benefit for literary things. There were fifteen other poets. We didn't tell anybody that McCartney was going to play. And we developed that riff really nicely. In fact, Linda made a little tape of our rehearsal. So then, we went onstage and knocked it out. There's a photo of us on the CD. It was very lively and he was into it. Linda likes my photos and she likes Robert Frank, who is my mentor. And I had taken some good photos of them at their place in Long Island when they were saying goodnight to me as I was going back to New York. We traded some photos. Paul was into poetry, and having his poetry published. So he asked me to look at his poetry and critique it. We got onto haiku, and Linda liked the form so she used those seventeen-syllable forms for her book of photos. Paul is also a painter and had published a little book of his paintings. I also wrote haikus for a book of 108 water paintings, one haiku for each painting. I showed it to him in Long Island and he was knocked out, and liked the form so he began working with that, also. So we had a rapport about technical things.

Didn't you see the Beatles play, and there's some poem you wrote about the event?

Yes! I saw them in Portland, Maine. I was up there with Gary Snyder, probably 1965, 1966. In my *Collected Poems* it's dated by a poem describing the Beatles playing in Portland. I was with a couple of little children. I had gotten tickets and was sitting way out in the bleachers, and John Lennon came out and said, "We understand that Allen Ginsberg is in the audience. So three cheers. So now we'll have our show." He saluted me from the stage, which amazed me and made me feel very proud with all these young kids at my side. Then I knew Lennon and Yoko Ono lived in New York and visited them on and off. I was involved in some political things with them occasionally.

In the late Sixties or early Seventies I visited McCartney in London. I was on TV that day, a "Pro Pot" rally in Hyde Park, and the cops had stopped me from playing a harmonium or talking on a microphone. So I came down from my ladder from where I was talking and gave the cop a flower. That was kind of a knockout for everybody in London at that time, that I did that rather than getting mad. And I was watching that on TV with Mick Jagger at McCartney's house. And McCartney was painting a satin shirt and he gave it to me as a "performance shirt." We talked a little. We met each other over the years and then we met again when he did *Saturday Night Live,* and he greeted me like an old lost buddy.

What did Paul McCartney add to your recording of "Skeletons"?

He reacts to the words in an intelligent way. You can hear it on the tape. Like if I say on the recording, "What's cooking," all of a sudden he brings in the maracas to get that really funny excitement. When I say, "Blow Nancy Blow," he blows on the Hammond organ. He added a lot of enthusiasm and a lot of interpretation. And sometimes when I made a flub, he covered it. He left his lead sheet in his guitar case, so we had to share my lead sheet [at the gig], which was fun. After the Tibet House benefit, Danny Goldberg [president of Mercury Records], who was in the audience at Carnegie Hall, called up my office 'cause he heard it and liked it and said "Do you want to record it?" I got together Marc Ribot, Lenny and David Mansfield. And Lenny was the session-maker. Lenny has worked with Patti, a poet, and he has worked with Jim Carroll, a poet, and John Giorno, a poet. So he's very literate and encouraging. And I didn't know if he'd pay attention to me, but at the Carnegie Hall benefit we all did together—when he stepped in, he was right on the spot, and helpful. Then we did it again at a benefit out in Ann Arbor, Michigan, with Patti Smith. Lenny was there and we did it again with a local bassist, and he played a fantastic solo. Since he knew how to get things together, and he knew people at the label like Danny Goldberg, he was the natural person to take over.

We made a basic track and McCartney had said, "If you record it, I'd like to work on it. It would be fun." So we did a twenty-four-hour overnight mail to him, and he got it and listened to it after a few days. He spent a day on it. He put on maracas, drums and Hammond organ, trying to sound like Al Kooper. And guitar, which was very strong. Then the day it arrived, Philip Glass was in town, and he volunteered because he thought it was my hit, so he wanted to do something with it. He added piano, very much in his style, which fit perfectly onto the rest of the tape. Then Hal Willner wound up mixing it and brought out McCartney's role and the very nice, dramatic structure that McCartney had given to it. I had planned that after "Blow Nancy Blow" you would have four consecutive choruses of instrumentals. McCartney and I had planned the breaks the first time, and varied it a little.

You also did a rewritten version of "Amazing Grace" on the flip side?

About three years ago, Ed Sanders asked all of his friends to write new verses of "Amazing Grace" for one evening of "Amazing Grace" at St. Mark's Church. A lot of people from the Naropa Institute wrote. Anne Waldman, Tuli Kupferberg and I heard of a Zen master who was working with the homeless, who had a sitting meditation on the Bowery with a lot of his students, including Anne Waldman. And they reported that in midwinter it was terrible sleeping in cardboard boxes. The worst thing was that people would pass them by and not acknowledge

their existence—shutting them out. The sense of alienation and helplessness, and being ignored. No eye contact. People were scared of them. And that's what turned me on. Keep them—acknowledge them. That was the inspiration. Keep them in human contact. The verses I wrote seem to be full of heart, to the point, compassion.

And now something you began as a poem, "Skeletons," has evolved into a recording collaborative. Have you considered the expanded audience?

Yeah, but when you write a poem like that, it runs through your mind—who is going to listen to it? President Clinton is going to hear this. I'll send it to [George] Stephanopoulos, who I know. [Senator Bob] Dole will probably hear of it, or someone around Dole will hear it. Rush Limbaugh will probably hear it because it's me and it's nasty to him. Young college kids will hear it. I wonder what Dylan will think? I wonder what McCartney will think? So all those people are present in my mind, inevitably, 'cause I know them. My father. My mother. My brother. What is Robert Creeley gonna think? What is Gary Snyder gonna think? What is *People* magazine gonna think? What is God gonna think? What's Buddha gonna think? But literally, what will my Tibetan lama teacher think? Is this too aggressive, or is this helpful? Things like that.

Is there a reason you used the skeleton as a metaphor throughout the poem?

I'm Buddhist, and you look at these issues through the grave, and also setting them up as skeleton puppets, setting up the military people, the advertising people, the network people, the talk-show junkies, Big Brother. Setting them up as skeletons, as puppets. Setting them up as transparent phantoms, and looking at the issues out of the grave. The idea of putting all the present factions and seeing them from the grave as walking skeletons.

Do *you feel the music people coming to your work now? Fans as well as musicians who have enjoyed your books and previous records?*

All that, and a lot of these musicians have grown up on my poetry. So some, like Marc Ribot, once heard me read, and liked it. It's just an accumulation of experience with my poetry, and it seems at this point I'm able to work with any musician who I'd like to.

I did a collaboration three months ago with Ornette Coleman for French television. They sent a limousine, and I did it with Gregory Corso and the late Herbert Huncke, and we went to Ornette's studio. Huncke died at the ripe old age of eighty-one. He died the way he wanted, surrounded by friends and full of morphine from the doctors.

I read some poems and Ornette punctuated them with saxophone. We did a monochordal chant, ending in three chords. Ornette was totally great. Gregory would read a poem, or get up and make some comment, and Ornette answered with sax. They were talking back and forth.

I've noticed some alternative and college radio stations will often pair you up with Patti Smith.

Patti is coming from the St. Mark's Poetry Project and Anne Waldman as a mentor, and Burroughs, who she loves a lot, so our paths have crossed that way quite often. I think I first really saw her at the Burroughs Nova Convention in 1978, in New York. I really picked up on her there. Her improvisation onstage and her vulnerability and her sort of informality and at the same time her bravery. That was real interesting. And I've been watching her since. We've done a few shows together to raise money for a heart center. We've done it three years at a big theater which holds four thousand people, and we filled it. Patti's inclined toward a Rimbaud kind of Buddhist thing, and I was interested in her Rimbaud connection and her Rimbaud behavior. When she retired from the whole thing, that was very interesting, that someone could drop the whole theme and passion to take care of her children and have a family, and come back renewed. And when she came back, she was friends with a friend of mine, who introduced her to Oliver Ray, who is now playing with her.

I *know that Burroughs introduced you to some key books in the mid-Forties that were influential to your thoughts and writing, and Kerouac, around the same time, when you were attending Columbia University, maybe 1950, had been into some form of Buddhism and spontaneous prose, but an older generation of writers had an impact on your eventual voice. I mean, today, I said as far as New Jersey goes, it's you, Bruce Springsteen and Frank Sinatra, but you added, "William Carlos Williams," whom you met at age seventeen.*

I knew him from my hometown of Paterson, New Jersey. He actually innovated the idea of listening to the way people talked and writing in that way—using the tones of their voice and using the rhythmical sequences of actual talk instead of dat dat dat dot dot dot. "This is the forest . . ." Instead of a straight square metronomic arithmetic beat, there's the infinitely more musical and varied rhythmic sequences of conversation as well as the tones. 'Cause if you notice, most academic poetry is spoken in a single solitary moan tone that maybe doesn't have the variety of when you are talking to your grandmother or baby.

It happens every one hundred or one hundred fifty years. It did in the days of Wordsworth, who in his preface to lyrical ballads, suggested that poets begin writing in the words and diction of men of intelligence, or talk to each other intelligently, instead of imitating another century's literary style. So, I think what happened is that we followed an older tradition, a lineage, as the modernists at the turn of the century continued their work into idiomatic talk and musical cadences and returned poetry back to its original sources and actual communication between people. That was picked up generation after generation up to people like U2, who are very much influenced by Burroughs in their presentation of visual material, or Sonic Youth—Thurston Moore and Lee Ranaldo are interested in poetry. I actually am working with them now.

Artists from new generations, alternative rock bands, still keep discovering your work and acknowledging your influence.

It's fun. You always learn from younger people. I learned a lot from William Carlos Williams, and the elders of my generation—people who were much older than me when I was young. And that intergenerational amity is really important because it spreads myths from one generation to another of what you know, and all the techniques and the history. At the same time, Williams learned from his connection with Corso and myself and [Peter] Orlovsky—renewed his lease, so to speak. And the advent of the Black Mountain/Beat Generation/San Francisco poetry renaissance really renewed his poetic life, in a sense, brought him out to the public. All of a sudden, with the phalanx of younger people following his lead, he became the sage that he was, rather than the eccentric jerk from New Jersey. And I think it gave him a lot of gratification to realize he had been on the right track, and that it wasn't in vain.

And I get the same thing whenever I work with younger people. And I learn from them. I don't think I would have been singing if it wasn't for the younger Dylan. I mean he turned me on to actually singing. I remember the moment it was. It was a concert I went to with Happy Traum in Greenwich Village. I suddenly started to write my own lyrics, instead of using Blake's poetry. Dylan's words were so beautiful. The first time I heard them, I wept. I had come back from India, and at a welcome home party in Bolinas, Charlie Plymell, a poet I liked a lot, played me

Dylan singing "Masters of War" from *Freewheelin' Bob Dylan*, and I actually burst into tears. It was a sense that the torch had been passed to another generation. There's a young poet now, Jeffrey Manaugh, a senior at Chapel Hill [North Carolina], and he's about twenty, and he's a great poet, I think. I sent Ferlinghetti some of his pamphlets, and Ferlinghetti asked him to send a manuscript to consider for City Lights. At the age of twenty, that's rare. So there's always, every generation, somebody comes along and knocks your heart open.

*W*hy has there been a Beat Generation literary renaissance and Eighties/Nineties new appreciation now of audio/video Beat writing/performing activities?

Audiences now are really interesting. It's about a quarter young kids from the ages of fourteen to eighteen, due to the retro renaissance of Beat interest. Maybe it's the actual expression of emotion that interests people who have been deprived of emotion, and not really able to express their erotic joy or grief for a long time, under the Reagan and Bush repression era. Also, in the Eighties, the renaissance might have been a reaction against the mid–Seventies disco music, which was totally mechanical and characteristic of that retreat from feeling. The generation now feels a sense of alienation, voidoid, grunge, Kurt Cobain, so what is really needed is another shot of emotion and a renaissance of people being able to express their emotions in music or in poetry. And, that's one thing that I think my new recording collection is really useful for musically as well as verbally. So, I'm glad to show my heart. People now want to say what they really think because they are faced in every direction by plastic, corporate protrusion of fear, and the substitution of violence, kitsch, stereotype, discontinuity, and no sense of ground. But, there is real ground in everybody, and there is longing and desire. Desire for affection, desire for tenderness, desire for love, desire for security and safety, desire to be cuddled. And that was mocked for so many years by the Malthusian idea of "I'm all right." "Dog eat dog." "I got mine, Jack." The Darwinian competition as the keynote. Trilllions of dollars in debt that we will never climb out of. Spending, S and L's, the military wasting money to show off.

People are now more receptive to candor, cheerfulness and some kind of openness and reality against the pessimistic, negative FBI in the closet, J. Edgar Hoover secrecy. We were proposing a better world, not denouncing this world, and I think the media got so upset that their notion of the world was being questioned by a vision of maybe something that was better. They decided [then] that we were negative. I think you'll find sympathy in "Howl." In fact, I remember when Kerouac was asked on the William F. Buckley TV show in the Sixties what the Beat Generation meant, Kerouac said, "*Sympathetic.*"

© MELLON 1998

BY GREIL MARCUS

[Rolling Stone 761, May 29, 1997]

"GO FUCK YOURSELF WITH YOUR ATOM BOMB."

That's the fifth line of "America," a poem Allen Ginsberg wrote in Berkeley in 1956, just as he was finding his voice, and if you don't think it's funny maybe you're not an American. Certainly you don't live in the same country that was invented by tall-tale tellers — crafty and sly, indomitable and bitter—like Davy Crockett, Abraham Lincoln, Mark Twain, William Faulkner, Ralph Ellison, Cassius Clay, Bob Dylan and Allen Ginsberg. That was always Ginsberg's country, whether in "A Western Ballad," a perfectly still, empty-desert song he composed in Paterson, New Jersey in 1948—

> When I died, love, when I died
> there was a war in the upper air:
> all that happens, happens there

—or in a not so famous line from the famous "Howl," so famously debuted at the Six Gallery in San Francisco in 1955: "the cosmos instinctively vibrated at their feet in Kansas." The line confused me when I first came across it—so I made fun of it ("Kansas?") to a friend who'd seen a lot more of the country than I had, as Ginsberg had. "Look," said the late Sandy Darlington, a writer and folk singer from Washington state, in words Ginsberg's Kansan comrades Bruce Conner and Michael McClure might have used, "anyone can run off to Japan like Gary Snyder and get the cosmos to vibrate at their feet at the top of

Allen Ginsberg, Cherry Valley, New York, 1973
MELLON

Mt. Fuji. To get the cosmos to vibrate at your feet in Kansas—well, then you know you really *got* it."

Like "Howl," like the 1966 "Wichita Vortex Sutra" (perhaps Ginsberg's greatest poem, certainly his most expansive, his most American-geographical: The cosmos doesn't vibrate at his feet in this Kansas, America itself does), "America" is, among other things, a comic rant. Its cadences are simple, blunt, and in perfect balance, so much so that the lines of the poem seem less made than found, picked up off the street, one-liners anybody else might have thrown away that only Ginsberg has a use for. Whether you hear the poem on the page; on Ginsberg's four-CD set *Holy Soul Jelly Roll*, as Ginsberg in stand-up-comedy-drag recited the piece to a laughing Berkeley audience in 1956; or as collected on the three-CD set *The Beat Generation* in a more somber recording Ginsberg made in 1959, the same qualities are present, and they take the poem out of the time from which it emerged, connecting it to all-American time. There's a bemused but finally baffled—almost defeated—reverence toward the enormity and impenetrability of this thing, this America, this terrible looming witch-hunting Godzilla of infinite hope and charm (in 1956 Ginsberg performs the poem as if all of America's crimes against him, against *itself*, are a kind of shaggy-dog story, just like the poem itself). There's an instinctive, soon enough cultivated impiety toward any or all of America's priests. And at rock bottom there is embrace, the impossibility of separation or exile or even pulling away: America as the tar baby and Ginsberg's hand stuck. Whenever I hear Ginsberg say *America go fuck yourself with your atom bomb* I see him grinning with pleasure—the pleasure of telling your own country to go fuck itself, to be sure, but also the thrill of Slim Pickens riding his atom bomb at the end of *Dr. Strangelove*, wahooing himself and everybody else into oblivion.

If Ginsberg had reformed himself, renounced a few past errors, smiled through a bit of youthful excess, he too might have been present at Bill Clinton's first inauguration, along with such dubious characters as Bob Dylan and Michael Jackson: On that day in 1993 the barrier of legitimacy was very low. As it happened, though, Ginsberg never renounced anything, in the same way that a statement often offered by elders never passed his lips: "There's nothing new under the sun." When I met him last fall he seemed most excited by plans for his own *Unplugged* special "with Dylan, Paul McCartney, and Beck!" In all of his gestures of quietude or vehemence, basking in celebrity while at the same time raising old grudges from the dead, he was as he'd always

been, spreading the word, promoting the cause, honoring his fellows, casing the room.

Even shaking hands for the first time, Ginsberg was cruising. Not well, moving very carefully, dressed like a retired, respectable Jewish bookseller from his parents' generation, he was a dirty old man in the guise of a clean old man, like the "clean old man" in *A Hard Day's Night*—unless it was the other way around. "Fuck the Beatles, fuck the songs, fuck the cute direction and Marx Brothers comparisons," as the late Lester Bangs wrote: "it's BLATANTLY OBVIOUS that the most rock 'n' roll human being in the whole movie is the fucking grandfather!" So speaking softly, like a rabbi, Ginsberg spent a solid hour giving me hell for once calling Jack Kerouac a phony. Not because he knew him and I didn't, but because I hadn't read all there was to read, hadn't heard all there was to hear ("You don't know *Mexico City Blues*, do you? I didn't think so. I've just recorded it. I'll send you a copy"). Sitting there with Ginsberg, the America he had so often evoked so eloquently and so completely—seemed small enough to see whole, and too hot to touch.

Allen Ginsberg Dying
April 4, 1997

BY LAWRENCE FERLINGHETTI

Allen Ginsberg is dying
It's in all the papers
It's on the evening news
A great poet is dying
But his voice
        won't die
His voice is on the land
In Lower Manhattan
in his own bed
he is dying
There is nothing
to do about it
He is dying the death that everyone dies
He is dying the death of the poet
He has a telephone in his hand
and he calls everyone
from his bed in Lower Manhattan
All around the world
late at night
the telephone is ringing
"This is Allen"
        the voice says
"Allen Ginsberg calling"
How many times have they heard it
over the long great years
He doesn't have to say Ginsberg
All around the world
in the world of poets
there is only one Allen
"I wanted to tell you" he says
He tells them what's happening
what's coming down
on him

Death the dark lover
going down on him
His voice goes by satellite
over the land
over the Sea of Japan
where he once stood naked
trident in hand
like a young Neptune
a young man with black beard
standing on a stone beach
It is high tide and the seabirds cry
The waves break over him now
and the seabirds cry
on the San Francisco waterfront
There is a high wind
There are great whitecaps
lashing the Embarcadero
Allen is on the telephone
His voice is on the waves
I am reading Greek poetry
The sea is in it
Horses weep in it
The horses of Achilles
weep in it
here by the sea
in San Francisco
where the waves weep
They make a sibilant sound
a sibylline sound
Allen
       they whisper
            Allen

Dear Allen

BY PATTI SMITH

Dear Allen

There are 785,000 copies of Howl in print in America
There is only one read by your side as you lay beneath
a portrait of Walt Whitman in your death sleep

There is only one that beheld a humble blue
curtain flutter above your pillow as faithful monks
chanted and friends softly shuddered and Peter
discreetly attended and a universe of children kept
spinning prayers into songs in the form of little
blue cloths the size of even smaller skies
peopled with tiny stars whispering
you are dead

There are 785,000 copies of Howl but only one
bearing fragile sketches of your handsome face
so poorly executed
as you would not
even in death
stop moving

There is only one bathed
in Gregory's small sigh
oh my allen

Only one wrapped in Buddhist gauze
housing this pause this solemn regret
that you are nothing
now save the last
beat the last moan
of your own blues

Oh Allen Allen Ginsberg
oh see what you have done
see see Allen
see what you have done
you took us in
from everywhere
and made us all
as one

Editor's note: *The following tributes, recollections and good-byes—written and oral—ran in a special section devoted to Allen Ginsberg in* ROLLING STONE *761, May 29, 1997.*

THE FIRST TIME I SAW ALLEN Ginsberg, he was at a party standing over by the fireplace, and nobody was talking to him. This was after "Howl" but before his big pinnacle. And this woman went over to him and said, "I can't talk to you; you're a legend." And he said, "Yeah, but I'm a friendly legend."

He was able to make peace in ways that no one else could, except John Lennon who had the quality of bringing peace wherever he went. I have three memories of Ginsberg really using these powers.

Back in '65, we took the bus up to Berkeley for Vietnam Day. The day before the big rally, the Hell's Angels said they were going to protest Vietnam Day by pounding the shit out of the protesters. Since we kind of knew the Angels, we went over to Oakland, to [Angels leader] Sonny Barger's house. Ginsberg went with us, right into the lion's mouth with his little finger cymbals. *Ching, ching, ching.* And he just kept talking and being his usual absorbing self. Finally they said, "Okay, okay. We're not going to beat up the protesters." When he left, one of the Angels, Terry the Tramp, says, "That queer little kike ought to ride a bike." From then on, he had a pass around the Angels. They had let all the other Angels know "he's a dude worth helping out." They were absolutely impressed by his courage.

About fifteen years ago, we had a poetry festival at the University of Oregon, which we held on their basketball court; we invited big names to be headliners at the evening event. During the day, aspiring headliners performed outside to see if they'd make it into the show. As the day went on, people began to drift in. At the end of the day, we had about three thousand people on the court, and no one had bought a ticket. Ginsberg said, "Let me get them." And he took his little harmonium. And he *om*'d, and pretty soon everybody was going "*om, om, om.*" At the height of the *om*, he just gestured for the door, and all three thousand people stood up and walked out so we could charge them five bucks to walk back through the door. *Power.*

And the third thing was a time when we were driving around. Ginsberg and some others were in the back [of the bus] on a mattress, and we got pulled over by a cop for a tail light or something. The cop looked in the back, and there was Ginsberg on top of this, well, boy, really. And the cop looked in and said, "What's going on?" "Sir," Allen said, "this boy is having an epileptic seizure. I have to hold him down." That was it. *Phew.*

Three examples of his courage and his humor. As this stuff comes up, I get all of these images of Ginsberg. I remember there was this picture of him in the newspaper, he'd been at a peace rally, and the cops beat him up. They were carrying him out on a stretcher, all pummeled, and he began flashing the V sign for the reporters taking pictures. Pretty soon, he had everyone laughing, even the cops. But he wasn't trying to inflame people. There was a time when if you weren't trying to inflame people, you were almost subversive.

I can't help but feel privileged to have really known Ginsberg, Timothy Leary and Jerry Garcia. These are three revolutionary heavies, and as time goes by and all this hysteria about drugs wears off, these guys will be re-evaluated in terms of their work and their effect on society. All three were real revolutionary leaders—like Benjamin Franklin or Thomas Jefferson—and it's the same revolution, the revolution of consciousness, without which the nation will not survive. We've got to be mature enough to incorporate everyone into this revolution. Its basis is mercy and justice and mercy before justice.

—KEN KESEY

A few months ago we were on the roof terrace of the Soho Grand, in New York, in the snow, and he sat down in the deck chairs and, for laughs, joking and taking the piss out of himself, put a hat and a blanket around himself. He looked like some old guy you'd see transplanted from Miami. And he recited the lyrics from "Miami," a song of ours, for this TV special we did, and it blew us all away. He gave it the full Ginsberg treatment:

> *Big girl with the sweet tooth*
> *Watches the skinny girl in the photo shoot*
> *Her eyes all swimmin' pool blue*
> *And she tastes of chlorine*

It's on film, and for some eerie reason it's in the same tempo as the song, so they cut it in—it's something. "Miami" sounded great coming out of his lips, sounded a lot better than it is, probably, as a lyric. I think to make other men poets is a gift, indeed.

The last I saw him was in his new place down in the East Village—his whole world was in boxes. And they were all numbered. And he had everything filed, every photograph he'd ever taken. He had some very smart people working for him. It was almost like he'd tidied everything up. I don't know if he knew then; he didn't tell us.

We were trying to buy him an Irish-tweed suit—because I knew he likes them, but he wouldn't let me. He said, "No, no, don't do that; I'll catch you in Ireland."

I wasn't a great friend of his or anything, just a fan, and he was good to me as a fan. When I left his apartment the other week, he just piled me up, a whole pile of rare editions of his books and the last one he gave me was his father's book of poetry.

Allen was extraordinary. There's a much more minimal style, sort of post-Carver sense for literature right now. But that drunk language still survives. If you think about it, the headiness of the Sixties and the dizziness of it all, I think his position is safe.

—BONO

The people in the Beat movement—myself, Gregory Corso, Allen, Jack Kerouac—we were quite different artistically. But we were together in the simple concept of openness and expanding awareness. Before anyone had begun to make a real breakthrough, there was Allen leading these outspoken readings in front of fraternity boys at Columbia. They were the people you'd expect to be the least receptive and most hostile to that kind of message, but he didn't seem to encounter much direct confrontation. He won them over with his absolute sincerity, his openness. There was that courage. Very definitely, he extended the area of artistic expression; he extended the area of what was artistic.

I admired very much the calm and dignity with which he met his death. The doctors told him two to four months, and he said, "I think much less." It was, of course, much less. He said to me, "I thought I'd be terrified when I heard that diagnosis. I'm not terrified at all. I'm exhilarated."

—WILLIAM S. BURROUGHS

I had just gotten out of Clinton prison at Dannemora, in New York, in November of '49, where I had been for robbery, and was spending time in the Village. I used to hang out at this lesbian bar, the Pony Stable, where a friend of mine did caricatures. One night this young man comes in. He had these eyes: deep black pools of light. I didn't know that he was gay then, that he was out cruising. But he was looking at me, so I went up and hustled a beer out of him. We started talking and poetry came up. I mean, I didn't know anybody like Allen. I'd been in prison. I had my prison poems with me and showed them to him. That was how we got to know each other. Then he introduced me to Kerouac and Burroughs; he said to them, "Look who I have found." That man became my brother, my Jewish grandmother, my teacher, my PR man. He pushed me like he pushed everybody. In the end, I guess he didn't teach me how to live too well. But he did teach me how to die. He let go so beautifully. The last thing he said to me: "Toodle-oo."

I think of him as the captain of a ship who brought in a great cargo, and deposited it here. He was the Beat Generation. He was a great, spirited man, a great, lifelong friend. I will miss him, dear Allen.

—GREGORY CORSO

The first reading of "Howl," in October 1955, was part of a very outspoken evening. There were between one hundred and two hundred people there: woman professors in old fox coats, anarchists, carpenters, workers from the docks, young poets. Jack [Kerouac] was there that night, making collections for jugs of wine, tapping on the jugs in time with us, yelling, "Go, go, go." What we all wanted to do with the Six Gallery reading was take the poetry off the page and deliver it to the ear and body and consciousness of the person there listening. What we were saying wouldn't be published, the kind of things we were saying had no publishers. So we did it right out loud. What we discovered was the people in the audience were there to hear exactly what we were doing. We were speaking for them. And Allen drew the line with "Howl." People left after that completely blown away. It was very immediately a revelation.

—MICHAEL MCCLURE

I remember walking away from the Six Gallery, in San Francisco, after Allen's first reading of "Howl," saying, "Poetry will never be the same. This is going to change everything." Everyone who attended was set back. It was the power of "Howl." He got right into the quandaries and complexities of the Eisenhower era, the personal lives of those who were marginalized and often in pain, and brought those voices forward. It was the beginning of the Beat Generation and, in a sense, the defining moment in all of our literary careers.

—GARY SNYDER

Allen Ginsberg, John Cage and La Monte Young were the first three figures of the New York avant-garde I met when I arrived in the city in 1963. The last time I saw him was during last month's Tibet House benefit concert at Carnegie Hall. Lenny Kaye and I played while Allen sang "Don't Smoke" with his wonderfully infectious, dribbly lilt mixed in with the melodic rhythm of the cantor.

In the period between the two events, Allen was the conscience of the underground/avant-garde to whom we all deferred.

—JOHN CALE

Allen was a pretty far-out cat. He was a highly intellectual guy who had a lot of bright ideas. And as he became older, he never stopped having them. He found a way to keep going, and to be at peace with himself. Once,

Allen had organized this recording session, where he'd be reciting the poetry of William Blake. He was a Blake scholar. We were all crowded into this small studio in Greenwich Village. He had Charlie Mingus, Larry Coryell and myself, and Allen was playing some kind of Middle Eastern double-reed instrument. We got to know each other very well when there were problems with the time signature for the cadence of the poetry. So I wrote out a chart for him with the time signature and gave him the cadence. He showed me that chart, like thirty years later: "This is what you wrote out for me!" I had written it out on a paper bag. He kept it all that time. So that's how we got to be good friends.

—ELVIN JONES

Allen and I first met in London, in '67. Through the years, whenever our paths crossed, he never ceased to impress me with his wisdom and sense of fun.

Allen was sexy in a way a mountain sometimes could be. He was gentle in a way a true friend could be. And he was intelligent in a way that influenced a whole generation. It's hard to believe that he's gone. In fact, I would like to think that I might still meet him somewhere.

—YOKO ONO

I can still see Allen oming through the tear gas in New Haven, in the early Seventies, when everybody was starting to freak out. Next thing you know, the tear gas was gone; everybody kept oming. That was courage. A lot of people don't realize that aside from writing good poetry, he pulled the covers down on the mean and the nasties. He'd bust them. And he never lost his great sense of humor. He was always more of a chuckler than a guffawer; he had a very intelligent wit. It was just such a pleasure to be around him.

—WAVY GRAVY

Allen got me to lecture at the Naropa Institute for a lyric-writing class and I got to watch him lecture about poetry. He taught Walt Whitman and knew about every reference in every poem. He was a brilliant lecturer (and I'm a connoisseur because my father was a lecturer and taught Dante) and Allen was erudite and totally serious but also very funny. He made scholarly sort of jokes that you'd have to be very clever to understand. Also, Allen was everyone's sort of very own Jewish mother. He made me countless dinners over the years, and he loved it; he was a great cook—and a terrible nag. Once I'd had a bit too much to drink and the next day he really let me have it. Oh, I was furious. But he was a very warm man; he had a great gift for friendship.

—MARIANNE FAITHFULL

His poetry was so American and so straightforward, so astute, and he had such a recognizable voice. Modern rock lyrics would be inconceivable without the work of Allen Ginsberg. It opened them up from the really mediocre thing they'd been to something more interesting and relevant. He was very brave, and he was also very honest—a no-bullshit person.

In the Fifties, Sixties, Seventies, Eighties, Nineties, Allen was everywhere; he was a part of everything, everybody's life. From the very beginning of the Velvet Underground, when people were saying how shocking we were, Allen was there dancing, playing Tibetan bells. The world's diminished now. But his spirit goes on though people and their work. And his poems will stand the test of time. He was a very inspiring guy, and on top of that, he was really nice. What a striking combination.

—LOU REED

The first time I met Allen was, I think, the winter of 1963–64, when I was nineteen years old. I'd driven into New York to pick up Gregory Corso and bring him back down to Princeton to do a poetry reading. When I got to his apartment, Corso told me his wife had just given birth to their first child that morning. He'd been up, so could he bring along another poet to read? Out of the next room stepped Allen Ginsberg, just back from India. As soon as the reading started, Gregory went off to a corner of the stage and fell asleep, and Allen did the entire gig. It was right when the Vietnam War was starting to get nasty, when he and Bob Dylan were starting to hook up. Allen seemed larger than life to me then—as he seems larger than death to me right now. Before he went onstage, he said he was cold, so I loaned him my sweater. After he gave it back, I wore it everyday for weeks because it had Allen's smell.

One hot July, ten years later, I was passing through Naropa Institute and stayed in the faculty apartments. Late one night I was rolling around in bed with a friend of mine when she went and woke up Allen, whose room was down the hall, and he came back naked and crawled into bed with us. I wasn't into it, so I climbed into a sleeping bag. As Allen and my friend caressed each other, Allen reached over and touched me on the forehead, and I came instantly. I thought of that the day after he died when I heard his poem "Death and Fame," in which Allen described his vision of his own funeral, a great public one at St. Patrick's Cathedral or St. Mark's Church or the largest synagogue in Manhattan, in which five decades of ex-lovers would testify that he gave great head.

"Old Courage-Teacher"—that's what Ginsberg called Walt Whitman. That's what Allen was for so many people. "He immortalized tenderness," Peter Leavitt, a poet-friend, said to me.

At the same time, Allen was a man of towering wraths—usually followed by anguished guilts. You couldn't write a poem like his "Pentagon Exorcism" without being able to focus your anger to a diamondlike intensity. When you think about the Fifties now, you think about Allen Ginsberg quicker than you think about Dwight David Eisenhower.

—LEWIS MACADAMS

Allen Ginsberg and I traveled at various times with Bob Dylan's Rolling Thunder Revue mid-Seventies, loosely dubbed "poets-in-residence." I was hired to contribute ideas to the movie (*Renaldo and Clara*)—the brothel scene filmed in Quebec City one of them, a visit to the Shakers another (never panned out, the Shakers were considered too old). Allen was in heaven with the energy of the scene, but yearned to be included onstage, always the frustrated rock & roller (close to death, he was hoping to complete an MTV *Unplugged*). I'd gone back to Boulder, Colorado, to teach/run our burgeoning Jack Kerouac School of Disembodied Poetics at the Naropa Institute that Allen and I had cofounded in 1974, but was lured to Fort Collins for the filming of the show that became the *Hard Rain* TV special. It was pouring. The musicians and roadies were grumpy and nervous about being electrocuted. Dylan had been promising Allen the moon. Yes, he'd be invited to read onstage, etc., etc. But when? During a long break I got my nerve up and marched into Bob's dressing room demanding, "Let the poet read in the rain!" A flurry of consultation. Okay. Allen took the stage, ever modest but commanding. A mere seven-line poem, "On Neal's Ashes." Allen held the crowd in thrall, his voice ringing out prophetic, clear, passionate for a rare transmuted tantric moment: "Delicate eyes that blinked blue Rockies all ash / Nipples, Ribs I touch w / my thumb are ash . . . asshole anneal'd to silken skin all ashes, all ashes again." And I thought more power at times in that lone naked human hungry voice than all the electrified amps in the world.

—ANNE WALDMAN

Allen and I got into the American Academy of Arts and Letters, in 1973—at the same time—and a guy from *Newsweek* called me and said, "So what does it feel like for a couple of outsiders like you to suddenly get taken into the establishment?" and I said—and Allen agreed with me—"If we aren't the establishment, then who is?" I was always very fond of Allen, always very glad to see him. His love was uncritical and utterly open and irresistible. He was a saint and he was the only politically effective poet of my lifetime.

—KURT VONNEGUT

In late '77, I was hired on as Allen's temporary secretary and then kept on. I started working out of Allen's apartment. It was amazing we got any work done at all: There would be people visiting all day. There were open house rules at Ginsberg's: You could eat anything in the refrigerator, especially if you were willing to replace it. Always use the towel on the wall under the peg with your name on it. That's how it was. I worked for him nineteen and a half years, and I never once lost respect for him as a person. Of all the time I spent with him, my favorite moments were when we'd have a few hours together driving in a car that didn't have a telephone. We could just talk. About literature, ideas, anything. His first name was Irwin, Irwin Allen Ginsberg, and I always called those moments time with Irwin.

—BOB ROSENTHAL

When most people think of Allen Ginsberg, they think of his effect on the Beat Generation. What many people don't realize is that he has also had a tremendous effect on kids today. I think Allen is not so much a symbol of intelligence but of love. I hope that his works will become more and more integrated into the curriculum of American high schools so that he can continue to challenge and inspire

future generations. To Allen, I say this: May you reincarnate as the tightest-assed, broadest-shouldered hulk in the universe!

—SEAN ONO LENNON

I knew Allen in so many ways. But what's most memorable to me are the times we performed together onstage. The passion and conviction of his performances were contagious. The day after he died, I had a concert in Chicago, it had all been arranged months before, and I didn't want to cancel. On the program I was to play "Hydrogen Jukebox," a piece we did together. I almost didn't play it, but I decided that I if didn't play it that night, I never would. The first twenty seconds were difficult, then I began to hear the voice, Allen's voice. I've incorporated him into my own being, both physically and consciously. It's not when I'm playing that I miss him, but when I'm not.

—PHILIP GLASS

The last evening I spent with Allen Ginsberg was over a year ago at the Naropa Institute, in Boulder, Colorado. As we talked Buddhism and listened to music, Allen kept snapping photos as if his camera was a musical instrument.

He led an exemplary public life, blending Old Testament prophecy with Buddhist centering, creating a monumental body of creative work while still finding time to teach the next generations (like my kid Vanessa, a writing student of his).

I called Allen last summer to invite him to a reunion of the survivors of the 1968 Democratic National Convention we were holding in Chicago during the 1996 Democratic convention. He wanted badly to come, but said his health was failing, and he needed the rest. During the convention he did appear on live hookup with several of us on *Larry King Live*. With great wit and delivery, he recited "The Ballad of the Skeletons," which I think ranks with "Howl" as a final, witty denunciation of the official and universal hypocrisy to which Allen never succumbed.

—TOM HAYDEN

He was a man with an immense number of sides, really a leader. In the early Sixties Allen and I were asked to appear on a television show to talk about the Beat Revolution. Allen was naturally brought up first, and then I was to speak. I had been on a few shows at that point, but this was Allen's first. He said to me, "Gee, I really feel out to sea. How should I behave?" I gave him what I thought was my acquired wisdom. Then the show started, and I said to myself that's the last time I'm ever going to give Allen Ginsberg advice. He just took over. He was everything. The interviewer was in a state of delight; he'd rarely had so good a guest; unexpected, startling, sensible, serious. Allen had instincts when it came to presenting himself in public with his ideas. Six months before the Democratic National Convention in Chicago in '68, we were having a drink together, and he asked if I was going to go to the convention. I told him I thought so, and he said he was going to go, too. He said, "There's going to be terrible trouble. I really have a very bad feeling about how bad it's going to be." When Chicago did come, there was Allen in the very center of it. He knew that it could blow up in his face. He had real guts that way. In the end, he was one of the four or five real leaders of all that went on there.

—NORMAN MAILER

Who else played such a high-profile, dynamic and germinal role across the Beat presence, the Haight's heyday and the present generation? He was equally at home with the roles of wise man and fool. His writing philoso-phy of "first thought—best thought" has influenced poetry today as deeply as did William Carlos Williams's earlier dictum: "No reality but in things." He now joins that company of phantom voices linked through the centuries who have left their visions like a gypsy's wares spread out on the grass of our minds.

—ROBERT HUNTER

I owe Allen Ginsberg a lot. He set me free. When I was a hick kid of fifteen and read "Howl," I found in it permission, even encouragement, to live an outsider's life. He described me to myself. I realized that I was not alone as one of those "angelheaded hipsters burning for the ancient heavenly connection to the starry dynamo in the machinery of night," and that I could now consider such aspirations a virtue rather than a sin. And so, with his distant midwifery, I became who I am.

Like Tim Leary, Allen did not want to punctuate his passionate life with whimpering horror and resolved instead to gather his friends about him and die in a civilized fashion, as people died when death was still domesticated, before science made it wild.

—JOHN PERRY BARLOW

When I first read Ginsberg in my teens, I remember very specifically feeling things open up and thinking about the life ahead of me as being a lot more open than growing up to be a refrigerator repairman in Akron, Ohio—not that that's a bad thing. But "Howl" and "Kaddish," they just gave me a sense of possibility. It's one of those magic things when you're a kid in Akron: You read William S. Burroughs, you read Allen Ginsberg and you listen to Ornette Coleman. You come to New York, and you end up meeting those guys—it was amazing. I was in awe the first time I met Ginsberg. I guess I'm still in awe.

—JIM JARMUSCH

Allen always stayed in touch with culture, with what was going on. He came to the first show I did with my band Pen Pal, a few years ago. It was just around the time when Larry Clark was filming *Kids*, and all these skateboard kids from the movie showed up, and there was Allen sitting there in the middle, attentively listening. Between songs, he would say, "You should enunciate more." He always pushed you to get the words out, to do the best you could.

—DAVID GREENBERG

His ability to keep his sense of humor made him a very attractive person. He was always laughing. He had a terrific warmth and happiness that he held onto until the day he died.

—DEBORAH HARRY

I first met Allen Ginsberg at an art opening. Ginsberg took my picture and asked me if I was gay and what was I doing that night. I said, "No, I'm not gay; I like girls." To switch topics I asked him if he'd ever heard of KRS-One, a hip-hop MC who reminded me of some of his poetry. He said no, but that he'd like to hear some of this hip-hop stuff. I told him I'd send him one of my mixed tapes. I never did find out what he thought of KRS-One, but I still like his poetry. I don't think that Ginsberg was the type to think of death as an occasion for mourning—I kind of think he would see it like loops, like beats transforming and being remixed. Some old "myth of the eternal return" type shit. Shit that would kind of challenge people's minds to open the fuck up. "Howl" on.

—DJ SPOOKY

I usually met Allen at some event. The last one was at Dan Berrigan's seventy-fifth birthday party last May. About a thousand people came: Catholics and Protestants, Jews and Muslims, probably some Marxists, and people who had no name for their philosophy. Allen recited a poem, and I got the crowd singing, "Where Have All the Flowers Gone." Afterward, Allen came up and gave me some new verses he'd written to be sung to "Amazing Grace." We always knew we were on the same side. We both were part of the anti-war effort, and I was strengthened by his courageous independence. Everybody was strengthened by his courageous independence. "Look what Allen's doing. Well, by gosh, more people should do that." Walt Whitman would have been delighted.

—PETE SEEGER

One year ago Allen invited me to play back-up guitar at a Princeton University reading. Although we had practiced beforehand in his hotel room, by the time of the performance I was distracted enough by the enormous crowd to forget how the first song went. I sat down next to Allen onstage, leaned over and told him, "maybe I should sit out the first song because I have forgotten it."

"Oh," Allen said calmly in front of the anticipating students, "well here, I'll teach it to you again, this is how it goes," and with the patience of a great teacher teaching the one student who was a little behind, he instructed me, "Da-da-da, da-da-da-dum. Da-da-da, da-da-da-dum." The three thousand now amused students were humming along as Allen repeated the phrasing, "Da-da-da, da-da-da-dum." Shaking my head that I was ready, we proceeded, and it really rocked the audience. The song was "The Ballad of the Skeletons."

—GUS VAN SANT

Working with Allen was a great joy: He was inspirational in his quest for excitement. The crazier we got playing, the more he liked it. At the sessions for "The Ballad of the Skeletons," he taught me and the other musicians the Buddhist walk—as you place your feet down, you feel the curvature of the earth. I always hope to remember that walk that he taught me and how it's done, and to keep on walking myself in those footsteps.

—Lenny Kaye

Some artists are very generous; they oblige us by having three selves. This way when they die, we've only lost their public and private face, and the work is left to us forever; left in a way that memory—which can serve us badly—can never do as well. And now that Allen's wonderfully public, clamorous self: artistic, antagonistic, pessimistic, optimistic, hedonistic, realistic, naturalistic . . . is gone, along with his private face: brilliant and goofy, sweet and grasping, loving and grating, aggressive and shy, gentle and rough . . . so *much* person. I wave. So long pal! It's been good to know ya. So generous to have left us so much.

—Alfred Leslie

Lion in your state—of the world—in chains. I did not know you well but whenever we met I could tell—who you were—a forest of fire barely breaking the surface every now-and-then—you were gone. We all want to be remembered and I will always hear you—in other words—goodbye—dear Allen.

—Graham Nash

Allen Ginsberg in his East 12th Street apartment, New York City, 1997
ANNIE LEIBOVITZ/CONTACT PRESS IMAGES

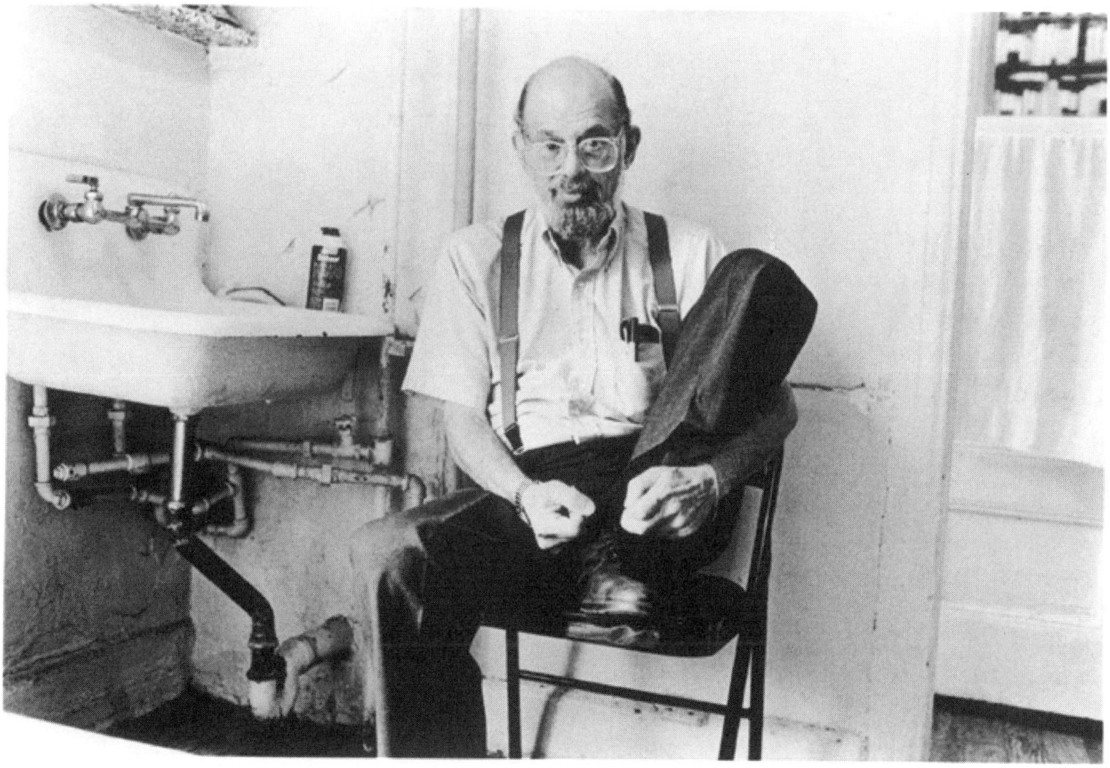

Herbert Huncke, 1940s
ALLEN GINSBERG COLLECTION

PART V

Beat Lights
Characters, Role Models and Others

The Originator:
Herbert Huncke

BY LYDIA LUNCH

SHORT-SHIFT HUSTLER, PETTY thief, con artist, convicted felon, parasitic leech, lifelong junkie. The unsung hero of the literary underground was a mesmerizing storyteller whose collected memoirs, beautifully rendered, are infused with heartbreaking detours, detailing life lived to the extreme. A life spent endlessly searching for a freedom whose very essence is fleeting, a freedom whose song at first sting, sings of release, of liberation, of a fraudulent utopia that quickly fades as the stranglehold of addiction takes root.

Herbert Huncke was THE original Beat. He inspired the damn phrase—from which the Unholy Trio of Burroughs, Ginsberg and Kerouac would forever profit: employing aliases in their thinly disguised portraits of him as "Herman" in *Junkie*, "Junky" in *The Town and the City*, "Elmo Hassel" in *On the Road* and "Huck" in *Visions of Cody*, etc. Even "Howl" used Huncke as a reference point.

Born in 1915, in Greenfield, Massachusetts, and raised in what would soon become Al Capone's Chicago, Huncke first hit the highway at the age of twelve, running away from a hysterical mother, doting granny and overbearing father. Got as far as Geneva, New York, before his outsider status gave him away. Picked up and shipped back to Mommy by a motorcycle cop, his first taste of freedom unleashed the beast within.

Herbert Huncke at the opening for the Beat Culture exhibit, the Whitney Museum, New York City, 1995
MELLON

At fourteen, Huncke got popped, in what would be a series of numerous drug busts. He was befriended by Elsie John—a hermaphrodite who worked the sideshow, peddling heroin to supplement kicks a circus salary couldn't cover. They both got popped. Charges against Huncke were dropped. He was still a minor.

Began hustling down at the lakefront. Chump change. Which didn't go far once the Great Depression hit. Took off, this time out West. Caught his first freight train in Reno. Nickel-and-diming it. The next decade finds our hero, as hobo, zigzagging across the country. Wherever the rails went. Hitchhiking when he got the itch. Walking if he had to. Back up to Chicago, down to New Orleans, Memphis, Nashville, Detroit. Living hand to mouth, hooked on the underbelly.

In '39 he hit 42nd Street. He was twenty-four. Did whatever it took to survive. Sold his sex to lecherous old men. Had a habit. Stole to provide for it. Started to get strung out. Sought comfort and companionship in the smoky jazz clubs on 52nd Street. Hung out with Billie Holiday. Charlie Parker. Fellow dopeheads. Shit, even committing a string of burglaries with Dexter Gordon. Boosting fur coats to hookers up in Harlem. And always taking notes. Gutter scribe. Scribbling riffs in dog-eared journals.

Money burns a hole in your pocket. Especially when you don't have any. And you're milking a heroin habit. Luck runs out. There's no one left to mooch off.

Huncke needed a break and, lured in by the song of the sirens, shipped out to sea during World War II. A quick escape he learned to embrace whenever times got too tight. Or the street got too hot. Or he thought he needed to kick. Although, he somehow always managed to score. Morphine, pot, pills. Whatever . . . Once a junkie, always a junkie.

The middle Forties found him banging it

back around in Times Square, being solicited by Dr. Alfred Kinsey, who paid Huncke a deuce a pop to pull in other hustlers whose horror stories would help to illustrate his groundbreaking studies on American sexual behavior. Even Burroughs was roped in on that con.

Huncke was suspicious of Burroughs. He had reason to be. Too damn straight, overeducated, living on a trust fund, dressed like the FBI. They met at Huncke's—"Old Bill" was trying to pawn off a shotgun and a gross of morphine. Drugs and a gun cemented the shaky relationship.

Burroughs used Huncke as intro to the underworld. Huncke gave him his first shot of dope after a lengthy discourse on the pros and cons of an altered reality versus screaming into the void while trying to kick at the invisible bitch of an addiction. Burroughs bought in. Soon following Huncke's lead. Took to small-time pickpocketing. With Huncke's assist, passed scripts for Dilaudid, morphine. Smoking, snorting or shooting as much shit as they could get their hands on. Selling the scraps on the black market. Burroughs took the fall when the heat closed in. Managed to land a suspended sentence.

Burroughs soon fled to an isolated farm outside of New Waverly, Texas, where he attempted to mastermind a small fortune in marijuana crops. Invited a junk-sick Huncke down to kick; he had just been released from a stint in a Bronx jail. Supposed to bring a jar of seeds to cultivate. Huncke was so out of it, he forgot them. Made it up to Burroughs by keeping the larder stocked with paregoric, Nembutals and Benzedrine pilfered from the local pharmacy. Tended the plants, but the crop was ruined when they neglected to cure it properly.

Not two years later and another bust for Huncke. Weaseled his way into Allen Ginsberg's life; the poet took pity on the delirious vagabond. Huncke was strung out and stealing to support his habit. Used Ginsberg's pad as warehouse for stolen goods. Both got busted for it.

Ginsberg to the nuthouse, Huncke to the Big House.

Most of the Fifties found Huncke locked down in Sing Sing, Dannemora, Riker's Island. Almost ten years of hard time got him cut off from and ignored by his buddies on the outside. Burroughs and Ginsberg used Huncke's hard luck stories to help further illustrate their own degeneracy and were getting published in the interim. Huncke cleaned up but couldn't write in prison. Most of his journals were lost in late night scrambles from one crash pad to another. But decades of drug use did nothing to dull Huncke's memory or attention to detail. With the help of Diane di Prima, he published his first book, *Huncke's Journal*, in 1965 (now included in *The Herbert Huncke Reader,* along with most of his other writings).

Prison couldn't completely cure his criminal tendencies. Junk saw to that. But the last stint in the Big House taught him how to refine his hustle. Got by now more on his wits. Supported himself as master storyteller. Spinning glorious tales of decadent America, one spanning the past six decades. Drifting back and forth from couch to couch. Trading a poem, some prose, a journal entry for a place to sleep, something to eat, a shot, a fix, a decent conversation. Sometimes pausing just long enough to jot it all down. Then on to the next gig. Managed to survive mainly on his notoriety. Genius.

Huncke died in 1996 at the age of eighty-one. The Grateful Dead paid the rent for his last few years spent in glorious squalor at the Chelsea Hotel. Heroin, Valium and cocaine cocktails kept coming, most likely by beautiful young men playing delivery boys. He was still writing. Still reminiscing. Still vital. Remembering more than most of us will ever live to forget.

I never met Huncke. But he still speaks to me in a voice of gentle desperation and compassionate understanding on the complexity and fragility of the human condition, generously revealing the stamina of his tortured soul, who in the face of all odds, was still desperate to communicate, to write, to reach out. Godfather of Beat, patron saint of the wretched, bohemian gypsy, dear Herbert Huncke, I hope the ether you now inhabit is the ultimate heavenly high.

Neal Cassady, 1952

CAROLYN CASSADY

Genesis Angel

BY ARAM SAROYAN

Editor's note: The following is an excerpt from 'Genesis Angels: The Saga of Lew Welch and the Beat Generation,' originally published by William Morrow in 1979.

I T'S A BEAT GENERATION SUNRISE THE day Denver's Neal Cassady blows into New York City, with his girlfriend Luanne, ready to dig and be dug—a friend of a friend of somebody's—but as history would have it, destined to plug in to the nuclear unit of Kerouac/Ginsberg/Burroughs plus others and it's now that this chemical compound combusts—that's Neal's contribution—and soon will take off on the road. Cassady is, you might say, the West's very own Ambassador of Joy to this informal convention of poets and seers.

And John Kerouac, still a bit stolid in his command of the comma and semicolon, and the great thunderous, river-deep mountain-high sentences of his first, now to be published book, *The Town and the City*, and perhaps even in danger of being lionized by the publishing industry into an early retirement to a leather-bound study, with a dutiful wife, three or four fine children, the National Book Award, the Pulitzer Prize, the friend of statesmen, the friend of Truman and Gore and Norman—but out of the racket, and off of the rock & roll and riot and riches of his prose written as an American nomad (although his mother always provided him a clean bed and good food when he needed to come home to sleep it off and write it down).

Think of it, if John never became Jack, and went on being a big Thomas Wolfe–type talent, never discovered goofing along for prose surprises and wild scribbled notebooks of shirt-pants-socks-shoes, hello world, glee. That was Jack,

touched by the angel and madman, bulging out of the Goodwill Jim Clinton suit, parking cars in a midtown parking lot for his money: Mr. Neal.

Now this is where it did combust because what happened was Jack saw Neal and listened to his wild, never-get-a-word-in-edgewise, spontaneous patter (make a Sixties disc jockey sound like Pat Paulsen or the Great Stone Face): This man was a rapid, word chasing man chasing word chasing man chasing time chasing space—look out! just like his driving—saved by exposure and the rare posture of ecstatic brotherhood. Neal was nervous. He was almost crazy. But he came for fun and love, or as much as he could manage. And Jack, who had recently fallen out of a short-term marriage, needed a life to lead as a writer about life, and Neal was willing to share everything: as they did in life, forever after.

And Allen Ginsberg fell in love with Neal, and they became lovers (because Neal wanted love and harmony and complete trust in everybody)—he was insecure and wanted love, too—and Jack was left wistful wondering about the deep day- and night-long conversations and ramifications of Neal and Allen in the Columbia apartment night.

The hungry generation.

And Bill Burroughs met the man and shook his hand. And Luanne got mad at Neal for always racing around like a lunatic, but he appeased her, too, by turning on the great sun-lamp of his attention and giving her a blast of it, undivided.

"Now, Luanne, we've known each other's

souls from many different exposures and angles, we've swept each other's floors, and put away each other's clothes, we've enjoyed perfect love and communion in the sexual dimension, and practiced through the wonders of driving through America in my beat-up Chevrolet, rehearsed every nook and cranny of our Golden Love, and this is New York, which we have carefully planned in advance, and I do have the important responsibility of parking the cars for money, and seeing Jack and Allen and the others for the important reason (which we've also discussed and agreed) of making my own contribution among these important American men of the arts. Also, honey, I have brought some weed home with me, and it is better than either of us have known up to this very moment. Smoked it with Allen last night, and now must smoke it with you. We have important points to establish freshly, and this will help us. Where are the matches—yes, yes, yes."

Neal was like W. C. Fields with an eight-cylinder engine—and handsome. All the paradoxes and collapses and Atom Bomb and Christmas Tree Birthday Party, cop on the corner, all the magazines combined: *Life Time True Confessions Confidential Movie World Car*: is Neal.

Allen and Jack took a long deep look and listen into the whole American day and night in their friend: They saw the absence and the presence he was, and they both loved him and laughed at his child joy and handsome man purpose and importance. Neal came out of the West to touch them with his . . . not his knowledge, but his *experience*. Neal didn't so much know it, as be it: He was the American fact, writ bold and clear in his own charged presence and haunted, yet ecstatic mind.

Ahab and Gatsby and Columbus himself (he parked with supernatural speed and precision, a car Columbus) in awkward friendly suit, with, as Kerouac once remarked in another context, slacks with peculiarities.

Nothing quite fit. The car didn't work—except it couldn't help but be fired and at times drive anyway under the enormous, comradely pressure of Neal's nervous system. This man really was worthy of much better toys, or deeper work, than the current social reality would seem to make available. But could he stop for a moment to make such a determination?

No.

Neal couldn't stop being Neal or he might perish in the extinguishing knowledge of the want and lack and crime and murder and sorrow in the lines of his own soul. But he rode the Life Principle all his life, keeping it together on a threadbare budget and honest work that blessed his deep restlessness with simple routines.

And Jack and Allen, who came from homes, after all, just said ah, and followed him into America.

Neal's Ashes

BY GINA BERRIAULT

[ROLLING STONE 119, October 12, 1972]

THE ASHES OF NEAL CASSADY are contained within a silver-gray rayon drawstring bag that fits within a crudely fancy box of varnished yellow wood shaped somewhat like a wedding cake on a platter, all of this weighing ten pounds on the bathroom scale of the woman who was his wife, the longest of three wives, in whose cupboard the ashes rest. Clutched in the arms of his last mistress, the ashes in their *Hecho en Mexico* box were conveyed back by bus from San Miguel where he was picked up unconscious beside the railroad tracks early one morning in 1968, a few days before his forty-second birthday. And all that *wild, yay-saying over-burst of American joy*, in Kerouac's words, all that joy that he embodied for the Beats and embodies now for the rock generation and for Sunday Supplement writers who have never, they figure, experienced joy—who have only read of how it's experienced by somebody else and who overdose Cassady with joy—was it so astoundingly there before the body was reduced to ashes?

"I think he's happy here. He always wanted to come home." Usually an offensive consolation that survivors parrot at gravesides, in this case it rings with the iron dolor of a bell in a Mexican cathedral. The wife Carolyn is a little woman with the fragility of body and the strength of mind that combine for an evangelical endurance. Heather grows by the door; there's a small lawn. The town is Los Gatos, a suburbia of ranch-style houses an hour or so from San Francisco, on acreage that used to be orchards. On the walls hang her pastel-toned oil paintings of the three Cassady children, all now in their early twenties. On the coffee table and on the shelves and away in the cupboards are some of the novels and periodicals that contribute to the Neal Cassady legend. She's writing her own story now.

"Allen came by to see the ashes and said he'd scatter them on the Ganges if we liked, and then he said, 'Ask your son,' and John said, 'What's the matter with them right here?' I was going to ask Hugh Lynn Cayce if there was any place at the Cayce Foundation where I could put them, because Neal was so wrapped up in Cayce, but I didn't get to talk with him, he was so busy last Saturday—all those people. I'd thought before about Unity, because they have a practice of scattering them on their rose gardens, but Neal wasn't Unity-sold. That teaching insists that you think of yourself as part of God, and Neal just couldn't do it, and every time I'd bring it up he'd get violent, he'd say, 'I read all that in prison.' As far as I know he loathed himself all the time. He couldn't think of himself as good, an expression of God. All that, even in the Cayce parts, he'd scourge. He didn't believe in a good God. He demanded proof, and to him the proof would be if God were stronger than his own will and his own desires. God could stop him, and then he would believe in Him."

Although the number of years of a marriage don't always add up to a greater knowledge of a mate, there was something to be gleaned from sixteen years and from the five years after the divorce when "he hung around like a shadow." She knew him as well as any of the many others who claim now to have known him so well, and yet who are unable to suspect a dark side to any heavenly body.

"So many of the young men who are enamored of the Neal myth, they feel a longing to imitate him. Obviously the image has a response in everybody's longings, and Kerouac's. But if you get down to what it was in essence, like liberty or lack of restriction or inhibitions or rules, whatever it is that Neal represented for them, like free-dom and fearlessness, Neal was fearless but he wasn't free. Neal wanted to die. So he was utterly fearless as far as chances went because he was asking for it all the time. I kept thinking that the imitators never knew and don't know how miserable

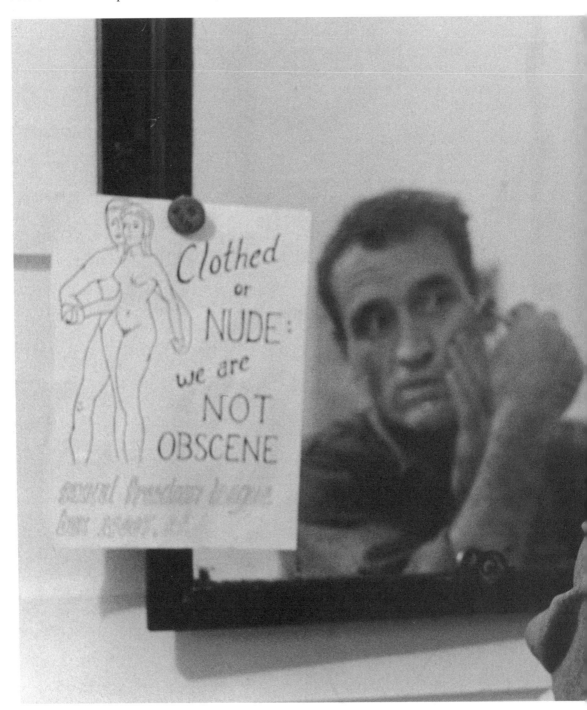

these men were, they think they were having marvelous times—joy, joy, joy—and they weren't at all."

It's not evident on her face or in her voice—the hard way she came to her knowledge of him.

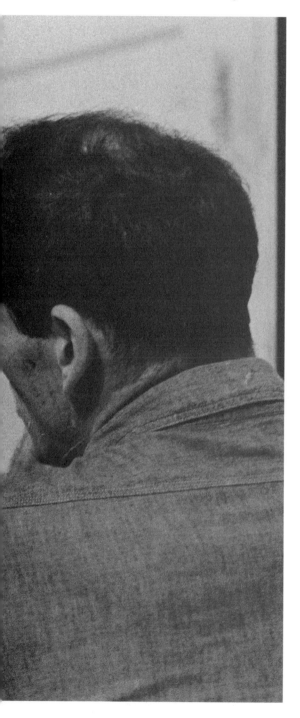

Rather, there's an attempt to make light of her experience as if she's still in the presence of very young children who must not be alarmed. He attempted suicide, he told her, a couple of times when he was in his teens.

"He said something about hiding under a bridge, I remember. I think he was going to drown himself. Then one day, back when we were living in San Francisco, he tried to do it with a gun. But I got the gun away from him and then he was ashamed of himself that he couldn't do it. But after that we ran into the Cayce thing about suicide and he wouldn't do it because of the penalty. There are as many different ways of paying for it as there are of doing it and motives for doing it, and some of the penalties that Cayce and other seers have mentioned—sometimes you spend a whole lifetime in frustration, sometimes you're killed right at the moment when you want to live the most. Because you misunderstood the value of life you must learn the value of life. He really took that to heart, but he got around it by sneaking around it. As long as his motive was not to destroy his life he felt he was conning God."

She gets up from the sofa to answer the phone. A social worker is calling about the sixteen-year-old runaway girl who has chosen to live with Carolyn, and the undertone of compassion in her low voice, as she talks on the phone, indicates who she was, for Cassady and for Kerouac, too, who spoke of her this way: *And I shudder sometimes to think of all that stellar mystery of how she is going to get me in a future lifetime, and I seriously do believe that will be my salvation, too. A long way to go.*

"I think they were trying to be something else to the other," she says of that famed comradeship.

Neal Cassady shaving at Allen Ginsberg's San Francisco apartment, 1965
LARRY KEENAN JR.

"Each one wanted the other to admire him. Jack, who was reticent, thought that Neal had this wonderful way of overcoming his own reticence and could just go ahead and sweep the women off their feet.

"Well, Neal never enjoyed it unless there was violence. He couldn't manage it any other way. The only times he was ever not able to do it was when I was offering or willing. It had to be rape. Until finally I only submitted because I was afraid of him. At last, then, I said, 'I can't stand it anymore, kill me or whatever,' and much to my surprise he was very nice about it, he seemed to understand. Of course, he had dozens on the outside anyway. Jack was very romantic and loving and not very good in bed, either. Apologetic. He was the other extreme. He felt he was doing something he shouldn't to a woman and I think that's why he preferred whores."

She was lover to Jack while married to Neal. "Neal always wanted it that way. He always passed on his girlfriends to Jack, it was a ritual. It happened to me and I had to work it through. I knew about LuAnne, Neal's first wife, that they'd shared her. In those days I thought she was a loose woman, that she didn't care who she slept with, and since they were all three traveling together. . . . I didn't think of it as Neal's sharing, as Neal's idea. But then when Jack was living with us— Jack who was very, very moral, oddly enough, and so straitlaced about other people's wives— Neal was called to go on a two-week hold-down on the railroad and when he left he said, 'My best pal, my best gal' and Jack and I were just perfect all the time he was gone, we hardly dared to be in the same room together. When Neal came back I said, 'Did you say that because you were afraid we were going to and you didn't want to be made a fool of, or did you say it because you really wanted it to happen?' He said, 'Oh, I thought it would be nice.' So I said to myself, 'If that's how you are then let's see how nice it is.' Because he

was really jealous and it was the only way I could keep him home. It worked like a charm. They both stayed home and watched each other. I had two husbands for a long time. It wasn't actually all that great as far as sex was concerned, there was nothing all that exciting in either one of them, but at least it made home life fun and we could all do things together where before they'd always gone out, and I was left. Or like one time, before, when they brought home a couple of whores.

"Jack first lived with us in 1952 and wrote some of *On the Road* and *Visions of Cody*. Then he came back the next year and we'd moved to San Jose, and he lived with us six months and worked on the railroad. So he'd be out and Neal would be home and Neal would be out and Jack would be home. We had a big house with an extra bedroom and that was Neal's idea, we always had to have a room for Jack. And one reason why it all quit was that we bought this house and realized afterwards there was no place for Jack, and he was quite hurt because he'd sort of worked out his life that he'd spend six months with us and a month or so in Mexico and then he'd go back to see his mother and then he'd come out with us. And this house, as well as fame and fortune, clobbered it—it all came at the same time. But they were thinking of putting a trailer in the backyard, it was just accepted that he'd live with us whenever he could. Of course, we were terribly discreet. Whenever Neal was around, Jack and I were perfectly proper. Even though Neal knew and offered this, he'd get fits of jealousy. But he seemed to like the idea, it was his way of showing Jack his love by sharing his women. No matter who it was he always offered her to Jack."

Whatever meanings are to be got from this giving, Kerouac in his novel about his breakdown, *Big Sur*, at last wonders why. He wonders in that novel about the possibility of envy and enmity in those friends he loved so well, and prefers to tell himself that he's lost his mind . . .

Gone the way of the last three years of drunken hopelessness which is physical and spiritual and metaphysical hopelessness you can't learn in school no matter how many books on existentialism or pessimism you read, or how many jugs of vision-producing Ayahuasca you drink, or Mescaline take, or Peyote goop up with ... The face of yourself you see in the mirror with its expression of unbearable anguish so haggard and awful you can't even cry for a thing so ugly, so lost, no connection whatever with early perfection and therefore nothing to connect with tears or anything.

Yet the sedentary adulators of Cassady, comparing him with his compadre Kerouac who closeted himself away in a corner of the continent and drank himself to death, now write in their columns of Cassady that he "stayed on the road of Life, the road of Kicks, the road of Now ... always on top of everything," and disallowing him anything but joy they attribute his last days' despondency, "if there had been any," only to the unavailability of speed down there in San Miguel.

Carolyn met Neal shortly after the war, when she was enrolled at the University of Denver. A mutual friend, a young man who frequented the campus and the pool halls, brought Neal up to her room. "The boy used to follow me around, always telling me about these fantastic exploits of his that turned out to be Neal's. So then he told me about Neal, he built up this great hero and I was abashed, I idolized him before I met him. We lived together a month and then he went off with Allen Ginsberg to Burroughs's ranch in Texas where he was growing acres of pot. I couldn't compete with that and came out to California. Allen has just sent me a lot of letters Neal wrote to him and they're passionate love letters, but it looks like Neal was just leading him on. He was down there in Texas for just a few days and he rejected Allen, and Allen asked him for one last night, but Neal got a girl, instead.

"Allen wrote a very poignant letter to Neal

about that sad night in a hotel room, it was his last night before he shipped out. Years later, when we were in San Jose, Allen came to see us and I found them making love . . . Neal was ambi to an extent. I think it was just any kind of sex because it was such a masochistic thing. He even got a kick out of allowing men to do it to him. He didn't like men, didn't seek them, he just would let them once in a while. Sex was his real devil, because he masturbated constantly if he wasn't with a woman, until in later years he preferred it instead of hassling with a woman. But he loathed himself for it, he did it to punish himself and every time he'd be nauseated. Probably because of his Catholic beginnings he took the 'miserable worm' part to heart, he felt he was cursed with that need."

Yet someone else, a friend of the Cassadys', an elderly astrologer, likens him to a legendary figure called the Love Apple, a handsome man who gave of himself to all who desired him in order to assuage their human loneliness.

Seeking spiritual salvation, the couple tried the Past Lives route, much traveled in those years, and ran into more trouble. Carolyn describes the impact: "What was interesting about the first tape of Past Lives reading—he had a horrendous experience, being castrated. By an enemy officer. He was in the Babylonian army, a general of Nebuchadnezzar, and he was in battle with a Hebrew army, but he fell for a girl and without thinking he made her and she happened to be the wife of a Hebrew officer, who caught him and publicly castrated him. So he never went back to his family but he became the vice king of Babylon in an effort to show that he could be as much a man or as powerful as any. He became the chief of the underworld and mostly in violent things like bullfighting and bear baiting. And if that reading was true it seemed to tie in with the compulsion."

Not many people break their thumbs and it is likely that those thumbs that do get broken heal without complications. Cassady's bandaged thumb, which was granted a long paragraph in *On the Road*, was not without heavy consequences, unknown to Kerouac:

"Neal hit his first wife on the forehead and broke his thumb," according to Carolyn. "He was up in her hotel room and she wanted to be rid of him, she was waiting for her fiancé to get off a ship any day. Then he came back to me and I drove him to the hospital, and he couldn't do any work. It had this cast with a big traction hook because a thumb is particularly hard to set. So I let him take care of Cathy, who was four months old, and I went to work. Well, we had this crummy place on Liberty Street and he had to wash diapers in the sink and he probably wrung them with that hand and got urine in it. Then he went back to changing tires before it was healed, and he always drove himself so hard and fast, he not only had to be the best and the most amazing worker, but it was like flagellation, and the cast was just mash. The bone got infected and I had to give him penicillin shots, but he left for New York, and in the end they had to cut off the tip of his thumb.

"And later on, more than ten years later, the same medium who gave us the Past Lives readings was doing a thing she'd invented on the theory that the thumbprint is directly connected with the pituitary gland. She'd done these fantastic experiments, printing the thumbprint on some kind of crystal stuff, and she made photographic slides and got these amazing color pattern—each print is like an aura. Neal wanted one done and then we realized that the thumbprint on his dominant hand was amputated. It seemed spooky to him because his connection with the pituitary, which occultly is like the highest mind, was shot. It seemed terribly significant, it meant that he had been crippled in the spiritual realm."

No matter how many persons engage in the attempt to divulge and delineate a particular person, it seems an impossibility to know, at last, that chosen one. The mystery only deepens.

"Neal was known as a woman beater. He couldn't stay with one woman and some of them couldn't be true to one man and so they tortured him in the same way. [His girlfriend] Natalie Jackson was paranoid. She threatened to kill herself and it looks as if she did—she slipped off a roof trying to get away from the police, but she'd already cut her throat with a piece of glass from a broken skylight. That's the kind of girl he took up with.

"They lost $10,000 on the races, it was part of what we got for that accident when he was working on the railroad, he fell off a boxcar and mangled his foot. Some of the money went to buy this house and the rest went down the drain. She forged my signature. . . . It doesn't diminish from the man any, from the goodness of him, because the thing that appealed to people was his enormous kindness and compassion. I was impressed with his standards which were true Christian standards that everybody else put down. In other words, I always felt deeply that he had ideals that were stronger than most men's, than sterling citizens'. He had convictions and beliefs that were bigger than the social values. He couldn't do those values at all, but the deep down spiritual values. . . . He could talk and would talk with anybody and instantly they felt that he really cared about them. How many people do you know who give of their whole selves when you first meet them? And it was a powerful thing because he was so perceptive and intelligent that he could meet them right where they were. Now part of that became conning, he learned how to use that to con. He was a master at getting you to think that he knew exactly where you were and what you needed and he could always supply it."

The gentle woman in the old sweater goes relentlessly on until you wonder if that legendary figure behind the wheel of the Merry Pranksters' bus—the man who they like to claim knew intuitively that the way was clear when he went around curves on the wrong side of the highway—wasn't the driver at all but some stranger they picked up, out there in the night.

"Before the bus trip, he threw himself down and burst into tears. He couldn't stand himself and the life he was living. He couldn't drop everybody, but he resolved that when he was with them he wouldn't be the clown anymore. But they'd all stand around and expect him to perform and he couldn't help it, he'd start off again and then he'd be lost. Everybody could recognize the brilliance of his mind, but you simply couldn't stay with it, your mind couldn't work that fast. It was astonishing the way his mind worked, but it drove you crazy. He'd take more and more drugs to keep it up and be what they expected him to be. I don't know whether they thought he was a sage or just weird. I used to think that they exploited him but I don't think so now. He liked doing it, it was an ego boost when people wanted him to perform. But he got sick of himself. Near the end he was at Kesey's farm in Oregon, and I guess it was in the middle of a big party and Neal couldn't stand it another minute and he rushed out without a jacket, without his cigarettes, and went to the highway and hitchhiked down and called me from a friend's house in Larkspur. They'd put him to bed, he'd collapsed. I got Al Hinkle to drive me up, and on the way home Neal was hanging onto my hand. I was in the front seat and he was lying in the backseat. He said he couldn't stand another minute the way he was living. Al talked to him about a job on the railroad again, he said the administration had changed and that maybe they'd be more sympathetic.

"Neal knew all along, I'm sure, that he couldn't do it but he was going along with it because there was nothing else to do. And when Al went home Neal started racing up and down the hallway. He'd throw himself on his knees by John's bed and rock and moan and groan and when I'd try to comfort him he'd say, 'No, it's all right,' and I'd back off and come in here and sit because I didn't know what was going to happen next, and he came racing in here. 'Where's John? Where's John? I killed my son. I killed my son.' He said he had to wash his hair or take a shower and I could hear the water running but he was pounding on the walls and yelling and I was terrified. Then he calmed down and sat at the table and opened his Bible which he carried with him all the time and started reading a passage which I can't find again, but it was something about bad companions. Then in a minute or two he went to bed and I thought he was dead.

"We were into Past Lives readings a lot and in a past life with John he was responsible for his son's being chopped up by knife blades on chariot wheels. They were both charioteers in Assyria, or somewhere, and Neal had invented knife blades for the wheels, for warfare, but the blades were on when they were racing, and John looked back and saw that Neal was losing his balance and they both fell and died, but Neal, as he died, watched his son cut to ribbons. We thought we'd never find anybody like Cayce, never anybody that good. There's this old lady in San Jose who's in touch with all these people, she has a big house and most of them stay there when they come to town, like the Cayce people, and she always kept us in touch with them. Then in 1963, I guess it was, this woman came to town. She was a medium, they call them channels now. She was supposedly a channel for a Seventh Plane Astral Teacher. She traveled around the country and gave Past Lives readings, so by the time we got to her there were a lot of tapes of other people's that we could hear and see whether we were interested, and the tapes were fantastic. They could have been made up and we weren't positive they were the gospel truth but we figured if those things hadn't happened then something very much like them must have, because we got a lot of vibes.

"This channel turns on the tape recorder and goes into a trance and the spirit guide, the person who's passed on to the other side, takes over and through her he gives you the lives that he feels relate to this one. Now the first tape you got, the first year, was supposed to be the physical and emotional lives, then the next year it was spiritual karma and another set of lives. And Neal's first reading was just awful. You never heard of such ghastly lives, they made this one look like a picnic. I'm sure they couldn't give everybody that information, not everybody could stand it. He ended up sobbing at the end of it, he was really broken up. That's the only thing I can connect that night with. He might have lived that life, he might have had some memory, but he always felt guilty about John, that he wasn't the father he would like to have been."

Was he in triple binds, then—the binds of the Self, and over that the binds of somebody else's Image of him in literature, an exaggeration he had to live up to, and over that the binds laid upon him by some Spirit Guide on the Other Side—the task of working off some mistakes and mishaps in previous existences?

"And in the morning he got up early, he went with a railroad conductor who was going to drive him to San Francisco to get his job back. He played the whole scene perfectly sanely, like he was going to do it, and he was going to come back that night and start all over. Everything was going to be great, you know. Then for two weeks we never knew what happened, we didn't hear a word, and then the kids saw him in the city, on a bus. They said he'd been arrested and been in jail for all the warrants out against him for driving without a license. Periodically at this point he was getting caught and if his friends didn't have the money to pay the fine he'd go to jail for the weekend or a week. His mind was gone. Jami said

he didn't recognize her, he kept talking to her girlfriend as if she were Jami. I didn't see much of him after that. Once or twice . . .

"He'd been going around with a girl in San Francisco, and she was urging Neal to go to Mexico and get well and write, etcetera. People say they quarreled terribly. The odd thing about her was that she heard voices and they told her he was going to be all well in six weeks. She said she could heal him, she said she had this house there. She was the daughter of a wealthy family in Philadelphia. I kept urging him to do it because of the warrants and I thought that maybe in the sun and quiet possibly he'd get well. He looked awful. She wrote to me when he died, and letters after, telling me about what transpired, but she gave me a couple of different versions and she was talking more and more in her letters about psychic phenomena, like each time she looked in the mirror she saw his face. She was strung out on drugs. He was in San Miguel only a couple of days and the last night he went to this wedding. He was on seconal all day and he didn't drink as a rule but he drank at the wedding. Whether he did it carelessly or whether he knew what he was doing, nobody will ever know. The only thing that came out of the autopsy was that the contents of the stomach had an alcoholic smell and everything was congested. It seems to have been the combination of seconal and alcohol, and he was already sick from speed.

"Of course, Hugh Lynn Cayce told him he would never be allowed out through suicide and he knew that himself, just from his own feelings—that he had this hard thing to do and he was going to have to live it. So you see, that's why I don't know about that last minute. I knew how he felt about suicide and yet his mind was so gone and he could have got to the point where he just couldn't stand it, and that was stronger than his belief about suicide. Or more likely, I feel that he just kind of went to hell, and didn't care. Risked it. In other words, he may have felt that since he'd been risking his life all along he might just as well take the drinks on a dare, and it worked this time. Not to purposely end it, because he may have felt that even *that* was going to be denied him. I know how desperate he was, he called me from Los Angeles before he went down to Mexico and said he was coming home. He kept saying, 'I'm coming home, I'm coming home,' on and on. So I know he was miserable. There was no place to turn, and he said, 'Well, maybe by my birthday,' and I didn't hear the rest of the sentence.

"So she brought the ashes all the way up, hugging them in her arms, on the bus, and got across the border. When she came here she didn't want to let them out of her arms, so first I just put them on a table, here, for that evening—she came at night—and when she went to bed I stashed them. She was so strange, she hung around all day. I painted and she sat beside me and rapped and then she'd start singing and then she'd break into laughter. She turned up at the door again a week later, she wanted to see the ashes and say good-bye. I guess she was hitchhiking."

Of the several women who were his wives and mistresses and who remain in touch with Carolyn, only one has a share of the ashes—the woman he lived with after he and Kerouac left for New York in that time, more than twenty years ago, of the bandaged thumb, when Cathy was still an infant and Carolyn was pregnant with Jami.

"She asked me if I'd get a divorce and I said if Neal will ask me. She wrote the letter and he signed it, and that hurt, too. She got pregnant and he did his duty. He went to Mexico for a quick divorce and then he married her, but he left the same day to come back here. I think he married her bigamously, I never got the divorce papers. Both other marriages were annulled, the first and that one, the third. She thought I ought to split the ashes with her and I finally gave her a tea-spoonful. I said, 'You knew him for one year and I've known him for twenty.' I put them in a little box and wrapped it in foil and she said they arrived on her husband's birthday, and her daughter by that marriage put them at her father's place at dinner, thinking it was a birthday package for him. She thought that was terribly funny.

"She'd call me up and tell me what she was going to do with them, she had all these ideas. First she was going to put them in her family plot in New Hampshire, then she called to say, 'Do you think I ought to buy a tree in Washington Square?' Then she said 'You know what I'm going to put with them? You remember that quarter that has an eagle on it, one way it looks like a cowboy with a hard-on? Don't you think that would be appropriate to put with the ashes?'

"Then I didn't hear from her for a while and finally she called and said she'd phoned Stella Kerouac, Jack's widow, in Florida, who'd never heard of her, and asked if she'd let her bury the ashes on Jack's heart. That was *it*. So Stella told her that when she sold the house in Florida she and Jack's mother were going back to Lowell and that she hadn't got Jack a proper headstone yet and when she did she'd meet her there and they could dig up the grave."

Carolyn brings out the fancy box containing the ashes and sets it on the coffee table. Stapled to a side of the box is a scrap of paper on which is typed *Contiene Cenizas Del Sr. Neal Cassady Jr.* in faint ink.

Another Pretty Face

BY LIZA WILLIAMS

WHAT I HAVE WRITTEN HERE is true to my memory.

Allen introduced me to Lucien up at Helen Parker's place in Truro in 1950. I had gone there with Eugene, a fellow painter I had met in New York at the Art Students League. We had come to Provincetown and were overwhelmed by the gay life that seemed to be a part of everything. When we went to a cabaret, we heard a man sing "lover back up to me" followed by "a hard man is good to find." I was amazed—that was the first overt homosexual entertainment I had ever seen. In the 1940s gay men were called fags, fairies, nelly boys, pansies and so on. Not much encouragement for being out.

Eugene had said he knew a woman in Truro, just down the Cape, and said let's go visit her. Helen Parker, whose house we had come to, was a tall, lovely, redheaded woman who—because I was twenty—I thought was much older. She had been engaged to John Dos Passos and then became the lover of a man whose name I recall as Prince Shavshevadsie, but then she left him to live on her own. Her houseguest was Allen Ginsberg. He had just been discharged from the new clinic at Columbia-Presbyterian Hospital that claimed it could change homosexuals into heterosexuals. Helen was helping him to test it out.

Allen came up to me and started to talk. I didn't know who he was, but I liked him because he was warm and open. He told me he was a poet and more, then he asked if I knew who was staying in the small tent on the lawn? He went on to tell me that it was Lucien Carr—a wonderful person who was very handsome and had recently come out of jail for murdering someone. I began to draw back. But Allen persisted, you should get to know him, he is a really nice person, why don't you go outside and meet him? Strange place, strange people, a murderer who was really nice, handsome . . .

I went outside and walked over to the tent. Hello I said, sticking my head inside to see, for it was dark in there. He looked up and after a minute said come in. So I crawled inside with the extraordinarily beautiful man, he made me think of Leslie Howard or Amelia Earhart. We talked and talked and I began to melt into love and never asked him who he murdered, I didn't suppose you could, really, not on first meeting. I can't remember what I said to Eugene, but he drove away.

Lucien and I stayed together in the tent that night and became lovers. The next day we went to the beach where we lay side by side sharing a towel over our head. I thought it was a bit like the tent. I told him my mother lived in Oaxaca where she had gone after her divorce to marry an engineer. When she met him again she found out he supported the Korean War so she didn't marry him because she was a communist, but had stayed on in Oaxaca to paint. Lucien told me he had a good friend in Mexico City who he had been wanting to visit. Maybe, since he had the next weeks off, we should just get in his car and go to

Jack Kerouac (left) *and Lucien Carr, Columbia University students, 1944*
ALLEN GINSBERG

Mexico together. I was delighted, I was thrilled at the thought of the trip and with him, it seemed a total wonderment. The next day with encouragement from Allen and Helen, we put some stuff in the car and took off.

Mexico, which I had been to as a child with my parents, was as I remembered it: beautiful people with deep dark eyes, churches that were baroque inside and out. One evening we drove by a church that had flickering lights moving up its façade; they turned out to be young boys with lit candles scrappling up the curlicues. Fiestas, Saint's Day, we did not know, but as I write that fifty years later, the moving lights still reflect in my memory. First we went to Mexico City to see Bill Burroughs and wife Joan. For me, it was a hideous experience of which I've written before. Then we drove to Oaxaca to see my mother. We stayed a few days, and when we left, my mother said, "I was in the room next to you and could hear you crying at night." "It's alright, Mama," I said, "we will work it out. I was crying because Lucien wouldn't make love to me."

When we got back to New York City, we went to my loft and Lucien moved his stuff in. Lucien Lucien how I loved him with the romantic passion of a twenty-year-old whose main source of experience in relationships was the movies. If Lucien didn't make love to me, it must be my fault in some way. I would figure it out and my beautiful Lucien would want me again. Meanwhile there was the fact that when he came home to me he was usually drunk, and that Allen was always around to keep me company while he waited to see Lucien. It was a strange sort of life, which fascinated me, and most of all I loved Lucien entirely.

We met some loft people who lived on our street and most intriguing to me was Billy Cannastra. Lucien and he got along and we would sometimes invite him to come to see us. I, in particular, loved Billy, because he knew about merriment and wit and laughed and talked about books

and had interesting friends such as Chester Kallman who was Wystan Auden's lover. Dylan Thomas visited the loft when he was traveling in America and in a drunken moment threw Billy's beautiful leatherbound *Beowulf* out the window. There were also various poets and *Partisan Review* staff and, most remarkably, a large African-American woman named Winnie who would show up some evenings. She would come in the door and take off her clothes and, from a can she had brought, shake talcum powder all over her body, smoothing it down as she went. Then Winnie would join in, sitting there like a huge white black woman.

Billy Cannastra had a lot of troubles. He had graduated Harvard Law a couple of years before, but he didn't want to practice. So to his mother's fury, he had fled Boston for a loft in Manhattan. He did wonderful things to his loft like putting in freestanding bookshelves supported on piping. For his eating area, there was a big Con Edison wooden spool for a table and around it back-seats from cars. I had never seen either of these innovations—which later became quite common—and was elated to be in such an environment. His life seemed enthralling, but the troubles dimmed everything. After he finished a drink, Billy would chew on the martini glass, letting shards of glass fall out of his mouth. Billy would hang outside of windows, holding onto the small and often-rusted safety bars. Once, he jumped out a second-story window and landed on the roof of a car. The roof was dented, but Billy was okay and just came up and had another drink. These mini-suicides confused me, because he could seem so lighthearted. I did not understand them, I guessed he was a homosexual, though he never talked to me about it.

One night, when he phoned from the Village and said he was coming to visit, we waited a long time and he never showed up. That wasn't like him, and we felt perturbed though we knew he drank a lot and maybe that had interfered. I don't know why I can't remember who told us, but someone phoned us later that night to tell us Billy was dead. He had been on the subway and just past Bleecker Street, he had climbed out a window and been decapitated by a subway pillar. His mother, who had been furious with him and his lifestyle, came down to his loft to clear it out and, while there, piled up his Japanese silk kimono collection and burned it. She wouldn't let any of us come to his funeral, and we heard that she refused to play his favorite Bach cantata.

A while later Jack Kerouac moved into Billy's loft to be with his new wife Joan, who'd been living with Billy. She was nice and pretty and from an ordinary sort of family in Albany. I liked her a lot and we spent time together. She wanted to introduce her husband to her mother, so it was decided that Lucien and I, Allen of course, and Jack and Joan would drive up to Albany for this event. I don't think Albany is more than 150 miles from New York City, but it took us four drunken days to get there. It's hazy, the trip, though I remember much getting in and out of the car to go into bars. Joan and I hardly drank, nor did Allen, we must have been a sort of cover for the drunken men. Joan's mother lived in a most ordinary house on a street of ordinary houses. Joan opened the door and our group of hungover drunks burst in. Joan's mother was sitting on her sofa looking apprehensive. Joan introduced her to Jack, who looked a wreck and didn't seem to care, while the rest of us milled around.

In New York Jack and Joan stayed to themselves or sat with their friends in a bar somewhere drinking and telling stories. I went along with Lucien sometimes. Most people treated Jack as a mentor and crowded around him. I found him cold and gruff, wanting to control others with his masculinity. It was not possible for me to become his friend, so I had practically no real contact with him. I felt he looked at me with indifference because I was not a pretty girl. So I often stayed at home on the occasions that included Jack.

Lucien only slept with me a dozen or so times during the year and a half he lived with me in the loft, but I got pregnant anyway. The only abortionist he knew of was in Chicago, and he gave me the money to go by myself on the train. When I came back, no one met me, I felt pretty sick, took a taxi back to the loft only to find Lucien drinking with his cohorts.

Lucien worked a night editor's job at United Press. He would go to work at 7:00 p.m. and get out at 2:00 a.m. Almost every night Allen would show up to wait for Lucien. When it got to just before 2:00 a.m., Allen would go with me to meet Lucien, then we'd go to a nearby bar where Lucien would drink whiskey until the bar closed at four. A few times Lucien left us to go to Hoboken where the bars remained open until 6:00 a.m. Sometimes a bartender would give him a Coke bottle filled with whiskey to take home. One night, when we had not met him, he didn't come home. I got very anxious and called several emergency rooms and even the police. Later the next morning Lucien phoned me from his mother's apartment. The police tried to pick him up for disorderly conduct and he had run away. The police chased him, so he went into a church for sanctuary. The police didn't respect that and hit him, breaking a bone in his shoulder. He decided to run again and had escaped to his mother's where she wanted him to stay until he healed. I wanted to go and visit him, but he said not to, his mother wouldn't let Jews in the house.

When I asked Lucien about the murder for the first time—having the feeling that it was indelicate to ask a murderer to tell you how or why he killed—he told me about David Kammerer. He said David was homosexual and he wasn't. He followed him around all the time when he was still in high school back in St. Louis. One time, he told me, they had driven to some beach in Mexico and gone surfing. Supposedly, David broke his neck in the surf so Lucien got him into the car to take him to the hospital.

Then, Lucien paused, and said, you know there was a hospital about three miles away, but I decided to take him to a hospital thirty miles away, and all the time he was making noises. I started out, the dirt road was full of ruts and potholes, and it made his head bounce around. We got there eventually . . . he survived.

It seemed obvious to me he wanted David to die, though he didn't say that. He managed, however, to do that some years later, after David followed him to New York City. And Lucien, just how did he kill him? He hadn't killed him driving his broken neck over Mexican rutted roads—but in New York City, where he didn't want him as a lover. I suppose it didn't seem to him that he would ever get David to leave him alone. His story wasn't too explicit when he finally told me. I don't remember his exact words so I will paraphrase, but not invent: There was this man who followed me from St. Louis where he had been bothering me all through high school. I wanted to go to Columbia and I didn't want him around so when he showed up in New York City I was very angry. I kept telling him to leave me alone, to go away, to keep away from me. Finally one night I was drinking with Jack, and David came in and I couldn't take it anymore. I told David I wanted to talk to him and he should come with me down to the lawn by the river where it would be quiet. We went down there and he reached for me, I went mad and took my pocket knife and stabbed him. Then I went back and talked to Jack. I told him I had just killed David. Jack didn't believe me. I took David's eyeglasses from my pocket and handed them to Jack. Then he believed me and told me to stay there and we could drink and later I could turn myself in and that's what I did.

When the trial took place, Lucien said that David had tried to molest him, thus using homophobia as a defense. I think Lucien—as with so many men at that time facing homosexual feelings—chose denial. And I was a part of that. Looking back, fifty years later, I realize that everyone in this story suffered because of homophobia. I regret that even with all the time that has passed, this prejudice still persists.

Hipsters, Flipsters and Skin-Poppin' Daddies:
The Way-Out, Sick, Beat Humor of Lord Buckley and Lenny Bruce

BY DON WALLER

ANY SERIOUS DISCUSSION OF "Beat humor" starts with the late Lord Buckley and Lenny Bruce. Funnily enough, they weren't Beats and they weren't "beatniks"—they were predecessors and contemporaries of both. Which means that everybody who ever knew the difference between "hip" and "hep" was pickin' up on the sounds these too-hip clowns were puttin' down from way back *previously*, Jim. And ever since.

The key connection between Buckley, Bruce and the Beats comes through jazz. Not just the jazz scene—although musicians were among the first to discover Buckley and Bruce, when they were all working the same club circuit—but the emphasis placed on spontaneity and improvisation. It's no great leap from Jack Kerouac's pounding his way through endless rolls of paper in imitation of oh, say, Sonny Stitt's solos to Bruce's manic verbal spritzing as learned at the feats of nonperforming New York comedy legend Joe Ancis. Buckley and Bruce's relentless verbal inventiveness also dovetails with the Beat poetic aesthetic: Poetry should be read aloud, and the Romantic *slanguages* spoken by society's outsiders (jazz musicians, junkies, gays, hobos, Jews, African-Americans, criminals, poets, et al.) are the true sounds of America singing. According to composer-musician David Amram, who knew both Kerouac and Buckley, the author could quote the comic's routines from memory. Lawrence Ferlinghetti, too, has acknowledged Buckley's influence on his poetry, and his City Lights Books published a compendium of Buckley's routines, *Hiperama of the Classics*, in 1960.

One of the last surviving L.A. Beat poets John Thomas (the model for the "John Montgomery" character in Kerouac's *The Dharma Bums*) has vivid memories of Buckley's and Bruce's presence: "Of course, we all knew about Lord Buckley. I used to visit Buckley when he was living in Topanga Canyon and saw him perform locally many times. I remember hearing a reel-to-reel tape that someone had of Buckley performing 'The Raven' with musical accompaniment, and you could hear his wife and baby talking and making noise in the background. Same with Lenny Bruce. I remember his mother, Sally Marr, used to have a strip club in West L.A., near the Troubadour, and we used to go there to see Lenny. I also remember Lenny kissing [legendary Beat scenester] Hube the Cube's BLESSED BLESSED OBLIVION tattoo at the Enigma Sandwich Shop near Columbus Avenue in San Francisco."

One of the big reasons that Bruce's and Buckley's humor resonated so deeply among the Beats is that it came from *within* the hip community rather than making fun of it from the outside, like all those countless *New Yorker* beatnik cartoons. Bruce's lengthy eviscerations of showbiz conventions (his epic, twenty-minute routine about a hack comic bombing at "The Palladium" finds the would-be funnyman boasting, "I've got my 'hep-smoke-a-reefer' bit for the musicians!") and jazz-film clichés ("The Sound," featuring the unforgettable aside, "So you thought by hangin' around the men's room, you'd make it in show business?") are built entirely on an insider's perspective. Meanwhile, in the long years before the proliferation of ersatz "How to Speak Hiptionaries," Buckley's entire act was all but incomprehensible to those who weren't intimately familiar with the latest African-American slang.

As lords of personal excess, skin-poppin' Bruce and joint-smokin' Buckley were natural nonconformists. Of course, they believed racism was a drag, organized religions had strayed far from the teachings of Christ and Moses, and the repressive morality of the times was an insidious sham, but they came by these attitudes through years of experience (working mob joints, being hassled by the police, crossing the tracks of a segregated society)—not because they smelled a quick buck.

In other words, their humor had a point of view. And that's precisely what makes Bruce and

Lenny Bruce
ARCHIVE PHOTOS/METRONOME

Lord and Lady Buckley
ARCHIVE PHOTOS/THE PLATT COLLECTION

Buckley so eternally cool—their deep underlying humanism. Bruce wasn't using so-called obscenities for simple shock value or spouting racial epithets to reinforce existing prejudices, but to lance the boils of hypocrisy that covered the body politic of mid-Fifties America. Similarly, when Lord Buckley reworked the teachings of Christ into an outrageous hipster's slang, his real purpose was to underscore just how hip the true message of J. C. actually was.

The other thing is—they were both so god-damned *funny*. So who were these guys?

Back on April 5, 1906, in Toulumne, a California mining town in the foothills of the Sierra Nevada, Richard Buckley was born part Native American and full-time poor. He lit out for San Francisco, chasing work as a dishwasher, truck driver and lumberjack. Somewhere along the line he got into vaudeville, where grand orators and dialect-comics were part of a long tradition, mak-

ing his stage debut at San Antonio's Million Dollar Aztec Theater in the mid-Twenties. By the Thirties, he was performing at Al Capone–owned speakeasies in Chicago. Visiting a bankrupt circus, he liberated a glass-jewel-encrusted robe from a backstage trunk, draped it around his shoulders, and promptly rechristened himself Lord Buckley.

Buckley's Forties career highlights included USO tours and Ed Sullivan shows, where he dragged unsuspecting audience members onstage to pantomime his black-dialect routines. While appearing in a Broadway play, he met 'n' married one of the dancers (Elizabeth Hanson, now Lady Lisbeth Buckley), who encouraged him to concentrate on the act for which he became famous. To wit:

> Hipsters, flipsters and finger-poppin' daddies
> Knock me your lobes!
> I came here to lay Caesar out,
> Not to hip you to him.
> The bad jazz that a cat blows,
> Wails long after he's cut out
> The groovy is often stashed
> With their frames
> So don't put Caesar down . . .

So begins Buckley's translation of Mark Antony's Funeral Oration from William Shakespeare's *Julius Caesar* into what his Lordship referred to as the "hipsemantic" idiom. And yea, verily, a stiffer riff hath never been blown.

Buckley's ability to recast familiar stories —Shakespeare, the Bible, histories, biographies— into a mind-boggling *slanguage* knew no bounds. Buckley rings more changes on *Hamlet* ("To Swing or Not to Swing"), *Macbeth* ("Is This the Sticker") and the Bard himself ("Willie the Shake") than Charlie Parker's fabled high-speed deconstruction of "Cherokee" in some impossible key.

Getting biblical on y'all, Buckley offers

"Jonah and the Whale," wherein the leviathan expels our hero for smoking pot in his belly, and turns the story of Jesus Christ into "The Nazz." The latter is probably Buckley's best-known work, having inspired a Yardbirds' song title ("The Nazz Are Blue"), as well as the name for Todd Rundgren's first band.

His Lordship's hysterical histories stretch from "Nero" to the "Gettysburg Address" to "The Bad-Rapping of the Marquis de Sade, King of the Bad Cats." While Buckley's defense of the notorious libertine—on the grounds of consenting adult behavior and the capacity for evil within us all— still raises hackles 'n' shackles, his take on obscure Spanish explorer Alvar Nunez de Vaca ("Cabenza de Gasca, the Gasser") speaks to nothing less than Divine inspiration as manifested in the inexplicable power of love.

Whether essaying such dark literary lights as Edgar Allan Poe's "The Raven" and Cleveland poet Joseph Newman's "Black Cross" (there are bootlegs of "Black Cross" being performed by Bob Dylan, whose *Bringing It All Back Home* album features a 1963 Lord Buckley LP in its cover photo) or transforming the words of Robert W. Service's "The Shooting of Dan McGrew" into "A bunch of the studs was swingin' it up at the old Red Dog Saloon / And a cat he was rockin' the eight eight and blowin' 'How High the Moon'," there was clearly no muzzle on Lord Buckley's doggerel.

While "James Dean's Message to the Teenagers" describes a meeting between Buckley and the young actor that took place at Jazz City in Hollywood, his Lordship's most memorable real-people pieces are based on Mahatma Gandhi ("The Hip Ghan") and Albert Einstein ("The Hip Einie"). The latter "had so much wiggage, he was gigless," Buckley coolly observes.

Buckley also recorded about sixteen original bits, several of which—notably the tale of a temperate man who, when entrusted with his brother-in-law's still, becomes "God's Own Drunk" (which Jimmy Buffett has covered)—are rendered straight, rather than translated into the "hipsemantic." Two of the weirdest ("The Train" and "Governor Slugwell") feature Buckley vocalizing all sorts of sound effects—locomotive whistles, brass bands, peanut vendors, ticket-takers, etc.—to flesh out these cutting slices of American life.

David Amram recalls the night he played piano behind Buckley at a November 1960 party thrown by George Plimpton: "Buckley turned to me and said, 'Play me some "Shakespeare in the Park," and we'll turn these cats on to the sweet sounds of the groovy Bard.' " Opening with "Marc Antony's Funeral Oration" and "The Nazz," Buckley kept swinging for a solid hour, improvising madly, all while being heckled by a drunken Norman Mailer. The performance was designed to showcase Buckley's act for TV execs, because his New York City cabaret club card had been suspended for failure to report an ancient public drunkenness conviction. In ill health and unable to get work, Buckley was in dire need of benefactors. It was too late, however; he died the very next day (November 12) of a stress-related stroke. One measure of the high esteem in which musicians held his Lordship at the time of his death: Dizzy Gillespie and Ornette Coleman performed at Buckley's funeral.

Buckley wasn't recorded until 1951, and his first discs—mostly singles and EPs—weren't issued until 1955. Sadly, only one LP, *Way Out Humor*, was released before his untimely demise. Buckley's influence, however, extends all the way to George Harrison, whose 1977 song "Crackerbox Palace" was inspired by the tiny Hollywood house where Buckley lived in the Fifties. (The "Mr. Greif" namechecked in the tune was once Buckley's manager, and the line about "The Lord is well inside you" refers to the earthly—not the heavenly—divinity.)

Shared values aside, other than living in Los Angeles and working West Coast clubs to much of the same audience, there's no evidence of any personal connection between Lord Buckley and Lenny Bruce, although Amram remembers Bruce asking him if he was familiar with Buckley's work. Bruce—born Leonard Schneider on October 13, 1925—adopted his stage name in the late Forties. A 1948 appearance on *Arthur Godfrey's Talent Scouts* notwithstanding, Bruce wound up playing Los Angeles burlesque clubs, sometimes with his stripper wife Honey Harlowe, while he pursued a film career. Bruce wrote and starred in 1954's *Dream Follies* and *Dance Hall Racket*, a pair of ultra-low-budget weirdies. In the former, he played a henpecked, sex-obsessed husband, in the latter a nattily dressed, switchblade-snapping mob enforcer. Both are currently available on video through specialty retailers.

Hanging out with jazzmen and junkies, Bruce developed a habit and a reputation for making the band laugh. Sound engineer Wally Heider taped Bruce opening for Woody Herman's band at the Peacock Lane in Hollywood. Upon hearing the tape, Bay Area jazz critic Ralph J. Gleason championed Bruce's San Francisco debut, which led to the recording of his first album, *The Sick Humor of Lenny Bruce*, in 1959. Two years later, Bruce was headlining Carnegie Hall.

But then Bruce was busted for obscenity on October 4, 1961, while performing at the Jazz Workshop in San Francisco. (He'd already been popped for drugs in L.A. and Philadelphia.) The obscenity charges centered around three specific bits:

1) When relating a story about a local club's attempt to hire him, he quoted a showbiz buddy's report that he was preceded at the club by a gay revue: ". . . a bunch of cocksuckers."

2) Fantasizing about having a crazy father

who pursued him from coast to coast, harassing club owners, Bruce riffed: "And once in Detroit, he posed as a customer and he leaned against the booth so the ticket seller could not see him, and he was exposing himself, and he had a sign hanging from it, saying: 'When we hit $1500, the guy inside the booth is going to kiss it.'"

3) When Bruce closed his show with the infamous "*To* Is a Preposition, *Come* Is a Verb" routine, he comically dramatized how such innocuous words can be commonly used by a couple having sex, and pointed out the absurdity: "If anyone in this room or the world finds those two words decadent, obscene, immoral, amoral, asexual . . . If you think I'm rank for saying it to you, you, the beholder, think it's rank for listening to it, you probably can't come! And then you're of no use because that's the purpose of life, to re-create it."

A San Francisco municipal judge found Bruce guilty, but a second trial, by jury, reversed the verdict. Bruce would endure five more obscenity busts, including three times within five weeks in Los Angeles, where the cases were bundled together and ended in a hung jury. Chicago found him guilty in 1963, so did New York City in 1964. (In New York, Allen Ginsberg circulated a petition on Bruce's behalf that was signed by Ferlinghetti, Amram, Dylan, Gregory Corso and almost everyone else whose name appears in this book.) Both verdicts were eventually overturned.

All these trials were similar, pitting the concept of "community standards" as defined by police, prosecutors and judges (no paying customer ever filed a complaint) against whether the First Amendment rights established by the U.S. Supreme Court with regard to works of art extended to nightclub performances. Bruce's defense was always that, like a novelist, he should have the right to mirror the true speech patterns of his subjects; that the suppression of specific words—be they ethnic slurs or scatological refer-

ences—was the source of their power; that there's nothing inherently dirty about any given word ("If we take this toilet and boil it and it's clean, I can never tell you specifically a dirty joke about this toilet"); and that he wasn't a "dirty" comic ("I don't do motel jokes").

What Bruce meant by that last remark was that everything from Friars Club roasts to Las Vegas nightclubs to sleazy burlesque houses were filled with comics doing so-called "blue" material, ranging from cheap double-entendre gags about "little dingeys" to hoary sex jokes. Since comedy records didn't become big business until the late Fifties, not much of this foolishness ever made it to disc, but it's worth noting that nobody ever busted Rusty Warren, Belle Barth, Pearl Williams, B. S. Pully, Woody Woodward, Bert Henry, Rae Bourbon or Redd Foxx—to name a few of those who made what are euphemistically called "party records"—for obscenity. Of course, these comics didn't get mainstream media attention (Bruce, however, was dubbed "the most successful of the newer sickniks" by *Time*), and they weren't doing "subversive" routines such as Bruce's "Religions, Inc.," which portrayed America's spiritual leaders from the Pope on down as a cynical bunch of showbiz hucksters: "Johnny, baby, what's shakin', sweetie? Billy [Graham] wants to know if you can get him a deal on one of them dago sports cars."

All this courtroom wrangling, along with additional drug busts, eventually took its toll on Bruce's finances as well as his psyche. His legal battles became an all-consuming obsession, and he gradually jettisoned his comic set pieces in favor of free-form lectures on the law and language. Although often highly amusing, these diatribes were somewhat insular in appeal. Bruce's death from an overdose on August 3, 1966, made him a martyr, and the 1974 combination of a big-screen biopic (*Lenny*, starring Dustin Hoffman) and Albert Goldman's warts 'n' all hardcover

(*Ladies and Gentleman, Lenny Bruce!!*) cemented his legend. Bruce's not-to-be-trusted 1963 autobiography, *How to Talk Dirty and Influence People*, and a compendium of his routines, *The Essential Lenny Bruce*, remain in print as well.

Translating Bruce's slashing, shtick-to-the-ribs, sociological/scatological satire from the nightclub stage to the printed page isn't easy. David Amram, for example, recalls being mortified when Modern Jazz Quartet bassist Percy Heath first played him Bruce's "How to Relax Your Colored Friends at Parties" routine. Heath, however, gave props to the routine, explaining that African-Americans had to put up with the exact same behavior that Bruce was mercilessly skewering "everywhere we go." (The bit starts with an obnoxious suburbanite chummily noting "That Joe Louis was a helluva fighter" and ends with "Let's see that roll of tarpaper you've got there, Chonga!") The real painful humor here comes when you realize that today Bruce's bit would undoubtedly run afoul of the self-appointed czars of "political correctness," and you can hear more four-letter words while channel surfing through an average cable-TV comedy special. Now you know why Richard Pryor keeps a photograph of Lenny Bruce in his bedroom.

Lord Buckley. Lenny Bruce. The modern worlds of comedy and spoken word would be unthinkable without them.

BUCKLEY AND BRUCE ON THE RECORD

Only two Lord Buckley albums are currently available on CD:

His Royal Hipness (Discovery, 1992) contains the majority of his earliest and most famous material.

A Most Immaculately Hip Aristocrat (a recent Rhino reissue) sports tracks that were first waxed in '56, but remained unreleased until the late Frank Zappa issued them on his Straight label in 1970.

Four Lenny Bruce albums are available on CD via a pair of Fantasy twofer packages:

The Lenny Bruce Originals, Volume 1 and Volume 2.

A fifth LP, *The Carnegie Hall Concert*, which remained unreleased until 1972, was reissued on World Pacific in 1995. The rest of Bruce's largely posthumous catalog, including the LPs issued on Phil Spector's Philles and Spector and Zappa's Bizarre labels, is presently out of print.

Gregory Corso in his room at the Beat Hotel, 9 rue Gît-le-Coeur, Paris, 1957
ALLEN GINSBERG

Gregory Corso

BY WALTER RAUBICHECK

NEARLY MIDWAY THROUGH Kerouac's *Desolation Angels*, Jack Duluoz (Kerouac) stands in a San Francisco phone booth talking to Raphael Urso, who reads him "this long insane poem over the phone . . . as he yells and reads (and I take in every word, every meaning of this Lower East Side New York Italian genius reborn from the Renaissance) I think 'O God, how sad!—I have poet friends who yell me their poems in cities . . .'" For many readers of Beat literature this is their introduction to one of the essential voices of the movement, the voice of Gregory Corso.

A wonderful character, Urso in *Desolation Angels* is boyish, spontaneous, full of the most explosive energy; he is also the artist by whom Duluoz never ceases to be amazed, whether he is reciting or spontaneously picking out chords and melodies on a piano. At one key point in the novel, Urso gives Duluoz a silver crucifix to wear, which Jack treasures as a sign of the inherent spirituality of his own mad life. Later Jack rhapsodizes about "the greatness of Raphael—the greatness of his purity, and the purity of his regard for me— and letting me wear the Cross." In this road novel, Raphael in effect surpasses Cody Pomeray (Neal Cassady) as the friend/hero.

Gregory Corso has always embraced the ancient Greek role of the poet—the prophet, the messenger from the realm of spirit. Unlike Kerouac's immersion in Mahayana Buddhism and Catholicism, Ginsberg's avocation of Hinduism and Tibetan Buddhism and Ferlinghetti's espousal of anarchism, Corso tends to reject all ideologies. The spiritual insights and social commentary in

his poems flow naturally from his confidence that his perspectives—on such subjects as "Power," "Army," "Clown," "Death" and "Bomb," for example—are genuinely inspired and should be shared by all who feel the call of the imagination, of the creative spark within. Ginsberg once called him "Captain Poetry exampling revolution of Spirit," and indeed the revolution his poems generate in his readers is nothing less than a new way of seeing the world.

From his emergence as a poet in the mid-Fifties until today, Corso's public persona has always fit the archetype of the rebel artist. He was born on March 26, 1930, in New York's Greenwich Village to a very young woman who soon deserted him and returned to her native Italy. Much of his childhood was spent in foster homes and his adolescence in reformatories and prisons. He received no formal education after the sixth grade. Corso didn't drop out of middle-class society—he was never in it. During his three years at Clinton Prison in upstate New York, Corso devoured great works of literature as well as the dictionary. Later, he dedicated his second book of poetry, *Gasoline*, to "the angels of Clinton Prison who, in my 17th year, handed me, from all the cells surrounding me, books of illumination." (His devotion to the study of words has contributed to the occasional archaisms and elaborate diction that mark his work: "icy campanili," "autochthonic spirit.") Unkempt, boisterous and ill-mannered—he's been known to drunkenly insult his audience—Corso fulfilled the expectations of the 1950s mainstream media who assumed the Beats were primitive reprobates.

Even within the Beat world, Corso has always been perceived as a difficult case: At readings and the occasional symposium on the Beat Generation, he alternates between being amusing and obstreperous.

Yet his poetry shows no trace of his image, except perhaps for the poem "Clown," in which Corso says of himself "You have always been you, clown! /—a graft of lunacy on heaven's diadem." Unfortunately, Corso the clown has often obscured Corso the poet, and his work has still not achieved its proper recognition. Ginsberg and Kerouac, however, never doubted their friend's genius. In 1958 Ginsberg wrote, "He's probably the greatest poet in America, and he's starving in Europe." When asked in the late Sixties about his assessment of contemporary poets, Kerouac said, "For my taste, it's Gregory." Since the 1970s, Ginsberg and Kerouac (posthumously) have become accepted by the literary establishment and academia, but Corso remains an outsider. In a poem from the late Seventies, Corso explained his exclusion by joking that "Me, I'm still considered an unwashed beatnik sex commie dope fiend."

Corso's impressive first book, *Vestal Lady on Brattle*, was published in 1955 by friends he had met while living in Cambridge, Massachusetts, but it was not until 1958 and the publication of *Gasoline* by City Lights Press that he exploded onto the burgeoning Beat literary scene. By then, he was living in Paris at the infamous Beat Hotel on rue Gît-le-Coeur with Ginsberg and Burroughs. *Gasoline* introduces Corso's mature style: a unique mix of surrealistic images, colloquial language and absurdist humor. Like the great romantic writers he has always revered, Corso is a devotee of beauty, but even his hero Shelley never worshipped with such mad flights of imagination: "Rose is my visionic eyehand of all Mysticdom / Rose is my wise chair of bombed houses / Rose is my patient electric eyes, eyes, eyes, eyes / Rose is my festive jowl / Dali Lama Grand Vicar Glorious Caesar Rose!" The exuberance of Corso's verse is matched only by the audacity of his images, which stretch metaphors to their limits without losing the intuitive logic that unifies each poem. *Gasoline*, like Kerouac's *Mexico City Blues*, Ginsberg's *Howl* and Ferlinghetti's *A Coney Island of the Mind*, quickly became one of the seminal texts of Beat poetry. In a 1985 interview Bob Dylan cited it as one of the first books of poetry that influenced him. Certainly the imagery and the world view of Dylan's masterful mid-Sixties work are directly inherited from the poetry of Ginsberg, Kerouac, Ferlinghetti and Corso.

Corso's next two books, 1960's *The Happy Birthday of Death* and 1962's *Long Live Man*, are his most sustained achievements. The former contains his widely anthologized poem "Marriage," which satirizes middle-class values without spiteful malice: "Should I get married? Should I be good? / Astound the girl next door with my velvet suit and faustus hood? / Don't take her to movies but to cemeteries / tell all about werewolf bathtubs and forked clarinets." *Happy Birthday* also contains the controversial poems "Bomb" and "Power." In the former, Corso ridicules the late Fifties paranoia about atomic warfare, declaring "I do not know just how horrible Bombdeath is . . . / Yet no other death I know has so laughable a preview . . ."; in the latter, he redefines the word "power" to redeem it from all negative connotations and reassert its primal connection to freedom and the human will: "The angel is not as powerful as looking and then not looking." In these poems Corso applies the logic of imagination—as opposed to the logic of the intellect—to both contemporary social issues and perennial philosophical debates. Rather than assert a position, he provides the transcendent insight of the poet who is only and always on the side of spirit: "I 'ave no particular Power but that of Life."

At times, Corso's resistance to taking "sides" has placed him in opposition to more politically minded figures in the Beat Community. Because he disliked what he considered to be Corso's acceptance of "fascist" attitudes, Ferlinghetti refused to publish "Power" for City Lights Press; Corso published his subsequent books with New Directions. Likewise, unlike many leftists in the early Sixties, Corso refrained from celebrating (or condemning) Castro's revolution in Cuba, claiming in "Upon My Refusal to Herald Cuba" (*Long Live Man*) that it's "Best to tease all sides with awakening vibrations."

Long Live Man bears eloquent testimony to Corso's prolonged residence in Europe in the late Fifties through the Sixties. French, Italian, English and especially Greek settings reflect Corso's direct encounters with the memorials of Western cultural tradition, "aging my modern vision on winged lions," as he writes in a 1960 poem. In another poem inspired by his first visit to the Acropolis, Corso reports that "pressed face against a pillar I cried/Cried for my shadow that dear faithful sentry/Splashed across the world's loveliest floor." Though some critics of the Beats have complained their work had roots no deeper than the writers' own personal rebellion against 1950s conformity, Corso's European poems, like many of Ginsberg's from the same period, clearly illustrate how Beat literature emerged from such older continental sources as English Romanticism and French surrealism.

After 1962, Corso's poetic output faltered due in part to a long bout with heroin addiction. Only two volumes were published over a twenty-year period: 1970's *Elegiac Feelings American* and 1981's *Herald of the Autochthonic Spirit*. Both contain major work, such as his powerful elegy for Kerouac in *Elegiac Feelings* and several poems announcing his rededication to his calling in *Spirit*. In *Spirit's* opening poem, the Muse demands "'Do you favor heroin more than you do me?'" and Hermes cries "'You have failed to deliver the Message!'" The poet finally insists, "'I swear to you there is in me yet time/to run back

through life and expiate/all that's been sadly done ... sadly neglected ...'" In another *Spirit* poem he reports that "A Hellene happiness pervades the peace/and the gift keeps on coming..."

Mindfield, a 1989 collection of new and selected poems with forewords by Ginsberg and Burroughs, contains most of Corso's best work, as well as poems from the late Eighties in which he addresses social issues (homelessness, capital punishment) and personal issues (aging and death) with his usual inventive imagery and wit. In "Window" he insists in Whitman-like fashion that the essence of life (spirit) is indestructible, remaining uninterrupted by death: "People are unreliable/and your parents your priest your guru are people/and it is they who tell you must die .../To believe that life dies with the body/is to be spirit-sick." The word "autochthonic" in *Herald of the Autochthonic Spirit* means "sprung from the earth," and indeed the spirit for Corso is inseparable from the beauty of the natural and human worlds he inhabits: "Last night was the nightest/The moon full-mooned a starless space/Sure as snow beneath snow is whitest/Shall the god surface the human face."

Corso has participated in many of the Beat movement's seminal events. He "stars" along with Ginsberg and others in 1959's *Pull My Daisy*, the Robert Frank/Alfred Leslie film that captures the Beat lifestyle and humor better than any other visual document. In 1965, at London's Royal Albert Hall, Corso joined Ferlinghetti and Ginsberg at the International Poetry Reading, a gathering of renowned world poets. He also immortalized another famous Beat reunion in "Columbia U Poesy Reading—1975," an event that featured Corso with Ginsberg, William Burroughs and Peter Orlovsky: "Dear Audience/we early heads of present style & consciousness/... did climb the towers of the Big Lie/and boot the ivory apple-cart of tyrannical values/into illusory oblivion/without spilling a drop of blood." During the opening of the "Beat Culture and the New America" exhibition at the Whitney Museum in New York in 1995, Corso and Ginsberg sat together on a staircase overlooking the proceedings, two friends taking photographs, chatting amiably and smiling down at this particular tribute to the cultural revolution they created with their friend Kerouac.

As the Twentieth Century draws to a close, the orphan Corso is the sole survivor of his adopted Beat family and brother poets. In a recent poem he complains "I've yet to be smart about old age." But when this modern-day Hermes gains that wisdom, he will certainly deliver it: "There is no tell / throughout the ages / that a Messenger-Spirit / ever stumbled into darkness."

Rub Out
the Word

BY STEPHEN DAVIS

BRION GYSIN WAS THE CON-
summate bohemian outsider. Though
Gysin, who died in 1986 at age seventy, didn't consider himself part of the Beat
movement, his influence is still deeply felt among
the surviving Beats and their artistic descendants.
"Brion Gysin let the mice in," wrote his collaborator and spiritual brother William Burroughs,
which meant that for fifty years Gysin's subversive
aesthetic experiments opened psychic doors
through which poured enough alternative art
movements—from the Sixties counterculture
through Seventies punk, Eighties minimalists and
the Nineties alternative/rap scene—to last into
the millennium. No doubt, Gysin eventually will
be seen as one of the most important artists of the
Twentieth Century.

Gysin was born in England in 1916, schooled
in Canada and England and went to the Sor-
bonne in 1934, where he fell in with Gertrude
Stein's salon and began to paint. In the mid-
Thirties he was to exhibit with the Surrealists, but
his work was pulled off the gallery walls by hardcore Surrealist honcho André Breton at the last
moment. (Breton was apparently offended by
Gysin's openly gay life.) Gysin was in New York
during World War II, working as a shipyard
welder before joining the Canadian army, which
sent him to study Japanese. This sparked a lifelong
interest in calligraphy that combined with his
love of Arabic script to form Gysin's symbol-
obsessed pictographic painting style.

While in New York, Gysin researched and
wrote two works on black history. *To Master, A
Long Goodnight* was the biography of Josiah Hen-
son, the ex-slave who was the model for Uncle

Tom in *Uncle Tom's Cabin*. (He escaped to Canada
where he founded a colony of fugitive slaves.)
After Gysin published his monumental *History of
Slavery in Canada*, he was awarded one of the first
Fulbright fellowships in 1949 and set off for
Europe to seek his fortune.

In Paris the following year, Gysin ran into
Paul Bowles, who he had known in New York.
Bowles's first novel, *The Sheltering Sky,* was a best-
seller, and the mysterious Bowles was returning
to his adopted home in Tangier and urged Gysin
to come along and see Morocco.

"I went for the first time in 1950 with Paul,"
Gysin recalled. "In New York he was known as a
composer because he wrote a great deal of theatrical music for Broadway—Tennessee Williams,
Lillian Hellman, William Saroyan. Top of the line
stuff. Paul had perfect pitch, extraordinary ears,
and he taught me a lot about music. And of
course I owe him Tangier, because he told me:
'Look, I've bought this house in the medina of
Tangier; why don't you spend the summer there
while I go to New York and work.'

"But he ended up staying and we lived
together in his house and I pretty much stayed in
Tangier for twenty-three years. And Paul, of
course, is still there. What happened was that
Tangier was really happening, Paul is very interesting, I had my restaurant going, and gradually
people started coming to visit. There was quite a
nice little scene going for a while."

Tangier is a sunny white city perched on
the northwest shoulder of Africa. When
the wind is right, the call of the *muezzins* from
the mosques can drift five miles across the Strait

319

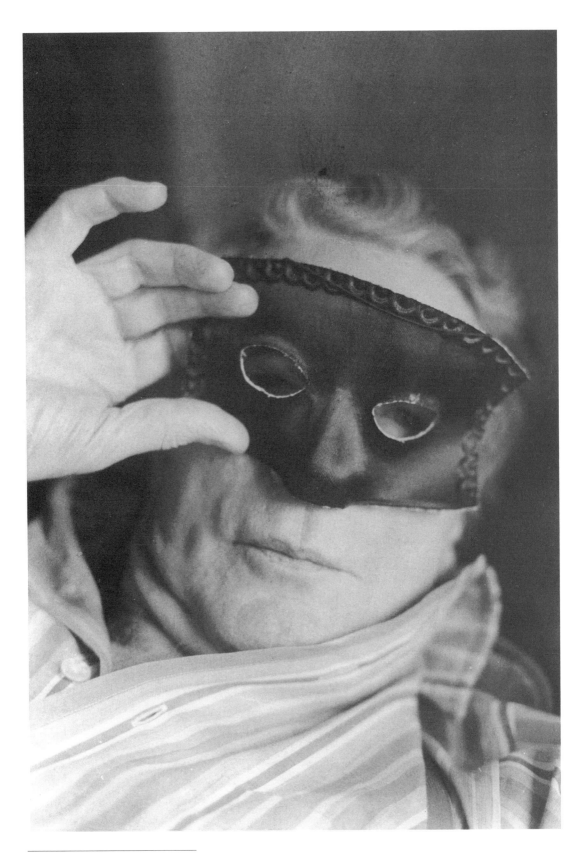

of Gibraltar and be heard in Andalusia, on Spain's southern tip. Since the days of the Roman Empire, Tangier has been the place where Europe and Africa uneasily intersect—both a haven for the notorious Barbary pirates and an oasis of European civilization on the wild North African shore. Moroccan sultans, ruling from Marrakesh, left Tangier alone, as the French and Spanish gradually colonized the city. In the 1830s Delacroix was the first European artist to discover the stunning light and old Morocco's Orientalist dreamscape. Next came Henri Matisse around the turn of the century, followed by a wave of expatriates, creating a tranquil international haven in Tangier that somehow survived World War II intact. After the war, ruled as a recognized "International Zone" by its foreign embassies, Tangier became the world capital of Anything Goes. With Europe in ruins and America constipated by the Cold War, Tangier had easygoing banking laws, no taxes, an open door to anyone with even a false passport. There were no cops to speak of, and no questions were asked. "People came to Tangier to have fun," Paul Bowles told me. "They came to enjoy themselves, and it was easy because *everything* was available for a price, and the price was always cheap. You could live like a rajah on a few hundred dollars a year."

Plus the climate was soft, the Moroccans were friendly, and there was plenty of *kif*, the ancient Moroccan blend of marijuana and black tobacco that gives the user a friendly blast of cannabis clarity; it helped empower Bowles over the next fifty years to one of the most illustrious careers in American lit. If you didn't like to smoke, you could eat *majoun*, a savory candy made from honey and hashish paste. Morphine, speed and the entire pharmacopoeia were available over the counter. French existentialist heroes like Jean Genet loitered in the cafés along the Boulevard

Brion Gysin, circa 1977
IRA COHEN

Pasteur or sipped mint tea in the Soco Chico, a tiny square deep in the medina. Tangier was as far out as you could get and still be on the fringe of familiar Western civ. In almost every respect, Tangier was a perfect incubator for disaffected American artists and angelheaded hipsters like the early Beats to hatch their brain-fevered, howling eggs.

Not long after they arrived in Morocco, Gysin and Bowles went to a religious festival near the Caves of Hercules on the Atlantic coast. There Gysin heard the keening wooden oboes of the Jajouka musicians for the first time. He told Bowles, "That's the music I want to hear every day for the rest of my life." Within a year he made contact with the musicians and visited Jajouka itself, a mountain village where, Gysin discovered, age-old rituals were preserved that stretched back to the religious rites of pagan Rome, Carthage and even further back to Arcadian Greece. But Jajouka was losing its valuable stock of hereditary musicians as young men left for the cities. To help the tribe, Gysin opened a restaurant in Tangier where rotating groups of musicians from the village could play for a stable clientele of expatriates and tourists. Gysin's place, the 1001 Nights, became *the* hangout during the Tangier of the 1950s. It lasted until Moroccan independence in 1956 reclaimed Tangier from the foreigners, and the city came once again under desultory Moroccan rule.

After the restaurant closed, Gysin began to experiment with avant-garde techniques for subverting the rules of language and reading. Driven by an iconoclastic desire to smash the linear and the square, Gysin eventually joined up with a new Tangier friend, a furtive but brilliant American dope fiend named William S. Burroughs.

Burroughs had come to Tangier to write, lured by the open city and the presence of renegade artists like Bowles and Gysin. He lived on the ground floor of the Villa Muniria and tapped out unspeakable sex and dope dreams on a tiny portable typewriter between trips to *la pharmacia* up on the Boulevard. In 1957 Tangier saw an influx of the proto-Beats: Jack Kerouac, Allen Ginsberg, Peter Orlovsky; all of whom crashed at the Muniria and, with the help of Alan Ansen, began to gather and edit the stained and trampled papers that had fallen out of Burroughs's typewriter. Working like hip copyist monks in an abbey from hell, the group collated and organized the manuscript of what would eventually become the hilarious, patently obscene novel *Naked Lunch* in 1959.

"I met Brion soon after my arrival in Morocco in the winter of 1953–54," Burroughs remembered, "at an exhibition of his paintings, but we didn't become friends while we were in Tangier. Then in 1958 we became neighbors at the Beat Hotel in Paris and from that time forward we formed what became the most important artistic friendship of my life."

The Beat Hotel, at 9 rue Gît-le-Coeur in the then slightly seedy Marais district in Paris, became a legendary Beat laboratory when Gysin and Burroughs found themselves staying there once post-independent Tangier became temporarily inhospitable. While Burroughs continued to pound out his twisted sci-fi scenarios, Gysin kept looking for ways of skewing the traditional presentation of both prose and poetry, to smash the tyranny and limitations of language, to "rub out the word." Literature's equivalent of Charlie Parker falling through the chord changes of "Cherokee" and discovering bebop occurred in the Beat Hotel one day in September 1959 when Gysin was cutting a mat for a new drawing in his third-floor atelier. The blade of his sharp Stanley knife sliced through the mat board and cut up some papers and magazines lying underneath. Gysin noticed that when he randomly matched cut-up clips from the *New York Herald Tribune* with other sliced columns from the *London Observer* and *Life* magazine's recent article on the Beat Generation, whole new meanings began

to take shape, some of them revelatory, slightly eerie and synchronistically cool. Gysin began to assemble new cut-ups—treating segmented pages of text as collage fragments—as a different kind of metapoetry that relied on chance pairings of dissimilar texts to impart a "third mind," a new way of (dis)ordering text to find secret or hidden meanings in randomly shape-shifting patterns of words.

"Eventually I took some of these and showed them to William," Gysin remembered, "and he liked some of the effects and started to work on them himself. Then a BBC producer took an interest in my first cut-up poem: 'Minutes to Go' was broadcast by the BBC and then published in a pamphlet with Burroughs and Gregory Corso."

"I was in Paris in the summer of 1960," Burroughs said. "This was after the publication of *Naked Lunch*. I was interested in the possibilities of Brion's technique and began experimenting myself with the cut-up collage. I'd seen it tried before, by T. S. Eliot, by Tristan Tzara. John Dos Passos used the same idea in 'The Camera Eye' sequences in *U.S.A.* I felt I had been working toward the same goal, so it was a major revelation to me when I actually *saw* it being done by Brion Gysin." Burroughs appropriated cut-ups and used them in the sequence of novels that made his name in the 1960s after the scandal of *Naked Lunch* subsided: *The Soft Machine, Nova Express* and especially *The Ticket That Exploded.*

I talk a new language," Gysin wrote in one of his many manifestos about messing with the Word. "You will understand. I talk about the springs and traps of inspiration."

In 1960, leaving cut-ups to Burroughs, Gysin began working with a new form of word-art that he called Permutations. Take a single phrase and reprogram it to run through every possibility of order, making apparent new shades of meaning and ideas. (RUB OUT THE WORD, OUT WORD THE RUB, THE OUT RUB WORD, etc.) This led to a series of experiments with audiotape—some of them broadcast by the BBC—involving cut-up and permutated spoken pieces by Gysin that linked word, voice and silent interval in intriguing and sometimes magical juxtaposition. (Not everyone appreciated Gysin's ideas. Samuel Beckett told Burroughs that the cut-up technique was a waste of time. Paul Bowles thought it was a cheap trick, or "colored lights" as he put it. Even Gregory Corso thought it wasn't poetry at all.)

By 1961, the Beats were back in Tangier for what came to be known as the "psychedelic summer." Harvard's Dr. Timothy Leary brought along a load of LSD tabs and Gysin, Burroughs, Ginsberg and Bowles took their initial trips into so-called consciousness expansion. While Gysin was initially fascinated with LSD, he was vehemently opposed to drugs like heroin and gradually became interested in reproducing the positive effects of psychedelics and even narcotics by using nondestructive mechanistic means. This led to Gysin's development of the legendary Dreamachine.

In 1958, while riding in a bus in the South of France, Gysin noticed that the stroboscopic effect of low sunlight flickering through a long lane of roadside trees began to induce hallucinatory visions and vivid memories even though his eyes were closed. Back in Paris, working with a young English mathematician Ian Sommerville, Gysin built a tall spinning cylinder pierced by regularly patterned shapes with a light source inside. When the viewer gazes at this "kinetic sculpture" with eyes closed, preferably accompanied by highly rhythmic music, intense patterns of light and color are produced on the back of the eyelids, affecting the alpha rhythms of the brain and allowing access to occluded mental processes.

Gysin designed the Dreamachine to stimulate cerebral images similar to (or better than) those produced by dreaming. But in the early Sixties, as the rising popularity of drug-induced dream-states began to catch on, the Dreamachine received little notice beyond elite art circles. Later in the decade, when publicized by Burroughs, Gysin's Dreamachine helped inspire the psychedelic light-show movement, when every local rock palace had its own throbbing, strobe-driven display flashing behind the band. That was only the beginning of Gysin's connection to the rock world.

In 1968 Gysin took Rolling Stone Brian Jones up to Jajouka to hear the enchanted flute music of the goat god, Pan, preserved in the old rituals of the hill tribe Ahl Serif. Jones made some recordings that were released in 1971 on the Stones' new label. So began an important linkage between Gysin/Burroughs and a new generation of artists interested in the same ideas that tantalized the Beats: sex, drugs and social control. The Stones, Lou Reed, Sting, Jimmy Page and Patti Smith all talked about the influence that Gysin, Burroughs and cut-ups had on their work. The epochal film *Performance* (starring Mick Jagger) was shot and edited using cut-up sequences to enter the narrative from different angles. Groups including Soft Machine and Steely Dan took their names from Burroughs riffs. A dialogue between David Bowie and Burroughs was published in the pages of ROLLING STONE. Later pop movements like hip-hop and the proliferation of music video owed a lot of their techniques and immediacy to cut-ups.

Brion Gysin left Tangier in 1973 and lived in Paris for the rest of his life. In an extremely cool studio overlooking the Constructivist masterpiece that is the Beaubourg museum, he continued to create as long as he lived. His novels include *The Process* (1969) and his wild and wooly *The Last Museum* (published posthumously in 1986), in which he caricatures the world of "deceptual art" and memorializes the days of the Beat Hotel. He and Burroughs lectured and exhibited together, skirting the worlds of art and literature. (It was no accident, many who knew both men believe, that Burroughs began his lucrative career as a ballistically inspired splatter artist only after Gysin's death. Otherwise Gysin might have died laughing.) Gysin recorded and played in Europe during the early 1980s with fellow expat Steve Lacy's avant-jazz ensemble, setting his cut-up world-weary lyrics to neobop arrangements that also had an element of collage. Always short of money, and feeling he'd been denied prestige and credit for his innovations, Gysin was nonetheless the hippest man in the world and the best conversationalist one could find anywhere. His last years were spent painting a huge series of canvases entitled "Calligraffiti of Fire," which he left to the city of Paris, along with the rest of his work. Before he died in 1986, the French government knighted him Chevalier of Arts and Letters. He liked to wear the official ribbon and its medal around his studio in his last days, savoring the recognition that seemed to come only as he was about to enter the next world.

Gysin and Burroughs are gone now. A French literary review occupies Gysin's old pad at 135 rue St. Martin. Still in Tangier as of this writing, Paul Bowles is almost ninety, and might serve tea to the odd pilgrim who finds him at home in the late afternoon and in a receptive mood. Tangier remains dramatic, though slightly shabby, full of hustlers and rough trade, but the sex and dope free-for-all is history. The room where Burroughs wrote *Naked Lunch* is now the bar of the Muniria, full of tourists off cruise ships. As the memories of legendary Beat conclaves fade and the older expats die off, all that remains of Beat Tangier are echoes and shadows, and an old Miles Davis sketch of Spain riding on the wind off the Strait. But the artistic innovations created there by Gysin (as well as by Burroughs and Bowles) will continue to provide the psychic template onto which other artists—even other generations of artists—impose their own visions of alternative worlds, and new ways of living in them.

I sum on the Little Folk: music from the Moroccan hills proves the great god Pan are not dead. I cast spells: all spells are sentences spelling out the word-lock that is you. Stop. Change. Start again. Lighten your own life sentence.

In the beginning, Word. You in the word and the word in You—Time ...

—BRION GYSIN

A Beat Book Review

BY LEE EISENBERG

[ROLLING STONE 58, May 14, 1970]

The Mad Cub by Michael McClure, Bantam, 171 pp., 75¢

H E HAS BEEN DRIFTING IN AND out of American novels continuously and is probably best known by his Fifties name, Holden Caulfield. We have made an art form out of him—the cracked-up, the disintegrated, the unreachable, the freak-out. He is forever misunderstood, alienated, yet desperate for emotional contact. This time around he comes out of the closet stoned, hung-up on toes and mildly funny. As usual, he is innocent.

"I am like a lost cub and somebody is always threatening me and wanting to injure me. If they realize that I have boyish innocence they wouldn't treat me the way they do."

The hero, addled by chloral hydrate, peyote and at least a six-year grass high, is the first-person narrator of Michael McClure's new novel, *The Mad Cub*. Faintly reminiscent of Richard Fariña's notable contribution to the disintegration obsession in our culture (*Been Down So Long It Looks Like Up to Me*), it tells of a soul's chase after feeling, commitment and communication. Captain Nowhere, as he calls himself, self-sorrowfully wants to be like "the wild beautiful creatures who are not out of place—the shining huge and furious fish in the seas and the wild animals on the tops of mountains waiting to become extinct."

Although *The Mad Cub* fits the requirements of the "What a Tempting but Depressing Scene This Is, Screwing Myself Up Like This" section of your favorite bookstore, it is something more than that. McClure is best known for his play *The Beard*, which was busted for its final scene (an explicit example of McClure's literary style known as cunnilinguistics). In *The Mad Cub* he amplifies the feelings of the characters of that play. There were only two: Billy the Kid and Jean Harlow. They represented American myths, but also the velvety soft eroticism of alienation and despair.

Without warning, Captain Nowhere says, "Billy the Kid was a seer, a mystic . . . a visionary—whatever you want to call it. He looked off into the space of the Western plains and frontier and he saw the horror that it is possible to see in space."

A few lines later, he states, "Jean Harlow died stinking in bed of uremic poisoning like the stink of a rat's cage all around her. Everybody is a mass of contradictions. . . . She was incredible and velvety and pure. . . . Novels are written to show you that there is psychological sense to actions but there isn't—only soul reasons and spirit reasons."

The mad cub (sure of himself as a cub—not as mad) wanders through a maze of shadow people. He is obscured by drugs, alcohol, incandescent personality trips. He is seventeen, religious, sex-obsessed, cynically together. He is twenty-three, morbid, prosaically self-questioning. At the end he finds salvation. The final sentence of the book is "Yes."

A Beat Book Review

BY DAVID SJOSTEDT

[ROLLING STONE 90, September 2, 1971]

Regarding Wave by Gary Snyder, New Directions, 84 pp., $1.75

> Once at Cold Mountain,
>   troubles cease—
> No more tangled, hungup mind.
> I idly scribble poems on the rock
>   cliff,
> Taking whatever comes, like a
>   drifting boat.

GARY SNYDER'S been adrift since the Fifties and his craggy translation of Zen lunatic Han-Shan's Cold Mountain poems.

His latest book vibrates a peaceful Chinese quality, with a profound simplicity and a satori-like awareness.

> No trail
>   can't be followed:
> Where are we the hill
> Goes up.

Snyder's longtime concern with ecology fills much of the book, as in "Civilization," an almost shruglike realization of world-ending:

> Those are the people who do
>   complicated things.
>
> They'll grab us by the thousands
>   and put us to work.
> World's going to hell, with all
>   these
>   villages and trails.
> Wild duck flocks aren't
>   what they used to be . . .
>
> When creeks are full
> The poems flow
> When creeks are down
> We heap stones.

Snyder spent most of 1956–68 in Japan studying Zen, gardening and shell-fishing, living off the land physically and spiritually.

> Waves
>   and the
>   prevalent easterly
>   breeze.
>   whispering into you
>   through us,
>   the grace

One of the co-conspirators in the Beat Poetry Renaissance in San Francisco in 1955 ("He's a head, peyotlist . . . warm-hearted and hungup on Indians," writes Ginsberg in his journal), Snyder has fused what he found of value in the Beat era with his later Eastern training. "Today we have many exploring the Ways of Zen, Vajrayana, Yoga, Shamanism, Psychedelics . . . toward the end of liberating a few dedicated individuals from psychological hang-ups and cultural conditionings." The goal being awareness, natural high, earth insight, present tense. In "What You Should Know to Be a Poet," Snyder concludes:

> all you can about animals as
>   persons.
> the names of trees and flowers
>   and weeds.
> names of stars, and the movements of the
>   planets and the moon.
>
> your own six senses, with a
>   watchful, and elegant mind.
>
> dreams.
> the illusory demons and illusory shining gods . . .
>
> the wild freedom of the dance,
>   extasy
> silent solitary illumination, en-
>   stasy
>
> real danger. gambles. and the
>   edge of death.

Snyder's been there.

Robert Frank
and the Beat Aesthetic

BY STEVE APPLEFORD

Alfred Leslie (left) *and Robert Frank on the set of 'Pull My Daisy,' 1959*
JOHN COHEN

THE PICTURES WERE UGLY. YES, photographs of the great forty-eight, from sea to shining sea, this land and your land, one nation under God himself, as grim as a funeral march. Not very funny at all, especially coming from this foreigner Robert Frank, who'd spent a year on the highway with a trunk-load of film and cameras, aiming to cut through America's glorious Norman Rockwell vision of itself. These were supposed to be the good times, back in '55 and '56, especially if your name was Ike or Bing. But not if you were a disheveled-looking Jew with a funny accent, driving through the great American outback, stopping at factories, soda fountains and parade routes, all in search of some darker truth about these United States.

Anyone like that passing through Arkansas or Detroit soon found himself arrested and interrogated at the community lockup, answering pointed questions about passports and spies and communists. Which is exactly what happened to Frank more than once in his travels. Not that anyone could have guessed what his true intentions were. Those wouldn't emerge until he published *The Americans*, a 1958 collection of eighty-three images in stark black and white, raw grainy scenes populated by your fellow Americans, your neighbors, yourself, who were now shown as somehow grotesque. Here were photographs of tensions between the races, the classes, the old and new worlds. A dark mood right out of Eastern Europe. And everywhere were jukeboxes, in the

pictures a glowing, beckoning, dominating presence, a ubiquitous messenger of pop culture, decades before the stuff permanently invaded hearts and minds via MTV and a thousand cable outlets. In his introduction to the 1959 U.S. edition of Frank's book, Jack Kerouac wrote, "You end up finally not knowing any more whether a jukebox is sadder than a coffin."

Robert Frank was as Beat as anyone, a true citizen of Bohemia, a Beat intimate. Over the years Frank photographed many of the movement's key figures, even took a road trip or two with Kerouac down south, and codirected *Pull My Daisy*, the farcical Beat film. But Frank's reputation never depended on that association, and so he was never remade into one of the movement's icons. Not even Allen Ginsberg fully understood the value of Frank's work until the photographer began tutoring him in the mid-1980s on the documentary value of the poet's own vintage snapshots of his now-famous pals. Frank remained too much of an individualist to join anyone's cast of characters.

Years later, the man was sharing a cab with colleague Danny Lyon when Frank declared: "You have to be a little crazy to be a photographer." His meaning wasn't entirely clear, but Frank's intentions were illustrated in his maddening documentary pictures, which remain his best-known work. He was twenty-two years old when he arrived in 1947 at the height of the American century, in a still-young nation flush with cash and righteous attitude after the end of World War II. Frank was a stranger from the polite and permanently neutral Switzerland, less a rebel than a youngster genuinely out to dissect and understand the great society around him. *The Americans* was not a formal photographic essay in the tradition of *Life* magazine, with a chronological series of images easily digested at the kitchen table. Instead, his pictures were raw, the focus sometimes uncertain, the blur disorienting and filled with tension.

Frank certainly had his champions, notably photographers Walker Evans and Edward Steichen, and magazine art directors Alexey Brodovitch at *Harper's Bazaar* and Alexander Leiberman at *Vogue*, all of whom served as references for his two Guggenheim grants. Frank's aims weren't specifically political, but he aimed his 35mm cameras with a critical eye at the new world. Mainstream critics were enraged. One wrote in a 1960 issue of *Popular Photography*: "He is a liar, perversely basking in the kind of world and the kind of misery he is perpetually seeking and persistently creating."

The years have been kinder to Frank's legacy. By the 1960s, his work was embraced as a key resource by a new generation of photographers. "He's able to sum up feeling and atmosphere in such an extraordinary way that it's hard not to be inspired by him," says Mary Ellen Mark, who discovered Frank's pictures while a student in the early Sixties. She's mined similarly grim scenes on the American landscape through her own documentary work and portraiture. "He has a very unique vision. It's a combination of style and content, atmosphere, very free and yet in a very beautiful and controlled frame."

The Americans was the single most influential work of photography since Walker Evans joined James Agee a generation earlier to document Dust Bowl survivors for the book *Let Us Now Praise Famous Men*. Frank filled his own pictures with shadowy scenes of people confronting and conforming to modern American society, crowded by new machines and manners. Subjects were often caught off-guard, off-balance, even irritated by the camera's presence. Happiness is a distant memory here, and with none of *On the Road*'s moments of jazz euphoria.

The impact was immediate, and Frank was soon confronted by new photographers aping his style. Frank could see this clearly enough to abandon still photography as a full-time endeavor by 1959. Beginning that year with *Pull My Daisy*, he became a filmmaker, guiding the likes of Ginsberg, poet Gregory Corso and painter Larry Rivers through improvised scenes of Beatnik monkeyshines. Frank and codirector Alfred Leslie cast their friends to act out an episode of pleasant chaos, goofing and pondering through a twenty-eight-minute film loosely based on the third act of an unproduced Kerouac play called *The Beat Generation*. In the film, a young bishop visits a gathering of poets—at a home inspired by that of Neal and Carolyn Cassady—who ask the poor befuddled man questions like: "Is baseball holy? Is the American flag holy? Is your sister holy? Are you holy? What is holy?" Kerouac's narration, added after the film was edited, is pure spontaneous prose, riffing blissfully across the spare jazzbo score of David Amram. Here within this choppy, 16mm film, Frank had captured the Beat ideal. It was the first of more than twenty-five increasingly personal films and documentaries.

Most notorious was *Cocksucker Blues*, which documented the 1972 Rolling Stones tour with graphic scenes of rock & roll decadence and decay, naked groupies and intravenous drug use. One momentous shot unfolds aboard the band's private jet, where Frank's camera finds the Stones jamming urgently on percussion instruments as their roadies strip women passengers for laughs and on-camera humping. The film also captures moments of wild musical euphoria, including a fiery duet between Mick Jagger and Stevie Wonder on "(Can't Get No) Satisfaction." But the Stones were so alarmed with the finished film they had commissioned, the band blocked its general release to the public. The film has been seen only infrequently ever since. "What goes on on the tour was worse than what you see," Frank said at a 1976 screening. The tour, he continued, "was a hard trip to survive, but I was never disgusted. I didn't follow the whole tour—you get involved in a trip like this and you get so strung out it's impossible to work . . . And it shows."

Frank's earliest film efforts were partly responsible for establishing a viable American independent film industry; in 1960 he joined other indie filmmakers in New York to create A New American Cinema, a group dedicated to experimental films. Their work encouraged a dynamic personal vision that can be seen in the later commercial work of such filmmakers as Jim Jarmusch and Gus Van Sant.

After a decade devoted mainly to filmmaking, Frank began exploring still photography again. What then emerged in the Seventies wasn't more gritty documentary photography in the style of *The Americans*, but a series of deeply personal collages that was less about seeing than probing within himself. The death in 1974 of his twenty-one-year-old daughter, Andrea, in a small plane crash near Tikal, Guatemala, is a recurring, wrenching theme. In 1995 Frank's son, Pablo, committed suicide while in his early forties, after years of physical and mental ailments. Other friends and family have left him, leading Frank to a more painful, naked vocabulary in death, sorrow and isolation. He turned to multiple images in his work, with desperate messages scrawled onto the film, messages both abstract and emotionally explicit.

Pictures were now impaled, drilled, nailed, defaced or ripped apart and reassembled. One dual photograph from 1978 shows a toy skeleton reflected in a mirror, with the words "Sick of Goodby's" splashed across in paint. By then, Frank was spending many of his days in Mabou, Nova Scotia, where the absence of neighbors led him to incorporate the emptiness of the inscrutable rural landscape into his work. In the corner panel of "Andrea, Mabou, 1977," the faded and scratched letters of his daughter's name hover above the icy, empty water offshore.

Frank has continued to dabble in the single-frame photography that launched his career: the 1984 Democratic Convention in San Francisco; Japan and the Middle East in the Nineties. And yet it is the more difficult collage work that dominates his later work in still photography. "Many artists believe their own myths, and they keep creating work that people expect of them, that made them famous," says Nan Goldin, renowned for her blunt photographic diary, and whose own move toward multiple images was at least partly inspired by Frank's example. "He did what was true to him at the time, regardless of anybody's expectations or wishes of what he would do. *The Americans* wasn't really supported at the time, and then everyone considers it his greatest work. But he has always continued to do what's true to him, rather than what any audience or any of his admirers or dealers might want him to do."

Among the last active survivors of the Beat era, Frank divides his time between Mabou and New York, listening to Van Morrison, the blues and Bob Dylan, lighting up the occasional spliff. His work is archived in the National Gallery of Art in Washington, D.C., but he lives much as he did in the Beat Fifties. No self-respecting artiste of the road would spend his golden years in some uptown paradise. He still keeps his studio on Bleecker right off the Bowery, down the street from the CBGB's noise palace, around the corner from Nan Goldin. "I've often seen him on the street," she says, "and I see that as an omen of good luck for that day."

No Shortcuts

BY MELLON

I MET ROBERT FRANK ON NEUTRAL ground. He is a kind of outsider and so am I. Photographers are often on the edges of things looking in. The place was Chautauqua Lodge in Boulder, Colorado, where in 1982 the survivors of the Beat Generation were invited by Allen Ginsberg and the Naropa Institute to celebrate the twenty-fifth anniversary of the publication of Jack Kerouac's *On the Road.* My husband, John Tytell, was invited to the event because he wrote *Naked Angels,* one of the first histories of the Beat Generation. As a young photographer, I had been lucky enough to photograph some of these angels and this work was included in a group show at the Boulder Center for the Arts.

It just seemed to happen that I spent most of my time with Robert, watching him in the process of making a film to commemorate the occasion. It's all I was really interested in doing, it happened naturally, and we got along fine.

I really didn't know much about Robert then, except that he seemed to be a mysterious figure. Everyone had strong opinions about him, some worshipful and others resentful or jealous or confused. Simply, he inspired awe, both positive and negative.

I tried to stay out of his way and become invisible while I watched him at work. Every time he pointed his camera at me I moved away. I don't like to be photographed. But when I saw the first screening of *This Song's for You, Jack,* Robert had somehow slipped me into several scenes. What surprised me was that though I had often changed clothes that week, on film he managed to catch me in the same outfit, which I had

actually worn on days spaced far apart. This was magic in my eyes, and through the years that I have known Robert, the magic is still powerfully there.

Recently, having tea on St. Mark's Place in New York City in the dead of winter, I mention to Robert how, in small ways, I have affected his work. His photograph "Like a Dog," for example. He looks at me with his soulful sad eyes and I see my reflection there.

"That's natural, I find things from the people I spend time with."

Robert's inscription, written in my copy of *The Americans,* says "to the lucky Mellon"; I feel very lucky and thankful to experience firsthand, from time to time, his special being. It is a joyful experience to be with Robert — his warmth, unusual humor, generosity. I am learning a lot along the way.

While at Jack's Spectra on Christopher Street in the Village, getting some laser copies of photos of Robert for this essay, I noticed a woman peering over my shoulder. She exclaims, "What an interesting looking man! Should I know who he is?" To most people, Robert remains anonymous, not a celebrity at all.

In 1994 the National Gallery of Art in Washington, D.C., presented a large retrospective of Robert's work—he was the first living photographer to be so honored by the museum. The opening reception was a dream, with Robert beaming modestly in a green silk shirt, hands thrust deeply in corduroy pants, solid to the ground. June, his wife, looked radiant in a long satin and velvet evening gown, her Eskimo beautiful face visibly pleased. All this happened under a giant Calder mobile, a dinner-jacketed musician playing Debussy at a grand piano, a lovely feast being served.

I ask Robert what it's like to be a legend.

"It's like getting dessert when you don't want it."

Though Robert's work is mostly personal, he is a very private person. He is extremely kind, in a special way, with a certain loyalty to his friends, his memories. But the past—his friendship with Jack Kerouac, Allen Ginsberg and others from his youth—is sad for him too. Perhaps it makes him sad to be known as a Beat, when he is so much more.

Especially because he acknowledges his roots in Switzerland and wants to give something back to where he was born. Yes, Robert is very Suisse underneath the Beat. Just watch how precisely he works, like fixing the gears on a bicycle. Listen to

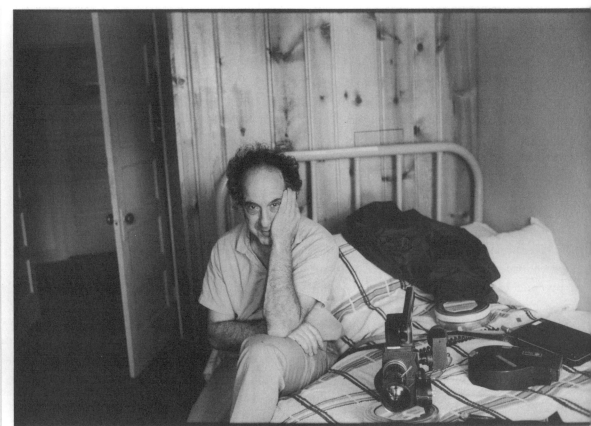

In 1982, I was very wild. "You have to be tamed," Robert told me, "but don't do stories that are too close to reality."

Robert Frank at Chautauqua Lodge, Boulder, Colorado, 1982

MELLON

him converse in Suisse Deutsch with Max, his buddy from Zurich, and imagine two bears grunting in a pine forest on a snowy mountain.

Above all, Robert clings to the Present, and struggles to focus on just what's in front of his nose. Right now he's troubling over the process of recutting his film about Peter and Julius Orlovsky, *Me and My Brother.* I ask what the problem is.

> "How to proceed, do it right, give it more life, more strength. There are no shortcuts."

I show him some of my work. I want to try making a video of my adventurous life in photography.

> "Don't think you are always doing a masterpiece. Just do it and put everything outrageous in it, don't be self-conscious. Put in shots of your dog, go back and forth, make it spontaneous, then edit it. You'll always get something good."

Robert doesn't plan far in advance. I guess that's Beat. When I call him, he thinks that I want

Walking with my dog Hunter on Bond Street, Robert is on the lookout "to see if the magic is there." ©MELLON 1998

Robert Frank on Bond Street, New York City, 1996
MELLON

to see him *now.* Sometimes he says "I'm busy, too busy" or "I'll be finished in ten days" or "Come over in two hours."

What's also Beat about Robert is that he is in touch with his sadness. His life isn't Disney, Hollywood, *Harper's Bazaar,* a cartoon of glossed-over emotions, retouched, denied.

"Art comes from a well of pain. Anything else is not authentic. Artists are inspired by sadness. If not, it's preaching, it's a lie."

In *Moving Out,* the catalogue from the National Gallery show, under each reproduction are the words "printed out." I ask him what that means.

"It's bullshit, just to make it seem more important. I used to sell my photographs for forty and fifty dollars, the same ones that are so famous now."

Robert also thinks he is very lucky to make a lot of money—he is not a jerk. But the world of photography has become "obscene," and that makes him angry. There is a great deal of slick and bland work being done, surface stuff, boring.

"The best way is the simple and truthful way."

That's what Robert's after. And that's the goal of his Andrea Frank Foundation, a charitable foundation supporting artists and the visual arts.

Robert does not often throw a tantrum when things go wrong. Sure, he aims for perfection, but when he makes mistakes, he doesn't beat himself up. He just goes on. Keeps on moving. Once, as he was signing a vintage print, a big blob of ink spewed from the tip of his Japanese pen. I gasped.

"It's just a picture, a piece of paper, isn't it?"

I learn from Robert by osmosis. Being with him is like a transmission, as Kazuko, a friend, always says. Today is what is important—and the infinity surrounding Robert as he tries to make order from the chaos. Robert wrote to me on a postcard emblazoned with a dancing Indian goddess, which he sent from Mabou, his home in Nova Scotia.

"Be calm, follow your inspiration coming from your heart—and not to get side-tracked (confused) by blinking lights."

It's vital to be straightforward, an attribute he affectionately associates with Jack Kerouac. And acknowledging what's deep inside one's being. *Frank* is the best way to describe Robert, really. On another card he writes,

"It's all feeling, maybe better than looking."

That's why we are so moved when we see his work. We see the feeling, the center of feeling. And the movement of feeling, which is the brilliance of Robert, the sequences of images, the magic of the Rainbow.

Robert makes a face when he hears the word *manipulation.* There's manipulation that works, that's intrinsic to the feeling, and manipulation that is surface. Robert manipulates his photographs by scratching words into his negatives, painting over the images, even letting his electrician friend Gunther drill a big hole into a pile of prints. In his recent films he uses such new technology as a digital video camera, but he often gets disgusted and returns to his camera that's thirty years old.

July 17, 1998. I just spoke to Robert who's in Mabou. He is flying to Taormina, Sicily, to screen the new version of *Me and My Brother* at a film festival. There are good days and bad days for Robert. Today is a good day. This morning he was up in a willow tree trimming branches with a chainsaw. Now he is lying down, enjoying the feeling of having done something. I am calling Robert to let him know that Holly from Rolling Stone Press asked me to write an essay for *The Rolling Stone Book of the Beats* on what I've learned from him. "Well, use your brain," he says. I am surprised at his response—somehow I didn't think he would be happy about this. He dislikes journalism, and thinks that 99 percent of what's been written about him is "null." "I don't like stories about me," he says. So I hope this is not coming out as a story, but a thank you, like *Thank You*, his wonderful little book of illustrated correspondence.

[A Journal Entry]

Father's Day, May 10th, 1997

Dear Robert, you are my spiritual father and I *am* lucky to know you. On a broader note, you are also a father to so many people, young and old. Papa Soul. I hope you realize that you are as loved as a garden of wild irises and roses.

PART VI

Keeping the Beat
The Legacy

Robbie Robertson, Michael McClure, Bob Dylan and Allen Ginsberg
(from left), North Beach, San Francisco, December 5, 1965
LARRY KEENAN JR.

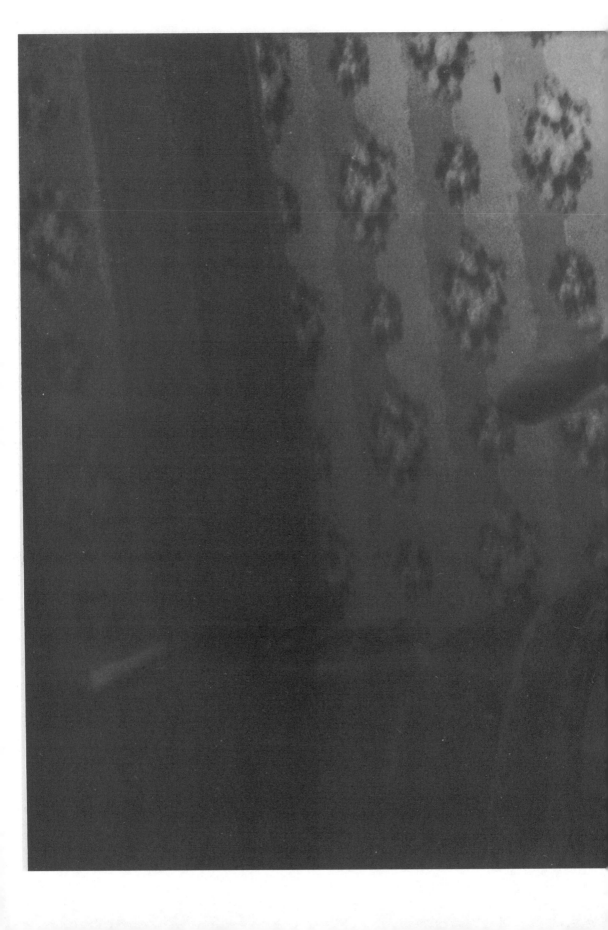

Spontaneity Through Time:
Why the Beats Have Lasted

BY ANTHONY DeCURTIS

WHY HAVE THE BEATS SURVIVED? This country, the sanctified, vilified subject of so much of the Beats' writing, is hardly known for preserving its literary movements. If they endure at all, they endure on their own power among a carefully cultivated cognoscenti. Any movement as subversive and insistently of its moment as the Beats would seem to be an ideal candidate for that most American of all fates, the fate of so much of the consumer-driven culture the Beats rose up against: obsolescence.

The Beats, however, have not merely survived, but thrived. The movement's central figures—Jack Kerouac, Allen Ginsberg and William Burroughs—have become icons. They're almost certainly better known throughout the world now than at any previous point. True, it would be worse than naive to suggest—with all due respect to the scale of both their output and their achievement—that the Beats have lasted for purely aesthetic reasons. Survival for artists in America is far more complex than that.

In a way that amuses and delights every sympathetic soul who was around when the Beats first straggled onto the cultural scene—their very existence a rebuke to any orthodoxy of appearance—personal style has as much to do with Beat going on as anything else. In the two decades immediately following the end of World War II —the era of "the man in the gray flannel suit" and the "organization man"—the Beats were a punchline in the mainstream culture, parodied as "beatniks," routinely denounced for their proudly, determinedly unkempt appearance. In the Nineties, however, when poet Allen Ginsberg was rarely seen not wearing a suit, every frat boy with the slightest pretension to flair sports a goatee. Kerouac wore khakis, an advertisement informs us. Ginsberg himself did a clothing ad, as did, incredibly enough, the entirely incorrigible William Burroughs, who, admittedly, always did cut a flashy figure.

It is hardly just a contemporary phenomenon to ponder the terms on which the Beats have gained acceptance. Even figures that had been associated with the movement found reasons to question its proliferation relatively early on. "Here you have a cafe in a California beach town or an identical cafe in Vancouver, B.C., or an identical cafe in Marseilles, or an identical cafe in Tokyo, and here are people in beards and bare feet busy sitting around writing poetry," said poet Kenneth Rexroth in 1960. "Well, these people are simply status seekers. This is a struggle for in-group prestige. It fulfills all the definitions that the sociologists have elaborated to take care of the most conventional, the most commercialized behavior."

Such complaints are common, of course, when any underground phenomenon begins to claw its way to the surface of broader recognition. And, it is important to note, style and imagery are only part of the reason for the Beats' ubiquitousness these days; those things are mere

(Previous pages) *William Burroughs and Jack Kerouac engage in a little horseplay in New York City, Fall 1953*

ALLEN GINSBERG

symptoms or superficial expressions that, for better and worse, overlay the deeper ways in which the Beats have penetrated our culture. No one would have thought to use them to sell products—the highest honor this age of marketing accords—if they didn't carry mighty symbolic weight. In a way that is perfectly suited to an era in which the memoir has become the definitive literary form, the Beats' lives have grown so throughly entangled with their work as to be inseparable in the popular imagination. Quite simply, as people and as artists, the Beats suit the tenor of our times.

In addition, the Beats have become cultural signifiers for the promise of personal freedom, and the drama of their story intensifies as that promise, at least in part, proves illusory and crashes against the borders of what reality will allow. For this reason the Beats have become a rite of passage for literate young people who hope to elude the grimmer aspects of socialization. In your teens and early twenties, regardless of your upbringing, society begins to turn the vise. Looming ahead is the corporate life, that minimum-wage job, marriage, children, a life-long fate among the "neat, neck-tied producers and commuters of America and steel civilization . . . ," as Kerouac wrote, people who lack "even enough time to be disdainful."

The Beats had energy to burn and plenty of time to be disdainful. Different as they are from each other, they stand collectively as a wild, alternative vision to the soul-deadening track of conformity. More wonderfully, as contrary as their vision might initially seem, it resonates deep in the American soul and the American past. In that vision, commuter trains transform into railroads that can carry you out beyond any limits, and highways, far from being conveyor belts for people moving to and from jobs, become routes to the end of the blissed-out American night. Dean Moriarty and Sal Paradise taking off and heading

west in Kerouac's On the Road, the essential Beat text, revives an image that pulses at the restless heart of this country's literature and history. "But I reckon I got to light out for the Territory ahead of the rest," declares Huck Finn at the end of the novel that bears his name, "because Aunt Sally she's going to adopt me and sivilize me and I can't stand it." Being "sivilized" is akin to the feeling that propelled Sal Paradise's journey in On the Road, the "feeling that everything was dead." Huck couldn't stand it, and neither could Dean and Sal.

The rolling thunder of Ginsberg's lines echo those of Walt Whitman, the Nineteenth-Century bard who, in singing himself, sang America. "What thoughts I have of you tonight, Walt Whitman," Ginsberg wrote in "A Supermarket in California, "for I walked down the sidestreets under the trees with a headache self-conscious looking at the full moon / . . . I saw you, Walt Whitman, childless, lonely old grubber, poking among the meats in the refrigerator and eying the grocery boys."

If the Beats drew inspiration from the most boisterous, romantic voices in the American literary tradition, they in turn have inspired every alternative movement that followed them. Primarily, the relationship between the Beats and the counterculture of the Sixties is undeniable. Neal Cassady—Kerouac's Dean Moriarty—drove the bus into the mystic for Ken Kesey's Merry Pranksters. Ginsberg played a dynamic role in the political protests of the Sixties, and the psychedelia of that era—particularly the lyrics of Bob Dylan and Jimi Hendrix—would have been unthinkable without Ginsberg's swirling, rhapsodic verses.

It's a tribute to the many-leveled aspects of the Beats' work that they helped launch the cultural revolution of the Sixties, as well as the succeeding countermovements to that time. As evidenced from his 1974 ROLLING STONE interview with William Burroughs (reprinted in this book), David Bowie may have been entirely unaware of the enormous debt he owed the Beats when he started out. That debt is no less profound, however, for Bowie's being unconscious of it—he certainly knows about it now—nor for its indirectness. Virtually all of Bowie's early lyrics derive from the parody of hipster slang in Anthony Burgess's novel, *A Clockwork Orange*, and its accompanying movie. Burroughs's cut-up techniques and caustic subject matter also were crucially important for Lou Reed, Iggy Pop and Richard Hell, and he directly collaborated with Kurt Cobain, R.E.M. and Laurie Anderson. Ginsberg, for his part, was a primary literary source for Patti Smith's bardic rantings, and he recorded with the Clash, Philip Glass and Hal Willner. More broadly, a complex, sexually ambiguous, defiantly poetic figure like Morrissey would be unimaginable without the earlier breakthroughs made by Ginsberg.

What the Beats accomplished stylistically and experimentally as writers looks far easier than it is—which is, of course, another reason for their ongoing popularity. Though it by no means diminishes the soaring brilliance of his own work—or that of the many great writers he also influenced—Kerouac's "Essentials of Spontaneous Prose" has probably been responsible for more bad writing over the past half century than any other work of literary instruction. Most famously, he insists on "no revisions (except obvious rational mistakes, such as names or calculated insertions in act of not writing but inserting). . . . If possible write 'without consciousness' in semi-trance."

Those suggestions have convinced thousands of impressionable people that, as a process, writing consists of hopping in a car with your buddy, getting high and documenting your free-associative observations in a notebook. Similarly, Burroughs's cut-ups have led innumerable young

writers to believe that ripping up a page from a newspaper or magazine and randomly reconstructing it is a sure way to escape the prison-house of language, the "mind-forg'd manacles" that William Blake indicted in his "Songs of Experience."

What those notions fail to take into account, however, is the degree to which Kerouac, who was in his mid-thirties when *On the Road* changed his life, had done all the hard work required to make his spontaneous gestures meaningful. And in a 1987 interview with Robert Palmer, Burroughs dismisses the idea that anyone can use the cut-up technique intelligently. "But of course, anyone can't," he says. "If two people cut up the same material, the results will be quite different, and there's always the fact of selection. If I cut something up, I don't use it all, and I select what I use."

The major figures of the Beat movement are now all dead. Toward the end of their lives, they, as all writers do, wondered how they would be remembered. Though their personal lives often—but certainly not always—fell far short of the values they espoused, their best work has lost none of its boldness, none of its urgency, none of its lust for transcendence. Their ardent conviction that every moment can be the opportunity for spontaneous reinvention, for a purifying whirl of creative motion, will never lose its ability to thrill.

It's true that the Beats have been romanticized—and even sentimentalized—far too much. But we must never succumb to what Joyce Carol Oates has described as "pathography," the reduction of artists' lives to their flaws, neuroses and illnesses. That's nothing more than a cheap, smug way of making ourselves feel superior—conveniently, without the burden of having to produce work of such significance that it would make us the object of the same type of unforgiving public scrutiny.

For all their spiritual aspirations, the Beats

were tough and eminently of this world. They can withstand even the harshest inquiries into their lives with no apology. While defending William Burroughs against obscenity charges, Allen Ginsberg wrote, "A naked lunch is natural to us, / we eat reality sandwiches. / But allegories are so much lettuce. / Don't hide the madness." The Beats didn't, and in that fearlessness stands their meaning—for their time, ours and the future.

When the Beatniks Were Social Lions

BY HUNTER S. THOMPSON

Editor's Note: ROLLING STONE's very own gonzo journalist wrote this piece for the April 20, 1964, issue of 'The National Review.'

WHATEVER HAPPENED TO the Beat Generation? The question wouldn't mean much in Detroit or Salt Lake City, perhaps, but here it brings back a lot of memories. As recently as 1960, San Francisco was the capital of the Beat Generation, and the corner of Grant and Columbus in the section known as North Beach was the crossroads of the "beat" world.

It was a good time to be in San Francisco. Anybody with half a talent could wander around North Beach and pass himself off as a "comer" in the new era. I know, because I was doing it, and so was a fellow we'll have to call Willard, the hulking, bearded son of a New Jersey minister. It was a time for breaking loose from the old codes, for digging new sounds and new ideas, and for doing everything possible to unnerve the Establishment.

Since then, things have died down. The "beatnik" is no longer a social lion in San Francisco, but a social leper; as a matter of fact, it looked for a while as if they had all left. But the city was recently startled by a "rent strike" in North Beach and as it turned out, lo and behold, the strikers were "beatniks." The local papers, which once played Beat Generation stories as if the foundation of The System were crumbling before their very eyes, seized on the rent strike

Gregory Corso and Allen Ginsberg on the set of 'Pull My Daisy,' 1959

JOHN COHEN

with strange affection—like a man encountering an old friend who owes him money, but whom he is glad to see anyway.

The rent strike lasted only about two days, but it got people talking again about the Beat Generation and its sudden demise from the American scene—or at least from the San Francisco scene, because it is still very extant in New York. But in New York it goes by a different name, and all the humor has gone out of it.

One of the most surprising things about the rent strike was the fact that so few people in San Francisco had any idea what the Beat Generation was. An interviewer from a radio station went into the streets seeking controversy on "the return of the beatniks," but drew a blank. People remembered the term, and not much more.

But the Beat Generation was very real in its day, and it has a definite place in our history. There is a mountain of material explaining the sociological aspects of the thing, but most of it is dated and irrelevant. What remains are the people who were involved; most of them are still around, looking back with humor and affection on the uproar they caused, and drifting by a variety of routes toward debt, parenthood and middle age.

My involvement was tangential at best. But Willard was in there at the axis of things, and in retrospect he stands out as one of the great "beatniks" of his time. Certainly San Francisco has good cause to remember him; his one and only encounter with the forces of law and order provided one of the wildest Beat Generation stories of the era.

Before San Francisco, he had been in Germany, teaching English and cultivating an oriental-type beard. On his way out to the coast he stopped in New York and picked up a mistress with a new Ford. It was *de rigeur*, in those days, to avoid marriage at all costs. He came

to me through the recommendation of a friend then working in Europe for a British newspaper. "Willard is a great man," said the letter. "He is an artist and a man of taste."

As it turned out, he also was a prodigious drinker in the tradition of Brendan Behan, who was said to have had "a thirst so great it would throw a shadow." I was making my own beer at the time and Willard put a great strain on the aging process; I had to lock the stuff up to keep him from getting at it before the appointed moment.

Sadly enough, my beer and Willard's impact on San Francisco were firmly linked. The story is a classic, and if you travel in the right circles out here you will still hear it told, although not always accurately. The truth, however, goes like this:

Willard arrived shortly before I packed up and left for the East; we had a convivial few weeks, and, as a parting gesture, I left him a five-gallon jug of beer that I did not feel qualified to transport across the nation. It still had a week or so to go in the jug, then another few weeks of aging in quart bottles, after which it would have had a flavor to rival the nectar of the gods. Willard's only task was to bottle it and leave it alone until it was ready to drink.

Unfortunately, his thirst threw a heavy shadow on the schedule. He was living on a hill overlooking the southern section of the city, and among his neighbors were several others of the breed, mad drinkers and men of strange arts. Shortly after my departure he entertained one of these gentlemen, who, like my man Willard, was long on art and energy, but very short of funds.

The question of drink arose, as it will in the world of art, but the presence of poverty cast a bleak light on the scene. There was, however, this five-gallon jug of raw, unaged home brew in the kitchen. Of course, it was a crude drink and might produce beastly and undesired effects, but . . . well . . .

The rest is history. After drinking half the jug, the two artists laid hands on several gallons of blue paint and proceeded to refinish the front of the house Willard was living in. The landlord, who lived across the street, witnessed this horror and called the police. They arrived to find the front of the house looking like a Jackson Pollock canvas, and the sidewalk rapidly disappearing under a layer of sensual crimson. At this point, something of an argument ensued, but Willard is six feet four, and 230 pounds, and he prevailed. For a while.

Some moments later the police came back with reinforcements, but by this time Willard and his helper had drunk off the rest of the jug and were eager for any kind of action, be it painting or friendly violence. The intrusion of the police had caused several mottos to be painted on the front of the house, and they were not without antisocial connotations. The landlord was weeping and gnashing his teeth, loud music emanated from the interior of the desecrated house, and the atmosphere in general was one of hypertension.

The scene that followed can only be likened to the rounding up of wild beasts escaped from a zoo. Willard says he attempted to flee, but floundered on a picket fence, which collapsed with his weight and that of a pursuing officer. His friend climbed to a roof and rained curses and shingles on the unfriendly world below. But the police worked methodically, and by the time the sun set over the Pacific the two artists were sealed in jail.

At this point the gentlemen of the press showed up for the usual photos. They tried to coax Willard up to the front of his cell to pose, but the other artist had undertaken to rip the toilet bowl out of the floor and smash it into small pieces. For the next hour, the press was held at

bay with chunks of porcelain, hurled by the two men in the cell. "We used up the toilet," Willard recalls, "then we got the sink. I don't remember much of it, but I can't understand why the cops didn't shoot us. We were out of our heads."

The papers had a field day with the case. Nearly all the photos of the "animal men" were taken with what is known among press photographers as "the Frankenstein flash." This technique produces somewhat the same impression of the subject as a flashlight held under his chin, but instead of a flashlight, the photographer simply holds his flash unit low, so that sinister shadows appear on the face of a subject, and a huge shadow looms on the wall behind him. It is a technique that could make Casper Milquetoast look like the Phantom of the Opera, but the effect, with Willard, was nothing short of devastating; he looked like King Kong.

Despite all the violence, the story has a happy ending. Willard and his friend were sentenced to six months in jail, but were quickly released for good behavior, and neither lost any time in fleeing to New York. Willard now lives in Brooklyn, where he moves from one apartment to another as the walls fill up with paintings. His artistic method is to affix tin cans to a wall with tenpenny nails, then cover the wall with lumpy plaster and paint. Some say he has a great talent, but so far he goes unrecognized except by the long-suffering San Francisco police, who were called upon to judge what was perhaps his most majestic effort.

Willard was as hard to define then as he is now; probably it is most accurate to say he had artistic inclinations and a superabundance of excess energy. At one point in his life he got the message that other of his type were gathering in San Francisco, and he came all the way from Germany to join the party.

Since then, things have never been the same. Life is more peaceful in San Francisco, but infinitely duller. That was pretty obvious when the rent strike cropped up; for a day or so it looked like the action was back in town, but it was no dice.

One of the "strikers," an unemployed cartoonist with a wife and a child and a rundown apartment for which he refuses to pay rent, summed up the situation. His landlady had declined to make repairs on the apartment, and instead got an eviction order. In the old days, the fellow would have stayed in the place and gotten tough. But the cartoonist is taking the path of least resistance. "It takes a long time to get people evicted," he says with a shrug, "and we're thinking of splitting to New York on a freight train anyway."

That's the way it is these days in the erstwhile capital of the Beat Generation. The action has gone East, and the only people who really seem to mourn it are the reporters, who never lacked a good story, and a small handful of those who lived with it and had a few good laughs for a while. If Willard returned to San Francisco today, he probably would have to settle for a job as a house painter.

Visuals: How the Beats Begat the Freaks

BY THOMAS ALBRIGHT

[ROLLING STONE 9, April 27, 1968]

Editor's Note: ROLLING STONE was less than six months old when it published this essay, comparing the Haight-Ashbury counterculture to its North Beach forbears.

BACK IN THE MID-FIFTIES, everyone was talking about San Francisco as the center of a new Renaissance—of literature, art and jazz; it faded mistily into old newspaper clips, surviving mostly in dim memories of the "Beat Generation."

Ten years later, the action shifts from Grant Avenue to Haight Street, and history seemingly repeats itself, but more so: a regenerative burst of liberation and creativity, followed by an inundation of publicity, commercialization, nowhere imitators and hangers-on, police harassment and violence.

Almost everyone seems to take for granted a certain link between the "Beat" era of the Fifties and the "Hip" generation of today, if only for the sake of contrast. Yet, in a McLuhanesque age that measures generations in terms of changing attitudes and lifestyles rather than how long it takes to reach working age, ten years is a lot longer than it once was. Not much is ever said about the "Beat Generation," and even less is any effort made to place today's scene in any kind of historical perspective.

The word "underground" is so bad it's good. Those within it resent and disclaim the label, not to mention its numerous distortions; yet everyone has a reasonably sharp picture of what it means: a movement alienated, or separate, from the Establishment, the academies and the powers that be. The same is true for the labels "beat" and "hippie." There used to be all kinds of bickering over the meaning of "beat"—was it upbeat, downbeat, or deadbeat?—as well as over who it fit, who transcended it, who qualified as a "beatnik," a real bohemian, weekend bohemian, fringee or plainclothes priest. Ten years later, such distinctions blur into an impressionistic picture of the spirit of the time—a picture in which even the Gray Line tourists and hostile critics have their place. Today, argument revolves about "hippies," "original hippies," "teeny-boppers" and other labels. The distinctions exist, but there is a broad validity to the popular notion that lumps them all together, in a growing revolutionary army, the underground spirit of the Sixties.

Even at this date, it's impossible to look back at the "Beat" era except through a thick cloud of myth and distortion; whatever problems "hippies" have faced, they have won an infinitely more sympathetic hearing from the "Establishment" than the Beats ever did, and the hostility persists, inspired largely by concentrating on the celebrities and camp followers and ignoring the vast area between.

A great gulf exists between the Beat and hippie generations, just as it amounts to a long leap between jazz and rock. Yet the latter hang together on an alternating current of progression and reaction, and between the Beat and hippie eras the lines of continuity are as broad as the contrasts are sharp.

From the infinitely complex tapestry, one can unravel certain major strands.

1. Sociologically speaking, the Beats formed the first large-scale, self-conscious and widely publicized group of middle-class dropouts—this, at a time when the standard transition was from Boy Scout uniform to army khaki to gray flannel suit. The Establishment was appropriately enraged, and the Beats were understandably ago-nized and torn within themselves; they were killing the Buddha, and their stance alternated between manic nihilism and despairing pes-simism. These were the McCarthy, and then the Eisenhower years, and the Beats often seemed to parody the general apathy.

For the most part, the Beats functioned

within the Establishment—hung out in Establishment bars, donned suits to pick up unemployment checks or work in Establishment jobs; no other facilities existed, the Beats were relatively few in number and isolation was a key fact of existence. There was a greater sense of community than the Beats are generally now given credit for but organization was anathema, and such community as there was was informal, an encounter and then a drawing apart, activism centered on such spur-of-the-moment issues as raising bail for someone the cops had hauled away.

At the same time, the Beats were, psychologically, much more intensely and programmatically alienated from the Establishment than are the hippies, with all their subculture; such relations as were necessary—paying a cover charge, perhaps working—were accepted with the irony accorded such facts of life as going to the john. But there was no move at all toward a rapprochement (except to put on an inquiring journalist) and, especially in the area of art, any success with the Establishment was scornfully regarded as a sell-out. The Beats dislodged their cultural roots by reveling in urban rootlessness with its outcast subcultures. The hippies, a truly rootless generation, seek roots in nature, in the cult of the American Indian, in the ancient traditions of Oriental thought.

Sociologically, and psychologically, the main contrasts between the Beat and the hippie eras are in terms of isolation vs. community, opposition vs. separate-but-equal relationship to the Establishment, social apathy vs. activism and pessimism vs. optimism. No one can begin to explain these changes in terms of particular causes, but part of the reason certainly lies in the difference of sheer numbers—the coming of age of the postwar baby boom—and in a group consciousness fostered in the first generation to be reared in front of a television set. There was the fact of Kennedy, who galvanized the entire nation from apathy to activism—between the Beat and hippie periods came the brief but important era of the Berkeley

Gary Snyder, Michael McClure and Allen Ginsberg (from left) *onstage at the Human Be-In, 1967*
LISA LAW

militants and the folk revival—and there is an optimism that survived the assassination, although forced upon itself by the frustrations of the Johnson years.

And there has been a parallel change in the Establishment itself—shaken by a series of crises, from Korea and the Beats to civil rights and Vietnam. Over the years, the walls have cracked to admit many of the rebels of the Fifties—jazz fans, appreciators of abstract expressionism, pot-smokers, a number of the Beats themselves, sometimes in such influential roles as college professors. And the thing that the Beats had started captured the imagination of successive waves of self-aware and disenchanted youth, who in succeeding years developed and modified the lifestyle into the hippie community of today.

2. Philosophically, the Beats were the end product of postwar European existentialism, plus varying doses of Oriental thought—mostly Zen —though rarely from original sources, and mostly interpreted through popularizers like Alan Watts or European authors like Herman Hesse. There were dashes of magic and alchemy, Ouspensky and Gurdjieff.

It was the variety of existentialism that emphasized alienation and risk, with its alternate possibilities of despair or total experience, either of which might end as total insanity, but either preferable to the rationalistic tradition that had produced such insanities of its own as wars, prejudice and little houses of death in suburbia.

Alienation was cultivated, and total experience was pursued, in vast amounts of booze, in sex, occasionally in heroin, frequently in grass; peyote had relatively wide use, as did primitive forms of speed like inhalers; later on came methedrine.

Besides the mind expanders—mild in comparison with acid and more recent drugs—Oriental thought and art forms like haiku provided a certain unifying, synthesizing tendency in Beat philosophy. But few Beats ever approached satori;

the dualism of Western philosophy and religion prevailed—"he's an evil cat" was a favorite compliment—hang-ups were explained most recently in Freudian, rather than Jungian terms, and the unity of Oriental thought was seen mostly as a fragilely beautiful, but rarely attainable, light on the other side of a dark tunnel. Irony was a key attitude toward the conflict of what should be and what was.

The big difference today is the extent to which the old dualism has actually yielded before a more unifying attitude. This does not mean that all hippies have uncovered the atman, but think of how the Beats would react to the idea of loving everybody.

The philosophical contribution of the Beats was largely destructive, but necessarily so: It razed some of the strongest parts of the materialistic citadel and laid at least some of the groundwork upon which the activists and hippies have developed more durable, livable values.

3. If the Beats laid to waste all the other old values, they replaced them with the worship of Art, in true romantic tradition; you might say the Beats were the last of the bohemians.

In art, as in so much else, the Beat attitude was schizoid. One of the era's most revolutionary achievements was taking art out of the academies, museums and concert halls into the streets, coffeehouses and nightclubs—Beat poets declaimed on street corners and tabletops, Beat paintings hung in bars and shop windows and jazzmen in noisy clubs perfected an art form by freely improvising on the basic structures of Tin Pan Alley popular songs.

Improvisation broke down the rigid distinctions between creative and performing arts that had solidified since the end of the Baroque era; Kerouac and others wrote nonstop, unedited prose manuscripts, and performance entered the visual arts through action painting.

Yet, such traditional artistic concepts as exclusiveness, monumentalism and immortality lingered in sometimes weird ways. Art was in the streets and clubs, but the street was mostly Grant Avenue; the audience was hardcore and zealously antisquare; art was an instrument of warfare. The revolutions in prose, poetry and the visual arts were primarily in terms of content and presentation; there actually was little formal innovation. Many jazzmen were intensely preoccupied with extended forms, which almost invariably turned out to be classical; however sardonically, they fretted about the status of jazz as an art form.

Deep down, everyone who scribbled in notebooks, sketched portraits in charcoal or blew sax with his back to the audience, wanted someday to Make It; however personal and direct the expression, they were playing for history, if not for the grandstands. The Beats carried to an extreme the idea of the artist as isolated, agonized seeker, mad seer, accusatory prophet and self-destructive martyr—the tradition of Rimbaud, Van Gogh and Dylan Thomas. Their heroes were the Nelson Algren heroes—Negroes, junkies, madmen, people who had seen too much and suffered too deeply. To the Beats, art was life, but life could never be art, as it is to the hippies, except in its most absurd, exaggerated forms.

The jazz session is symbolic of the Beat era: The musicians straggled in, blew together for a moment and then left, back to the private hells of their own pads. The same was true of the long conversations in the Coexistence Bagel Shop, of encounters on the street, of love-making. It's a world away from today's rock groups who live together, practice together, travel together and play for large audiences at the Fillmore and Avalon, usually even showing up on time; for all its superficial bizarreness, the hippie lifestyle has a strange quality of domesticity. You can contrast the eras in terms of their use of publications: The Beats' major effort was a journal called *Beatitudes*, an anthology of poetry, fiction and an occasional essay; hippie publications are mostly journalistic, combining factual pieces on topics like drugs and

police, and self-improvement articles; Alan Watts has dubbed the Haight Street *Oracle* the "Hindu-Science Monitor."

Beat art always balanced the aesthetic of rugged individualism and personal expression with an abiding sense of history, mostly Western; hippie art carries the idea of art as personal expression to an extreme, yet individualism often blurs into tribal anonymity—it recalls certain historic styles, but often wholly by accident; western history is replaced by the latest thing in exotica. The commercialism that the Beats shunned, the hippies have developed into a sub-Establishment where the line between commercialism, art and personal expression no longer exists.

As in other areas, in art the hippies have progressed to an unprecedented degree beyond the Beats' hang-up with traditional values; in the hippie subculture, art and life have become synonymous. Almost as in primitive societies, everyone is an artist—maybe because he draws, paints flowers on his car or plays guitar, but even if not, because he does his thing, like wearing bells, or being beautiful.

Their artistic expression really represents a radical departure from the Beats. In keeping with McLuhanism, there is not much going on in creative literature and poetry; what there is, is less angry or despairing, more exalting—mantras, chants, love poetry that recalls the Song of Solomon.

Musically, rock is primarily a development of the folk-soul reactions against the overcerebral dead-end that jazz had reached by the late Fifties—a thing that never happened in North Beach, by the way, where funk generally remained as the prevailing style, and where the beginnings of a soul revival had already developed.

But what a fantastic development the rock scene represents. Composition, at a low ebb in the jazz days, has been restored; groups and individuals everywhere are creating tunes in which the distinction between pop and art song has been completely obliterated. At the same time, performances retain the creativity of jazz; they are electric, in both senses of the word. The true poetry of the age is in the song lyrics; sometimes, as in Dylan, they still reflect some of the old nightmare anger; mostly, they are fresh statements on old subjects like love or such long-neglected things as the Dionysian celebration of the universe.

Hippie art is flowing, lyrical, expansive, organic and realistic, at least to the psychedelic vision. A return to figure painting had begun back in the Beat era, where both abstract expressionism and dramatic, direct and highly personal realism that grew out of it remained as parallel art styles. Hippie art grows partly out of the current mainstream styles of op, pop and camp (which is simply pop of an older era), but it remains apart from Establishment art, except insofar as it has been adopted for commercial purposes. Finally there is everything related to film—which has expanded earlier ideas of underground filmmaking into engulfing environmental art forms.

Beat art, rooted in a dramatic sense of emotional experience, has yielded to an art of sensation—sound, color, and shape for their sakes, documentaries of the psychedelic trips.

The Beats, actually, were a relative instant in history: Their art was personal, urgent, tense and separate from life, possibly so much so that the Beats could not survive. Hippie art, by contrast, is functional, integrated entirely into the daily life of the subculture. It lacks the individuality of most of the old Beat art, but as an art movement, it will probably last much longer.

The Beats and the Birth of the Counterculture

BY PARKE PUTERBAUGH

"America when will you be angelic /
When will you take off your clothes?"

ALLEN GINSBERG ISSUED THAT challenge in his poem "America" while ensconced in San Francisco in the late Fifties. The peripatetic poet wrote those words while habituating a city that has functioned as a new frontier for anarchists, free-thinkers, bohemians, writers, painters and musicians for much of this century. The Bay Area has been the staging area for movements in arts and letters, among them the Berkeley Renaissance of the Forties and the San Francisco Renaissance of the late Fifties. The latter was ignited, in part, by the Six Gallery poetry reading on October 13, 1955, at which Ginsberg debuted "Howl," his epic poem that railed at America's fascistic mindset with unrepressed rage. San Francisco at that time was in America but not completely of it, providing a base of enlightened skepticism from which one could launch bilious grenades.

Time and again, San Francisco has stood naked before the world at the ramparts of free speech and artistic expression, and one can endlessly speculate why this is so. For one thing, its hilly, zigzagging streets and chilly, fog-shrouded weather provide a nurturing isolation for a community energized by contact with nature yet also driven indoors to pursue the life of the mind. For another, there has been a long tradition of liberal thinking in the Bay Area, including anarchist workingmen's circles and the creative remnants of a conscientious objectors' camp in Waldport, Oregon, who filtered down after World War II. Berkeley and San Francisco State have attracted liberal faculties and student bodies that have helped shaped the intellectual tenor of life in the Bay Area.

Most important, there have been periodic instances where a local scene suddenly achieved a critical mass, like a star erupting into a supernova, energizing not only those in the vicinity but drawing people from outside with its irresistible gravity. Poet Michael McClure has referred to such events as "spiritual occasions." In the late Fifties, San Francisco served as headquarters for the Beat Generation. It was primarily a literary movement of poets with spiritual and ecological dimensions and an ear for jazz. The world they created at coffeehouses, poetry readings, literary soirees and jazz dens provided the launching pad for a broader-based movement of youth who, emboldened by their Beat elders, forged a psychedelic subculture that defined itself in vigorous opposition to the American mainstream.

While the Beat poets and caricatured "beatniks" who followed had been based in North Beach, hippies took up residence in the cheaply rented old Victorian mansions of Haight-Ashbury. To a degree, they embraced the literary precepts of the Beats. However, they also dove headlong into an LSD-fueled world of expanded consciousness that brought heady innovations to rock music, light shows, poster art and comic books. They adopted different modes of dress (from antiquarian clothing to low-maintenance denim and long hair), an appreciation of handcrafted jewelry and leather goods, radical

Gary Snyder signals the beginning of the Human Be-In by blowing the conch shell, while Allen Ginsberg chants "We are one!," January 14, 1967 GENE ANTHONY

approaches to politics and spirituality, and alternative models for living (Native American, Rabelaisian, Buddhist, whatever).

The counterculture fully blossomed in San Francisco from 1965 to 1967. Certain of the Beats—especially Ginsberg, McClure and Gary Snyder—provided direct mentoring to the embryonic counterculture. At least one cornerstone event—the Human Be-In, a daylong festival of music, poetry and celebration held in Golden Gate Park on January 14, 1967—was largely conceived and planned by the above-mentioned Beat troika, who also read their poetry in between sets by Quicksilver Messenger Service, the Grateful Dead and other San Francisco bands. The counterculture persisted to the end of the decade, although the petals of flower power wilted rapidly. By 1970, the community's spirit had been broken and its most charismatic and creative figures were dispersed, leaving little more than a smoking crater of hard drugs and scuffling squalor in Haight-Ashbury. But the achievements of the counterculture while it prospered have outlived the years of decay that followed, and attempts to proclaim the era a failure miss the point. As Michael McClure wrote in his introduction to photographer Gene Anthony's cultural history *The Summer of Love*, "Those who believed in the Tribe knew in some secret place in their awareness that it didn't matter whether it lasted or not; a spiritual occasion has a set of laws other than the ones that extend the life of the one-dimensional society."

The living legacy of those days includes the priorities placed on equality and the environment. Moreover, owing to that legacy one is free to choose viable alternatives in America in this day and age, whereas that has typically not been the case. One can pursue an alternative lifestyle, listen to alternative music, hold alternative political views and so forth. While the hippies

pioneered such breakthroughs on a large scale, they were in many ways building on seeds first sown by the Beats.

It's not only fair but necessary to point out that the counterculture couldn't have taken the form it did if not for its Beat forebears. That statement would be valid if only for the influence the Beats had on one of the keystone bands of the San Francisco scene, the Grateful Dead, who themselves were largely responsible for the spread of the counterculture and its perpetuation over time. While the Dead are principally associated with Ken Kesey and the Merry Pranksters, having provided an acid-blues soundtrack as the house band for the anarchic Acid Tests, their ties to the Beats actually date back further, at least in Jerry Garcia's case.

According to Garcia, the transient life of touring that gave rise to the Deadhead phenomenon was largely inspired by *On the Road*: "I read it and fell in love with it, the adventure, the romance of it, everything. . . . I owe a lot of who I am and what I've been and what I've done to the beatniks from the Fifties and to the poetry and art and music that I've come in contact with."

Bob Weir, the Dead's rhythm guitarist, likewise forged a kinship with the Beats, albeit less with its literary manifestations than the freewheeling lifestyle embodied by such figureheads as Kesey and the Pranksters, especially Neal Cassady. The Pranksters were fond of saying, "You're either on the bus or off the bus," alluding to the ever-sharpening line between hip and straight in America, and Weir quite literally boarded the bus. It's his own story he's telling in "That's It for the Other One," from the Dead's acid-rock symphony *Anthem of the Sun*, when he sings: "The bus came by and I got on / That's where it all began." The bus was the Pranksters' riotously painted means of conveyance, the driver Neal Cassady.

At some of the earliest counterculture events, Weir recalls Cassady being set up "with a tower of scaffolding on rollers with microphones, cameras and all kinds of stuff where he could go around and interview people. Sometimes he would just take the stage, and he and his girlfriend had a sort of standup routine where they'd rave at each other. It was pretty free-form, but it was also—I hate to use the word cosmic, but I don't know how else to describe it. We were together in this big mind meld, and he would be having a conversation with what was going on in your head and going through your head. Cassady kept developing. Kerouac, from what I've read of his writings, only caught the budding Neal Cassady but never caught him in full bloom. He amounted to a whole lot more than Kerouac was ever around to document. Kerouac was gone even before we [the Dead] got started."

Gary Duncan of Quicksilver Messenger Service also got turned on to the bohemian community that began with the Beats and carried over to the counterculture. The Haight-Ashbury scene "was basically an outgrowth of the Beat Generation in North Beach," Duncan recalls. "I first started hanging out there when I was about fourteen, back when there were no hippies. There were beatniks and little crash pads around town—just a whole scene going on. Poets and painters, every kind of drug imaginable and every kind of crazy motherfucker in the world."

The cultural revolt espoused by the Beats against the status quo of the Fifties was picked up by the musical counterculture in the Sixties, which struck its own blows against the empire. In that sense, the Haight-Ashbury musicians inherited the revolutionary zeal of the Beat Generation. "I think it was a reaction against the Fifties," theorizes Grace Slick, "which were extraordinarily boring and stiff. Compared to the Sixties, it was like being asleep. Our generation was the best-educated one before or since, and we had

the opportunity to read books that gave us a scenario. We got a chance to observe and experiment with different ideas and art forms."

San Francisco, in other words, functioned as a crucible in which different elements of thought and expression flowed together and interacted across time. Certain Beat Generation figureheads such as Allen Ginsberg, Neal Cassady, Gary Snyder and Michael McClure were witnesses to and participants in both the beatnik and hippie eras. Other Beat titans, notably Jack Kerouac and Kenneth Rexroth (who, incidentally, became bitter adversaries), were uninterested in or incapable of relating to the changes that attended the rise of the counterculture. To Allen Ginsberg, however, the hippie insurgency was not a challenge to the waning authority of San Francisco's Beat literati but part of a continuous thread woven into the cultural landscape of this century.

"A lot of people in San Francisco got together in the Sixties just like the grunge kids get their own gangs together on Avenue A in New York City today," Ginsberg observed a few months before his death in 1997. "They have their own culture, their own community, their own friendships. Except we were doing it at a time when it was less well-known to do that. There were precedents, like the Modernists of the Twenties—Ezra Pound, James Joyce and T. S. Eliot in Paris. The whole gang around Gertrude Stein, Ernest Hemingway and F. Scott Fitzgerald and all that was a similar thing. So Haight-Ashbury was a continuation, another manifestation of things that had happened before in history. It was just gangs of friends getting together."

Although it is tempting to describe a linear progression from poet-spewing Beats to guitar-thrashing hippies, it wasn't quite that cut and dried. The Beat Generation and the counterculture were not neatly linked as a parent to a child, and the latter wasn't only about music any more than the former was only about poetry. Moreover, the influence didn't proceed in one direction only, from old to young or from writers to musicians. San Francisco in the Sixties was actually a fluid scene in which influences traveled across permeable borders in all directions. Thus, the progression from beatniks to hippies wasn't so much a segue but, as Michael McClure puts it, "what is called an interpenetration in Buddhism."

"It's not happening on just one front," McClure notes of the counterculture. "This is people who have known each other for a long time coming together in different ways. A huge, fluid scene is developing with a philosophy and an attractive, strange newspaper to go with it and a new art form, rock music, that's very catchy. It's a simultaneous permeability of people overlapping each other from what had been a number of separate existences: jug-band scenes or poet groups or painter cliques."

The same principle of disparate elements holds true even for the Beat poets who'd been banded together under the rubric of the San Francisco Renaissance. Conjoined in the aftermath of a defining event (the Six Gallery poetry reading), they were actually a small but heterogeneous grouping of cliques. Various figures were as likely to clash with each other as conspire to advance a common cause. As Steven Watson put it in *The Birth of the Beat Generation*, "The Renaissance can best be described as overlapping constellations of poets who chose San Francisco for their home."

Within their ranks there were sage first-generation elders (Kenneth Rexroth, Robert Duncan, William Everson, Philip Whalen); wild-eyed East Coast Beats (Kerouac, Ginsberg, Gregory Corso, Robert Creeley); hip, "myriad-minded" younger voices (Gary Snyder, Michael McClure, Lew Welch); and several visionary poet-mystics who stood apart from the crowd (Philip Lamantia, Bob Kaufman, Kenneth Patchen). Then, of

course, there were Ken Kesey and Neal Cassady, who aren't grouped with the Renaissance men but were both writers and, more important, characters whose Prankster-ish, performance-art existences served as the most direct links between the Beat Generation and the counterculture.

Despite their differences, a galaxy of shared concerns bound the various poetic constellations together, at least during the latter half of the Fifties. They generally read the same authors, espoused pacifism, studied Eastern religion and held leftist/anarchist views. They regarded mainstream American society with wary indifference, if not outright disdain. This is why Ginsberg's Six Gallery reading of "Howl," a vocal articulation of rage against the machine that restored to American poetry its "prophetic consciousness," by the author's own reckoning, was such a powder keg whose reverberations carried over into the 1960s.

The real legacy of Beats and beatniks, from the point of view of Haight-Ashbury in the Sixties, had less to do with passing along stylistic approaches to music, art and literature—because the forms and emphases were radically different—than with offering a bold, forthright template for revolt and uncensored self-expression. Poet Lawrence Ferlinghetti, whose City Lights bookshop and publishing imprint were critical to disseminating Beat Generation writings, maintains, "All the main tenets of the hippie counterculture were first articulated by the Beat writers of the Fifties: the turn toward Far East, Buddhist philosophy and mysticism in general, ecological consciousness, political positions. Further parallels were pacifism and antiwar positions, and generally the fact that both were youth revolts, maybe the first revolts of the Twentieth Century against mechanization and industrialization. What hasn't been said enough is that the counterculture was a youth revolt that, it seems to me, began with the Beats."

Another parallel between Beats and hippies,

Ferlinghetti continues, is that "for the first time since the Nineteenth Century, American writers and artists were turning on with psychedelics rather than alcohol. Writers of the Twenties were all alkies. When Beats came along in the late Forties, the established writers were all drinkers. The Beats were the first writers since Poe and Ludlow who used psychedelics for creative purposes."

Likewise, the musicians and artists of Haight-Ashbury found doors to creativity unlocked by psychedelics, especially pot and acid. "We took a lot of drugs," admits Gary Duncan of Quicksilver. "That period of time in the Sixties was an up type of music. It may not have been the best technically, but the feeling in all the music was very up, because everybody was taking acid."

As was the case with the Beat poets, the rock bands of the San Francisco scene were less drawn to fame and fortune than to breakthroughs on the level of consciousness, creativity and an unfettered lifestyle. Duncan could have been speaking for the whole Haight-Ashbury community when he says, "We didn't really have that drive to go and be stars. We were more concerned with making sure we always had enough dope. We weren't going to play the game. We were beatniks."

Beats and Hippies:
A Tabular Synopsis

BY PARKE PUTERBAUGH

Category	Beats	Hippies
Adversary	the Establishment	the Establishment
Censorship	Ginsberg's *Howl*	Lenore Kandel's *Love Book*
Charismatic spirit	Neal Cassady	Neal Cassady
Conscience	remnants of C.O. camp, Waldport, Ore.,	The Diggers
Culmination	*Black Mountain Review* #7 (Fall 1957)	Human Be-In (Feb. 14, 1967)
Decade	Fifties	Sixties
Defining event	Six Gallery reading (poetry)	A Tribute to Dr. Strange (concert/dance)
Favorite hangout	Coexistence Bagel Shop	Psychedelic Shop
Gathering places	coffeehouses	ballrooms
High priest		
& organizer	Allen Ginsberg	Allen Ginsberg
Literary patriarch	Kenneth Rexroth	Ken Kesey
Medium	literature	music
Musical preference	bebop jazz	acid rock
Neighborhood	North Beach	Haight-Ashbury
Non-alcoholic beverage	coffee	electric Kool-aid
Periodical	*Beatitude*	*Oracle*
Political satirist	Lenny Bruce, Lord Buckley	Paul Krassner, Abbie Hoffman
Presidents	Eisenhower	Johnson and Nixon
Psychedelic drug	peyote	LSD
Religion	Buddhism, mysticism	Buddhism, mysticism
Rituals	poetry readings	rock concerts
Seminal events	Poets Follies	Acid Tests
Shared voices	Gary Snyder, Michael McClure	Richard Brautigan, Allen Ginsberg
Transcendent capitalists	Lawrence Ferlinghetti (City Lights)	Chet Helms (Family Dog/Avalon Ballroom)
Visual arts	figurative artists	poster artists
War	Korea	Vietnam

Ken Kesey (with flute) *and his Merry Pranksters
descend on New York City, June 1965*
DAVID GAHR

Beat
Pharmacopoeia

BY CARLO McCORMICK

IT IS PERHAPS STILL TOO EARLY TO tell exactly how the primal howl and rambling road trip that came out of American letters in the Fifties will be treated by history. What is certain is that the formidable differences from mainstream America that the Beats manifested—the high-bohemian vernacular unleashed by Jack Kerouac, Allen Ginsberg's embrace of alternative values and identity—has become common currency among scores of youth who haven't even read their work. For all the myriad ways the Beats' obvious transgression from and subversion of convention can be registered—an explicit queerness, radical politics or iconoclastic, idiosyncratic otherness—one of the most evident and consistent surely has to be the major role drugs played in their life and work.

Bohemian drug use—the crucial means by which the creative spirits of that era transmogrified quotidian experience—would in fact come to signify a complex set of intricate social, political and psychological attitudes that have held a mesmerizing and lasting effect on the Beats' followers. Much of this can be directly attributed to the art itself as well as to the personal statements made by the Beats, who have been alternately romanticized or vilified because of it. The projection on them of attitudes, identities, ideologies and agendas perpetrated by the ever-shifting perspectives of society render even the most fundamental distinctions of life and art a highly subjective muddle.

William S. Burroughs
(from a color Mylar photograph), *1970*
IRA COHEN

The positive and negative forces drugs exerted on the Beats, the prominence intoxicants have in their very best work, and the dramatic changes that such an involvement subsequently wrought on society, have made it an unavoidable issue for even the most academic studies of that era. What is "truth" or fiction, or that various substances held different priorities according to each writer, or even that the Beats were hardly the first artists to get high (maybe among the earliest to consistently proselytize the process), is ultimately subordinate to the significance of how their relationship to drugs has been registered by American culture as a whole since then.

In the 1950s, as the United States settled down into a great period of prosperity and growth, the country's nearly pathological dedication to normalcy was at a level of national identity compelling and comprehensive enough to verge on patriotic necessity. With television, movies and music promoting a pop-culture pablum of suburban bliss and mundane predictability, and the Cold War enshrining these new American values as a program of paranoid intolerance so widespread and extreme that McCarthyism seems in retrospect more a symptom than a cause, it was perhaps inevitable that something would have to give. A society in such complete and utter denial of everything about itself that wasn't white, modern, middle-class, hard-working, God-fearing, flag-saluting and American as Mom's apple pie was beyond all else delusional and schizophrenic. For those of us who weren't around then, it's hard to imagine how outnumbered, ostracized and alone those outsider visionaries who didn't subscribe to the authority of this reality were. In historical reconsideration, we can only thank the gods below for giving us that odd lot of alcoholics, speed-freaks, potheads, junkies, psychedelic shamans, perverts and all-around commie, nigger-loving Jew homos, so that now when it comes to America we don't have to love it or leave it to Beaver.

And, really, that's what's so damn seminal about the Beats. The fact that society by and large rejected their hallucination of another world — one that was hep, bohemian, nomadic, innovative, spontaneous, cool and deeply informed by the magic medicine of the indigenous ancients who had worshipped mushrooms and peyote; the loco weed of the field Negroes; and the miracles of modern chemistry that gave us heroin and LSD — is precisely why they remain so appealing today. They played the first chords of a discordant heterodoxy that has only expanded in time to fugue-like proportions. And as long as America must cling to its hegemony of moral majority it will always need to define itself by what it is *not*.

Essential to the vitality of what is new — as true of the Beats' emergent drug culture as it is of much cultural novelty — is an often less-than-evident connection to ancient traditions. Such a lineage may be drawn from the earliest of Beat drug encounters, such as Gary Snyder's partaking of the American Indian sacrament peyote in Oregon in the late Forties, and Burroughs's and Ginsberg's individual South American quests for the psychoactive shaman brew ayahuasca (their correspondence comparing notes was later collected in *The Yage Letters*). Native peoples weren't the only earlier explorers into this largely unknown territory to whom the Beats could look. Marijuana, the archetypal Beat mind and mood enhancer, can be directly tied to the purveyors of jazz and blues, another huge influence. In the 1940s, Mezz Mezzrow first wrote about this connection, which dates back to

the Twenties. As the first white subculture to extol the virtues of smoking grass, the Beats were indebted to the hip jazz of bop, particularly that of Charlie Parker (to whom we might also give the dubious credit of influencing some to enter the opiated realm of heroin). Smoking tea resulted in the collective loosening of rigid mindsets, allowing exploration of other realities and leading to the linguistic equivalent of jazz improvisation.

Grass, wine, beer and cigarettes were a large part of the San Francisco Beat scene, recalls experimental filmmaker and assemblage artist Bruce Conner, who also observed firsthand the Bay Area's pill culture, speed craze and phenomenal psychedelic explosion. Today Conner abhors chemicals and, rather, considers the only worthwhile "additives" to be "Native-American drugs" like peyote and mushrooms, which offer a "spiritual dimension." The recently re-released Conner film short *Looking for Mushrooms*, which in its many permutations evolved over a period from 1958 to 1967, provides one of the most cogent and hypnotic bridges between the mind expansion of the Beats to the psychedelia of the hippie Sixties. Conner's fast-cut editing and layered montage film techniques are imbued with transcendental, trance-like qualities similar to the drug experience, and would later influence Peter Fonda and Dennis Hopper's *Easy Rider*, psychedelic light shows, early Beatles films and art-punks Devo (who collaborated with Conner on music videos). Conner points out that legal drugs (coffee, cigarettes and alcohol) were dominant among his contemporaries, yet the availability of then-legal psychedelics contributed to their adoption by the Beats.

Given the Beats' remarkable candor regarding their drug use, it is easy to forget how alien, dangerous and taboo such a position was. Michael Horowitz, an archivist, historian and antiquarian book dealer who specializes in drug literature (and whose encyclopedic font of information has been invaluable to this essay), cites a 1965 photograph of Allen Ginsberg carrying a placard announcing POT IS A REALITY KICK at a rally for LeMAR [LEgalize MARijuana], as evidence of how outspoken despite the risk some Beats were in regard to drugs, particularly marijuana. Journalist Al Aronowitz, who conducted an extensive interview with Jack Kerouac in 1959, describes marijuana as "the glue that held the Beat Generation together underground—you'd get together and smoke a joint like hanging out on the corner drinking wine." Aronowitz, who later turned on to pot several of the Sixties' most prominent rock artists, suggests the key role played by the jazz community—"the potheads who preceded the Beats."

Poet and photographer Ira Cohen traveled to Morocco in 1961, following the path of Kerouac before him on the same Yugoslavian freighter for a ninety-dollar fare. Describing the black tobacco and hasish concoction, kif, as "a door opener for artists," Cohen made Morocco his home for four years, leading the way for what was to become the hippie invasion of that region. His *Hashish Cookbook* (penned under the name Panama Rose) offers up "the goblet of dreams, majoun" and a recipe for making "the fabled white cookie of Marrakesh" that has evolved into the popular "spacecakes" available in Amsterdam today. Bridging the gap between the prosody of the Beats and the visuals of psychedelia, Cohen wrote some of the Sixties' best doped-out, visionary poetry and created an immensely popular series of Mylar-distorted photographs of trans-generational contemporaries from Burroughs to Hendrix.

While kif, mushrooms, marijuana and peyote brought with them the mysticism and non-Western ways of thinking that would greatly influence the Beats and their followers, synthetic drugs offered a shortcut to accessing new realities. The speed and alcohol cocktail, which accounts for both the best and worst of Kerouac's work, served as a great lubricator for his binge writing and also as a consciousness-altering tool due to its sleep-deprivation effects.

Warhol film star Taylor Mead took up the Beat mantle when, in the mid-Sixties, he relocated to Europe, spending three years doing Quaaludes. Using relatively new medical substances to access ancient states, Mead recalls one night in the late Sixties being zonked on STP (a psychedelic-amphetamine mixture), wandering into New York's West Village after an all-nighter, and seeing "Washington Square Park [melting] into three-thousand-year-old ... Persia in the most amazing transference I ever experienced."

Heroin, introduced to the Beats by Herbert Huncke, has perhaps been the most controversial drug brought to our attention by that movement. Appropriated, like marijuana, from black jazz artists, heroin would make the career of Burroughs and destroy the muse for Lenny Bruce, Gregory Corso (temporarily) and countless others in the Beat orbit. Huncke got hold of it through his lowlife contacts in Times Square and certainly did a good job of spreading the word. But if one considers the opiated visions of Nineteenth-Century England, particularly within the literature of Thomas DeQuincey and Samuel Taylor Coleridge, narcotics weren't new —the willingness of artists to openly discuss heroin was novel. One such social realist and brilliant Beat contemporary, Hubert Selby Jr., author of *Last Exit to Brooklyn*, is still writing today but in sadly diminished health, partially due to years of drug addiction. On the subject of heroin and creativity, Selby bitterly laments that the only thing drugs ever truly taught him was that he couldn't do them and live.

Eighty-year-old Dr. Oscar Janiger, who conducted the early tests for an experimental drug, LSD-25, from the Sandoz laboratory, still believes acid has great research possibilities. During the 1950s, Dr. Janiger did an extended research project that confirmed some of the "extraordinary perceptual effects of the drug." (Subjects of his LSD studies included Jack Nicholson, Andre Previn, Anaïs Nin, Christopher Isherwood, Cary Grant and James Coburn.) Janiger's work provided further understanding of that unknown territory encompassing creativity, perception and the mind. No one among his eight hundred subjects (including cousin and close friend Allen Ginsberg) ever "denied or backed off their original position that LSD was a remarkable and heuristically significant drug," according to Janiger. Extremely powerful in its capacity to create dramatic shifts in both perception and imagination, LSD, says Janiger, seemed to be most effective or more catalytic or have a more dramatic effect on his subjects who were creative professionals because they were the most capable and willing to undergo such a transformative experience. Working in what he describes as "a pristine time, when people could take the medicine without all that other social baggage that has become attached to it," Dr. Janiger found that few ever experienced a bad reaction, and for artists, by their own testimony (Ginsberg and his cohorts included), "it helped them tremendously to understand the creative process." After taking LSD, his subjects made statements like "this is worth four years in art school" and "now I finally understand the nature of abstract art," according to Janiger, who theorizes that "drugs for a jazz musician, artist or writer [can] provide a situation where you give up some of the technique for freer creative expression."

The Beats, of course, created innovative literary techniques while expanding their minds through drugs. For that we can thank them, as well as for their role in introducing these new tools to so many of us. And please, rather than listening to the thought police, read the books listed in Michael Horowitz's invaluable sidebar. When it comes to drugs, take my word for it, they're the greatest gift to human consciousness.

Key Works of
Beat Drug Literature

COMPILED BY MICHAEL HOROWITZ

Dates indicate first publication in book form, or in a periodical if that was the only appearance.

AUTHOR	TITLE	YEAR	DRUG
Mezzrow, Mezz	*Really the Blues*	1946	marijuana, opium
Burroughs, William S.	*Junkie*	1953	heroin
Kerouac, Jack	*On the Road*	1957	marijuana, benzedrine
Lamantia, Philip	*Narcotica*	1959	heroin, opium, cocaine, marijuana
McClure, Michael	"Peyote Poem"	1959	peyote
Rubington, Norman	*Fuzz Against Junk* by "Akbar del Piombo"	1959	heroin
Burroughs	The *Naked Lunch* Trilogy	1959,1961,1962	heroin and other drugs
Gelber, Jack	*The Connection*	1960	heroin
Green, Jack	"Peyote"	1960	peyote
Kerouac	*Tristessa*	1960	morphine
Trocchi, Alex	*Cain's Book*	1960	heroin
Ginsberg, Allen	"from *Journals*, 1952"	1960	peyote
Ginsberg	"Laughing Gas" in *Kaddish & Other Poems*	1961	nitrous oxide
Ginsberg	"Mescaline" in *Kaddish & Other Poems*	1961	mescaline
Ginsberg	"Lysergic Acid" in *Kaddish & Other Poems*	1961	LSD
Ginsberg	"Magic Psalm"; "The Reply"; "The End" in *Kaddish & Other Poems*	1961	ayahuasca
Bowles, Paul	*A Hundred Camels in the Courtyard*	1962	kif
Bruce, Lenny	*Stamp Help Out*	1963	marijuana
Burroughs & Ginsberg	*The Yage Letters*	1963	ayahuasca
McClure	"The Mushroom" in *Meat Science Essays*	1963	psilocybin
McClure	"Drug Notes: Peyote, Heroin, Cocaine" in *Meat Science Essays*	1963	peyote, heroin, cocaine
Burroughs	*Nova Express*	1964	heroin
Cholst, Seymour	"Notes on the Use of Hashish"	1965	marijuana/hashish
Fainlight, Harry	"Mescaline Notes"	1965	mescaline
Johnson, Kay	"LSD-748"	1965	LSD
Andrews, George	*Burning Joy*	1966	LSD
Cohen, Ira	*The Hashish Cookbook* by "Panama Rose"	1966	marijuana/hashish
Rosenthal, Irving	*Sheeper*	1967	marijuana
Ginsberg, Allen	*Wales — A Visitation*	1967	LSD
Kandel, Lenore	"Peyote Walk" in *Word Alchemy*	1967	peyote
Kandel, Lenore	"Junk/Angel"; "Blues for Sister Sally" in *Word Alchemy*	1967	heroin

AUTHOR	TITLE	YEAR	DRUG
Southern, Terry	"Red-Dirt Marijuana" in *Red-Dirt Marijuana*	1967	marijuana
Southern, Terry	"The Blood of a Wig" in *Red-Dirt Marijuana*	1967	dexedrine
Ferlinghetti, Lawrence	"Through the Looking Glass" in *The Secret Meaning Of Things*	1968	LSD
Mead, Taylor	*On Amphetamine and in Europe*	1968	amphetamine
Bremser, Bonnie	*Troia*	1969	psilocybin, peyote
Gysin, Brion	*The Process*	1969	kif
Waldman, Anne	"13 Tanka: In Praise of Smoking Dope"	1969	marijuana
Burroughs, William, Jr.	*Speed*	1970	amphetamine
Cohen, Harvey	*The Amphetamine Manifesto*	1970	amphetamine
McClure	*The Mad Cub*	1970	various drugs
Burroughs, William, Jr.	*Kentucky Ham*	1973	heroin
Olson, Charles	"Under the Mushroom" in *Muthologos,* Vol.1	1978	psilocybin
di Prima, Diane	"The Holidays at Millbrook—1966" in *Shaman Woman, Mainline Lady*	1982	LSD
Huncke, Herbert	*Guilty of Everything*	1990	heroin, marijuana, benzedrine

My Beat Journal

BY ERIC ANDERSEN

'D BEEN LUCKY TO BE THIRTEEN and see and hear Elvis Presley perform in his gold suit at my hometown of Buffalo, New York's Memorial Auditorium in 1956. Now, I was in my English class sleepwalking through *Cry the Beloved Country*, waiting with lidded eyes for the bell to ring so I could go home to the radio. Then one late spring day, something crazy happened. There came along a book named "Howl." The angry, screaming stanzas hit the eye hard, with an impact rivaling the first time I heard "Rock Around the Clock." A time bomb dropped. Yet who were the "angelheaded hipsters . . . destroyed by madness, hysterical, naked . . . looking for an angry fix?" Who was Allen Ginsberg? Even the book looked different: A pocket paperback with a generic black-and-white cover. It was new and outrageous, with an unbelievable rage that transcended the tongue-in-cheek sneer of "Don't Be Cruel."

Soon, other books surfaced: Gregory Corso's *Gasoline* and Lawrence Ferlinghetti's *A Coney Island of the Mind*. Finally, Jack Kerouac's *On the Road* appeared. I began reading the pages with the same sense of complicity that I'd had discovering Rimbaud and Baudelaire's poetry (written a hundred years earlier), as if the words were a road map to my soul. *On the Road* had joy and tenderness and sex and speed. It swept me away. It was new and it was American. It was dream-inducing nectar to my young eyes. I was hooked. I was sixteen.

Circulating at the time were rumors of "beatniks." (Once, at a Miles Davis Quintet concert in Buffalo, I had spotted some ghostlike faces peering out above black turtlenecks.) I learned fast what the word meant to parents—something unsavory that put a smirk on the lips. (Note: "beatnik," a pejorative term coined in the mid-Fifties by *San Francisco Chronicle* columnist Herb Caen, was a cross between sputnik [read: communist] and beaten down and seedy [read: Eastern European Jews].) These allusions of disgust made our little gang perk up.

When I left home, San Francisco and New York would furnish the chemical and spiritual underpinnings of a Beat lifestyle I would make my own. That was during the crack of time between the Beats and the hippies, when the civil rights movement and the Vietnam War were heating up. Later on, I would learn that the real cultural revolution in America didn't start in the Fifties or Sixties, as so many believed. It really began in the mid- to late Forties. Its roots didn't spring from the ashes of postwar Europe; they were homegrown, fresh out of the vast vernacular wetlands of Walt Whitman and Henry Miller and Billie Holiday.

After World War II, America was suddenly on the move. Regional borders cracked, leaving wide-open spaces of economic possibilities for an eager populace ready to ascend. My dad had moved our family from Pittsburgh to Buffalo, where he got a new job. While our parents were socializing to Sinatra, we kids were busy awaiting the arrival of our first TV. Meanwhile, new developments in blues, R&B, jazz, Beat writing and action painting were approaching critical mass, having progressed up the rivers and across the vast plains states to urban backstreet neighborhoods. These scattered eruptions detonated almost simultaneously—spewing visual, verbal

374

and musical ideas to feed a new, fiery cauldron encompassing the momentum of the Beat writers' coast-to-coast migrations; the southern Delta electric blues peregrinations; the East Coast bebop jazz explorations; and the first abstract-expressionism painting experiments. Within five years, the pot would come to a boil. Put it this way: Woody Guthrie, Jack Kerouac, Muddy Waters, Charlie Parker and Jackson Pollock were in full swing before the popularity of Elvis or transistor radios came into existence.

After the Second World War, America was spiritually unmapped; a potential wasteland of consumers was easy prey for the slick engines of consumerism. Corporate America leered at us from highway billboards and green TV tubes, with a jeering taunt of: "Can't you afford this? Everyone can. It's easy. Can't you?"

I remember as a kid, my dad's work buddies dumping him off following hours of after-work bar-hopping. I can still see them laughing awkwardly, as I looked up at their embarrassed flushed faces, like it was some kind of joke, while I hauled my dad's heavy drunken body in from the car. I'd be alone with Dad in the kitchen—when my mom couldn't bear the sight of him—feeding him Campbell's chicken-noodle soup to sober him up. Then I'd put him to bed to sleep it off—my mom secretly hoping he wouldn't miss another day of work. I remember wanting things other kids had that my parents couldn't afford. My young America could smell fear. It was stumbling in a housecoat, struggling in a new subdivision; a smiling, fearful, drunken, argumentative, expectant, Juicy Fruit–cracking world that would soon be heavily injected with lethal doses of material dreams, conformity, McCarthyism,

Mexico City, 1956: Gregory Corso, Lafcadio Orlovsky (front row, from left); *Jack Kerouac, Allen Ginsberg, Peter Orlovsky* (back row, from left)

ALLEN GINSBERG

blacklists, political paranoia and Cold War propaganda.

If America's sudden taste for life was based on shallow, quick consumer gratification, the Beats' swollen hunger was stimulated by other things—what they explored or saw, heard or read, fixated on and talked about. The newfound word patterns of Kerouac, Ginsberg and Burroughs would sing out with the immediacy of great jazz improvisations while laying open profound human emotions. Their language would communicate music, spirit and poignancy. It had something to do with the sheer grace of their humanity. They were resolved to be firsthand witnesses to a new postwar world. And for them, life manifested a spiritual realm. In the face of growing political repression, they remained remarkably cool-headed and unafraid. They weren't intimidated by the system and wrote what they pleased. "Write what you want bottomless from bottom of the mind," Kerouac wrote. Ginsberg, the socialist, stood up to authority, and patrician Burroughs gave it the finger. It had very little to do with making money or gaining material security.

In the meantime, my parents struggled with their lives—the jobs and the bills. And my new shoes might come "next month."

Although at the dawn of the Forties, Ginsberg, Kerouac and Burroughs attended privileged universities, with blue-chip names like Harvard and Columbia; their postgraduate studies quickly took them to the nether-realms of Times Square. Gathering knowledge, keeping records, they haunted the shadowy streets, bars and alleys of New York, Denver, New Orleans, San Francisco and Mexico City. Though similar to orphaned criminal saints like Jean Genet, their voices were American, with literary influences extending from Blake and Dostoyevsky to Whitman; from Balzac to Wolfe; Spengler to science fiction.

In 1913 Ezra Pound, the poet-master of the

literary epigram, exclaimed: "Make it new." By 1949, these writers were fast on their way to fulfilling Pound's decree that *the artist is the antenna of the race*. If words can possess the power to transcend the present and retain the magic to conjure the spirits of the future, then the words of Kerouac, Ginsberg and Burroughs deftly qualified for what Pound had in mind, when he declared: "Literature is news that stays news."

New York's Times Square and the streets of Greenwich Village, in the Forties, weren't the café-lined boulevards of Paris in the Twenties. In glaring contrast to the rivalry and guarded correspondence of Fitzgerald, Dos Passos and Hemingway, Kerouac, Ginsberg and Burroughs weren't afraid to remain open with each other and maintain close personal and artistic ties throughout their lives, illustrated by the abundance of correspondence amassed among them. Over travel and time, this confederation had a core and a glue sorely missed in my own circles. It shared uncanny dimensional spaces consisting of enthusiasm for language, deep lasting friendships, yen for adventure and spiritual odysseys into mystical worlds—and on some occasions, the scoring of drugs. But the Beats' line remained: Never compete.

Jack Kerouac, Allen Ginsberg, William Burroughs, Gregory Corso and Lenny Bruce became America's new language models. Their word machinery still operates, miraculously withstanding rust and oblivion. On an earth swamped by processor chips, pocket phones, telecommunications satellites and life-defying precision equipment like stealth bombers, their words survive—words still highly charged with living information that will not soon self-destruct into some Zip-driven–zero obsolescence. And now looking back on Burroughs, he may have added a new definition of the word *stealth*.

Kerouac wrote that life was "a dream already ended." And if his sweet-sad rhythmical prose and poems taught us to see the colors around us, William Burroughs showed what they could reveal. With brutal honesty, scalpel pen and cool surgical eye, Burroughs peeled back the skin on issues no other American novelist had ever dared to address: America's addiction to paranoia and control. He didn't try to conceal his own personal addiction to drugs, nor did he romanticize it. From researching his own problem, he extrapolated bigger theories about addiction and control. He set to work with the clinical exactness of a scientist. Except *his* investigations and field-trip expeditions led him to the tawdry back streets of New York and Mexico City, South American jungles and rivers in search of the hallucinogen yage, and Tangier's Soco Chico, to return eventually to a room where he would assemble the material, within the lab of his own skull. In *Naked Lunch* he utilized much of the imagery he gleaned from his exotic wanderings to chilling effect, with real landscapes merging effortlessly with those created by his phantasmagorical mind. With exceptional powers of observation, a sharp ear for vernacular speech, a keen sense of telepathy and a scathing wit, Burroughs assembled the shards of a multiprism world with awesome skill. The master of shock comedy and he hilarious liberator of *noir*, he is arguably the most lucid prose writer in the language since James Joyce.

The Beat writers' language mixed shocking directness with sweet ingenuity. A feeling of a fresh new literary landscape lay over the horizon advancing ideas that totally eclipsed the grain. New lifestyle concepts emerged. The Beats re-examined the tired precepts, reset a few things and, in the process, tipped the scale of normalcy. Their lifestyle defied an insecure, conforming, homophobic, drug-fearing, competitive, anxiety-ridden, worried America. In the Fifties of *Naked Lunch*, William Burroughs struck a buried chord that has resonated across the decades: "But there's no drag like U.S. drag. You can't see it, you don't know where it comes from . . . you walk in and it hits you. But where does it come from?" Then there was the matter of the strange war in Korea and the ongoing (and expensive) battle with communism. In the 1950s, books with titles like *The Man in the Gray Flannel Suit* and *The Organization Man* topped the best-seller lists. Sinatra's songs about "broads" were tolerated with a wink, and the neurosis of Tennessee Williams's theatrical rape of Blanche DuBois was almost acceptable—but not the "holy cocks" of Ginsberg's "Howl" or Kerouac's mad-hatter scroll of *On the Road* or Burroughs's detailed description of shooting up ("red orchid bloomed at the bottom of the dropper," "watching the liquid rush into the vein as if sucked by the silent thirst of his blood . . .") in *Naked Lunch*.

Never cagey with words, the Beats didn't try to be coy. Nor was their literary intent merely to shock the reader (though that was fun, too). With language, they were generous, precise, often graphic, but always exposing what they meant. They never masked anything, no matter where the ink might spill.

The Beats traveled incognito—dressed as railyard workers or flannel-shirted lumberjacks. Indeed, their trademark style was no style at all. They could blend into the common American patchwork; think like Pascal; withdraw like Buddha; or criss-cross the Great American Night like invisible men. The ordinary was their disguise. It wouldn't occur to the real Beats to grow a goatee, wear a black beret or buy a straw-wrapped Chianti bottle just for the sake of stuffing a candle into it. That was Left Bank stuff. They usually had too many other things on their minds.

If Eisenhower's America could project its playful/rebellious fantasies onto Marilyn Monroe and James Dean, laugh at Bob Newhart's air-hostess jokes and weep over the loss of a marlin in *The Old Man and the Sea*, it still wasn't ready to become the human sacrifice of Lenny Bruce's lacerating wit ("There's no such thing as dirty

words, just dirty minds"). It wasn't seriously interested in heroin addiction, homosexuality, Zen satori or outlaw drunken amphetamine-crazed binges. That was nuthouse, pulp-fiction stuff. (Burroughs's first book, *Junkie*, would be published in 1953 in that format, with the guileful subtitle disclaimer—*Confessions of an Unredeemed Drug Addict*.)

Rather, a sensitive literary discussion of the hour might be about how Holden Caulfield ever managed to escape the appalling clutches of that insipid boarding school. America's great William Faulkner had been in decline (until he was rescued from neglect and oblivion to be awarded the 1949 Nobel Prize). Perhaps some had read (or seen the movie of) Nelson Algren's *The Man With the Golden Arm*. There were rumors about addiction in the jazz world (read: Negro). But those problems were for mainstream Americans, "other people, dope fiends, not people like us." By the late Sixties, America still couldn't even begin to fathom, much less face, what had been routine sexual practices and substance-intake realities for the Beats since the late Forties.

The Beats were a faithful compass, a beacon that shone over the American wasteland. But there was a harrowing, dark flipside to the Beat coin, going back to the beginnings of the "outlaw writers," as Burroughs would later call them. In 1944, the Beats' friend Lucien Carr stabbed a man to death and Kerouac was arrested as an accessory; Burroughs later rolled drunks in subways for drug money, was arrested for forged prescriptions in New York, had a marijuana bust in New Orleans and accidentally shot his wife dead in Mexico in a drunken game of William Tell. At twenty-one, in 1949, Ginsberg was arrested for possession of stolen goods after a high-speed Keystone Cops car chase–and-crash caper involving hipster and addict-thief Herbert Huncke. Ginsberg was sent to a mental asylum (as his mother had been before him), which later inspired "Howl." When Kerouac sought the Holy Grail of a Merciful Life through the road and Buddhism, he couldn't see it through. He died a bitter alcoholic reactionary with a liver that finally backed up and killed him at age forty-seven. Neal Cassady tried using fast cars to outrace the ghost of death, or gun it down, only to have it madly pursue him and catch him alone one night, leaving him cold on the ground beside some Mexican railroad tracks. And the stories continue . . .

Young Greenwich Village thief Gregory Corso found Beauty in books and reinvented himself in a cell, serving three years for robbery at Dannemora State Prison. William Burroughs had earlier warned him in Paris, "heroin is poison," but Corso later battled the narcotic demons. Yet his sense of beauty as projected in his poetry remained unscathed and unsurpassed. Boston's supreme poet John Weiners was often in and out of mental hospitals, enduring painful electric-shock therapies; yet he continued to compose his beautiful, fragile, incandescent elegies of despair and love.

The dark side cast its shadows. The Beats enjoyed each other's youthful company, but none could handle having kids of his own. Burroughs and Kerouac spent little time with their children, who died before reaching middle age. Once, when Corso tried to show Kerouac his newborn baby in New York, Kerouac responded, "Why would you show me something that was going to die?" Corso was confused and hurt. Better to be unborn or "safe in heaven dead," was Kerouac's unspoken reply; free and safe away from the great "meat wheel" of this sad, temporal, suffering world. Life was hurting Kerouac.

Buffalo was a long way from the realm of the Beats. In 1963 I had big dreams. After I quit college, I hitched to San Francisco with a notebook and my guitar. I got a job playing in the Coffee Gallery in North Beach, a place where John Weiners had swept the floors six years before. My first objective was to meet the Beat

poets. One afternoon, David Meltzer, a local poet who moonlighted at City Lights Books, introduced me to Allen Ginsberg and Lawrence Ferlinghetti. Allen, dressed in a *dhoti*, the white sari-like robe of a holy man, had just returned from a long trip to India and Southeast Asia.

Several weeks later I saw him again at a Haight-Ashbury poetry reading, this time dressed in black. It was a surreal scene; people were scared and on edge because it was the night JFK was assassinated. Afterward I went to Ferlinghetti's house to a party. Bottles of cheap jug wine cluttered the tables, and Ginsberg, bearded and completely naked, was sitting on a woman's lap next to me. In front of the fridge was a glazed-eyed Neal Cassady. Quiet, standing still, he held a shoebox full of clean-sifted weed he'd just brought up from Mexico. I remember David's wife, Tina, rolling cigar-size joints from tissue-thin sheets of a Chinese newspaper. People sat around talking quietly among themselves like a family reunion. I didn't say much. The party ran all night—as if nothing had happened that day in Dallas. Very kind to everyone, Allen appeared almost courtly. I saw him get sick that night from too much wine.

I kept in contact with Allen over the years. I'd check in with him from time to time, visit him, or he'd come down to a gig of mine. Once, while leading his Beat seminar at Brooklyn College, he called to invite me to meet William Burroughs, who was reading and speaking to the class that day. Afterward Allen and Burroughs signed an old copy of *Naked Lunch* someone had given me.

Allen did another very thoughtful thing six years ago. He sent over to my home in Norway a copy of the limited-edition facsimile-transcript version of "Howl," something he knew interested me very much. He remembered the conversation we'd had at a party, talking about the original manuscript of Eliot's "The Waste Land," which I'd just seen at the New York Public Library. Ezra Pound had done a major editing job on the poem by crossing out the first fifty-five lines. Pound's ruthless act had made it a masterpiece. I had asked Allen about his own editing of "Howl," which was illustrated in the new book. He said he would send it to me and I could see for myself. When it arrived, I experienced a new understanding of "Howl," through its seven drafts and revisions. By viewing Allen's process of correcting the typescripts with annotations, I saw how it finally evolved.

Tucked in among copies of correspondence, photographs and other related texts was a remarkable little essay by Carl Solomon on Artaud. On the book's front page, Allen sketched a childlike drawing of a sighing "black-eyed Buddha" in a lotus position with two halos encircling the body and head, holding a string of beads in his hands. Above and below were scribbled stars and a small close-eyed skull with a flower jutting out of the mouth. At the bottom were the date and his loopy scrawled inscription, "long delayed memento . . . Allen." Allen, more than anyone, knew one ideal the Beats stood for: Do not forget your friends.

The spirit of the Beats has never deserted me. They taught me new ways to see and a new way to live. Their words have freed and inspired my own writing with as much intensity as any reality that surrounds me. The recently departed souls of Allen Ginsberg, Herbert Huncke, William Burroughs—and the souls preceding them, Neal Cassady and Jack Kerouac—remain vital to my life. I miss them. They are as indispensable as the living ones today: poets like Gregory Corso, New York's great profound bard and raging Beauty-hunter; John Weiners, the poet of radiance and rare poignant brilliance, from Boston's Beacon Hill. And the other apostles of truth and meaning: Bob Dylan, Joni Mitchell and Lou Reed.

These are the writing Buddhas. They remain the guardians whose pens write straight and true lines—not twisted and bent by sorrow. Their lives and writings have sustained me and given me confidence. Their words are my treasures, as they were my dad's, when he was alive. They are the eyes of the jewel. I am lucky to have gotten to meet and know some of them. They are spirits who illuminated my path, who provided the lantern I carry within, in the hope that one day a light will shine for others, as these great souls have shone for me.

(*This is dedicated to the memory of Robert Palmer.*)

Children
of the Beats

BY DANIEL PINCHBECK

AS A CHILD, BROWSING through the bookshelves in my mother's apartment on Manhattan's Upper West Side, I occasionally found strange pieces of paper and scrawled notes inside the pages of old books on Zen Buddhism and magazines with names like *Big Table* and *The Evergreen Review*. The notes were from Jack Kerouac, who had been involved with my mother, Joyce Johnson, for a few years in the late 1950s, long before I was born. These accidentally unearthed scraps provided me with insight into the ghostlike fragility of an artist's physical legacy. They also introduced me to the Beat Generation's work, which I began to read even before I entered high school.

From time to time, figures from my mother's mysterious past would appear in our living room—such as Allen Ginsberg, Abbie Hoffman or Lawrence Ferlinghetti. As a teenager, I felt somewhat shy in their presence, imagining a depth of history between them and my mother that I couldn't share. I also saw a certain wariness in these poets and avatars, a certain tension, similar to what soldiers might feel after a long military campaign. It later seemed to me that decades of public attention and media

Diane di Prima and family,
San Francisco, 1972
GERARD MALANGA

scrutiny—often negative or accusatory in tone, especially in the early years—had taken a toll on them, made them somewhat inflexible, alert to invisible dangers hidden in the air like radio frequencies.

Kerouac's insidiously catchy phrase "mad to live, mad to love, mad to be saved, desirous of everything at the same moment . . ." was the message that my mother paid to have inscribed in my high school yearbook upon graduation in 1984. I saw it, even then, as both an encouragement and a reproach—a reproach because I already suspected that something lodged in my consciousness, as well as in the world that I belonged to, didn't allow for such a fervent pursuit of experience and ecstasy. The cynicism of the Reagan years had seeped into the atmosphere. When my friends and I sought parallels to the 1950s counterculture, we found ourselves unsatisfied. What we wanted no longer existed, or continued to exist only as style, parody, pastiche.

My marginal relationship to Beat history made me wonder what became of the children of the group's central figures. From the safe vantage point of my middle-class adolescence, I loved the movement's original testimonies, but I had been spared the chaos of their creators. In 1995, I went on a journey to speak to their children to see how they had been shaped by the values of that distant era—had their parents' live-for-the-moment ethos inspired them? Had it hindered or harmed them? Some of both, I discovered.

The Gramercy Park Hotel is a gloomy place that attracts traveling salesmen, rootless dowagers, tourists and low-level heavy-metal bands. A hastily assembled press conference, held in a plain, gray-carpeted suite, had been called by Jan Kerouac, the forty-three-year-old only child of Jack Kerouac, to announce litigation against her father's estate.

The meeting started late. Waiting around the coffee dispenser, lawyers in shiny gray suits smelling of cologne and hair spray chatted with frowzy-looking women journalists from the wire services, while notebook-toting writers wearing beads and T-shirts—most of them having no discernible press affiliation—drank bitter coffee from plastic cups. Jack Micheline, a "street poet" who had made something of a career based on his friendship with Kerouac in the Fifties, held court in one corner. In another, an enormously fat, brown-bearded man in a psychedelic jacket and a priest's collar gave out photocopies of his own confused manifesto. Finally, Jan appeared amid a small pack of journalists and advisers; she looked terrified and fluttery in a white linen dress. She walked to the front of the room and joined her supporters seated behind a cafeteria-style table and a microphone.

Jan's lawyer, Thomas A. Brill, a stiff-faced, blond-haired man in pinstripes, spoke first at the conference. "We hope to demonstrate," he said, "that the signature of Gabrielle Kerouac, Kerouac's mother, was forged on her last will in 1973, while she lay dying in a nursing home." That will left sole title of the estate to Kerouac's last wife, Stella Sampas Kerouac, who died in 1990, and not to his daughter, whom Gabrielle Kerouac never really knew. Jan received royalty checks from her father's estate. But his physical property—manuscripts, letters, clothes—belonged to the Sampas family. The scroll on which Kerouac wrote *On the Road* during a three-week breakthrough into spontaneous prose might sell for more than one million dollars at auction, with each of his other manuscripts worth perhaps a third of that price. Everything that Kerouac touched or wore has become sanctified with value.

In his work, Kerouac often avowed a horror of procreation, of "the wheel of the quivering meat conception" that turns in the void, "expelling human beings, pigs, turtles, frogs. . . ." He could never accept Jan as his own contribution to "that slaving meat wheel." He once showed my mother a photograph of a little girl in pigtails. Even in the snapshot, my mother could see that the girl looked like him, sharing his tan skin and solid jaw. "This isn't my daughter," said Kerouac, explaining that a former wife, Joan Haverty—Jan's mother—had been impregnated by another man while they were married.

Jan had met her father only twice before his death in 1969: when she was nine and a court ordered blood tests to determine whether Kerouac should pay child support, and when she was fifteen and had run away from home. She had published two novels, *Baby Driver* and *Trainsong*, chronicling her early life, before she became seriously ill. Alcoholism led to kidney failure, and she now had to administer dialysis to herself four times each day.

When Jan spoke, she told of her final meeting with her father. She had driven to his house in Lowell, Massachusetts, on her way to Mexico with her boyfriend, pregnant with a child that would be stillborn. In his dreary, desperate drunkenness, Kerouac said to her: "Yeah, you go to Mexico. Write a book. You can use my name." Her voice breaking and her eyes often failing so that she frequently stalled in mid-sentence, Jan also described her life on the road after she left home, living on a commune in California, then working as a stablehand and a waitress. As the audience shifted uneasily, she discussed her drinking, her years of poverty, her unhappy relationships. "For some reason," she said, "I kept being attracted to men who would abuse me."

When we met for breakfast a few days later at the Gramercy, Jan wore blue jeans and a baseball cap backward. "I hope to live for another ten years," she said to me.

Her small hands were thick and tough, like the hands of a farm laborer. Her eyes, however, were clear blue and guileless, almost childlike. "My dream is to buy my own house in New Mexico, but at the moment, I'm broke, almost

completely penniless," she said. "The checks from the estate seem to arrive very erratically." (In fact, it turned out that royalty checks came regularly from Kerouac's agent, Sterling Lord.)

The huge bearded man who wore a priest's collar at the press conference hovered protectively at a nearby table.

"Who's that?" I asked.

"Oh, that's Buddha," Jan said, and waved at him.

"He calls himself Buddha?"

"Yeah. Buddha's a fan of my work. He lives in Lowell and visits my father's grave every day. He offered to act as my bodyguard while I'm in New York."

Jan said that she received about $60,000 a year from the Kerouac estate, and had another lawyer investigating to see whether she deserved more. "I didn't even know I was entitled to any royalties until 1985, and Stella fought tooth and nail to stop me from getting them. But this case is not about getting more money for me." Her dream was to have a Kerouac house "like the Hemingway house in Florida, where people can visit and scholars can go to examine my father's manuscripts, letters and books."

On the Road closed with Kerouac's alter ego Sal Paradise musing on his lost friend and hero: "I think of Dean Moriarty, I even think of old Dean Moriarty, the father we never found, I think of Dean Moriarty." For Jan, Kerouac was also "the father we never found," his absence sentencing her to a kind of permanent exile.

Speaking to her, I thought of William Burroughs Jr.—the son of Burroughs and Joan Vollmer, whom Burroughs killed in Mexico in 1951 when he drunkenly tried to shoot a glass off her head and missed—who had also endured a childhood in exile. While his father traveled the world, searching for the mystical drug yage in South America and then living in Tangier, Billy grew up with his grandparents in Florida. He followed his father into drug addiction, writing two autobiographical novels, *Speed* and *Kentucky Ham*, before a liver transplant failed. "I've always wanted to continue beyond X point," Billy wrote in *Speed*. "That is, I've always been kind of dumb." He died in 1981, at the age of thirty-four. Jan Kerouac would die a year after I met her of liver and kidney failure.

Unlike the Kerouac legacy, the estate of the Beat poet Bob Kaufman is not exactly a money machine. "We get a check for around $200 a year in royalties," said Parker Kaufman, the poet's thirty-six-year-old son, named after Charlie Parker. I met Parker in San Anselmo, a sunny suburban town at the foot of the mountains outside San Francisco, where he lived in a small residential hotel—what a hard-boiled writer in a previous era would have unhesitatingly called a "fleabag," with ratty carpets on the floor, bathrooms in the hallway and a laminated tree stump lodged in the dingy downstairs lobby instead of a bench.

He had a long, fine-featured face with a jagged scar running along one edge of his jaw. Tall and thin, wearing a Paula Abdul T-shirt and blue jeans, he carried a knapsack filled with schoolbooks over his slumped shoulders—he had just begun attending a small college nearby. As we shook hands, I noticed his faint grimace of reluctance. Several people, including Parker's mother, Eileen Kaufman, had warned me that he hated to talk about his father; setting up a meeting at all had been a delicate matter.

"They tell me that my dad's world-renowned and famous, but I can't see any reason to be interested in him," said Parker. "I never thought he amounted to much. Most of the times that I remember, he was totally incoherent."

Bob Kaufman was a legendary figure on the West Coast and in Europe, where he was known as the "American Rimbaud." The term "beatnik" was originally adopted to describe Kaufman after one of his spontaneous readings in the Coexistence Bagel Shop in San Francisco during the late Fifties. A street in North Beach was named after Kaufman, and his face was painted next to Baudelaire's on the mural against the wall of City Lights Books, which faces Jack Kerouac Alley. Part black, part Jewish, Kaufman was less well-known on the East Coast and in academic circles, perhaps because he had been ignored by what Lawrence Ferlinghetti, the poet and publisher of City Lights Books, has called "the East Coast Beat establishment." Other people ascribe his exclusion from the canon to racism.

It is also true that Kaufman chose to be obscure. Not long before his death in 1989, he told a scholar who sought him out in a bar around North Beach: "I don't know how you get involved with uninvolvement, but I don't want to be involved. My ambition is to be completely forgotten." Some of his poems reflect this desire, including "I Am a Camera," one of his last:

> THE POET NAILED ON
> THE HARD BONE OF THIS WORLD
> HIS SOUL DEDICATED TO SILENCE
> IS A FISH WITH FROG'S EYES,
> THE BLOOD OF A POET FLOWS
> OUT WITH HIS POEMS, BACK
> TO THE PYRAMID OF BONES
> FROM WHICH HE IS THRUST
> HIS DEATH IS A SAVING GRACE
> CREATION IS PERFECT.

Kaufman's life story suggests a certain chaotic helplessness. Invited to read at Harvard in 1960, he got waylaid instead in the underground world of New York City, where he became addicted to amphetamines, served time in prison and received shock therapy. When he returned to San Francisco in 1963, he began a ten-year vow of silence during which he wrote nothing. His silence lasted until the end of the Vietnam War.

"I don't really remember the silent treatment

thing too well," Parker said. "The main thing I remember is when I was like fourteen, we went out to the park together and it took Dad somewhere between a half hour and forty-five minutes to hit a ball out to me. He was so wasted from all of the years of self-abuse that he couldn't swing a bat."

After his initial reluctance faded, Parker was eager to talk—his San Anselmo life, it seemed, was isolated and friendless. He led me to a coffee shop decorated in imitation of a Fifties diner, its shiny tin walls adorned with photographs of Elvis. "In San Francisco, everyone identifies me as Bob Kaufman's son," he told me. "I only want to be known for myself." Most of his early childhood was spent in North Beach where, as a toddler, he appeared with his parents and Taylor Mead in Ron Rice's experimental film *The Flower Thief*. His parents split up during Kaufman's decade of speechlessness, and Parker traveled with his white hippie mother to Mexico, Morocco and Ibiza, Spain. In Ibiza, Eileen let Parker, who was then ten, go off with a wealthy English family that was traveling around the world. She was not to hear from him again for more than two years.

"I was with my second family in the mountains of Afghanistan near Kabul when war broke out and we couldn't get across the Khyber Pass," Parker recalled. "We were trapped in this house, under two hundred feet of snow. We had to tunnel out to buy vegetables or food; we had no heat. If we were out in the streets after 5:00 p.m., starving attack dogs would chase us. This situation lasted for one and a half years."

In North Beach in the early Seventies—before Parker and his second family were rescued by a scouting party—Eileen was reunited with her husband. When Kaufman found out that Parker was missing, he broke his vow of silence only once, to say: "You lost our son." After Parker returned home, his parents were remarried in a

ceremony on Mount Tamalpais, in California. But Parker found it impossible to relate to his father.

"It's frustrating when everyone's telling you, 'How dare you talk back to your dad? He's a genius,'" Parker said. "Meanwhile, it's okay for him to sleep on the sofa all day, drinking beer and smoking four packs of cigarettes."

Parker opened up a leather portfolio of his modeling and acting photographs, most of them at least a decade old. He had appeared in a few movies, including *The Right Stuff*, and in some television shows, including *Midnight Caller*, and was working on his acting career—"it was getting to the point where I was beginning to get paid"—when he was beat up and knifed at a club where he was working.

"Sometimes I just think I have bad karma," he said. He told me that he and his mother were currently destitute. "I don't know where my next meal is coming from. It's *that* bad." His elderly mother rode the bus to see him every few days, wearing a bright blue cape and bringing him lunch meat and bread. He was out of cigarettes, and I guiltily got him a couple of packs of Marlboros at a convenience store.

"Right now, I'm like this close to ending it all," he said between bites of a cheeseburger I bought him. "I was walking across the Golden Gate Bridge and I looked over and thought how easy it would be just to leap over the ledge." He sighed. "I am trying to come to terms with the possibility that I won't do anything spectacular with my life. My main goal at this point is just to be able to provide for my family someday. I want to have what we never had."

Although he never published his own creative writing, Lucien Carr was an important and original member of the Beats. He rolled the young Kerouac home in a beer barrel one drunken night, and introduced Kerouac and

Ginsberg to William Burroughs. In an incident that is part of the peculiarly violent prehistory of the Beat movement, Carr stabbed David Kammerer to death in Riverside Park in New York in 1944. An older man who had fallen obsessively in love with Carr as his Boy Scout master in Missouri, Kammerer had pursued Carr to Columbia, even taking a job as a janitor at the university to be near him. Carr was found guilty of manslaughter and was sent to a state reformatory in Elmira, New York, for two years before he was pardoned by the governor. (He later became an assistant managing editor of United Press International, and is now retired.) Two of Carr's sons are Caleb Carr, the best-selling author of *The Alienist* and *Angel of Darkness*, and Simon Carr, an abstract painter.

I visited Simon Carr in his Lower East Side studio, crowded with abstract paintings of swirls rendered with a Cézanne-like palette. Slender and handsome, with brown hair going gray, Simon wore round gold-framed intellectual-style glasses, and his eyes looked gentle behind the lenses. He showed me a catalogue from his last SoHo exhibition, "Chromaticism and Joy."

Simon credited his father with giving him and his siblings "the sense that you were definitely going to do something—that you had to express it to say it. My dad was a great talker—he and his friends would talk all night." But he said he gravitated to fine art because "it's the opposite of talking: The bottom line of great painting is silence."

Simon's wife Cristina worked as a conservator at the Metropolitan Museum of Art; they had three children in private schools in the city. He made a living teaching at various colleges and art schools around New York; he was also running a special studio class for unwed mothers at Manhattan Community College. "I associate the Beats with the more difficult times we had as a family," he said. "There was a lot of wild drinking, a lot of

people disappearing and then coming back. It was a difficult time for a ten-year-old trying to hold his world together. You might have a wild time one night and then wake up the next morning and you don't know what to eat for breakfast because there's no food around and everyone's asleep."

His brother Caleb agreed: "What's extremely romantic for adults may be disruptive and frightening for children," he said when I reached him by phone. "The Beats were so concerned with breaking molds and creating new lifestyles that they threw the baby out with the bathwater—they threw out the social framework needed to maintain a family. If any element got lost in the Beat equation, it was the idea of children."

Caleb's novel *The Alienist* was about as un-Beat a book as it is possible to imagine—as clammy as the Beats were heated—and I wondered if this was intentional. I saw personal messages in lines like this: "He probably had a troubled relationship with one or both parents early on, and eventually grew to despise everything about them—including their heritage."

I think the Beats were extremely dysfunctional people who basically had no business raising children," said Christina Mitchell, the daughter of John Mitchell—a Beat entrepreneur who started many of the original coffeehouses in Greenwich Village, including the Fat Black Pussy Cat and the Figaro. Christina was also the daughter of Alene Lee. Part black, part Cherokee Indian, Lee appeared in Kerouac's novel *The Subterraneans* as Mardou Fox, the gorgeous dark-skinned woman that Leo Percepied loved and lost and mourned for: "No girl had ever moved me with a story of spiritual suffering and so beautifully her soul showing out radiant as an angel wandering in hell." Lee was the only woman and the only black person included in an early essay by Kerouac, defining the Beat movement by the spiritual epiphanies that the group experienced: "A.L.'s vision of everything as mysterious electricity."

During the years Christina was growing up, she and her mother lived with Lucien Carr. Her mother's relationship with Carr, Christina recalled in a voice filled with incantatory rage, was "ten years of fighting, screaming, hitting, going to the police station in the middle of the night, going to Bellevue, wandering the streets, watching Mom and Lucien beat each other to a pulp." Their narcissism was all-consuming, she thinks now. "I was basically a nonperson to them. I don't think they knew I was there."

She said she never read *The Subterraneans* or any of the other manifestoes of the group. The only Beat she really respected was Allen Ginsberg. "Most of the Beat people disappeared from our lives, but when my mother died, Allen was by her bedside. He was one of the few people to value a human being beyond their fame or status."

Christina stumbled out of her adolescence—"I was either shy or catatonic"—and joined the Reverend Sun Myung Moon's Unification Church. "I spaced out for five years. I entered the group because I wanted the stability of a family— what they talked about—one happy world. The whole time I was with them my mother never told me to come back." She finally left the Moonies and resurfaced in Denver, where she attended a community college and began to rebuild her life.

When I spoke to her, Christina was thirty-seven, living in Upstate New York and majoring in English literature. As a reaction to the horror that she feels was her own childhood, she admitted to being perhaps overly protective of her six-year-old son and infant daughter: "I am compulsive with my kids. I feel that it is a really shitty world and I want to keep the shit off of them." She accompanied her son to the first day of his first-grade class, despite the teacher's objections. "I hope my compulsion to protect them won't destroy them."

Despite her anger at her mother, Christina believed that Lee was an extraordinary person. "She went out with all of them, didn't she? Kerouac, Corso, Lucien. But she never capitalized on her involvement with the beatniks. She had no interest in having her fifteen minutes of fame. My mother was a woman who could not be typecast, stereotyped or dismissed. I think they were all a little bit in awe of her."

I see that generation as kind of like a brilliant child," said Tara Marlowe, the twenty-seven-year-old daughter of the anarchist Beat poet Diane di Prima. "They did whatever they wanted."

Di Prima, a ferocious individualist, was the mother of five children by four different men. She reared her brood in San Francisco's rough Fillmore district. "We got chased a lot," Tara recalled the day I met her in the East Village, where our mothers had once lived. Tara's father, Alan Marlowe, was a former male model who spent his last years at the Rocky Mountain Buddhist Center. "Dad thought women were for breeding and men were for fucking." Tara didn't visit him when he was dying. "I don't regret that decision," she said. "A dying asshole is still an asshole."

Tara was short and stocky—she resembled her mother except for her long, polished fingernails and the silver chain around her neck. Frank and eloquent about her past, she said she grew up "like a kid in a potato patch. I've never met anyone poorer than we were. When I was a kid, my mother once told us that she was going on strike —she wasn't going to be the mother and cook for us anymore. She's still on strike."

"What did that mean to you?"

"It meant that no one ever taught me table

manners," she said, "or how to dress or that I should clean myself, so I walked around like a filthy ragamuffin with matted hair." At thirteen, Tara left home and moved to Mendocino, where she met a seventeen-year-old coke-dealer boyfriend. "I got involved in sexual relationships that to me weren't sexual. I was basically in a rage most of the time. Now I'm sort of a born-again virgin." She lived as an "emancipated minor" in a converted chicken coop near the alternative school she was attending. Eventually, she returned home. "At our house, the drug dealers were the good guys," she recalled. "They brought Christmas presents — the whole Robin Hood thing. The poets were these icky guys with foam at the side of their mouths."

In college, Marlowe wrote poems and even published her own poetry magazine, *Dissociated Press*. She said as an adult she drinks only occasionally, noting that when she does drink, "there's not enough alcohol in the world to make me feel better." She lived in the Williamsburg section of Brooklyn, working as a freelance graphic artist. "For the first time, I'm beginning to enjoy my life," she said. "I still feel like some kind of space alien, a complete outsider from middle-class culture. It sometimes seems as if the world is this big office party and I'm the uninvited guest."

Some of my earliest memories are of visiting Hettie Jones, my mother's best friend from her blackstocking days, and her daughters, Kellie and Lisa, on the Bowery. When I was a child, Hettie's creaky, crooked and labyrinthine apartment seemed almost organic to me, as if it had grown outward from her vibrant personality to fill the space around her. I faintly recall crowded holiday parties with a cheerful mix of poets, painters and jazz musicians drinking and laughing, jammed up against each other in the narrow hallways. Growing up, I regretted that my mother put that bohemian world behind us,

moving away from downtown to the more bourgeois boundaries of the Upper West Side.

"I don't know much about the Beat period," said Lisa Jones, the daughter of Hettie and the poet LeRoi Jones. "I never read the books—the writers of the Harlem Renaissance had a much greater influence on me. I guess I was trying to divorce myself from that history, from my parents' story."

A *Village Voice* columnist, Lisa had published a book of essays called *Bulletproof Diva*. She had also worked with Spike Lee and written movie and television scripts. Her older sister, Kellie, had become a curator and art historian. Lisa's father left the family early in her childhood to join the Black Nationalist movement, changing his name to Amiri Baraka. "People like my mom were already talking about a different idea of family back then," Lisa said. "We belonged to a tight community. I hate the idea that growing up with one parent automatically means you have to be dysfunctional. Though my parents weren't together, we spent time with both of them and were loved and nurtured by both of them. My grandparents were always there and they were a strong force.

"As a kid, it never struck me that we were that bohemian," Lisa said emphatically. "We had chores and curfews—although my mom might disagree. I always referred to myself as a B. A. P.— a Bohemian American Princess."

Some people found in the Beat quest for personal freedom not an excuse for nihilism or bad behavior, but a way to develop new models of commitment. For instance, the Beat poet Michael McClure's daughter, Jane McClure, followed the thread of her father's interest in naturalism to study molecular biology and eventually became a doctor. Of her life on Haight-Ashbury she recalled "nothing was scary —everything was interesting." Her father's friendships with Jim Morrison and the Hell's Angels caused no injury and seemed to leave no particular impression.

Allen Ginsberg's life demonstrated his Buddhist-Beat ethos of compassion and responsibility. Although he never had his own kids, he continued to help members of his huge community as well as their children. Many of the children I spoke to had memories of Allen's generosity. At various times, he bailed Burroughs's son, Billy, out of jail, let Jan Kerouac live at his house in Boulder, and put up Cassady's son Curtis Hansen at his apartment in New York. Treating the Beats as an extended family, Allen nursed his friends back to health when they were sick, put them up when they ran out of money, supported their work and used his influence to help whenever possible. His empathetic behavior offers a contrast to the self-centered concerns of most artists today.

The children of Neal Cassady, the Beat Generation's most famous icon of perpetual adolescence and sexual craving, grew up as well. Cassady and his "wild yea-saying over burst of American joy" inspired some of Kerouac's and Ginsberg's best work in the Fifties. A decade later, he led the Merry Pranksters psychedelic charge across the continent. The son of a Denver wino, Cassady wasn't much of a writer, but he played the role of Socrates to the counterculture, inspiring others by his manic example.

I met John Allen Cassady, the son of Neal and Carolyn Cassady, for several pints of beer at a bar in the North Beach section of San Francisco. John Allen told me that he found *On the Road* dull going. "A lot of that Beat stuff is so obtuse," he said. He was an expansive man with a white beard and bright blue eyes, friendly and talkative. "My friends used to call me the albino wino." He was living in San Jose, California, working for a computer company that manufactured optical scanners; he answered customers' queries about the product. Years before, he had made dulcimers and sold them at country fairs; he was also something of a Deadhead.

"Neal had such a capacity for everything," John Allen said. "I think he was a very evolved soul. I've inherited his wheel karma. Dad had eighteen cars in the back of our yard; I've got about six in mine. We must have been charioteers in ancient Rome." As John Allen spoke, I sensed that he had told some of his stories many times in other pubs, for other occasions, and I began to suspect that sadness lurked beneath his surface gregariousness.

John Allen said that his father wrote other books besides *The First Third*, an early childhood memoir published by City Lights. He added: "There was a *Second Third* and a *Third Third*, Neal told me. He wrote them on reams and reams of yellow notebook paper but, unfortunately, he had all of the papers in the backseat of this old jalopy, which he left at Ken Kesey's place. He went away for a couple of weeks, and when he came back he found that some punk kids had stolen the car. That was it—his whole life's work gone. He was really upset about that."

John Allen also told me that Billy Burroughs, the son of William, had lived with him in Santa Cruz, California, for three months in 1976, after he received a liver transplant. "That guy was hell-bent on self-destruction. His attitude was, 'Hey, I got a new one to burn.' Toward the end, he started getting pretty unintelligible." John Allen was glad when Billy moved on—he had already witnessed his own father's unraveling a decade earlier.

"By the Sixties, Dad was so burned out, so bitter," John Allen said. "He told me once that he felt like a dancing bear, that he was just performing. He was wired all the time, talking nonstop. I remember once, after a party, about 2:00 a.m., he went in the bathroom, turned on the shower and just started screaming and didn't stop. I was about fifteen then and I knew he was in deep trouble, that he was really a tortured soul. He died not too long after that."

Maybe you can explain what all the fuss was about," said Curtis Hansen, John Allen's half-brother and Neal Cassady's other son. Curtis, forty-five when I met him, never really knew his father. Curtis's mother, Diana Hansen, was a Barnard graduate who fell in love with Cassady while working at an advertising agency in the late Forties; she ended up with a walk-on in *On the Road.* "What did those guys do that was so amazing?"

"Um, well, I suppose they offered some kind of antidote to the repression of the Cold War period," I said, hesitating at the English-lit-class banality of the phrases. "They encouraged people to find new ways of living, to rediscover America."

Curtis paused thoughtfully. "Cassady had a great public-relations department, I guess," he said, "always surrounding himself with all those phenomenal writers and so on."

A former disc jockey, Curtis was programming director for WICC-AM, a radio station in Bridgeport, Connecticut, and for WEBE-FM in Fairfield County. We drove in his Japanese compact through the city's rainy, eerily empty streets to the radio station's impersonal glass office tower. Solidly good-looking in a jungle-print tie and tan pants—he looked like a somewhat stockier version of Cassady—Hansen gave off a strong positive vibe that suggested a disposition inherited from his father. The only thing of Neal's that he owned was a sheaf of yellowing handwritten letters that Cassady wrote to Diana Hansen in the early Fifties, when he was trying to convince her to move to one town away from his wife, Carolyn, so he could continue the sexual triangulation that was one of his life's driving obsessions.

"The letters have some pretty wild stuff in them," Curtis said. "He talks about cunt hair and

all the sex they're going to have when they get together. You can tell they had a real good sexual relationship."

"What did your mom tell you about Cassady?" I asked.

"Oh, she said that he was a jailbird—that I should stay away from him. I was real embarrassed when he went to prison in the late Fifties—that's why we changed my name to Hansen."

"What did you think of *On the Road?*"

"That book they wrote together?" he said. "I thought it was *boring*," he says. "I never really understood what that whole shtick was about."

Yet Hansen was inspired by the father he never knew and the book he didn't care for to go on the road himself, driving across country in 1969, after he was "invited to leave" college on suspicion of selling mescaline and for having a girl in his room. "That trip across the country is one of the things I'm proudest of in my life," he said. "Cassady had just died, I got laid for the first time, got high and took off. It was definitely a symbolic journey."

"I imagine that it must have been difficult to be Cassady's son," I offered.

"Well, I used to feel I had a lot to live up to," he said in his effusive, former-DJ voice. "I wish my dad had been around so I could have asked him about girls. I used to have a lot of trouble in that area."

In a few weeks, he and his wife, a receptionist at his office, were due to visit Salt Lake City for a creative visualization workshop. "This is definitely the dawning of the Age of Aquarius," he said. "I'm totally in favor of—what do they call it? —'popular spirituality.' Just because it's popular doesn't mean it's wrong."

At his office, Hansen excitedly showed me the computer that creates each day's playlist—it was all based on market research, studying the demographic reaction to song "burnout" and likability among baby-boomer women. "We don't want to upset our audience or they'll turn the dial," he explained, gesturing with his hands as he speaks. "We try to use only good words on the air, like 'free' and 'special offer.'"

We walked past the darkened soundstages, where insectile-looking headgear and metal protuberances dangled from the ceiling. Technicians hurried past, many of them wearing 1960s-style beards and ponytails. "Ronald Reagan once sat here," Hansen said, pointing at a bare wooden table. "There used to be a plaque but I guess it fell off."

Listening to the drone of a Michael Bolton song in Hansen's office, where windows overlooked the gray panorama of Bridgeport, I thought about how radio once encouraged the outsider expression of someone like Alan Freed, who promoted rock & roll in its early days. In the Forties and Fifties, Symphony Sid's shows of jazz and bebop had inspired Kerouac and Cassady on their manic jaunts across the continent.

"Does it bother you that radio has become so corporate?" I asked Hansen.

"No, that's what's so great about our time," he said. "What I think has happened is that the counterculture and the mainstream have merged." He waved his hands excitedly in the air as he continued. "You don't have to listen anymore to the songs you don't like—you only listen to the songs that the *majority* of the people like. You see what I mean? The mainstream has become the new frontier." From his desk, he turned up the volume on the live feed from the soundstage down the hall, and the voice of Michael Bolton grew louder and louder until it momentarily seemed to envelop us.

Talkin' 'Bout Our Generations

BY JOYCE JOHNSON AND DANIEL PINCHBECK

Editor's note: How do a mother and son, both active in New York's Downtown literary scenes—the former in the Fifties and the latter in the Nineties—take stock of the Beats' influence on writing and culture? Here, Joyce Johnson and Daniel Pinchbeck compare notes.

Daniel Pinchbeck: What do you think makes the Beats still relevant today?

Joyce Johnson: I think we're in a period that's psychically similar to the 1950s. There's a lot of money around, there's a kind of cultural blandness, there's a conservatism in terms of morals. Also, there's a sense that people's lives are on set tracks, that the future isn't a wide-open possibility. People are still attracted to the Beats because they hold out the promise or illusion of freedom.

DP: When you say "illusion," do you mean that what the Beats stood for was counterfeit in any way?

JJ: In *On the Road,* not even Dean Moriarty or Sal Paradise find absolute freedom; it's their *pursuit* of it that we identify with. There are certain illusions we need—they're energizing, change-bringing forces. For Kerouac, the road was always more hopeful than the destination.

We have to separate what was authentic about the Beat movement from the superficial imitations of the Beat lifestyle. Almost as soon as the word *beatnik* was coined, you could see *Beat* losing its original meaning. I remember Greenwich Village suddenly becoming flooded with kids in beatnik outfits shortly after the publication of *On the Road*. You couldn't get down MacDougal Street on a Saturday night. There was even a do-it-yourself beatnik kit manufactured with a beret, fake goatee and a pair of shades. I found one recently at a flea market.

DP: Do you think that there could be a scene as concentrated and vibrant as the Beat scene today?

JJ: It can't be created by looking backward. The Beats weren't trying to imitate the rebellion of the Lost Generation. Their reaction against the repressive atmosphere of the postwar years went hand in hand with their deliberate break with literary tradition. When you have this extraordinary fusion of content and form, you have the makings of a powerful artistic and cultural movement.

DP: You say this is a conservative time, yet in many of the areas that the Beats helped to break open, the society remains broken open. I'm thinking about sexuality, drugs, even the attitudes toward "multiculturalism." In these areas it seems the Beats helped create a permanent shift in consciousness.

JJ: That's true, but we're certainly experiencing a backlash now. Probably one reason for this is that the drug culture that blossomed in the Sixties has been so destructive.

DP: Have you run into much Beat-influenced writing in the fiction workshops you've taught?

JJ: I have seen some road novels, and of course the Beats opened up previously forbidden subject matter for all writers. It could be said that Kerouac and Ginsberg initiated the confessional memoir. As for spontaneous prose, some inexperienced writers have been seriously misled by that idea. They forget that Kerouac's breakthrough in voice came after he had been writing for years; he also had an extraordinary memory that he could tap into, which made his high-velocity writing possible.

DP: You've never been attracted to Beat-influenced work yourself, to the New York Downtown fiction scene of Kathy Acker, for instance.

JJ: My biggest influence was the very un-Beat Henry James because of the way he communicated the subtleties of relationships and because of his empathy for women and his fascination with sexual repression. I was, however, powerfully attracted to Allen's voice and Jack's voice and dazzled by their fearlessness and energy. When I wrote my memoir of the 1950s, *Minor Characters,* I think I attempted to evoke the voice of that period. I went back and reread a lot of the original sources, and the style of the Beats had a delayed effect on me that was beneficial.

DP: As I get older, what I admire about the Beats has changed considerably. I now appreciate their experiential approach, and their openness toward life and spirituality, more than their experimentalism and sometimes adolescent posturing. They roamed far and wide, worked on ships and railroads. The lifestyle of most white middle-class writers today seems a little embalmed by comparison, and that lack of experience is reflected in their fiction.

I was always attracted to the Beat model of artistic community, but I now think that such a community may be impossible to create in this climate. The pressures on life in New York, for example, are too intense, the need to make so much money just to stay in place kind of kills the experimental spirit.

JJ: In the Beat period, it was much easier to get along on very little—you could pay a very low rent and still live with some grace. In the artistic community there wasn't much conspicuous consumption. A loft was just a working space with a bed in one corner and a coal stove to keep the place warm. Dinner parties were organized around big pots of spaghetti. A glass of beer in the

Five Spot was twenty-five cents, and you could nurse it along and hear Coltrane or Thelonious Monk. If you needed clothes, you went to the Salvation Army or thrift shops.

DP: Is that where you shopped?

JJ: Sometimes. Also, Hettie Jones and I learned to sew. We made some pretty snazzy shift dresses.

DP: A few years before his death, Harold Brodkey wrote that people engaged in the literary world today are always trapped in an act of transvestitism, dressing up in the clothes of dead writers or literary figures of the past. I edit a literary magazine, *Open City,* and the venture seems slightly nostalgic. It is not in tune with the "make it now!" self-promotional mentality of the present.

JJ: Now *you're* in danger of idealizing the past. Kerouac certainly had the desire to "make it now" when he was in his twenties. In fact, he was terribly jealous of the success of his friend John Clellon Holmes when *Go* came out before Jack could deal with the same material. His seven obscure, impoverished years between the publication of *The Town and the City* and *On the Road* broke his spirit and embittered him permanently. Ginsberg was far more resilient, and his intuitive understanding of how to promote himself and the other unpublished writers in his circle ultimately helped bring the Beats to public attention.

DP: But now the cultural situation is even more confusing and complex.

JJ: In the 1950s there was a sense that literature and writing had a burning importance—that you could write a book or paint a painting and change the world. That kind of faith seems to be lacking now. Literature has been pushed toward the sidelines of the culture. There isn't that sense of centrality or permanence to the written word —everything seems more disposable.

DP: I actually think part of the problem is the expanded population and the increased scale of everything. In the 1960s there were perhaps a hundred galleries in New York, and just a few important ones. Now there are a thousand, featuring every kind of work, and it is impossible to determine which are important. Even though the number of major publishing houses keeps shrinking, there are more books being published than ever before.

JJ: How important are the Beats to writers of your generation?

DP: A lot of my closest writer friends have very little interest in them. The influence of the Beats filtered through someone like Thomas Pynchon seems to have a wider effect. In a sense, the Beat influence is simultaneously everywhere and nowhere. It has been pointed out to me that even the confessional style of TV talk shows or Internet discussions owes a debt to the Beats. It seems to me—perhaps I'm wrong—that since the 1950s literature has become increasingly a rarefied pursuit reserved for the upper-middle and affluent classes in America. Many fiction writers today don't have the perspective to appreciate or understand why the Beats attempted to incorporate

outsider voices as well as working-class culture in their writings.

JJ: The French-Canadian, white working-class culture that Jack came from had a great deal of vitality and color. Literature was still venerated, and a gifted kid like Jack could find his way to it, even in a factory town like Lowell. Now everything is permeated and leveled out by the mass media.

When I went to Russia ten years ago, I was surprised by how literate people were. Even a park attendant in Novgorod knew Akhmatova's work. Now that our popular culture is infiltrating Russia, I doubt you'd find a guy like that reading her poetry.

DP: Well, that may be true. But I do think it is necessary to resist nostalgia to a certain extent. The cultural situation changes constantly, and suddenly out of what seems like a total void who knows if a surprising Renaissance won't bloom? As Kerouac said in one of my favorite quotes of his, "Look for diamonds in the sidewalk."

The Recorded Legacy
of the Beats

BY JAMES AUSTIN

M Y FASCINATION WITH JACK Kerouac and the Beat Generation actually began in the late 1950s. A pop culture phenomenon simply known as "the beatniks" had infiltrated such popular media as television, print and audio recordings. At first I thought it was something manufactured by Hollywood as a form of entertainment, like cowboys, hot rods and Howdy Doody. (Hey, I was nine years old. What did I know? Anything on television other than a test pattern or soap operas was good enough for me.) In reality there were millions of young, impressionable minds soaking up whatever was being filtered through TV and radio. And as we got older, most of us found Kerouac and Company. By the time we set foot on a college campus, *On the Road* was a cultural rite of passage. As we matured, we understood how pop-culture America and Madison Avenue homogenizes it all and spits it back out in movies and the like.

By 1987, when I began working at Rhino Records, a fairly established independent label that specialized in Fifties and Sixties pop and rock & roll reissues, I had read nearly all of Jack Kerouac's books, and his elusive recordings had become my passion. At this time, recordings by Kerouac and Ginsberg were long out of print, and there were no audio compilations of the Beats. It nagged at me that I couldn't purchase Kerouac's legendary recordings on Hanover and Verve; on the collector's market these highly prized recordings fetched between $100 and $200, depending on the condition. All I had were third-generation cassettes.

So in 1990 I decided to approach my company with the idea of doing a Kerouac box set. By then, Dylan's *Biograph* and Clapton's *Crossroads* had been released, both of which had garnered significant sales and publicity, while establishing a new format: a twelve-by-twelve-inch box including a lavish booklet containing liner notes, discography, sessionography and rare photos. No one had done anything like this in the realm of spoken word, however. Here was the opportunity to create a sumptuous presentation that made a larger statement than any single-CD package could accomplish. At first, the idea was viewed as too extravagant for a spoken-word project. I insisted that a "best of," eighteen-track collection was not ambitious enough. Well, I finally got my way, and a three-CD Kerouac box set was in the works.

The recordings for *The Jack Kerouac Collection* featured Jack in a relaxed setting reading solo, accompanied by pianist Steve Allen and backed by saxophonists Al Cohn and Zoot Sims. For jazz and poetry fans, the albums *Poetry for the Beat Generation* (1959), *Blues and Haikus* (1959) and *Readings on the Beat Generation* (recorded in 1959, released in 1960) were real breakthroughs. Jack understood jazz and how to combine his voice with music, which positively influenced his recitation. He didn't read his compositions—he *performed* them. His voice became the equivalent of Charlie Parker's alto saxophone or Dizzy Gillespie's trumpet. The phrasing and the understated emotive quality were completely seductive and sounded virtually effortless. Despite his reputation as an alcoholic, he seemed in control—never boozy or incoherent. Jack had chops, like a master on his instrument. His combination of poetry and jazz spawned imitators, but also inspired his peers; Lenny Bruce later performed "Psychopathia Sexualis" to parody the poetry and jazz phenomena as presented on television shows and in the likes of *Mad* magazine in the late Fifties.

In the beginning, the only raw material with which to compile the Kerouac box set were two cassettes. I wanted the anthology to have exceptional sound quality, but the existence of master tapes for *The Jack Kerouac Collection* was questionable. When I made inquiries about the original tapes, all I heard was, "Don't count on it." If tapes existed, they would be stored at Abbey Road Stu-

dios in England. Coincidentally, Rhino had two independent tape archivists researching those very vaults. Every week I made calls to see if the tapes had been found, but it was always: "Not yet." As deadlines approached for the project, it became evident that I would soon need to give up on master-tape recordings and concentrate on find-

ing LPs in good condition—not an easy task. At one point I got so discouraged that I walked down the street, a block from the offices at Rhino, to St. Anne's Church in Santa Monica. Well, I thought, if Catholicism was good enough for Jack, it is good enough for me. Since then, I've coined the term "Crisis Catholicism"—when you really want anything you're willing to pray for, the prayer always starts with "Oh please, God." In this case it was the elusive master recordings that I was after. The very next day, I received a call from Bob Hyde, the archivist working in England. To my astonishment, he had found tapes for one of the albums, complete with two outtakes and a studio conversation. These became the highlight of our box set.

The Jack Kerouac Collection was released in 1990 to favorable reviews, excellent sales and my (and Rhino's) first Grammy Nomination for Best Historical Package. The collection also brought me into contact with Jan Kerouac, William Burroughs, Allen Ginsberg and Jerry Garcia. I located Jan with the help of Beat historian and writer Stephen Ronan, and she and I became quite close. Not only did she pen the introduction to the box, but she also went on our publicity junket to New York to speak with television and radio press. Her devotion to her father was very touching, and the collection seemed to rejuvenate her. A new phase had begun in her life, and we spent hours going back and forth to New York together, talking about her dad and the cast of characters making up what we know as the Beat Generation. There were times while producing the project that I felt as if Jack was nearby —a sort of reissue guardian angel. Jan and I remained friends until her tragic and untimely death in 1996. I miss her very much.

Jack Kerouac listening to himself
on the radio, 1959
JOHN COHEN

Due to the success of Jack's spoken-word recordings, Rhino gave me the go-ahead to produce a three-CD set of various Beat-related recordings spanning the years 1959 to 1973. I conspired with Stephen Ronan and audio archivist Gordon Skene to include everything from Jack and company to Ken Nordine, Lord Buckley and Dizzy Gillespie to Tom Waits and Rod McKuen. We wanted to reflect the whole gamut of the movement, from its roots in 1940s bop-era jazz to the kooky, exaggerated beatnik caricatures invented by the media. I wanted this eclectic collection to capture that whole era of disengagement and experimentation with both reverence and humor.

The pop-culture image of the beatniks, of course, bore little resemblance to the literary Beat movement. But it was pop culture's twisted exaggeration that first inspired my own personal foray into the Beat Generation, eventually leading me—and I'm sure countless others—to the real thing. Our kitschy tour guide was a regular character on the TV sitcom *The Many Loves of Dobie Gillis*, Maynard G. Krebs, who sported a goatee and threadbare sweatshirt and avoided the hardworking ("work!?") ethos of blue-collar America in favor of part-time scholastic pursuits and full-time "goofing off." Now, for all to view on national television, he came to represent the Beat movement and the literary Beat Generation suffered a slap by this.

Hollywood also capitalized on the Beats. Mostly B movies became the next means of cultural exploitation, including such titles as *The Beat Generation*, *Greenwich Village Story* and ultra-campy *The Rebel Set*, with the requisite, tantalizing movie poster that screamed: "Those Beatniks! Living in hobo love. Hunting for strange kicks! Dealing in startling crime!" Though *On the Road* has yet to make it to the screen, a 1960 sanitized version of *The Subterraneans* starred George Peppard and French actress Leslie Caron as Mardou Fox.

Also cashing in on this new craze were truly inspired Beat barons like Fred McDarrah, a *Village Voice* photographer who got work for his friends with his Rent-a-Beatnik party "entertainment" service in 1959. Fred McDarrah and buddies like black street-poet Ted Joans were among the first hipsters to straddle the line, one foot in the Greenwich Village literary world, the other in Madison Avenue satire.

We tried to capture all this with *The Beat Generation* box set, since even the clichéd showbiz versions can tell us something about our culture. Generally the set was well received, but there were those who misunderstood the collection. Some like Allen Ginsberg thought the kitsch aspect destabilized the legitimate Beat content. Allen feared that someone listening to John Drew Barrymore reciting "Christopher Columbus Digs the Jive" would not be able to distinguish that from, say, Allen himself, William Burroughs and the other authentic Beats. My impulse was that Jack Kerouac didn't take the Beat identification too seriously by the time the neophyte beatniks arrived. He appreciated the humor in fads, trends and pop culture in America, and we know he dug Elvis, James Dean and TV.

Still, Allen was interested in our creating a box set of his own recordings, which got under way prior to the release of *The Beat Generation* box. Allen had graciously written a beautiful tribute to Jack for the Kerouac collection. We soon became friends and continued to discuss the idea of a Ginsberg box set, but for this to come to fruition, it meant that Allen had to acquire the rights to his recordings, many of which were owned by major record labels. With the indomitable spirit and expertise of his archivist Bob Rosenthal, the task of assembling this unique collection began. We needed a coproducer to work with Allen in culling more than forty years' worth of his recordings, and Hal Willner was the perfect choice. Allen had tremendous respect for Hal, who had produced his 1989 album *The Lion for Real*, in addition to numerous other jazz and spoken-word projects for various artists. Hal, it turned out, had often dreamed of producing just such a project. His enthusiasm for Kerouac and the Beat Generation helped him to face the daunting task of sifting through literally hundreds of hours of Allen's spoken-word in every format you could imagine. Willner's devotion not just to the project but to Allen himself was inspiring and touching. I don't believe there could have been anyone as patient, diplomatic and persistent —all requirements for working with Ginsberg— as was Hal. In spite of his heavy agenda working as music consultant for *Saturday Night Live* and on Robert Altman's film *Short Cuts*, Hal's passion prevailed, and the four-CD set *Holy Soul Jelly Roll: Poems and Songs 1949–1993* was released in 1994.

At a party celebrating the release, Allen was speaking with a few admirers when I turned to ask him a question. He excused himself from the group saying, "I need to speak with my boss." Trust me, except for his God, Allen never had a boss. He had charm and warmth to balance his sometimes irascible nature. And his role in American culture and literature connecting the Beat Generation to the hippie movement through to current times is nothing short of astounding. Do the words *no compromise* mean anything to you?

They certainly did to Allen. Carrying the Beat torch with strength and conviction, he compelled you into his world, sharing his feelings about his family, his religion and his loves with honesty and the "supernatural brilliance of the soul." Undaunted by the changing political climate over the five decades of his career, Allen stood by his beliefs. Those moments his light shone brightest for me was when he read his poetry. Then he became larger than life. You might not have always agreed with what he said, but you had to admire his passion.

There's no doubt about it; Beat culture helped create the history that came after it. To say that we owe a debt of wisdom and joy to the antimaterialist, nonconformist Beats (or the goofy but charming beatniks) is an understatement. Trends and fads, however, are cyclical. If, these days, you don't see anyone with a goatee or hear the words *cool*, *dig* or *what a trip*, it just means that the beatific subculture of America has returned underground for a while. Maybe it will resurface in a movie, in a Broadway play or on the back of a cereal box. But it will be back, just you wait and see.

Oh those Beatniks, living in bohemian love pads and hunting for strange kicks ... count me in!

In the House
of Language

BY LEE RANALDO

Editor's note: *This review of the box set 'The Jack Kerouac Collection' originally ran in the October 1990 issue of 'Forced Exposure.'*

[letter excerpt] I love telephone poles all strung together and filing off into the distance, and giant steel power-line towers standing like aliens in ochre fields. All the roads rushing, rushing, the burnt fields, lakes, farm buildings, fabulous cities. I like to write in the car because the process is so like the action—a stream of images unraveling like a ribbon (like a film).

I have to show you the really handsome circa 1950 photos of him, so dashing as he stood poised to be taken seriously as an author, at last, suit and tie, hair slicked, beautiful innocent face. The thing I value in his writing is that he could really SEE, even in his later cloudy state, his condition and situation (c.f. Big Sur, Vanity), retaining w. a cinematic clarity the essence of each phase of his life, the places and people and feelings.

He could see the reasons to strive, to try; yet also the reasons why none of it matters, "… and anyway I wrote the book because we're all gonna die …" The futility of achievement, the sad fact that no matter how much one accomplishes, it's not going to save us. He had believed, early on, as we all did, that heroic deeds and great words/thoughts COULD save us, and set us free. There he was, life in uproar, his brother, father, best friend dead, loved ones distant, his dreams, even when fulfilled, not adding up to salvation. All his youth gone, his youthful desires accomplished somewhat and well done too and yet, what of it?

I half-heartedly attempted a Carver article last year, just for myself, and wrote all this stuff, but ultimately I realized that he meant so much to me that it was beyond the logic of explanations, and exposition, it was completely emotional, intuitive, non-conveyable. So I put all those writings in a file and left them. I have tapes of him reading, which I really want you to hear …

Jack Kerouac rambling by Tompkins Square Park, New York City, 1953

ALLEN GINSBERG

So now we have the tapes of Jack's voice, available to any who might want them. I can give up my search for those beat-up, old, impossible-to-find-and-then-$150-when-you-do Hanover and Verve releases. His voice as familiar as my friend Thom's at this point, and that means pretty close. I'm wondering, now: Who wants to listen? Are there still people willing to take this stuff to heart? Poets? Idea-visionaries? People with backgrounds and hometowns and new lives, mothers, fathers, lovers and their attendant sadnesses, troubles, friends, broken-down old cars, riotous insane good times, the love of maps, the Madonna Inn, full suitcases, Las Vegas, the big questions, confusion, longing, desire, goofing, silliness, indulgence, despair, cinemas, bedroom eyes, rowboats, bookstores?

> what about the 'jazz' comparison?
> his mother?
> his drinking
> patricide
> his bisexuality (c.f. *Memory Babe*)
> impotence
> his grave marker: HE HONORED LIFE
> his beaut. handsome face
> the sound (rolling) of his voice
> Charlie Parker
> his great wit
> his vision?

Somewhere in the pages of *Vanity of Duluoz* we find our man Jack talking about the genealogy of his surname, *Kerr* stemming from the Cornish Celtic word for "house," and *Uack* meaning "language of." Thus: *In the House of Language*. He had found for himself the most perfect life-affirmation! Beyond family beyond religion beyond the road: The word and nickel notebooks full were what Jack believed in—they constituted the true furnishings in his head-house. For better or worse he was damned to thought-dreams and the written word as memory, the printed page as history.

These three records were all recorded in 1959; there were none before or later, although Jack had long kept a tape recorder by his side, to record his drunken Sinatra imitations, sure, but also because he recognized that which he was about: language, how it sounds, how it is spoken, how it rolls off the mind's tongue. The spontaneous head-spew that appears before the mind can apply logic and reason. These pieces may be spontaneously writ and recited, but it's obvious how much preparation has come first, how much attention to rhythm, to punctuation, to tone.

Poetry for the Beat Generation: Everyone has got their own cryptic mass of buzzwords that contain their thoughts, express their feelings. When you decipher the code, you may enter into the landscape, move around inside a world-view and decide if it's someplace you'd like to linger, and explore.

I'm listening to Mike Watt's new demo tape now, and his world is *econo, flannel, pedro* and *righteous*. Nick Cave's world these days is full of bibles and preachers and emotional trials. He has adopted the imagery of rolling trains, barnyards and swamps.

Jack's was redbrick, *mad* and *gone*, all that road going, red wine and *tea* and pomes, Christianity and Buddhism. Trying to make sense out of things that one shouldn't necessarily try to make sense out of, namely, well, everything. How to understand our own lives in light of a wheatfield, the billion stars at night, TV shows, paintings, Kmarts, pop music, plutonium, eight-track tapes, a beautiful face looking straight into yrs, history, etc. How to fit into it, see yrself on the end of its line.

Jack was haunted by history, by events. Why did things happen the way they did? Have you ever asked yrself this? How did I get *HERE*?

How from football star to notorious beatnik scribe, from pure three-yr-old boy to whirl-winded misunderstood famous thirty-yr-old King of the Beats, and the blur beyond. Drunk. How are these dots connected? Jack wanted to know, to understand the futility of banging his head against the world, trying to make sense of his own life. So he spewed forth, hoping that maybe the thoughts he assembled—the specific memories and created images which he chose to signify in his work—would shed some light on these questions.

Leafing through an old *Evergreen Review*, the second issue, the San Francisco issue, I found Jack's "October in the Railroad Earth." It's also the first track on his beautiful first record, one I've heard many times and am quite familiar with. It's a wonderful piece on tape, but it's one of his stories that has always remained somewhat impenetrable to me in print—these dense wordimages (". . . how'd'ya like'ta oolyakoo with me, mon?") not always adding up. Reading those opening paragraphs again, which my ears have grown so familiar with, I realized that the words as written move somehow too slowly, the images don't come across fast enough to flash cinematic; but as Jack reads aloud it really rolls, the images knocking rhythmic tip, tup, bip, bop into one another, pushing the thing forward at a great clip. All the word-pictures falling into place. Listen to his voice: the sound of it as well as the meanings. His voice on these discs opens up the words, elucidates and sets the scene, the mindset, in which these thoughts roam.

It's only recently I'm struck by the terribly tacky lounge-piano accompaniment that Steve Allen provides here, vamping on "What Kind of Fool Am I" and "Stormy Weather." *Gheesh!* (But it doesn't matter.) Jack, end of "MacDougal Street Blues": ". . . I just wanna be sincere." And that he is, I can feel it on this one.

Blues and Haikus: My least favorite record in this collection, this one seems thrown-off, unfocused, a bit off all around despite some nice passages. The booklet claims that Al Cohn and Zoot Sims didn't even care afterwards to hear playback, but went for drinks, leaving Jack dismayed. It sort of sounds like that. There is less mood on this disk. Too spontaneous(!). This is indulgent babbling, riffing with no place to go, on the part of all the players. Too loose. Occasionally a flash of Jack's vision, a phrase or sentence rises out of the murk. This record makes little sense to me. I can't really listen to it, esp. next to the other two.

The Steve Allen Show Bonus Cut: This is what it's all about, an essential blast, encapsulated. (Seek this on video!) ". . . All the stories I wrote were true, because I believed in what I saw."

> I'm in love. What more can I say? In love with an image of crooked Slavic telephone poles, knowing I can get that across to you, of blue shower spray steaming soft skin; Cinemascope love, wide-screen, beautiful with a green face, and words writ perfectly and endlessly on long pages. A 1924 magazine beauty with gray eyes staring up from beneath the surface, drowning eternal.
>
> I'm hiding behind the screen, unwilling to look at this room. Unable to look at you and know how I feel. The room is rushing up at me, thought-dreams flashing like strobes, one after the next, no time to pull them up from the well. I'm spinning words not deeds. Blowing a hollow horn.

Readings by Jack Kerouac on the Beat Generation: Late night now, I'm thinking of so many different things, the loft is quiet, I'm flashing images as the house sleeps. Jack is talking, there's no music on this one, just his voice. I'm not listening to the stories right now, I know them by heart anyway (ev'n the never-heard ones). His voice is the music now, I hear his occasional punctuation— "Neal," "Third and Howard (S.F.)," "Colorahda,"

"I love Allen Ginsberg, let that be recorded in Heaven's unchangeable heart" (and when did you love a friend enough to proclaim it unabashedly to the world, without fear?), "Mardou" (how sad and carefully he tells of his failed love), all the rolling and dripping language, comforting, familiar as rain on a porch.

It has been pointed out how this last disc, unaccompanied, is startlingly the most musical of all. After the over-casual air of *Blues and Haikus,* this is a serious record: I can feel Jack alone in the studio ("... and in the BarOQUE periodof-theThreeStooges ..."), telling it, and he's seen it clear. Impressions, stories, emotions, everything that's important. We ride along knowing we're somewhat tangential to his need to tell it. The Three Stooges as a Twentieth-Century metaphor, in seriousness, and throwing his best friend in their midst, what could be more perfect?

The Extra Track: He gets onstage, right?, and is to address this ridiculous topic: "Is There a Beat Gen?" (a critic's idea, natch), and he stands up and says "The question is very silly because we should be wondering tonight 'Is There a World' ... there really is no world, you know, sometimes I'm walking on the ground and I see right through the ground ... there is really no world ... you'll find out ..."

Now he says this with utmost seriousness, it's his premise, his belief, and it seems to go right by everyone. It doesn't even get an uneasy laugh. That's where he's coming from, but the audience is waiting to be entertained with funny stories and drunken episodes. Missing the point. THERE IS NO WORLD, he says. There Is No World.

"And here is a poem I wrote about Harpo Marx," he says, "Harpo! I'll always love you! ..."

"This poem," he says, "I dedicate to human suffering and human salvation! You're not listening!!"

NOT LISTENING, NOT LISTENING, *STILL NOT LISTENING* . . . .

The Beat Goes On

BY GRAHAM PARKER

ONE SPRING DAY IN 1969, Dave, Mick and I handed in our notices at the Animal Virus Research Institute. Deliberately staggering our appearances in the boss's office for maximum effect, we caused the fat, baffled Northerner (after the third young evacuee had submitted his resignation) to bellow to no one in particular, "What's going on here?"

The three of us had hatched a shocking scheme to leave our comfortable homes and jobs for daring, mold-breaking lives picking tomatoes on the island of Guernsey, and watching the startled reactions of the Institute's boss and his dullard staff was the first step in our nascent adventure. Mick's uncle lived in Guernsey, the second largest land mass among the islands located in the English Channel. According to Mick, a tall burly bumpkin of a youth, honest as the day is long, his uncle resided in a massive stone house and ran a tidy little tomato business that cried out for able young men of no fixed abilities.

Not long before our rebellious caper was formulated, Dave, a moon-faced longhair who fancied himself a bit of a bohemian, had given me a copy of *Junky* by William Burroughs. Burroughs's lifestyle, which apparently consisted of lying around staring at his foot for months on end whilst ensconced in a funky garret in some exotic locale, appealed to me immensely, even though drug addiction seemed patently stupid and unnecessary (brown ale was the strongest stimulant I'd tasted at that point in my life), and I had begun to think that perhaps a steady job, the promise of a lumpen wife and an early bedtime might not be all that life had to offer. As if on cue, Jack Kerouac's *Lonesome Traveler* dropped into the

epicenter of my doubt, and the desire to escape the stifling, Formica-coated world of the English suburbs became fixed in my soul.

We ferried over to Guernsey and duly took up tomato-picking duties, craning our necks while we plucked the heavy, greenhouse-grown monsters from their thick dust-shedding vines. It was grueling, filthy work, and Dave and I heaved sighs of relief when Mick's uncle used our drunken, late-night sojourns as an excuse to eject us from his premises, although we knew full well that it was our long hair that pissed him off. (Mick, straight arrow that he was, remained with his uncle and those gigantic tomatoes.)

The nights of mild inebriation in which Dave and I indulged hardly matched the epic excesses of Burroughs or Kerouac, but it was a start. And with our departure from the mansion on the hill and Mick's beady-eyed uncle, we finally had left behind the security of a parental figure and the constraints that came with it. Before us lay the railroad earth and all the Beat fellaheen that the lonesome world could throw at us.

Dave, as it happens, didn't last long. Deep down, he had his sights set on a plump wife and a semi-detached in Crowthorne or some similar Tupperware hell, and he returned to England and the straight and narrow (at nineteen years of age the idea of regular sex can subvert even the most adventurous young man). But I was hooked on the freedom of the open road, despite the fact that I wasn't yet quite on it. Within six months, I had returned to England to live with my cousin and his wife (going back to my parents would have been cheating), secured a job at the Chichester Rubber Glove Factory and finally saved enough money to get me to the serious fellaheen universe: Morocco.

Stepping off the ferry into France (a real foreign country and the obvious starting point on the budding hitchhiker's route to North Africa), I felt that I was at last approaching lonesome, dirt-poor hobohood. I quickly made it to Paris, where I spent an indeterminate amount of time residing in a gloomy high-ceilinged pension. Here, I lived a thoroughly beat existence, surviving on croque-monsieurs and baguettes that I actually did tap on lamp posts (the baguettes, not the croques) in the French manner as I walked back to my desolate digs in wonderfully depressing St. Michel. Playing my no-brand guitar on the banks of the Seine, surrounded by the youthful flotsam of Europe and America, I was poignantly happy. Wary of attachment, however, I eventually loaded my rucksack with bread and pushed on toward Spain and finally Morocco, the beatest place on the whole planet.

Though I had many surreal experiences in Morocco, I didn't exactly follow Burroughs's path: I fortunately never managed to stick a needle in my arm, and the only contact I had with Arab boys was to tell them to piss off when they followed me around begging for dirhams. In addition, I never read or even heard of Ferlinghetti, Orlovsky or Ginsberg; Flaubert and

Rimbaud are to this day just names I can't pronounce. But I wrote plenty of stream-of-consciousness lyrics and lonesome dirges to the road.

I sometimes wonder if Jack—had he avoided his downward spiral and lived to enjoy his continuous recognition—would have started traveling again. Would he have performed for people all over the world with book tours and TV appearances, staying in nice hotels, and getting paid for the privilege? Why not? It may seem decidedly unBeat, but Burroughs and Ginsberg worked well into their old age.

That explosion of talent that formed the Beat movement was arguably as influential on Twentieth-Century culture as any key rock & roll wellspring, from Robert Johnson to Chuck Berry, Bob Dylan to the Beatles. Not to the masses perhaps, but the masses only pick up the scraps anyway. Time has proven that the work of Kerouac and Burroughs, et al., although forever categorized in what often seems a stifling, sycophant-encircled genre, will just not go away.

To this day, I derive inspiration from this powerful source and from that period in my life most affected by it. Thirty years later, in varying degrees, the Beat ethic continues to inform my work. And—I'm still traveling.

The Washington Squares
and Our Beat Quest

BY LAUREN AGNELLI

PERCEPTION COLORS EVERYTHING: As New York City's neo-Beat rock-folk trio of the Eighties, the Washington Squares (Tom Goodkind, Bruce Paskow and *moi*), we were perceived as beatniks—sort of. And we thought beatniks were cool, because they were rebels, bohemians, artists. But as soon as we did our vital research, we learned the term "beatnik" was a spin on "Sputnik" and more a cartoonish appellation and put-down instead of a real cool, real gone cat. So then it became with us: *Out with the beatnik! In with the Beats!* and with it a beautiful, round (not square!) world of grand iconoclast tradition: Art! Liberty! Fraternity!

Vestiges of New York's Fifties art scene could be found in the early Eighties at Chinese Chance restaurant, a.k.a. One University Place, a Mickey Ruskin establishment (Mickey ran Max's Kansas City in its artist hangout heyday). While I was waitressing there in 1983, two strange guys (named Tom and Bruce) wearing black slacks and striped shirts and berets started coming in and chatting me up. Concerned for their hunger, I would slip the two, who turned out to be erstwhile punk musicians, as much gratis soup and bread and soda as I could while juggling tables belonging to Art World luminaries such as John Chamberlain, Nathan Josephs, Jim Dine, Don Christianson and a host of occasional bohos, including Joni Mitchell. Chinese Chance's walls were crowded with art by many of the patrons (who in turn got bar/restaurant tabs for their pieces) and by regulars who'd contributed to the colorful scene, like Paul Butterfield and Taylor Mead. What better atmosphere in which to form a new musical group with bohemian ideals? Tom,

Bruce and I actually came up with our name, the Washington Squares, on a cocktail napkin at One U, sipping cokes and coffee after brainstorming on a Village walk.

We loved dressing the part in our "appurtenances of Beat," the berets, the goatees (except *pour moi, la femme*), the Ray-Ban shades, black turtlenecks. While we would espouse striped shirts (à lá French sailors, I suppose), we would for some other arcane reason eschew the sandals. As any fashion maven will tell you, revisionist vintage is the sincerest form of flattery. The image, while fun to re-create, was just the tip of the beret. For at heart, each of us Squares was a nonconformist reactionary, up against the lifeless, machine-driven rock music of the early Eighties (nascent techno, Duran Duran, Human League, et al.). We wanted to make something REAL, and so naturally the Beats appealed to us on account of their knee-jerk nonconformity. A big NO! to the Bourgeois, with kudos to the Artist, who would no doubt create that Brave New Utopia for each new generation.

As it happens, "New Generation" was one of our signature Washington Square songs (by Bruce Jay Paskow). And in Bruce's "D Train Line," he takes "a train in a hole to a job I hate / Ridin' on the D Train Line." Pure Maynard G. Krebs ("*Work*?!"), eh? Inspired by another dark night of the soul was Tom Goodkind's "Daylight": ". . . Asks why I dig deep / I hide, try to go back to sleep . . . Daylight you better get the hell on out of here!" One of my signature Washington Square songs, "Charcoal," was an homage to the sublime poet William Blake, who was universally revered by the Beats ("Some do search for gold /

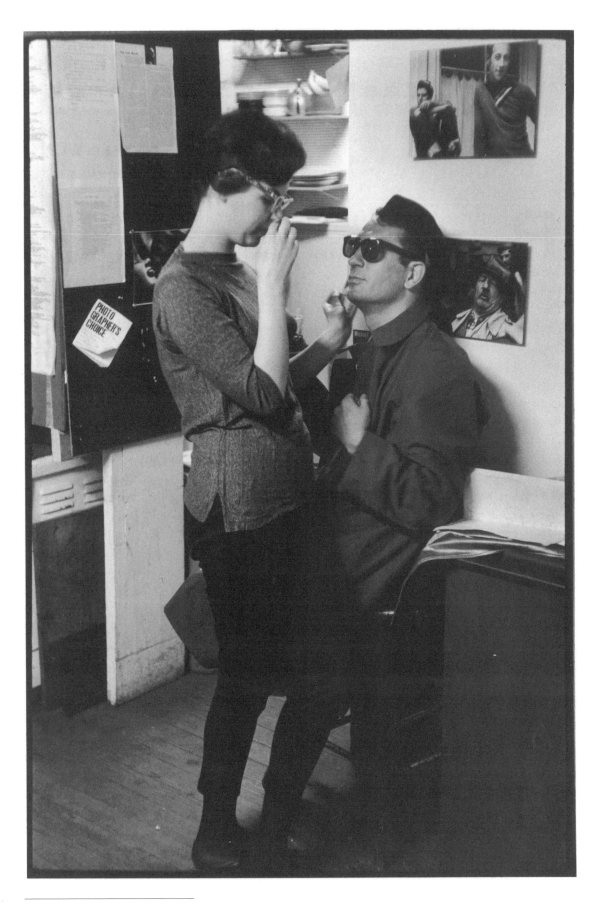

What is the purpose? / Yellow smiles or warm souls / I'll take the Charcoal . . ."). In Blake's day, he would hold gatherings in his home where he set his poetry to music—early hootenannies if you will. In the late Sixties, Allen Ginsberg would set Blake's words to music on the recording *Songs of Innocence and Experience*. More Squares' *tours de force* gleefully touting the rebel Beat were "Neal Cassady Died," "You Can't Kill Me" and "La Roue de Fortune" ("Just lift your head and live for now"). When we played "Greenback Dollar" live as our finale, we hammered home with 50,000 Watts of Folk (as we would jest) a passionate balls-to-the-wall paean to our perception of the Beat Ideal: to be hip, rebellious, a nonconformist loner. "Well, I don't give a damn about a greenback–a dollar / I spend it fast as I can / For a wailing song and a good guitar / The only things that I understand."

In the Squares, we also had attitudes belonging to the Red Diaper Baby and the hippie-dippie too, but, hey, a lot of pop culture transpired between the Fifties and the Eighties and we sure as hell weren't purists: We were impressionable songwriters, musicologists and fiery performers.

Now some of you might think, "Rock and folk? The real Beats, man, they were into bebop and jazz!" Sure, we knew that, and would from time to time throw jazz "quotes"—musical riffs on guitar and piano—into the musical mixture, like a little of Horace Silver's "Song for My Father" in "You Can't Kill Me." Being only the sum of our influences (summer camp folk music, rock & roll, pop music and—*gasp!*—the Beatles and the Stones, for Chrissakes), we created the catchy vocal-harmonied musical hybrid, the Washington Squares.

I would compare our Beat nostalgia (or wannaBeatism) to the way Nineties kids affect the style of the punks or the hippies or the whatevers. They know the look, and may even be sympa-thetic to the cause. However, how purist can *any* of us be, having not lived it? And as much fun as it was to run around the world in my Washington Squares beatnik togs ("the REAL Village People," we would say, and even made and sold "beatnik kits" for a short while, tastefully done for his and hers—*hilarious*), the perception of us as hip "Squares" surpassed reality. The truly mythic part, for us, was reading, then meeting and hanging out with some amazing Beat writers and the musicians and scenesters who were part of their orbit: Allen Ginsberg, Peter Orlovsky, Lawrence Ferlinghetti, comedian Professor Irwin Corey, *Village Voice* writer Howard Smith, writer/scenester Larry "Ratso" Sloman, DJ/musician Oscar Brand, David Amram, the Kingston Trio's Dave Guard and John Stewart, former Limeliter Lou Gottlieb, Peter, Paul and Mary (especially Peter Yarrow), folkie Tom Rush. How are folkies connected to the Beats? The coffeehouse scene initiated by the Beats became a folk-music scene as the Beats' bohemianism evolved into the folkrock movement's egalitarian activism; the lyrics to the folk songs became the poetry of the folkies.

Nowadays I keep the Beat crusade alive in small ways—remaining nonconformist, still committed to my music and writing, still in love with art, life, freedom—and coffee. I also smile to myself that the Beats are alive in this every-corner-a-cappuccino coffee craze and in microbreweries, vividly recalling how Howard Smith regaled us one steamy Village night, with tales of beatnik glory over cups of tea and wine: "We would get drunk on beer at the Kettle of Fish on MacDougal, then go down to the Figaro on Bleecker and get all jazzed up on espressos, then run right back and do it all over again." Those were the days, my friend; and the Washington Squares in our day were happy to bring them back.

Jack Kerouac making a new friend at a New York City loft party, 1959   BURT GLINN/MAGNUM PHOTOS INC.

Kerouac, Ginsberg, the Beats and Other Bastards Who Ruined My Life

BY JOHNNY DEPP

THERE I WAS, AGE THIRTEEN, EYES shut tight listening intently to *Frampton Comes Alive* over and over again, as some kind of pubescent mantra that helped to cushion the dementia of just how badly I wanted to whisk Bambi, the beautiful cheerleader, away from the wedge of peach melba that was the handsome hunky football hero . . .

I was daydreaming of taking her out behind the 7-11 to drink Boone's Farm strawberry-apple wine and kiss until our mouths were raw. *ZZZ-ZRRRIIIPP!!* was the sound I heard that ripped me from that tender moment. My brother Danny, ten years my senior and on the verge of committing fratricide, having had more than enough of "Do you feel like we do?," promptly seized the vinyl off the record player and with a violent heave chucked the sacred album into the cluttered abyss of my room.

"No more," he hissed. "I can't let you listen to that shit anymore!"

I sat there snarling at him in that deeply expressive way that only teens possess, decompressing too fast back into reality. He grabbed a record out of his own collection and threw it on.

"Try this . . . you're better than that stuff. You don't have to listen to that shit just 'cause other kids do."

"Okay, fucker," I thought, "bring it on . . . let's have it!"

The music started . . . guitar, fretless stand-up bass, flutes and some Creep pining away about " . . . venturing in the slipstream . . . between the viaducts of your dreams. . . ." Fuck this, I thought, this is pussy music—they're not even plugged in! Those guitars aren't electric! The song went a bit

further, "Would you find me . . . would you kiss my eyes . . . to be born again . . ." The words began to hit home; they didn't play that kind of stuff on the radio, and as the melody of the song settled in, I was starting to get kind of used to it. Shit! I even liked it. It was a sound I hadn't really ever given any attention to before, because of my innate fear of groups like America, Seals and Crofts and, most of all, the dreaded Starland Vocal Band. I didn't give half a fuck about a horse with no name, summer breezes or afternoon delights! I needed space to be filled!!! Filled with sound . . . distorted guitars, drums, feedback and words . . . words that meant something . . . sounds that meant something!

I found myself rummaging and rooting wildly through my brother's record collection as if it were a newfound treasure, a monumental discovery that no one—especially no one my age—could know about or understand. I listened to it all! The soundtracks to *A Clockwork Orange* and *Last Tango in Paris*, Bob Dylan, Mozart and Brahms . . . The whole shebang! I couldn't get enough. I had become like some kind of junkie for the stuff and in turn became a regular pain in the ass to my brother. I wanted to know all that he did. I wanted to know everything that rotten white-bread football brute didn't. I was preparing to woo that fantastic little ra-ra girl out of the sunlight of the ice-cream parlor and into my nocturnal adolescent dreamscape.

And so began my ascension (or descension) into the mysteries of all things considered *Out-side*. I had burrowed too deep into the counter-culture of my brother's golden repository, and as years went by, he would turn me on to other areas of his expertise, sending me even further into the dark chasm of alternative learning.

One day he gave me a book that was to become like a Koran for me. A dog-eared paperback, roughed up and stained with God knows what. *On the Road*, written by some goofball with a strange frog name that was almost unpronounceable for my teenage tongue, had found its way from big brother's shelf and into my greedy little paws. Keep in mind that in all my years of elementary school, junior high and high school, possibly the only things I'd read up to that point were a biography of Knute Rockne, some stuff on Evel Knievel and books about WW II. *On the Road* was life changing for me, in the same way that my life had been metamorphasised when Danny put Van Morrison's *Astral Weeks* onto the turntable that day.

I was probably about fifteen by this time, and the cheerleader had begun to fade from my dreams. I didn't need her now. I needed to wander . . . whenever and wherever I wanted! I'd found myself at the end of my rope as far as school was concerned; there seemed no particular reason for me to stay. The teachers didn't want to teach, and I didn't want to learn—from them. I wanted my education to come from living life, getting out there in the world, seeing and doing and moving amongst the other vagabonds who had had the same sneaking suspicion that I did, that there would be no great need for high-end mathematics, nope . . . I was not going to be doing other people's taxes and going home at 5:37 p.m. to pat my dog's head and sit down to my one meat and two vegetable table waiting for *Jeopardy* to pop on the glass tit, the Pat Sajak of my own private gameshow, in the bellybutton of the universe, Miramar, Florida. A beautiful life, to be sure, but one I know I was destined not to have, thanks to big brother Dan and the French-Canadian with the name Jack Kerouac.

I had found the teachers, the soundtrack and the proper motivation for my life. Kerouac's

train-of-thought writing style gave great inspiration for a train-of-thought existence—for better or for worse. The idea to live day-to-day in a "true pedestrian" way, to keep walking, moving forward, no matter what. A sanctified juggernaut.

Through this introduction to Kerouac, I then learned of his fellow conspirators Ginsberg, Burroughs, Corso, Hunke, Cassady and the rest of the unruly lot. I dove into their world full on and sponged up as much as I possibly could of their works. The "Howl" of Ginsberg left me babbling like an idiot, stunned that someone could regurgitate such honesty to paper. Burroughs's *Naked Lunch* sent me into fits of hysterical laughter, with the imagery of talking assholes and shady reptilian characters looming, always not far behind. Cassady's *The First Third* rants on beatifically like a high-speed circular saw. The riches I was able to walk away with from these heroes, teachers and mentors is not available in any school that I've ever heard of. Their infinite wisdom and hyper-sensitivity were their greatest attributes and in some cases—as I believe it was with Kerouac—played a huge part in their ultimate demise.

I had the honor of meeting and getting to know Allen Ginsberg for a short time. The initial meeting was at a soundstage in New York City, where we were both doing a bit in the film *The United States of Poetry*. I was reading a piece from Kerouac's *Mexico City Blues*, the "211th Chorus," and as I was rehearsing it for camera, I could see a familiar face out of the corner of my eye: "Fuck me," I thought, "that's Ginsberg!!!" We were introduced, and he then immediately launched into a blistering rendition of said chorus, so as to show me the proper way for it to be done.

"As Jack would have done it!" he emphasized.

I was looking straight down the barrel at one of the most gifted and important poets of the Twentieth Century, and with all the truth and guts I could muster up, I said in response, "Yeah, but I'm not reading it as him, I'm reading it as me. It's my interpretation of his piece."

Silence—a *LONNNGG* silence. Tick tock tick tock tick tock . . .

I was smiling nervously, my eyes sort of wavering between his face and the floor. I sucked down about half of my five-thousandth cigarette of the day in one monster drag and filled the air around us with my poison. It was at that point that I remembered his "Don't Smoke!" song . . . oops . . . too fucking late now, boy, you done stepped in shit! I looked at Ginsberg, he looked at me, and the director looked at us both as the crew looked at him, and it was quite a little moment, for a moment there. Allen's eyes squinted ever so slightly and then began to twinkle like bright lights. He smiled that mystic smile, and I felt as though God himself had forgiven me a dreadful sin.

After the shoot, we took a car back to his apartment on the Lower East Side and had some tea. He was gracious enough to speak to me about the early years with Kerouac, Cassady and the others. We spoke of many things, from the cost of a limo ride to the high-pitched voice of Oscar Wilde; he actually had a recording of Wilde reading "The Ballad of Reading Gaol." He flirted unabashedly and nonstop for the duration of my visit, even allowing me to smoke, as long as I sat next to the kitchen window and exhaled in that direction. He kindly signed a book to me and a couple of autographs (one for my brother, of course), and then I made my way back to the hotel, only to have already received a call from him, inviting me to some kind of something or other.

From that day forward, we stayed in touch with each other over the next few years, and even spent time together from time to time. Our communication continued until our final conversation, which was just three days before he passed on. He called me to say that he was dying, and

Johnny Depp and Allen Ginsberg on the set of 'The United States of Poetry.'
CHRIS BUCK/COURTESY JOHNNY DEPP AND WASHINGTON SQUARE FILMS

that it would be nice to see each other again before he checked out. He was so calm and so peaceful about it that I had to ask how he felt given this situation. He gracefully said that it was like a ripple on a sea of tranquility. He then cried a little, as did I; he said, "I love you," and so did I. I told him I would get to New York as soon as possible, and fuckin' A, I was gonna go—the call came only days later.

Ginsberg was a great man, like his old pals, who had paved the way for many, and many more to come. The contribution of these people goes way beyond their own works. Without *On the Road*, "Howl" or *Naked Lunch,* for example, would we have been blessed with the likes of Hunter S. Thompson and Bob Dylan? Or countless other writers and poets of that caliber who were born out of the Fifties and Sixties? Where would we be without modern classics like *Fear and Loathing in Las Vegas* or "The Times They Are a-Changin'"?

So much has happened to me in the twenty years since I first sat down and took that long drag on Kerouac's masterpiece. I have been a construction laborer, a gas station attendant, a bad mechanic, a screen printer, a musician, a telemarketing phone salesman, an actor, and a tabloid target—but there's never been a second that went by in which I deviated from the road that ol' Jack put me on, via my brother. It has been an interesting ride all the way—emotionally and psychologically taxing—but a motherfucker straight down the pike. And I know that without these great writers' holy words seared into my brain, I would most likely have ended up chained to a wall in Camarillo State Hospital, zapped beyond recognition, or dead by misadventure.

So in the end, what can *anyone* . . . scholar, professor, student or biographer . . . really say about these angels and devils, who once walked among us, though maybe just a bit higher off the ground?

Beat Generation in the
Generation of Beats

BY MARK KEMP

Ted Joans gives a poetry reading at the Café Bizarre, Greenwich Village, 1959

BURT GLINN/MAGNUM PHOTOS INC.

CHUCK D LOOKED AT ME QUIZZI-cally, his furrowed brow barely show-ing beneath the bill of his black Raiders cap. "Sure," the rapper said as I handed him a yellowed copy of Allen Ginsberg's *Howl.* "I'll read it. Sounds interesting."

The year was 1994 and I had caught up with Public Enemy's commanding frontman backstage at Dodgers Stadium in Los Angeles, where his group was about to open for U2's Zoo TV Tour. For months I had been trying to facilitate a dis-cussion between Chuck, the most compelling wordsmith of late-Eighties hip-hop, and Gins-berg, the most influential poet of the Beat Gener-ation. This transgenerational summit meeting would be published for posterity in the pages of *Option,* the alternative-culture magazine that I edited at the time. Why did I wish to foist a young African-American rapper who once declared Louis Farrakhan a prophet onto a sexa-genarian, homosexual, Jewish poet? Well, because I believed these two men had more in common than most people might expect.

Take Public Enemy's 1988 bombshell of a song "Night of the Living Baseheads," in which Chuck D laments how freebase cocaine had weakened the hopes of his generation: "My man Daddy-O once said to me / He knew a brother who stayed all day in his Jeep / And at night he went to sleep / And in the mornin' all he had was / The sneakers on his feet / The culprit used to jam and rock the mike, yo / He stripped the Jeep to fill his pipe / And wander around to find a place / Where they rocked to a different kind of bass!" Rewind thirty-four years earlier, when Ginsberg, in "Howl," so graphically and yet so tenderly voiced his similarly existential view of wasted youth: "I saw the best minds of my generation destroyed by / madness, starving hysterical naked, / dragging themselves through the negro streets at dawn / looking for an angry fix . . ."

Rather than try to follow in the Beat's footsteps, hip-hop artists simply *are* their modern-day equivalents. The Beats' work expressed existential self-awareness through participation in the here and now—a message also found within the colliding beats, samples and rhythms of hip-hop. The soul of Beat lingers in the rhymes of the rappers, whose often willfully antagonistic language conveys—in the parlance of Norman Mailer in his 1957 essay "The White Negro"—the idea that "in a bad world there is no love nor mercy nor charity nor justice unless a man can keep his courage . . ."

You can draw a line from the original Beats to the New Beats—as writer S. H. Fernando Jr. dubbed hip-hop culture in his 1994 book *The New Beats: Exploring the Music, Culture, and Attitudes of Hip-Hop* — following each movement's linkage of jazz to spoken-word poetry. Contemporary practitioners include the Blue Note beats of Us3, the bebop badness of Digable Planets, the boombastic big-band sound of the Dream Warriors, as well as the Native Tongues collective (the Jungle Brothers, A Tribe Called Quest, De La Soul) and the avant-garde playfulness of the Disposable Heroes of HipHoprisy, the Beastie Boys and Beck.

But Beat attitude, Beat consciousness, the Beat lifestyle is more about *ir*reverence than obligatory jazz references or self-consciously arty literary devices, although those elements were surely part of the rebelliousness of the original Beats. The Beat Generation's essence, for instance, reverberates in Public Enemy's "Black Steel in the Hour of Chaos"—the ability to survive in the face of hopelessness and despair. As Jack Kerouac once wrote and recited backed by the jazz playing of pianist Steve Allen, "Anyway, I wrote the book because we're all gonna die."

The original Beats surfaced just after the explosion of the atom bomb. The New Beats peaked as crack and AIDS had begun corroding an entire generation. So for the hip-hop generation, the phrase "keeping it real" became the mantra du jour, much as "be here now" was used by the post-Beat hippie generation. Keep it real for yourself. Keep it real for your circle of friends. Keep it real for the survival of your culture. And most of all, don't trust the Man. It is a concept so nihilistic it's downright spiritual—like Kerouac's spirituality in the hour of his own generation's chaos. It's no wonder that the most foul-mouthed gangsta rappers routinely thank God on their album credits. The idea is, we're gonna party now, defend ourselves and live the lives we choose in this very moment, because at any time—to paraphrase wannaBeat Jim Morrison—the whole shithouse might come falling down.

With a hip, hop, the hipit, the hipidipit, hip, hip, hopit, you don't stop ...

—"Rapper's Delight,"
SUGAR HILL GANG

In 1979 the Sugar Hill Gang first bumrushed the *Billboard* charts, selling two million copies of a goofy little single called "Rapper's Delight." Back then, hip-hop culture, like the Beat Generation in the 1940s, was still a very underground New York phenomenon. DJs and MCs knew each other, traded rhymes, participated in mock feuds over who were the best lyricists in the neighborhood. They were friends and sparring partners, they name-checked each other in song.

The style had come from an earlier form of rap that had begun in the dance clubs of the Caribbean, where DJs would chatter over the records they played. In the book *Reggae, Deep Roots Music,* one of those DJs, Machouki, explained that "sometimes when we listen to the record and find that music is wanting, we would inter-serve something like 'Get on the ball . . .' and cover the weakness in the record. It was live jive and it really made people feel happy." The same philosophy prevailed during rap's earliest days in New York. But with competition growing among DJs, that talk soon developed into the onomatopoeic poetry of "Rapper's Delight" and the reality verse of Grandmaster Flash and the Furious Five's ghetto documentary "The Message."

By the mid-1980s, numerous groups were creating this new style of Beat poetry—RunDMC, L.L. Cool J, the Beastie Boys—and taking it to the pop charts, where it began competing with traditional pop and rock & roll. By the latter part of the decade, hip-hop had splintered into so many different varieties that new subgenres were invented, although the denizens of hip-hop culture, like the close-knit members of the Beat Generation in the 1950s, remained in strong solidarity.

Meena-meena-meena-meena-meena
 (say what?)
Meena-meena-meena-meena-meena
 (say what?) ...
Fly buddy (buddy),
Don't you know you make me go nutty
 (nutty)?
I'm so glad that you're not a fuddy-duddy
 (duddy).
Not too skinny and not too chubby

(chubby).
Soft like Silly Putty (Putty) ..."

—"Buddy"
DE LA SOUL WITH A TRIBE CALLED QUEST,
JUNGLE BROTHERS, QUEEN LATIFAH
AND MONIE LOVE

When groups like De La Soul, A Tribe Called Quest and the other members of hip-hop's self-defined Native Tongues collective trade rhymes and complete each other's thoughts in their Beat wordplay, they are continuing a tradition of freestyle spoken word that goes back to the New York and San Francisco coffeehouses of the 1950s. When Greg Tate writes about hip-hop culture, his prose dances and sings just as Kerouac's did when he wrote about jazz. In his 1988 essay, "Homeys on the Rage: Public Enemy," Tate characterizes a typical hip-hop audience: "The latest floor craze is hyperkinetic — neck, head, elbows, and feet spasmodically jerking and shuffling every which way. Electric boogie meets lindy bop." A more recent member of hip-hop culture, New York's DJ Spooky, even took his alias, "The Subliminal Kid," from the character in William S. Burroughs's *The Ticket that Exploded* and *Nova Express* who distorts reality by exposing the world to cut-up films and tapes of past and present cultures.

Indeed, the looping rhythms of hip-hop contain the very core of the "Beat" in Beat Generation: More than any popular youth counterculture since the 1960s—save for the most obscure fringes of the avant-garde —hip-hop's cut-and-paste interpretation of modern life can be directly traced to Burroughs. Moreover, the swinging, bopping cadence of its words juxtaposed against the thump-thump-thump of the music have kept alive the spirit of Kerouac's readings backed by jazz musicians. Another aspect of hip-hop that recalls early Beat writing is its name-dropping of fellow rappers. Just as Kerouac's novels were populated by thinly disguised versions of Ginsberg, Cassady and other friends, Chuck D's quoting his buddy "Daddy-O" of Stetsasonic in "Night of the Living Baseheads" exemplifies this.

Harlem is vicious
modernism. BangClash ...
Can you stand such beauty?
So violent and transforming.
The trees blink naked, being so few.

—"Return of the Native,"
AMIRI BARAKA

In the 1990s hip-hop has taken Beat consciousness into white suburbia in a way that would positively stun Jack Kerouac. Its beats and attitude rule MTV; its clothing colors runways from New York to Paris. No longer do fresh-faced white kids have to wait until freshman year of college to face the existential panic of living alone, without a safety net. Instead, they can listen to Tupac Shakur's "All Eyez on Me" on the radio: "Was hyper as a kid, alone, as a teenager, on the mobile / Calling big shots on the scene major / Packing hundreds in my drawers, Fuck the law / Bitches I fuck with a passion, livin' rough and raw / Catchin' cases at a fast rate, ballin' in the fast lane / Hustle 'til the morning, never stopped until the cash came / I live my life as a Thug nigga / Until the day I die." The clipped cadence of Shakur's words and the self-conscious disrespect of the "bitches I fuck" hark back to Kerouac's speed-crazed writing in *The Subterraneans*: ". . . he pushed a violinist queer into a doorway and I pushed another one in, he slugged his, I glared at mine, I was 18, I was a nannybeater and fresh as a daisy too . . ."

Shakur's stark images of contemporary urban life have galvanized millions of white suburban youths just as the passion of jazz galvanized the small circle of white Beat writers who had come together at Harlem's neighboring Columbia University during the 1940s. The romance of hopelessness. The idea of the dread of self-discovery that inspired Mailer's "The White Negro": "So no wonder that in certain cities of America . . . this particular part of a generation was attracted to what the Negro had to offer. In such places as Greenwich Village, a menage-a-trois was completed — the bohemian and the juvenile delinquent came face-to-face with the Negro, and the hipster was a fact in American life." Mailer's group of young white outcasts came to the realization that, "Any Negro who wishes to live must live with danger from his first day, and no experience can ever be casual to him, no Negro can saunter down a street with any real certainty that violence will not visit him on his walk." The difference between those outcast white bohemians of the Fifties and the white suburban hip-hop consumers of the Nineties is that the group is no longer small, nor does it merely consist of outcasts.

There always was a crucial missing link in the Beat Generation, though. That missing link was the black poet himself. LeRoi Jones (now known as Amiri Baraka, and a strong adherent of young, contemporary African-American poets and rappers) held the key to the insights that might have rendered the Beat Generation a great literary force rather than just an enduring influence on popular culture. Behind the hype surrounding Kerouac, Burroughs, Ginsberg and the rest were black poets whose words were every bit as powerful as Charlie Parker's bop that so inspired Kerouac's writing style. But until recently, we've known little about such fringe figures as Ted Joans, Bob Kaufman and Iceberg Slim (who inspired rapper Ice-T's moniker).

Foremost among the earliest music-backed black spoken-word artists were Los Angeles' Watts Prophets, formed in 1967, followed a year later by New York's Last Poets. The black musician, writer and spoken-word artist who took this new jive Beat style to FM radio was Gil Scott-Heron, whose 1974 musical poem, "The Revolution Will Not Be Televised," was one of the earliest well-known rap songs, though the genre had not yet been named. As influential as all of these protorappers were, however, it wasn't until Public Enemy shouted "Bring the Noise" that the message of the Black Beats reached a more mainstream audience.

In the end, my dream meeting between Chuck D and Allen Ginsberg never happened. Public Enemy's political style of rap gave way to a new wave of New Beats—the West Coast gangsta rappers. Ginsberg died of cancer. And yet, in the ensuing years, the link between the Beat Generation and the Hip-Hop Nation has only grown stronger and more pervasive in our culture. In retrospect, I realize that Chuck D and Allen Ginsberg were destined *not* to have that meeting. The New Beats are themselves, not tied to the white sages of old. From Sugar Hill Gang to Public Enemy, De La Soul to Tupac Shakur, the New Beats create their own work with words that live in the here and now, not bound by tradition. Words that break rules. These artists are Beats if for no other reason than because they refuse to bow down to the mantle of Beat.

The Beats
and Alt.Culture

BY STEVE APPLEFORD

THE ROAD GOES ON FOREVER, the road and the myth of Jack and Neal, those desperate travelers, a pair of holy dreamers in search of some impossible existential nirvana. And by 1979, a full three decades after their first journey, that myth was a powerful draw for young Jennifer Joseph, just one more itinerant coed, aspiring poet and would-be rocker to make the endless journey from New York to San Francisco too many times with some friends in her $400 jalopy, a fabulous '71 Mercury Marquis. She'd heard the stories, read the books. Now the road beckoned. Go! Go! Go!

"Jen, *On the Road* is fiction," her mother had told Jennifer, then standing in some far-flung phone booth. "Fiction, okay?"

Perhaps so, but the secret naked doodlings of Kerouac and Burroughs and Ginsberg mattered as much to Joseph as they had to any previous generation. The Beats set a standard for intellectual adventurism, one rooted in experience, in the road. They explored extremes in sex and drugs. And their happy destitution became so ingrained in American culture that in later decades Bohemia was just another neighborhood, a lifestyle choice for hipsters, neither shocking nor particularly dangerous. The legend of Kerouac's seven years on the road launched not only crazy-headed college girls across deserts and swamplands, but vanloads of punk rockers, invading

Photographer Allen Ginsberg shoots Lee Ranaldo reading from 'On the Road' during NYU's marathon reading of the novel, Beat Generation conference, May 22, 1994.
© GORDON BALL

your town with guitars and amplifiers on highways newly paved with the efforts of an alternative culture headed by the likes of Black Flag and Sonic Youth. Get in the van, get in the van . . .

The same DIY ethic that once encouraged ravaged street raconteur and doper Herbert Huncke to become a writer ultimately informed all things alternative. In the Nineties, that influence even touched commercial ventures like Lollapalooza and the music of Kurt Cobain and Beck, the latter of which emerged like some crazymad folk poet, a coffeehouse troubadour with a leaf-blower and flaming acoustic guitar. R.E.M.'s Michael Stipe has borrowed from Burroughs's cut-up technique, which slices and rearranges text into new forms, new words and meanings. Theirs was just one more generation inspired and ruined by the legacy of the Beats, a legacy that prevails because the work somehow retains its revolutionary, anti-establishment edge.

"This is the real thing," declares Joseph, now owner of Manic D Press, a San Francisco publisher of new poetry and literary fiction. "A lot of the work, whether it's *On the Road*, 'Howl' or *Naked Lunch*, it was good thirty years ago, it's good today, it will be good in thirty years, it will be good in three hundred years. The poem 'Howl' is not going to go away. It's a damn good poem."

That work remains a key resource for the members of Sonic Youth, which emerged from the New York punk scene with an atonal blend of tortured guitar tone, pop culture obsession and a lingering Beat aesthetic. Their music offers a flurry of ideas and textures, unpolished and unkempt, sometimes aimless and somehow pure. This isn't pop. In the East Village apartment guitarist Thurston Moore shares with wife and guitarist-bassist Kim Gordon, volumes on the Beats crowd shelf space shared with punk history books. And guitarist Lee Ranaldo coproduced a 1997 Kerouac tribute CD, *Kerouac—kicks joy darkness*, that matched the writer's words with

music and spoken-word performance by the likes of Stipe, Patti Smith, Joe Strummer and Jeff Buckley.

For Ranaldo, the Beats still matter. "As the first young generation to come of age in the wake of the atomic age," Ranaldo says, "they were looking at life and society with a new perspective: the knowledge that for the first time it was a real possibility that the whole shithaus could go up at any minute, and that one had better 'live for today,' as the saying goes, and grab at life whilst one could. No previous generation lived under this specter. They were among the first to break out of the mid-century conservative molds, and strike out for new territory, new mental/psychedelic awareness. Also, they were among the first generation to grow up with a greater worldwide information awareness, which has grown through today into our info-overloaded culture."

For Kerouac's nephew Jim Sampas, the folk singer and producer who oversaw the *kicks joy darkness* tribute, the tradition that alternative culture shares with the Beats can be found within Kerouac's own source material: bop jazz and confessional literature. "A lot of the lyrics in alternative music tend to be very introspective, as Kerouac's work was, and very freestyle, not clichéd," says Sampas. "They're talking about what happens in their lives, they're talking about what's happening with themselves, and trying to reflect upon it—as opposed to trying to create a song that's just going to sell a lot of albums."

Joseph understood. After her college graduation in 1982, she migrated to San Francisco, settling in the same North Beach neighborhood where nearly thirty years earlier Allen Ginsberg first howled manic obscene truths to an astonished populace. Joseph sang and played guitar in the Furies, an all-girl outfit with a weakness for pop songs about art (and which included future Sleater-Kinney drummer Janet Weiss). And she watched as poet and City Lights publisher

Lawrence Ferlinghetti strolled past her living room window every morning on his way to the office. Manic D Press was soon modeled after Ferlinghetti's own City Lights publishing house, which was the first to champion the work of Beat writers on both coasts on any broad scale. "Each generation has to take responsibility for its own culture," she says.

By then, underground literary culture was emerging in unexpected places. In the early Nineties, MTV began airing brief moments of spoken word, performed by poets culled from the Nuyorican Cafe in Manhattan. Poetry became so firmly absorbed into pop culture that it was used in commercials for Nike sneakers. Then, in 1994, the Lollapalooza festival enlisted poets from across America to read at different stops on the tour. Joseph gathered ten San Francisco poets to read at dates scattered from Las Vegas to Vancouver. "In Las Vegas it was 110 degrees, so we always had a great crowd inside the poetry tent," she says with a laugh.

The cumulative effect of all this was the creation of a national poetry scene that continued for years afterward. Not that the connection between poetry and rock was anything new. Many artists from the mid-Seventies Blank Generation began as writers, and turned to punk as a new forum for expression. Both Patti Smith and Jim Carroll were established writers before releasing their first albums. Both debut records were compelling, even revolutionary statements, made when punk meant more than simple Neanderthal pop.

In Los Angeles, the punk band X emerged from a poetry workshop at Venice's Beyond Baroque literary center. That trend was reversed in the Eighties when Henry Rollins stepped away from Black Flag to perform intense readings from his journals, before turning to a more improvisational style. In that, Rollins was vaguely following the Beat dictum: first thought, best thought. Kerouac's commitment to spontaneous prose found

its inspiration in bebop's healing squealing solos, and master Jack seeing Buddha in the inscrutable round face of Charlie Parker. (Another form could be found in Ginsberg's historic testimony at the Chicago 7 trial: "Ohhhhhhhmmmmm-mmm . . . .")

In 1997 Patti Smith recorded an epic eleven-minute improvisation called "Memento Mori," where her band wound itself into an edgy, expansive mood as Smith narrated a Vietnam parable (". . . and Johnny never went marching home . . . You are remembered!") that also translated into a declaration of love for her fallen Beat mentors.

Bohemia isn't everyone's fantasy come true. "I'm trying not to live that way right now," says Mary Timony, singer-guitarist of the noise-pop band Helium. She appreciates the reckless, absurd beauty in Kerouac's work, the strange wisdom between the lines. Helium even appeared on *kicks joy darkness*, making soft, haunted sounds behind the benign narration of Ferlinghetti. "But I cannot stand glorifying bohemian culture. I hate it. It makes me very anxious, because it's sort of an anxious lifestyle: the drugs, and traveling all over the place. I don't feel like I'm a musician because it's really cool to be a musician. I'm doing it because it's something I enjoy. I just hate when the alternative lifestyles are glorified."

Henry Rollins read *On the Road* once in 1982 and wasn't impressed. By then, Rollins had been sing-shouting with Black Flag for a year, hurtling between distant punk-rock gigs in a no-frills van, usually broke and sleeping on floors. Kerouac's tales of joy rides and Spanish girls seemed like some distant fantasy. "I was living on the road in those days, and his experiences that I remember reading in the book didn't jive with my reality, which was more violent and less intellectual and way more a furious and gnarly ride," Rollins says. "So it didn't inspire me to read anymore."

Fans are always giving him books, however.

Burroughs's *Naked Lunch* is a common gift (along with Ayn Rand's *The Fountainhead*), but Rollins has never bothered to read it. He's read little of Ginsberg. ("I saw Ginsberg on television whacking two drum sticks together, saying 'Don't smoke!' over and over again," says Rollins. "I thought that was pretty cool.") He finds more direct inspiration in the blunt narrative of vagabond Henry Miller and post-Beat hyperrealist Hubert Selby Jr., and yet Rollins's career is like the ultimate manifestation of the DIY ethic and Beat tradition, spewing uncensored episodes from his sorry life on stages worldwide. His 2.13.61 publishing company, originally designed to print and distribute only a single-stapled volume of his own writing, has since expanded to publish

poetry, fiction and photography by a variety of new-school outcasts. In that, Rollins's production is not unlike how Ferlinghetti's City Lights created a venue for his own generation.

"I go out there and let it rip," says Rollins. "I just go out there and tell it like I see it, fully realizing there's lots of room to disagree. Which is

good and healthy I reckon. I try not to mess with it or overthink it."

Underground culture and the commercial expectations of pop music is rarely a comfortable mix, leaving many rockers from the Nineties ambivalent and uncomfortable with success. Cobain was moved to scrawl "Corporate Magazines Suck" across his T-shirt while posing for ROLLING STONE. Meanwhile, the newest literary generation finds meaningful mainstream attention hard to come by. "There's some incredibly great work being written," notes Joseph, "and hopefully today's writers can get out from under the shadow of the beatniks. This generation doesn't have a name. "

Nothing is sadder than last year's hep. Looking back tends to inspire more embarrassment than enlightenment. What survives intact from the Beat era is not the surface stereotypes, all the bongos and berets and the white Negro hipster-speak. Ginsberg remained a compelling figure through the decades, up until his death in 1997, by remaining true to his work without retreating from contemporary culture. The Beats somehow kept their cool, without the self-importance of Sixties youth culture.

"They're wilder and more free-spirited than a lot of people of the hippie age that I know," says Frank Black, who did not discover the Beats until he found his own success with the Pixies and as a solo artist. "They're definitely a lot more: 'Oh yeah! I was growing pot up in Topanga in '52!' They're kind of wild people. Well-educated people too."

In their last years, Ginsberg and Burroughs found new collaborators in the Nineties. Cobain provided frayed guitar feedback on Burroughs's

Kim Gordon and Michael Stipe
visiting William Burroughs in his Lawrence, Kansas,
backyard, 1996
LEE RANALDO

The "Priest" They Called Him spoken-word CD. Burroughs was also cast as an aging junkie and defrocked priest by director Gus Van Sant in *Drugstore Cowboy*, which was part road movie, part junkie manifesto and outlaw diary, with Matt Dillon capturing all the same restlessness and aimlessness of the Beat era. And Van Sant directed the video to "The Ballad of the Skeletons," Ginsberg's grand final statement, with musical backing from Paul McCartney, Philip Glass and Lenny Kaye.

The passing of Ginsberg and Burroughs has ended their prolific production. But not even death will likely end their influence. For Exene Cervenkova, who didn't discover their work until after she was already a poet and a singer-songwriter with X, their presence will continue to be felt. "When Allen Ginsberg died it was the first time in my life that I thought there must be life after death because he has to go somewhere," says Cervenkova. "With everyone else it was just tragic. But with him it was, Okay, what now?"

Beat Bibliography
Selected Books About the Beats

Ash, Mel. *Beat Spirit: The Way of the Beat Writers As a Living Experience.* New York: Putnam Publishing Group, 1997.

Beaulieu, Victor-Lévy. Translated by Sheila Fischman. *Jack Kerouac: A Chicken-Essay.* Toronto, Canada: The Coach House Press, 1975. Original French edition: Montreal: Editions du Jour, 1972.

Cassady, Carolyn. *Heart Beat: My Life with Jack and Neal.* New York: Pocket Books, 1976.

Cassady, Carolyn. *Off the Road: My Years with Cassady, Kerouac, and Ginsberg.* New York: William Morrow and Company, 1990.

Felver, Christopher. *Felinghetti Portrait.* Utah: Gibbs-Smith, 1998.

French, Warren. *Jack Kerouac.* New York: Macmillan, 1986.

Gifford, Barry, and Lawrence Lee. *Jack's Book.* Original edition: New York: St. Martin's Press, 1978. Reprint: New York: St. Martin's, 1988.

Ginsberg, Allen. *Snapshot Poetics: A Photographic Memoir of the Beat Era.* San Francisco: Chronicle Books, 1993.

Johnson, Joyce. *Minor Characters: A Young Woman's Coming of Age in the Beat Generation.* New York: Doubleday, 1994. Original edition: Boston: Houghton Mifflin Company, 1983.

Johnson, Kent and Craig Paulenich, eds. *Beneath a Single Moon: Buddhism in Contemporary American Poetry.* Boston: Shambhala Publications, 1991.

Jones, Hettie. *How I Became Hettie Jones.* New York: Grove Press, 1990.

Krim, Seymour, ed. *The Beats.* Greenwich, Connecticut: Fawcett Publications, 1960.

Lee, A. Robert, ed. *The Beat Generation Writers.* United Kingdom: Pluto Press, 1996.

Mahoney, Denis, Richard L. Martin and Ron Whitehead, eds. *A Burroughs Compendium: Calling the Toads.* Mystic, Connecticut: Hozomeen Press, 1998.

Maynard, John Arthur. *Venice West: The Beat Generation in Southern California.* New Brunswick, New Jersey: Rutgers University Press, 1993.

McDarrah, Fred W. and Gloria S. *Beat Generation: Glory Days in Greenwich Village.* New York: Schirmer Books, 1996.

McDarrah, Fred W. *Kerouac & Friends: A Beat Generation Album.* New York: William Morrow and Company, 1985.

McNally, Dennis. *Desolate Angel: Jack Kerouac, the Beat Generation, and America.* New York: Random House, 1979. McGraw-Hill, 1980.

Miles, Barry. *William Burroughs: El Hombre Invisible.* New York: Hyperion, 1993.

Miles, Barry. *Ginsberg: A Biography.* New York: Simon & Schuster, 1989.

Milewski, Robert J. *Jack Kerouac: An Annotated Bibliography of Secondary Sources, 1944–1979.* Metuchen, New Jersey: The Scarecrow Press, 1981.

Morgan, Bill. *The Beat Generation in New York: A Walking Tour of Jack Kerouac's City.* San Francisco: City Lights Books, 1997.

Nicosia, Gerald. *Memory Babe: A Critical Biography of Jack Kerouac.* Berkeley and Los

Angeles: University of California Press, 1994.
First edition: New York: Grove Press, 1983.

Phillips, Lisa, ed. *Beat Culture and the New America: 1950–1965*. New York: Whitney Museum of American Art, 1995.

Plummer, William. *The Holy Goof: A Biography of Neal Cassady*. New York: Marlowe & Co., 1994.

Ronan, Stephen. *Disks of the Gone World: An Annotated Discography of the Beat Generation*. Lanham, Maryland: Scarecrow Press, 1999.

Sandler, Irving. *The New York School: The Painters & Sculptors of the Fifties*. New York: Harper & Row, 1978.

Sterritt, David. *Mad to Be Saved: The Beats, the '50s, and Film*. Carbondale, Illinois: Southern Illinois University Press, 1998.

Saroyan, Aram. *Genesis Angels: The Saga of Lew Welch and the Beat Generation*. New York: William Morrow and Company, 1979.

Tonkinson, Carole, ed. *Big Sky Mind: Buddhism and the Beat Generation*. New York: Riverhead Books, 1995.

Turner, Steve. *Jack Kerouac: Angelheaded Hipster*. New York: Viking Penguin, 1996.

Tytell, John. *Naked Angels: The Classic Account of Three Who Changed America's Literature*. Original Edition, 1976. Second Edition: New York: Grove Press, 1991.

Watson, Steven. *The Birth of the Beat Generation: Visionaries, Rebels, and Hipsters, 1944–1960*. New York: Pantheon Books, 1995.

Whalen, Philip. *Off the Wall: Interviews with Philip Whalen*. Donald, Allen, ed. San Francisco: Four Seasons Foundation, 1978.

"The Neal Cassady Issue." *Spit in the Ocean*, Number 6, 1981.

Selected Anthologies of Beat Writers

Ball, Gordon, ed. *Allen Verbatim*. New York: McGraw-Hill, 1974.

Burroughs, William, James Grauerholz, and Ira Silverberg. *Word Virus: The Willam S. Burroughs Reader*. New York: Grove Press, 1998.

Cassady, Neal. *The First Third*. Original Edition, San Francisco: City Lights Books, 1971. Expanded Edition: San Francisco: City Lights Books, 1981.

Cassady, Neal. *Grace Beats Karma: Letters from Prison, 1958–1960*. New York: Blast Books, 1993.

Charters, Ann, ed. *Jack Kerouac: Selected Letters*. New York: Penguin Books, 1996. First Edition: New York: Viking Penguin, 1995.

Charters, Ann, ed. *The Portable Beat Reader*. New York: Viking Penguin, 1995.

Charters, Ann, ed. *The Portable Jack Kerouac*. New York: Viking Penguin, 1995.

Feldman, Gene, and Max Gartenberg, eds. *The Beat Generation and the Angry Young Men*. Original edition: New York: The Citadel Press, 1958. Reprint edition: New York: Ayers, 1977.

Gifford, Barry, ed. *As Ever: The Collected Correspondence of Allen Ginsberg & Neal Cassady*. Berkeley: Creative Arts Book Company, 1977.

Ginsberg, Allen. *Collected Poems, 1947–1980*. Original Edition: New York: Harper & Row, 1984. Reprint edition: New York: Harper Collins, 1988.

Harris, Oliver, ed. *The Letters of William S. Burroughs, 1945–1959*. New York: Viking Press, 1993.

Kerouac, Jack. *Some of the Dharma*. New York: Viking Press, 1997.

Kherdian, David, ed. *Beat Voices: An Anthology of Beat Poetry*. New York: Henry Holt & Co., 1995.

Knight, Brenda. *Women of the Beat Generation: The Writers, Artists and Muses at the Heart of a Revolution*. Berkeley: Conari Press, 1996.

McClure, Michael. *Lighting the Corners: On Art, Nature, and the Visionary*. Albuquerque: University of New Mexico Press, 1993.

Padgett, Ron, and David Shapiro, eds. *An Anthology of New York Poets*. New York: Random House, 1970.

Peabody, Richard, ed. *A Different Beat: Writings by Women of the Beat Generation*. London: Serpent's Tail, 1997.

Rosset, Barney, ed. *Evergreen Review Reader, 1957–1966*. New York: Blue Moon Books, 1993.

Schafer, Benjamin, ed. *The Herbert Huncke Reader*. New York: William Morrow and Company, 1997.

Welch, Lew. *I Remain: The Letters of Lew Welch and the Correspondence of His Friends, Vol. I*. Donald Allen, ed. San Francisco: Grey Fox, 1980.

Selected Beat Documentaries

The Source, written, directed and produced by Chuck Workman (Calliope, 1999, distributed by WinStar Cinema).

What Happened to Kerouac?, directed and produced by Richard Lerner and Lewis MacAdams (New Yorker Films, 1986, distributed by WinStar Entertainment).

Selected Beat Recordings

William S. Burroughs

Burroughs, William S. *Dead City Radio*. Island, 1990.

Burroughs, William S. *Spare Ass Annie and Other Tales*. Island, 1993.

Burroughs, William S. *Call Me Burroughs*. Word Beat/Rhino, 1995.

Burroughs, William S. *The Best of William Burroughs* [four-disc box set]. Mouth Almighty/Mercury, 1998.

Allen Ginsberg

Ginsberg, Allen. *Holy Soul Jelly Roll: Poems and Songs 1949–1993* [four-disc box set]. Los Angeles: Rhino, 1994.

Ginsberg, Allen. *Howl*. Fantasy, 1959.

Ginsberg, Allen. *The Lion for Real*. 1989.

Jack Kerouac

Kerouac, Jack. *The Jack Kerouac Collection*. Word Beat/Rhino, 1989.

Kerouac, Jack. *Readings by Jack Kerouac on the Beat Generation*. Verve, 1998.

Kerouac, Jack. *Jack Kerouac Reads on the Road*. Rykodisc, 1999.

Parker, Graham with music by David Amram. *Visions of Cody*. Penguin Audiobooks, 1996.

Various. *A Jack Kerouac Romnibus* [CD-ROM]. Mind in Motion/Penguin Electronics, 1995.

Various. *Kerouac: kicks joy darkness*. Rykodisc, 1997.

Miscellaneous

Amram, David. *Pull My Daisy . . . and other Jazz Classics*. Premier/Empire, 1995.

Various. *The Beat Generation*. Rhino, 1992.

Various. *Beat: The Beat Experience* [CD-ROM]. The Red Hot Organization/Voyager, 1995.

Various. *Howls Raps and Roars*. Fantasy, 1992.

Contributor Biographies

A cutting-edge bohemian and artist from the get-go, **Lauren Agnelli** has contributed her evocative vocals and songcraft to more than sixty CDs to date, including those by the Washington Squares (whose 1988 release was nominated for a Grammy), Brave Combo, aGNELLI & rAVE and the forthcoming NY Movies. Her writing—sometimes under the nom de plume Trixie A. Balm—has appeared in the *Village Voice* and *Creem*. She is also the author of lyrics, poems, works of fiction and liner notes. To paraphrase Leonard Cohen, since Agnelli has never married her generation, she will never be a widow in the next.

Thomas Albright wrote art criticism, provocative columns and hard news coverage for *the San Francisco Chronicle* as well as *Artnews*, ROLLING STONE, various art publications and fine art catalogs. Before his death at age forty-nine in 1984, he had authored the widely acclaimed *Art in the San Francisco Bay Area, 1945–1980* (UC Press), in addition to some 3,000 articles and reviews. In 1989, Chronicle posthumously published a collection of his articles, *On Art and Artists*. Lawrence Ferlinghetti heralded Albright's writings as covering "events that no one else could cover as an insider." Albright had been a contemporary of Ferlinghetti's during the Fifties in North Beach, where they experienced firsthand the Beat scene.

Barry Alfonso is a songwriter and journalist currently residing in Nashville. Among his credits as a Beat scholar are contributing liner notes to *The Beat Generation* box set and *To Call*

Me Burroughs, both released by Rhino Records. In addition, he has appeared as a performance poet at assorted American venues under the nom de plume Lou Minatti.

Musician, composer, conductor, author, father and farmer, **David Amram** collaborated with Kerouac on the first-ever jazz/poetry reading in New York City in 1957. He wrote the musical score and the title song for the groundbreaking Kerouac film *Pull My Daisy* in 1959. He also acted in the film. His symphonic works include excerpts from Kerouac's *The Lonesome Traveler* in his cantata, *A Year in Our Land—Four Seasons in America*. Since being chosen by Leonard Berstein as the New York Philharmonic's first composer in residence in 1966, Amram has written over a hundred orchestral, choral and chamber works, as well as two operas. He scored the films *Splendor in the Grass* and *Manchurian Candidate*. Amram is currently at work on the book *Collaborating with Kerouac*, and has been recently commissioned by James Galway to write a flute concerto, *Giants of the Night*, dedicated to Charlie Parker, Dizzy Gillespie and Jack Kerouac. He continues to tour the world, conducting symphonies and playing with his quartet.

Eric Andersen is a writer and musician who has recorded twenty-one albums of his own songs. His 1964 experiences are chronicled in his twelve-minute song "Ghosts Upon the Road" on the album of the same name. For the Jack Kerouac spoken-word tribute album *kicks joy darkness,* Andersen recorded the last verse of the unpublished Kerouac poem "Brooklyn Bridge Blues" while walking across the Brooklyn Bridge. He has recently written about William Burroughs for the National Norwegian Theatre, and his most recent album is *Memory of the Future*. He divides his time between New York and his home outside Oslo, Norway.

Steve Appleford is a Los Angeles–based writer and photographer. His work has appeared in the *Los Angeles Times*, *Spin*, ROLLING STONE, *Option*, the *Philadelphia Inquirer*, *Entertainment Weekly*, *George*, *TV Guide*, *L.A. Weekly* and *Los Angeles Reader*. He is currently features editor at *Bikini* magazine.

James Austin is senior director of A&R and special projects for Rhino Records. He is the executive producer of the Atlantic Jazz reissue series and supervises Rhino's Word Beat label. He produced the box sets *The Beat Generation*, *The R&B Box*, *Songs of the West* and the Grammy-nominated *Genius & Soul: The Ray Charles Collection* and *Jack Kerouac Collection*, among other projects.

Gordon Ball managed Allen Ginsberg's upstate New York farm from 1968 to 1971; shot a movie of it (*Farm Diary*, distributed by Filmmakers' Cooperative); edited three books, including two volumes of journals, with the poet; and between 1968 and 1971 took a thousand photographs of Ginsberg and his Beat colleagues, some of which have appeared in numerous books and periodicals, including *DoubleTake* and the *New York Times*. In 1999, Coffee House Press published Ball's memoir, *'66 Frames*. He teaches film and Beat literature at the Virginia Military Institute.

Lester Bangs was an editor at *Creem* for five years and wrote about rock from 1969—when his first reviews appeared in ROLLING STONE— to his death in 1982, at the age of thirty-three.

He is the author of *Blondie* (Simon & Schuster/ Delilah) and a collection of essays, *Psychotic Reactions and Carburetor Dung* (Knopf/Vintage).

Novelist, reporter and scriptwriter **Victor-Lévy Beaulieu** is the founder and current head of the Canadian book publishing house Éditions Trois-Pistoles. Among his fifty-eight books are *Jack Kerouac: a chicken-essay*, *A Quebecois Dream*, *Don Quixote in Nighttown* and *Two Solicitudes* (with Margaret Atwood).

Henry Cabot Beck is a freelance journalist, based in Manhattan, who, like, frequently contributes to *Interview* magazine and other periodicals. Man.

Gina Berriault's latest book, *Women in Their Beds*, won the 1997 National Book Critics Circle Award for Fiction, the PEN-Faulkner Award and the Commonwealth Club gold medal. Two of her short novels, *The Son* and *Afterwards*, are again in print (Counterpoint Press, 1998).

Artist and writer **Rick Bleier**, a native New Yorker who has lived in Boston and Berkeley, has knocked about the country extensively, drawing and writing about the people he has encountered. He was awarded two grants to show his collection "Lowell Celebrates Kerouac," which has been exhibited at Artists Space, the Queens Museum and other galleries. He is also a contributing artist at the *Village Voice* and a drawing and painting instructor at a number of arts organizations.

Douglas Brinkley is a professor of history at the University of New Orleans and the director of the Eisenhower Center for American Studies. He is the editor of a forthcoming collection of Jack Kerouac's journal writings and the author of a forthcoming Kerouac biography. His most recent book is the *American Heritage History of the United States* (Viking, 1998).

Carolyn Cassady grew up in Nashville, where she won prizes for set designs and sold her first portrait at sixteen. After graduating from Bennington College in Vermont in 1944 with a B.A. in Stanislavsky drama, she served as an air raid warden in New York, then became an occupational therapist for the U.S. Army in Palm Springs, California. She then worked as a teaching assistant at the University of Denver while studying for her M.A. in fine and theater arts, and started a theater arts department for the Denver Art Museum. In 1947, she met Neal Cassady, Allen Ginsberg and Jack Kerouac, marrying Cassady the following year in San Francisco, where they had three children. In 1970, Doubleday gave her a contract to write *Off the Road,* a memoir of her life with Cassady, Kerouac and Ginsberg. (It is available now in Penguin editions in the UK and U.S.) Cassady has lived in England for fifteen years.

Ann Charters is the author of the first biography of Jack Kerouac, *Kerouac: A Biography,* one of the early volumes published by Straight Arrow Books in 1973. She is also the editor of *The Portable Beat Reader* (Viking/Penguin, 1992) and *The Selected Letters of Jack Kerouac* (Viking/Penguin, 1995).

Craig Copetas described himself as "the former poet laureate of Pittsburgh, now living in self-proclaimed exile in Europe" when he mediated the 1974 discussion between David Bowie and William Burroughs that appears in this book. He obtained a degree in political philosophy from the University of East Anglia.

Stephen Davis is a veteran journalist and the author of *Jajouka Rolling Stone* and many other books.

Anthony DeCurtis is a contributing editor at ROLLING STONE and the author of *Rocking My Life Away: Writing About Music and Other Matters.*

He is the editor of *Present Tense: Rock & Roll and Culture* and coeditor of *The Rolling Stone Illustrated History of Rock & Roll* and *The Rolling Stone Album Guide.*

Johnny Depp is not a writer; he is a professional liar and has been for fifteen years, at least. He writes nothing for no one, contributes nothing to nothing and likes it that way. He is currently transient and likes it *that* way. His future is questionable and his past even more. He enjoys smoking, hates skiing, and fears only the dark place.

Ann Douglas is a Parr Professor of comparative literature at Columbia University. She holds a B.A. from Harvard (1964), a B.Phil. from Oxford (1966) and a Ph.D. from Harvard (1970). Douglas taught at Princeton from 1970 to '74 and was the first woman to teach in its English department. She has published numerous essays, articles and book reviews on American culture in the *New York Times* and *The Nation,* among other publications; introductions for *Little Women, Uncle Tom's Cabin* and *Charlotte Temple* in Penguin editions; and *Word Virus,* a William Burroughs anthology (Grove, 1998). The author of *Terrible Honesty: Mongrel Manhattan in the 1920's* (Farrar, Straus, 1995), she is currently at work on *If You Live, You Burn: Cold War Culture in the United States 1939–1965.*

Eric Ehrmann was a twenty-three-year-old contributing editor to ROLLING STONE in 1969 when his report on Kerouac's funeral ran in the magazine. His columns on political affairs have appeared in the *Boston Globe,* the *Chicago Tribune,* the *Christian Science Monitor,* the *New York Times* and *USA Today.* He has lectured at the Indiana University School of Journalism and at the University of Virginia and was writer in residence at the University of New Mexico. He is a member of PEN West.

Lee Eisenberg is the former editor of *Esquire* and now a consulting editor at *Time*. He is the author of numerous articles and books.

Lawrence Ferlinghetti is the author of *A Coney Island of the Mind*, one of America's most enduring and best-selling volumes of poetry. Since the 1950s, his bookstore, City Lights, has been "a beacon of avant-garde literature and left-wing political thought," says the *Los Angeles Times*. His City Lights Press has published some of America's most provocative works, including the original edition of *Howl*. In 1998 he was named San Francisco's poet laureate.

Holly George-Warren is the coeditor of *The Rolling Stone Album Guide, The Rolling Stone Illustrated History of Rock & Roll, Rolling Stone: The '70s and The Rolling Stone Encyclopedia of Rock & Roll*. Her writing appears *in The Rolling Stone Book of Women in Rock, The Encyclopedia of Country Music* and *Traditions: New York*, among other books. She also has written for a variety of publications, including ROLLING STONE, the *New York Times* and the *Village Voice*.

Mikal Gilmore is a ROLLING STONE contributing editor and the author of *Shot in the Heart*.

John Grissim Jr. was ROLLING STONE's books and sports editor in the late Sixties. He was a frequent contributor until the mid–Seventies when his interests turned to the sea. He lives in northern California and is the editor and publisher of *Marine Watch*, a magazine about ocean events.

Brian Hassett hitchhiked from Vancouver, Canada, to the 1982 Kerouac conference in Boulder and has been on the road ever since. He's performed his poetry with the Beats and written about their pious frenzy for the *Village Voice, DHARMA beat*, the *Toronto Star, Relix* and numerous other publications. He is still

cruising with the top down in his karmacoupe @aol. com.

Richard Hell is the author of the novel *Go Now* as well as several other books. His albums include *Blank Generation, Destiny Street* and *R.I.P.* He's at work on a second novel.

Michael Horowitz has been a drug historian for nearly thirty years. One of the founders and directors of the Fitz Hugh Ludlow Memorial Library, the world's largest collection of drug-related literature, he has published widely in the field, including *Moksha: Aldous Huxley's Writings on Psychedelics and Visionary Experience* (1977); *The High Times Encyclopedia of Recreational Drugs* (1978); *Shaman Woman, Mainline Lady: Women's Writings on the Drug Experience* (1982) and *An Annotated Bibliography of Timothy Leary* (1988). He is currently owner of Flashback Books, specializing in rare and out-of-print drug and counterculture literature (e-mail: flashbks@nbn.com).

Joyce Johnson is the author of *Minor Characters*, a memoir about her involvement with the Beat Generation, which won a 1983 National Book Critics Circle Award. Her other books include *What Lisa Knew: The Truths and Lies of the Steinberg Case, Come and Join the Dance, Bad Connections* and *In the Night Cafe*. She has written for *The New Yorker, Mirabella* and *Vanity Fair*. During her many years as a book editor, she was responsible for the publication of Jack Kerouac's neglected masterpiece, *Visions of Cody*, as well as important Beat-related books by LeRoi Jones, Allen Ginsberg and John Tytell.

Hettie Jones's memoir of the Beat scene, *How I Became Hettie Jones*, is now available from Grove Press. She is also the author of *Drive*, a collection of poems (Hanging Loose), *Big Star Fallin' Mama: Five Women in Black Music* (Puffin) and other work. She lives in Manhattan's East Village and teaches writing at Parsons, the 92nd Street Y

Poetry Center and the Bedford Hills Correctional Facility.

Mark Kemp is vice president of music editorial at VH1. A former music editor at ROLLING STONE, he was the editor of *Option* magazine for five years and has written for various publications, including *Spin* and the *New York Times*. He is currently working on a book about Southern culture as told through music.

Harvey Kubernik was the project coordinator of *The Jack Kerouac Collection* box set and has produced more than fifty albums of words and music, including recordings by Ray Manzarek, Paul Kantner, Henry Rollins and Exene Cervenka, and live reading events for Allen Ginsberg, Michael McClure, Wanda Coleman and Harry E. Northup. A music journalist since 1972, he has written for *Crawdaddy, Melody Maker, Mojo, Musician, New Times, L.A. Weekly* and the *Los Angeles Times.*

More than twenty years ago, **Lydia Lunch** baptized herself a confrontationalist, commencing at age sixteen as primal screamer and guitar guerrilla for the seminal no-wave band Teenage Jesus and the Jerks. She has continued her assault on complacency via music, film, writing, spoken word, photography and sculpture and has recorded her own music as well as with Kim Gordon, Clint Ruin, Rowland S. Howard, Thurston Moore and her bands Eight Eyed Spy and 13.13. She has also recorded several spoken-word albums, the most recent with Exene Cervenka *(Rude Hieroglyphics)* and appeared in many underground films, including Richard Kern's *The Right Side of My Brain* and *Fingered.* Her most recent written work is her novel *Paradoxia,* published in 1997. She continues to tour and exhibit her work in many forms.

Lewis MacAdams is the author of ten books of poems and stories, a former director of the

Poetry Center at San Francisco State and two-time winner of the World Heavyweight Poetry Championship. He coproduced and codirected the documentary *What Happened to Kerouac?* He is currently working on a book for Simon & Schuster, *The Birth of the Cool.*

Greil Marcus is a contributing editor of ROLLING STONE. He is the author of *Invisible Republic, Lipstick Trace*s and *Mystery Train.*

Michael McClure is an award-winning poet and playwright who wrote "Mercedes Benz" with Janis Joplin. In 1999, Shambhala Books is publishing his collection of Zen dharma poems, *Touching the Edge.* Among his recent books is *Huge Dreams* (Viking/Penguin), a collection of his poems from the early Beat and San Francisco period. He lives in the Bay Area with his wife, sculptor Amy Evans McClure.

Carlo McCormick is senior editor of *Paper* magazine. His writing has been published in *Art Forum, High Times* and *Spin.* He also has contributed essays to art books and exhibition catalogs.

Mellon takes pictures and writes. A selection of her photos of the Beats will appear in *Paradise Outlaws* (William Morrow, 1999). A Body in Motion, she Keeps the Fire Going, Tries to Be Quiet and Waits for What's Next.

Richard Meltzer, the author of *The Aesthetics of Rock* (1970), has produced ten or eleven book-length heaps of inspired prose, including *Gulcher, Richard Meltzer's Guide to the Ugliest Buildings of Los Angeles, L.A. Is the Capital of Kansas* and the 1995 novel *The Night (Alone),* as well as a pair of poetry collections, *17 Insects Can Die in Your Heart* and *Tropic of Nipples.* In addition to service in the literary trenches, he has done time as a visual artist, filmmaker, garbage picker, boxing authority (as a consultant for the PBS documentary *Down for the Count*), rock lyricist (Blue

Öyster Cult's million-selling "Burnin' for You"), punk-rock singer and DJ. Currently at work on a *very* smutty second novel, he remains a towering figure of Anglo-American culture, et cetera.

Robert Palmer, a longtime contributor to ROLLING STONE, was once described by the magazine as the nation's preeminent music critic. He was the first fulltime pop music critic for the *New York Times* and in his lifetime published five books, including *Deep Blues* and *Rock and Roll: An Unruly History*. Palmer held teaching posts at a number of universities, including Yale and the University of Mississippi; produced blues albums for Fat Possum; wrote, narrated and directed several films; and acted as chief consultant for a multipart television history of rock & roll jointly produced by PBS and the BBC. In the 1960s he played clarinet with the Insect Trust and remained an active musician for most of his life. At the time of his death in 1997, at the age of fifty-two, he was working on two books, a memoir of his thirty-year career as a music journalist and an account of his years in Morocco.

Graham Parker released his first album, the raw and compelling *Howlin' Wind*, in 1976. More than a dozen critically acclaimed LPs have followed. In his spare time, Parker writes short stories. He has also been involved in spoken-word tributes to Jack Kerouac, including CD-ROMs, books on tape and public readings.

Daniel Pinchbeck is a writer based in New York City. His work has appeared in the *New York Times Magazine*, *Esquire* and the *Village Voice*. He is currently the editor of *Open City*, an art and literary journal.

Music writer **Parke Puterbaugh** is a longtime contributor to ROLLING STONE and a coeditor of *I Want to Take You Higher: The Psychedelic Era*

1965–1969 (Chronicle, 1997). He has also served as a curatorial consultant to the Rock and Roll Hall of Fame and Museum.

As a member of Sonic Youth, **Lee Ranaldo**'s newest album is *A Thousand Leaves*; his latest solo release is *Amarillo Ramp (for Robert Smithson)*. He also wrote the text of the chapbook *Moroccan Journal: Jajouka Excerpt* and is at work with photographer Leah Singer on a larger book about Morocco.

Walter Raubicheck teaches English at Pace University in New York and has published a number of articles on detective fiction, rock music and American literature that have appeared in various books and journals.

Michael Rogers is a novelist who has also been a writer and editor for ROLLING STONE, *Outside* and *Newsweek*. He is now vice president of Washingtonpost.Newsweek Interactive and editor and general manager of Newsweek.com.

Marshall Rosenthal wrote book reviews for ROLLING STONE in the early Seventies.

Aram Saroyan's most recent book is *Day and Night: Bolinas Poems* (Black Sparrow Press, 1998). He is the author of "lighght," the controversial one-word poem that became the subject of ongoing government and public debate after it was chosen by Robert Duncan in 1968 for a National Endowment for the Arts poetry award.

A freelance writer for thirty years, **David Sjostedt** has contributed reviews to ROLLING STONE the *Boston Phoenix* and numerous Northern California newspapers. His fiction and poetry have been published in *Kuksu, First Leaves* and *The Dickens*. He lives in Sonoma County, California, and is at work on a novel.

Born in Chicago, December 30, 1946, the poet and musician **Patti Smith** released her first album, the seminal *Horses*, in 1975, and as of this writing is in the studio with her band recording her eighth. Her books include *Babel, Early Work, The Coral Sea* and *Patti Smith: Complete.* She is currently at work on a book about Robert Mapplethorpe's formative years as an artist, which will be published by Doubleday.

John Swenson has been a syndicated music columnist for United Press International since 1986, a ROLLING STONE contributor since 1975 and the author of numerous books on music. He is also editor of *The Rolling Stone Jazz and Blues Album Guide* (Random House, 1999).

Hunter S. Thompson is a humble man who writes for a living and spends the rest of his time bogged down in strange and crazy wars. He is the author of many violent books and brilliant political essays, which his friends and henchmen in the international media have managed for so many years to pass off as Gonzo Journalism.

John Tytell is the author of *Naked Angels* (Grove Press, 1976), *Ezra Pound: The Solitary Volcano* (Doubleday, 1987), *Passionate Lives* (Carol, 1991), *The Living Theater: Art. Exile and Outrage* (Grove Press, 1995) and *Paradise Outlaws: Remembering the Beats* (William Morrow, 1999). He is a professor of English at Queens College at the City University of New York.

David L. Ulin is the author of *Cape Cod Blues* (Red Dust, 1992), a chapbook of poems. His work appears in the *Los Angeles Times*, the *Los Angeles Weekly*, the *Chicago Tribune*, *Newsday* and *Salon*. Currently, he is writing a book about Jack Kerouac for the University of California Press and editing a collection of Southern California literature for City Lights Books.

Don Waller is the author of *The Motown Story* (Scribner, 1985) and contributed a chapter to

Make the Music Go Bang! (St. Martin's Press, 1997). He has written thirty-five sets of album liner notes, and his byline has graced *USA Today*, *Billboard*, *Mojo* and the *Los Angeles Times*. Cooking is his hobby; music is his life. Waller likes double espressos, fine Irish whiskey, Dunhill cigarettes and custom-tailored silk suits.

Born Liz Lehrman in 1928 (evolved into **Liza Williams** by 1962—usual story). Raised and educated in Greenwich Village by communist parents. Thrown out of Party at age seventeen for reading Koestler's *Darkness at Noon* and associating with a Trotskyite. Thus inoculated against stupid power and boring political tracts, dropped out of college and set out to see the world. Hitchhiked through Western Europe with friend, spent six months in Paris, six in London, then accepted invitation to Cape Town (free ticket) and ended up marrying speed-freak concert pianist and living in South Africa over eleven years. Years of meaningful anti-Apartheid activity culminating in five months underground during state of emergency. Had to leave, returned to live on mother's floor in L.A. Culture Schock and then a receptionist job at Pacifica Radio, columnist for *L.A. Free Press* (seven years), rock & roll publicist Capitol Records, hired away by Island Records to run L.A. office. Became manic and quit to go to Mexico with Dr. Gonzo (fear and loathing), equally berserk. Putnam's published collection of columns (*Up the City of Angels*, 1971), hung around Hollywood and was offered an assistant professorship by General Honors at Cal State University–Long Beach. Due to being a dropout, was qualified with experimental equivalency. Wow, best job ever! Eventually, to her detriment, became manic again, and it's been shuck and jive to stay alive ever since.

Index

Page numbers in *italics* refer to captions.